THE COMPLETE
STEP-BY-STEP
COOK
BOOK

THE COMPLETE
STEP-BY-STEP
COOK
BOOK

MORE THAN 800 RECIPES IN FULL COLOR

SALAMANDER

Published by Salamander Books Limited
8 Blenheim Court
Brewery Road
London N7 9NT
United Kingdom

3 5 7 9 8 6 4 2

ISBN 1 84065 032 X

A member of **Chrysalis** Books plc

CREDITS
Project managed by: Anne McDowall
Recipes selected by: Hilaire Walden
Typeset by: SX Composing DTP
Printed in Spain

Half-title page: Asparagus Niçoise (page 35)
Title page: Lemon & Honey Chicken (page 100), Bass with Ginger & Lime (page 72),
Nectarine Meringue Nests (page 382)
Below: Victoria Sponge Cake (page 403)

CONTENTS

INTRODUCTION

The Complete Step-by-Step Cookbook is a unique collection of more than 800 recipes that have been created and written by experienced cookery authors and that are suitable for cooks of all tastes and all levels of abilities and with varying amounts of time and money available. Novice cooks will find instructions for how to make simple recipes such as white sauce or victoria sponge, while experienced cooks and food-lovers of all culinary abilities will find plenty of recipes to inspire and tempt them.

The Complete Step-by-Step Cookbook is both an attractive book and an extremely practical one. Each dish is shown in a full-colour photograph, and clear, concise, step-by-step instructions, accompanied by helpful step-by-step photographs, show how to make it.

The Complete Step-by-Step Cookbook contains authentic recipes from some of the most popular of the World's cuisines, including French, Italian, Spanish, Greek, Turkish, North African, Thai, Vietnamese, Chinese, Japanese, American and British. To help you to find out a little more about some of the ingredients that may be unfamiliar, useful glossaries of Mediterranean and Eastern ingredients (on pages 472–475) give descriptions, preparation, cooking and storing instructions, plus recommendations for suitable substitutes where applicable.

You will find many popular recipes in *The Complete Step-by-Step Cookbook*, whether you are looking for a mouthwatering dish to feed the family for lunch, tea or supper, provide a special meal for friends or serve for a more formal dinner party. There are recipes for every occasion and every type of cooking, from breakfasts to baking, from a festive dinner to a barbecue. Classic dishes – chocolate brownies, English trifle, roast turkey, paella, tiramisu, to name but a few – are accompanied by plenty more unusual ideas that will enable you to extend your repertoire, safe in the knowledge that the recipes will work, and with the reassuring "helping hand" of the step-by-step instructions and photographs.

SOUPS

CLEAR BEET SOUP

VICHYSSOISE

1 onion, coarsely grated
1 large carrot, coarsely grated
1 lb. raw beets, peeled, coarsely grated
Fresh parsley sprig
1 bay leaf
4 cups chicken stock
1 egg white
Juice ½ lemon
Salt and pepper to taste
Thin lemon slices to garnish

In a large saucepan, combine vegetables, parsley, bay leaf and stock. Bring to a boil, cover and simmer 30 minutes. Strain soup in a colander set over a bowl.

Clean pan and return liquid to pan. To clear soup, bring to a boil. Whisk egg white in a small bowl, then stir into soup. Simmer gently 15 minutes.

2 tablespoons butter
3 medium-size leeks, trimmed, sliced, washed
1 shallot, finely chopped
8 ozs. potatoes, sliced
3 cups light chicken stock
Pinch ground mace or grated nutmeg
Salt and pepper to taste
⅔ cup half and half
Snipped chives to garnish

Melt butter in a large saucepan. Cook leeks and shallot in butter, covered, over low heat 10 minutes without browning. Add potatoes, stock and mace. Bring to a boil, cover and simmer 20 minutes.

In a food processor fitted with a metal blade or a blender, process mixture to a purée. Strain puree through a sieve set over a bowl. Season with salt and pepper.

Strain soup through a muslin-lined sieve set over a bowl. Stir in lemon juice. Cool and refrigerate until chilled. Season soup with salt and pepper. Garnish with lemon slices.

Makes 4 to 6 servings.

Cool and stir in ⅔ of half and half. Refrigerate until ready to serve. Swirl in remaining half and half. Garnish soup with snipped chives.

Makes 6 servings.

FENNEL & PEAR SOUP

2 fennel bulbs
2 tablespoons butter
3 ripe pears
3¾ cups chicken or vegetable stock
⅔ cup crème fraîche or thick sour cream
Salt and freshly ground pepper
Crème fraîche or thick sour cream and chopped
    fennel leaves to garnish

Trim fennel, cut lengthwise into quarters and coarsely chop. Melt butter in a saucepan, add fennel and cook 5 minutes, stirring occasionally, until beginning to soften.

Peel pears, cut into quarters and remove cores. Coarsely chop pears and add to pan. Stir in stock. Bring to a boil, reduce heat, cover and simmer 15 minutes or until fennel and pears are tender.

Purée soup in a blender or food processor. Return to rinsed-out pan and stir in crème fraîche or sour cream, salt and pepper. Refrigerate at least 2 hours. Serve in chilled bowls, or reheat and serve hot. Garnish with a swirl of crème fraîche or sour cream and fennel leaves.

Makes 6 servings.

GAZPACHO

1½ lbs. beefsteak tomatoes
½ Spanish onion, chopped
1 green bell pepper, chopped
1 red bell pepper, chopped
2 garlic cloves, chopped
2 slices firm white bread, crusts removed, broken
    into pieces
1¼ cups tomato juice
3 tablespoons extra-virgin olive oil
2 tablespoons sherry vinegar
Salt and black pepper
About 8 ice cubes to serve
ACCOMPANIMENTS:
1 diced small red bell pepper, 1 diced small green bell
    pepper, 1 diced small onion, 1 chopped hard-
    cooked egg and croutons

With a sharp knife, peel, seed and chop tomatoes. In a blender or a food processor with the metal blade, combine tomatoes and remaining soup ingredients, except ice cubes. Process until smooth. Pour soup through a nylon strainer, pressing down well on contents of strainer. If necessary, thin soup with cold water, then cover and refrigerate until chilled.

Place accompaniments in separate bowls. Adjust seasoning of soup, if necessary, then pour into cold soup bowls. Add ice cubes and serve with accompaniments.

Makes 4 servings.

Variation: Do not strain the soup if more texture is preferred.

ZUCCHINI & TOMATO SOUP

CURRIED PARSNIP SOUP

2 tablespoons butter
1 medium-size onion, finely chopped
12 ozs. zucchini, coarsely grated
1 garlic clove, crushed
2½ cups vegetable stock
1 (14-oz.) can chopped tomatoes
2 tablespoons chopped fresh mixed herbs, if desired
Salt and pepper to taste
¼ cup whipping cream and fresh basil leaves to
   garnish

Melt butter in a large saucepan. Cook onion
in butter over medium heat until soft. Stir in
zucchini and garlic and cook 4 to 5 minutes.

Stir in stock and tomatoes with juice. Bring
to a boil and simmer 15 minutes.

3 tablespoons butter
1 medium-size onion, chopped
1 teaspoon chopped gingerroot
1 teaspoon curry powder
½ teaspoon ground cumin
1 lb. parsnips, chopped
1 medium-size potato, chopped
3¾ cups beef stock
⅔ cup plain yogurt
Salt and pepper to taste
Lemon peel strips to garnish
CURRIED CROUTONS:
½ teaspoon curry powder
Squeeze lemon juice
2 tablespoons butter
2 thick slices bread

Melt butter in a large saucepan. Gently cook
onion in butter until onion is soft. Stir in
gingerroot, curry powder and cumin and
cook 1 minute. Add parsnips and potato and
stir over medium heat to coat vegetables with
spicy butter. Pour in stock and bring to a
boil. Simmer 30 minutes or until vegetables
are very tender. In a food processor fitted
with a metal blade or a blender, process mixture to a purée. Clean pan and return purée
to clean pan. Ladle a small amount of purée
into a bowl. Whisk in yogurt, then pour back
into purée.

Stir in herbs, if desired, and season with salt
and pepper. Garnish with dollops of whipping cream and basil leaves.

Makes 4 servings.

Season soup with salt and pepper and gently
reheat. To prepare croutons, preheat oven to
400F (205C). In a small bowl, beat curry
powder, lemon juice and butter. Spread on
bread. Remove crusts and cut in cubes. Place
cubes on a baking sheet and bake in preheated oven until crisp and golden. Garnish
soup with croutons and lemon peel strips.

Makes 4 to 6 servings.

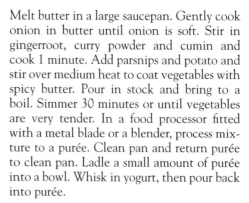

ONION SOUP

⅓ cup butter
1½ lbs. large onions, thinly sliced
4½ cups beef stock
1¼ cups dry white wine
Large pinch of mixed dried herbs
Pinch of freshly grated nutmeg
Salt and freshly ground pepper
6 slices French bread
5 ozs. (1¼ cups) shredded Gruyère cheese
Flat-leaf parsley sprigs to garnish

Melt butter in a large, heavy saucepan, add onions, stir to coat with the butter and lay a piece of waxed paper on top.

Cook over very low heat, without stirring, 20 to 30 minutes or until onions are soft and rich golden brown. Add stock, wine, dried herbs, nutmeg, salt and pepper and bring to a boil. Reduce heat, cover and simmer 45 minutes. Meanwhile, preheat oven to 350F (180C). Arrange bread slices on a baking sheet and bake 10 to 15 minutes or until dried but not browned.

Preheat broiler. Divide soup among heat-proof soup bowls. Float a slice of bread on top and sprinkle with cheese. Broil until cheese is bubbling and golden. Garnish with flat-leaf parsley sprigs and serve immediately.

Makes 6 servings.

ROASTED BELL PEPPER SOUP

6 large tomatoes
1 garlic clove, chopped
⅓ cup olive oil
Salt and freshly ground pepper
4 red bell peppers, quartered
1 onion, finely chopped
6 ozs. potatoes, cut into ¾-inch cubes
Shredded basil leaves, to garnish
BASIL PURÉE:
1 small bunch of basil
2 tablespoons olive oil
1 teaspoon lemon juice

Preheat oven to 350F (180C). Oil two roasting pans. Cut tomatoes in half.

Place tomatoes, cut side up, in one of the roasting pans. Scatter garlic and drizzle 2 tablespoons of the oil over tomatoes. Season with salt and pepper. Place bell peppers in the other pan. Drizzle with 2 tablespoons of the oil. Put tomatoes and bell peppers in oven and cook tomatoes 45 to 60 minutes or until beginning to blacken around edges. Cook bell peppers, turning occasionally, until their skins are charred and blistered. Put bell peppers into a plastic bag and leave until cool enough to handle. Peel bell -peppers and coarsely chop.

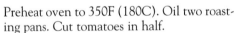

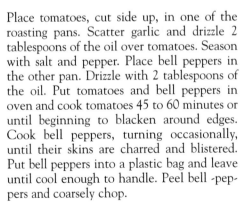

Heat remaining oil in a large saucepan. Add onion and cook, stirring occasionally, 5 minutes or until soft. Add potatoes, bell peppers and 3¾ cups water. Cover and simmer 20 minutes. Transfer to a blender or food processor, add tomatoes and purée. Press through a strainer, return to rinsed-out pan and heat through. Season. Pound basil leaves with a large pinch of salt. Stir in oil and lemon juice. Drizzle basil purée on to soup, garnish and serve.

Makes 6 servings.

HERBED PEA SOUP

¼ cup unsalted butter
1 leek, finely chopped
1 small head butter lettuce, separated into leaves
About 3¾ cups vegetable or chicken stock or water
Several sprigs of chervil
Few sprigs of parsley
1 lb. fresh or frozen green peas
Salt and freshly ground pepper
Half and half, to garnish

CREAM OF MUSHROOM SOUP

¼ cup butter
12 ozs. mushrooms, finely chopped
½ cup all-purpose flour
2 cups chicken stock
⅔ cup milk
1 tablespoon chopped fresh parsley
1 tablespoon lemon juice
Salt and pepper to taste
⅔ cup half and half
¼ cup plus 1 tablespoon whipping cream
1 tablespoon finely chopped watercress
Watercress leaves to garnish

Melt butter in a saucepan, add leek and cook, stirring occasionally, 5 minutes or until soft. Add lettuce and cook 1 or 2 minutes or until leaves have wilted.

Melt butter in a large saucepan. Gently cook mushrooms in butter 5 minutes.

Add stock or water, chervil, parsley and peas. Bring to a boil, reduce heat and simmer 10 minutes if using fresh peas. If using frozen peas, simmer 5 minutes or until peas are tender.

Stir in flour, then gradually add stock and milk. Bring to a boil, then simmer 10 minutes. Add parsley and lemon juice. Season with salt and pepper. Stir in half and half and reheat gently.

Purée soup in a blender or food processor and return to rinsed-out pan. Add salt and pepper and reheat gently without boiling. If soup is too thick, add some boiling stock or water. Swirl in half-and-half and serve.

Makes 4 servings.

In a small bowl, whip cream until soft peaks form. Stir in chopped watercress. Top each portion of soup with watercress chantilly. Garnish with watercress leaves.

Makes 4 servings.

CARROT & CILANTRO SOUP

1 lb. carrots
2 tablespoons olive oil
1 small onion, finely chopped
1 garlic clove, crushed
1 teaspoon coriander seeds, crushed
1 teaspoon ground coriander
3¾ cups vegetable stock
Salt and pepper to taste
⅓ cup dark raisins, chopped
1 tablespoon chopped fresh cilantro
SESAME CROUTONS:
1 thick slice bread, crusts removed
1 tablespoon butter
1 tablespoon sesame seeds

Dice 2 carrots and set aside. Chop remaining carrots. Heat oil in a large saucepan. Gently cook chopped carrots, onion and garlic in oil 10 minutes. Stir in crushed coriander seeds and ground coriander and cook 1 minute. Pour in 3 cups of stock. Cover, bring to a simmer and cook 15 minutes or until carrots are tender. Meanwhile, in a small saucepan, simmer diced carrots in remaining stock until carrots are tender.

In a food processor fitted with a metal blade or a blender, process mixture to a purée. Clean pan and return purée to clean pan. Stir cooked diced carrots with stock and raisins into purée. Season with salt and pepper. Reheat gently, to prepare croutons, toast bread on each side until golden. Cool, spread with butter and sprinkle with sesame seeds. Toast until golden. Cut toast in small cubes. Stir chopped cilantro into soup. Garnish soup with sesame seed croutons.

Makes 4 servings.

SOUPE AU PISTOU

½ cup dried haricot beans, soaked overnight
1 onion, finely chopped
5 ozs. pumpkin, chopped (optional)
1 stalk celery, sliced
2 small leeks, chopped
2 baby turnips, diced
6 ozs. small green beans, cut into 1-inch pieces
5 ozs. shelled broad beans or lima beans (about 1 cup)
3 ripe tomatoes, peeled and chopped
2 ozs. fine vermicelli
Salt and freshly ground pepper
PISTOU:
Handful of basil leaves
3 garlic cloves
6 tablespoons olive oil
¾ cup grated Parmean cheese

Drain haricot beans. Put into a large saucepan with onion, pumpkin, if using, and 7½ cups water. Bring to a boil and boil rapidly 10 minutes. Cover and simmer 1 hour. Add celery, leeks and turnips and cook 10 to 15 minutes. Add remaining ingredients. Cook 10 minutes or until beans and vegetables are tender.

Meanwhile, make the pistou. Coarsely chop basil. Using a pestle and mortar, pound garlic with the basil, then gradually add oil, stirring until well blended. Stir in Parmesan cheese and 1 or 2 tablespoons of hot soup. Pour the soup into warmed bowls, spoon a little pistou into each serving, garnish with Parmesan shavings and serve.

Makes 6 servings.

MINESTRONE

2 tablespoons olive oil
2 ozs. lightly smoked streaky bacon, diced
2 large onions, peeled and sliced
2 garlic cloves, skinned and crushed
2 medium carrots, peeled and diced
3 stalks celery, trimmed and sliced
1¼ cups dried haricot beans, soaked
1 (14½-oz.) can chopped tomatoes
10 cups beef stock
4 ozs. frozen green peas
12 ozs. potatoes, peeled and diced
6 ozs. small pasta shapes
8 ozs. green cabbage, thinly sliced
6 ozs. green beans, trimmed and sliced
3 tablespoons each chopped fresh parsley and basil
Salt and freshly ground pepper

Heat oil in a large saucepan and add bacon, onions, and garlic. Cover and cook gently for 5 minutes, stirring occasionally until soft but not colored. Add carrots and celery and cook 2 to 3 minutes until softening. Drain beans and add to the pan with tomatoes and stock. Cover and simmer 1 to 1½ hours, until beans are nearly tender.

Add peas and potatoes and cook for a further 15 minutes, then add the pasta, cabbage, beans and chopped parsley and cook for a further 15 minutes. Stir in the basil, adjust seasoning and serve.

Makes 8 servings.

Note: Serve with freshly grated parmesan cheese, if desired.

BLUE CHEESE & BROCCOLI SOUP

6 ozs. potatoes
2 tablespoons butter
1 onion, finely chopped
4½ cups chicken stock
12 ozs. broccoli
Salt and freshly ground pepper
4 ozs. blue cheese
GARLIC CROUTONS:
2 slices white bread, crusts removed
2 tablespoons sunflower oil
1 tablespoon butter
1 garlic clove, finely chopped

Peel potatoes and cut into 1-inch cubes.

Melt butter in a large saucepan over medium heat. Add conion and cook, stirring occasionally, 5 minutes or until soft. Add stock and potatoes, bring to a boil, reduce heat, cover and simmer 10 minutes. Cut broccoli into flowerets and add to pan. Return to a boil, reduce heat, cover and simmer 10 minutes or until vegetables are tender.

Meanwhile, make croutons. Cut bread into shapes with a pastry cutter. Heat oil, butter and garlic in a skillet and fry bread shapes on both sides until golden and crisp. Remove with a slotted spoon and drain on paper towels. Purée soup in a blender or food processor. Return to rinsed-out pan, add salt and pepper, then crumble in cheese. Reheat gently without boiling, until cheese has melted. Garnish with croutons and serve.

Makes 6 servings.

MEDITERRANEAN FISH SOUP

¼ cup olive oil
1 large onion, finely chopped
2 garlic cloves, crushed
1 small fennel bulb, chopped
2 lbs. mixed fish and shellfish
2 tomatoes, peeled and chopped
Several parsley sprigs, chopped
3 sprigs each thyme and basil
Pinch of saffron strands
Strip of orange peel
Salt and freshly ground pepper
About 4½ cups fish stock

Heat oil in a saucepan, add onion, garlic and fennel and cook 5 minutes or until soft.

Cut fish into 1½-inch pieces. Add tomatoes, herbs, saffron, orange peel, salt and pepper to saucepan. Lay fish on top and add just enough stock to cover fish. Bring to barely simmering and cook over low heat, uncovered, 8 minutes.

Add shellfish and cook 5 minutes or until fish and shellfish are tender. Skim any scum from surface of soup and serve.

Makes 4 to 6 servings.

Note: For best results use a selection of white fish such as haddock, cod or whiting. Don't use oily fish such as mackerel as it gives a bitter taste to the soup.

CREAMY FISH SOUP

STOCK:
1 lb. fish heads, bones and trimmings
5 cups water
1 small onion, quartered
1 carrot, sliced
1 stalk celery, chopped
Bouquet garni
Salt to taste
6 black peppercorns
1 bay leaf
Lemon slice
SOUP:
12 ozs. white fish fillets, skinned
3 tablespoons butter
⅓ cup all-purpose flour
⅔ cup half and half
Salt and pepper to taste
Lemon slices, chopped fresh dill or chervil sprigs and paprika to garnish

To prepare stock, combine fish bits, water, vegetables and bouquet garni in a large saucepan. Season with salt. Add peppercorns, bay leaf and lemon slice. Bring to a boil over low heat and skim off any scum that rises to surface. Simmer 20 minutes. Strain stock, without pressing it, through a colander set in a bowl. Clean pan and measure 3¾ cups of stock into pan (any remaining can be frozen). Add fish and poach until it flakes.

In a food processor fitted with a metal blade or a blender, process fish and a small amount of stock to a purée. Clean pan and melt butter in pan. Stir in flour and cook 1 minute without browning. Gradually add remainder of stock, then stir until boiling. Simmer 10 minutes. Whisk in fish purée and half an half. Season with salt and pepper. Garnish with lemon slices, chopped dill and paprika.

Makes 4 to 6 servings.

SEAFOOD & COCONUT SOUP

3 stalks lemon grass, cut into 2-inch lengths
1 (2-inch) piece of galangal, thinly sliced
1 (1-inch) piece of ginger root, thinly sliced
2 teaspoons finely chopped red chile
4½ cups coconut milk
10 kaffir lime leaves
7 ozs. boneless, skinless chicken breast, cut into
   1-inch cubes
5 tablespoons fish sauce
Juice of ½ lime
7 ozs. raw unpeeled jumbo shrimp, peeled and
   deveined
7 ozs. firm white fish fillets, cut into 1-inch cubes
Small handful each cilantro and Thai basil leaves
Cilantro springs to garnish

In a saucepan, put lemon grass, galangal, ginger and chile. Add 2 cups water. Bring to a boil then simmer for 5 minutes. Add coconut milk and lime leaves. Simmer for 10 minutes. Add chicken, fish sauce and lime juice to pan. Poach for 5 minutes. Add shrimp and fish. Poach for a further 2-3 minutes until shrimp turn pink.

Add cilantro and basil to pan. Stir, then ladle into warm soup bowls. Remove and discard lemon grass and lime leaves before eating. Garnish with cilantro.

Makes 4 servings.

NEW ENGLAND CLAM CHOWDER

2 (10-oz.) cans clams
3 slices bacon, diced
1 medium-size onion, finely chopped
1 lb. potatoes, diced
1¼ cups fish stock
1¼ cups milk
⅔ cup half and half
Pinch dried leaf thyme
Salt and pepper to taste

Drain clams, reserving liquid. Chop clams and set aside.

Fry bacon in a large saucepan over high heat until fat runs and bacon is lightly browned. Add onion and saute until soft. Stir in reserved clam liquid, potatoes, stock and milk. Bring to a boil and simmer about 20 minutes or until potatoes are tender.

Stir in clams, half and half, and thyme. Season with salt and pepper. Reheat a few minutes, but do not allow to boil.

Makes 6 servings.

RICH COUNTRY CHICKEN SOUP

3 tablespoons butter
4 ozs. button mushrooms, chopped
1/3 cup all-purpose flour
2½ cups strong chicken stock
2½ cups milk
12 ozs. cooked chicken, diced
2 egg yolks
2/3 cup half and half
Salt and pepper to taste
WATERCRESS DUMPLINGS:
1 cup self-rising flour
½ teaspoon salt
Pinch mixed dried leaf herbs
2 ozs. shredded suet
1 bunch watercress, trimmed, finely chopped
1 small egg, beaten
1 tablespoon water
Chicken stock for cooking dumplings

Melt butter in a large saucepan. Gently cook mushrooms 4 to 5 minutes. Stir in flour, then gradually add stock and milk. Bring to a boil, stirring constantly. Cover and simmer 15 minutes. Meanwhile, to prepare dumplings, sift flour into a medium-size bowl. Mix in salt, herbs, suet and watercress. Add egg and water and mix to a dough. Roll dough in 24 balls. In a large saucepan, bring stock to a boil. Drop dumplings into stock, cover and simmer 10 minutes.

Remove soup from heat and stir in chicken. In a small bowl, beat egg yolks and half and half. Ladle in a small amount of soup into half and half mixture and mix quickly. Pour back into soup and heat gently without boiling until thick. Season with salt and pepper. Using a slotted spoon, remove dumplings from stock and add to soup to serve.

Makes 6 servings.

CHICKEN & MUSHROOM SOUP

2 garlic cloves, crushed
4 cilantro sprigs
1½ teaspoons peppercorns, crushed
1 tablespoon vegetable oil
4½ cups chicken stock
5 pieces dried Chinese black mushrooms, soaked in cold water 30 minutes, drained, coarsely chopped
1 tablespoon fish sauce
4 ozs. chicken, cut into strips
2 green onions, thinly sliced
Cilantro sprigs to garnish

Using a pestle and mortar or a small food processor, pound or mix garlic, 4 cilantro sprigs and peppercorns to a paste. In a wok, heat vegetable oil, add paste and cook, stirring, 1 minute. Stir in stock, mushrooms and fish sauce. Simmer 5 minutes.

Add chicken, reduce heat so liquid simmers and cook gently 5 minutes. Scatter green onions over surface and garnish with cilantro sprigs.

Makes 4 servings.

COCK-A-LEEKIE

2 large chicken quarters
5 cups chicken stock
Bouquet garni
1 lb. leeks
12 prunes, soaked in water 1 hour
Salt and pepper to taste
Leek stems to garnish
OATY DUMPLINGS:
¾ cup regular oats
1 cup whole-wheat bread crumbs
1 tablespoon chopped fresh herbs
Salt and pepper to taste
¼ cup margarine, softened
2-3 tablespoons cold water

In a large saucepan, drop chicken into stock and add bouquet garni.

Bring to a boil, then simmer 30 minutes. Remove chicken from stock and cool. Remove bouquet garni and skim off any fat from surface of soup. Trim coarse leaves from leeks, then cut lengthwise. Wash thoroughly and cut in 1-inch pieces. Add leeks and prunes to soup. Simmer 25 minutes. Cut chicken in small pieces and add to soup. Season with salt and pepper.

To prepare dumplings, combine oats and bread crumbs in a medium-size bowl. Stir in herbs. Season with salt and pepper. Cut in margarine. Add cold water and mix to a dough. Divide in small balls and drop into soup. Cover and simmer 15 minutes. Garnish with leek stems.

Makes 6 servings.

HOT & SOUR SOUP

1 teaspoon chopped gingerroot
1 tablespoon chopped lemon grass
2-3 small fresh red chiles, seeded and chopped
3 cups chicken broth
2-3 tablespoons lime juice or vinegar
3 tablespoons fish sauce
1 tablespoon dried shrimp, soaked and rinsed
1 (8-oz.) cake tofu, cut into small cubes
1 oz. bean thread vermicelli, soaked and cut into short lengths
2 tablespoons soaked black fungus, coarsely chopped
¼ cucumber, thinly shredded
4-6 ozs. cooked peeled shrimp
Salt and freshly ground white pepper
Cilantro leaves to garnish

Using a pestle and mortar, pound the ginger, lemon grass and chiles to a fine paste. Bring the broth to a rolling boil in a pan, add the lemon grass mixture with the lime juice or vinegar, fish sauce and dried shrimp. Bring back to a boil, then add tofu, vermicelli and black fungus. Simmer mixture about 2 minutes.

Add cucumber and shrimp, bring back to a boil once more, then season with salt and plenty of pepper. Serve the soup hot (see Note), garnished with cilantro leaves.

Makes 4-6 servings.

Note: This soup must be served piping hot – warm both serving tureen and soup bowls.

HARIRA

2 tablespoons vegetable oil
12 ozs. boneless lean lamb, cut in small cubes
1 medium-size onion, sliced
2 teaspoons ground coriander
½ teapoon ground tumeric
½ teaspoon cayenne pepper
½ teaspoon ground ginger
½ teaspoon ground cumin
8 ozs. tomatoes, peeled, chopped
1 garlic clove, crushed
2½ cups water
1 (14-oz.) can garbanzo beans, drained
Salt and pepper to taste
Juice of 2 limes or 1 lemon
1 tablespoon chopped fresh cilantro
¼ teaspoon ground cinnamon to garnish

Heat oil in a large saucepan. Fry lamb in oil quickly until evenly browned all over. Reduce heat and add onion. Cook 5 minutes, stirring constantly. Stir in all spices. Cook 1 minute and add tomatoes, garlic and water.

In a small bowl, mash ¾ of garbanzo beans. Add mashed and whole beans to soup. Season with salt and pepper. Bring to a boil and simmer 40 minutes or until lamb is tender. Just before serving. Stir in lime juice and cilantro and simmer 2 minutes. Sprinkle soup with cinnamon.

Makes 4 to 6 servings.

SPICY CHICKPEA SOUP

1⅓ cups (8 ozs.) chickpeas, soaked overnight, then drained
¼ cup olive oil
1 slice bread, crusts removed
1 Spanish onion, finely chopped
8 ozs. chorizo, thickly sliced
3 beefsteak tomatoes, peeled, seeded and chopped
1 tablespoon paprika
¼-½ teaspoon cumin seeds, finely crushed
1 pound fresh spinach, chopped
3 garlic cloves

Cook chickpeas in 1½ times their volume of boiling water 1½ to 2 hours or until tender.

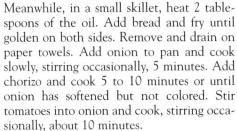

Meanwhile, in a small skillet, heat 2 table-spoons of the oil. Add bread and fry until golden on both sides. Remove and drain on paper towels. Add onion to pan and cook slowly, stirring occasionally, 5 minutes. Add chorizo and cook 5 to 10 minutes or until onion has softened but not colored. Stir tomatoes into onion and cook, stirring occasionally, about 10 minutes.

In a saucepan, heat remaining oil. Stir in paprika and cumin, then add spinach. Cook until spinach has wilted. Using a mortar and pestle, pound garlic with a pinch of salt. Add fried bread and pound again. Drain chickpeas, reserving liquid. Stir chickpeas into spinach with tomato and garlic mixtures and ¾ cup chickpea liquid. Cover pan and simmer about 30 minutes; add more liquid if mixture becomes too dry.

Makes 4 servings.

SCOTCH BROTH

2 lbs. neck of lamb, cut in pieces
6 cups light stock
¼ cup pearl barley
Salt and pepper to taste
1 large onion, chopped
2 leeks, trimmed, chopped
2 stalks celery, chopped
1 small turnip, diced
1 large carrot, sliced
Bouquet garni

In a large saucepan, combine lamb and stock. Bring slowly to a boil and skim off any scum that rises to surface.

Add barley and season with salt and pepper. Cover and simmer 2 hours. Remove meat from lamb bones. Discard fat and return meat to stock.

Add remaining ingredients to stock and bring back to a simmer. Cook 30 minutes or until vegetables are tender. Discard bouquet garni. Season again with salt and pepper, if necessary.

Makes 6 servings.

MULLIGATAWNY

1 lb. boneless beef stew meat, cut in pieces
7½ cups water
1 (2-inch) piece gingerroot, peeled
2 bay leaves
1 medium-size onion, chopped
1 teaspoon turmeric
½ teaspoon chile powder
2 teaspoons coriander seeds, crushed
2 teaspoons cumin seeds, crushed
8 black peppercorns, crushed
1 small cooking apple, peeled, cored, chopped
1 carrot, sliced
2 tablespoons red lentils
2 garlic cloves, chopped
Salt to taste
1 tablespoon lemon juice
GARLIC CROUTONS:
2 thick slices bread
¼ cup plus 2 tablespoons vegetable oil
3 garlic cloves, crushed

In a large saucepan, cover beef with water. Bring to a boil. Skim surface and add remaining ingredients except lemon juice. Simmer very gently 2½ to 3 hours or until beef is tender. Meanwhile, to prepare croutons, cut off crusts from bread and dice bread. Heat oil in a medium-size skillet. Fry diced bread and garlic, turning bread constantly until crisp and golden. Remove with a slotted spoon and drain on a paper towel.

Remove beef and set aside. Pour stock through a sieve set over a bowl, rubbing vegetables through. Discard pulp. Cool, then refrigerate meat and stock until chilled. Remove solidified fat from surface of soup. Pour into a pan and reheat. Cut beef in small pieces. Add beef and lemon juice to soup and season again with salt, if necessary. Simmer 5 minutes. Garnish soup with croutons.

Makes 4 to 6 servings.

TUSCAN BEAN SOUP

¾ cup dried red kidney beans, soaked overnight and
  drained
¾ cup dried haricot beans, soaked overnight and
  drained
2 tablespoons olive oil
1 large onion, finely chopped
2 garlic cloves, crushed
4 stalks celery, thinly sliced
1 (14-oz.) can crushed tomatoes
3¾ cups vegetable or ham stock
Salt and freshly ground pepper
1 tablespoon chopped fresh marjoram
Marjoram sprigs to garnish

MUSHROOM & BARLEY BROTH

⅓ cup barley, soaked overnight in cold water to cover
4½ cups vegetable stock
¼ cup dried cep mushrooms
⅔ cup boiling water
3 tablespoons olive oil
3 shallots, finely chopped
2 teaspoons chopped fresh thyme
5 cups sliced mixed fresh mushrooms
⅔ cup hard cider
1 bay leaf
1 teaspoon Dijon-style mustard
Salt and pepper

Put kidney and haricot beans in a large
saucepan and cover with cold water.

Bring to a boil and boil rapidly 10 minutes.
Cover and simmer 45 minutes, or until beans
are tender. Drain beans, reserving cooking
liquid. Put half the beans and some of the
cooking liquid in a blender or food processor
and purée until smooth.

Drain barley. Into a large pan, place barley
and add stock. Bring to a boil, then reduce
heat, cover and simmer 45 minutes. Soak
dried ceps in boiling water 20 minutes. Drain
ceps, reserving liquid, and chop.

Heat oil in a large saucepan. Add onion,
garlic and celery and cook over low heat,
stirring occasionally, 5 minutes or until soft.
Stir in bean purée, tomatoes, stock, and
remaining beans. Bring to a boil, reduce
heat, cover and simmer 30 minutes. Add
enough reserved cooking liquid, if necessary,
to give desired consistency. Season with salt
and pepper. Stir in marjoram, garnish with
marjoram sprigs and serve.

Makes 6 servings.

In a large pan, heat oil. Add shallots and
thyme; cook 5 minutes. Add ceps and fresh
mushrooms. Stir-fry over medium heat 5
minutes or until golden. Add cider and boil
rapidly until liquid is almost evaporated.
Add barley with stock, reserved cep liquid,
bay leaf and mustard to pan. Simmer,
covered, 1 minutes. Season with salt and
pepper and serve with whole-wheat rolls.

Makes 6 to 8 servings.

SPICY LENTIL SOUP

2 tablespoons olive oil
½ teaspoon cumin seeds
1 medium-size onion, chopped
1 garlic clove, crushed
2 carrots, chopped
2 stalks celery, chopped
½ teaspoon chile powder
½ teaspoon turmeric
1 teaspoon ground coriander
6 ozs. red lentils, washed
5 cups vegetable stock
1 bay leaf
Salt and pepper to taste
Fried onion rings and fresh tarragon sprigs to garnish

Heat oil in a large saucepan over medium heat. Add cumin seeds. When seeds begin to pop, add onion and cook until golden. Add garlic, carrots and celery and cook gently 10 minutes. Stir in all spices and cook 1 minute, then add lentils.

Pour in stock. Add bay leaf and bring to a boil. Reduce heat and simmer 1 hour. Remove bay leaf. In a food processor fitted with a metal blade or a blender, process soup to a purée. Clean pan and return purée to pan. Season with salt and pepper. Gently reheat. Garnish with fried onion rings and tarragon sprigs.

Makes 6 servings.

DUTCH PEA SOUP

8 ozs. yellow split peas, soaked overnight
6 cups water
Bouquet garni
1 bay leaf
8 slices bacon, diced
1 onion, chopped
2 leeks, chopped
1 large carrot, chopped
2 stalks celery, chopped
Salt and pepper to taste
1 (4-oz.) piece spicy or garlic sausage, diced
2 tablespoons chopped fresh parsley

Drain peas. In a large saucepan, combine peas, water, bouquet garni and bay leaf.

Bring to a boil, cover pan and simmer 2 hours. Stir in diced bacon and vegetables and simmer 1 hour.

Remove bouquet garni and bay leaf. In a food processor fitted with a metal blade or a blender, process soup to a purée. Clean pan and return purée to clean pan. Season with salt and pepper. Stir in sausage and reheat soup. Stir in chopped parsley.

Makes 6 servings.

COLD
FIRST
COURSES

TAPÉNADE

7 ozs. small ripe olives, pitted
2 ozs. capers
4 anchovy fillets
1 or 2 garlic cloves, crushed
1 tablespoon Dijon mustard
½ cup olive oil
1 teaspoon chopped fresh thyme
½-1 teaspoon fresh lemon juice
Freshly ground pepper
8 slices French bread
Chopped fresh chives to garnish

Using a pestle and mortar, pound olives, capers, anchovies, garlic and mustard to a smooth paste.

Work in a little oil, a drop at a time, then gradually add remaining oil, pounding constantly. Stir in thyme, lemon juice and pepper to taste. If necessary, adjust the consistency by adding more oil (it should be a thick, spreadable paste).

Toast bread on both sides. Spread with tapénade, garnish with chopped chives and serve.

Makes 4 to 6 servings.

Note: Tapénade can be kept in a covered container in the refrigerator for up to five days. Serve at room temperature.

ANCHOVY SPREAD

2 garlic cloves, crushed
2 (2-oz.) cans anchovies in olive oil, drained
1½ tablespoons chopped fresh basil
⅓ cup olive oil
2-3 teaspoons red wine vinegar
2 teaspoons tomato paste
Freshly ground pepper

Using a pestle and mortar, pound garlic and anchovies to form a smooth paste.

Pound in basil. Work in a little oil, a drop at a time, then gradually add remaining oil, pounding constantly.

Stir in vinegar and tomato paste and season with pepper. Serve with crudités and country bread.

Makes 4 to 6 servings.

Note: Anchovy spread can be stored in the refrigerator in a glass jar for up to five days. Stir and adjust the level of vinegar and basil to taste before serving.

HUMMUS

TZATZIKI

2 teaspoons cumin seeds
1 (15-oz.) can chickpeas, drained
¼ cup ground almonds
1 garlic clove, crushed
⅔ cup regular plain yogurt
1 tablespoon olive oil
2 teaspoons chopped fresh mint
Juice of ½ lemon
Salt and freshly ground pepper
Olive oil and cayenne pepper, to garnish
Crudités and pitta bread to serve

Heat a small heavy skillet and add cumin seeds. Dry fry, shaking pan, until seeds begin to smell aromatic.

Reserve a few cumin seeds for garnish and put remainder in a food processor or blender. Add chickpeas, ground almonds, garlic, yogurt, olive oil, mint, lemon juice, salt and pepper. Process to form a slightly grainy paste.

Transfer to a serving dish and let stand 30 minutes. Drizzle with a little olive oil and sprinkle with cayenne pepper and reserved cumin seeds. Serve with crudités and fingers of pitta bread.

Makes 4 servings.

1 cucumber
2½ teaspoons salt
1 garlic clove
1 tablespoon chopped fresh mint
1 cup plain yogurt, sheep's milk preferred
Pepper
Mint leaves to garnish
Pitta bread to serve

With a sharp knife, peel cucumber and cut into small dice. Place in a colander, sprinkle with 2 teaspoons salt and let drain 1 hour.

Pat cucumber dry with paper towels. Crush garlic with remaining salt until creamy.

In a bowl, mix together garlic, chopped mint and yogurt. Season with pepper. Stir in diced cucumber. Transfer to a serving bowl. Garnish with mint leaves and serve at once with pitta bread.

Makes 6 servings.

CREAM CHEESE WITH HERBS

TARAMASALATA

8 ozs. well-drained fromage blanc or low-fat cream
  cheese
1 tablespoon chopped fresh parsley
1 tablespoon chopped fresh chives
1 tablespoon finely chopped shallot
1 tablespoon olive oil
2 tablespoons dry white wine
1 teaspoon white wine vinegar (optional)
Salt and freshly ground pepper
¼ cup crème fraîche or whipping cream
Parsley sprigs and fresh chives to garnish

¼ pound smoked cod's roe
3 slices white bread, crusts removed
2 garlic cloves, crushed
Juice of 1 lemon
⅓ cup extra-virgin olive oil
¼ cup plain yogurt
½ teaspoon paprika
½ small onion, grated
30 to 40 cherry tomatoes and slivered ripe olives to
  serve

With a sharp knife, scrape cod's roe from skin and put into a blender or food processor fitted with the metal blade.

Beat cheese 2 or 3 minutes to lighten it. Beat in parsley, chives, shallot, oil, wine, vinegar, if using, and salt and pepper.

Soak bread in a little water, then crumble into blender or processor. Process until smooth. With the motor running, add garlic, lemon juice, olive oil, yogurt and paprika. Add more lemon juice or olive oil if necessary for flavor or consistency. Finally add onion. Process until smooth.

Lightly beat crème fraîche or cream and fold into cheese mixture. Spoon into serving bowl, cover and refrigerate. Garnish with parsley sprigs and chives and serve with crudités.

Makes 4 servings.

Cut tops off tomatoes and carefully scoop out flesh and seeds. Leave upside down on paper towels 30 minutes. Spoon taramasalata into tomatoes. Top each one with a sliver of ripe olive.

Makes 6 servings.

HERB & FETA BALLS

1 cup cream cheese (8 ozs.), softened
¾ cup crumbled feta cheese (3 ozs.)
1 garlic clove, crushed
1 teaspoon chopped fresh parsley
1 teaspoon chopped fresh mint
2 tablespoons sesame seeds, 1 tablespoon finely
   chopped fresh parsley and 1 tablespoon finely
   chopped fresh mint, to garnish
Grape leaves to serve
Kumquat or yellow tomato wedges to garnish

In a small bowl, mix together cream cheese and feta cheese until smooth. Stir in garlic, parsley and mint.

Roll cheese into 20 balls. Chill at least 1 hour. Meanwhile, toast sesame seeds for garnish: put in a skillet and heat until seeds are golden-brown, stirring frequently. Let cool.

To garnish, mix together chopped parsley and chopped mint. Roll half of the cheese balls in herbs and half in toasted sesame seeds. Serve on grape leaves and garnish with kumquat or yellow tomato wedges.

Makes 20.

PEARS WITH STILTON SAUCE

3 large pears
1 tablespoon lemon juice
Chervil leaves, to garnish
STILTON SAUCE:
½ cup crème fraîche
2 tablespoons milk
3 ozs. Stilton cheese
1 or 2 teaspoons fresh lemon juice
2 teaspoons poppy seeds
Salt and freshly ground pepper

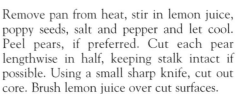

To make sauce, put crème fraîche and milk into a saucepan and heat gently. Crumble in Stilton cheese and stir until melted.

Remove pan from heat, stir in lemon juice, poppy seeds, salt and pepper and let cool. Peel pears, if preferred. Cut each pear lengthwise in half, keeping stalk intact if possible. Using a small sharp knife, cut out core. Brush lemon juice over cut surfaces.

Divide sauce among six serving plates. Slice each pear half lengthwise and arrange on top of sauce, in a fan shape. Garnish with chervil leaves and serve.

Makes 6 servings.

CHEESE & HERB TRIANGLES

¼ lb. feta cheese
½ cup cottage cheese
½ beaten egg
1 tablespoon chopped fresh parsley
1 tablespoon chopped fresh mint
1 tablespoon snipped fresh chives
Pepper
4 sheets filo pastry
¼ cup butter

Into a bowl, crumble feta cheese. Add cottage cheese, egg, parsley, mint, chives and pepper. Blend together with a fork.

Preheat oven to 375F (190C). Butter a baking sheet. Lay the sheets of dough in a pile on a work surface. Keep covered while working with one sheet at a time. In a small saucepan melt butter. Brush one sheet of dough with butter. Cut it into 4 long strips.

Place a teaspoon of filling in one corner of dough strip. Fold a corner of dough over filling. Turn triangle over and over to the end of the strip. Repeat with remaining dough. Brush tops of triangles with butter. Bake in the oven 10 to 12 minutes or until crisp and brown.

Makes 16.

RICOTTA MOLDS

1½ cups ricotta cheese (12 ozs.)
1 tablespoon finely chopped Italian parsley
1 tablespoon chopped fennel tops
1 tablespoon snipped fresh chives
1 tablespoon unflavored gelatin powder
3 tablespoons water
⅔ cup mayonnaise
Salt and freshly ground pepper
Fresh herb sprigs to garnish
BELL PEPPER SAUCE:
2 large red bell peppers, broiled, peeled and choppped
3 tablespoons extra-virgin olive oil
Few drops of balsamic vinegar
Salt and freshly ground pepper

In a bowl, mix together cheese and herbs. Oil 6 (about ½-cup) molds. In a small bowl, soften gelatin in water 5 minutes. Place bowl over a saucepan of simmering water and stir until dissolved. Cool slightly, then stir into cheese mixture with mayonnaise, salt and freshly ground pepper. Divide among oiled molds, cover and refrigerate until set.

To make sauce, put bell peppers and oil in a food processor or blender and process until smooth. Add balsamic vinegar to taste, and season with salt and freshly ground pepper. Pour into a small bowl, and refrigerate until required. Turn out ricotta molds onto individual plates and serve with sauce. Garnish with herb sprigs.

Make 6 servings.

CELERIAC RÉMOULADE

⅔ cup mayonnaise
2-3 teaspoons Dijon mustard
1 teaspoon fresh lemon juice
Salt and freshly ground pepper
1 lb. celeriac
2 tablespoons chopped fresh chervil or parsley
Lettuce leaves to serve

Put mayonnaise into a large bowl, add mustard and lemon juice to taste and season with salt and pepper. Peel and coarsely grate celeriac.

Add celeriac to a large saucepan of boiling water and cook 30 to 60 seconds. Drain celeriac and rinse under cold running water. Drain again and dry on paper towels.

Mix celeriac into mayonnaise. Spoon into lettuce leaves. Sprinkle with chervil or parsley and serve.

Makes 4 servings.

Variation: Celeriac tastes better if briefly blanched in this way, but it can also be eaten raw.

RED PEPPER VINAIGRETTE

4 red bell peppers
4 hard-cooked eggs, halved
1 (2-oz.) can anchovies in olive oil, drained
2 tablespoons capers
2 tablespoons chopped fresh flat-leaf parsley
VINAIGRETTE:
2½ tablespoons red wine vinegar
½ cup olive oil
Salt and freshly ground pepper

Preheat broiler. Place whole bell peppers on broiler rack and broil, turning occasionally, until charred and blistered all over.

Leave until cool enough to handle, then peel, working over a bowl to catch the juices. Cut bell peppers in half and discard cores and seeds. Arrange bell pepper halves on serving plates and add juices from bowl.

To make vinaigrette, whisk together vinegar, oil, salt and pepper and pour over bell peppers. Remove egg yolks from whites. Chop egg whites and scatter over bell peppers. Arrange anchovies on top and sprinkle with capers. Press egg yolks through a strainer over bell peppers, sprinkle with chopped flat-leaf parsley and serve.

Makes 4 servings.

LEEKS VINAIGRETTE

12 small leeks, white parts only
1½ tablespoons chopped fresh parsley
1 hard-cooked egg, chopped
Dill sprigs and red bell pepper strips, to garnish
VINAIGRETTE:
1 tablespoon white wine vinegar
½ teaspoon Dijon mustard
Salt and freshly ground pepper
4-5 tablespoons olive oil

Arrange leeks in a steamer, cover and steam 5 to 10 minutes or until tender. Drain on paper towels.

To make vinaigrette, whisk together vinegar, mustard, salt and pepper. Slowly add oil, whisking constantly. Transfer leeks to serving plates, add vinaigrette and let cool slightly. Sprinkle leeks with parsley and egg, garnish with dill sprigs and bell pepper strips and serve.

Makes 4 servings.

MUSHROOMS À LA GRECQUE

2 tablesppons olive oil
1 onion, finely chopped
1 garlic clove, chopped
1 tablespoon coriander seeds
1¼ cups red wine
1 tablespoon tomato paste
Bouquet garni
1 lb. button mushrooms
1¼ lbs. ripe tomatoes, peeled, seeded and chopped
Salt and freshly ground pepper
Flat-leaf parsley sprigs to garnish

Heat oil in a large skillet, add onion and garlic and cook, stirring occasionally, 7 minutes or until beginning to color.

Stir in coriander seeds, wine, tomato paste and bouquet garni. Add mushrooms, tomatoes, salt and pepper.

Bring to a boil, reduce heat and simmer 10 minutes or until mushrooms are just tender. Transfer to a bowl and let cool. Cover and refrigerate for several hours. Remove bouquet garni. Garnish with flat-leaf parsley and serve.

Makes 4 servings.

Note: A bouquet garni is a bunch of fresh herbs used to flavor a dish but removed before serving. The herbs may vary but it always includes parsley, thyme and a bay leaf.

PRAWN CRYSTAL ROLLS

8 ozs. cooked peeled shrimp
4 ozs. cooked pork, coarsely chopped
4 ozs. cooked chicken meat, coarsely chopped
2 tablespoons grated carrot
2 tablespoons chopped water chestnuts
1 tablespoon chopped preserved vegetable
1 teaspoon finely chopped garlic
2 green onions, finely chopped
1 teaspoon sugar
2 tablespoons fish sauce
Salt and freshly ground pepper
10-12 sheets dried rice paper
Flour and water paste
Fresh mint and cilantro leaves
Iceberg or leaf lettuce leaves
Spicy Fish Sauce (page 311)

Cut any large shrimp in half. In a bowl, mix shrimp, pork, chicken, grated carrot, water chestnuts, preserved vegetable, garlic, onions, sugar, fish sauce, salt and pepper. Fill a bowl with warm water, then dip the sheets of rice paper in the water one at a time. If using large sheets of rice paper, fold in half then place about 2 tablespoons of the filling onto the long end of the rice paper, fold the sides over to enclose the filling and roll up, then seal the end with a little of the flour paste. The roll will be transparent, hence the name crystal.

To serve, place some mint and cilantro in a piece of lettuce leaf with a crystal roll and wrap into a neat parcel, then dip the roll into the Spicy Fish Sauce before eating.

Makes 4 servings.

MARINATED MUSHROOMS

1 oz. dried Chinese mushrooms, soaked in hot water
   20 minutes
4 ozs. oyster mushrooms
4 ozs. button mushrooms
1 tablespoon sunflower oil
2 tablespoons light soy sauce
2 stalks celery, chopped
2 garlic cloves, thinly sliced
1 whole cinnamon stick, broken
Chopped celery leaves to garnish
MARINADE:
3 tablespoons light soy sauce
3 tablespoons dry sherry
Freshly ground pepper

Drain Chinese mushrooms and squeeze out excess water. Discard stems and thinly slice caps. Slice oyster and button mushrooms. Heat oil in a nonstick or well-seasoned wok and stir-fry all the mushrooms 2 minutes.

Add remaining ingredients except marinade and garnish and stir-fry 2 or 3 minutes or until just cooked. Transfer to a shallow dish and let cool. Mix together marinade ingredients and pour over cooled mushroom mixture. Cover and chill 1 hour. Discard cinnamon stick, garnish and serve on a bed of bean sprouts and shredded napa cabbage.

Makes 4 servings.

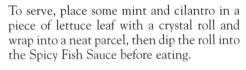

EGGS WITH ANCHOVY DRESSING

3 ozs. arugula or other lettuce leaves
4 hard-cooked eggs, halved
1 teaspoon finely chopped Italian parsley
1 teaspoon snipped fresh chives
ANCHOVY DRESSING:
5 anchovy fillets canned in oil, drained
⅓ cup mayonnaise
3-4 tablespoons milk
Freshly ground black pepper

To make dressing, put anchovy fillets in a small bowl. Mash with a fork, then blend in mayonnaise, adding milk to give a creamy consistency. Season with freshly ground black pepper.

Arrange lettuce leaves and egg halves on a serving plate. Spoon dressing over and around eggs and sprinkle with herbs.

Makes 4 servings.

SHRIMP-STUFFED EGGS

4 hard-cooked eggs, peeled
¼ cup mayonnaise
2 ozs. shelled cooked shrimps, chopped
Salt, red (cayenne) pepper and lemon juice to taste
Lettuce leaves to serve
Whole shrimp, paprika and fresh parsley sprigs to garnish

With a sharp knife, slice eggs in half lengthwise. Using a teaspoon, scoop the yolks into a bowl, reserving the whites.

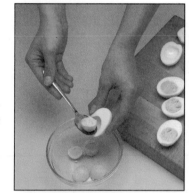

Add mayonnaise to yolks and, using a fork, mash with the yolks and shrimp. Add salt, cayenne and lemon juice.

Divide shrimp mixture among egg whites. Arrange on lettuce leaves and garnish with whole shrimp, paprika and parsley sprigs.

Makes 4 servings.

FENNEL & DOLCELATTE

3 medium-size fennel bulbs
1 tablespoon fennel seeds, lightly crushed
¼ cup extra-virgin olive oil
Juice of ½ lemon
Pinch of sugar
Salt and freshly ground pepper
1 cup crumbled dolcelatte cheese

Trim fennel, reserving green feathery tops. Add whole bulbs to saucepan of boiling salted water. Cook 5 minutes, then drain. Refresh under cold running water, drain well and pat dry with paper towels. Set aside. Chop reserved fennel tops and set aside.

In a small skillet over medium heat, dry-fry seeds 2 to 3 minutes to brown and release aroma. Remove from heat and stir in olive oil, lemon juice, sugar, salt and freshly ground pepper.

Thinly slice fennel bulbs and arrange in a shallow serving dish. Add oil and fennel seed mixture. Sprinkle with cheese and reserved fennel tops. Let stand 30 minutes. Toss lightly before serving.

Makes 4 to 6 servings.

GINGERED MELONS

½ honeydew melon
½ cantaloupe melon
1 (4-oz.) can water chestnuts, rinsed
1 (1-inch) piece fresh gingerroot, peeled and finely
  chopped
¼ cup dry sherry
4 pieces stem ginger in syrup, sliced
2 tablespoons dried melon seeds

Using a spoon, scoop out the seeds from both melons. Cut in half, peel away skin and thinly slice melon flesh. Slice water chestnuts.

Arrange melon slices on serving plates and top with sliced water chestnuts.

Mix together chopped ginger, dry sherry and stem ginger with its syrup and spoon over melon and water chestnuts. Cover and chill 30 minutes. Sprinkle with melon seeds and serve.

Makes 4 servings.

GREEN & GOLD ROULADE

1 lb. carrots, sliced
½ cup cream cheese, softened
Salt and freshly ground pepper
1 lb. frozen chopped spinach
4 eggs, separated
Large pinch of grated nutmeg
Flat-leaf parsley sprigs and carrot ribbons to garnish
HERB SAUCE:
¾ cup crème fraîche
1 tablespoon chopped fresh parsley
3 tablespoons chopped fresh chives
Chopped fresh chives to garnish

Cook carrots in a saucepan of boiling salted water 15 minutes or until tender. Drain.

Purée carrots in a blender or food processor. Add cream cheese, salt and pepper and process until well blended. Set aside.

Preheat oven to 400F (205C). Lightly oil a 13- x 9-inch jelly roll pan and line with parchment paper. Lightly oil parchment paper. Cook spinach according to package directions. Drain well, pressing out as much water as possible. Place in a bowl and let cool slightly. Stir in egg yolks, nutmeg, salt and pepper.

In a large bowl, whisk egg whites until soft peaks form, then fold into spinach mixture. Gently spread into prepared pan and bake 15 to 20 minutes or until firm.

Meanwhile, make herb sauce. Mix together crème fraîche, parsley and chives, cover and refrigerate until required. Gently reheat carrot mixture without boiling. Turn spinach roll onto a sheet of parchment paper, peel off lining paper and spread spinach roll with carrot mixture.

Roll up by gently lifting parchment paper. Garnish herb sauce with chopped chives. Garnish roulade with flat-leaf parsley and carrot ribbons, slice and serve on warmed plates with herb sauce.

Makes 6 servings.

ASPARAGUS NIÇOISE

1 tablespoon lemon juice
1 lb. asparagus spears
8 ozs. cherry tomatoes, halved
12 black olives, pitted and halved
Basil sprigs, to garnish
DRESSING:
1 teaspoon Dijon mustard
1 tablespoon white wine vinegar
Salt and freshly ground pepper
⅓ cup extra-virgin olive oil
1 hard-cooked egg, finely chopped

Add lemon juice to a saucepan of boiling salted water. Snap tough ends from asparagus. Tie spears in a bundle.

Stand bundle upright in pan so that tips stand out of water. Cover with a dome of foil and simmer 10 minutes or until tender. Drain well and let cool. Take 16 stalks and cut in half lengthwise, cutting as far as bottom of tip so that tip remains intact. Cut remaining stalks into 1-inch lengths and put in a bowl with tomatoes and olives.

Arrange four asparagus spears on each of four serving plates to make a square, with a tip at each corner and halved stalks splayed out at right angles. To make dressing, whisk together mustard, vinegar, salt and pepper then whisk in oil. Stir in chopped hard-cooked egg. Pour dressing over tomato and asparagus mixture and toss together. Arrange mixture in center of asparagus squares. Garnish with basil sprigs and serve.

Makes 4 servings.

AVOCADO & RED CURRANTS

3 ripe avocados
Red currants, to garnish
DRESSING:
6 ozs. red currants
2 tablespoons balsamic vinegar
½ cup light olive oil or sunflower oil
Salt and freshly ground pepper
½ to 1 teaspoon sugar

To make dressing, purée red currants in a blender or food processor. Press through a nylon strainer to remove seeds.

Return red currant purée to blender with vinegar. With motor running, gradually pour in oil. Season with salt and pepper and add sugar to taste.

Halve avocados lengthwise. Remove pits and peel. Thinly slice flesh lengthwise. Fan out slices on serving plates. Stir dressing and pour around avocados. Garnish with red currants and serve immediately.

Makes 6 servings.

Note: Be sure to use a nylon strainer as a metal one may taint the flavor of the red currants.

CAPONATA

2 eggplant
Salt and freshly ground pepper
½ cup olive oil
1 onion, finely chopped
1 garlic clove, chopped
4 stalks celery, sliced, leaves reserved for garnish
1 (14-oz.) can crushed tomatoes
2 teaspoons sugar
2 tablespoons balsamic vinegar
1 tablespoon pine nuts, lightly toasted
1 tablespoon capers
12 pitted ripe olives, halved

Cut eggplant into ¼-inch thick slices.

Place eggplant in a colander, sprinkle generously with salt and leave 1 hour. Preheat oven to 300F (150C). Heat 2 table-spoons olive oil in a saucepan, add onion and garlic and cook, stirring occasionally, 5 minutes or until soft. Add celery and cook, stirring occasionally, another 5 minutes. Stir in tomatoes, sugar and vinegar and bring to a boil. Simmer, uncovered, 15 to 20 minutes or until thickened. Season with salt and pepper and stir in pine nuts, capers and olives.

Rinse eggplant thoroughly and pat dry with paper towels. Arrange in a shallow oven-proof dish. Spoon a little tomato mixture onto each eggplant slice. Drizzle remaining oil over and around eggplant. Cover with foil and cook in oven 45 to 60 minutes or until eggplant are tender. Let cool. Garnish with celery leaves and serve at room temperature.

Makes 6 servings.

PÂTÉ DE CAMPAGNE

12 ozs. veal or chicken, finely chopped
1½ lbs. lean unsmoked bacon, finely chopped
8 ozs. calf or lamb liver, finely chopped
2 tablespoons butter
2 small onions, finely chopped
10 ozs. ham, chopped
3 or 4 garlic cloves, finely chopped
2 tablespoons chopped fresh parsley
2 teaspoons herbes de Provence
2 teaspoons freshly ground pepper
2 teaspoons salt
½ teaspoon ground allspice
½ cup dry white wine
2 tablespoons brandy

Put veal or chicken, bacon and liver into a bowl. Melt butter in a saucepan and cook onions, stirring occasionally, 7 minutes or until lightly browned. Add onions to meats with all remaining ingredients and mix well. Cover and refrigerate 2 hours. Preheat oven to 325F (165C).

Pack pâté mixture into a 7½-cup terrine. Cover with foil. Put into a roasting pan and pour in enough boiling water to come three-quarters of the way up sides of terrine. Bake 1½ hours. To test if cooked, insert a skewer in center and count to 5. If skewer feels hot when withdrawn, the pâté is cooked. Remove from roasting pan and let cool. Put weights on top and refrigerate for a few hours. Turn out, slice and serve.

Makes 10 to 12 servings.

RATATOUILLE TERRINE

12 large spinach or Swiss chard leaves
Salt and freshly ground pepper
3 yellow bell peppers, quartered
3 red bell peppers, quartered
1 garlic clove, crushed
½ cup olive oil
2 eggplant
4 zucchini
Red and yellow bell pepper strips and flat-leaf parsley
 sprigs to garnish
2 tomatoes, peeled, seeded and diced, to serve
TOMATO VINAIGRETTE:
1 large ripe tomato
4 teaspoons balsamic vinegar
½ cup olive oil

Put a layer of yellow bell peppers in bottom of lined terrine, then add a layer of red bell peppers, followed by layers of eggplant, zucchini, red bell pepper, eggplant, zucchini, finishing with a layer of yellow bell pepper. Lightly season each layer with salt and pepper.

Remove spinach stems and rinse leaves thoroughly. Blanch spinach in boiling water 1 minute. Drain, rinse in cold water and drain again. Spread spinach leaves on a clean dish towel, place another dish towel on top and pat dry. Line a 4½-cup terrine or loaf pan with plastic wrap. Line terrine with blanched spinach leaves, leaving ends overhanging sides of terrine. Season lightly with salt and pepper.

Fold overhanging spinach over top of terrine. Cover with plastic wrap. Press down with a weight and refrigerate 8 hours.

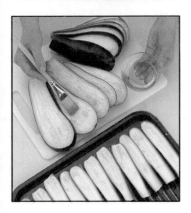

Preheat broiler. Broil and peel bell peppers. Mix together garlic and olive oil. Cut zucchini and eggplant lengthwise into ½-inch slices. Brush with garlic oil and broil on both sides until soft and beginning to brown.

To make tomato vinaigrette, put tomato, vinegar, olive oil, salt and pepper in a blender or food processor and process until smooth. Press through a strainer. Turn terrine onto a serving dish and remove plastic wrap. Garnish with bell pepper strips. Slice terrine with a very sharp knife, garnish with flat-leaf parsley and serve with tomato vinaigrette and diced tomato.

Makes 6 to 8 servings.

TUNA PÂTÉ

3 tablespoons butter
4 green onions, white part only, chopped
2 celery stalks, finely chopped
1 (7-oz.) can tuna in water, drained
2 tomatoes, peeled, seeded and chopped
2 tablespoons mayonnaise
1 teaspoon lemon juice
1 teaspoon white wine vinegar
Salt and freshly ground pepper
Chopped Italian parsley, parsley leaves and pitted
  green olives to garnish
Crusty bread or toast to serve

Melt butter in a small skillet over low heat. Add green onions and celery; cook 5 minutes to soften. Let cool.

Put green onion mixture in a blender or food processor with remaining ingredients, except garnish and bread. Process until fairly smooth. Transfer to a serving dish, cover and refrigerate at least 30 minutes. Garnish with chopped parsley, parsley leaves and green olives and serve with crusty bread or toast.

Makes 4 to 6 servings.

SMOKED TROUT MOUSSE

1¼ lbs. thinly sliced smoked salmon
5 ozs. cream cheese, softened
⅔ cup regular plain yogurt
Juice of ½ lemon
Salt and freshly ground pepper
Pinch of cayenne pepper
Tarragon sprigs to garnish
CUCUMBER VINAIGRETTE:
⅓ cup light olive oil
Juice of lemon
1 tablespoon chopped fresh tarragon
⅛ cucumber, seed and finely diced

Line 6 (½-cup) ramekins with plastic wrap. Line with half the smoked salmon.

Put remaining smoked salmon into a blender or food processor with cream cheese, yogurt, lemon juice, salt and cayenne. Process until smooth. Spoon into lined ramekins, cover and refrigerate at least 4 hours.

To make vinaigrette, whisk together oil and lemon juice. Stir in tarragon, cucumber, salt and pepper. Turn each mousse out onto a serving plate and remove plastic wrap. Garnish with garragon sprigs and serve with cucumber vinaigrette.

Makes 6 servings.

POTTED SHRIMP

¾ lb. shelled cooked small shrimp
Salt
Red (cayenne) pepper, to taste
1 teaspoon lemon juice
½ teaspoon ground ginger
¾ cup butter
1 tablespoon finely chopped fresh chives
Chives to garnish
French bread or buttered toast to serve

SALMON MILLE FEUILLES

¾ cup plain yogurt, chilled
¾ teaspoon chopped dill
Salt and pepper
8 sheets filo pastry dough
Melted butter
4 ozs. smoked salmon trimmings, ground
2 tablespoons heavy cream, well chilled
1 bunch chives, roughly snipped
12 large slices smoked salmon
Dill sprigs to garnish
Lemon wedges to serve

If using thawed, frozen shrimp, pat dry with paper towels.

In a bowl, mix together half of the yogurt, the dill, salt, and pepper. Cover and chill. Preheat oven to 425F (220C). Cut twenty-four 3-inch circles from filo pastry. Lay half the circles on a baking sheet, brush with melted butter, then cover each circle with another. Brush with melted butter and bake 5 minutes until golden. Transfer to a wire rack to cool. Into a blender or food processor, put salmon trimmings. With motor running, slowly pour in cream and remaining yogurt until just evenly mixed. Add chives and pepper to taste.

In a bowl, combine shrimp, salt, cayenne, lemon juice and ginger. Cover and refrigerate. In a saucepan, melt butter over very low heat. Pour the clear liquid into a bowl, leaving the milky residue in pan to be discarded. Stir chopped chives into clear liquid. Let stand 20 minutes.

Divide shrimp among 6 small ramekin dishes. Spoon chive butter over, pressing shrimp down until covered with butter. Cover and refrigerate until firm. Garnish with chives, and serve with French bread or toast.

Makes 6 servings.

Cut salmon into twelve 3-inch circles. Place pastry circle on a plate, spread with 1/12 of the smoked salmon cream, then cover with a smoked salmon circle. Repeat twice more to make one mille feuille. Make 3 more mille feuille in the same way. Chill. Serve garnished with dill sprigs and accompanied by sauce and lemon wedges.

Makes 4 servings.

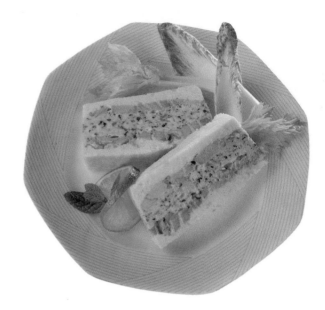

LAYERED FISH TERRINE

1 lb. salmon, skinned and boned
Salt and white pepper
⅔ cup medium-dry white wine
2 small bunches watercress, trimmed
1 tablespoon butter
1 shallot, finely chopped
1 lb. firm white fish, such as hake, monkfish, or cod,
    skinned, boned, and cubed
2 egg whites
1 cup whipping cream, chilled
Lime slices and mint sprigs to garnish

In a small saucepan, melt butter. Add shallot and cook over low heat until softened but not browned. In a blender or food processor, purée shallot with fish. Add egg whites and season with salt and pepper. Process 1 minute, then, with motor running, slowly pour in cream. Remove and reserve two-thirds of fish mixture. Add watercress to blender or food processor and purée briefly. Chill both mixtures 30 minutes.

Cut salmon into long strips. Put salmon strips into a dish. Season with salt and white pepper and pour wine over salmon. Cover and refrigerate about 1 hour.

Preheat oven to 350F (175C). Lightly oil a 10- x 3½-inch terrine pan. Spread half the plain fish mixture in the bottom of the pan, then half the salmon strips followed by all the green mixture. Cover this with remaining salmon strips, then remaining white mixture.

Meanwhile, bring a saucepan of lightly salted water to a boil. Add watercress and blanch 1 minutes. Drain watercress, rinse under cold running water, and drain again. Dry on paper towels; set aside.

Cover terrine with foil. In a roasting pan, place terrine and pour in enough boiling water to come halfway up sides of terrine. Bake about 40 minutes until a skewer inserted in center comes out clean. Transfer terrine to a wire rack to cool slightly, then refrigerate. Cut into slices and serve garnished with lime slices and sprigs of mint.

Makes 4 to 6 servings.

CHICKEN WITH GREEN SAUCE

SPINACH ROLL

1 lb. cooked chicken breasts
Mixed lettuce leaves
Italian parsley sprigs to garnish
SAUCE:
1 bunch Italian parsley
8 basil sprigs
1 (2-oz.) can anchovy fillets in oil, drained
1 shallot, chopped
2 garlic cloves, crushed
3 tablespoons white wine vinegar
1 teaspoon Dijon-style mustard
¼ cup fresh bread crumbs
Freshly ground pepper
½ cup extra-virgin olive oil

1 tablespoon garlic-and-herb-flavored butter
1 (8-oz.) package frozen spinach, thawed, drained
Salt and pepper
Freshly grated nutmeg
2 large eggs, separated
2 tablespoons grated Parmesan cheese
FILLING:
¼ cup mayonnaise
1 tablespoon creamed horseradish sauce
1⅓ cups finely shredded smoked chicken
1 teaspoon finely grated lemon peel
1 large red bell pepper, chopped
Watercress to garnish

To make sauce, using a blender or food processor, process all sauce ingredients, except olive oil, to a smooth paste. With motor running, slowly pour in oil to make a thick but pourable consistency.

Preheat oven to 400F (205C). Grease a 13- x 9-inch baking pan; line with greased parchment paper. In a saucepan, melt butter. Add the spinach and cook 1 minute, then season with salt, pepper and nutmeg. In a blender or food processor, process spinach mixture until puréed. Add egg yolks; process to combine. In a small bowl, beat egg whites until stiff; gently fold into spinach mixture. Into prepared pan, spoon spinach mixture and level surface. Bake 7 to 10 minutes until springy to the touch.

Slice the chicken and arrange with lettuce leaves on a serving plate or individual plates. Pour sauce over and around the chicken. Garnish with parsley sprigs.

Makes 4 to 6 servings.

Sprinkle Parmesan cheese over a large piece of parchment paper. Turn out roll onto parchment paper, remove lining paper, trim roll edges and roll up loosely. Let cool. In a small bowl, mix together mayonnaise, horse-radish, chicken, lemon peel and chopped pepper. Unroll roll, spread with the chicken filling and re-roll. Cut into slices to serve. Garnish with watercress.

Makes 4 servings.

PROSCIUTTO WITH FIGS

12 paper-thin slices prosciutto
4-6 ripe figs
Fresh Italian parsley leaves or mint sprigs to garnish

ITALIAN MEAT PLATTER

4 ozs. thinly sliced mixed salamis
2 ozs. thinly sliced mortadella
2 ozs. thinly sliced prosciutto or coppa
2 ozs. thinly sliced bresaola
2 large pickles
1 small bunch radishes, trimmed
6 ozs. cherry tomatoes
¾ cup ripe olives or green olives
Lettuce leaves
Italian parsley leaves to garnish
DRESSING:
5 tablespoons extra-virgin olive oil
2 tablespoons lemon juice
1 tablespoon red wine vinegar
1 teaspoon Dijon-style mustard
Salt and freshly ground pepper

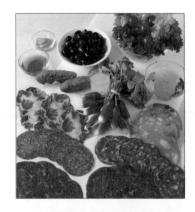

Arrange prosciutto on a platter or individual plates.

Arrange meats on a large platter. Thinly slice pickles on the diagonal and add to platter with radishes, tomatoes, olives and lettuce leaves.

Halve figs lengthwise, then cut into quarters, and arrange beside ham. Serve garnished with parsley leaves or mint sprigs.

Makes 4 servings.

To make dressing, mix all ingredients together in a small bowl and serve with meat platter. Garnish with parsley leaves.

Makes 6 to 8 servings.

Note: The selection of meats can be varied to include your favorites. Serve with crusty bread, bread rolls or bread sticks.

CHICKEN LIVER PÂTÉ

1 lb. chicken livers
1 cup unsalted butter
1 garlic clove, crushed
2 tablespoons brandy
2 tablespoons port wine
Salt and pepper
2 tablespoons red currant jelly

Soak chicken livers in cold water 1 hour. Drain and remove membranes. In a skillet, heat 2 tablespoons of the butter. Add livers and fry 2 minutes, then add garlic and cook 2 to 3 minutes or until livers are cooked through, but still pink in center.

Cut remaining butter into cubes. Add to pan. Remove pan from heat. Leave butter to melt over livers. Meanwhile, into a small pan, put brandy and port wine. Boil rapidly about 1½ minutes or until the liquid is reduced to a syrup; do not burn or the flavor of the pâté will be ruined.

Add wine mixture to livers. Season with salt and pepper and cool 15 minutes. Into a food processor or blender, put liver mixture. Blend until you have a smooth pâté. Pour into 8 individual ramekins or 1 large serving dish. Melt red currant jelly and pour over pâté. Cover and refrigerate at least 3 to 4 hours before serving.

Makes 8 servings.

PORK & LIVER PÂTÉ

12 ozs. bacon slices
8 ozs. lean pork, chopped
8 ozs. pork liver, chopped
8 ozs. pork sausage
1 small onion, finely chopped
2 garlic cloves, chopped
1 tablespoon chopped thyme
1 tablespoon chopped oregano
3 tablespoons Marsala wine
Salt and freshly ground pepper
Thyme and oregano sprigs to garnish

Preheat oven to 325F (165C). Grease an 8- x 4-inch loaf pan. Lay bacon slices flat on a board and stretch using the back of a knife.

Line the loaf pan, with the bacon slices, reserving a few slices to cover the top. Place pork in a blender or food processor and process until finely chopped. Add remaining ingredients and process briefly until well blended but not smooth. Put pork mixture into loaf pan, smooth top and cover with reserved bacon. Cover tightly with oiled foil.

Place loaf pan in a roasting pan half-filled with boiling water. Cook in preheated oven 1½ to 1¾ hours until firm. Remove foil. Cover pâté with waxed paper, then put a plate or board and a heavy weight on top; refrigerate overnight before turning out. Slice to serve and garnish with herb sprigs.

Makes 6 to 8 servings.

CHICKEN & HAM MOUSSE

LAYERED COUNTRY TERRINE

1⅓ cups finely ground cooked chicken
1 cup finely ground cooked ham
1 tablespoon fresh lemon juice
1 tablespoon chopped fresh parsley
1 tablespoon snipped fresh chives
⅔ cup mayonnaise
2 teaspoons unflavored gelatin powder
3 tablespoons chicken stock
⅔ cup whipping cream
Chives and lemon wedges to garnish

In a bowl, mix chicken with ham, lemon juice, chopped herbs and mayonnaise.

In a small pan, sprinkle gelatin over chicken stock; leave 5 minutes to soften. Over low heat, melt very gently until gelatin dissolves. Remove from heat; cool. Fold into ham and chicken mixture.

In a medium-size bowl, with an electric mixer, lightly beat cream to form soft peaks. Carefully fold into chicken and ham mixture. Pour mixture into a 4½-cup mold; cover and refrigerate 2 to 3 hours or until set. Unmold carefully on a plate and garnish with chives and lemons. Serve with hot crusty rolls.

Makes 4 servings.

8 bacon slices
4 ozs. chicken livers
4 ozs. ground pork
4 ozs. pork sausage
1 garlic clove
1 onion, finely chopped
3 tablespoons chopped fresh parsley
½ cup fresh white bread crumbs
¼ cup brandy
1 egg, beaten
¼ teaspoon freshly grated nutmeg
1 teaspoon finely grated lemon peel
Salt and pepper
2 skinned and boned chicken breast halves
1 bay leaf
Parsley to garnish

Preheat oven to 350F (175C). On a chopping board, place bacon. Stretch with the back of a knife. Use 4 of the slices to line a 5-cup loaf pan, reserving 4 slices for top. With a sharp knife, roughly chop chicken livers. Mix together with pork, sausage, garlic, onion and parsley. In a small bowl, soak bread crumbs in brandy, then add to meat mixture. Beat in egg, nutmeg, lemon peel, salt and pepper.

Over bacon in pan, spread one-third of the meat mixture. Cut chicken into thin slices; layer half over meat mixture. Cover with half the remaining meat mixture, then cover with remaining chicken and remaining meat mixture. Lay reserved bacon on top and add bay leaf. Cover with foil. In a baking pan three-quarters full of boiling water, place terrine. Bake 1½ hours. Remove from oven and cool. Cut into slices; garnish with parsley. Serve with crusty bread.

Makes 4 to 6 servings.

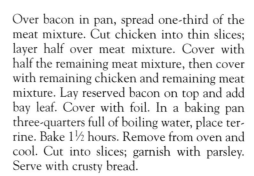

HOT
FIRST
COURSES

GOAT CHEESE SOUFFLÉS

BAKED EGGS WITH RICOTTA

Scant cup milk
1 shallot, finely chopped
1 bay leaf
6 black peppercorns
3 tablespoons butter
⅓ cup all-purpose flour
4 ozs. goat cheese
3 eggs, separated
1 tablespoon chopped fresh chives
Salt and freshly ground pepper
⅔ cup whipping cream
¼ cup coarsely grated Parmesan cheese
Mâche and hazelnuts to garnish

2 tablespoons butter, melted
½ cup ricotta cheese
2 teaspoons snipped fresh chives
4 eggs
½ cup whipping cream
Salt and freshly ground pepper
Whole chives to garnish

Preheat oven to 350F (175C). Use butter to grease 4 small individual heatproof dishes. Divide ricotta cheese among dishes, levelling surface with a teaspoon. Sprinkle cheese with chives.

Preheat oven to 350F (180C). Butter 6 (⅔ cup) ramekins. Put milk, shallot, bay leaf and peppercorns into a saucepan and bring slowly to a boil. Strain into a cup. Melt butter in a saucepan, add flour and cook, stirring, 2 minutes. Remove from heat and gradually stir in warm milk. Simmer 3 minutes. Crumble in goat cheese and stir until melted. Stir some sauce into egg yolks. Stir yolk mixture, chives, salt and pepper into sauce. Remove from heat. Whisk egg whites until holding soft peaks and fold into sauce.

Break an egg into each dish and top with cream. Season with salt and freshly ground pepper.

Spoon into prepared ramekins. Stand dishes in a roasting pan and pour boiling water into pan to come one-third up sides of ramekins. Bake 15 to 20 minutes or until firm. Let cool. When ready to serve, preheat oven to 400F (205C). Run a knife round sides of ramekins and turn soufflés into a shallow ovenproof dish. Add cream, sprinkle with Parmesan cheese and bake 10 to 15 minutes or until golden. Garnish with mâche and hazelnuts and serve.

Makes 6 servings.

Place dishes in a shallow baking pan half-filled with warm water. Bake in preheated oven 10 to 12 minutes until eggs are cooked as desired. Garnish with whole chives.

Makes 4 servings.

FETA & HERB POPOVERS

1 tablespoon vegetable oil
Scant cup milk
1 tablespoon melted butter
2 eggs, beaten
¾ cup all-purpose flour
2 teaspoons chopped fresh chives
2 teaspoons chopped fresh parsley
Salt and freshly ground pepper
4 ozs. feta cheese, cut into 24 cubes
Flat-leaf parsley and chopped fresh chives to garnish
MANGO SAUCE:
2 tablespoons mango chutney
¾ cup regular plain yogurt

FAVA BEANS WITH GOAT CHEESE

¼ cup extra-virgin olive oil
1 onion, chopped
2 lbs. fresh fava beans, shelled, or 12 ozs. frozen
   fava beans, thawed
1 tablespoon chopped rosemary
Salt and freshly ground pepper
2 heads Belgian endive or 1 head radicchio
1 (8-oz.) goat cheese log, sliced
Rosemary sprigs to garnish

Heat oil in a large skillet, add onion and cook over medium heat about 10 minutes until soft and golden. Stir in beans and rosemary.

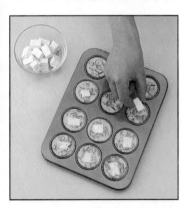

Preheat oven to 425F (220C). Brush cups in 2 (12-cup) mini muffin pans with oil and put into the oven to heat. Stir milk and melted butter into eggs. Sift flour into egg mixture and whisk together to make a smooth batter. Stir in chives, parsley, salt and pepper. Fill each muffin cup with batter. Put a cube of feta cheese in the center of each one and bake 20 to 25 minutes or until puffed and golden.

Add enough water to just cover beans and season with salt and freshly ground pepper. Bring to a boil, reduce heat, cover and simmer 12 to 15 minutes, stirring frequently, until beans are very tender and liquid is absorbed.

Meanwhile, make mango sauce. Put mango chutney in a bowl, chopping any large pieces of fruit. Stir in yogurt. Arrange popovers on serving plates. Garnish with flat-leaf parsley and chives and serve with mango sauce.

Makes 6 servings.

Preheat broiler. Slice endive or radicchio and stir into hot beans. Lay cheese slices on top of bean mixture. Put skillet under hot broiler 2 to 3 minutes until cheese is browned. Serve hot garnished with rosemary sprigs.

Makes 4 to 6 servings.

CARROT & GINGER SOUFFLÉS

½ cup blanched almonds, finely ground and toasted
2 cups chopped carrots
1 tablespoon olive oil
1 small onion, finely chopped
2 teaspoons grated gingerroot
3 tablespoons butter or margarine
3 tablespoons all-purpose flour
1 cup milk
2 cups shredded vegetarian Cheddar cheese
½ cup shredded vegetarian Cheshire cheese
3 eggs, separated

Preheat oven to 375F (190C); lightly oil 8 (1-cup) ramekins.

Sprinkle inside of each ramekin with ground almonds to coat sides. Shake out excess and reserve. In a pan of boiling water, cook carrots 15 minutes or until soft. In a small pan, heat oil. Add onion and gingerroot; cook 10 minutes or until softened. Drain carrots. In a blender or food processor, purée carrots and onion mixture until smooth.

In a small pan, melt butter. Stir in flour and cook 1 minute. Gradually add milk; cook, stirring, until thickened. Remove from heat. Stir in cheese. Cool and beat in egg yolks, carrot purée and remaining almonds. Stiffly beat egg whites and fold into cheese mixture. Spoon into prepared ramekins. Place in a roasting pan and add enough boiling water to come two-thirds the way up sides of dishes. Bake 30 minutes or until browned, then serve at once.

Makes 8 servings.

PARMESAN ASPARAGUS

¼ cup olive oil
1½ teaspoons coarse sea salt
1½ lbs. asparagus
Freshly ground pepper
2 hard-cooked eggs, chopped
2 ozs. Parmesan cheese
Lemon wedges

Preheat oven to 350F (180C). Grease an ovenproof dish with a little of the olive oil. Sprinkle with half the salt.

Snap woody ends off asparagus stalks and peel tough skin from bottom 2 inches of stalks, if necessary. Arrange asparagus in prepared dish and drizzle with remaining oil. Turn asparagus in oil and sprinkle with remaining salt. Roast 10 to 15 minutes or until tender. Transfer to warmed serving plates.

Season with pepper and sprinkle with chopped eggs. Using a vegetable peeler, shave curls of Parmesan over asparagus. Serve immediately with lemon wedges.

Makes 6 servings.

BAKED EGGPLANT LAYERS

2 large eggplant
Salt
2 red bell peppers, peeled
⅓ cup olive oil
10 ozs. mozzarella cheese, thinly sliced
Oregano leaves, to garnish
TOMATO SAUCE:
2 tablespoons olive oil
2 garlic cloves, crushed
1½ lbs. plum tomatoes, peeled and chopped
2 teaspoons chopped fresh oregano
Salt and freshly ground pepper

Preheat broiler. Rinse eggplant well, drain and dry thoroughly with paper towels. Arrange on a rack in a baking pan. Brush with ¼ cup of the olive oil and broil on both sides until soft and beginning to brown.

Cut eggplant into ½-inch-thick slices. Place in a colander, sprinkle generously with salt and leave 1 hour. Cut bell peppers into thin strips.

Preheat oven to 350F (180C). Place half the eggplant slices on a baking sheet. Arrange mozzarella slices on top, cutting to fit if necessary. Top with half the pepper strips. Place remaining eggplant slices on top. Drizzle with remaining olive oil.

To make tomato sauce, heat olive oil in a skillet. Add garlic and cook a few minutes or until soft. Add tomatoes, oregano, salt and pepper and cook over low heat, stirring, 2 minutes, without allowing tomatoes to lose their texture. Keep warm.

Bake 3 to 5 minutes or until heated through, but do not allow cheese to melt. Arrange remaining strips of bell pepper on top, garnish with oregano leaves and serve with tomato sauce.

Makes 6 servings.

EGG & SPINACH CUPS

½ lb. spinach
2 tablespoons butter or margarine, diced
1 cup vegetarian blue cheese, crumbled
½ cup whipping cream
Pinch of grated nutmeg
Salt and pepper
4 eggs
4 dill sprigs, to garnish
French bread slices to serve

Preheat oven to 375F (190C); lightly butter 4 ramekins. Rinse spinach and discard any thick stems.

In a large pan, cook spinach with only the water that clings to leaves 1 to 2 minutes or until just wilted. Drain, squeeze out excess liquid and chop finely. Transfer to a bowl. Beat in butter and cheese until melted, then stir in ⅓ cup of the cream, the nutmeg, salt and pepper.

Divide mixture among ramekins. Make a small hollow in center of each one. Break an egg into each hollow and spoon remaining cream over eggs. Place in a roasting pan. Pour in enough boiling water to come two-thirds up sides of ramekins. Bake 20 to 30 minutes or until eggs feel firm to the touch. Serve hot with French bread and garnish with dill sprigs.

Makes 4 servings.

WATERCRESS CUSTARDS

2 red bell peppers
2 tablespoons olive oil
½ cup vegetable stock
1 tablespoon butter or margarine
4 cups watercress leaves
3 eggs
¾ cup whipping cream
½ cup finely shredded vegetarian Cheddar cheese
1 teaspoon Dijon-style mustard
Salt and pepper

Preheat oven to 400F (205C). Roast peppers 20 to 25 minutes until skins are lightly charred. Transfer to a plastic bag and let cool 30 minutes. Peel peppers, discard seeds, reserving any juices. In a blender or food processor, purée peppers and juices with oil and stock to form a smooth sauce. Press purée through strainer into a small pan. Reduce oven temperature to 350F (165C); grease 6 molds.

In a skillet, melt butter. Add watercress; cook 1 minute or until just wilted. In a blender or food processor, purée watercress. Add eggs, cream, cheese, mustard, salt and pepper; process until smooth. Pour into molds. Place in a roasting pan and pour in enough boiling water to come two-thirds up sides of molds. Bake 25 minutes or until firm in centers. Let rest 5 minutes, then unmold. Serve warm with reheated pepper sauce.

Makes 6 servings.

MUSHROOMS WITH ANCHOVIES

½ cup crumbled fresh bread without crusts
¼ cup milk
1 lb. medium-size flat button mushrooms
4 bacon slices, finely chopped
4 canned anchovy fillets, finely chopped
1 garlic clove, finely chopped
1 egg, beaten
3 tablespoons finely chopped fresh parsley
Pinch of chopped fresh oregano
Salt and pepper
¼ cup dry bread crumbs
¼ cup olive oil
Fresh oregano to garnish

Preheat oven to 400F (205C). Oil a large baking sheet. Into a small bowl put bread. Add milk and let soak. Remove stems from mushrooms and chop finely. Put into a bowl with bacon, anchovy fillets, garlic, egg, parsley, oregano, salt and pepper. Squeeze soaked bread dry, add to bacon mixture and mix together well.

Divide bread mixture among mushrooms, piling mixture into small mounds. Place on baking sheet and sprinkle with bread crumbs. Drizzle oil over mushrooms. Bake on top shelf of oven 20 to 30 minutes or until top of stuffing is crisp. Let stand a few minutes before serving; garnish with oregano.

Makes 4 to 6 servings.

ZUCCHINI TIMBALES

1½ lbs. zucchini
3 eggs, beaten
1 tablespoon chopped fresh basil
½ cup ricotta cheese
Salt and freshly ground pepper
TOMATO SALSA:
12 ozs. tomatoes, peeled and diced
1 red onion, finely chopped
1 tablespoon chopped fresh basil
1 tablespoon olive oil
1 teaspoon lime juice

To make tomato salsa, mix together tomatoes, onion, basil, olive oil, lime juice, salt and pepper. Refrigerate until required.

Oil 6 (½-cup) ramekins. Trim ends from zucchini. Using a vegetable peeler, cut very thin ribbons from two of the zucchini. Cut remaining zucchini into slices. Steam ribbons over boiling water 2 minutes or until soft. Spread on paper towels and pat dry. Steam sliced zucchini 3 to 5 minutes or until soft. Preheat oven to 400F (205C).

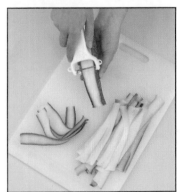

Press out as much moisture as possible from zucchini slices and place in a blender or food processor with eggs, basil, ricotta, salt and pepper. Process to a coarse purée. Line ramekins with zucchini strips. Fill with purée, fold ends of zucchini strips over filling and cover with foil. Place ramekins in a roasting pan and pour in ½-inch boiling water. Bake 10 to 15 minutes or until set. Leave 5 minutes, turn out and serve with tomato salsa.

Makes 6 servings.

BAKED MUSHROOMS

⅓ cup shredded coconut
6 large open cap mushrooms
⅓ cup butter or margarine, softened, or olive oil
1 garlic clove, crushed
Grated peel and juice of 1 lime
½ teaspoon grated gingerroot
1 tablespoon chopped fresh cilantro
Salt and pepper
Lemon slices and cilantro leaves to garnish

Preheat oven to 400F (205C). On a baking sheet, place coconut. Bake 2 to 3 minutes or until browned. Remove from oven and cool slightly.

Trim mushrooms, discarding stems. In a large roasting pan, place mushrooms trimmed-side up. Cream butter, coconut and remaining ingredients together. Spread over inside of mushrooms. Cover loosely with foil. Bake 15 to 20 minutes or until mushrooms are tender. Serve hot with fresh bread to soak up the juices. Garnish with lemon slices and cilantro leaves.

Makes 4 servings.

BAKED STUFFED ARTICHOKES

4 large artichokes
1 tablespoon butter
5 tablespoons olive oil
3 slices lean bacon, chopped
1 small onion, finely chopped
2 celery stalks, finely chopped
2 medium-size zucchini, finely chopped
1 garlic clove, crushed
1 tablespoon chopped sage or 1 teaspoon dried sage
1 tablespoon chopped Italian parsley
Salt and freshly ground pepper
3 tablespoons fresh bread crumbs
¼ cup shredded pecorino cheese (1 oz.)
Juice of 1 lemon
Italian parsley sprigs to garnish

Preheat oven to 400F (205C). Cook artichokes in a saucepan of boiling salted water 30 minutes. Remove and place upside down to drain. Pull away and discard outer leaves and, using a teaspoon, remove central hairy choke. Heat butter and 2 tablespoons of the olive oil in a saucepan. Add bacon, onion, celery, zucchini and garlic and cook 5 minutes, stirring frequently, until vegetables are just soft. Stir in herbs. Purée half the mixture in a blender or food processor fitted with the metal blade. Return to pan. Season with salt and freshly ground pepper.

Place artichokes close together in baking dish. Fill center of artichokes with vegetable mixture. In a small bowl, mix together bread crumbs and cheese. Pile on top of filling. Sprinkle with lemon juice and remaining 3 tablespoons olive oil. Cover with foil and bake in preheated oven 15 minutes. Remove foil. Bake 10 minutes until lightly browned. Garnish with Italian parsley sprigs.

Makes 4 servings.

EGGPLANT NAPOLETANA

1½ lbs. medium-size Japanese-type eggplant
Salt
1 cup all-purpose flour
1 cup peanut oil
1 cup olive oil
½ cup extra-virgin olive oil
6 anchovy fillets in oil, drained and mashed
1 tablespoon sun-dried tomato paste
3 tablespoons red wine vinegar
8 Italian parsley sprigs
2 garlic cloves
Freshly ground pepper
Italian parsley sprigs to garnish

Preheat peanut oil and olive oil together in a saucepan or deep-fryer to 375F (190C). Deep-fry eggplant in batches in the hot oil about 4 minutes until golden-brown. Transfer to paper towels to drain. Keep hot.

Peel the eggplants and cut into 1-inch slices. Spread eggplant out on a large plate and sprinkle with salt. Leave 30 minutes, then rinse thoroughly under cold running water to remove salt, drain and pat dry with paper towels.

In a small saucepan, gently warm the extra-virgin oil over low heat. Stir in anchovies, tomato paste and vinegar and simmer, stirring, 2 minutes.

Put flour into a large plastic bag, add eggplant and toss to coat. Remove coated eggplant and discard excess flour.

Finely chop together the parsley sprigs and garlic. Transfer eggplant to a warmed serving plate. Top with anchovy sauce and season with salt and freshly ground pepper. Sprinkle with chopped parsley and garlic and serve immediately garnished with Italian parsley sprigs.

Makes 4 to 6 servings.

FRIED EGGPLANT

2 small eggplants
Salt
Vegetable oil for frying
2 lemons, cut into quarters
BATTER:
1 cup all-purpose flour
Pinch of salt
2 tablespoons butter, melted
¾ cup lukewarm water
1 egg white

To make batter, into a large bowl, sift flour and salt. Add melted butter and water, beating to form a smooth, creamy batter. Let stand 1 hour.

Slice eggplants into ¼-inch slices. Place in a colander, sprinkle with salt and let drain 30 minutes. In a bowl, whisk egg white until stiff but not dry. Fold into batter. Pat eggplant slices dry with paper towels.

In a skillet, heat ½ inch oil. Dip eggplant slices into batter. Fry in batches 2 minutes, then turn over and fry a further 2 minutes until crisp and golden on both sides. Drain on paper towels. Keep warm while frying remaining slices. Serve at once, with lemon quarters.

Makes 6 servings.

IMAM BAYALDI

2 small eggplants
Salt
¼ cup extra-virgin olive oil
1 large onion, chopped
1 garlic clove, crushed
1 red bell pepper, seeded and chopped
2 tablespoons tomato paste
2 ozs. sun-dried tomatoes in oil, drained and chopped
½ teaspoon sugar
1 teaspoon wine vinegar
Pepper
Toasted pine nuts and cilantro leaves to garnish

Cut eggplants into ¼-inch slices. Sprinkle with salt and put into a colander to drain 30 minutes. Preheat oven to 350F (175C). In a skillet, heat 2 tablespoons of the olive oil, add onion, garlic and bell pepper. Cook about 10 minutes until onion is soft. Add tomato paste, sun-dried tomatoes, sugar, vinegar and pepper.

Pat eggplant slices dry with paper towels. Arrange slices in a baking pan. Put a teaspoonful of tomato mixture onto each eggplant slice. Drizzle remaining olive oil over and around eggplants. Cover pan and bake 40 to 50 minutes until eggplants are tender. Serve garnished with toasted pine nuts and cilantro leaves.

Makes 6 servings.

STUFFED ZUCCHINI RINGS

½ cup bulgur wheat
6 zucchini, each about 6 inches long
1 tablespoon extra-virgin olive oil
1 small onion, finely chopped
2 teaspoons tomato paste
1 teaspoon chopped fresh mint
Salt and pepper
2 tablespoons fresh lemon juice
Fresh grape leaves to serve
Fresh herbs to garnish

BROILED RADICCHIO

2 large heads of radicchio
6 anchovies in olive oil
2 garlic cloves, cut into slivers
⅓ cup olive oil
Salt and freshly ground pepper
4 ozs. mozzarella cheese, thinly sliced
Lemon slices to garnish

Put bulgur wheat into a bowl. Pour in enough boiling water to come well above the wheat. Let soak 1 hour. Drain thoroughly.

Cut radicchio lengthwise in half. Drain anchovies, reserving oil, and chop.

Preheat oven to 350F (175C). Cut rounded ends off zucchini. With a small apple corer, carefully remove centers from zucchini. In a small skillet, heat oil. Add onion and cook until soft. Remove from heat. Stir in bulgur wheat, tomato paste, mint, salt and pepper. Press stuffing firmly into hollowed-out zucchini.

Push garlic and anchovy pieces between radicchio leaves. Heat half olive oil in a flameproof dish. Put radicchio halves, cut side up, in dish and cook over low heat 5 minutes or until underside of radicchio softens and begins to brown. Remove from heat.

Place zucchini in a baking dish. Pour lemon juice and ¼ cup water over zucchini. Cover dish and bake 45 minutes, or until zucchini are tender but still firm enough to slice neatly. With a sharp knife, cut zucchini into ⅛-inch slices. Serve on a plate lined with grape leaves. Garnish with fresh herbs.

Makes 6 servings.

Preheat broiler. Season radicchio with salt and pepper. Drizzle with a little anchovy oil and remaining olive oil. Arrange mozzarella slices on top of radicchio and broil until mozzarella is bubbling and beginning to brown. Garnish with lemon slices and serve immediately.

Makes 4 servings.

BROILED VEGETABLES

1 red bell pepper
2 baby zucchini
2 baby eggplants
1 fennel bulb
8 baby corn-on-the-cob
Salt and pepper
Zucchini flowers and basil sprigs to garnish
MARINADE:
⅔ cup extra-virgin olive oil
2 garlic cloves, crushed
1 teaspoon chopped fresh parsley
1 teaspoon chopped fresh mint
1 teaspoon chopped fresh oregano

To make marinade, in a bowl, mix together olive oil, garlic, parsley, mint and oregano. Cut bell pepper lengthwise into quarters. Remove seeds and core. Cut zucchini in half lengthwise. Cut eggplants in half lengthwise. Cut fennel bulb into quarters. Put pepper, zucchini, eggplants, fennel and corn into the bowl with the marinade. Leave at least 1 hour.

Preheat broiler or grill. Broil vegetables about 10 minutes, or until tender. Turn them every few minutes and brush with marinade. Season with salt and pepper. Garnish with zucchini flowers and basil sprigs.

Makes 8 servings.

Variation: A wide variety of vegetables can be prepared this way. Try mushrooms, tomatoes, Belgium endive, onion and squashes.

VEGETABLE CROSTINI

1 zucchini
1 small eggplant
1 small red bell pepper
1 small fennel bulb
2 garlic cloves, crushed
1 teaspoon chopped fresh thyme
¼ cup olive oil
Salt and freshly ground pepper
12 slices ciabatta, toasted
10 ozs. mozzarella cheese
Thyme sprigs to garnish

Cut zucchini, eggplant and bell pepper into ½-inch pieces. Coarsely chop fennel.

Preheat broiler. In a bowl, mix together zucchini, eggplant, bell pepper, fennel, garlic, thyme, oil, salt and pepper. Spread vegetables in a broiler pan and broil 12 to 15 minutes, turning frequently, until tender and beginning to brown at edges.

Slice cheese and arrange on toasted ciabatta. Pile broiled vegetables on top of cheese. Broil 2 or 3 minutes or until cheese is beginning to bubble. Garnish with thyme sprigs and serve at once.

Makes 6 servings.

MUSHROOM BRIOCHES

6 small brioches
⅓ cup olive oil
1 garlic clove, crushed
2 shallots, finely chopped
12 ozs. mixed mushrooms, sliced
1 teaspoon Dijon mustard
2 tablespoons dry sherry
1 tablespoon chopped fresh tarragon
⅔ cup whipping cream
Salt and freshly ground pepper
Watercress to garnish

Preheat oven to 400F (205C). Pull tops off brioches and scoop out insides of each brioche to make a hollow case.

Brush insides of brioches with 3 tablespoons of the olive oil. Arrange brioches on a baking sheet and bake 10 to 12 minutes or until crisp. Meanwhile, heat remaining oil in a saucepan, add garlic and shallots and cook, stirring occasionally, 3 minutes or until soft. Add mushrooms and cook over low heat, stirring occasionally, 5 minutes.

Stir in mustard, sherry, tarragon, cream, salt and pepper. Cook for a few minutes or until cream reduces and thickens slightly. Fill brioche cases with mushroom mixture, garnish with watercress and serve at once.

Makes 6 servings.

CRISPY WON TONS

1 red bell pepper
1 carrot
5 green onions
4 ozs. each button mushrooms and bean sprouts
2½ cups sunflower oil
1 teaspoon grated gingerroot
1 teaspoon sugar
1 teaspoon each soy sauce and sesame oil
2 teaspoons sherry
24 won-ton skins
DIPPING SAUCE:
6 tablespoons fresh lime juice
2 teaspoons sugar
1 teaspoon Thai fish sauce
1 teaspoon finely chopped green onion
1 fresh green chile, cored, seeded and chopped

To make dipping sauce, mix together lime juice, sugar, fish sauce, green onion and chile. Stir until sugar has dissolved. Set aside. Cut bell pepper and carrot into thin matchsticks. Shred green onions, reserving a few shreds for garnish. Thinly slice mushrooms. heat 2 tablespoons of the sunflower oil in a wok and stir-fry bell pepper, carrot, green onions, mushrooms, bean sprouts and gingerroot 1 minute. Add sugar, soy sauce, sesame oil and sherry and cook, stirring, 2 minutes. Turn into a strainer and leave to drain and cool.

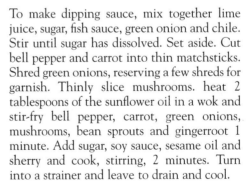

Put 1 teaspoon vegetable mixture in the middle of each won-ton skin. Gather up corners and twist together to seal. In a wok or deep-fat fryer, heat oil to 350F (180C) or until a cube of bread browns in 60 seconds. Fry won tons, a few at a time, 1 or 2 minutes, until crisp and golden. Remove with a slotted spoon and drain on paper towels. Keep warm while frying remaining won tons. Garnish with reserved green onion shreds and serve with dipping sauce.

Makes 6 servings.

DIM SUM

2½ cups all-purpose flour
1 cup ground pork
3 green onions, 1 reserved for garnish, 2 chopped, including some green
2 large Chinese cabbage leaves, shredded, plus extra leaves for lining steamer basket
1 (1-inch) piece of gingerroot, grated
1 tablespoon cornstarch
1 tablespoon each light soy sauce and rice wine
2 teaspoons dark sesame oil
½ teaspoon sugar

Sift flour into a bowl. Make a well in center and slowly pour in 1 cup boiling water. Mix in flour with a fork or chopsticks.

Continue to mix to form a rough dough, adding more flour, if necessary. Cover bowl and leave for 1 minute, to cool. Using your hands, form dough into a soft, loose ball. Knead on a lightly floured surface for about 5 minutes until smooth and elastic. Cover and leave to rest for 30 minutes. In a bowl, combine remaining ingredients using chopsticks or a fork. Set aside.

Divide dough in half. Roll each half to a 9-inch cylinder. Using a floured sharp knife, cut each cylinder into 12 thick slices. Cover with a damp cloth.

Roll each slice into a ball then roll out to a 4-inch circle, making edges slightly thinner than center. Place 1 tablespoon filling in center. Brush edges of circle with a little water.

Lift wrapper around filling, gathering and pinching wrapper to form a purse shape. Put on a tray and cover with a damp cloth. Repeat with remaining dough and filling.

Place some dim sum in a steamer basket lined with cabbage leaves, without crowding dim sum. Cover with a lid. Steam over simmering water for 12-15 minutes until tender but chewy. Garnish with reserved green onion and serve warm with soy sauce mixed with shredded fresh red chile for dipping.

Makes 6 to 8 servings.

VIETNAMESE SPRING ROLLS

FILLING:
2 ozs. bean thread vermicelli, soaked then cut into
  ½-inch pieces
2 tablespoons black fungus, soaked then coarsely
  chopped
8 ozs. ground pork
4 ozs. raw peeled shrimp, chopped
1 small onion, finely chopped
2 green onions, finely chopped
1 teaspoon finely chopped garlic
2 tablespoons fish sauce
Salt and freshly ground black pepper
ASSEMBLING AND FRYING:
10-12 sheets dried rice paper
1 egg, beaten
Oil for deep-frying

SERVING ACCOMPANIMENTS:
Iceberg or leaf lettuce
Fresh mint and cilantro leaves
Spicy Fish Sauce (page 311)

Separate the lettuce into single leaves and arrange on a serving platter with the mint and cilantro leaves.

Combine the filling ingredients in a medium bowl. Set aside. Soften the rice papers, one at a time. If using square ones, cut each in half; if using round ones, leave whole. Place about 2 tablespoons of the filling at one end of the paper, fold over and tuck in both sides and roll over. Seal the end with a little beaten egg and set aside. Repeat to fill all the rolls.

Cut the cooked spring rolls in half and arrange on the platter with the lettuce leaves, mint and cilantro leaves. Place a saucer of the Spicy Fish Sauce in the center for dipping. (The dipping sauce can be served in individual saucers, if preferred.)

Heat the oil in a wok or deep-fat fryer to about 350F (180C) and deep-fry the rolls, in batches, 5-7 minutes until golden brown. Remove and drain. (If they are not to be served at once, they can be kept in a very low oven up to 3 hours until needed.)

To serve, place half a spring roll with a mint and cilantro leaf on a lettuce leaf, then wrap it into a neat parcel. Holding it with fingers, dip into the fish sauce before eating.

Makes 4 to 6 servings.

Variation: To make vegetarian spring rolls, substitute 8 ozs. bean sprouts, 1 grated carrot and 1 (8-oz.) cake tofu for the pork and shrimp.

PROSCIUTTO BASKETS

2 sheets filo pastry, 16- x 12-inch rectangles
2 tablespoons butter, melted
1 tablespoon olive oil
1 red onion, finely chopped
1 teaspoon sugar
5 ozs. prosciutto, coarsely chopped
10 sun-dried tomatoes, coarsely chopped
7 ozs. salad leaves
DRESSING:
¼ cup olive oil
2 teaspoons white wine vinegar
Salt and freshly ground pepper

Preheat oven to 375F (190C). Cut filo pastry into 24 (4-inch) squares.

Lightly brush a 12-cup muffin pan with butter. Brush 12 sheets of pastry with butter. Line each cup with a square of pastry. Brush remaining sheets of pastry with melted butter and place on top, arranging them so that the points are like petals. Bake 10 minutes or until golden. Keep warm. Heat oil in a saucepan, add onion and cook, stirring occasionally, 5 minutes, until soft. Add sugar and cook 3 minutes. Stir in prosciutto and sun-dried tomatoes. Heat over low heat to warm through.

To make dressing, put olive oil, wine vinegar, salt and pepper in a large bowl and whisk together. Add salad greens and toss well. Arrange salad on six serving plates. Fill tartlet cases with prosciutto mixture. Arrange on serving plates, garnish with basil leaves and serve.

Makes 6 servings.

CHICKEN LIVER CROSTINI

8 ozs. fresh chicken livers
2 tablespoons olive oil
2 medium leeks, white parts only, washed and finely chopped
1 stalk celery, finely chopped
1 tablespoon balsamic or sherry vinegar
2 tablespoons capers in brine, drained
⅓ cup chicken stock
1 tablespoon chopped fresh thyme
Salt and freshly ground pepper
12 slices French bread, toasted on both sides
Thyme sprigs to garnish

Rinse livers, removing gristle or discolored bits. Dry on paper towels.

Heat olive oil in a nonstick frying pan, add leeks and celery and cook 5 minutes until soft but not colored. Add chicken livers and fry them with the vegetables about 5 minutes. Sprinkle with the vinegar and allow it to evaporate over the heat.

Stir in the capers, chicken stock and thyme and bring to a boil. Season well with salt and pepper. Reduce heat and simmer 10 to 15 minutes until thickened and creamy, stirring all the time. Spread the mixture on the warm toasted bread and serve at once, garnished with thyme sprigs.

Makes 6 servings.

NUTTY CHICKEN STRIPS

12 ozs. skinned and boned chicken breast meat
½ cup blanched almonds, finely ground
Fresh white bread crumbs
2 teaspoons finely chopped fresh parsley
¼ cup all-purpose flour
Salt and pepper
1 large egg, beaten
Vegetable oil for deep-frying
2 tablespoon fruit chutney
1 tablespoon mayonnaise
1 teaspoon finely grated orange peel
1 tablespoon orange juice
Parsley and orange slices to garnish

Cut chicken into thin strips. In a bowl, mix almonds, bread crumbs and parsley.

Into a large plastic bag, put flour, salt, pepper and chicken. Shake well. Dip chicken strips into beaten egg, then roll in bread crumb mixture to coat completely. Freeze 15 to 20 minutes. Pour about 3 inches of oil into a deep pan. Heat to 375F (190C) or until an 1-inch bread cube browns in 40 seconds. Add chicken strips, a few at a time; fry 3 to 4 minutes until golden-brown. Drain well on paper towels and keep warm while frying the remaining chicken.

In a small bowl, mix together chutney, mayonnaise, orange peel and juice. Spoon into a small serving dish. Garnish chicken with parsley and orange slices. Serve the sauce for dipping.

Makes 4 servings.

GARLIC & LEMON SHRIMP

8 ozs. small to medium raw shrimp
Salt and freshly ground pepper
4 tablespoons olive oil
2 tablespoons sunflower oil
3 large cloves garlic, coarsely chopped
1 dried red chile pepper, stem and seeds removed, chopped
Fresh lemon juice
2 tablespoons chopped fresh parsley
Crusty bread to serve

Shell shrimp and pat dry on paper towels. Lay shrimp in a dish and sprinkle lightly with salt.

Heat the oil in a nonstick frying pan, add garlic and chile and fry 1 to 2 minutes until garlic is golden. Immediately add shrimp and cook over high heat for 2 minutes until the shrimp are just pink. Add lemon juice to taste and season with pepper.

Stir in chopped fresh parsley, then serve the shrimp in ramekins, hot or cold with plenty of crusty bread.

Makes 4 servings.

SHRIMP & FETA PURSES

3 tablespoons butter, melted
4 ozs. cooked, peeled shrimp, thawed if frozen
6 ozs. feta cheese, crumbled
1 oz. sun-dried tomatoes, roughly chopped
1 teaspoon chopped fresh chives
1 teaspoon chopped fresh fennel
Salt and freshly ground pepper
6 sheets filo pastry, about 16- x 12-inch
Fennel leaves and lemon twists to garnish

CHILE SHRIMP BALLS

1 lb. cooked, peeled large shrimp, thawed and dried,
    if frozen
1 fresh red chile, seeded and chopped
3 green onions, finely chopped
Grated zest of 1 small lemon
2 tablespoons cornstarch
1 egg white, lightly beaten
Salt and freshly ground pepper
Strips of fresh red chile to garnish

Preheat oven to 400F (200C). Brush a baking sheet with melted butter. Dry shrimp on paper towels and roughly chop.

Place all the ingredients except the garnish in a blender or food processor and process to form a firm dough-like mixture.

Mix together shrimp, feta cheese, sun-dried tomatoes, chives, fennel, salt and pepper. Cut each sheet of filo pastry into twelve squares. Brush each square with melted butter and layer three more squares on top, arranging them at different angles to form petals.

Divide the shrimp mixture into 12 portions and form each portion into a smooth ball, flouring the hands with extra cornstarch if necessary, to prevent sticking.

Place a spoonful of shrimp mixture in middle of pastry. Pull up edges of pastry and pinch together at top to form a purse. Put on baking sheet and brush with melted butter. Cook in oven 10 to 15 minutes or until golden brown. Garnish with fennel leaves and lemon twists and serve.

Makes 6 servings.

Bring a wok or large saucepan of water to a boil, arrange shrimp balls on a layer of parchment paper in a steamer and place over water. Cover and steam 5 minutes or until cooked through. Garnish with sliced chile and serve on a bed of shredded napa cabbage and watercress.

Makes 4 servings.

TUNA CROQUETTES

1 (15½-oz.) can tuna in water
About 1 cup milk
2 tablespoons olive oil, plus extra for deep-frying
¼ Spanish onion, finely chopped
4 tablespoons all-purpose flour
1½ tablespoons finely chopped fresh parsley
2 tablespoons lemon juice
3 eggs, beaten
Salt and pepper
3 cups fresh bread crumbs
Lemon wedges and watercress to serve

Drain tuna and add enough milk to liquid to make 1½ cups. Flake tuna; set aside.

In a small saucepan, heat 1 tablespoon of the olive oil. Add onion and cook about 4 minutes or until soft but not colored. Stir in flour and cook, stirring, 2 minutes. Remove from heat and slowly stir in half the milk mixture. Return to heat and bring to a boil, stirring in remaining milk mixture. Simmer 8 minutes, stirring occasionally. Remove from heat; stir in tuna, parsley, lemon juice, 1 egg, salt and pepper.

Into a shallow dish, pour tuna mixture. Cool, cover and refrigerate 2 to 3 hours. Put remaining eggs and the bread crumbs into separate bowls. Lightly beat eggs. Dip small balls of tuna mixture first in egg, then bread crumbs to coat evenly. Half fill a deep-fryer with oil and heat to 350F (175C). Fry tuna balls in batches 2 to 3 minutes until crisp and golden. Using a slotted spoon, transfer to paper towels to drain. Serve hot with lemon wedges and watercress.

Makes 4 servings.

STUFFED SQUID

1½–2 lbs. small squid
4 anchovy fillets, canned in oil, drained
2 ozs. blanched almonds, toasted and chopped, or 6 ripe olives, pitted and chopped
1 garlic clove, crushed
1½ tablespoons mixed chopped fresh parsley and oregano
1 egg, beaten
1 tablespoon ground blanched almonds
Salt and paprika
3 tablespoons olive oil
Juice ½ lemon
Lemon slices, sliced pitted ripe olives and fresh herb sprigs, to garnish

Preheat oven to 350F (175C). To prepare squid, with a sharp knife, cut off fins. Pull bag and tentacles apart. Remove sword-shaped pen and viscera from bag. Cut head away from tentacles and discard. Rinse bag and tentacles thoroughly under cold running water. Chop tentacles finely and place in a small bowl. Using a fork, mix in anchovies, then chopped almonds or olives, garlic, herbs, egg and ground almonds. Season with salt and paprika.

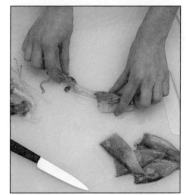

Fill squid with anchovy mixture, secure openings with wooden picks, then place in a single layer in a shallow baking dish. Sprinkle with salt and paprika, then pour the oil and lemon juice over the squid. Bake about 30 minutes or until tender. Serve garnished with lemon slices, ripe olives and herbs.

Makes 4 to 6 servings.

FISH FINGERS WITH PIQUANT DIP

BUTTERFLIED SHRIMP

1¼ lbs. frim white fish, such as hake, haddock, cod, skinned
Salt and pepper
1 egg, beaten
1 cup fresh bread crumbs
Olive oil for deep-frying
Lemon wedges and dill sprigs to garnish
DIP:
⅔ cup low-fat mayonnaise
6 tablespoons plain yogurt
3½ tablespoons finely chopped dill pickles
2 tablespoons chopped dill
1 tablespoon capers, drained and chopped if large
2 teaspoons Dijon mustard

1 lb. extra-large shrimp
Juice of 1 lemon
5 tablespoons extra-virgin olive oil
½ garlic clove, crushed
2 teaspoons sun-dried tomato paste
Pinch of red (cayenne) pepper
1 tablespoon chopped basil or 1 teaspoon dried leaf basil
Salt and freshly ground pepper
Basil sprigs to garnish

Remove and discard heads and legs from shrimp. Using sharp scissors, cut shrimp lengthwise almost in half, leaving tail end intact.

To make dip, in a bowl, beat all ingredients together. Pour into a serving bowl, cover, and refrigerate.

Place shrimp in a shallow dish and add half of the lemon juice and 2 tablespoons of the olive oil. Stir in garlic. Cover and marinate at least 30 minutes. Preheat broiler. Arrange shrimp in 1 layer on a rack and cook under hot broiler about 3 minutes until shrimp have curled and are bright pink.

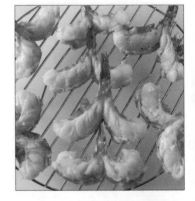

Remove bones from fish, then cut flesh into thin strips. Season strips. Dip in egg, then in bread crumbs to coat evenly. Half-fill a deep-fat fryer with oil and heat to 350F (175C). Add fish, in batches if necessary so pan is not crowded, and fry until crisp and golden. Drain on paper towels. Serve hot with wooden picks, accompanied by the dip. Garnish with lemon wedges and sprigs of dill.

Makes 4 servings.

Mix together the remaining lemon juice and the 3 tablespoons olive oil, the sun-dried tomato paste, cayenne, basil, salt and freshly ground pepper in a small bowl. Either spoon over shrimp or serve separately for dipping. Garnish shrimp with basil sprigs.

Makes 4 servings.

STUFFED MUSSELS

4 lbs. mussels, scrubbed and trimmed
3 thyme sprigs
HERB BUTTER STUFFING:
1 shallot, finely chopped
2 garlic cloves, finely chopped
1 tablespoon finely chopped fresh parsley
1 tablespoon finely chopped fresh chives
1 teaspoon chopped fresh chervil
1 cup fresh bread crumbs
⅔ cup butter, softened
1-1½ tablespoons fresh lemon juice
Salt and freshly ground pepper
Flat-leaf parsley sprigs to garnish

To make herb butter stuffing, mix together shallot, garlic, herbs and bread crumbs, then beat into butter. Add lemon juice, salt and pepper and set aside. Cover the bottoms of shallow ovenproof serving dishes with a thick layer of coarse sea salt or crumpled foil. Pour 1¼ cups water into a large saucepan. Bring to a boil, add mussels and thyme, cover tightly and cook over high heat, 4 minutes, shaking occasionally, until mussels open.

Preheat oven to 450F (230C). Drain mussels, discarding any that remain closed. Discard top shells of mussels and arrange mussels in dishes on top of salt or foil. Divide herb butter among mussels and bake 10 to 12 minutes or until sizzling and golden. Garnish with flat-leaf parsley and serve at once.

Makes 4 to 6 servings.

CAJUN CRABCAKES

1 small clove garlic, finely chopped
2 tablespoons finely chopped white and green parts
  of green onions
2 tablespoons finely chopped red bell pepper
1 egg, beaten
1½ tablespoons mayonnaise
1 lb. fresh white and brown crab meat, chopped
1 tablespoon chopped fresh parsley
2 cups fresh bread crumbs
Squeeze lemon juice
Salt and red (cayenne) pepper
Olive oil for shallow frying
Sour cream and snipped chives and crisp green salad
  to serve

In a mortar or small bowl, put garlic, green onions, bell pepper, and a pinch salt. Crush together using a pestle or end of a rolling pin. Stir in egg, mayonnaise, crab meat, parsley, and about half the bread crumbs to bind together. Add lemon juice, salt, and cayenne to taste.

Form crab mixture into 8 cakes, ¾-inch thick and 2½ inches round. Lightly press in remaining bread crumbs. Chill 1 hour. In a nonstick skillet, heat a thin layer oil. Add crab cakes in batches and fry 3 to 4 minutes on each side until golden. Serve warm with sour cream and chives, and a crisp green salad.

Makes 8.

SPICY JUMBO SHRIMP

2 garlic cloves, crushed
1 small bunch cilantro, finely chopped
Juice of 2 limes
1 fresh red chile, cored, seeded and finely chopped
⅓ cup sunflower oil
24 raw jumbo shrimp
GUACAMOLE:
1 garlic clove, crushed
4 tomatoes, peeled and finely chopped
1 fresh green chile, cored, seeded and finely chopped
Juice of 1 lime
2 tablespoons chopped fresh cilantro
Salt and freshly ground pepper
1 large ripe avocado

SIZZLING SHRIMP

½ cup olive oil
4 garlic cloves, finely crushed
1 small fresh red chile, seeded and chopped
¾ pound raw shrimp, shelled
Sea salt
2 tablespoons chopped fresh parsley
Lemon wedges and bread to serve

In a shallow nonmetallic dish, mix together garlic, cilantro, lime juice, chile and sunflower oil. Add shrimp and mix well. Cover and refrigerate 1 or 2 hours, turning occasionally. To make guacamole, put garlic, tomatoes, chile, lime juice, cilantro, salt and pepper into a bowl and mix well. Halve avocado lengthwise and remove pit. Using a teaspoon, scoop out flesh, taking care to scrape away dark green flesh closest to skin. Mash into tomato mixture.

In 4 individual flameproof dishes over high heat, heat oil. Add garlic and chile and cook 1 to 2 minutes, then add shrimp and sea salt.

Preheat broiler. Remove shrimp from marinade and arrange on broiler rack. Broil 2 or 3 minutes on each side, basting with marinade. Serve with guacamole and tortilla chips.

Makes 6 servings.

Note: Don't prepare the guacamole more than 30 minutes in advance or the avocado will discolor.

Cook 2 to 3 minutes, stirring occasionally. Stir in parsley. Serve quickly so the shrimp are sizzling in the oil, and accompany with lemon wedges and bread to mop up the juices.

Makes 4 servings.

Note: One large dish, or a skillet, can be used instead of individual dishes.

FISH

FISH & PESTO PACKAGES

2 sheets filo pastry dough, about 2 ozs.
Melted butter for brushing
2 fish fillets, such as turbot or salmon, about 5 ozs. each, skinned
2 ozs. cooked shelled shrimp, finely chopped
1 cup chopped button mushrooms
5 tablespoons fromage frais or low-fat cream cheese
2-3 teaspoons pesto sauce
Salt and pepper
Tossed salad to serve

Preheat oven to 400F (205C). Butter a baking sheet. Brush 1 sheet of filo pastry with butter. Place the other sheet on top and brush with butter, then cut in half. Place 1 fish fillet in center of each filo pastry square. Top with shrimp and mushrooms. Mix together fromage frais or cream cheese and pesto sauce. Season with salt and pepper. Spoon one-quarter of the pesto mixture onto each portion of mushrooms. Reserve remaining mixture.

Bring together 2 opposite edges of filo pastry and fold down over fish. Fold remaining edges over and tuck ends under fish. Brush with melted butter and place on baking sheet. Bake 15 minutes or until browned. Using a pancake turner, transfer fish to a warmed serving plate. Split open top of pastry and spoon in remaining pesto mixture. Serve with a tossed salad.

Makes 2 servings.

TURBOT PACKAGES

2 garlic cloves, unpeeled
2 large red bell peppers
2 teaspoons balsamic vinegar
1½ teaspoons olive oil
Salt and pepper
8 spinach leaves, stems removed
4 pieces turbot fillet, about 5½ ozs. each
Stir-fried mixed peppers to serve

Preheat broiler. Wrap garlic in foil and broil 5 to 7 minutes to soften. Broil peppers, turning frequently, until evenly charred and blistered.

Leave peppers until cool enough to handle, then remove skins. Halve peppers and remove seeds and cores. Peel garlic. In a blender or food processor, purée garlic with peppers, vinegar, and oil. Season with salt and pepper. To a saucepan of boiling water, add spinach leaves. Cook 30 seconds. Drain, and refresh under cold running water, then spread out on paper towels to dry.

Season turbot. Wrap each piece in 2 spinach leaves. In a steaming basket or colander, place wrapped fish and cover. Bring water to a boil in a saucepan. Place steamer basket on it and steam 5 to 6 minutes. Meanwhile, heat pepper sauce gently. Serve sauce with the turbot packages, accompanied by stir-fried mixed peppers.

Makes 4 servings.

FISH WITH MUSHROOM CRUST

3 cups finely chopped brown mushrooms
2 tablespoons lemon juice
2 tablespoons whole-grain mustard
2 tablespoons firmly packed fresh bread crumbs
3 green onions, finely chopped
1¼ tablespoons finely chopped fresh parsley
Salt and pepper
4 turbot fillets, about 5 ozs. each
Lemon slices and parsley sprigs to garnish
Zucchini and tomato sautéed together to serve

Preheat broiler. In a bowl, firmly mix together mushrooms, lemon juice, mustard, bread crumbs, green onions, 1 tablespoon of the parsley, and salt and pepper to taste.

Broil turbot, skin sides up, 2 minutes. Turn fish over, spread with mushroom mixture and pat it in.

Broil fish until mushroom mixture has set and fish flakes. Sprinkle with remaining chopped parsley. Garnish with lemon slices and sprigs of parsley and serve with zucchini and tomato sauté.

Makes 4 servings.

BAKED COD WITH LENTILS

3 tablespoons olive oil
3 shallots, finely chopped
2 garlic cloves, finely crushed
1 cup green or brown lentils
3½ teaspoons crushed coriander seeds
1¼ cups fish stock
1¼ cups dry white wine
2 tablespoons chopped fresh cilantro
1½ lbs. cod fillet, cut into 4 pieces
Pinch saffron threads, toasted and crushed
4 tomatoes, peeled, seeded, and chopped
Salt and pepper
Cilantro sprigs to garnish

In a saucepan, heat 1½ tablespoons oil. Add 2 of the shallots and the garlic and cook over low heat until softened. Stir in lentils and 3 teaspoons coriander seeds. Cook 2 minutes, stirring, then stir in stock and wine. Bring to a boil, then reduce heat and simmer, covered, 30 to 45 minutes until lentils are tender. Stir in chopped cilantro. Meanwhile, preheat oven to 450F (230C). In a nonstick roasting pan, heat 1 tablespoon oil. Add cod, skin sides down; cook 2 minutes. Transfer to oven and bake 8 minutes.

In a saucepan, heat remaining oil. Add remaining shallot and coriander seeds and the saffron and cook over low heat until softened. Add tomatoes and a little lentil cooking liquid, then season with salt and pepper. Simmer 5 minutes. Drain lentils and season. Serve cod on lentils, garnished with sprigs of cilantro and accompanied by the tomato relish.

Makes 4 servings.

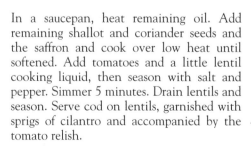

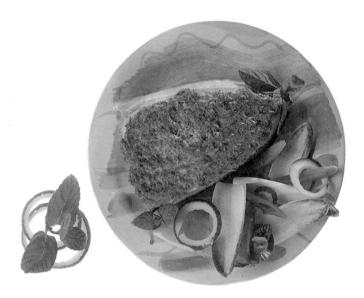

YOGURT-TOPPED HALIBUT

2 tablespoons cumin seeds
2 tablespoons coriander seeds
2 large green onions, chopped
2 garlic cloves, chopped
2 tablespoons chopped fresh mint
2 teaspoons dried dill weed
⅔ cup plain yogurt
1 teaspoon paprika
Salt and pepper
4 halibut steaks, about 6 ozs. each
Mint sprigs to garnish
Belgian endive, red onion, and mint salad to serve

Heat a small, heavy skillet. Add cumin and coriander seeds and heat until fragrant.

Into a mortar or small bowl, place seeds. Crush with a pestle or end of a rolling pin. Work in green onions, garlic, mint, and dill, then stir in yogurt and paprika. Season with salt and pepper.

Into a shallow baking pan, place fish in a single layer. Spread yogurt mixture over top of each steak, cover dish, and refrigerate 2 to 3 hours. Preheat broiler. Broil fish, basting occasionally, 10 to 15 minutes or until fish begins to flake and a crust has formed on yogurt topping. Garnish with sprigs of mint and serve salad.

Makes 4 servings.

FISH GRATINS

½ teaspoon Dijon mustard
1 tablespoon lemon juice
1 tablespoon olive oil
Pinch freshly grated nutmeg
Salt and pepper
4 cod or haddock steaks, about 5 ozs. each
½ cup finely shredded sharp Cheddar cheese
3 tablespoons freshly grated Parmesan cheese
2 tablespoons fine fresh bread crumbs
Paprika
Pattypan squash to serve
Basil sprigs to garnish

Preheat broiler. In a small bowl, beat together mustard and lemon juice using a fork, then gradually beat in oil. Add nutmeg and season with salt and pepper. Place fish in a broiler pan. Brush 1 side of each fish with mustard mixture, then broil, coated sides up, 2 minutes. Turn fish over, brush tops with mustard mixture, and broil 2 minutes longer.

Cover fish with Cheddar cheese. Mix together Parmesan cheese and bread crumbs, then sprinkle evenly over fish. Season generously with pepper. Broil until the top is golden and bubbling. Lightly sprinkle with paprika. Serve with pattypan squash, garnished with sprigs of basil.

Makes 4 servings.

FISH CAKES

1 lb. potatoes, cut into pieces and boiled
1 lb. cooked mixed fresh and smoked fish, such as
    haddock or cod, flaked
2 tablespoons butter, diced
3 tablespoons chopped fresh parsley
1 egg, separated
Salt and pepper
1 egg, beaten
About 1 cup bread crumbs made from day-old bread
Olive oil for frying
Lemon wedges and onion and avocado salad to serve
Dill sprigs to garnish

Drain potatoes. Gently heat potatoes in saucepan a few minutes over low heat, shaking pan occasionally.

Remove pan from heat. Mash potatoes, then beat in fish, butter, chopped parsley, and egg yolk. Season with salt and pepper. Transfer to a large bowl and mix well. Chill if the mixture is too soft to handle.

Divide fish mixture into 8 equal portions. With floured hands, form each portion into a flat cake. In a bowl, beat egg white with whole egg. Spread bread crumbs on a plate. Dip each fish cake in egg, then in bread crumbs. In a skillet, heat a thin layer of oil. Fry fish cakes about 3 minutes on each side until crisp and golden. Drain on paper towels. Serve hot with lemon wedges and salad, garnished with sprigs of dill.

Makes 4 servings.

HOT FISH LOAF

3 tablespoons butter
2 garlic cloves, crushed
2 teaspoons all-purpose flour
¾ cup milk
1¼ lbs. white fish fillets, such as cod or haddock,
    skinned and chopped
⅔ cup whipping cream
2 teaspoons anchovy extract
3 eggs and 1 egg yolk
Lemon juice
Salt and red (cayenne) pepper
4 ozs. cooked shelled shrimp
2 tablespoons chopped fresh basil
Lemon wedges and cilantro sprigs to garnish
Cheese, tomato, or broccoli sauce to serve (optional)

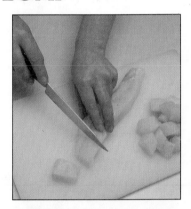

Preheat oven to 300F (150C). Butter and line bottom of a 6½-cup terrine or loaf pan. In a saucepan, melt butter. Add garlic and cook 1 minute. Stir in flour and cook, stirring, 1 minute, then gradually stir in milk. Bring to a boil, stirring. Reduce heat and simmer about 3 minutes, stirring occasionally. Pour sauce into a blender or food processor. Add fish, cream, anchovy extract, eggs, and egg yolk. Purée, then add lemon juice and salt and cayenne.

Spoon half the fish mixture into terrine or loaf pan. Finely chop shrimp, then sprinkle them evenly over fish with chopped basil. Spoon remaining fish mixture over top. Cover terrine or loaf pan tightly with parchment paper or foil. Place in a roasting pan and pour in enough boiling water to come halfway up sides. Bake about 1¾ hours. Onto a warm serving plate, invert terrine or pan. Tilt slightly to drain off juice. Garnish with lemon and cilantro and serve with sauce, if desired.

Makes 4 to 6 servings.

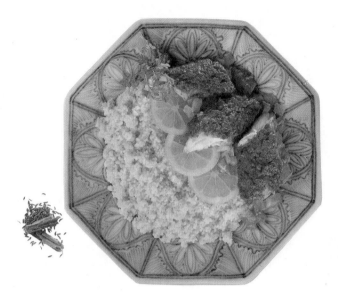

MIDDLE EASTERN MONKFISH

2 garlic cloves
1 (2½-inch) piece gingerroot
3 tablespoons olive oil
2½ tablespoons tomato paste
1½ teaspoons ground cinnamon
1 teaspoon caraway seeds, crushed
Salt and pepper
2¼ lbs. monkfish
½ onion, finely chopped
Couscous and lemon slices to serve

Finely chop garlic and gingerroot together. In a small bowl, stir oil into tomato paste. Stir in garlic mixture, cinnamon, and caraway seeds. Season with salt and pepper.

Remove fine skin from monkfish, then spread with spice mixture. Place fish into a shallow dish. Cover and refrigerate 1 to 1½ hours.

Preheat oven to 400F (205C). Cut a piece of foil large enough to enclose fish. Make a bed of chopped onion on foil. Place monkfish, and any spice paste left in dish, on onion. Fold foil loosely over fish and seal edges tightly. Bake monkfish 20 to 25 minutes. Open foil, baste fish, and bake 10 to 15 minutes longer or until fish flakes. Serve on a bed of couscous, garnished with lemon slices.

Makes 4 servings.

BASS WITH GINGER & LIME

2 shallots, finely chopped
1 (1½-inch) piece gingerroot, finely chopped
Juice of 2 limes
¼ cup rice wine vinegar
1 cup olive oil
2 tablespoons Chinese sesame oil
2 tablespoons soy sauce
Salt and pepper
6 to 8 bass fillets, about ½-inch thick each
Leaves from 1 bunch cilantro
Toasted sesame seeds to garnish
Stir-fried baby corn and sun-dried tomatoes to serve

In a bowl, mix together first 8 ingredients. Set aside.

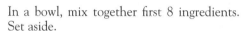

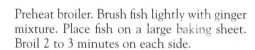

Preheat broiler. Brush fish lightly with ginger mixture. Place fish on a large baking sheet. Broil 2 to 3 minutes on each side.

Before serving, bring remaining ginger mixture to a full boil, then remove from heat. Chop cilantro, reserving a few leaves for garnish. Mix chopped cilantro into ginger mixture. Spoon some onto serving plates at room temperature, then place fish on top. Sprinkle with sesame seeds and garnish with reserved cilantro leaves. Serve with stir-fried baby corn and sun-dried tomatoes.

Makes 6 to 8 servings.

CURRIED TROUT

Seeds from 6 cardamom pods
2 teaspoons cumin seeds
¼ cup plain yogurt
1 large garlic clove, chopped
2 tablespoons lime juice
1 (1-inch) piece gingerroot, chopped
1 teaspoon curry powder
Pinch ground turmeric
¼ teaspoon red (cayenne) pepper
Salt
1 teaspoon red food coloring (optional)
2 trout, about 10 ozs. each
Vegetable oil for brushing
Rice with chiles and tomato and onion salad
Lemon and lime wedges and cilantro sprigs to
  garnish

BROILED FISH & CILANTRO

1½ lbs. gray mullet, porgy, or monkfish fillets
3 tablespoons olive oil
2 garlic cloves, crushed
1½ teaspoons toasted cumin seeds, ground
1 teaspoon paprika
1 fresh green chile, finely chopped
Handful cilantro leaves, finely chopped
3 tablespoons lime juice
Salt
Hot cooked rice to serve
Mint sprigs and lime wedges to serve

Heat a small, heavy pan. Add cardamom and cumin seeds and heat until fragrant. Into a mortar or small bowl, place seeds. Crush with a pestle or end of a rolling pin. Into a blender or small food processor, put yogurt, garlic, lime juice, all the spices, cayenne, and salt. Mix together to make a paste. Add food coloring, if using.

Place fish into a shallow, nonmetallic dish. In a bowl, mix together remaining ingredients, except rice, mint and lime wedges.

Spoon olive oil mixture over fish. Cover and refrigerate 3 to 4 hours, turning occasionally.

With the point of a sharp knife, make 3 deep slashes in each side of trout. Spread spice mixture over trout, working it into the slashes. Place trout into a shallow, nonmetallic dish in a single layer. Cover and marinate in refrigerator 4 hours. Preheat broiler. Brush broiler tray with oil. Sprinkle a little oil over fish and broil about 7 minutes on each side. Serve with rice, chiles, tomato and onion salad, garnished with lemon and lime wedges and sprigs of cilantro.

Makes 2 servings.

Preheat broiler. Place fish on a baking sheet. Broil fish about 4 minutes on each side, basting with cilantro mixture occasionally, until flesh flakes when tested with the point of a sharp knife. Serve warm on a bed or rice, garnished with sprigs of mint and lime wedges.

Makes 4 servings.

TROUT WITH ALMONDS

4 trout, each weighing 10 ozs., cleaned
Salt and freshly ground pepper
1/3 cup unsalted butter
1/2 cup sliced almonds
2 tablespoons fresh lemon juice
Dill sprigs and lemon wedges to garnish

Season trout inside and out with salt and pepper. Heat 1/4 cup of the butter in a large skillet.

Add trout to pan and cook, in batches if necessary, 12 to 15 minutes, turning once, until skin is crisp and flesh flakes easily. Drain trout on paper towels, transfer to warmed serving plates and keep warm.

Wipe pan with paper towels. Heat remaining butter in pan, add almonds and cook, turning occasionally, until lightly browned. Stir in lemon juice, salt and pepper. Quickly pour over fish, garnish with dill and lemon wedges and serve.

Makes 4 servings.

SOLE MEUNIÈRE

3 tablespoons all-purpose flour
Salt and freshly ground pepper
8 sole fillets, each weighing 3 ozs.
3/4 cup unsalted butter
Juice of 2 lemons
2 tablespoons finely chopped fresh parsley
Parsley sprigs and lemon wedges to garnish

Season flour with salt and pepper. Coat fish lightly and evenly in flour and set aside.

Gently heat 1/2 cup butter in a small saucepan until foamy. Wring a piece of cheesecloth out in very hot water, use to line a strainer and place over a bowl. Carefully skim foam from surface of butter and pour butter through cheesecloth, to remove white sediment.

Heat butter in a large skillet until sizzling. Add fish, in batches, and cook over medium heat 4 minutes on each side, until crisp but not brown. Transfer to warmed serving plates and keep warm. Pour off cooking juices and wipe pan. Add remaining butter to pan and heat until foaming and golden brown. Stir in lemon juice and parsley and immediately pour over fish. Garnish with parsley and lemon and serve.

Makes 4 servings.

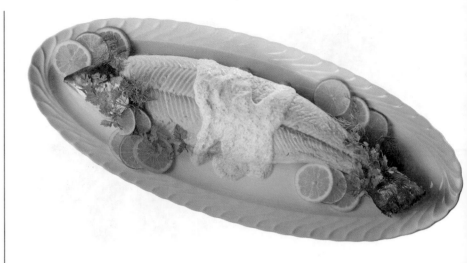

TUNA PEPERONATA

6 slices tuna, about 1-inch thick each
4 garlic cloves
1/3 cup olive oil
1 large onion, finely chopped
1 large red bell pepper, thinly sliced
1 green bell pepper, thinly sliced
14 ozs. tomatoes, peeled, seeded, and diced
1 tablespoon sun-dried tomato paste
3 sprigs thyme
1 bay leaf
Salt and pepper
Parsley sprigs to garnish

Cut slits in tuna. Cut 2 garlic cloves into slivers and insert in slits in tuna. In a large skillet, heat half the oil. Add tuna and cook until lightly browned on both sides. Remove tuna from skillet and set aside. In skillet, heat remaining oil. Add onion and bell peppers and cook over medium heat, stirring frequently, about 10 minutes or until soft.

Chop remaining garlic. Add to pan and cook 1 minute, then add tomatoes, tomato paste, thyme, and bay leaf. Simmer, uncovered, 15 to 20 minutes, stirring occasionally. Return tuna to pan and season with salt and pepper. Cover with buttered parchment paper and simmer 15 minutes. Serve garnished with sprigs of parsley.

Makes 6 servings.

SALMON WITH HERB SAUCE

1/2 onion, chopped
1 carrot, chopped
1 stalk celery, chopped
1 lemon, sliced
1 (3½-lb.) salmon
Bouquet garni of 2 bay leaves and sprig each
   rosemary, sage, and parsley
3/4 cup dry white wine
Salt and pepper
1 bunch watercress, roughly chopped
3 tablespoons chopped fresh parsley
2 tablespoons chopped fresh chervil
1 tablespoon chopped fresh dill
1 cup ricotta cheese or low-fat soft cheese
Lime and lemon slices and herb sprigs to garnish

Preheat oven to 435F (220C). Place a large piece of foil on a large baking sheet. Make a bed of all the vegetables and half the lemon slices on foil. Place salmon on vegetables and add bouquet garni and remaining lemon slices. Fold up foil. Pour in wine, season with salt and pepper, and seal edges of foil tightly. Bake 1 hour. Remove baking sheet from oven and cool fish in foil.

Strain cooking liquid, then boil it until reduced to about 1/3 cup. Add watercress and herbs and boil until softened. Pour herb mixture and liquid into a blender or food processor. Add cheese and purée. Season with salt and pepper. Pour into a serving bowl and refrigerate. Lift fish onto a rack. Carefully remove skin, fins, and fatty line that runs along spine. Transfer to a large serving plate, garnish with lime and lemon slices and sprigs of herbs and serve with sauce.

Makes 6 servings.

MACKEREL WITH MUSTARD

2 tablespoons Dijon mustard
1/4 cup finely chopped fresh cilantro
2 garlic cloves, finely crushed
2-3 teaspoons lemon juice
Salt and pepper
4 mackerel, about 10 ozs. each
Rolled oats
Tomato, fennel, and thyme salad to serve
Lemon wedges and cilantro sprigs to garnish

Preheat broiler. In a bowl, mix together mustard, cilantro, garlic, and lemon juice. Season with salt and pepper.

Using the point of a sharp knife, cut 3 slashes on each side of each mackerel. Spoon mustard mixture into slashes and sprinkle with a little oats. Wrap each fish in a large piece of foil and fold edges of foil together to seal tightly.

Place foil packages under hot broiler 5 minutes. Open foil, turn fish, reseal packages, and broil 2 to 3 minutes longer. Open foil, place fish under the broiler and broil 2 to 3 minutes or until cooked through and flesh flakes easily. Serve with a salad, garnished with lemon wedges and sprigs of cilantro.

Makes 4 servings.

HERRINGS IN OATS

About 1 tablespoon Dijon mustard
About 1 1/2 teaspoons tarragon vinegar
1/3 cup mayonnaise
1/3 cup plain yogurt
4 herrings, about 8 ozs. each, cleaned and heads and tails removed
Salt and pepper
1 lemon, halved
2/3 cup steel-cut oats
Rice and artichoke heart salad to serve
Lemon wedges and cilantro sprigs to garnish

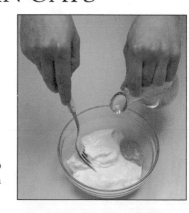

In a small bowl, beat mustard and vinegar to taste into mayonnaise and yogurt. Spoon into a small serving bowl and chill.

Preheat broiler. Working with 1 fish at a time, place fish on a board, cut-side down and open out. Press gently along backbone with your thumbs. Turn fish over and carefully lift away backbone and attached bones.

Season with salt and pepper and squeeze lemon juice over both sides of fish. Fold fish in half, skin side outward. Repeat with remaining fish. Coat each fish evenly in oats, pressing in well but gently. Place herrings on a broiler pan. Broil herrings 3 to 4 minutes on each side until brown and crisp and flesh flakes easily. Serve hot with the mustard sauce, accompanied by salad and garnished with lemon wedges and sprigs of cilantro.

Makes 4 servings.

MACKEREL & GOOSEBERRIES

1 lb. fresh or frozen gooseberries
1 teaspoon fennel seeds
2 (1-lb.) mackerel, each cut into 2 fillets
1 tablespoon olive oil
Salt and freshly ground pepper
1 tablespoon pastis (see Note below)
1 teaspoon sugar
2 tablespoons butter, diced
Parsley sprigs, to garnish

Put gooseberries and fennel seeds in a saucepan with just enough water to cover. Bring to a boil, reduce heat and simmer 7 to 10 minutes or until very soft.

Meanwhile, preheat broiler. With the point of a knife, make three slashes in each mackerel fillet. Season fish, brush with oil on each side and broil 10 minutes, turning once.

Reserve a few gooseberries for garnish. Press remainder through a nylon strainer into a saucepan, pressing hard to extract all the juice. Add pastis, sugar, salt and pepper and heat gently, gradually beating in butter. Pour sauce over fish, garnish with reserved gooseberries and parsley and serve with steamed vegetables.

Makes 4 servings.

Note: Pastis is an anise-flavored liqueur.

SEA BASS ROASTED WITH FENNEL

1 (2½-lb.) sea bass without head, ready to cook
4 rosemary sprigs and 4 oregano sprigs
3 large fennel bulbs
Salt and freshly ground black pepper
3 tablespoons olive oil
Juice of 1 lemon
4 tablespoons chopped fresh oregano and parsley
⅔ cup dry white wine
8 large green olives, pitted

Preheat oven to 425F (220C). Wash fish inside and out and pat dry on paper towels. Lay it in an oval ovenproof dish. Fill cavity with sprigs of rosemary.

Cut fennel bulbs in half lengthways, cut out core and slice the bulbs thickly. Blanch in boiling salted water 5 minutes. Drain. Whisk oil, lemon juice, chopped herbs, salt and pepper together in a medium bowl. Stir in the fennel, turning until coated. Spoon the fennel over and around the fish, and pour over any remaining marinade. Spoon the wine over top and scatter with olives.

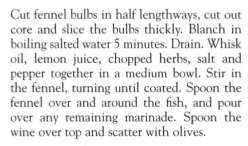

Bake 15 minutes, then spoon the cooking juices over the fish and gently stir the fennel around. Bake 15 minutes. Turn off the oven and leave fish 5 minutes before serving. Garnish with oregano sprigs and serve with mixed rice.

Makes 4 servings.

FISH WITH TAMARIND & GINGER

6 tablespoons vegetable oil
1 (2½-lb.) whole fish or 1 single piece, such as cod,
　bass or red snapper
1 small onion, finely chopped
6 green onions, thickly sliced
2 garlic cloves, crushed
1 tablespoon grated gingerroot
2 teaspoons fish sauce
1½ tablespoons light soy sauce
1 teaspoon crushed palm sugar
1 tablespoon tamarind water
Freshly ground pepper
Cilantro sprigs to garnish

Over medium heat, heat 4 tablespoons of the oil in a wok. Add fish and fry about 5 minutes on each side, until browned and flesh is opaque when tested with a knife. Meanwhile, heat remaining oil in a small saucepan over medium heat, add onion and cook, stirring occasionally, until browned. When fish is cooked, drain on paper towels. Arrange fish on a platter and keep warm.

Stir into wok the green onions, garlic and gingerroot. Stir-fry 2 to 3 minutes, then stir in fish sauce, soy sauce, sugar and tamarind water. Cook 1 minute, season with pepper, then pour over fish. Sprinkle fish with browned onions and garnish with cilantro sprigs.

Makes 4 servings.

SKATE WITH BROWN BUTTER

⅓ cup unsalted butter
2 skate wings, each weighing 8 ozs.
1 tablespoon chopped fresh parsley
Salt and freshly ground pepper
1 tablespoon fresh lemon juice or white wine vinegar
2-3 teaspoons capers
Lemon slices and flat-leaf parsley sprigs to garnish

Gently heat butter in a small saucepan until foamy. Wring a piece of cheesecloth out in very hot water, use to line a strainer and place over a cup. Pour butter through cheesecloth, to remove white sediment. Pour about half of butter into a large skillet.

Add skate and cook 4 or 5 minutes on each side. Drain on paper towels, then transfer to warmed serving plates. Sprinkle with parsley, salt and pepper and keep warm.

Pour remaining clear butter into a small saucepan and heat until golden brown and nutty smelling. Add lemon juice or vinegar and capers and immediately remove from heat. Pour over skate, garnish with lemon slices and parsley and serve.

Makes 2 servings.

SOLE WITH CHIVE SAUCE

½ cup cottage cheese, drained and pressed through a
  fine strainer
Grated peel and juice of 1 lemon
Salt and pepper
3½ ozs. cooked shelled shrimp, finely chopped
8 sole or flounder fillets, skinned
1 cup fish stock
1 small shallot, finely chopped
1 tablespoon dry white vermouth
6 tablespoons dry white wine
¾ cup whipping cream, fromage frais, or cream
  cheese
1½ tablespoons finely snipped fresh chives
Shrimp and snipped fresh chives to garnish
Broccoli to serve

Preheat oven to 350F (175C). Grease a shallow baking dish. In a bowl, beat together cottage cheese and lemon peel and juice. Season with salt and pepper. Stir in shrimp. Spread mixture on skinned side of fillets, then roll up neatly. Secure with wooden picks. Place fish in a single layer in dish, pour in stock to come halfway up the rolls, and add chopped shallot. Cover dish and cook in the oven about 20 minutes or until fish begins to flake. Meanwhile, in a small saucepan, boil vermouth and wine until reduced by half.

Transfer fillets to a warm plate and keep warm. Add stock and shallot to wines and boil until reduced by three-quarters. Stir in cream, if using, and simmer to a light creamy consistency. If using fromage frais or cream cheese, stir in and heat without boiling. Quickly pour sauce into a blender and mix until frothy. Add chives and seasoning. Pour some sauce over fish and serve rest separately. Garnish fillets with shrimp and chives and serve with broccoli.

Makes 4 servings.

CAJUN-STYLE RED SNAPPER

2 red snapper, 1¼ to 1½ lbs. each
2 tablespoons unsalted butter
2 tablespoons olive oil
SPICE MIX:
1 plump clove garlic
½ onion
1 teaspoon salt
1 teaspoon paprika
½ teaspoon red (cayenne) pepper
½ teaspoon ground cumin
½ teaspoon mustard powder
1 teaspoon each dried thyme and dried oregano
½ teaspoon pepper

With the point of a sharp knife, cut 3 slashes on each side of both fish.

To make spice mix, in a pestle and mortar or in a bowl using the end of a rolling pin, crush together garlic and onion with salt. Stir in remaining spice mix ingredients. Spread some spice mix over each fish, making sure it goes into the slashes. In a shallow dish, lay fish. Cover and refrigerate 1 hour.

In a large skillet, melt butter and heat oil until sizzling. Add fish and fry about 4 minutes on each side until fish is cooked through and flakes easily and spice coating has blackened.

Makes 2 servings.

Note: Serve with a colorful selection of tomato, lemon, and lime slices with thyme and parsley sprigs.

BAKED BASQUE COD

FIVE-SPICE SALMON

3 tablespoons olive oil
1 small green bell pepper, diced
1 onion, finely chopped
2 tomatoes, peeled and diced
1 garlic clove, crushed
2 teaspoons chopped fresh basil
4 cod fillets, skinned, each weighing 6 ozs.
Juice of ½ lemon
Salt and freshly ground pepper
Lemon slices to garnish

Preheat oven to 375F (190C). Brush four large squares of oil with a little oil.

Mix together bell pepper, onion, tomatoes, garlic and basil. Put a cod fillet on each piece of foil. Top each fillet with bell pepper mixture.

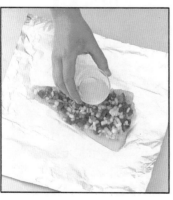

Drizzle with lemon juice and remaining oil. Season with salt and pepper then fold foil to make four parcels. Put packages on a baking sheet and cook in oven 20 to 30 minutes or until fish flakes easily when tested with a knife. Unwrap foil parcels and transfer fish, vegetables and cooking juices to warmed serving plates. Garnish with lemon slices and serve.

Makes 4 servings.

1 teaspoon sesame oil
3 tablespoons soy sauce
3 tablespoons dry sherry or rice wine
1 tablespoon honey
1 tablespoon lime juice or lemon juice
1 teaspoon five-spice powder
1½ lbs. salmon fillet, skinned and cut into 1-inch strips
2 egg whites
1 tablespoon cornstarch
1½ cups vegetable oil
6 green onions, sliced into 2-inch pieces
½ cup light fish stock, chicken stock or water
Dash hot pepper sauce (optional)
Lime wedges to garnish
Cooked rice to serve

In a shallow baking dish, combine sesame oil, soy sauce, sherry, honey, lime juice and five-spice powder. Add salmon strips and toss gently to coat. Allow to stand 30 minutes. With a slotted spoon, remove the salmon strips from marinade and pat dry with paper towel. Reserve marinade. In a small dish, beat egg whites and cornstarch until soft peaks form. Add salmon strips and toss gently to coat completely.

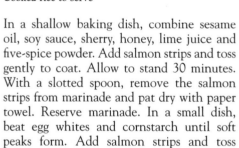

Heat vegetable oil in the wok until hot. Add the salmon in batches. Fry 2 to 3 minutes until golden, turning once. Remove and drain on paper towels. Pour oil from wok into heatproof bowl and wipe wok clean. Pour marinade into wok and add green onions, stock and pepper sauce, if using. Bring to a boil and simmer 1 to 2 minutes. Add fish and turn gently to coat. Cook 1 minute until hot. Garnish with lime and serve with rice.

Makes 4 servings.

STEAMED FISH

1 whole fish, such as sea bass or grouper, weighing
  about 2 lbs., cleaned and scored on both sides at
  1-inch intervals
Salt and freshly ground black pepper
1 teaspoon sugar
1 teaspoon chopped gingerroot
1 tablespoon each chopped white and green parts of
  green onion
1 tablespoon fish sauce
2 teaspoons sesame oil
1 tablespoon shredded gingerroot
1 tablespoon vegetable oil
1 tablespoon each black bean sauce and soy sauce
2 small fresh red chiles, seeded and shredded
Cilantro leaves to garnish

Rub the fish inside and out with salt and
pepper, then marinate in a shallow dish with
the sugar, ginger, white parts of green onion,
the fish sauce and sesame oil 30 minutes.
Place fish with marinade in a bowl in a
steamer, or on a rack inside a wok over boiling water, cover and steam 15-20 minutes.

Remove dish from the steamer or wok, place
the ginger and green part of green onion on
top of the fish. Heat vegetable oil in a small
saucepan, add black bean sauce, soy sauce
and chiles and stir-fry 30 seconds, then
drizzle it over fish. Garnish with cilantro and
serve with rice and a salad.

Makes 4 servings.

Note: If the fish is too big to fit into your
steamer or wok, cut it in half crosswise and
re-assemble it on a warmed plate to serve.

BROILED FLAT FISH

1¼ lbs. flat fish, such as flounder, cleaned
Salt and freshly ground black pepper
1 tablespoon vegetable oil, plus extra for brushing
½ teaspoon minced garlic
½ teaspoon chopped gingerroot
2 shallots, finely chopped
2-3 small fresh red chiles, seeded and chopped
1 tablespoon chopped green onion
2 tablespoons fish sauce and 1 teaspoon sugar
1 tablespoon tamarind water or lime juice
2-3 tablespoons chicken broth or water
2 teaspoons cornstarch

Score both sides of the fish at 1-inch intervals and rub with salt and pepper.

Let fish stand 25 minutes. Meanwhile, preheat broiler. Brush both sides of fish with oil
and broil under the hot broiler about 4
minutes each side until lightly brown but not
burned. Place on a warmed serving dish.

Heat the 1 tablespoon oil in a small pan and
stir-fry the garlic, ginger, shallots, chiles and
green onion 1 minute, then add the fish
sauce, sugar, tamarind water or lime juice
and broth or water. bring to a boil and simmer 30 seconds. Mix cornstarch with
1 tablespoon water and stir into sauce to
thicken. Pour the sauce over the fish. Serve
with carrots and snow peas, garnished with
cilantro leaves.

*Makes 2 servings on its own, or 4-6 servings
with other dishes as part of a meal.*

LIME BROILED FISH KEBABS

BAKED TROUT WITH GINGER

12 ozs. monkfish tails, skinned and cut into ¾-inch cubes
12 ozs. trout fillets, skinned and cut into ¾-inch pieces
2 limes
1 teaspoon sesame oil
Large pinch of five-spice powder
Freshly ground pepper
Strips of lime zest to garnish

Place monkfish and trout in a shallow dish. Juice one of the limes and grate the zest. Mix juice and zest with sesame oil and five-spice powder, pour over fish, cover and chill 30 minutes.

Soak 4 bamboo skewers in cold water. Halve and quarter remaining lime lengthwise, and then halve each quarter to make 8 wedges. Slice each piece of lime in half crosswise to make 16 small pieces.

Preheat broiler. Thread monkfish, trout and lime pieces onto skewers and place on broiler rack. Brush with marinade and season with pepper. Broil 2 minutes on each side, brushing occasionally with marinade to prevent drying out. Drain on paper towels, garnish with lime zest and serve with rice, vegetables and lime wedges.

Makes 4 servings.

2 trout, each weighing 10ozs., cleaned
Salt and freshly ground pepper
2 green onions, finely shredded
1 tablespoon chopped fresh cilantro
Strips of fresh red chile to garnish
SAUCE:
1 garlic clove, finely chopped
½-inch piece fresh ginger root, peeled and finely chopped
2 tablespoons white rice vinegar
2 tablespoons light soy sauce
2 tablespoons dry sherry
1 teaspoon salt
1 teaspoon chile powder
2 teaspoons sugar

Preheat oven to 350F (175C). Rinse trout and pat dry with paper towels. Season trout inside and out with salt and pepper. Fill the cavities with green onions and cilantro. Using a sharp knife, score flesh lightly in diagonal lines. Place trout in a nonstick roasting pan.

Mix together sauce ingredients and pour over trout. Cover loosely with oiled foil and bake 20 minutes, basting halfway through. Remove foil, baste, and bake, uncovered, 10 minutes. Skin trout and remove flesh from bones to give 4 fillets. Brush with cooking juices, garnish with strips of chile and serve with noodles and vegetables.

Makes 4 servings.

CRISPY FISH HOTPOT

12 ozs. zucchini, thinly sliced
2 Red Delicious apples, cored and thinly sliced
1 large onion, sliced
6 ozs. small green beans, cut into 1-inch lengths
1 teaspoon dried sage
1¼ cups fish stock
1½ lbs. cod fillet, skinned and cubed
Salt and freshly ground pepper
12 ozs. potatoes with skins on, thinly sliced
¾ cup (3 oz.) shredded Cheddar cheese

Preheat oven to 375F (190C). Arrange layers of zucchini, apples, onion and beans in an ovenproof casserole dish.

Sprinkle with sage and pour in stock. Cover and bake 30 minutes. Remove from oven, arrange fish on top and season with salt and pepper.

Arrange sliced potatoes on top, sprinkle with cheese and bake 35 to 40 minutes, or until potatoes are tender and cheese is melted and golden. Serve hot.

Makes 4 to 6 servings.

Variation: Any firm white fish fillets, such as whiting or haddock, can be used instead of cod in this recipe.

HADDOCK & SALMON PIE

¼ cup butter
½ cup all-purpose flour
1¼ cups milk
1¼ cups fish stock
12 shallots
1 lb. potatoes, diced
2 garlic cloves, crushed
2 tablespoons olive oil
1 tablespoon whipping cream
Salt and freshly ground pepper
2 tablespoons whole-grain mustard
¼ cup chopped fresh parsley
1 lb. salmon fillet, skinned and cubed
8 ozs. smoked haddock, skinned and cubed
12 small button mushrooms
1 egg, beaten

Melt butter in a flameproof casserole dish, add flour and cook over low heat, stirring, 2 minutes. Gradually stir in milk and fish stock, then add shallots. Bring to a boil, reduce heat and simmer 30 minutes. Meanwhile, cook potatoes and garlic in boiling salted water 20 minutes, or until potatoes are tender. Drain. Mash potatoes and garlic and stir in olive oil, cream, salt and pepper. Set aside. Preheat oven to 400F (205C).

Season shallot sauce with salt and pepper and add mustard and parsley. Add salmon, haddock and button mushrooms and simmer 10 minutes. Pipe or spoon potato on top of fish mixture and bake 10 minutes. Take out of oven and brush with a little beaten egg. Return to oven and bake 20 minutes, or until potato is golden.

Makes 4 to 6 servings.

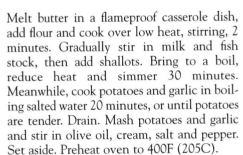

GREEK SEAFOOD CASSEROLE

CHUNKY FISH CASSEROLE

1 tablespoon olive oil
1 onion, chopped
1 garlic clove, crushed
1 stalk celery, chopped
Grated zest and juice of ½ lemon
4 large ripe tomatoes, peeled and chopped
2 tablespoons chopped fresh parsley
1 fresh bay leaf
1 teaspoon dried oregano
Salt and freshly ground pepper
12 ozs. monkfish fillet, skinned and cubed
8 ozs. cleaned squid, cut into rings
1 lb. mussels, cleaned
Chopped green olives to garnish

1 cup pasta shells
3 tablespoons olive oil
2 garlic cloves, finely crushed
½ cup pearl onions, halved
2 cups halved button mushrooms
1 lb. firm, white fish, such as cod or monkfish
8 ozs. trout fillets
3 tablespoons well-seasoned all-purpose flour
1⅓ cups fava beans
½ cup dry white wine
1¼ cups fish stock
Large bouquet garni
Grated peel and juice of 1 lemon
5 ozs. cooked shelled shrimp or cooked shelled
   mussels or clams
Chopped fresh herbs to garnish

Heat olive oil in a Dutch oven. Add onion, garlic and celery and cook 5 minutes or until soft. Add lemon zest and juice, tomatoes, parsley, bay leaf, oregano, salt and pepper. Bring to a boil, reduce heat, cover and simmer 20 minutes. Add monkfish to pan, adding a little water if necessary. Return to a boil, cover and cook 3 minutes.

Preheat oven to 350F (175C). In a large saucepan of boiling water, cook pasta three-quarters of time recommended on package. Drain and rinse under cold running water; set aside. In a skillet, heat half the oil. Add garlic, onions, and mushrooms and cook 3 to 4 minutes. Using a slotted spoon, transfer vegetables to a large, deep baking dish. Meanwhile, skin fish, if needed, and cut into 1-inch chunks. Toss in seasoned flour.

Stir in squid and place mussels on top. Return to a boil, reduce heat, cover tightly and cook 5 minutes or until fish is tender and mussels have opened. Discard any mussels that remain closed. Garnish with chopped olives and serve.

Makes 4 servings.

Heat remaining oil in a skillet. Add fish, in batches if necessary, and fry 2 to 3 minutes, turning pieces carefully. Transfer to dish. Add pasta and beans. Stir wine, stock, bouquet garni, and lemon peel and juice into skillet. Bring to a boil. Reduce heat and simmer a few minutes, then pour into dish. Cover and bake about 30 minutes. Add shrimp, mussels or clams, cover again, and bake about 5 minutes. Garnish with plenty of chopped herbs.

Makes 4 servings.

SHELLFISH

SHRIMP WITH GARLIC

2 tablespoons vegetable oil
5 garlic cloves, chopped
¼-inch slice gingerroot, very finely chopped
14 to 16 large shrimp, peeled, tails on, deveined
2 teaspoons fish sauce
2 tablespoons chopped cilantro
1-2 tablespoons water
Freshly ground pepper
Lettuce leaves, lime wedges and diced cucumber to
 serve

In a wok, heat oil, add garlic and fry until browned.

Stir in gingerroot, heat 30 seconds, then add shrimp and stir-fry 2 to 3 minutes until beginning to turn pink. Stir in fish sauce, cilantro, water and plenty of pepper. Boil 1 to 2 minutes.

Line a plate with lettuce; top with shrimp. Serve with lime wedges and diced cucumber.

Makes 4 servings.

SHRIMP IN YELLOW SAUCE

2 fresh red chiles, seeded, chopped
1 red onion, chopped
1 thick stalk lemon grass, chopped
1-inch piece galangal, chopped
1 teaspoon ground turmeric
½ cup water
1 cup coconut milk
14-16 raw large shrimp, peeled, deveined
8 Thai basil leaves
2 teaspoons lime juice
1 teaspoon fish sauce
1 green onion, including some green top, cut into
 thin strips

Using a small food processor, mix to a paste chiles, red onion, lemon grass and galangal. Transfer to a wok and heat, stirring, 2 to 3 minutes, then stir in turmeric and water and bring to a boil. Reduce heat and simmer 3 to 4 minutes until most of the water has evaporated.

Stir in coconut milk and shrimp and simmer, stirring occasionally, about 4 minutes until shrimp are just firm and pink. Stir in basil leaves, lime juice and fish sauce. Sprinkle green onion over shrimp.

Makes 4 servings.

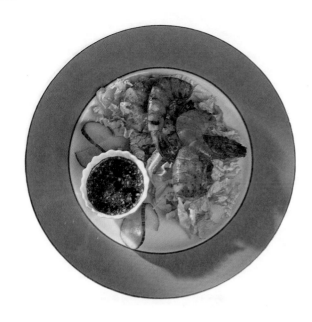

SHRIMP WITH ASIAN SAUCE

1½ lbs. raw jumbo shrimp
Lime wedges and basil sprigs to garnish
MARINADE:
Handful Thai or ordinary fresh basil, finely chopped
2 tablespoons finely chopped garlic
2 tablespoons finely chopped fresh gingerroot
2 tablespoons finely chopped green chiles
2 teaspoons rice wine or medium-dry sherry
2½ tablespoons peanut oil
1 teaspoon Chinese sesame oil
Salt and pepper

To make marinade, in a pestle or a small bowl, pound ingredients together using a mortar or end of a rolling pin.

Discard legs and heads from shrimp. Using strong scissors, cut shrimp lengthwise in half, leaving tail end intact. Remove dark intestinal vein. Rub marinade over shrimp, spoon any remaining marinade over them, cover, and refrigerate 1 hour.

Preheat broiler or grill. Cook shrimp in a single layer about 3 minutes until curled and bright pink. Garnish with lime wedges and sprigs of basil. Serve any remaining marinade separately.

Makes 4 to 6 servings.

SALT & PEPPER SHRIMP

16 uncooked large shrimp
1 teaspoon chile powder
1 teaspoon coarse sea salt
1 teaspoon Szechuan peppercorns, crushed
2 garlic cloves, finely chopped
1 tablespoon peanut oil
DIP:
½ teaspoon Szechuan peppercorns, toasted and ground
2 tablespoons light soy sauce
2 tablespoons dry sherry
1 teaspoon brown sugar

Cut off the heads of the shrimp. Use scissors to remove legs, leaving shells.

Rinse shrimp and pat dry with paper towels. In a bowl, mix together shrimp, chile powder, salt, peppercorns and garlic. Heat oil in a nonstick or well-seasoned wok until very hot and stir-fry shrimp 2 or 3 minutes or until shrimp are pink and cooked through. Drain on paper towels.

Mix together ingredients for dip. Serve the shrimp immediately with the dip and a salad.

Makes 4 servings.

Note: Serve with a finger bowl of water and lemon slices, to freshen the hands.

PACIFIC SHRIMP

2 tablespoons peanut oil
1 lb. raw medium-size shrimp, shelled and deveined
2 garlic cloves, finely chopped
1-inch piece gingerroot, peeled and finely chopped
2 celery stalks, sliced
1 red bell pepper, sliced
4 green onions, cut into thin strips
1 (8-oz.) can unsweetened pineapple chunks, drained, juice reserved
2 teaspoons cornstarch
2 teaspoons soy sauce
1 tablespoon lemon juice
Dash of hot pepper sauce
1 cup macadamia nuts, rinsed lightly if salted

Heat a wok until hot. Add 1 tablespoon of the oil and swirl to coat wok. Add shrimp and stir-fry 2 minutes or until shrimp turn pink and feel firm to the touch. Remove to a bowl. Add remaining oil to wok. Add garlic and gingerroot and stir-fry 30 seconds. Stir in celery, bell pepper and green onions and stir-fry 3 or 4 minutes or until vegetables are tender but still crisp. Stir in the pineapple chunks.

Dissolve cornstarch in the reserved pine-apple juice. Stir in soy sauce, lemon juice and hot pepper sauce. Stir into the vegetable mixture and bring to a simmer. Add reserved shrimp and macadamia nuts and stir-fry until sauce thickens and shrimp are heated through.

Makes 4 servings.

SHRIMP WITH LEMON GRASS

2 cloves garlic, chopped
1 tablespoon chopped cilantro
2 tablespoons chopped lemon grass
½ teaspoon black or white peppercorns
3 tablespoons vegetable oil
12-14 ozs. raw peeled shrimp, cut in half lengthwise if large
2 shallots or 1 small onion, sliced
2-3 small fresh chiles, seeded and chopped
2-3 tomatoes, cut into wedges
1 tablespoon fish sauce
1 tablespoon oyster sauce
2-3 tablespoons chicken broth or water
Cilantro leaves to garnish

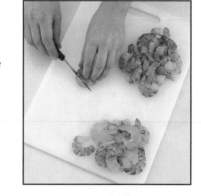

Using a pestle and mortar, pound the garlic, chopped cilantro, lemon grass and pepper-corns to a paste. Heat oil in a wok or frying pan and stir-fry the spicy paste 15-20 seconds until fragrant. Add shrimp, shallots or onion, chiles and tomatoes and stir-fry 2-3 minutes.

Add fish sauce, oyster sauce and broth, bring to a boil and simmer 2-3 minutes. Serve garnished with cilantro leaves.

Makes 4 servings.

LOBSTER WITH BASIL DRESSING

4 lobsters, 1 to 1¼ lbs. each
Mâche and lemon wedges to serve
DRESSING:
⅓ cup drained and chopped sun-dried tomatoes in
   olive oil
1 small bunch basil, chopped
4 tablespoons walnut oil
2 tablespoons sherry vinegar
Pepper

To make dressing, chop tomatoes and basil together. In a small bowl, beat together oil and vinegar, then stir in tomatoes and basil. Season with black pepper.

Using a large, heavy knife, and working from head to tail along the back, split lobsters in half. Remove and discard intestine that runs through center to tail, stomach from near head, and spongy gills.

Brush cut side of lobsters generously with dressing and set aside 15 minutes. Preheat broiler. Broil lobster about 3 minutes. Meanwhile, gently warm remaining dressing in a small saucepan. Brush lobster with dressing and serve with mâche leaves, and lemon wedges. Serve remaining dressing separately.

Makes 4 servings.

STIR-FRIED SHRIMP

10 ozs. raw peeled shrimp
3 tablespoons vegetable oil
1 teaspoon chopped garlic
½ teaspoon chopped gingerroot
1 tablespoon chopped green onion
4 ozs. straw mushrooms, halved lengthwise
2 ozs. water chestnuts, sliced
3 tablespoons fish sauce
1 tablespoon sugar
About 2-3 tablespoons chicken broth or water
1 teaspoon chile sauce (optional)
Salt and freshly ground black pepper
Cilantro leaves to garnish

Halve shrimp lengthwise. Heat oil in a wok or pan over high heat and stir-fry the garlic, ginger and green onion about 20 seconds. Add the shrimp, mushrooms and water chestnuts and stir-fry about 2 minutes.

Add fish sauce and sugar, stir a few times, then add broth or water. bring to a boil and stir 1 minute. Finally, add the chile sauce, if using, and season with salt and pepper. Garnish with cilantro leaves and serve at once.

Makes 4 servings.

Variation: This is a standard stir-fry recipe. If preferred, use different types of fish or meat, cut into small, thin slices, and cook with any other kind of vegetables.

CURRIED CRAB

SPICY CRAB

1½ lbs. cooked large crab claws, thawed and dried, if frozen
1 tablespoon sunflower oil
2 garlic cloves, thinly sliced
1 large green bell pepper, shredded
8 ozs. small broccoli flowerets
5 tablespoons Chinese Vegetable Stock (see glossary)
1 tablespoon ready-made Madras curry paste
1 tablespoon light soy sauce
1 teaspoon brown sugar

1 clove garlic, chopped
2 shallots or the white parts of 3-4 green onions, chopped
1 teaspoon chopped gingerroot
1 tablespoon chopped lemon grass
2-3 tablespoons vegetable oil
1 teaspoon chile sauce
1 tablespoon sugar
3-4 tablespoons coconut milk
About 2 cups chicken broth
3 tablespoons fish sauce
2 tablespoons lime juice or vinegar
Meat from 1 large or 2 medium cooked crabs, cut into small pieces
Salt and freshly ground black pepper
Cilantro leaves to garnish

Wrap the end of a rolling pin in plastic wrap and tap the main part of the crab claws until the shell cracks, leaving pincers intact. Peel away hard shell to expose crab flesh, leaving shell on pincers. Heat oil in a nonstick or well-seasoned wok and stir-fry crab and garlic 1 or 2 minutes or until crab is lightly browned. Drain on paper towels and set aside.

Using a pestle and mortar, pound the garlic, shallots or green onions, ginger, and lemon grass to a fine paste. Heat oil in Dutch oven, add the garlic mixture, chile sauce and sugar and stir-fry about 1 minute. Add the coconut milk, broth, fish sauce and lime juice or vinegar and bring to a boil.

Mix together remaining ingredients and add to wok. Simmer 5 minutes, stirring occasionally. Return crab and garlic to wok and simmer 2 or 3 minutes, stirring to coat crab with sauce. Serve immediately with rice, vegetables and lemon wedges.

Makes 4 servings.

Add the crabmeat and season with salt and pepper. Blend well and cook 3-4 minutes, stirring constantly, then serve hot, garnished with cilantro leaves.

Makes 4 servings.

Note: Uncooked crabs can be used for this dish, but increase the cooking time by about 8-10 minutes.

MALAY CURRIED CLAMS

MUSSELS WITH BASIL

24 steamer clams
1 tablespoon vegetable oil
1 tablespoon sesame oil
2 garlic cloves, finely chopped
1 (1-inch) piece gingerroot, peeled and finely chopped
1 tablespoon fermented black beans, rinsed and chopped
1 tablespoon curry paste or 2 tablespoons curry powder
1 cup light fish stock or chicken stock
¼ cup ketchup
2 tablespoons oyster sauce
1 tablespoon soy sauce
1 teaspoon Chinese chile sauce
2 teaspoons cornstarch dissolved in 3 tablespoons water
4 green onions, thinly sliced

1½ lbs. mussels in shells, cleaned, debearded and rinsed
1 large garlic clove, chopped
1 (3-inch) piece galangal, thickly sliced
2 stalks lemon grass, chopped
10 Thai basil sprigs
1 tablespoon fish sauce
Thai basil leaves to garnish
Spicy Fish Sauce (page 311)

With a stiff brush, scrub clams well. Cover with cold water and soak about 1 hour. With a Chinese strainer, carefully remove clams from soaking liquid to a colander. (This leaves any sand or grit on the bottom.) Discard any clams that are not tightly closed. Heat oils in a wok, swirling to mix oils and coat wok. Add garlic, gingerroot and black beans and stir-fry 30 seconds or until fragrant. Stir in curry paste and cook 1 minute, stirring constantly.

Place mussels, garlic, galangal, lemon grass, basil sprigs and fish sauce in a large saucepan. Add water to a depth of ½ inch. Cover pan, bring to a boil and cook about 5 minutes, shaking pan frequently, until mussels have opened. Discard any mussels that remain closed.

Stir in clams, stock, ketchup, oyster sauce, soy sauce and chile sauce. Bring to a boil, reduce heat, cover and simmer about 5 minutes or until clams open. Stir cornstarch mixture and stir into clams with green onions. Stir until sauce thickens and green onions turn a bright color. Discard any unopened clams. Serve immediately with steamed rice or noodles.

Makes 2 servings.

Transfer mussels to a large warmed bowl or individual bowls, and strain cooking liquid over mussels. Garnish with basil leaves. Serve with sauce for dipping.

Makes 2 to 3 servings.

MUSSELS IN TOMATO SAUCE

2 tablespoons olive oil
2 shallots, finely chopped
2 garlic cloves, crushed
⅔ cup medium-dry white wine
1½ cups peeled, seeded, and chopped tomatoes
Finely grated peel of 1 lemon
2 tablespoons capers, drained and chopped
3 tablespoons chopped fresh parsley
3 lbs. fresh mussels, cleaned
Salt and pepper
Crusty bread to serve

In a large saucepan, heat oil. Add shallots and garlic and cook gently until softened. Add wine, tomatoes, lemon peel, capers, and half the parsley. Bring to a boil.

To pan, add mussels. Cover and cook over high heat 3 to 4 minutes, or until mussel shells open, shaking pan frequently; discard any mussels that remain closed. Season with salt and pepper. Transfer to large bowls or soup plates, sprinkle remaining parsley over and serve with crusty bread.

Makes 2 to 3 servings.

MUSSELS IN WHITE WINE

1 tablespoon olive oil
1 small onion, finely chopped
2 plum tomatoes, peeled, seeded and chopped
Pinch of chile powder
2¼ cups dry white wine
3 lbs. mussels, scrubbed and trimmed
Salt and freshly ground pepper
1 tablespoon chopped fresh flat-leaf parsley

Heat oil in a flameproof casserole dish. Add onion and cook over low heat, stirring occasionally, 5 minutes, or until soft. Add tomatoes, chile powder and white wine.

Bring to a boil. Add mussels, cover tightly and cook over high heat, shaking dish occasionally, 3 or 4 minutes, or until mussels open. Discard any mussels that remain closed.

Season with salt and pepper, sprinkle with parsley and serve.

Makes 4 servings.

Note: Before cooking mussels, discard any that are open and do not close when tapped sharply.

SCALLOPS WITH CASHEWS

¼ cup dry sherry or rice wine
3 tablespoons ketchup
1 tablespoon oyster sauce
1 tablespoon white-wine vinegar
1 tablespoon sesame oil
1 teaspoon Chinese chile sauce (or to taste)
1 tablespoon each grated orange zest and orange juice
1 teaspoon cornstarch
1 tablespoon vegetable oil
½ lb. bay scallops, with roe (optional)
2 garlic cloves, finely chopped
4 green onions, thinly sliced
6 ozs. asparagus, cut into 1-inch pieces
5 ozs. cashew nuts, lightly rinsed

In a medium-size bowl, combine sherry, ketchup, oyster sauce, vinegar, sesame oil, chile sauce, orange zest, orange juice and cornstarch. Heat a wok until hot, add oil and swirl to coat wok. Add scallops and stir-fry 1 or 2 minutes or until they begin to turn opaque. Remove to a bowl.

Add garlic, green onions and asparagus to wok and stir-fry 2 or 3 minutes or until asparagus is bright green and tender but still crisp. Stir sauce ingredients and pour into wok. Bring to a simmer. Return scallops to wok and add the cashews. Stir-fry 1 minute or until scallops are heated through, tossing to coat all ingredients. Serve with rice garnished with strips of orange peel.

Makes 4 servings.

SCALLOPS WITH VEGETABLES

3 tablespoons vegetable oil
1 teaspoon chopped garlic
1-2 small red chiles, seeded and chopped
2 shallots or 1 small onion, chopped
2 ozs. snow peas
1 small carrot, thinly sliced
8 ozs. fresh scallops, sliced
2 ozs. sliced bamboo shoots
2 tablespoons black fungus, soaked and sliced
2-3 green onions, cut into short sections
2 tablespoons fish sauce
1 teaspoon sugar
About 2-3 tablespoons chicken broth or water
1 tablespoon oyster sauce
Salt and freshly ground black pepper
Cilantro leaves to garnish

Heat oil in a wok or pan over high heat and stir-fry garlic, chiles and shallots or onion for about 20 seconds. Add the snow peas and carrot and stir-fry about 2 minutes. Add scallops, bamboo shoots, fungus and green onions and stir-fry 1 minute.

Add fish sauce and sugar, blend well and stir 1 minute, then add the broth or water. Bring to a boil and stir a few more seconds. Add oyster sauce and season with salt and pepper. Garnish with cilantro leaves and serve at once.

Makes 4 servings.

STIR-FRIED SCALLOPS

THAI CURRIED SEAFOOD

1 lb. fresh bay scallops, cleaned and trimmed
8 ozs. baby corn
8 ozs. snow peas
1 tablespoon sunflower oil
2 shallots, chopped
1 garlic clove, finely chopped
1 (½-inch) piece fresh gingerroot, peeled and finely chopped
2 tablespoons yellow bean sauce
1 tablespoon light soy sauce
1 teaspoon sugar
1 tablespoon dry sherry

Rinse scallops and dry with paper towels.

Slice the baby corn in half lengthwise and remove ends from snow peas. Heat oil in a nonstick or well-seasoned wok and stir-fry shallots, garlic and ginger 1 minute.

Add scallops, baby corn and snow peas and stir-fry 1 minute. Stir in remaining ingredients and simmer 4 minutes or until scallops and vegetables are cooked through. Serve on a bed or rice.

Makes 4 servings.

Note: Scallops are sometimes sold with edible orange roe still attached.

2 tablespoons vegetable oil
1 lb. scallops, cut in half lengthwise
1 onion, chopped
1 (2-inch) piece gingerroot, peeled and finely chopped
4 garlic cloves, finely chopped
1 tablespoon curry paste or 2 tablespoons curry powder
1½ teaspoons each ground coriander and cumin
1 (6-inch) piece stalk lemon grass, crushed
1 (8-oz.) can chopped tomatoes
½ cup chicken stock
2 cups unsweetened coconut milk
12 mussels, scrubbed and debearded
1 lb. cooked, peeled shrimp, deveined
12 crab legs, meat removed, cut into ½-inch pieces
Chopped cilantro and shaved coconut to garnish

Heat a wok until hot and add 1 tablespoon of the oil, swirl to coat wok. Add scallops and stir-fry 2 or 3 minutes or until opaque and firm. Remove to a bowl. Add remaining oil to wok and add onion, gingerroot and garlic. Stir-fry 1 or 2 minutes or until onion begins to soften. Add curry paste, coriander, cumin and lemon grass. Stir-fry 1 or 2 minutes. Add tomatoes and stock. Bring to a boil, stirring frequently. Simmer 5 minutes or until slightly reduced and thickened. Add the coconut milk and simmer 2 or 3 minutes.

Stir mussels into sauce and cook, covered, 1 or 2 minutes or until mussels begin to open. Stir in shrimp, crab sticks and reserved scallops. Cook, covered, 1 or 2 minutes more or until all mussels open and seafood is heated through. Remove the lemon grass stalk and discard any mussels that have not opened. Garnish with chopped cilantro and shaved coconut.

Makes 6 to 8 servings.

CHICKEN & TURKEY

CHICKEN WITH TARRAGON

3 tablespoons finely chopped fresh tarragon
¼ cup butter, softened
1 (3½-lb.) chicken
Salt and freshly ground pepper
½ cup dry white wine
¼ cup whipping cream
Tarragon sprigs to garnish

Preheat oven to 400F (205C). Beat tarragon into butter, then push butter between chicken breast and skin.

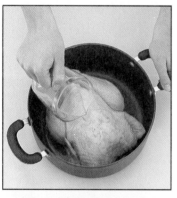

Season chicken with salt and pepper and put in a heavy Dutch oven. Add wine. Cover tightly and cook in oven 30 minutes. Reduce oven temperature to 350F (180C) and cook 1¼ to 1½ hours or until chicken is tender.

Transfer chicken to a warmed plate and keep warm. Tilt pan and spoon off the fat, leaving behind cooking juices. Boil cooking juices to thicken to a light sauce. Reduce heat, stir in cream and simmer to thicken slightly. Carve chicken, garnish with tarragon sprigs and serve with sauce.

Makes 4 servings.

COQ AU VIN

2 tablespoons butter
2 slices thick-cut smoked bacon, chopped
18 pearl onions
8 ozs. button mushrooms
Olive oil for frying (optional)
6 chicken legs
1 onion, chopped
1 carrot, diced
2 garlic cloves, crushed
1½ tablespoons all-purpose flour
2½ cups red Burgundy wine
¾ cup chicken stock
Bouquet garni
Salt and freshly ground pepper
Chopped fresh parsley to garnish

Melt butter in a heavy Dutch oven, add bacon and cook until crisp. Remove with a slotted spoon and drain on paper towels. Add pearl onions to pan and cook, stirring occasionally, until golden. Remove with a slotted spoon and drain on paper towels. Add mushrooms to pan, adding oil if necessary, and cook until lightly browned. Remove with a slotted spoon and drain on paper towels. Add chicken to pan and cook over medium to high heat until browned all over. Remove and drain on paper towels.

Add chopped onion and carrot to pan and cook until lightly browned, adding garlic towards end of cooking. Add flour and cook, stirring, 2 minutes. Stir in wine and stock and bring to a boil. Return all ingredients to pan, add bouquet garni, salt and pepper, cover and cook over very low heat 50 to 60 minutes. Remove chicken and vegetables, discard bouquet garni and boil sauce to thicken. Return chicken and vegetables to pan. Garnish with parsley and serve.

Makes 6 servings.

POULET PROVENÇAL

POULET BASQUAISE

10 garlic cloves
1 tablespoon finely chopped fresh thyme
1 tablespoon finely chopped fresh marjoram
Salt and freshly ground pepper
1 (3½-lb.) chicken, cut into 8 pieces
2 tablespoons fresh lemon juice
¼ cup olive oil
1 thyme sprig
1 small rosemary sprig
6 basil leaves, shredded
8 anchovy fillets, drained and chopped
4 beefsteak tomatoes, peeled, seeded and chopped
⅔ cup dry white wine
24 Niçoise olives
Chopped fresh herbs and basil sprigs to garnish

3 red bell peppers
1 (3-lb) chicken, cut into 8 pieces
Salt and freshly ground pepper
3 tablespoons olive oil
2 onions, thinly sliced
3 garlic cloves, chopped
½ fresh red chile, cored, seeded and chopped
4 beefsteak tomatoes, peeled, seeded and chopped
Bouquet garni
4 ozs. Bayonne ham or prosciutto, diced
½ cup dry white wine
Chopped fresh parsley to garnish

Preheat broiler. Broil bell peppers, until charred and blistered all over.

Crush 2 garlic cloves and mix with chopped herbs and a small pinch of salt. Cut small incisions in chicken and insert a little herb mixture into each incision. Rub with lemon juice and pepper and refrigerate 2 hours. Preheat oven to 325F (165C). Heat half the oil in a saucepan. Finely chop remaining garlic and add to pan with thyme, rosemary and basil. Cook, stirring occasionally, 5 minutes. Stir in anchovy fillets, tomatoes, wine and pepper. Bring to a boil, reduce heat and simmer 15 minutes.

Leave bell peppers until cool enough to handle, then peel. Halve remove cores and seeds and cut flesh into strips. Season chicken with salt and pepper. Heat oil in a heavy Dutch oven, add chicken and cook until browned all over. Remove with tongs or a slotted spoon, transfer to a large plate and set aside.

Heat remaining oil in a heavy Dutch oven, add chicken and cook until browned all over. Add sauce, cover and cook in the oven 45 minutes, turning chicken once or twice. Add olives and cook 15 minutes. Garnish with mixed herbs and basil sprigs and serve.

Makes 4 servings.

Note: Niçoise olives have a special flavor as they are marinated in oil and herbs. If you can't get them, use plain ripe olives instead.

Add onions and garlic to pan and cook, stirring occasionally, 5 minutes or until soft. Stir in chile, tomatoes and bouquet garni and simmer 15 minutes. Stir in ham, wine and bell peppers. Bring to a boil, add chicken and any juices on plate and season with pepper. Cover tightly and simmer 50 to 60 minutes or until tender. Transfer chicken to warmed serving plates. Boil sauce to thicken, pour over chicken, garnish with chopped parsley and serve.

Makes 4 servings.

CHICKEN CHASSEUR

POULET AU VINAIGRE

1 tablespoon olive oil
3 tablespoons butter
4 chicken quarters
3 shallots, finely chopped
1 garlic clove, finely chopped
1 tablespoon all-purpose flour
5 ozs. brown or shiitake mushrooms, sliced
1 cup dry white wine
2 beefsteak tomatoes, peeled, seeded and chopped
Several tarragon and parsley sprigs
Salt and freshly ground pepper
Tarragon sprigs to garnish

1 tablespoon vegetable oil
1 tablespoon butter
4 chicken legs
1 onion, finely chopped
Bouquet garni
4 tomatoes, peeled, seeded and chopped
2 teaspoons tomato paste
1¼ cups red wine vinegar
1¼ cups chicken stock
Salt and freshly ground pepper
Chopped fresh parsley to garnish

Heat oil and 2 tablespoons of the butter in a heavy Dutch oven, add chicken and cook until browned all over.

Heat oil and butter in a heavy Dutch oven. Add chicken and cook until lightly browned all over.

Remove chicken and set aside. Add shallots and garlic to pan and cook, stirring occasionally, 5 minutes or until soft. Add flour and mushrooms and cook, stirring, until flour has browned lightly. Stir in wine and tomatoes. Bring to a boil, stirring.

Remove chicken and set aside. Add onion to pan and cook, stirring occasionally, 5 minutes or until soft. Return chicken to pan, add bouquet garni, cover and cook over low heat 20 minutes, turning occasionally.

Return chicken to pan and add herbs, salt and pepper. Cover tightly and cook over low heat 50 to 60 minutes. Remove chicken with a slotted spoon, transfer to warmed plates and keep warm. Remove herbs from sauce and discard. Boil sauce to thicken slightly. Reduce heat and stir in remaining butter. Pour sauce over chicken, garnish with tarragon sprigs and serve.

Makes 4 servings.

Add tomatoes to pan, and cook, uncovered, until liquid has evaporated. Combine tomato paste and vinegar and add to pan. Simmer until most of liquid has evaporated. Add stock, salt and pepper and simmer until reduced by half. Sprinkle with parsley and serve.

Makes 4 servings.

GARLIC CHICKEN

CHINESE BARBECUE CHICKEN

1 bunch of thyme
1 (3½-lb.) chicken
2 heads of garlic, separated into cloves but not peeled
Salt and freshly ground pepper
¾ cup dry white wine
1 tablespoon butter, diced
Thyme sprigs to garnish

4 chicken quarters, each weighing 8 ozs.
2 garlic cloves, finely chopped
1-inch piece fresh gingerroot, peeled and finely chopped
¼ cup hoisin sauce
2 tablespoons dry sherry
1 teaspoon chile sauce
1 tablespoon dark soy sauce
1 tablespoon brown sugar
1 tablespoon chopped fresh chives to garnish

Preheat oven to 400F (205C). Put some thyme sprigs into cavity of chicken. Put chicken into a heavy Dutch oven just large enough to hold chicken, and tuck remaining thyme sprigs and a few cloves of garlic around it.

Add remaining garlic cloves and wine. Season chicken with salt and pepper. Bring to a boil, cover tightly and cook in the oven 30 minutes. Reduce oven temperature to 350F (180C) and cook 1¼ to 1½ hours or until chicken is very tender.

Remove skin and fat from chicken quarters. Rinse and pat dry with paper towels. Using a sharp knife, score the top of the quarters in diagonal lines.

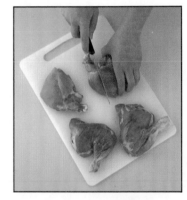

Place chicken in a shallow dish. Mix together all the remaining ingredients except the chives and spoon over the prepared quarters. Cover and chill overnight.

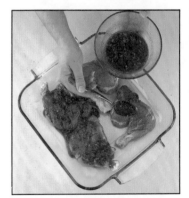

Transfer chicken and garlic to a warmed serving plate and keep warm. Discard thyme. Tilt pan and spoon off fat, leaving behind cooking juices. Boil cooking juices to thicken slightly. Remove from heat and stir in butter. Carve chicken, garnish with thyme sprigs and serve with garlic cloves and sauce.

Makes 4 servings.

Note: Garlic cooked in this way has a mild, sweet flavor. To eat, squeeze cloves out of skin and mash into sauce.

Preheat broiler or grill. Place chicken on broiler rack and cook 20 minutes, turning once, until cooked through. Garnish with chives and serve with rice and salad.

Makes 4 servings.

LEMON & HONEY CHICKEN

4 boneless chicken breasts, each weighing 4 ozs.
3 tablespoons honey
4 teaspoons light soy sauce
Grated zest and juice of 2 lemons
1 garlic clove, finely chopped
Freshly ground pepper
1 tablespoon sunflower oil
2 tablespoons chopped fresh chives
Thin strips of lemon zest to garnish

Remove skin and fat from chicken breasts. Using a sharp knife, score chicken breasts in a crisscross pattern on both sides, taking care not to slice all way through. Place in a shallow dish.

Mix together honey, soy sauce, lemon zest and juice, garlic and pepper. Pour over chicken, cover and chill 1 hour.

Heat oil in a nonstick or well-seasoned wok. Drain chicken, reserving marinade, and cook 2 or 3 minutes on each side, until lightly golden. Add marinade and simmer 5 minutes, turning frequently, until chicken is cooked through and sauce syrupy. Stir in chives, garnish with lemon zest and serve on a bed of noodles.

Makes 4 servings.

VIETNAMESE STIR-FRIED CHICKEN

8 ozs. boned and skinned chicken breasts
2 teaspoons cornstarch
2 teaspoons fish sauce
Salt and freshly ground pepper
2-3 tablespoons vegetable oil
½ teaspoon minced garlic
1 teaspoon finely chopped lemon grass
1 teaspoon chopped gingerroot
4-6 dried small red chiles
2 ozs. snow peas, trimmed
½ red bell pepper, cut into cubes
2 ozs. sliced bamboo shoots, drained
1 teaspoon sugar
1 tablespoon rice vinegar
2 tablespoons oyster sauce
½ teaspoon sesame oil

Cut chicken into bite-size slices or cubes. Mix cornstarch with 1 tablespoon water. Place chicken in a bowl with cornstarch paste and fish sauce. Season with salt and pepper and marinate 20-25 minutes. Heat oil in a wok or frying pan and stir-fry the garlic, lemon grass, ginger and chiles 30 seconds. Add the chicken pieces and stir-fry about 1 minute until the color of the chicken changes to white.

Add vegetables and cook 2-3 minutes, stirring constantly, then add sugar, vinegar, oyster sauce and 3-4 tablespoons water. Blend well, bring to a boil and add the sesame oil. Serve at once with flat rice noodles.

Makes 4 servings.

Variation: Use chicken broth instead of the 3-4 tablespoons water.

VIETNAMESE CHICKEN

1-2 cloves garlic, chopped
1-2 stalks lemon grass, chopped
2 shallots, chopped
1-2 small red or green chiles, chopped
1 tablespoon chopped cilantro
¼ cup fish sauce
6-8 chicken drumsticks, skinned
Lettuce leaves
Spicy Fish Sauce (page 311) to serve

Using a pestle and mortar, pound garlic, lemon grass, shallots, chiles and cilantro to a paste.

In a medium bowl, thoroughly blend pounded mixture with the fish sauce to a smooth paste. Add drumsticks and coat well with the paste. Cover the bowl and leave to marinate 2-3 hours in the refrigerator, turning drumsticks every 30 minutes or so.

Preheat grill or broiler. Cook the drumsticks over grill or under the broiler 10-15 minutes, turning frequently and basting with the marinade remaining in the bowl the first 5 minutes only. Serve hot on a bed of lettuce leaves with the Spicy Fish Sauce as a dip.

Makes 4-6 servings.

CHICKEN IN BLACK BEAN SAUCE

1 teaspoon cornstarch
4 teaspoons light soy sauce
1 (1-inch) piece gingerroot, finely chopped
1 garlic clove, crushed
12 ozs. skinned and boned chicken breasts
1 green bell pepper, seeded
8 canned water chestnuts, drained
4 green onions
2 tablespoons vegetable oil
½ cup cashews
5 tablespoons dry sherry
¾ cup bottled black bean sauce

In a bowl, mix together cornstarch, soy sauce, gingerroot and garlic. Slice chicken into thin strips. Coat chicken strips in cornstarch mixture and let stand 10 minutes. Dice green pepper. Cut water chestnuts in half. Slice green onions into 1-inch pieces. Set aside.

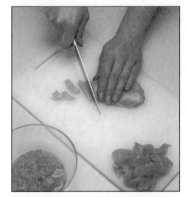

In a wok or large skillet, heat oil. Add chicken and stir-fry 2 minutes. Add bell pepper, green onions and water chestnuts and stir-fry 1 minute longer. Add cashews, sherry and black bean sauce. Stir-fry until sauce thickens.

Makes 4 servings.

PEPPERED CHICKEN KEBABS

1 lb. skinless, boneless chicken breasts, cubed
1 tablespoon rice wine
1 tablespoon dark soy sauce
Grated zest and juice of 1 lime
2 teaspoons brown sugar
1 teaspoon ground cinnamon
1 teaspoon sunflower oil
1 teaspoon Szechuan peppercorns, toasted and
    crushed
Strips of lime zest to garnish

Place chicken in a shallow dish. Mix together rice wine, soy sauce, lime zest and juice, sugar and cinnamon. Pour over chicken.

Cover chicken and chill 1 hour. Meanwhile, soak 8 bamboo skewers in cold water 30 minutes. Remove chicken pieces from marinade, reserving marinade, and thread chicken on to skewers.

Preheat broiler. Brush broiler rack lightly with oil and place skewers on rack. Brush with marinade and sprinkle with peppercorns. Broil 3 minutes, turn, brush again and broil another 2 or 3 minutes or until cooked through. Drain on paper towels. Garnish with lime zest and serve with wedges of lime and shredded napa cabbage.

Makes 4 servings.

CHICKEN FAJITAS

¼ cup dry white wine
Finely grated peel and juice of 2 limes
1 tablespoon Worcestershire sauce
2 teaspoons brown sugar
½ teaspoon dried leaf basil
½ teaspoon dried leaf oregano
1 garlic clove, crushed
4 skinned and boned chicken breast halves
2 tablespoons vegetable oil
8 green onions, sliced
1 red bell pepper, sliced
1 green bell pepper, sliced
8 flour tortillas, warmed
⅔ cup dairy sour cream
Avocado, chopped
Oregano sprigs to garnish

First prepare marinade for chicken. In a bowl, mix together wine, lime peel and juice, Worcestershire sauce, sugar, basil, oregano and garlic. Slice chicken breast into thin strips. Add to marinade. Mix well and marinate 30 to 40 minutes, stirring occasionally. In a skillet, heat 1 tablespoon of the oil. Add green onions and bell peppers; cook until onions are starting to brown, but the vegetables are still crisp. Remove from skillet and set aside. Drain chicken, reserving marinade.

In a skillet, heat remaining oil over medium-high heat. Add chicken (in several batches, if necessary) and fry quickly until golden-brown. Remove from pan with a slotted spoon and set aside. Add reserved marinade to pan and boil until thickened. Return chicken and peppers to skillet; mix well until all ingredients are coated. Put tortillas on a plate. Place spoonfuls of chicken mixture in middle of each tortilla; top with sour cream and avocado. Fold, garnish and serve.

Makes 4 servings.

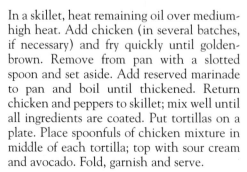

CHICKEN IN VINEGAR SAUCE

CHICKEN KIEV

4 boneless chicken breast halves
Salt and pepper
⅓ cup olive oil
12 garlic cloves
1 small onion, finely chopped
About 3 tablespoons sherry vinegar
1 tablespoon paprika
1½ tablespoons chopped fresh oregano
2 tablespoons fresh bread crumbs
1¼ cups chicken stock
Fresh herbs to garnish

Season chicken with salt and pepper. In a heavy pan, heat oil. Add chicken and cook 10 minutes.

Meanwhile, slice 4 of the garlic cloves. Add sliced garlic to pan with the onion and cook about 5 minutes or until chicken is lightly browned all over.

Remove chicken from pan, stir in vinegar and boil 2 to 3 minutes. Return chicken to pan. Pound remaining garlic with a little salt, the paprika and oregano, then stir in bread crumbs and a quarter of the stock. Pour over chicken, add remaining stock and cook about 20 minutes or until chicken is tender and sauce is fairly thick. Adjust seasoning and amount of vinegar, if necessary. Serve garnished with fresh herbs.

Makes 4 servings.

½ cup unsalted butter, softened
3 garlic cloves, crushed
Finely grated peel of ½ lemon
1 tablespoon chopped fresh parsley
Salt and pepper
4 skinned and boned chicken breast halves
2 eggs, beaten
3 cups fresh white bread crumbs
Vegetable oil, for deep frying

In a bowl, beat together butter, garlic, lemon peel, parsley, salt and pepper. Transfer to a pastry bag fitted with a plain ¼-inch tip.

On a cutting board, lay chicken breasts. Insert a sharp knife into breast to form a pocket. Pipe butter into pocket; do not over-fill or butter will burst through flesh. Refrigerate 25 minutes.

Dip a filled chicken breast half into beaten eggs, then roll in bread crumbs. Repeat, making sure chicken is well coated. Repeat with remaining chicken. Half-fill a deep-fryer or pan with oil. Heat to 375F (190C) or until an 1-inch bread cube browns in 40 seconds. Add chicken, 2 pieces at a time, and fry 8 to 10 minutes or until chicken is cooked through and golden-brown. Drain on paper towels. Serve immediately with a squeeze of lemon juice.

Makes 4 servings.

ROQUEFORT VERONIQUE

2 tablespoons butter
1 tablespoon vegetable oil
4 skinned and boned chicken breast halves
1 leek, chopped
2 teaspoons all-purpose flour
¾ cup milk
2½ ozs. Roquefort cheese
⅓ cup half and half
5 ozs. seedless green grapes, halved
Chopped fresh parsley to garnish

In a skillet, heat butter and oil. Add chicken; cook, turning, until golden on all sides.

Reduce heat. Stir in chopped leek. Cover and cook 30 minutes or until chicken juices run clear when chicken is pierced. Remove chicken from skillet; set aside on a warmed plate.

Sprinkle flour into pan; cook, stirring, 1 minute. Remove from heat; gradually stir in milk. Bring to a boil, stirring, and cook 2 minutes until thickened. Add cheese, half and half and grapes; cook, stirring, 5 minutes. Pour sauce over chicken and garnish with parsley.

Makes 4 servings.

BROILED CHICKEN & HERBS

4 chicken breast halves
2 garlic cloves, sliced
4 sprigs rosemary
6 tablespoons olive oil
Grated peel of ½ lemon
2 tablespoons dry white wine
Salt and pepper
½ teaspoon Dijon-style mustard
2 tablespoons balsamic vinegar
1 teaspoon sugar

With a sharp knife, make several incisions in chicken. Insert pieces of garlic and rosemary. Place chicken in a flameproof dish.

In a bowl, mix together 2 tablespoons olive oil with lemon peel and juice, wine, salt and pepper. Pour over chicken breast halves and marinate 45 minutes. Preheat broiler.

Place chicken breast halves, skin-sides down in dish. Broil 5 minutes. Turn chicken over and spoon marinade over chicken; broil 10 minutes longer or until skin is crisp and brown. Beat together mustard, vinegar, sugar, salt and pepper and remaining oil. Add any cooking juices from pan and spoon over chicken to serve.

Makes 4 servings.

TANDOORI CHICKEN

TIKKA KEBABS

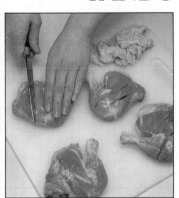

4 chicken leg quarters, skinned
Juice of 1 lemon
Salt
2 teaspoons ground turmeric
2 teaspoons paprika
1 teaspoon curry powder
1 teaspoon ground cardamom
½ teaspoon chile powder
Pinch of saffron powder
2 garlic cloves, crushed
2 teaspoons chopped gingerroot
1 tablespoon olive oil
¾ cup plain yogurt
Lemon wedges, parsley and salsa to garnish

Cut deep diagonal cuts in chicken flesh.

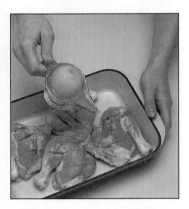

Sprinkle chicken with lemon juuice and a little salt. In a bowl, mix together remaining ingredients. Use to coat chicken quarters, cover and refrigerate 4 hours or overnight.

Preheat broiler. Cook chicken 25 minutes, brushing with any excess marinade and turning frequently until the chicken is tender and juices run clear when chicken leg is pierced with a knife. A slight blackening of the chicken gives an authentic look. Garnish with lemon wedges, parsley and salsa.

Makes 4 servings.

⅔ cup plain yogurt
1 tablespoon grated gingerroot
2 garlic cloves, crushed
1 teaspoon chile powder
1 teaspoon ground cumin
1 teaspoon turmeric
1 tablespoon coriander seeds
Juice of 1 lemon
½ teaspoon salt
2 tablespoons chopped fresh cilantro
12 ozs. skinned and boned chicken, cubed
RAITA:
⅔ cup plain yogurt
2 teaspoons mint jelly
¾ cup finely chopped cucumber
2 green onions, finely chopped

In a blender or food processor, process yogurt, gingerroot, garlic, chile powder, cumin, turmeric, coriander seeds, lemon juice, salt and cilantro until smooth. Pour into a bowl. Stir in chicken, cover and refrigerate overnight.

Preheat broiler. Thread chicken cubes onto skewers. Broil 15 to 20 minutes, turning frequently and brushing with any remaining marinade. In a small bowl, mix together Raita ingredients. Serve kebabs on a bed of pilaf rice. Garnish with mint springs. Pass Raita separately.

Makes 4 servings.

CHICKEN & CORN FRITTERS

1 ripe banana
1 egg
¾ cup finely chopped cooked chicken
1 (8-oz.) can whole-kernel corn, drained
2 green onions, finely chopped
½ teaspoon ground cumin
2 teaspoons chopped fresh cilantro
Salt and red (cayenne) pepper
¾ cup self-rising flour
Vegetable oil for frying
Chile sauce or chutney
Cilantro to garnish

Mash the banana in a bowl. Add egg, chcken, corn and green onions.

Stir in cumin, cilantro, salt and cayenne. Mix well. Add flour and mix to form a soft batter. In a heavy-bottomed skillet, heat oil. Add spoonfuls of chicken mixture. Cook about 1 minute, turning once.

Remove fritters from pan with a slotted spoon. Drain well on paper towels. Serve fritters warm with a chile sauce or chutney. Garnish with cilantro.

Makes 4 servings.

CHICKEN WITH SHERRY

¼ cup raisins
1 cup oloroso sherry
3 tablespoons olive oil
1 (3½-lb.) chicken, cut into 8 pieces
1 Spanish onion, finely chopped
1 garlic clove, finely chopped
1 cup chicken stock
Salt and pepper
4 tablespoons pine nuts

In a small bowl, soak raisins in sherry 30 minutes.

In a large pan, heat 2 tablespoons of the oil, add chicken and cook until lightly and evenly browned, about 10 minutes. Transfer to paper towels to drain. Add onion and garlic to pan and cook over low heat, stirring occasionally, until softened and lightly colored, about 7 minutes. Strain raisins, reserving sherry, and set aside.

Stir sherry into pan. Simmer until reduced by half. Add stock, chicken, salt and pepper, bring to a boil, then reduce heat and simmer until chicken is tender, about 35 minutes. In a small pan, heat remaining oil. Add pine nuts and cook until lightly colored. Drain on paper towels, then stir into pan with raisins. Transfer chicken to a warm serving dish. Boil liquid in pan to reduce slightly. Pour over chicken.

Makes 4 servings.

CHICKEN WITH SALSA VERDE

4 small skinless chicken breasts
½ cup chopped fresh parsley
1 clove garlic, finely chopped
¼ cup chopped fresh mint
1 tablespoon finely chopped capers
1 tablespoon finely chopped gherkins
Finely grated peel and juice of 1 lemon
⅓ cup olive oil
Salt and freshly ground black pepper

Place chicken breasts in a sauté pan, cover with water and bring to a boil. Simmer over low heat 15 to 20 minutes until cooked. Allow to cool completely in the water.

In a bowl, mix together the parsley, garlic, mint, capers, gherkins, lemon juice and peel. Gradually beat in olive oil and season with salt and pepper. Do not do this in a food processor or the texture will be ruined.

Thickly slice each chicken breast crosswise and arrange on a plate, spoon a little salsa verde over it and serve the rest separately. Serve with salad.

Makes 4 servings.

LEMON & CHILE CHICKEN

1 (3¼ to 3½-lb.) free-range chicken, cut into 8
pieces
4 ripe juicy lemons
8 cloves garlic
1 small red chile, split, seeds removed, and chopped
1 tablespoon honey
4 tablespoons chopped fresh parsley
Salt and freshly ground black pepper

Place chicken pieces in a shallow ovenproof baking dish. Squeeze juice from the lemons and pour into a small bowl. Reserve the lemon halves.

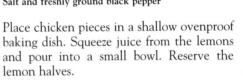

Remove skin from 2 of the garlic cloves, crush them and add to lemon juice with the chile and honey. Stir well and pour mixture over the chicken, tucking the lemon halves around pieces. Cover and refrigerate at least 2 hours, turning once or twice.

Preheat oven to 400F (205C). Turn the chicken skin-side up and place lemon halves cut-side down around the pieces with the remaining whole garlic. Roast in oven 45 minutes or until golden brown and tender. Stir in the parsley, taste and season. Garnish with the roasted lemon halves and serve with puréed potatoes.

Makes 4 servings.

MOROCCAN-STYLE CHICKEN

FLEMISH BRAISED CHICKEN

3 lbs. chicken, cut into 8 pieces
4 tablespoons olive oil
Grated peel and juice of 1 lemon
1 teaspoon each ground cinnamon, ground ginger
  and ground cumin
½ teaspoon salt
½ teaspoon red (cayenne) pepper or to taste
1 onion, chopped
3 or 4 garlic cloves, finely chopped
1 red bell pepper, diced
1 tomato, peeled, seeded and chopped
1 cup chicken stock or water
16 pitted prunes
¼ cup honey
1 large lemon, thinly sliced
Toasted almonds and chopped fresh parsley to garnish

¼ cup butter
1 (4-lb.) chicken
1 lb. leeks, sliced
8 ozs. carrots, sliced
½ head celery, chopped
4 ozs. button mushrooms, halved
2½ cups chicken stock
2 bay leaves
12 small new potatoes
1 cup dry white wine
⅓ cup whipping cream
2 egg yolks
Flat-leaf parsley sprigs and chopped parsley to garnish

Melt butter in a large flameproof casserole dish. Add chicken and brown all over.

In a large shallow baking dish, combine chicken pieces with 2 tablespoons of the olive oil, the lemon peel, lemon juice, cinnamon, ginger, cumin, salt and cayenne. Work the spice mixture into the chicken pieces, cover and marinate in the refrigerator 4 to 6 hours or overnight. Heat a wok until hot. Add 1 tablespoon oil and swirl to coat wok. Arrange marinated chicken pieces on bottom and side of wok in a single layer and stir-fry 6 to 8 minutes or until golden. Remove chicken pieces to a clean baking dish.

Remove from dish. Preheat oven to 400F (205C). Add leeks, carrots, celery and mushrooms to dish and stir well. Cover and cook 5 to 10 minutes, or until soft. Add stock and bay leaves. Bring to a boil and add chicken. Cover and bake 30 minutes. Add potatoes and cook 30 minutes. Lift out chicken and remove vegetables with a slotted spoon. Keep warm.

Add remaining oil, onion, garlic and bell pepper to wok. Stir-fry 2 or 3 minutes. Add tomato and stock and bring to a simmer, stirring. Return chicken and marinade to sauce. Simmer, covered, 20 minutes. Add prunes, honey and lemon slices. Simmer 20 minutes or until chicken is tender. Remove chicken to a serving dish, spoon sauce over chicken and sprinkle with almonds and parsley. Serve with couscous.

Makes 4 servings.

Add wine to dish and bring to a boil. Reduce to a simmer. In a large bowl, mix together cream and egg yolks. Pour some hot stock into cream mixture, stirring constantly. Return to dish and heat through. Do not boil. Return vegetables to dish. Carve chicken, garnish with parsley sprigs and chopped parsley and serve with vegetables and sauce.

Makes 6 servings.

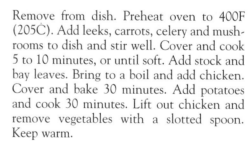

CILANTRO CHICKEN

2 teaspoons sunflower oil
1 garlic clove, finely chopped
1 shallot, finely chopped
12 ozs. lean cooked skinless chicken, diced
1 teaspoon ground coriander
2 teaspoons dark soy sauce
Freshly ground pepper
2 tablespoons chopped fresh cilantro
4 ozs. bean sprouts
1 large carrot, grated
1 oz. fresh cilantro leaves
2 nectarines, sliced
2 bananas, halved, sliced and tossed in juice of 1
   small lemon

Heat oil in a nonstick or well-seasoned wok and stir-fry garlic and shallot 1 minute. Add chicken, coriander, soy sauce and pepper and stir-fry 2 or 3 minutes or until chicken is lightly browned. Remove from heat and stir in chopped cilantro.

Mix together bean sprouts, grated carrot and cilantro leaves. Place on serving plates and top with warm chicken mixture. Arrange nectarine and banana slices around edge of each salad and serve immediately.

Makes 4 servings.

SPICY CHICKEN WINGS

1 tablespoon light soy sauce
1 tablespoon dry sherry or rice wine
2½ lbs. chicken wings, tips removed and wings cut
   into 2 pieces at joint
1 tablespoon peanut oil
1 (1-inch) piece gingerroot, peeled and finely chopped
2 garlic cloves, finely chopped
3 tablespoons fermented black beans, coarsely
   chopped
½ cup chicken stock
2 tablespoons soy sauce
1 teaspoon Chinese chile sauce
4-6 green onions, thinly sliced
6 ozs. small green beans, cut into 2-inch pieces
2 tablespoons chopped peanuts and fresh cilantro
   leaves to garnish

In a shallow baking dish, combine soy sauce, sherry and chicken wings. Toss well and marinate, covered, 1 hour. Heat a wok until hot. Add peanut oil and swirl to coat wok. Add gingerroot and garlic and stir-fry 1 minute. Add chicken wings and, working in 2 batches, stir-fry 3 to 5 minutes or until golden. Stir in black beans, stock, soy sauce and chile sauce. Return all chicken wings to wok.

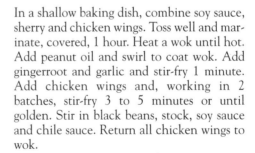

Bring to a boil, reduce the heat and cook 4 to 6 minutes, stirring frequently. Stir in green onions and green beans and cook 2 or 3 minutes more or until chicken is tender and juices run clear. Sprinkle with peanuts and garnish with cilantro leaves.

Makes 4 to 6 servings.

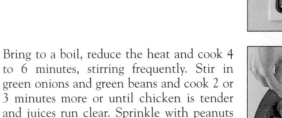

MOZZARELLA CHICKEN

4 skinless, boneless chicken breasts
2 teaspoons pesto
3 ozs. smoked mozzarella cheese, thinly sliced
4 slices prosciutto
2 tablespoons butter
3 ozs. shallots, very finely chopped
⅔ cup dry white wine
1 teaspoon Dijon mustard
Salt and freshly ground pepper
Basil sprigs to garnish

Cut a horizontal slit along each chicken breast to form a pocket. Spread a little pesto in each pocket.

Put mozzarella slices into pockets. Wrap a slice of prosciutto around each chicken breast. Tie with fine string or cotton. Melt butter in a skillet, add shallots and cook over low heat 3 minutes or until soft. Add chicken breasts and cook until lightly browned on each side. Pour in wine. Bring to a boil, reduce heat, cover and simmer 20 minutes or until chicken is cooked through and tender.

Remove chicken with a slotted spoon and keep warm. Stir mustard into pan. Season with salt and pepper and allow to bubble 1 minute. Remove string or cotton from chicken. With a sharp knife, slice each breast and arrange on warmed serving plates. Pour sauce over chicken, garnish with basil sprigs and serve.

Makes 4 servings.

Note: Use plain mozzarella if smoked variety is unavailable.

CHICKEN CRUMBLE

1 tablespoon olive oil
1 lb. skinless, boneless chicken breasts, cubed
1 leek, sliced
8 ozs. mushrooms, thinly sliced
4 ozs. frozen green peas
2 cups plain yogurt
2 teaspoons whole-grain mustard
Salt and freshly ground pepper
⅔ cup rolled oats
½ cup whole-wheat flour
¼ cup butter
1 cup fresh whole-wheat bread crumbs
1 tablespoon grated Parmesan cheese
2 teaspoons dried thyme
1 tablespoon sesame seeds
Thyme sprigs to garnish

Heat oil in a large flameproof casserole dish. Add chicken and cook, stirring, until golden on all sides. Add leek and cook, stirring occasionally, 10 minutes, or until leek is soft. Preheat oven to 400F (205C). Add mushrooms and peas to dish and cook 3 to 5 minutes, or until peas have thawed. Remove from heat and stir in yogurt, mustard, salt and pepper.

Put oats and flour in a bowl and cut in butter until mixture resembles bread crumbs. Stir in bread crumbs, Parmesan cheese, thyme and sesame seeds. Sprinkle mixture evenly over top of chicken and bake 40 to 45 minutes, or until topping is golden brown. Garnish with thyme sprigs and serve.

Makes 4 servings.

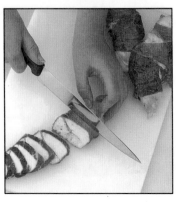

LEMON & CORIANDER CHICKEN

4 chicken thighs, skinned
4 chicken drumsticks, skinned
¼ cup vegetable oil
1 (2-inch) piece fresh gingerroot, grated
4 garlic cloves, crushed
1 green chile, seeded, finely chopped
½ teaspoon ground turmeric
1 teaspoon ground cumin
1 teaspoon ground coriander
Salt and red (cayenne) pepper to taste
½ cup water
Grated peel and juice of 1 lemon
4 ozs. cilantro, chopped
Cilantro leaves and lemon slices to garnish

Rinse chicken; pat dry with paper towels. Heat oil in a large skillet and add chicken. Fry, turning frequently, until browned all over. Remove from pan with a slotted spoon; set aside. Add gingerroot and garlic to skillet; cook 1 minute. Stir in chile, turmeric, cumin, coriander, salt and cayenne; cook 1 minute more.

Return chicken to pan, add water and lemon peel and juice. Bring to a boil, then cover and cook over medium heat 25 to 30 minutes, or until chicken is tender. Stir in chopped cilantro. Serve hot, garnished with cilantro leaves and lemon slices.

Makes 4 servings.

Variation: Substitute fresh parsley, or a mixture of parsley and mint for the cilantro, if preferred.

APRICOT & CHICKEN CURRY

2½-lbs. chicken pieces, skinned
½ teaspoon chile powder
1 tablespoon garam masala
1 (1-inch) piece fresh gingerroot, grated
2 garlic cloves, crushed
1 cup dried apricots
⅔ cup water
2 tablespoons vegetable oil
2 onions, finely sliced
1 (14-oz.) can chopped tomatoes
Salt to taste
1 tablespoon sugar
2 tablespoons white wine vinegar

Rinse chicken; pat dry with paper towels. Cut each piece into four pieces and put in a large bowl. Add chile powder, Garam Masala, gingerroot and garlic; toss well to coat chicken pieces. Cover and refrigerate 2 to 3 hours to allow chicken to absorb flavors. In a separate bowl, combine apricots and water; soak 2 to 3 hours.

Heat oil in a large heavy saucepan; add chicken pieces. Cook over high heat about 5 minutes, or until browned all over. Remove from pan and set aside. Add onions to pan and cook, stirring, about 5 minutes, until soft. Return chicken to pan with tomatoes, cover and cook over low heat 20 minutes. Drain apricots, add to pan with salt, sugar and vinegar. Simmer, covered, 10 to 15 minutes, until tender. Serve hot.

Makes 4 servings.

ARABIAN POUSSINS

SPICY CHICKEN PATTIES

2 tablespoons olive oil
1 small red onion, finely chopped
1¼ cups couscous
1½ cups chicken stock
¼ cup finely chopped dried apricots
2 tablespoons raisins
Grated peel and juice of lemon
¼ cup pine nuts, toasted
1 tablespoon chopped fresh mint
4 poussins (young chickens)
Salt and pepper
⅔ cup dry white wine
2 teaspoons mint jelly
Mint sprigs, to garnish

1¼ lbs. boneless chicken breasts, skinned
4 green onions, finely chopped
3 tomatoes, peeled, seeded, chopped
3 tablespoons chopped cilantro
1 (1-inch) piece fresh gingerroot, grated
1 garlic clove, crushed
1 teaspoon ground cumin
1 teaspoon garam masala
Salt and red (cayenne) pepper to taste
1 egg, beaten
1½ cups fresh bread crumbs
¼ cup vegetable oil
Tomato wedges and green onion brushes to garnish

Preheat oven to 350F (175C). In a pan, heat 1 tablespoon of the oil. Add onion; cook until softened. Put couscous into a bowl. Add 1 cup of the stock, the cooked onion, apricots, raisins and lemon peel and juice. Let stand 15 minutes. Stir in pine nuts and mint. Loosen skin around the breast of each poussin. Carefully push stuffing around meat, securing skin in place with a wooden pick. Place any excess stuffing under poussins in a roasting pan.

Rinse chicken breasts; pay dry with paper towels. Finely mince chicken and put into a large bowl with onions, tomatoes, cilantro, gingerroot, garlic, cumin, Garam Masala, salt, cayenne, egg and half of the bread crumbs. Mix thoroughly, then divide into 18 pieces and form into patties. Roll patties in remaining bread crumbs, to coat completely.

Brush poussins with remaining oil and sprinkle with salt and pepper. Roast 50 to 60 minutes, basting occasionally. Remove poussins from roasting pan and set aside. Pour remaining stock, the wine and mint jelly into pan and stir over high heat. Bring to a boil. Spoon over poussins and serve. Garnish with mint sprigs.

Makes 4 servings.

Heat oil in a large skillet. Fry patties in two or three batches 10 to 12 minutes, until crisp and golden brown and no longer pink in center. Drain on paper towels. Serve hot, garnished with tomato wedges and green onion brushes.

Makes 6 servings.

Variation: Use boneless turkey breast instead of chicken, if preferred.

Note: Patties can be prepared up to 12 hours in advance, chill until ready to cook.

STUFFED CORNISH GAME HENS

GINGER TURKEY & CABBAGE

4 Cornish game hens
Watercress sprigs to garnish
STUFFING:
2 cups fresh whole-wheat bread crumbs
2 ozs. dried apricots, chopped
1 small bunch watercress, chopped
½ cup hazelnuts, chopped
Salt and freshly ground pepper
1 egg yolk
WATERCRESS SAUCE:
1 onion, finely chopped
1 bunch watercress, chopped
½ cup dry white wine
1 tablespoon chopped fresh tarragon
1 teaspoon lemon juice
¼ cup plain yogurt

1¼ cups red wine
2 tablespoons red wine vinegar
⅔ cup raisins
8 ozs. dried apricots, halved
1 (1-inch) piece gingerroot, peeled and grated
2 garlic cloves, crushed
Salt and freshly ground pepper
4 turkey breast fillets, each weighing 6 ozs.
½ head red cabbage, shredded
Flat-leaf parsley sprigs, to garnish

In a large bowl, mix together red wine, vinegar, raisins, apricots, gingerroot, garlic, salt and pepper. Add turkey.

Preheat oven to 400F (205C). To make stuffing, mix together bread crumbs, apricots, watercress, hazelnuts, salt and pepper. Stir in egg yolk. Use to stuff cavity of each hen. Place hens in a shallow flameproof dish and roast 50 to 60 minutes, or until cooked through. To test, pierce thigh with a skewer: if juices run clear hens are cooked. Remove hens from dish and keep warm.

Cover and marinate in the refrigerator at least 2 hours or overnight. Preheat oven to 400F (205C). Arrange red cabbage in a shallow ovenproof dish. Remove turkey from marinade and mix marinade with cabbage. Place turkey on top.

To make watercress sauce, add onion to cooking juices in dish and cook over low heat, stirring occasionally, 5 minutes, or until soft. Add chopped watercress and stir well. Add white wine, tarragon and lemon juice and heat gently. Stir in yogurt and season with salt and pepper. Heat gently to warm through. Pour sauce on to warmed serving plates and place hens on top. Garnish with watercress and serve.

Makes 4 servings.

Bake 45 to 50 minutes, or until turkey is tender and cooked through. Garnish with flat-leaf parsley and serve.

Makes 4 servings.

CREAMY PAPRIKA TURKEY

TURKEY WITH BROCCOLI

4 tablespoons butter
1 onion, finely chopped
1 teaspoon paprika
1 cup whipping cream
1 tablespoon Dijon-style mustard
2 tablespoons chopped fresh dill
Salt and freshly ground pepper
1½ lbs. turkey cutlets, cut crosswise into 1-inch
   strips
6 tablespoons seasoned all-purpose flour
2 tablespoons vegetable oil
½ lb. tagliatelle or egg noodles
10 ozs. fresh or frozen peas
2 teaspoons caraway seeds
Fresh dill sprigs to garnish

1 tablespoon vegetable oil
1 lb. turkey cutlets, cut into thin strips
1 tablespoon sesame oil
1 lb. broccoli, stems and flowerets cut into 1-inch
   pieces
4 green onions, cut into 1-inch pieces
1-inch piece gingerroot, peeled and cut into julienne
   strips
2 garlic cloves, finely chopped
¼ cup dry sherry or rice wine
2 tablespoons light soy sauce
2 teaspoons cornstarch dissolved in 1 tablespoon water
¼ cup chicken stock
1 (8-oz.) can water chestnuts, rinsed and sliced
Cilantro to garnish
Cooked white rice and wild rice to serve

Heat wok until hot. Add 1 tablespoon of the butter and swirl to coat wok. Add onion and stir-fry 7 or 8 minutes. Add paprika and cook 1 minute. Add cream and bring to a simmer; cook 1 or 2 minutes or until slightly thickened. Add mustard and dill and season with salt and pepper. Pour into a small bowl; keep warm. Wipe wok clean. Dredge turkey strips in seasoned flour. Heat a wok until hot. Add vegetable oil and 1 tablespoon butter and swirl to coat wok. Add turkey strips, working in batches and stir-fry 2 or 3 minutes. Remove to a plate and keep warm.

Heat a wok until very hot but not smoking. Add vegetable oil and swirl to coat wok. Add turkey strips and stir-fry 2 or 3 minutes or until beginning to color. Remove to a bowl. Add sesame oil to wok. Add broccoli and stir-fry 2 minutes. Add green onions, gingerroot and garlic and stir-fry 2 or 3 minutes more or until broccoli is tender but still crisp.

Cook tagliatelle according to package directions; drain well. Heat a wok until hot. Add remaining butter, peas and caraway seeds. Stir-fry 2 or 3 minutes or until peas are tender. Stir in noodles and season. Stir in a spoon of the reserved sauce and toss to coat noodles. Turn out onto serving plate. Pour remaining sauce and turkey strips into a wok, tossing to coat. Cook 1 minute. Spoon turkey strips and sauce over noodles. Garnish with dill sprigs.

Makes 4 servings.

Add sherry and soy sauce and cook 2 minutes. Stir dissolved cornstarch and chicken stock together; stir into wok. Stir-fry 1 minute or until sauce bubbles and thickens. Add reserved turkey strips and water chestnuts, tossing to coat, and cook 1 minute or until turkey is heated through. Garnish with cilantro and serve with rice.

Makes 4 servings.

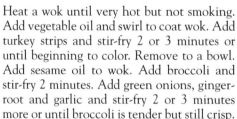

SZECHUAN TURKEY

1 lb. lean boneless turkey
1 egg white, lightly beaten
Large pinch of salt
1 teaspoon cornstarch
1 tablespoon sunflower oil
½ teaspoon Szechuan peppercorns, toasted and
  crushed
8 ozs. vegetable chow-chow, shredded
8 ozs. snow peas
1 (4-oz.) can water chestnuts, rinsed and sliced

Remove skin and fat from turkey. Cut into
thin strips about ¼-inch thick.

Place turkey strips in a bowl and mix with
egg white, salt and cornstarch. Cover and
chill 30 minutes.

Heat oil in a nonstick or well-seasoned wok
and stir-fry turkey with crushed peppercorns
2 minutes or until turkey is just colored. Add
remaining ingredients and stir-fry 3 minutes
or until just cooked through. Serve immediately.

Makes 4 servings.

SWEET & SOUR TURKEY

1 lb. lean skinless, boneless turkey
1 tablespoon sunflower oil
2 shallots, chopped
2 stalks celery, sliced
2 tablespoons light soy sauce
1 red bell pepper, sliced
1 yellow bell pepper, sliced
1 green bell pepper, sliced
1 (4-oz.) can bamboo shoots, drained
3 tablespoons plum sauce
2 tablespoons white rice vinegar
1 teaspoon sesame oil
2 tablespoons sesame seeds

Trim away any excess fat from turkey. Cut
into 1-inch cubes. Heat oil in a nonstick or
well-seasoned wok and stir-fry turkey, shallots and celery 2 or 3 minutes or until lightly
colored.

Add soy sauce and bell peppers and stir-fry 2
minutes. Stir in bamboo shoots, plum sauce
and vinegar and simmer 2 minutes. Stir in
sesame oil, sprinkle with sesame seeds and
serve.

Makes 4 servings.

ROAST STUFFED TURKEY

1 (8-lb.) oven-ready turkey with giblets
2½ cups water
STUFFING:
4¼ cups soft white bread crumbs
1 large onion, finely chopped
3 celery stalks, finely chopped
Finely grated peel and juice 1 lemon
8 plums, pitted, chopped
⅔ cup red wine
2 cups chestnut purée
1 tablespoon chopped fresh sage
1 tablespoon chopped fresh thyme
1 tablespoon chopped fresh oregano
Salt and pepper to taste
1 lb. bacon
½ cup all-purpose flour

Preheat oven to 375F (190C). Cover whole turkey with strips of bacon over breast bone, body, legs and wings to keep moist during cooking.

Remove giblets from turkey. Place in a saucepan with water. Bring to boil, cover and simmer 1 hour. Strain stock into a bowl; reserve liver. To prepare stuffing, place bread crumbs, onion, celery, lemon peel and juice, plums and wine in a saucepan. Bring to a boil, stirring constantly, and cook 1 minute. In a food processor fitted with a metal blade, process turkey liver, chestnut purée and herbs until smooth. Season with salt and pepper. Add bread crumb mixture and process until evenly blended.

Bake turkey in oven 2 hours. Remove bacon and cover turkey and pan with thick foil. Return to oven another 1 to 1½ hours or until turkey is tender and only clear juices run when pierced with a knife between the legs of turkey. Let stand in pan 20 minutes before removing. Remove any skewers or trussing string and place on a warmed serving dish. Chop crispy bacon finely.

Place ⅓ of stuffing into neck end of turkey. Pull over flap of skin and secure under turkey with skewers or string. Fill cavity of turkey with remaining stuffing. Pull skin over nose and secure with skewers or string. Truss turkey with string, securing wings and legs closely to body, and place in a roasting pan.

To prepare gravy, blend flour and some stock until smooth. Strain stock into a saucepan and stir in flour mixture. Bring to a boil, stirring until thickened. Cook 2 minutes. Taste and season with salt and pepper and pour into a gravy boat. Serve turkey with bread stuffing and chopped bacon.

Makes 10 servings.

Duck &
Game

DUCK WITH TURNIPS

1 (4- or 5-lb.) duck
Salt and freshly ground pepper
1 tablespoon olive oil
1 cup chicken stock
½ cup dry white wine
Bouquet garni
1¼ lbs. small turnips, halved or quartered
Pinch of sugar
Sage sprigs to garnish

Season duck generously inside and out with salt and pepper and prick fatty areas of breasts with a fork.

Heat oil in a heavy Dutch oven, add duck and cook over low heat, turning, until browned all over. Pour fat from pan, reserving 2 tablespoons. Add stock, wine and bouquet garni to pan, cover tightly and cook over low heat 30 minutes.

Meanwhile, heat reserved duck fat in a killet, add turnips, sprinkle with sugar and cook until browned all over. Add turnips to pan, baste with cooking liquid and cook, uncovered, 25 minutes or until duck and turnips are tender. Transfer duck and turnips to a warmed serving plate. Skim fat from sauce, then boil sauce to thicken slightly. Season with salt and pepper and remove bouquet garni. Carve duck, garnish and serve with turnips and sauce.

Makes 4 servings.

DUCK WITH ORANGE

2 boneless duck breasts, each weighing 6 ozs.
Salt and freshly ground pepper
1½ teaspoons chopped fresh thyme
2 oranges
1 teaspoon cornstarch
Juice of 1 lemon
¼ cup Cointreau
1 tablespoon unsalted butter
Orange twists and thyme sprigs to garnish

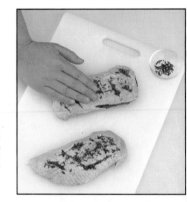

Using a sharp knife, score skin and fat on duck breasts in a crisscross pattern, taking care not to cut through flesh. Season with salt and pepper and rub with thyme.

Heat a heavy skillet over medium to high heat, add duck, skin side down, and cook 10 to 12 minutes, reducing heat a little if skin becomes too brown. Turn duck over and cook 5 minutes, or to taste. Transfer duck to a warmed plate and keep warm.

Meanwhile, remove 1½ tablespoons zest from oranges. Add to a small pan of boiling water and blanch 2 minutes. Drain, rinse in cold water and set aside. Squeeze juice from oranges. Pour most of fat from skillet. Stir cornstarch into pan, then add orange and lemon juice and orange zest. Bring to a boil, stirring, then add Cointreau, salt and pepper. Reduce heat and whisk in butter. Slice duck, arrange on serving plates, add sauce, garnish and serve.

Makes 2 servings.

DUCK WITH APPLES & PRUNES

1 tablespoon olive oil
4 (about 4-oz.) duck breasts
2 cooking apples, peeled and sliced
8 ozs. pitted prunes
2½ cups unsweetened apple juice
Salt and freshly ground pepper

Preheat oven to 400F (205C). Heat oil in a shallow flameproof casserole dish, add duck and cook 3 or 4 minutes on each side, until browned.

Cover with apple slices and prunes. Pour apple juice over duck and season with salt and pepper. Bring to a boil, cover with a lid or piece of foil and bake 55 or 60 minutes, or until duck is cooked through. Remove duck from dish with a slotted spoon, leaving behind apples and prunes, and keep warm.

Bring cooking juices in dish to a boil and boil 5 minutes, or until liquid has reduced and thickened. Pour sauce, apples and prunes over duck and serve.

Makes 4 servings.

VIETNAMESE ROAST DUCK

1 teaspoon minced garlic
2-3 shallots, finely chopped
2 teaspoons five-spice powder
2 tablespoons sugar
¼ cup red rice vinegar
1 tablespoon fish sauce
1 tablespoon soy sauce
4 quarter portions duck (2 breasts and 2 legs)
1 cup coconut milk
Salt and freshly ground black pepper
Watercress to serve
Cilantro leaves to garnish

In a bowl, mix garlic, shallots, five-spice powder, sugar, vinegar, fish and soy sauces.

Add duck pieces and marinate at least 2-3 hours or overnight in the refrigerator, turning occasionally. Preheat oven to 425F (220C). Remove duck portions from marinade and place, skin-side up, on a rack in a baking pan and cook in the oven 45 minutes, without turning or basting.

Remove duck and keep warm. Remove fat from the drip pan. Heat the marinade in the baking pan, add the coconut milk, bring to a boil and simmer 5 minutes. Season with salt and pepper, then pour sauce into a serving bowl. Serve duck portions on a bed of watercress, garnished with cilantro leaves.

Makes 4-6 servings.

Note: The duck portions can be chopped through the bone into bite-size pieces serving, if desired.

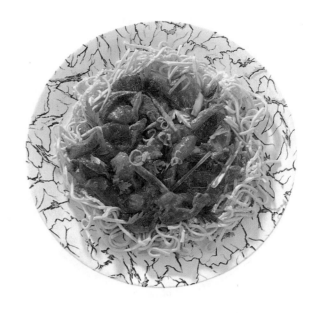

AROMATIC DUCK

2 half or 4 quarter portions of duck (2 breasts and 2 legs)
Salt and freshly ground black pepper
1 tablespoon five-spice powder
4-5 small pieces gingerroot
3-4 green onions, cut into short sections
3-4 tablespoons Chinese rice wine or dry sherry
12 sheets dried rice paper, halved if large
Fresh mint, basil and cilantro leaves
Spicy Fish Sauce (page 311)

DUCK WITH PLUMS

2 tablespoons vegetable oil
1½ lbs. duck breast fillets, skinned and excess fat removed, cut crosswise into thin strips
½ lb. red plums, pitted and thinly sliced
¼ cup port
6 teaspoons red-wine vinegar
Grated peel and juice of 1 orange
2 tablespoons Chinese plum sauce or duck sauce
4 green onions, cut into thin strips
1 tablespoon soy sauce
3-4 whole cloves
Small piece cinnamon stick
½ teaspoon Chinese chile sauce or to taste
Parsley and grated orange peel to garnish

Rub the salt, pepper and five-spice powder all over the duck portions.

In a shallow dish, mix ginger, green onions and rice wine or sherry, add duck portions and marinate at least 3-4 hours in the refrigerator, turning the duck pieces occasionally. Steam the duck portions with marinade in a dish in a steamer 2-3 hours. Remove the duck portions from the liquid. (The duck can be cooked up to this stage in advance, if desired.)

Heat a wok until hot. Add oil and swirl to coat wok. Add duck strips and stir-fry 3 or 4 minutes or until browned. Remove to a bowl. Add plums, port, vinegar, orange peel, orange juice, plum sauce, green onions, soy sauce, cloves, cinnamon stick and chile sauce to taste. Simmer 4 or 5 minutes or until plums begin to soften.

Preheat oven to 450F (230C) and bake the duck pieces, skin-side up, 10-15 minutes, then pull the meat off the bone. Meanwhile, soften dried rice paper in warm water. Place about 2 tablespoons of meat in each half sheet of rice paper, add a few mint, basil and cilantro leaves, roll into a neat bundle, then dip the roll in the Spicy Fish Sauce before eating it.

Makes 4-6 servings.

Return duck strips to wok and stir-fry 2 minutes or until duck is heated through and sauce is thickened. Garnish with parsley and grated orange peel. Serve with noodles.

Makes 4 servings.

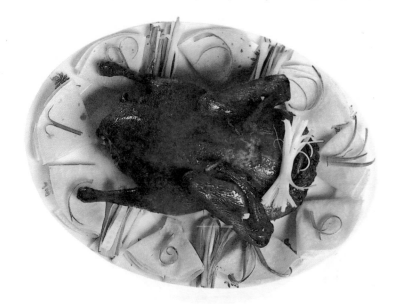

PEKING DUCK

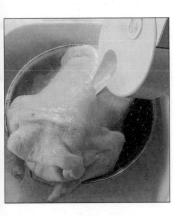

1 (4-lb.) oven-ready duck
1 tablespoon honey
3 tablespoons dark soy sauce
1 tablespoon sesame oil
Red food coloring, if desired
2 tablespoons water
PANCAKES:
3½ cups all-purpose flour
1 cup boiling water
⅓ cup cold water
1 teaspoon sesame oil
TO SERVE:
Hoisin sauce
6 green onions, cut into long shreds
½ cucumber, cut into long shreds

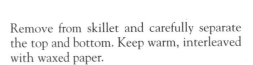

Place the duck in a colander in the sink. Pour boiling water over; repeat twice. Hang duck overnight in a cold airy place, or place on a rack in the refrigerator. Next morning, in a small bowl, mix together honey, soy sauce, sesame oil and coloring, if used. Place duck on a rack in a roasting pan, making sure the neck opening is closed. Brush evenly with honey mixture and let stand 1 hour. Preheat oven to 405F (205C).

Stir water into remaining honey mixture and pour through the vent, into the duck. With a meat skewer or wooden skewer, secure vent. Roast duck, 1½ hours, until juices run clear. Remove duck from oven and leave in a warm place 10 minutes before carving.

Meanwhile, make the pancakes. Sift flour into a bowl and gradually stir in boiling water; mix well. Stir in cold water to form a ball. On a floured surface, knead until smooth. Return to bowl, cover with a damp cloth and let stand 15 minutes.

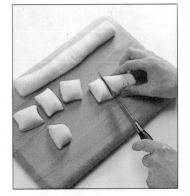

Divide dough in half; on a lightly floured surface, roll each half to a long roll 2 inches in diameter. Cut into 1-inch lengths. Flatten each piece with the palm of the hand. Lightly brush tops with sesame oil and place two pieces together, oiled-sides facing. Roll out each pair to 6-inch pancakes. Place a dry, non-stick skillet over medium heat and fry each pancake 20 to 30 seconds until beginning to bubble. Turn pancake over and cook a further 10 to 15 seconds until lightly browned.

Remove from skillet and carefully separate the top and bottom. Keep warm, interleaved with waxed paper.

Serve the carved duck on a warm plate with the stack of pancakes, and with hoisin sauce, green onions and cucumber in separate bowls.

Makes 4 servings.

DUCK WITH KIWI FRUIT

2 boneless duck breasts, each
½-inch piece fresh gingerroot, peeled and finely
    chopped
1 garlic clove, finely chopped
2 tablespoons dry sherry
2 kiwi fruit
1 teaspoon sesame oil
SAUCE:
¼ cup dry sherry
2 tablespoons light soy sauce
4 teaspoons honey

Remove skin and fat from duck breasts. With a sharp knife, score flesh in diagonal lines. Beat with a meat tenderizer until ½-inch thick.

Place duck breasts in a shallow dish and add ginger, garlic and sherry. Cover and chill 1 hour. Peel and thinly slice kiwi fruit and halve crosswise. Cover and chill until required. Preheat broiler. Drain duck breasts and place on broiler rack. Brush with sesame oil and cook 8 minutes. Turn and brush again with oil. Cook 8 to 10 minutes until tender and cooked through.

Meanwhile, put the sauce ingredients in a saucepan, bring to a boil and simmer 5 minutes or until syrupy. Drain duck breasts on paper towels and slice thinly. Arrange duck slices and kiwi fruit on serving plates. Pour sauce over duck and serve with rice and vegetables.

Makes 4 servings.

PIGEON WITH CRISP POLENTA

2 tablespoons chopped fresh sage
1 tablespoon chopped fresh rosemary
Salt and freshly ground black pepper
Scant 1 cup quick-cook polenta
8 pigeon breasts or 4 boneless chicken breast halves
Pinch of ground allspice
1 tablespoon olive oil
1 recipe Basic Tomato Sauce (page 307)
Rosemary and sage sprigs to garnish

Bring 2½ cups water to a boil with chopped herbs, salt and pepper. Sprinkle in the polenta, whisking to prevent lumps forming.

Reduce heat and simmer the polenta 5 to 10 minutes, stirring constantly until very thick. Turn out onto a wooden board and shape into a loaf with a spatula. Cool, cover and chill 1 hour. Preheat the broiler. Cut the polenta into 4 thick slices. Brush with some of the olive oil and broil on each side until crisp and golden. Keep warm.

Rub pigeon breasts with the allspice, then brush with a little olive oil. Place skin-side up on broiler pan and broil for 4 minutes. Turn over and broil 2 minutes. Top each polenta slice with 2 pigeon breasts. Garnish with rosemary and sage sprigs and serve with the fresh tomato sauce.

Makes 4 servings.

SPICY BROILED QUAIL

ROASTED GUINEA FOWL

1 garlic clove
Salt
1 teaspoon each ground cumin and coriander
½ small onion, coarsely chopped
1 tablespoon chopped fresh cilantro
Pinch of red (cayenne) pepper
⅓ cup extra-virgin olive oil
8 quail
Grape leaves, parsley and lemon slices to garnish

Into a food processor, put all the ingredients except quail and garnish.

Process to make a paste. Spread paste over quail. Cover and refrigerate 2 hours. Meanwhile, preheat broiler.

Broil quail 10 to 15 minutes, turning frequently, until cooked through and slightly charred on the outside. Serve quail on grape leaves, garnished with parsley and lemon slices.

Makes 4 servings.

Variation: Baby poussins or chicken portions can be cooked in this way.

Note: The quail are particularly good grilled on a barbecue.

1 tablespoon olive oil
2 guinea fowl
4 slices bacon, chopped
6 ozs. button mushrooms
6 ozs. shallots
2 tablespoons brandy
1 cup red wine
2½ cups chicken stock
3 tablespoons red currant jelly
Salt and freshly ground pepper
Majoram sprigs to garnish

Preheat oven to 350F (180C). Heat oil in a flameproof casserole dish. Add guinea fowl and brown all over.

Cover and bake 35 to 40 minutes or until tender. Remove and keep warm. Add bacon, mushrooms and shallots to dish and cook, stirring, 4 or 5 minutes, or until golden brown. Remove with a slotted spoon and keep warm. Add brandy, wine, stock and red currant jelly to cooking juices and stir well. Bring to a boil, stirring, and boil 20 to 25 minutes, stirring occasionally, until sauce is reduced and thickened.

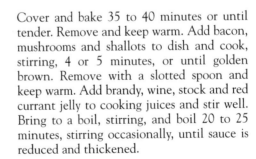

Return guinea fowl, bacon, mushrooms and shallots to dish and season with salt and pepper. Bring to a boil, reduce heat and simmer 4 or 5 minutes to warm through. Cut guinea fowl in half with kitchen scissors or a sharp knife. Garnish with marjoram sprigs and serve.

Makes 4 servings.

PHEASANT IN PARSLEY SAUCE

¼ cup butter
2 pheasants, ready to cook
1 bunch fresh parsley
3 onions, thinly sliced
¼ cup all-purpose flour
1¼ cups chicken stock
⅔ cup crème fraîche
Salt and freshly ground pepper
Flat-leaf parsley sprigs to garnish

Preheat oven to 350F (180C). Melt butter in a large flameproof casserole dish. Add pheasants and cook until browned all over. Remove and keep warm.

Separate thick parsley stalks from leaves and tie stalks together with string. Chop leaves and set aside. Add onions to dish and cook, stirring occasionally, 7 minutes, or until soft and lightly colored. Add flour and cook, stirring, 1 minute. Gradually add chicken stock, stirring constantly until smooth. Bring to a boil and add bundle of parsley stalks. Add pheasants, cover and bake 1 hour or until tender.

Remove pheasants from dish and keep warm. Remove and discard parsley stalks. Add chopped parsley and crème fraîche to sauce and season with salt and pepper. Heat gently to warm through. Cut pheasants in half with kitchen scissors. Garnish with flat-leaf parsley sprigs and serve with parsley sauce.

Makes 4 servings.

BROILED QUAIL

4 cleaned quail, each split down the backbone and pressed flat
Salt and freshly ground black pepper
1 teaspoon minced garlic
1 tablespoon finely chopped lemon grass
1 teaspoon sugar
1 tablespoon fish sauce
1 tablespoon lime juice or vinegar
1-2 tablespoons vegetable oil
Lettuce leaves
Cilantro leaves to garnish
Spicy Fish Sauce (page 311) to serve

Rub the 4 quail all over with plenty of salt and pepper.

In a medium bowl, blend garlic, lemon grass, sugar, fish sauce and lime juice or vinegar. Add quail, turning to coat in the mixture, then marinate 2-3 hours in the refrigerator, turning over occasionally.

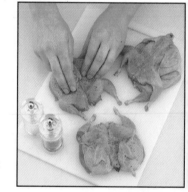

Preheat grill or broiler. Brush quail with oil and cook over grill or under broiler 6-8 minutes each side, basting with remaining marinade during first 5 minutes of cooking. Serve quail on a bed of lettuce leaves, garnished with cilantro leaves, accompanied by Spicy Fish Sauce as a dip.

Makes 4 servings.

PHEASANT WITH SULTANAS

⅓ cup sultanas
½ cup medium sherry
¼ cup olive oil
1 young pheasant
Salt and freshly ground pepper
1 oz. pine nuts

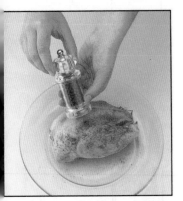

Preheat oven to 375F (190C). Put sultanas in a small bowl, add sherry and leave to soak. Rub 2 tablespoons of oil over pheasant and season with salt and pepper.

Put pheasant in a roasting pan and roast 30 to 45 minutes or until cooked through and tender. Just before pheasant is ready, drain sultanas, reserving sherry. Heat remaining oil in a skillet and cook pine nuts until golden. Add sultanas and cook 1 minute.

Carve pheasant and arrange on warmed serving plates. Scatter with pine nuts and sultanas and keep warm. Pour reserved sherry into roasting pan and heat, stirring to incorporate any sediment. Pour over pheasant and serve.

Makes 2 or 3 servings.

QUAIL WITH FIGS & ORANGES

3 tablespoons olive oil
8 quails
1 onion, thinly sliced
2 stalks celery, thinly sliced
⅔ cup dry white wine
⅔ cup hot chicken stock
Salt and freshly ground pepper
2 oranges
4 figs

Preheat oven to 325F (160C). Heat 2 tablespoons olive oil in a heavy pan. Add quails and cook until browned all over. Remove and set aside.

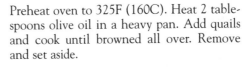

Add onion and celery to pan and cook over low heat 7 minutes or until soft and lightly browned. Replace quails and add wine and hot stock. Season with salt and pepper. Cover and cook in oven 30 to 40 minutes or until quails are cooked through. Just before end of cooking time, preheat broiler. Peel oranges, removing all pith and cut each one into four thick slices. Cut figs in half.

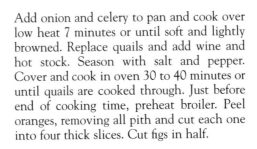

Brush orange slices with olive oil and broil 2 or 3 minutes. Turn, add figs and broil cut sides 2 minutes. Set aside and keep warm. Transfer quails, onion and celery to a warmed serving dish. Add cooking juices, arrange oranges and figs around birds and serve.

Makes 4 servings.

SPANISH PARTRIDGES

2 partridges, cut in half lengthwise
2 tablespoons brandy
Salt and pepper
3 tablespoons olive oil
1 Spanish onion, chopped
3 garlic cloves, finely chopped
2 tablespoons all-purpose flour
¼ cup red-wine vinegar
1 cup red wine
1 cup chicken stock
6 black peppercorns
2 whole cloves
1 bay leaf
2 carrots, cut into short lengths
8 shallots
1 oz. chocolate, grated

Stir vinegar into pan and boil 1 to 2 minutes. Add wine and boil 1 to 2 minutes, then add stock, peppercorns, cloves, bay leaf and partridges. Heat to a simmer, cover tightly and simmer 40 minutes. Add carrots and shallots, cover again and simmer 20 minutes.

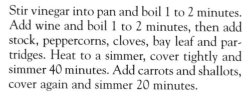

Rub partridges with brandy, salt and pepper and set aside 30 minutes. In a heavy pan into which the birds fit snugly, heat oil. Add onion and cook, stirring occasionally, 3 minutes. Stir in garlic and cook 2 minutes.

Transfer partridges, shallots and carrots to a warm dish. If necessary, boil the cooking juices until reduced to 1¼ cups, then purée in a blender or food processor with the metal blade.

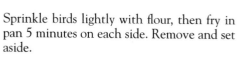

Sprinkle birds lightly with flour, then fry in pan 5 minutes on each side. Remove and set aside.

Return juices to pan over low heat and stir in chocolate until melted. Return partridges and vegetables to pan and turn them over in the sauce to coat.

Makes 4 servings.

PROVENÇAL RABBIT

3 ozs. pancetta
2 tablespoons olive oil
1 onion, chopped
4 rabbit portions
1 tablespoon seasoned flour
3 tablespoons tapénade (page 24)
1¾ cups chicken stock
⅔ cup dry white wine
2 fresh bay leaves
2 sprigs of thyme
Salt and freshly ground pepper
1 small fennel bulb, roughly chopped
Black olives and fennel leaves, to garnish

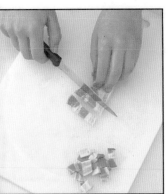

Preheat oven to 350F (180C). Roughly chop half pancetta.

Heat half oil in a Dutch oven. Add onion and chopped pancetta and cook 3 minutes. Remove with a slotted spoon and set aside. Dust rabbit portions with seasoned flour. Heat remaining oil in pan, add rabbit and cook until browned all over. Mix together tapénade, stock and wine and pour over rabbit. Add onion, pancetta, bay leaves and thyme. Season with salt and pepper and bring to a boil. Cover and cook in oven 45 minutes.

Add fennel and cook 45 minutes or until rabbit is cooked through and tender. Broil remaining pancetta until crisp then snip into small pieces. Scatter pancetta over rabbit. Garnish with olives and fennel leaves and serve.

Makes 4 servings.

Note: If you don't have time to make your own tapénade (page 24), it can be bought ready made, in small jars.

VENISON RAGOÛT

1 tablespoon all-purpose flour
Salt and freshly ground pepper
2 lbs. venison chuck, cubed
1 tablespoon olive oil
1 garlic clove, chopped
1¼ cups beef stock
1 tablespoon balsamic vinegar
8 juniper berries
8 black peppercorns
4 whole cloves
1 (14-oz.) can crushed tomatoes
8 ozs. baby carrots, trimmed
4 ozs. button mushrooms
1 tablespoon chopped fresh parsley

Preheat oven to 350F (180C). Season flour with salt and pepper and use to coat venison. Heat oil in a large flameproof casserole dish. Add venison, remaining seasoned flour and garlic and cook, stirring, 4 or 5 minutes.

Add stock, vinegar, juniper berries, peppercorns, cloves, tomatoes and carrots. Bring to a boil, cover and bake 1 hour or until venison is tender. Add mushrooms and cook 15 minutes. Sprinkle with chopped parsley and serve hot.

Makes 6 to 8 servings.

RABBIT STIFADO

2 tablespoons all-purpose flour
Salt and pepper
1½-2 lbs. rabbit pieces
⅓ cup extra-virgin olive oil
1 lb. tiny pearl onions
1 garlic clove, crushed
1 tablespoon tomato paste
1¼ cups red wine
1¼ cups chicken stock
1 bay leaf
2 fresh thyme sprigs
2 bread slices, crusts removed
2 tablespoons chopped fresh parsley

On a plate, mix together flour, salt and pepper. Toss rabbit pieces in seasoned flour. In a skillet, heat half the oil. Fry rabbit pieces until brown on both sides. Transfer to a flameproof casserole dish. Add onions to skillet and cook until they begin to brown. Add garlic and tomato paste to pan, then stir in wine and stock. Add bay leaf, thyme, salt and pepper. Add to casserole dish, cover and cook over low heat 1½ to 2 hours or until rabbit is tender.

Cut each slice of bread into 4 triangles. In a skillet, heat remaining oil. Fry bread until golden-brown on both sides. Dip one edge of each triangle into chopped parsley. To serve, place rabbit on a shallow plate and arrange onions around edge. Pour the sauce over the rabbit and garnish with fried bread.

Makes 6 servings.

RABBIT IN MUSTARD SAUCE

¼ cup butter
8 rabbit pieces
1 cup dry white wine
½ cup Dijon mustard
1 thyme sprig
Salt and freshly ground pepper
½ cup plain yogurt
Chopped fresh flat-leaf parsley and thyme sprigs to garnish

Melt butter in a flameproof casserole dish. Add rabbit and cook 5 to 10 minutes, turning, until browned all over. Remove with a slotted spoon.

Stir in wine, mustard, thyme, salt and pepper and bring to a boil. Return rabbit to dish, cover and simmer 25 minutes or until tender. Remove rabbit with a slotted spoon and keep warm.

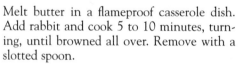

Boil sauce until reduced by half. Remove and discard thyme sprig and stir in yogurt. Warm through over low heat. Garnish rabbit with chopped parsley and thyme sprigs, add sauce and serve.

Makes 4 servings.

BEEF & VEAL

STEAK WITH BÉARNAISE SAUCE

4 beef sirloin steaks, about 1-inch thick
Salt and freshly ground pepper
BÉARNAISE SAUCE:
½ cup unsalted butter, diced
3 stalks each tarragon and chervil
2 teaspoons chopped shallot
4 black peppercorns, crushed
2 tablespoons dry white wine
2 tablespoons white wine vinegar
2 egg yolks
1 teaspoon each chopped fresh tarragon, parsley and chervil

Preheat broiler. Oil broiler rack, add steaks and season with pepper.

Broil 1 to 3 minutes on each side, according to taste. Meanwhile, make sauce. Melt butter in a small saucepan. Put tarragon and chervil stalks, shallot, peppercorns, wine and vinegar in a small saucepan, bring to a boil and boil until reduced to 2 teaspoons. Strain.

Put egg yolks into a blender or food processor with 2 teaspoons water and process briefly to combine. With motor running at low speed, pour in reduce liquid. With motor still running at low speed, pour in melted butter in a slow, steady stream, to make a thick sauce. Add herbs, salt and pepper and serve immediately with steaks.

Makes 4 servings.

Note: Use only very fresh, uncracked eggs for sauce.

PROVENÇAL BEEF DAUBE

1 large onion, chopped
1¼ cups red wine
3 garlic cloves, crushed
2 fresh bay leaves
1 sprig of thyme
Salt and freshly ground pepper
2¼ lbs. lean beef chuck, cubed
2 tablespoons olive oil
6 ozs. bacon, diced
1 tablespoon all-purpose flour
2 tablespoons balsamic vinegar
2 ripe tomatoes, chopped
6-inch strip pared orange zest
12 black olives, pitted and halved
1¼-2½ cups beef stock

Put onion, wine, garlic, bay leaves, thyme, salt and pepper in a large shallow dish and mix well. Add beef and stir well to coat. Cover and leave in a cool place overnight. Preheat oven to 325F (160C). Remove beef from marinade, reserving marinade, and pat beef dry on paper towels. Heat oil in a Dutch oven, add bacon and cook until golden. Remove with a slotted spoon and set aside.

Add beef to pan and cook until browned all over. Sprinkle on flour and cook 1 minute, stirring. Add reserved marinade and vinegar. Add tomatoes, orange zest and olives. Pour in enough stock to cover beef and season with salt and pepper. Cover tightly and cook in oven 3 hours or until beef is tender. If necessary, add more stock during cooking. Discard bay leaves, thyme and orange zest and serve.

Makes 4 to 6 servings.

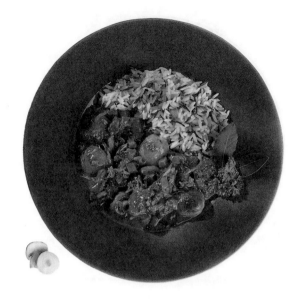

SPICY BRAISED BEEF

2 garlic cloves, crushed
½ teaspoon ground cinnamon
¼ teaspoon ground cloves
Salt and freshly ground pepper
1 (3-lb.) lean beef top round roast
3 tablespoons olive oil
4 onions, thinly sliced
½ cup red wine
2 tablespoons tomato paste
1 lb. spaghetti
1 tablespoon balsamic vinegar

Mix together garlic, cinnamon, cloves, salt and pepper. Make incisions in beef and push in garlic mixture.

Leave in a cool place 1 hour. Heat oil in a pan into which meat will just fit. Add meat and cook, turning, until browned all over. Remove from pan. Add onions and cook over low heat until soft and lightly browned. Replace meat, add wine and enough water to barely cover. Mix tomato paste with a little water. Stir into pan. Season, cover and simmer, turning meat frequently, about 1½ hours or until tender.

Bring a large saucepan of salted water to a boil. Cook spaghetti according to package instructions until just tender. Drain. Remove meat from pan and keep warm. Add vinegar to sauce. Boil over high heat until reduced to a smooth glossy sauce. Slice beef and arrange on warmed serving plates. Pour a little sauce over beef, stir remainder into spaghetti and serve with beef.

Makes 6 servings.

BOEUF BOURGUIGNON

1-2 tablespoons olive oil
2 slices thick-cut bacon, chopped
12 each pearl onions and button mushrooms
2 lbs. beef chuck steak, cubed
1 large onion, finely chopped
1 carrot, finely chopped
3 garlic cloves, chopped
1 tablespoon all-purpose flour
3 cups red Burgundy wine
Bouquet garni
Salt and freshly ground pepper
Chopped fresh parsley, parsley sprigs and bay leaves to garnish

Heat 1 tablespoon oil in a heavy Dutch oven, add bacon and cook 2 or 3 minutes.

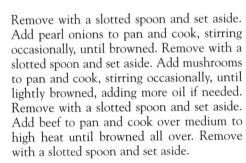

Remove with a slotted spoon and set aside. Add pearl onions to pan and cook, stirring occasionally, until browned. Remove with a slotted spoon and set aside. Add mushrooms to pan and cook, stirring occasionally, until lightly browned, adding more oil if needed. Remove with a slotted spoon and set aside. Add beef to pan and cook over medium to high heat until browned all over. Remove with a slotted spoon and set aside.

Add chopped onion and carrot to pan and cook, stirring occasionally, until beginning to brown. Return bacon and beef to pan, add garlic and stir in flour. Stir in wine, bouquet garni, salt and plenty of pepper. Heat until almost simmering, cover and cook over very low heat 2¾ hours, stirring occasionally. Add reserved onions and mushrooms, cover and cook 10 minutes, to warm through. Garnish with parsley and bay leaves and serve.

Makes 4 servings.

STIR-FRIED BEEF WITH LEEKS

1 lb. lean beef round or sirloin steak
1 tablespoon dark soy sauce
1 teaspoon sesame oil
Freshly ground pepper
1 tablespoon dry sherry
2 teaspoons cornstarch
1 lb. leeks
4 ozs. green onions
2 teaspoons sunflower oil
2 teaspoons sugar
⅔ cup Chinese Beef Stock (see glossary)
2 tablespoons chopped fresh chives
Fresh chives to garnish

Trim any fat from the beef and cut into ¾-inch pieces. Place in a bowl and mix in soy sauce, sesame oil, pepper, sherry and cornstarch. Cover and chill 30 minutes. Trim leeks and discard any coarse outer leaves. Slice thinly and wash well to remove any soil. Trim and shred green onions.

Heat oil in a nonstick or well-seasoned wok and stir-fry beef mixture 1 or 2 minutes or until beef is browned. Add leeks, green onions and sugar and stir-fry 3 or 4 minutes or until browned. Pour in stock and simmer 5 minutes, stirring occasionally, until thickened. Stir in chopped chives, garnish with chives and serve with noodles.

Makes 4 servings.

GARLIC BEEF CASSEROLE

1 lb. lean beef chuck, trimmed and cut into ¾-inch cubes
1 tablespoon peanut oil
2 shallots, chopped
4 garlic cloves, thinly sliced
2 large carrots, sliced
6 ozs. baby corn, halved lengthwise
8 ozs. button mushrooms
1¼ cups Chinese Beef Stock (see glossary)
2 tablespoons dark soy sauce
1 tablespoon rice wine
2 teaspoons five-spice powder
2 tablespoons hoisin sauce
1 teaspoon chile sauce

Heat oil in a nonstick or well-seasoned wok and stir-fry beef, shallots, garlic, carrots, baby corn and mushrooms 5 minutes. Add remaining ingredients and bring to a boil. Reduce to a simmer, cover and simmer 1 hour.

Remove from heat and blot surface with paper towels to absorb surface fat. Increase the heat and boil 10 minutes to reduce and thicken sauce. Serve with rice.

Makes 4 servings.

STIR-FRIED BEEF STEAK

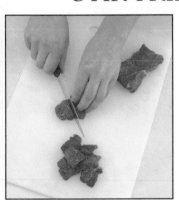

8 ozs. beef steak, cut into small, thin slices, about
  1 inch square
¼ teaspoon freshly ground black pepper
1 teaspoon sugar
1 tablespoon fish sauce
2 tablespoons vegetable oil
1 clove garlic, chopped
1 small onion, sliced
1 green bell pepper, cut into cubes
4 ozs. sliced bamboo shoots, drained
1 firm tomato, cut into 8 wedges
2 green onions, cut into short lengths
2 tablespoons soy or oyster sauce
2 teaspoons cornstarch

Mix beef with black pepper, sugar and fish sauce and marinate 15-20 minutes. Heat oil in a wok or frying pan over high heat and stir-fry garlic and onion about 1 minute. Add the beef and stir-fry 1 minute.

Add the bell pepper, bamboo shoots, tomato and green onions. Stir-fry 2-3 minutes, then blend in the soy or oyster sauce. Mix the cornstarch with 1 tablespoon water and stir into mixture. Cook, stirring, until thickened. Serve with rice noodles.

Makes 4 servings.

SZECHUAN BEEF

1 lb. lean beef fillet
1 tablespoon sunflower oil
1 garlic clove, finely chopped
1 (½-inch) piece fresh gingerroot, peeled and finely
  chopped
4 green onions, finely chopped
1 tablespoon hoisin sauce
1 teaspoon Szechuan peppercorns, toasted and
  ground
4 ozs. vegetable chow-chow
1 teaspoon sugar
Shredded green onions to garnish

Trim any fat and silver skin from beef. Cut beef into very thin slices.

Heat oil in a nonstick or well-seasoned wok and stir-fry beef, garlic, ginger and green onions 1 minute or until beef is browned.

Add remaining ingredients except the garnish and stir-fry 3 or 4 minutes or until beef is just cooked through. Garnish with shredded green onions and serve with rice.

Makes 4 servings.

BEEF-STUFFED CABBAGE

2 onions
5 tablespoons vegetable oil
3 garlic cloves, crushed
2 green chiles, seeded, chopped
1 (3-inch) piece fresh gingerroot, grated
1 lb. ground beef
¼ teaspoon ground turmeric
2 teaspoons garam masala
1 savoy cabbage
1 (14-oz.) can chopped tomatoes
2 tablespoons lemon juice
Salt and pepper to taste
⅔ cup water
Lemon slices to garnish

Chop 1 onion and slice the other.

Heat 2 tablespoons oil in a heavy saucepan, add chopped onion and cook, stirring, over medium heat about 8 minutes, until soft and golden brown. Add garlic, chiles and one-third of the gingerroot; cook 1 minute, then remove with a slotted spoon and set aside.

Add beef to pan and cook, stirring, until browned and well broken up. Stir in turmeric and Garam Masala, cook 1 minute, then add onion mixture.

Cover and cook 20 to 30 minutes, stirring occasionally, until cooking liquid is absorbed; cool. Remove core from cabbage with a sharp knife. Cook whole cabbage in boiling salted water 8 minutes, then drain and rinse in cold water. Leave until cool enough to handle, then carefully peel off 12 to 16 outside leaves, keeping them whole. Finely shred rest of cabbage.

Make sauce, heat remaining oil in a heavy saucepan, add sliced onion and cook, stirring frequently, 5 minutes, or until soft, but not brown. Add shredded cabbage, tomatoes, remaining gingerroot, lemon juice, salt, pepper and water. Bring to a boil and simmer 5 minutes.

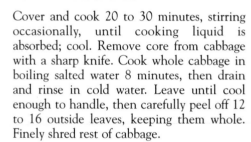

Preheat oven to 375F (190C). Put about 2 tablespoons beef mixture on each cabbage leaf, fold sides in and roll up neatly. Pour a little sauce into bottom of a casserole dish, add cabbage rolls and pour over rest of sauce. Cover and bake 40 to 50 minutes, until cabbage is tender. Serve hot, garnished with lemon slices.

Makes 4 servings.

BEEF WITH TOMATO SAUCE

GARLIC BEEF

2 garlic cloves, thinly sliced
1 tablespoon finely chopped fresh thyme
1 tablespoon finely chopped fresh marjoram
1 (1½-lb.) beef chuck steak
2 tablespoons olive oil
TOMATO SAUCE:
2 tablespoons olive oil
8 garlic cloves, chopped
1 fresh thyme sprig
2 fresh marjoram sprigs
3 fresh parsley sprigs
1 (14-oz.) can chopped tomatoes
8 canned anchovy fillets, drained and chopped
¾ cup dry white wine
24 small ripe olives, pitted
Salt and pepper

2 tablespoons olive oil
1 (4-oz.) piece slab bacon, cut into 2-inch cubes
1 (2-lb.) beef chuck steak, cut into 1½-inch cubes
1 Spanish onion, chopped
1 head garlic, divided into cloves
1 cup red wine
2 whole cloves
Bouquet garni of 1 fresh marjoram sprig, 1 fresh
  thyme sprig, 2 fresh parsley sprigs and 1 bay leaf
Salt and pepper

To make the sauce, in a saucepan, heat oil. Add garlic and herbs and simmer 5 minutes. Add tomatoes with their juice, then stir in anchovies, wine and olives. Simmer 15 minutes. Season to taste with salt and pepper.

In a large pan, heat oil. Add bacon and cook over low heat until bacon is almost crisp. Increase heat, add beef and cook about 5 minutes, stirring occasionally, until browned all over. Using a slotted spoon, transfer beef and bacon to a bowl.

Meanwhile, mix garlic with chopped herbs. Using the point of a sharp knife, cut small slits in beef and push the herb-covered slices of garlic deep into slits. In a large pan, heat oil. Add beef and cook 10 minutes until evenly browned. Add sauce, cover tightly and simmer about 1½ hours, turning beef occasionally, until beef is tender.

Makes 4 servings.

Stir onion and garlic into pan and cook 6 minutes, stirring occasionally. Stir in wine, cloves, bouquet garni, salt and pepper. Return meat to pan, cover tightly and simmer 2 hours, stirring occasionally, until meat is very tender. Add a little water if mixture gets too dry. Discard bouquet garni.

Makes 6 servings.

BEEF WITH WATER CHESTNUTS

1 lb. lean beef round or sirloin steak
1 tablespoon dark soy sauce
1 tablespoon dry sherry
1 teaspoon chile sauce
2 teaspoons brown sugar
2 teaspoons cornstarch
8 ozs. broccoli
1 (4-oz.) can water chestnuts, drained
1 tablespoon sunflower oil
Salt and freshly ground pepper
Strips of fresh red chile to garnish

Trim any fat from beef and cut into ¾-inch pieces.

Place beef in a bowl, and mix with soy sauce, sherry, chile sauce, sugar and cornstarch. Cover and chill 30 minutes. Meanwhile, cut broccoli into small flowerets. Bring a small saucepan of water to a boil and cook broccoli 3 minutes. Drain and rinse in cold water. Halve water chestnuts.

Heat oil in a nonstick or well-seasoned wok. Add beef mixture and stir-fry 2 or 3 minutes. Add broccoli and water chestnuts, season with salt and pepper and stir-fry 3 minutes. Garnish with red chile strips and serve with noodles.

Makes 4 servings.

SHREDDED BEEF & GINGER

1 tablespoon cornstarch
¾ cup beef stock
¾ cup dry sherry
2 teaspoons sugar
Salt and freshly ground pepper
2 teaspoons olive oil
2 carrots, cut into matchstick strips
2-inch piece fresh gingerroot, peeled and finely chopped
2 garlic cloves, crushed
12 ozs. lean beef round steak, cut into thin strips
6 ozs. snow peas

In a bowl, blend cornstarch with stock, sherry, sugar, salt and pepper and set aside. In a large skillet or wok, heat oil over high heat and stir-fry carrots, ginger and garlic 2 minutes. Add steak and stir-fry 3 minutes, until the meat is browned all over and cooked through. Add snow peas and stir-fry 1 minute.

Add cornstarch mixture and bring to a boil over high heat, stirring continuously 1 or 2 minutes, until sauce is thickened and glossy. Serve immediately with freshly cooked fusilli.

Makes 3½ cups or 4 servings.

LIGHT BEEF SATAY

1 lb. lean beef round or sirloin steak
MARINADE:
1 shallot, finely chopped
1 (1-inch) piece fresh gingerroot, peeled and finely
  chopped
2 garlic cloves, finely chopped
Zest and juice of 1 lime
2 teaspoons garam masala
Salt and freshly ground pepper
1 teaspoon light soy sauce
SAUCE:
6 tablespoons unsweetened shredded coconut
2 tablespoons crunchy peanut butter
1 tablespoon brown sugar
1 teaspoon sunflower oil
2 garlic cloves, finely chopped
1 fresh red chile, seeded and chopped
1 tablespoon dark soy sauce
Strips of fresh red chile to garnish

Soak 8 bamboo skewers in cold water to prevent the beef sticking to them. Trim any fat from the beef and cut into ¼-inch strips. Place in a shallow dish.

Mix together the marinade ingredients and pour over the beef. Mix well, cover and chill 2 hours.

Meanwhile, make the sauce. Place shredded coconut in a bowl and pour 1 cup boiling water over coconut. Leave for 30 minutes. Place a fine strainer over a bowl and pour the mixture through the strainer, pressing the coconut with a spatula or spoon to extract all the water. Discard coconut.

Blend coconut water with the peanut butter and brown sugar. Heat oil in a nonstick or well-seasoned wok and stir-fry garlic and chile 1 minute. Stir in peanut butter mixture and soy sauce and bring to a boil. Reduce heat and simmer 10 minutes, stirring occasionally, until thickened. Set aside.

Thread beef strips along each skewer in the shape of an S. Preheat broiler. Cover ends of skewers with foil to prevent burning. Broil beef 3 or 4 minutes on each side. Drain on paper towels. Reheat peanut sauce. Garnish with strips of red chile. Serve skewers on a bed of rice with the peanut sauce, lime wedges and a green salad.

Makes 4 servings.

THAI BEEF WITH NOODLES

¼ cup rice wine or dry sherry
2 tablespoons light soy sauce
2 garlic cloves, finely chopped
1-inch piece fresh gingerroot, peeled and finely
 chopped
½ teaspoon dried crushed chiles
1 lb. sirloin or tenderloin steak, 1-inch thick, cut
 crosswise into ½-inch strips
12 ozs. ramen noodles or thin spaghetti
1 tablespoon sesame oil
4 ozs. snow peas
4-6 green onions, cut into 2-inch pieces
2 teaspoons cornstarch, dissolved in ¼ cup water
2 tablespoons chopped cilantro
Cilantro leaves and lime slices to garnish

THAI BEEF CURRY

2 tablespoons vegetable oil
3 tablespoons ready-made Thai red curry paste
12 ozs. lean beef, cut into cubes
1 stalk lemon grass, finely chopped
4 ozs. long beans, or green beans, cut into 1½-inch
 lengths
About 8 pieces dried Chinese black mushrooms,
 soaked 20 minutes, drained and chopped
3 tablespoons roasted peanuts
1 fresh green chile, seeded and chopped
¼ cup water
1 tablespoon fish sauce
2 teaspoons crushed palm sugar
15 Thai mint leaves

In a shallow baking dish, combine rice wine, soy sauce, garlic, gingerroot and chiles. Add steak to dish and marinate 30 minutes, covered, turning once. Cook noodles according to package directions, drain and set aside. Heat wok until very hot. Add sesame oil and swirl to coat wok. Remove steak from marinade, scraping off any gingerroot and garlic and reserving marinade. Pat steak dry with paper towels. Add steak to wok and stir-fry 4 minutes or until browned. Remove and keep warm.

In a wok, heat the oil, add curry paste and stir 3 minutes. Add beef and lemon grass and stir-fry 5 minutes. Add beans and mushrooms, stir-fry 3 minutes then stir in peanuts and chile.

Add snow peas and green onions to any oil remaining in wok and stir-fry 1 minute. Stir cornstarch mixture and stir into wok with reserved marinade. Bring to a boil, stirring. Add reserved noodles and chopped cilantro. Add beef. Toss to coat well. Divide among 4 plates. Garnish with cilantro leaves and lime slices.

Makes 4 servings.

Stir for 1 minute then stir in water, fish sauce and sugar and cook about 2 minutes until beans are crisp-tender. Transfer to a warmed serving dish and sprinkle with mint leaves.

Makes 3-4 servings.

MANGO BEEF WITH CASHEWS

1 lb. lean beef round or sirloin steak
1 garlic clove, finely chopped
1 tablespoon light soy sauce
1 tablespoon rice wine
1 teaspoon cornstarch
Salt and freshly ground pepper
2 ripe mangoes
1 tablespoon sunflower oil
2 tablespoons chopped fresh cilantro
1 oz. unsalted cashew nuts, coarsely crushed

Trim any fat from the beef and cut into ¼-inch strips.

Place in a bowl and mix with garlic, soy sauce, rice wine, cornstarch, salt and pepper. Cover and chill 30 minutes. Peel the mangoes and slice flesh off the large flat pit in the center of each mango. Cut flesh into thick, even slices, reserving a few small strips garnish.

Heat oil in a nonstick or well-seasoned wok and stir-fry beef mixture 3 or 4 minutes until beef is browned all over. Stir in sliced mango and cook over low heat 2 or 3 minutes to heat through. Sprinkle with chopped cilantro and crushed cashews, garnish with reserved mango and serve on a bed of rice.

Makes 4 servings.

SPICY SESAME BEEF

1 tablespoon cornstarch
3 tablespoons light soy sauce
1 lb. beef sirloin steak, cut crosswise into thin strips
12 ozs. broccoli
2 tablespoons sesame oil
1 (1-inch) piece gingerroot, peeled and cut into julienne strips
2 garlic cloves, finely chopped
1 fresh hot red chile, seeded and thinly sliced
1 red bell pepper, thinly sliced
1 (14-oz.) can baby corn-on-the-cob, drained
½ cup beef stock, chicken stock or water
4-6 green onions, cut into 2-inch pieces
Toasted sesame seeds to garnish
Noodles or rice to serve

In a bowl, combine cornstarch and soy sauce. Add beef strips and toss to coat well. Let stand 20 minutes. Cut large flowerets from the broccoli and divide into small flowerets. With a vegetable peeler, peel the stalk and cut diagonally into 1-inch pieces. Heat a wok until very hot. Add sesame oil and swirl to coat. Add beef strips and marinade and stir-fry 2 or 3 minutes or until browned.

With a slotted spoon, remove beef strips to a bowl. Add gingerroot, garlic and chile to the wok and stir-fry 1 minute. Add broccoli, bell pepper and baby corn and stir-fry 2 or 3 minutes or until broccoli is tender but still crisp. Add the stock and stir 1 minute or until sauce bubbles and thickens. Add green onions and reserved beef strips and stir-fry 1 or 2 minutes or until beef strips are heated through. Sprinkle with sesame seeds and serve with noodles or rice.

Makes 4 servings.

GINGER BEEF WITH PINEAPPLE

1 lb. lean beef round or sirloin steak
Salt and freshly ground pepper
1 tablespoon sweet sherry
1 (1-inch) piece fresh gingerroot, peeled and finely
  chopped
1 garlic clove, finely chopped
1 teaspoon cornstarch
8 ozs. fresh pineapple
1 tablespoon sunflower oil
2 red bell peppers, thinly sliced
4 green onions, chopped
2 tablespoons light soy sauce
1 piece stem ginger in syrup, drained and thinly
  sliced

Trim any visible fat from the beef and cut into ¼-inch strips. Place in a bowl and season. Add sherry, chopped ginger, garlic and cornstarch and mix well. Cover and chill 30 minutes. Meanwhile, peel and core the pineapple and cut into 1-inch cubes.

Heat oil in a nonstick or well-seasoned wok, add beef mixture and stir-fry 1 or 2 minutes or until beef is browned all over. Add bell peppers and stir-fry for another minute. Add green onions, pineapple and soy sauce and simmer 2 or 3 minutes, to heat through. Sprinkle with stem ginger and serve on a bed of noodles.

Makes 4 servings.

DRY-FRIED BEEF STRIPS

2 tablespoons sesame oil
1 lb. beef round or sirloin steak, cut crosswise into
  julienne strips
2 tablespoons rice wine or dry sherry
1 tablespoon light soy sauce
2 garlic cloves, finely chopped
1 (½-inch) piece gingerroot, peeled and finely
  chopped
1 tablespoon Chinese hot bean sauce
2 teaspoons sugar
1 carrot, cut into julienne strips
2 celery stalks, cut into julienne strips
2 or 3 green onions, thinly sliced
¼ teaspoon ground Szechuan pepper
White and wild rice mixture to serve

Heat a wok until very hot. Add oil and swirl to coat wok. Add beef and stir-fry 15 seconds to quickly seal meat. Add 1 tablespoon of the rice wine and stir-fry 1 or 2 minutes or until beef is browned. Pour off and reserve any excess liquid and continue stir-frying until beef is dry.

Stir in soy sauce, garlic, gingerroot, bean sauce, sugar, remaining rice wine and any reserved cooking juices and stir to blend well. Add carrot, celery, green onions and ground Szechuan pepper and stir-fry until the vegetables begin to soften and all the liquid is absorbed. Serve with rice.

Makes 4 servings.

TERIYAKA STEAKS

SPICY BEEF WITH PEPPERS

¼ cup mirin or dry sherry sweetened with 1
 teaspoon sugar
¼ cup light soy sauce
1 (½-inch) piece gingerroot, peeled and minced
1 garlic clove, finely chopped
1 teaspoon sugar
½ teaspoon red pepper sauce or to taste
4 beef sirloin or tenderloin steaks, cut into strips
2 tablespoons sesame oil
4 green onions, thinly sliced
Cilantro leaves to garnish
Marinated cucumbers and rice to serve

In a shallow baking dish, combine mirin, soy
sauce, gingerroot, garlic, sugar and red pepper sauce to taste.

1 tablespoon cornstarch
¼ cup water
¼ cup light soy sauce
1 tablespoon honey or brown sugar
1 teaspoon Chinese chile sauce
2 tablespoons vegetable oil
1 lb. beef round or sirloin steak, cut crosswise into
 thin strips
1 tablespoon sesame oil
2 garlic cloves, finely chopped
1 fresh hot red chile, seeded and thinly sliced
1 onion, thinly sliced
1 each red, green and yellow bell pepper, cut into
 thin strips
Rice to serve

Add the meat and turn to coat well. Let
stand 1 hour, turning strips once or twice.

In a small bowl, dissolve cornstarch in the
water. Stir in soy sauce, honey and chile
sauce until blended. Set aside. Heat a wok
until very hot. Add vegetable oil and swirl to
coat wok. Add beef strips and stir-fry 2 or 3
minutes or until beef is browned. With a
slotted spoon, remove beef to a bowl.

Heat a wok until very hot. Add sesame oil
and swirl to coat wok. Drain meat, reserving
marinade, and add to wok. Stir-fry 2 or 3
minutes or until browned on all sides. Add
marinade and green onions. Cook 3 to 5
minutes or until meat is cooked to desired
doneness and most of marinade has evaporated, glazing the meat. Garnish with
cilantro and serve with marinated cucumbers
and rice.

Makes 4 servings.

Add sesame oil to the wok and add garlic
and chile. Stir-fry 1 minute or until fragrant.
Add onion and bell pepper strips and stir-fry
2 or 3 minutes or until beginning to soften.
Stir cornstarch mixture, then stir into mixture in wok and stir until sauce bubbles and
begins to thicken. Add beef strips and any
juices and stir-fry 1 minute or until beef is
heated through. Serve with rice.

Makes 4 servings.

BEEF IN OYSTER SAUCE

1 tablespoon cornstarch
1½ tablespoons soy sauce
1½ tablespoons soy wine or dry sherry
1 lb. beef round, sirloin or tenderloin steak, cut
  crosswise into thin strips
2 tablespoons sesame oil
½-inch piece gingerroot, peeled and chopped
2 garlic cloves, finely chopped
4 stalks celery, sliced
1 red bell pepper sliced
4 ozs. mushrooms, sliced
4 green onions, sliced
2 tablespoons oyster sauce
½ cup chicken stock or water
White and wild rice mixture to serve

In a bowl, combine 2 teaspoons of the corn-starch with soy sauce and sherry. Add beef strips and toss to coat well. Let stand 25 minutes. Heat a wok until very hot. Add oil and swirl to coat wok. Add beef strips and stir-fry 2 or 3 minutes or until browned. With a slotted spoon, remove to a bowl. Add gingeroot and garlic to oil remaining in wok and stir-fry 1 minute. Add celery, bell pepper, mushrooms and green onions and stir-fry 2 or 3 minutes or until vegetables begin to soften.

Stir in oyster sauce and combine remaining cornstarch with the stock, then stir into mixture in wok and bring to a boil. Add reserved beef strips and cook, stirring, 1 minute or until sauce bubbles and thicken and beef is heated through. Serve with rice.

Makes 4 servings.

BEEF STROGANOFF

2 tablespoons peanut oil and 1 tablespoon butter
1 lb. beef tenderloin or boneless sirloin steak, cut
  crosswise into ½-inch strips
1 onion, thinly sliced
½ lb. mushrooms, thinly sliced
Salt and freshly ground black pepper
1 tablespoon all-purpose flour
½ cup beef stock or veal stock
1 tablespoon Dijon-style mustard (optional)
1 cup dairy sour cream
2 tablespoons chopped dill
Pinch of red (cayenne) pepper
Rice to serve

Heat a wok until very hot. Add oil and swirl to coat wok. Add half of the beef strips.

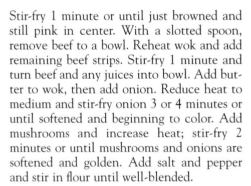

Stir-fry 1 minute or until just browned and still pink in center. With a slotted spoon, remove beef to a bowl. Reheat wok and add remaining beef strips. Stir-fry 1 minute and turn beef and any juices into bowl. Add butter to wok, then add onion. Reduce heat to medium and stir-fry onion 3 or 4 minutes or until softened and beginning to color. Add mushrooms and increase heat; stir-fry 2 minutes or until mushrooms and onions are softened and golden. Add salt and pepper and stir in flour until well-blended.

Add beef broth and bring to a boil, then simmer 1 minute or until sauce thickens. Stir in mustard, if using, and gradually add the sour cream. (Do not allow sour cream to boil.) Return beef strips and any juices to sauce, stir in chopped dill and simmer 1 minute or until beef is heated through. Sprinkle a little cayenne. Serve with rice.

Makes 6 servings.

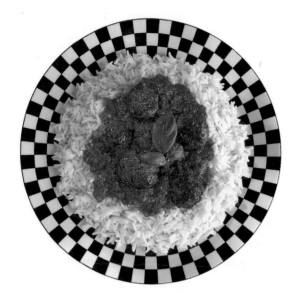

MEATBALLS IN TOMATO SAUCE

¼ cup milk
1 egg, beaten
½ teaspoon freshly grated nutmeg
1 slice white bread
2 onions, finely chopped
2 garlic cloves, crushed
1 teaspoon dried thyme
2 tablespoons chopped fresh parsley
1 lb. lean ground beef
1 tablespoon olive oil
1 (14-oz.) can crushed tomatoes
2 tablespoons tomato paste
Salt and freshly ground pepper
Basil leaves to garnish

In a shallow dish, mix together milk, egg and nutmeg. Add bread and soak 5 minutes. In a bowl, mix half of the onions and garlic with thyme, parsley and ground beef. Squeeze liquid from bread and add bread to beef mixture. Mix well and shape into 30 balls. Heat oil in a flameproof casserole dish. Add meatballs in batches and cook, turning, about 8 minutes, or until browned all over. Remove with a slotted spoon, drain on paper towels and keep warm.

Add remaining onion and garlic to dish with crushed tomatoes, tomato paste, salt and pepper. Bring to a boil and cook over medium heat, stirring constantly, until reduced and thickened. Add meatballs and heat gently to warm through. Garnish and serve.

Makes 4 servings.

BOBOTIE

1 cup milk
1 thick slice white bread
1 tablespoon olive oil
1 large onion, chopped
2¼ lbs. ground beef
2 teaspoons apricot jelly
¼ cup lemon juice
½ cup raisins
10 dried apricots
2 tablespoons mild curry powder
12 blanched almonds, roughly chopped
1 teaspoon salt
Freshly ground pepper
6 bay leaves
2 eggs

Preheat oven to 350F (180C). Put half of the milk in a shallow dish, add bread and soak 5 minutes. Heat oil in a flameproof casserole dish. Add onion and cook, stirring occasionally, 5 minutes, or until soft. Squeeze milk from bread and add bread to dish with all remaining ingredients except eggs and remaining milk. Mix well then level surface with a spoon. Bake 30 minutes.

Beat together remaining milk and eggs and pour over meat. Return to oven and bake 20 to 25 minutes, or until custard has set.

Makes 6 to 8 servings.

Note: This dish is particularly good served with a fruit chutney.

BELGIAN HOTCHPOTCH

BEEF GOULASH WITH CHILE

8 ozs. beef brisket, cubed
8 ozs. lamb shoulder, cubed
3 ozs. pork shoulder, cubed
2¼ cups chicken stock
2 bay leaves
Salt and freshly ground pepper
4 ozs. rutabaga, diced
10 small onions
8 ozs. Brussels sprouts
1½ lbs. potatoes, diced
1 large carrot, diced
8 ozs. pork chipolata sausages
⅔ cup crème fraîche

Put meat into a large flameproof casserole dish; pour in stock.

2 tablespoons olive oil
1 onion, sliced
1 garlic clove, crushed
2 teaspoons paprika
1½ lbs. lean beef chuck, cubed
Pinch of caraway seeds
2 bay leaves
1 tablespoon balsamic vinegar
2 cups beef stock
Salt and freshly ground pepper
1½ lbs. potatoes, diced
2 green bell peppers, sliced
1 fresh green chile, seeded and sliced
1 (14-oz.) can crushed tomatoes
2 tablespoons tomato paste

Add 2¼ cups water, bay leaves and 1 teaspoon salt. Bring to a boil, skimming any froth from surface. Cover tightly and simmer 2 hours. Add vegetables and cook 30 minutes, or until meat is tender. Remove meat and vegetables from dish with a slotted spoon and keep warm. Put sausages into dish and cook 10 minutes. Remove with a slotted spoon and add to meat and vegetables.

Heat oil in a flameproof casserole dish. Add onion, garlic and paprika and cook, stirring, 2 minutes. Add beef and cook 3 or 4 minutes, or until onion is soft and beef has browned. Add caraway seeds, bay leaves, vinegar and half of the stock. Season with salt and pepper and bring to a boil. Reduce heat, cover and simmer 1 hour.

Bring sauce to a boil and boil until reduced by one-third. Season with salt and pepper, stir in crème fraîche and heat gently to warm through. Pour sauce over meat and vegetables and serve.

Makes 4 to 6 servings.

Stir in remaining stock, potatoes, bell peppers, chile, tomatoes and tomato paste. Bring to a boil, reduce heat, cover and simmer 30 to 40 minutes, or until meat and vegetables are tender. Remove and discard bay leaves.

Makes 4 servings.

CHILE BEEF WITH NACHOS

POT ROAST OF BRISKET

1 tablespoon olive oil
1 onion, chopped
1 garlic clove, crushed
1 lb. lean ground beef
1 (15-oz.) can red kidney beans, drained
1 green bell pepper, chopped
2 tablespoons tomato paste
2 teaspoons mild chile powder
5 ozs. tortilla chips
1 cup (4 ozs.) shredded mozzarella cheese
1-2 teaspoons paprika

1 (3-lb.) brisket of beef
2 leeks, thickly sliced
1 bay leaf
2 parsley stalks
1 celery leaf
1 lb. carrots, thickly sliced
1 lb. sweet potatoes, cut into chunks
¼ cup cider vinegar
½ head cabbage, thickly shredded
Salt and freshly ground pepper

Heat a large flameproof casserole dish over medium heat, add beef and cook, turning, 3 or 4 minutes, or until browned all over.

Heat oil in a flameproof casserole dish. Add onion and garlic and cook, stirring occasionally, 5 minutes, or until soft. Add beef and cook 6 to 8 minutes, or until brown. Stir in kidney beans, bell pepper, tomato paste, chile powder and ⅔ cup water. Cover and simmer 10 to 15 minutes. Preheat oven to 400F (205C).

Remove from dish. Add leeks to dish. With a piece of string, tie together bay leaf, parsley stalks and celery leaf and add to dish with carrots and sweet potatoes. Stir well. Add vinegar and ½ cup water. Put beef on top.

Uncover and cook 5 minutes, or until sauce is reduced and thickened. Arrange tortilla chips over top, sprinkle with mozzarella cheese and paprika and bake 20 minutes or until cheese is melted and golden. Serve hot.

Makes 4 servings.

Cover and simmer 2½ hours or until beef is tender. Remove beef from dish and keep warm. Remove vegetables with a slotted spoon and keep warm. Bring sauce to a boil and add cabbage. Season and simmer 5 minutes. Carve beef and serve with vegetables.

Makes 6 to 8 servings.

DEVILED STEAKS

1 tablespoon olive oil
4 beef fillet steaks, about 4 ozs. each
Salt and freshly ground pepper
2 tablespoons sherry vinegar
6 tablespoons dry red wine
4 tablespoons beef stock
2 cloves garlic, chopped
1 teaspoon crushed fennel seeds
1 tablespoon sun-dried tomato paste
Large pinch chile powder
Chopped fresh parsley and parsley sprigs to garnish

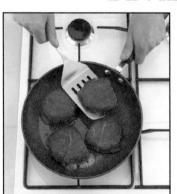

Heat oil in a nonstick frying pan until smoking, then add the steaks.

Cook 2 minutes, turn over and cook 2 minutes for medium/rare steaks. Cook a little longer if well-done steaks are preferred. Remove from the pan, season and keep warm while making sauce. Pour vinegar, red wine and stock into the pan and boil 30 seconds. Stir in garlic and fennel seeds. Whisk in the sun-dried tomato paste and chile powder, to taste. Simmer until the sauce is syrupy.

Place steaks on warm plates. Pour any juices into the sauce, bring to a boil, taste and season. Pour sauce over the steaks. Garnish with chopped parsley and parsley sprigs and serve with grilled tomatoes and roasted diced potatoes.

Makes 4 servings.

STEAK WITH TOMATO & OLIVES

4 (4-oz.) beef minute steaks
2 tablespoons olive oil
2 cloves garlic, chopped
1 medium onion, thinly sliced
1 carrot, finely diced
1 (14½-oz.) can chopped tomatoes
1 teaspoon balsamic vinegar
½ teaspoon dried oregano
1 tablespoon chopped fresh basil
Salt and freshly ground black pepper
12 Greek-style ripe olives, pitted
Basil leaves to garnish

Lightly brush both sides of the steaks with a little of the olive oil. Set aside.

In a nonstick saucepan, heat remaining oil and add garlic. Cook over low heat until golden. Add onion, carrot and 2 tablespoons water. Cover saucepan and simmer 10 minutes until onion is soft, stirring once. Stir in the tomatoes, vinegar, herbs, salt and pepper, then simmer, uncovered, 15 minutes until thick and reduced. Stir in the olives and keep warm.

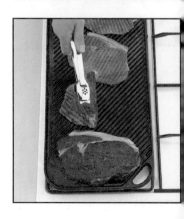

Heat a ridged griddle until smoking and grill steaks 1 minute per side. Remove to 4 warm plates and season with salt and pepper. Serve with the tomato and olive sauce. Garnish with basil leaves and serve with roasted sliced potatoes and broccoli.

Makes 4 servings.

BEEF IN BAROLO WINE

ITALIAN MEATBALLS

1 (2¼-lb.) beef round roast
6 cloves garlic, crushed
1 onion, roughly chopped
1 carrot, chopped
1 stalk celery, chopped
2 bay leaves
2 large thyme sprigs
2-3 peppercorns, lightly crushed
2 cloves
2 allspice berries, crushed
½ cup Barolo wine, or other full-bodied red wine
2 tablespoons tomato paste
⅔ cup beef stock
Salt and freshly ground black pepper

6 tablespoons low-fat milk
1 slice bread, crusts removed
1½ lbs. lean ground beef or lamb
6 green onions, chopped
1 clove garlic, chopped
2 tablespoons freshly grated Parmesan cheese
Freshly grated nutmeg
Salt and freshly ground pepper
2 tablespoons olive oil
⅔ cup dry white wine
1 (14½-oz.) can chopped tomatoes

Sprinkle milk over the bread in a shallow dish and let soak a few minutes.

Place meat in a large plastic bag with the garlic, onion, carrot, celery, bay leaves, thyme, peppercorns, cloves, allspice and wine. Shake the bag, seal and refrigerate several hours or overnight, turning meat occasionally. Next day, preheat oven to 325F (165C). Open bag, remove the meat from marinade and pat dry. Heat oil in a Dutch oven and brown the meat all over. Pour in reserved marinade, tomato paste and stock. Cover tightly and bake 2 to 3 hours until beef is tender.

Preheat oven to 350F (175C). Put meat into a large bowl and add soaked bread, green onions, garlic, cheese, nutmeg, salt and pepper to taste. Work together until well mixed and smooth. With wet hands, roll into 30 to 36 even-size balls. Heat the oil in a large nonstick frying pan and brown the meatballs in batches, then transfer them to a shallow ovenproof dish. Pour wine and tomatoes into frying pan and bring to boil, scraping up any sediment from the bottom of the pan.

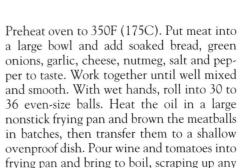

Lift meat out of pan and keep warm. Skim off any fat, remove bay leaves from the sauce. Purée in a blender or food processor until smooth. Taste and season. The sauce should be quite thick; if it is not, boil to reduce it. Slice the meat thinly and serve with the sauce, accompanied by snow peas and polenta.

Makes 8 servings.

Pour the sauce over the meatballs, cover and bake 1 hour until tender. Serve with buttered noodles.

Makes 8 servings.

VEAL SCALOPPINE

4 (4-oz.) veal or turkey scallops
2 tablespoons all-purpose flour
Salt and freshly ground pepper
3 tablespoons olive oil
3 tablespoons fresh lemon juice
6 tablespoons white wine
2 tablespoons chopped fresh parsley
Lemon wedges to garnish

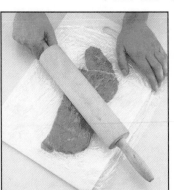

Trim veal of any gristle around edge. Place the veal between sheets of plastic wrap and pound out thinly without tearing. Coat in the flour seasoned with salt and pepper.

Heat the oil in a nonstick frying pan. Add veal and fry over high heat about 2 minutes per side, pressing them down with a spatula to keep them flat. Remove from the pan and keep warm.

Add the lemon juice and wine to the frying pan, stirring and scraping to dislodge any sediment. Boil 1 minute, then taste and season. Stir in parsley and pour the lemon sauce over veal. Garnish with lemon wedges and serve at once, with potatoes and stir-fried vegetables.

Makes 4 servings.

SALTIMBOCCA

8 (2-oz.) veal or turkey scallops
8 thin slices Parma ham
Salt and freshly ground pepper
8 fresh sage leaves
1 tablespoon olive oil
2 tablespoons butter
1/3 cup dry Marsala or sherry
Fresh sage leaves to garnish

Trim veal of any gristle around edge. Place between sheets of plastic film and pound out thinly without tearing. Trim Parma ham of any fat and cut to same size as veal.

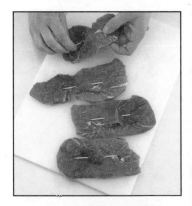

Season veal with a little salt. Place a sage leaf on top of each piece and cover with a slice of ham. Secure each one through the middle with a wooden pick, as if taking a large stitch. These are not rolled up.

Heat the oil and butter in a nonstick frying pan and fry the veal in batches, on both sides for about 2 minutes until golden and tender. Remove and keep warm. Add the Marsala to the pan, stir and bring to a boil, then boil 1 minute. Spoon the sauce over veal, garnish with sage and serve with green beans and noodles.

Makes 4 servings.

LAMB

TARRAGON LAMB NOISETTES

LAMB WITH ROSEMARY

1 tablespoon olive oil
¼ cup butter
8 boneless lamb chops, about 1-inch thick
Salt and freshly ground pepper
¼ cup brandy
3 tablespoons whipping cream
2 tablespoons chopped fresh tarragon
Tarragon sprigs and flat-leaf parsley to garnish

Heat oil and half the butter in a heavy skillet until sizzling.

Add lamb and cook 2½ or 3 minutes on each side, until well-browned but still pink in the center. Remove with tongs, transfer to warmed serving plates, season with salt and pepper and keep warm.

Add remaining butter to pan. When melted, add brandy, stirring to release browned bits, and bring to a boil. Stir in cream and tarragon and boil until thickened. Season with salt and pepper, pour over lamb, garnish with tarragon sprigs and flat-leaf parsley and serve.

Makes 4 servings.

1 (4½-lb.) leg young lamb
3 rosemary sprigs
2-3 garlic cloves, cut into slivers
Salt and freshly ground pepper
¼ cup butter
⅔ cup red or white wine

Preheat oven to 450F (230C). Cut small incisions in lamb with the point of a sharp knife.

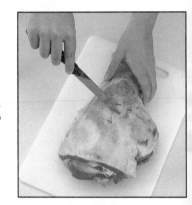

Remove leaves from one of rosemary sprigs. Insert leaves and garlic slivers into incisions. Season lamb with salt and pepper, put the remaining rosemary sprigs on top and dot with butter. Put into a roasting pan and roast 15 minutes. Reduce oven temperature to 350F (180C) and roast another 40 to 60 minutes or to desired doneness.

Leave lamb in oven, with door propped open, 15 minutes, to rest. Remove lamb from roasting pan and transfer to a serving plate. Tilt roasting pan and spoon off most of fat. Add wine, stirring to release browned bits. Bring to a boil over medium heat, reduce heat and simmer briefly. Season with salt and pepper. Carve lamb, garnish with rosemary sprigs and serve with sauce.

Makes 6 servings.

LAMB & FLAGEOLET BEANS

4 lamb shanks, each weighing 8 ozs.
4 garlic cloves, thinly sliced
2 tablespoons olive oil
1 onion, finely chopped
1½ cups dried flageolet beans, soaked overnight
1¼ lbs. tomatoes, peeled, seeded and chopped
1 tablespoon tomato paste
⅔ cup red wine
Bouquet garni
Salt and freshly ground pepper
1 small bunch of parsley, chopped
Flat-leaf parsley and bay leaves to garnish

Cut 4 incisions in each lamb shank. Insert a slice of garlic in each incision.

Heat oil in a heavy Dutch oven, add shanks and cook until browned all over. Remove and set aside. Add onion and remaining garlic to pan and cook, stirring occasionally, 5 minutes or until soft but not browned.

Drain and rinse beans and add to pan with tomatoes, tomato paste, wine, bouquet garni, salt and pepper. Return lamb to pan, cover tightly and cook over low heat 1½ to 2 hours or until lamb and beans are tender. Discard bouquet garni and stir in parsley. Garnish and serve with béarnaise sauce.

Makes 4 servings.

LAMB BOULANGÈRE

1 (4½-lb.) leg of lamb
4 garlic cloves
Salt and freshly ground pepper
3 tablespoons butter
2 lbs. potatoes, thickly sliced
1 Spanish onion, thinly sliced
1 bay leaf
2 thyme sprigs
About 1¼ cups veal or vegetable stock or water
1 tablespoon olive oil
Flat-leaf parsley to garnish

Cut small incisions in lamb. Thinly slice 2 of the garlic cloves and insert into incisions.

Season lamb with salt and pepper; set aside. Preheat oven to 325F (165C). Use 1 tablespoon of the butter to coat a shallow baking dish. Crush remaining garlic. Arrange layers of potatoes, onion, garlic, herbs, salt and pepper in the buttered dish. Add enough stock or water to just cover, dot with remaining butter, cover with foil and bake 1 hour.

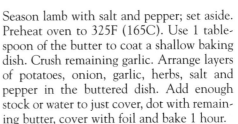

Heat oil in a heavy skillet, add lamb and cook quickly until lightly browned all over. Put lamb on top of potatoes and cover with foil. Increase oven temperature to 375F (190C) and bake lamb and potatoes 1¼ to 1½ hours, uncovering 15 minutes before end, to brown. Carve lamb, garnish with flat-leaf parsley and serve with potatoes.

Makes 6 servings.

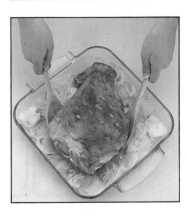

NAVARIN OF LAMB

MOROCCAN LAMB

1 tablespoon olive oil
2¼ lbs. boneless lamb, cubed
1 onion and 1 large carrot, finely chopped
Pinch of sugar
2 teaspoons all-purpose flour
½ cup dry white wine
2½ cups veal or chicken stock
Bouquet garni
Salt and freshly ground pepper
3 tomatoes, peeled, seeded and chopped
3 small turnips, quartered
12 pearl onions
12 small new potatoes
12 baby carrots, halved or quartered
5 ozs. shelled fresh green peas (about 1 cup)
Parsley sprigs to garnish

1 cup dried apricots
2 tablespoons olive oil
1 large onion, chopped
2¼ lbs. boneless shoulder of lamb, cubed
1 teaspoon ground cumin
½ teaspoon each ground coriander and cinnamon
Salt and freshly ground pepper
Grated zest and juice of ½ orange
1 teaspoon saffron strands
1 tablespoon ground almonds
About 1¼ cups lamb or chicken stock
1 tablespoon sesame seeds
Flat-leaf parsley sprigs to garnish

Cut apricots in half and put in a bowl.

Heat oil in a heavy Dutch oven, add lamb and cook until browned all over. Remove with a slotted spoon and set aside. Add chopped onion and carrot and cook, stirring occasionally, 10 minutes or until browned. Sprinkle with sugar and flour and cook, stirring, until lightly browned. Add wine, stock, bouquet garni, salt and pepper. Add tomatoes and bring to a boil, stirring. Return lamb to pan, cover tightly and cook over low heat 30 minutes.

Cover with ⅔ cup water and leave to soak overnight. Preheat oven to 350F (180C). Heat olive oil in a Dutch oven. Add onion and cook over low heat 10 minutes or until soft and golden. Add lamb, cumin, coriander, cinnamon, salt and pepper and cook, stirring, 5 minutes.

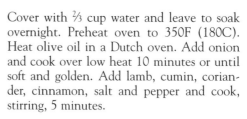

Add turnips, onions and potatoes, cover and cook 20 minutes. Add baby carrots and cook 10 minutes. Add peas and cook 5 to 7 minutes or until lamb and vegetables are tender. Remove lamb and vegetables with a slotted spoon, transfer to a warmed bowl and keep warm. Boil cooking juices to thicken slightly. Return lamb and vegetables to pan and turn in sauce. Garnish with parsley and serve.

Makes 4 servings.

Add apricots and their soaking liquid. Stir in orange zest and juice, saffron, ground almonds and enough stock to cover. Cover and cook in oven 1 to 1½ hours or until meat is tender, adding extra stock if necessary. Heat a skillet, add sesame seeds and dry fry, shaking pan, until golden. Sprinkle sesame seeds over meat, garnish with parsley and serve.

Makes 4 to 6 servings.

LAMB WITH RIPE OLIVES

¼ cup olive oil
1½ lbs. lean lamb, cut into small cubes
1 (4-oz.) piece unsmoked bacon, cut into small strips
2 garlic cloves, sliced
½ to 1 teaspoon chopped fresh oregano
¾ cup full-bodied white wine
1 fresh red chile, seeded and finely chopped
12-15 ripe olives, pitted
Fresh herbs to garnish

In a wide, shallow pan, heat oil. Add lamb, pork and garlic and cook over high heat to seal and brown meat.

In a small saucepan, boil oregano and wine 2 to 3 minutes. Stir into pan, cover and simmer 30 minutes.

Stir chile and olives into pan. Cover again and cook about 30 minutes or until lamb is tender. If necessary, uncover pan toward end of cooking time so liquid can evaporate to make a thin sauce. Garnish with herbs.

Makes 4 servings.

SPICE-COATED LAMB

4 garlic cloves
¼ teaspoon cumin seeds
1 tablespoon paprika
¼ teaspoon saffron threads, crushed
Salt and pepper
1½ lbs. lean lamb, cut into 1-1½-inch cubes
3 tablespoons olive oil
⅔ cup full-bodied dry white wine

Using a mortar and pestle, pound together garlic, cumin, paprika, saffron, salt and pepper.

Into a bowl, put lamb. Add spice mixture and stir well but gently to coat lamb. Set aside 30 minutes.

In a large pan, heat oil. Add lamb and cook 5 to 6 minutes, stirring occasionally, until lamb has browned. Stir in wine and heat to a simmer. Cover tightly and simmer 30 to 40 minutes or until meat is tender and sauce thickened.

Makes 4 servings.

RED-COOKED LAMB FILLET

1 lb. lean lamb fillet
3 tablespoons dry sherry
1 (½-inch) piece fresh gingerroot, peeled and finely
    chopped
2 garlic cloves, thinly sliced
1 teaspoon five-spice powder
3 tablespoons dark soy sauce
1¼ cups Chinese Vegetable Stock (see glossary)
2 teaspoons sugar
2 teaspoons cornstarch mixed with 4 teaspoons
    water
Salt and freshly ground pepper
Shredded green onions to garnish

Trim any excess fat and silver skin from lamb
and cut lamb into ¾-inch cubes.

Cook lamb in a saucepan of boiling water 3
minutes. Drain well. Heat a nonstick or well-
seasoned wok and add lamb, sherry, ginger,
garlic, five-spice powder and soy sauce. Bring
to a boil, reduce heat and simmer 2 minutes,
stirring. Pour in stock, return to a boil, then
simmer 25 minutes.

Add sugar, cornstarch mixture, salt and
pepper and stir until thickened. Simmer 5
minutes. Garnish with shredded green
onions and serve on a bed of rice.

Makes 4 servings.

STIR-FRIED SESAME LAMB

12 ozs. lean lamb fillet
1 tablespoon sunflower oil
4 ozs. shallots, sliced
1 red bell pepper, sliced
1 green bell pepper, sliced
1 garlic clove, finely chopped
1 tablespoon light soy sauce
1 teaspoon white rice vinegar
1 teaspoon sugar
Freshly ground pepper
2 tablespoons sesame seeds

Trim any fat and silver skin from lamb fillet.
Cut fillet into ¼-inch cubes.

Heat oil in a nonstick or well-seasoned wok
and stir-fry lamb 1 or 2 minutes or until
browned. Remove with a slotted spoon and
set aside. Stir-fry shallots, bell peppers and
garlic 2 minutes or until just soft.

Return lamb to wok with all the remaining
ingredients except the sesame seeds. Stir-fry
2 minutes. Sprinkle with sesame seeds and
serve with rice and vegetables.

Makes 4 servings.

LAMB IN HERB SAUCE

2 tablespoons olive oil
1½ lbs. lean boneless lamb, cut into pieces
1 Spanish onion, chopped
2 green bell peppers, chopped
3 garlic cloves, crushed
¾ cup dry white wine
⅔ cup water
1½ teaspoons chopped fresh thyme
Salt and pepper
1 small head lettuce, sliced
2 tablespoons chopped fresh parsley
2 tablespoons chopped fresh mint
2 ozs. pine nuts
Mint sprigs and pine nuts to garnish

In a large pan, heat oil. Add lamb and fry, stirring occasionally, until evenly browned. Using a slotted spoon, remove lamb and set aside. Stir onion into pan and cook about 4 minutes, stirring occasionally, until softened but not browned. Stir in bell pepper and garlic and cook 2 to 3 minutes, then stir in wine. Boil 1 minute.

Pour in water and bring to a boil. Reduce heat so liquid just simmers, then add lamb, thyme, salt and pepper. Cover and simmer about 1 hour. Stir in lettuce, parsley, mint and pine nuts, cover and cook 10 to 15 minutes. Serve garnished with mint sprigs and pine nuts.

Makes 4 servings.

STIR-FRIED MEATBALLS

1 (1-lb.) eggplant
¼ cup salt
1 tablespoon sunflower oil
2 tablespoons rice wine
1 (4-oz.) can bamboo shoots, drained and cut into
  strips
4 green onions, finely chopped, to garnish
MEATBALLS:
12 ozs. lean ground lamb
4 green onions, finely chopped
2 garlic cloves, finely chopped
2 tablespoons chopped fresh chives
Salt and ground white pepper
1 teaspoon ground cinnamon
2 teaspoons cornstarch
1 egg white

Cut eggplant into ¼-inch slices and layer in a bowl, sprinkling generously with salt. Set aside 30 minutes. Meanwhile, mix together meatball ingredients. Divide mixture into 24 portions and roll into balls, flouring the hands with extra cornstarch. Set aside. Transfer eggplant to a colander and rinse well under cold running water, pressing gently to remove all salt and bitterness. Drain well and pat dry with paper towels.

Heat oil and rice wine in a nonstick or well-seasoned wok and stir-fry eggplant 2 or 3 minutes or until softened. Add meatballs and carefully stir-fry 5 minutes. Add bamboo shoots and stir-fry 2 minutes. Remove meatballs and vegetables with a slotted spoon. Garnish with chopped green onions and serve with a salad.

Makes 4 servings.

LAMB WITH ONIONS

1½ lbs. lamb shoulder
1 teaspoon ground turmeric
1 teaspoon ground cumin
1 teaspoon ground coriander
1 (1-inch) piece fresh gingerroot, grated
2 garlic cloves, crushed
3 tablespoons vegetable oil
1 tablespoon superfine sugar
4 large onions, sliced into thin rings
1 lb. potatoes, cut into large chunks
1 cup water
Salt and red (cayenne) pepper to taste
1 teaspoon garam masala
Rosemary sprigs to garnish

Wipe lamb with a damp paper towel, trim off excess fat and cut into 1½-inch cubes.

Put lamb in a non-metal bowl. Mix together turmeric, cumin, coriander, gingerroot and garlic; add to lamb. Stir well, then cover loosely and refrigerate 2 to 3 hours. Heat oil in a heavy saucepan until smoking. Stir in sugar, then add onions and cook over medium-high heat 10 minutes, until a rich brown, stirring frequently. Remove onions with a slotted spoon and set aside.

Add lamb to pan; cook until browned all over. Add potatoes and cook, stirring, 2 minutes. Return onions to pan; add water, salt and cayenne. Bring to a boil. Reduce heat, cover and simmer 1¼ hours, or until lamb is tender, stirring occasionally. Stir in Garam Masala and serve, garnished with rosemary sprigs.

Makes 4 servings.

SAGE LAMB COBBLER

2 lbs. neck of lamb, boned and cubed
¼ cup all-purpose flour
1 tablespoon olive oil
1 large onion, chopped
¼ cup dried peas, soaked overnight
8 ozs. each carrots and rutabaga, diced
2¼ cups chicken stock
Salt and freshly ground pepper
Large pinch of paprika
TOPPING:
2 cups all-purpose flour
1½ teaspoons baking powder
¼ cup butter
1 teaspoon dried sage
1 egg
2 tablespoons milk, plus extra for brushing

Preheat oven to 325F (160C). Coat lamb in flour. Heat oil in a flameproof casserole dish. Add lamb and cook, stirring, until browned. Remove and set aside. Add onion and cook, stirring occasionally, 7 minutes, or until lightly browned. Return lamb and add peas, carrots and rutabaga. Pour in stock and season with salt, pepper and paprika. Bring to a boil, cover and bake 2 hours. Sift flour, baking powder and salt into a bowl. Cut in butter until mixture resembles fine brread crumbs.

Stir in sage. Add egg and milk and stir to a soft dough. Knead on a lightly floured surface and roll out to ½-inch thickness. Using a pastry cutter, cut out 1½-inch rounds. Arrange rounds on top of dish and brush with milk. Increase oven temperature to 400F (205C). Return dish to oven and cook, uncovered, 15 to 20 minutes, or until biscuits are risen and golden. Serve.

Makes 6 to 8 servings.

CURRIED LAMB WITH RAITA

STUFFED EGGPLANT

3 tablespoons olive oil
2 onions, finely chopped
1 (½-inch) piece gingerroot, peeled and grated
3 garlic cloves, crushed
1 teaspoon mild chile powder
1½ teaspoons turmeric
1½ teaspoons ground coriander
½ teaspoon each ground cumin and garam masala
1 lb. lean lamb, cubed
½ cup plain yogurt
Salt and freshly ground pepper
Mint sprigs to garnish
RAITA:
1¼ cups plain yogurt
1 cup diced cucumber
1 tablespoon chopped fresh mint

3 eggplants
Salt and pepper
Extra-virgin olive oil
1 onion, finely chopped
1 lb. ground lamb or beef
2 tomatoes, peeled and chopped
1 tablespoon tomato paste
1 tablespoon chopped fresh oregano
½ teaspoon ground cinnamon
¼ cup dry white wine
CHEESE SAUCE:
2 tablespoons butter
¾ cup all-purpose flour
1¼ cups milk
¾ cup grated kefalotiri cheese (3 ozs.)

Heat oil in a flameproof casserole dish. Add onions and cook, stirring occasionally, 5 minutes, or until soft. Add gingerroot, garlic, chile powder, turmeric, coriander, cumin and garam masala and cook, stirring, 2 minutes. Add lamb and cook, stirring, 2 minutes, or until browned.

Cut eggplants lengthwise, from stem, sprinkle with salt and let drain 1 hour. In a saucepan, heat oil. Add onion and cook until soft. Add lamb and stir until brown. Add tomatoes, tomato paste, oregano, cinnamon, salt, pepper, wine and ¼ cup water. Cover and simmer 15 minutes, stirring occasionally. Remove lid and cook until mixture is dry, stirring frequently. Pat eggplants dry with paper towels. Scoop out pulp. Chop half and mix with meat mixture (reserve other half for another dish).

Add yogurt, ½ cup water, salt and pepper and stir well. Bring to a boil, reduce heat and simmer 45 minutes. Meanwhile, make raita. Mix together yogurt, cucumber and chopped mint. Season with salt and pepper. Refrigerate until required. Garnish lamb with mint sprigs and serve with raita.

Makes 4 servings.

Preheat oven to 350F (175C). To make the sauce, in a saucepan, melt butter. Stir in flour and cook 2 minutes, stirring, over low heat. Remove from heat. Gradually stir in milk. Return to heat. Stir until thick and smooth. Simmer 5 minutes, stirring. Season with salt and pepper. Stir in two-thirds of cheese. Fill each eggplant shell two-thirds full of meat mixture. Place in a casserole dish. Top with sauce. Sprinkle with remaining cheese. Bake 20 minutes or until cheese is lightly browned.

Makes 6 servings.

BRAISED LAMB & VEGETABLES

1 lb. firm, yellow potatoes, cut into ¼-inch slices
2 garlic cloves, pounded to a paste
6-8 green onions, thinly sliced
2 medium or large artichoke bottoms, sliced
3 cups chopped brown mushrooms
Handful of parsley, finely chopped
1 tablespoon chopped mixed herbs
Salt and pepper
3 tablespoons olive oil
4 lamb shoulder or loin chops
¾ cup full-bodied dry white wine
Fresh parsley sprigs to garnish

Preheat oven to 375F (190C). In a bowl, combine potatoes, garlic, green onions, artichoke bottoms, mushrooms, parsley, mixed herbs, salt and pepper. In a heavy large pan, heat half the mixture. In a skillet, heat oil. Add lamb and brown on both sides. Drain on paper towels, then season with salt and pepper and place in pan.

Over the heat, stir wine into skillet to dislodge cooking juices, bring to a boil and pour over the lamb. Cover with remaining vegetables and add enough water to almost cover vegetables. Bring to a boil. Cover and cook in the oven about 30 minutes. Uncover and cook 1 hour or until lamb is tender. Add a little water if it seems too dry. Garnish with parsley.

Makes 4 servings.

LAMB WITH LEMON & GARLIC

3 tablespoons olive oil
2 lbs. lean, boneless lamb, cut into 1-inch pieces
1 Spanish onion, finely chopped
3 garlic cloves, crushed
1 tablespoon paprika
3 tablespoons finely chopped fresh parsley
3 tablespoons fresh lemon juice
Salt and pepper
3 tablespoons dry white wine (optional)

In a heavy large pan, heat oil. Add lamb and cook, stirring occasionally, until lightly browned. Do this in batches if necessary so the pieces are not crowded. Using a slotted spoon, transfer meat to a plate or bowl and reserve.

Stir onion into pan and cook about 5 minutes, stirring occasionally, until softened. Stir in garlic and cook 2 minutes, then stir in paprika. When well blended, stir in lamb and any juices on plate or in bowl, the parsley, lemon juice, salt and pepper. Cover tightly and cook over very low heat 1¼ to 1½ hours, shaking pan occasionally, until lamb is very tender. If necessary, add wine or 3 tablespoons water.

Makes 4 to 6 servings.

LAMB EN PAPILLOTTE

4 lamb leg steaks, each weighing 6 ozs.
1 tablespoon Dijon mustard
4 green onions, sliced
1 teaspoon chopped fresh rosemary
Salt and freshly ground pepper
1 lb. sweet potatoes, cut into chunks
1 lb. zucchini, thickly sliced
1 tablespoon olive oil
Rosemary sprigs to garnish

Preheat oven to 400F (205C). Cut four large squares of foil and place a lamb steak on each one. Spread lamb with mustard and sprinkle with green onions and rosemary. Season with salt and pepper.

Bring foil up over steaks to make a package and twist edges together to seal. Put packages in an ovenproof dish. Arrange sweet potatoes and zucchini around packages.

Drizzle vegetables with oil and season with salt and pepper. Bake 1 hour, basting and turning vegetables at least twice. Remove lamb from foil, garnish with rosemary and serve with vegetables.

Makes 4 servings.

LAMB CHILINDRON

¼ cup olive oil
1½ lbs. lean lamb, cubed
Salt and black pepper
1 Spanish onion, chopped
2 garlic cloves, chopped
3 red bell peppers, cut into strips
4 beefsteak tomatoes, peeled, seeded and chopped
1 dried red chile, chopped
Chopped fresh herbs to garnish

In a large pan, heat oil. Season lamb with salt and black pepper and add to pan.

Cook, stirring, until evenly browned, then using a slotted spoon, transfer to a bowl. Add onion to pan and cook about 4 minutes, stirring occasionally, until softened but not colored. Stir in garlic, cook 1 to 2 minutes, then stir in peppers, tomatoes and chile. Simmer 5 minutes.

Return lamb and any juices that have collected in bowl to pan. Cover tightly and simmer about 1½ hours, or until lamb is tender. Taste for seasoning and adjust if necessary. Serve garnished with chopped herbs.

Makes 6 servings.

LAMB YOGURTLU

2 pitta breads
3 tablespoons olive oil
1 lb. boneless leg of lamb, cubed
12 ozs. tomatoes, peeled and coarsely chopped
Salt and freshly ground pepper
1¼ cups regular plain yogurt, at room temperature
1 oz. pine nuts
2 tablespoons chopped fresh parsley

Split pitta breads in half and cut each half into four triangles. Heat half oil in a skillet. Add lamb and cook until browned all over.

Reduce heat and cook 10 minutes or until cooked through. Remove with a slotted spoon and keep warm. Toast pitta bread triangles and keep warm. Heat remaining oil in a skillet. Add tomatoes and cook briefly until just softened but still retaining their shape.

Reserve four pitta triangles and put remainder on warmed serving plates. Pour tomatoes and their juice over triangles and season with salt and pepper. Spoon most of yogurt over tomatoes. Arrange lamb on top and spoon remaining yogurt over. Sprinkle with pine nuts and chopped parsley, arrange reserved pitta triangles at side and serve.

Makes 4 servings.

SOUVLAKIA

2 garlic cloves, crushed
¼ cup lemon juice
2 tablespoons olive oil
¼ cup chopped fresh oregano
Salt and freshly ground pepper
1 lb. lean lamb fillet, cubed
6 fresh bay leaves, halved
Oregano sprigs to garnish
TOMATO AND OLIVE SALSA:
6 ozs. mixed green and black olives, pitted and finely
  chopped
1 small red onion, finely chopped
4 plum tomatoes, finely chopped
2 tablespoons olive oil

In a shallow dish, mix together garlic, lemon juice, olive oil, oregano, salt and pepper. Add lamb and mix well. Leave in a cool place 2 hours. To make salsa, put olives, onion, tomatoes, olive oil, salt and pepper in a bowl and mix together. Refrigerate until required.

Remove lamb from marinade and thread on to skewers, adding bay leaves to skewers at regular intervals. Broil over a grill or under a hot broiler, turning occasionally, 10 minutes or until lamb is brown and crisp on outside and pink and juicy inside. Garnish with oregano sprigs and serve with tomato and olive salsa.

Makes 4 servings.

SPICED RACK OF LAMB

1 tablespoon all-purpose flour
Salt and pepper
2 racks of lamb
1 garlic clove, finely chopped
2 tablespoons extra-virgin olive oil
1 lb. tomatoes, coarsely chopped
½ lemon, chopped
1 cinnamon stick
3 whole cloves
1 small red chile, seeded and chopped
½ cup dry white wine
2 tablespoons tomato paste
Lemon slices to garnish

Preheat oven to 350F (175C). Mix together flour, salt and pepper. Rub over lamb. Press garlic into gaps between bones. In a roasting pan, heat oil. Put lamb, skin-side down, in oil to brown. Remove lamb. Add tomatoes, lemon, cinnamon, cloves and chile to roasting pan. Return lamb, skin-side up, to pan.

In a bowl, mix together wine, ½ cup water and tomato paste. Pour over lamb. Cover pan loosely with foil. Roast 1 hour. Remove foil and roast 30 minutes or until lamb is cooked to desired doneness. Cut lamb into individual chops and keep warm. Place roasting pan on heat and boil liquid to reduce to a thick sauce. Pour over meat. Garnish with lemon.

Makes 6 servings.

ROAST LEG OF LAMB WITH WINE

1 (2¼-lb.) lean leg of lamb
2 tablespoons olive oil
1 (2-oz.) can salted anchovies, boned and rinsed
2 cloves garlic, chopped
1 tablespoon chopped fresh rosemary
8 juniper berries
2 tablespoons balsamic vinegar
Salt and freshly ground pepper
⅔ cup dry white wine

Trim lamb of any excess fat. Heat oil in a large pan in which the lamb will fit snugly. Add the lamb and brown all over. Remove and set aside.

In a mortar, pound the anchovies, garlic, rosemary and 4 of the juniper berries to a paste. Stir in vinegar. Make small incisions all over the lamb with a small sharp knife. Spread paste all over lamb, working it into the slits. Season. Replace lamb in pan, and pour in wine. Crush remaining juniper berries and add to the pan. Cover and simmer 1½ to 2 hours, until very tender, turning lamb every 20 minutes.

Carefully remove lamb from pan and keep warm. Skim fat from sauce. Add a little water, if necessary, and bring to a boil, scraping the bottom of the pan to mix in the sediment. Serve the sauce with the lamb, accompanied by potatoes, carrots and snow peas.

Makes 8 servings.

MOUSSAKA

1½ lbs. eggplant
Salt and pepper
1 tablespoon extra-virgin olive oil plus extra for frying
2 onions, finely chopped
1½ lbs. ground lamb or beef
2 tomatoes, peeled and chopped
2 tablespoons tomato paste
1 tablespoon chopped fresh oregano
1 teaspoon ground cinnamon
½ cup dry white wine
WHITE SAUCE:
¼ cup butter
½ cup all-purpose flour
2 cups milk
⅔ cup plain yogurt
¼ cup grated kefalotiti cheese (1 oz.)

Thinly slice eggplant and put into a colander. Sprinkle with salt and let drain 1 hour. In a saucepan, heat 1 tablespoon oil. Add onions and cook until soft. Add lamb and stir until brown. Add tomatoes, tomato paste, oregano, cinnamon, salt, pepper, wine and ½ cup water. Cover; simmer 30 minutes. Remove lid and cook until mixture is dry. Pat eggplants dry with paper towels. Heat ½ inch oil in a skillet. Fry eggplants, turning once, until beginning to brown. Drain on paper towels. Preheat oven to 350F (175C).

To make sauce, melt butter. Stir in flour and cook 2 minutes over low heat. Remove from heat. Gradually stir in milk and yogurt. Return to heat. Stir until thick and smooth. Simmer 5 minutes. Season with salt and pepper. Put a layer of eggplant in a baking dish. Cover with half of meat mixture, then half of remaining eggplant slices. Cover with remaining meat and eggplant slices. Pour sauce over top. Sprinkle with cheese. Bake 40 minutes or until brown.

Makes 6 servings.

BAKED LAMB WITH VEGETABLES

1 leg of lamb, about 4½ lbs.
3 garlic cloves, cut into slivers
Salt and pepper
1 eggplant, sliced
1½ lbs. potatoes, peeled
1 large onion, thinly sliced
1 lb. tomatoes, sliced
¼ cup white wine
1 tablespoon chopped fresh oregano

Preheat oven to 425F (220C). Cut slits in meat and insert slivers of garlic. Rub generously with salt and pepper. Place lamb in a large roasting pan and put in oven.

Reduce heat to 350F (175C) and roast 1½ hours for slightly pink meat or 2 hours for medium-well done. Meanwhile, slice eggplant into ¼-inch slices, place in a colander and sprinkle with salt. Let drain 30 minutes, then rinse and pat dry.

One hour before the end of cooking time, remove any fat from roasting pan and add vegetables. Add wine, season with salt and pepper and sprinkle with oregano. Return to the oven. Turn vegetables over during cooking to cook them evenly in juices. Carve lamb into slices, adding any meat juices to vegetables. Serve lamb with the vegetables and meat juices.

Makes 6 servings.

PORK

PORK WITH HERB SAUCE

½ cup fresh white bread crumbs
2 tablespoons white-wine vinegar
2 garlic cloves
2 canned anchovy fillets, drained
¼ cup chopped fresh parsley
2 teaspoons capers, drained
1 hard-cooked egg yolk
1 cup extra-virgin olive oil
Salt and pepper
4 boneless pork loin chops, about 1-inch thick

In a small bowl, soak bread crumbs in vinegar.

Meanwhile, using a mortar and pestle, crush garlic with anchovy fillets, parsley, capers and egg yolk. Squeeze vinegar from bread crumbs, then mix bread crumbs into mortar. Slowly stir in oil to make a creamy sauce. Add salt and pepper to taste. Set aside.

Preheat broiler. Broil chops about 12 minutes on each side until lightly browned and cooked through but still juicy in center. Season chops with salt and pepper and top with some of sauce. Serve remaining sauce separately.

Makes 4 servings.

PORK IN CIDER & ORANGE

3 tablespoons olive oil
Flour for coating
Salt and pepper
1 (1½-lb.) boned and rolled pork loin roast
1 small Spanish onion, sliced
1½ cups hard cider
Juice of 1 large orange
Zest of ¼ orange, cut into fine strips
Pinch of ground cinnamon
Pinch of sugar, if desired
Thin orange slices, herb sprigs and toasted slivered almonds to garnish

In a heavy large pan, heat oil. Put flour on a plate and season with salt and pepper. Roll pork in seasoned flour to coat evenly and lightly. Add to pan and brown evenly, about 10 minutes. Remove and keep warm. Stir onion into pan and cook over low heat about 20 minutes, stirring occasionally, until very soft and lightly browned. Stir in cider, orange juice and zest strips and cinnamon. Bring to a boil, reduce heat and simmer 2 to 3 minutes.

Return pork to pan, turn it in sauce, cover and simmer about 45 minutes or until pork is tender and juices run clear when tested with the tip of a knife. Transfer pork to a serving dish and boil sauce, if necessary, to thicken lightly. Taste for seasoning and add a pinch sugar, if necessary. Pour sauce over pork and garnish with orange slices and slivered almonds.

Makes 4 servings.

SPICED PORK LOIN

1 tablespoon paprika
3 garlic cloves, finely crushed
1 teaspoon chopped fresh oregano
½ teaspoon finely crushed cumin seeds
1 bay leaf, crushed
Salt
3 tablespoons extra-virgin olive oil
1 (1½-lb.) boned and rolled pork loin roast
2 tablespoons olive oil
¼ cup full-bodied dry white wine
Pitted green olives to serve

In a small bowl, mix together paprika, garlic, oregano, cumin seeds, bay leaf and salt. Stir in olive oil.

Rub spice mixture well into pork. Place in a non-metallic dish, cover and refrigerate 2 to 5 days. Bring pork to room temperature 30 minutes before cooking.

Cut pork into 4 slices. In a skillet over medium-high heat, heat oil. Add pork and brown quickly on both sides, then reduce heat and cook 4 to 5 minutes on each side until cooked through. Transfer slices to a warm serving plate. Stir wine into cooking juices, boil 2 to 3 minutes, then pour over pork. Scatter green olives over the top.

Makes 4 servings.

THAI PORK CURRY

½ cup coconut cream
1 onion, chopped
1 garlic clove, finely crushed
2 tablespoons ready-made fragrant curry paste
2 teaspoons fish sauce
½ teaspoon crushed palm sugar
12 ozs. lean pork, diced
3 kaffir lime leaves, shredded
25 Thai basil leaves
1 long fresh red chile, seeded, cut into strips, and Thai basil sprigs to garnish

In a wok, heat ⅓ cup of the coconut cream until the oil begins to separate. Stir in onion and garlic and cook, stirring occasionally, until lightly browned. Stir in curry paste and cook, stirring, about 2 minutes. Stir in fish sauce and sugar, then add pork and stir to coat. Cook 3 to 4 minutes.

Add lime leaves and basil leaves and cook 1 minute. If necessary, add a little water, but final dish should be dry. Drizzle remaining coconut cream over finished dish and garnish with chile strips and basil sprigs.

Makes 3 servings.

FLORENTINE ROAST PORK

1 (2¼-lb.) pork loin, boned
2 tablespoons chopped fresh rosemary leaves
2 cloves garlic, chopped
Salt and freshly ground black pepper
3 tablespoons olive oil
⅔ cup dry white wine

BARBECUED SPARERIBS

2 tablespoons chopped cilantro stems
3 garlic cloves, chopped
1 teaspoon peppercorns, cracked
1 teaspoon grated lime peel
1 tablespoon ready-made Thai green curry paste
2 teaspoons fish sauce
1½ teaspoons crushed palm sugar
¾ cup coconut milk
2 lbs. pork spareribs, trimmed
Green onion brushes to garnish

Preheat oven to 325F (165C). Using a flat skewer, make deep incisions all over the meat. Mix rosemary and garlic together with plenty of salt and pepper. Push the rosemary mixture into the incisions. Rub any remaining mixture into flap where the bones have been removed.

Season with salt and pepper and tie up neatly with string. Rub meat all over with olive oil and place in a roasting pan. Pour in white wine and roast in oven 1½ hours, basting frequently and turning the roast each time. If you have a spit or rotisserie, roast it on the spit, basting frequently.

Using a pestle and mortar or small food processor, pound or mix together cilantro, garlic, peppercorns, lime peel, curry paste, fish sauce and sugar. Stir in coconut milk. Place spareribs in a shallow dish, pour spiced coconut mixture over ribs, cover and refrigerate 3 hours, basting occasionally.

Transfer pork to a serving dish and keep warm. Skim fat off pan, and add a little water to the juices. Scrape up sediment and bring to boil, taste and season. Carve the pork into thick slices, garnish with rosemary sprigs and serve with the sauce, carrots and brown lentils.

Makes 6 servings.

Preheat a barbecue or a moderate broiler. Cook ribs about 10 minutes per side until cooked through and browned, basting occasionally with coconut mixture. Garnish with green onion brushes.

Makes 4 to 6 servings.

Note: The ribs can also be cooked on a rack in a roasting pan in a preheated 400F (205C) oven 45 to 60 minutes, basting occasionally.

MARINATED SPICED PORK

PORK WITH PRUNES

1 tablespoon olive oil
1 (3½-lb.) boneless pork leg, skin and fat removed
4 ozs. brown or shiitake mushrooms, sliced
Thyme sprigs and celery leaves to garnish
Salt
MARINADE:
2 tablespoons olive oil
1 onion, finely chopped
1 carrot, finely chopped
1 stalk celery, chopped
2 cups full-bodied red wine
6 juniper berries, crushed
8 black peppercorns, crushed
¼ teaspoon ground allspice
Bouquet garni

5 ozs. large pitted prunes
2½ cups dry white wine
3 tablespoons butter
4 pork chops
1 each onion, carrot and celery, chopped
1 cup veal or pork stock
Bouquet garni
Salt and freshly ground pepper
Squeeze of lemon juice

Combine prunes and half the wine in a bowl;
let soak overnight

To make marinade, heat oil in a heavy skillet,
add onion and carrot and cook, stirring
occasionally, 5 minutes. Add celery and
cook, stirring occasionally, until vegetables
are browned. Add wine, juniper berries,
peppercorns, allspice, bouquet garni and salt.
Let cool. Put pork into a nonmetallic dish,
add marinade, cover and refrigerate 24
hours, turning occasionally. Preheat oven to
350F (180C). Remove pork and vegetables
with a slotted spoon, drain pork on paper
towels and reserve vegetables. Strain marinade and set aside.

Heat 2 tablespoons of the butter in a heavy
Dutch oven, add chops and cook quickly
until browned on both sides. Remove and set
aside. Add vegetables to pan and cook, stirring occasionally, 5 to 7 minutes or until
lightly browned. Stir in remaining wine,
bring to a boil and boil 2 or 3 minutes. Add
stock and bring to a boil. Return chops to
pan, add bouquet garni, salt and pepper,
cover tightly and cook over low heat 45
minutes.

Heat oil in a heavy Dutch oven just large
enough to hold pork, add pork and cook until
browned all over. Remove and set aside. Add
mushrooms and cook 5 minutes. Add reserved vegetables and put pork on top. Add
marinade. Heat until almost simmering,
cover and cook in oven, turning occasionally,
2 to 2½ hours or until pork is tender. Transfer
to a warmed plate. Skim fat from sauce, then
boil to thicken. Season with salt. Carve pork,
garnish and serve with sauce.

Makes 4 to 6 servings.

Add prunes and soaking liquid to pan, bring
to a boil, cover and cook 30 minutes or until
pork is tender. Transfer pork and prunes to
warmed serving plates and keep warm.
Discard bouquet garni and boil sauce to
thicken slightly. Reduce heat and gradually
stir in remaining butter. Add lemon juice to
taste, pour sauce over pork and prunes and
serve.

Makes 4 servings.

PORK WITH CIDER

2 tablespoons butter
4 pork chops
1 onion, finely chopped
2 teaspoons Calvados or brandy
1¼ cups unsweetened apple juice
1 bay leaf
Salt and freshly ground pepper
2 small cooking apples, peeled, cored and sliced
1 tablespoon fresh lemon juice
2 tablespoons crème fraîche or sour cream
Salt and freshly ground pepper
Thyme sprigs and leaves to garnish

Melt butter in a heavy Dutch oven, add chops and cook quickly until browned on both sides. Remove and set aside.

Preheat oven to 350F (180C). Add onion to pan and cook, stirring occasionally, 5 minutes or until soft. Add Calvados or brandy and set alight. When flames die down, stir in apple juice and bring to a boil. Return chops to pan, add bay leaf, salt and pepper, cover tightly and bake 20 minutes.

Toss apples in lemon juice. Add to pan, cover again and cook 10 to 15 minutes or until pork and apples are tender. Remove pork and apples from pan with a slotted spoon, transfer to warmed plates and keep warm. Boil cooking liquid until lightly syrupy. Stir in crème fraîche or sour cream, pour over pork and apples, garnish with thyme and serve.

Makes 4 servings.

PORK WITH PEARS

2 tablespoons extra-virgin olive oil
2 onions, chopped
2 lbs. boned lean pork, cut into cubes
1 cup red wine
Grated zest of ½ orange
½ cinnamon stick
Salt and pepper
1¼ cups water
2 pears
2 teaspoons honey
Chopped fresh cilantro leaves, orange peel strips and pita bread, to garnish

In a flameproof casserole dish, heat oil. Add onions and cook until soft. Push to side of pan, turn up heat and brown meat in batches.

Add wine, orange zest, cinnamon stick, salt, pepper and water. Bring to a simmer, then cover casserole and cook 1 hour.

Peel, core and slice pears and place on top of meat. Drizzle honey over pears. Cover pan and simmer 30 to 40 minutes or until meat is tender. Garnish with chopped cilantro leaves, strips of orange peel and pita bread.

Makes 6 servings.

Note: This recipe is traditionally made with quinces. If quinces are available, use them instead of pears.

PORK WITH WATER CHESTNUTS

PORK WITH BASIL

1½ tablespoons vegetable oil
4 garlic cloves, chopped
2 fresh red chiles, seeded, finely chopped
12 ozs. lean pork, cubed
10 water chestnuts, chopped
1 teaspoon fish sauce
¼ cup water
Freshly ground pepper
3 tablespoons chopped cilantro
6 green onions, chopped
3-4 green onion brushes to garnish

9 ozs. thin egg noodles
4 tablespoons olive oil
1¼ lbs. pork tenderloin, cut into shreds
1 red onion, cut lengthwise in half, and thinly sliced
¼ cup shredded fresh basil leaves
2 tablespoons balsamic vinegar
3 tablespoons pine nuts, toasted
Salt and freshly ground pepper
Basil leaves to garnish

In a large saucepan of boiling water, cook egg noodles according to package directions. Drain, turn into a large bowl and toss with 2 tablespoons of the olive oil. Keep warm.

In a wok, heat oil, add garlic and chiles and cook, stirring occasionally, until garlic is golden.

Heat a wok until very hot. Add remaining olive oil and swirl to coat wok. Add shredded pork and stir-fry 2 or 3 minutes or until pork is golden. Add onion and toss with the pork, then stir-fry 1 minute.

Stir in pork and stir-fry about 2 minutes until almost cooked through. Add water chestnuts, heat 2 minutes, then stir in fish sauce, water and add plenty of pepper. Stir in cilantro and green onions. Garnish with green onion brushes.

Makes 3 to 4 servings.

Stir in shredded basil, the balsamic vinegar and pine nuts and toss to mix well. Add noodles to the wok, season to taste and toss with pork mixture. Turn into a shallow serving dish and garnish with basil leaves.

Makes 4 servings.

PORK & BEAN STIR-FRY

2 tablespoons vegetable oil
6 garlic cloves, chopped
12 ozs. lean pork, finely chopped
12 ozs. long beans or small green beans
12 water chestnuts, sliced
4 ozs. cooked peeled shrimp
1 tablespoon fish sauce
½ teaspoon crushed palm sugar
Freshly ground pepper
About 3 tablespoons water

In a wok, heat oil, add garlic and fry, stirring occasionally, until golden.

Add pork and beans and stir-fry 2 minutes, then add water chestnuts.

Stir 1 minute, then add shrimp, fish sauce, sugar, plenty of pepper and water. Boil 1 to 2 minutes, then transfer to a warmed serving plate.

Makes 4 servings.

SPICY PORK WITH PEAS

1 lb. pork tenderloin, cut crosswise into thin slices
1½ tablespoons soy sauce
2 tablespoons cider vinegar
1 tablespoon vegetable oil
1-inch piece gingerroot, peeled and finely chopped
2 garlic cloves, finely chopped
1 fresh hot red chile, seeded and thinly sliced
½ lb. fresh or frozen green peas or sugar snap peas
1 head radicchio or ½ head small red cabbage, thinly shredded
Rice pilaf to serve

In a small baking dish, sprinkle pork slices with soy sauce and vinegar. Toss to coat well. Let stand 15 to 20 minutes.

Heat a wok until hot. Add oil and swirl to coat wok. Add pork slices and stir-fry 2 minutes. Push to one side and add gingerroot, garlic and chile and stir-fry 1 minute to mix.

Add peas and radicchio and stir-fry 2 or 3 minutes or until vegetables are tender but still crisp. Serve with rice pilaf.

Makes 4 servings.

PORK SATAY

12 ozs. lean pork, cubed
Juice of 1 lime
1 stalk lemon grass, finely chopped
1 garlic clove, finely chopped
2 tablespoons vegetable oil
SAUCE:
4 tablespoons vegetable oil
½ cup raw shelled peanuts
2 stalks lemon grass, chopped
2 fresh red chiles, seeded, sliced
3 shallots, chopped
2 garlic cloves, chopped
1 teaspoon fish paste
2 tablespoons crushed palm sugar
1½ cups coconut milk
Juice of ½ lime

Divide pork among 4 skewers and lay in a shallow dish. In a bowl, mix together lime juice, lemon grass, garlic and oil. Pour over pork, turn to coat, cover and refrigerate 1 hour, turning occasionally.

Preheat broiler. Remove pork from dish, allowing excess liquid to drain off. Broil pork, turning frequently and basting, 8 to 10 minutes.

Meanwhile, make sauce. Over a high heat, heat 1 tablespoon of the oil in a wok, add nuts and cook, stirring constantly, 2 minutes. Using a slotted spoon, transfer nuts to paper towels to drain. Using a pestle and mortar or small food processor, grind nuts to a paste. Remove and set aside.

Using a pestle and mortar or small food processor, pound or mix to a smooth paste lemon grass, chiles, shallots, garlic and fish paste.

Heat remaining oil in wok, add spice mixture and cook, stirring, 2 minutes. Stir in peanut paste, sugar and coconut milk. Bring to a boil, stirring. Reduce heat so sauce simmers, add lime juice and simmer, stirring, 5 to 10 minutes, until thickened. Serve in a bowl to accompany pork.

Makes 4 servings.

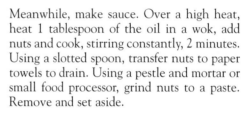

AFELIA

1¼ lbs. pork tenderloin
1 teaspoon coriander seeds
1 teaspoon brown sugar
Salt and pepper
1 tablespoon extra-virgin olive oil
1 cup red wine
Fresh cilantro leaves to garnish

With a sharp knife, cut pork into ½-inch slices. Place slices between 2 sheets of waxed paper and beat with a mallet or rolling pin to flatten slightly.

With a mortar and pestle, lightly crush coriander seeds with sugar and salt and pepper to taste. Sprinkle crushed mixture onto both sides of pork. Let stand in a cool place at least 30 minutes.

In a skillet, heat oil. Add pork in batches and brown on both sides. Return pork to skillet, pour in the wine, boil 1 minute, then reduce heat and cook, uncovered, 20 to 30 minutes or until pork is tender. The liquid should have reduced to a syrupy consistency. If not, transfer pork to a serving dish and keep hot. Boil liquid until reduced, then pour it over the meat and garnish with cilantro leaves.

Makes 4 servings.

COCONUT PORK WITH LIME

6 pork cutlets, about 4 ozs. each
1 (½-inch) piece gingerroot, peeled and grated
2 teaspoons ground cumin
1 teaspoon ground coriander
1 teaspoon chile powder to taste
1 teaspoon paprika
½ teaspoon salt
2 tablespoons vegetable oil
1 onion, cut lengthwise into thin wedges
3 or 4 garlic cloves, finely chopped
1¼ cups unsweetened coconut milk
Grated peel and juice of 1 large lime
1 small bok choy, shredded
Lime slices and cilantro leaves to garnish
Noodles to serve

Place cutlets between 2 sheets of waxed paper. Pound to ¼-inch thickness. Cut pork into strips. In a large shallow dish, combine gingerroot, cumin, coriander, chile powder, paprika and salt. Stir in pork strips and let stand 15 minutes. Heat a wok until very hot. Add oil and swirl to coat wok. Add pork and stir-fry 2 or 3 minutes or until cooked through. Remove to a plate and keep warm. Pour off all but 1 tablespoon oil from wok.

Add onion and garlic to wok and stir-fry 2 or 3 minutes or until onion is softened. Slowly add coconut milk. Bring to a simmer but do not boil. Stir in lime peel, lime juice and bok choy cabbage. Simmer 5 to 7 minutes, stirring frequently, or until bok choy is tender and sauce slightly thickened. Add pork and cook, covered, 1 or 2 minutes or until heated through. Arrange pork mixture on plates and garnish with lime slices and cilantro. Serve with noodles.

Makes 6 servings.

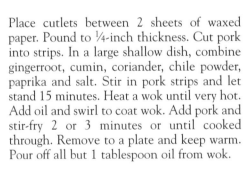

PORK & PRUNE MEDLEY

1 lb. pork tenderloin, cut into thin slices
2 tablespoons soy sauce
2 tablespoons balsamic vinegar or cider vinegar
2 tablespoons olive oil
2 zucchini, sliced
1 onion, cut lengthwise into thin wedges
1 red bell pepper, cut into thin strips
4 ozs. mushrooms, sliced
4 ozs. snow peas
4 ozs. asparagus, cut into 2-inch pieces
½ cup walnut halves
6 ozs. pitted prunes
Salt and freshly ground black pepper

In a shallow baking dish, sprinkle pork slices with soy sauce and vinegar and toss to coat well. Let stand 30 minutes. Heat a wok until hot. Add olive oil and swirl to coat wok. Add pork slices and stir-fry 3 to 5 minutes, or until golden on all sides. With a slotted spoon, remove to a bowl.

Add zucchini, onion, bell pepper, mushrooms, snow peas, asparagus, walnut halves and prunes and stir-fry 2 or 3 minutes until coated with oil. Add 2 tablespoons water to wok and cover wok quickly. Steam 1 or 2 minutes or until vegetables just begin to soften. Uncover wok, return pork to wok and toss to mix. Season with salt and pepper. Stir-fry 1 or 2 minutes or until pork is heated through.

Makes 4 servings.

INDONESIAN-STYLE PORK

1 tablespoon all-purpose flour, seasoned
1¼ lbs. pork tenderloin, cut into small cubes
2 or 3 tablespoons vegetable oil
1 onion, cut lengthwise in half and thinly sliced
2 garlic cloves, finely chopped
1 (1-inch) piece gingerroot, peeled and cut into julienne strips
½ teaspoon sambal oelek (see Note) or Chinese chili sauce
¼ cup Indonesian soy sauce or dark soy sauce sweetened with 1 tablespoon sugar
Cilantro leaves to garnish

In a bowl, combine seasoned flour and pork; toss to coat. Shake to remove excess flour.

Heat a wok until very hot. Add 2 tablespoons of the oil and swirl to coat wok. Add pork cubes and stir-fry 3 or 4 minutes or until browned on all sides, adding a little more oil if necessary. Push pork to one side and add onion, garlic and gingerroot and stir-fry 1 minute, tossing all the ingredients.

Add sambal oelek, soy sauce and ⅔ cup water; stir. Bring to a boil, then reduce heat to low and simmer, covered, 20 to 25 minutes, stirring occasionally, or until pork is tender and sauce thickened. Garnish with cilantro and serve with fried rice.

Makes 4 servings.

Note: Sambal oelek is a very hot, chile-based Indonesian condiment available in speciality or oriental food shops.

RATATOUILLE-STYLE PORK

SPICY PORK & LEMON GRASS

1 tablespoon olive oil
4 (1-inch-thick) boneless loin pork chops, about
   1¼ lbs. total, trimmed of fat
1 onion, coarsely chopped
2 garlic cloves, chopped
1 small eggplant, cut into 1-inch cubes
1 red or green bell pepper, diced
2 zucchini, thickly sliced
1 (8-oz.) can chopped tomatoes
1 teaspoon chopped fresh oregano or basil or
   ½ teaspoon dried leaf oregano or basil
½ teaspoon dried thyme leaves
Salt and freshly ground black pepper
Flat leaf parsley, to garnish
Fresh noodles to serve

1 clove garlic, chopped
2 shallots, chopped
3 tablespoons chopped lemon grass
1 tablespoon sugar
1 tablespoon fish sauce
Salt and freshly ground black pepper
12 ozs. pork fillet, cut into small, thin slices
2-3 tablespoons vegetable oil
2-3 stalks celery, thinly sliced
4 ozs. straw mushrooms, halved lengthwise
4 small red chiles, seeded and shredded
2 green onions, shredded
1 tablespoon soy sauce
About ¼ cup chicken broth or water
2 teaspoons cornstarch
Cilantro leaves to garnish

Heat a wok until very hot. Add olive oil and swirl to coat wok. Arrange pork chops on bottom and side of wok, in a single layer. Fry 4 or 5 minutes or until well browned on both sides, turning once and rotating during cooking. Remove to a plate. Add onion and garlic to remaining oil in wok and stir-fry 1 minute or until onion begins to soften. Add eggplant and bell pepper and stir-fry 3 to 5 minutes to brown and soften.

Using a pestle and mortar, pound the garlic, shallots and lemon grass to a paste. Transfer to a medium bowl and add the sugar, fish sauce, salt and pepper. Blend well, then add the pork slices, turning to coat them with the mixture, and marinate 25-30 minutes.

Add zucchini, chopped tomatoes and their juice, oregano, thyme and season with salt and pepper. Stir well and return pork chops to wok, covering them with the ratatouille mixture. Reduce heat and cook, covered, 6 to 8 minutes, shaking wok occasionally to prevent sticking. Uncover and cook 2 or 3 minutes to thicken sauce slightly. Garnish with parsley. Serve with noodles.

Makes 4 servings.

Heat oil in a wok or frying-pan and stir-fry pork slices 2 minutes. Add the celery, straw mushrooms, chiles, green onions and soy sauce and stir-fry 2-3 minutes. Use the broth to rinse out the marinade bowl and add to the pork. bring to a boil. Mix cornstarch with 1 tablespoon water and add to sauce. Cook, stirring, until thickened. Garnish with cilantro and serve at once with a mixture of rice and wild rice.

Makes 4 servings.

STUFFED PORK SHOULDER

1 (3-lb.) rolled pork roast
Salt and freshly ground pepper
1 lb. potatoes, cut into chunks
1 lb. rutabaga, cut into chunks
1 lb. parsnips, cut into chunks
1 tablespoon olive oil
1 tablespoon cornstarch
2¼ cups vegetable stock
1 tablespoon mango chutney
Sage leaves, to garnish
STUFFING:
1 (6-oz.) can corned beef, finely chopped
2 cups fresh white bread crumbs
1 onion, finely chopped
1 teaspoon dried sage
1 tablespoon mango chutney

Preheat oven to 350F (180C). Open out pork and flatten. To make stuffing, mix together corned beef, bread crumbs, onion and sage. Add chutney and stir together. Spread stuffing along center of inside of pork. Roll pork to enclose stuffing and tie securely with kitchen string. Season with salt and pepper. Put in a flameproof casserole dish, cover with a lid or piece of foil and bake 2 hours, basting meat every 45 minutes. Increase oven temperature to 400F (205C).

Place potatoes, rutabaga and parsnips around meat. Drizzle vegetables with oil and season with salt and pepper. Cook, uncovered, 45 to 55 minutes, turning vegetables occasionally, until meat and vegetables are tender. Remove meat and vegetables and keep warm. Mix cornstarch with a little cold water and stir into cooking juices. Stir in stock and bring to a boil, stirring. Add chutney and simmer 3 or 4 minutes. Slice pork, garnish and serve with vegetables and sauce.

Makes 6 to 8 servings.

CARAWAY POT ROAST

1 tablespoon olive oil
1 (2¾-lb.) pork shoulder roast
2 large onions, chopped
1 lb. parsnips, cut into chunks
3 tablespoons caraway seeds
½ teaspoon freshly grated nutmeg
Salt and freshly ground pepper
1 cup chicken stock
1 cup red wine
Thyme sprigs to garnish

Preheat oven to 350F (180C). Heat oil in a large flameproof casserole dish. Add pork and cook until browned all over.

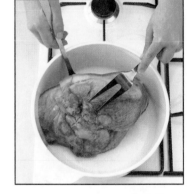

Remove pork from dish. Add onions and parsnips and cook, stirring occasionally, 7 minutes, or until golden. Lay pork on top of vegetables. Mix together caraway seeds and nutmeg and sprinkle on top of pork. Season with salt and pepper. Pour stock and wine around pork. Cover tightly and bake 2 hours, or until pork is cooked through and tender. Remove pork from dish and keep warm.

Remove vegetables from dish with a slotted spoon. Bring sauce to a boil and boil until reduced and thickened. Skim any fat from surface of sauce. Season with salt and pepper. Slice meat, garnish with thyme sprigs and serve with vegetables and sauce.

Makes 6 to 8 servings.

PROVENÇAL PORK CHOPS

2 teaspoons capers, chopped
¼ cup pitted ripe olives, chopped
8 sun-dried tomatoes, chopped
1 (2-oz.) can anchovies, drained and chopped
Juice of 2 lemons
2 garlic cloves, crushed
⅓ cup olive oil
¼ cup chopped fresh parsley
Salt and freshly ground pepper
4 pork loin chops, each weighing 6 ozs.
Basil sprigs to garnish

Mix together capers, olives, tomatoes, anchovies and lemon juice. Add garlic, all but 1 tablespoon of olive oil, parsley, salt and pepper. Heat remaining oil in a flameproof casserole dish. Add chops and cook 10 minutes on each side, until cooked through.

Pour tomato mixture over chops and bring to a boil. Simmer 5 minutes. Garnish with basil sprigs and serve.

Makes 4 servings.

PORK WITH APPLES

2 tablespoons olive oil
4 boneless pork loin chops, each weighing 6 ozs.
1 lb. onions, sliced
2 garlic cloves, crushed
12 plum tomatoes, peeled and chopped
⅔ cup beef stock
¼ cup red wine vinegar
1½ lbs. crisp apples
2 tablespoons lemon juice
Salt and freshly ground pepper

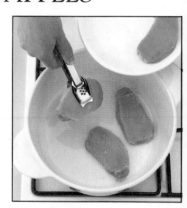

Preheat oven to 350F (180C). Heat olive oil in a flameproof casserole dish. Add chops and cook 3 minutes on each side, until browned.

Remove chops and keep warm. Add onions to dish and cook, stirring occasionally, 5 minutes, or until soft. Add garlic and tomatoes. Return chops to dish and pour in stock and red wine vinegar. Bring to a boil. Meanwhile, peel apples and use a melon baller to cut out ball-shaped pieces. Put apple balls into a bowl of water with lemon juice, to prevent apple discoloring. Chop remaining apple and add to dish. Cover and bake 1 hour.

Remove chops from dish and keep warm. Pour sauce into a blender or food processor and process 1 minute. Season with salt and pepper. Return to dish with chops and apple balls. Cook over low heat 15 minutes, or until apple balls are just tender. Serve hot.

Makes 4 servings.

BARBECUE SPARERIBS

2¼ lbs. pork spareribs
1 large onion, finely chopped
3 garlic cloves, crushed
2 bay leaves
1 teaspoon ground cumin
1 teaspoon mild chile powder
3 tablespoons cider vinegar
2 tablespoons tomato ketchup
1 tablespoon soy sauce
2 tablespoons honey
1 (14-oz.) can crushed tomatoes
Salt and freshly ground pepper

Preheat oven to 400F (205C). Put spareribs into a flameproof casserole dish and bake 30 minutes.

Remove ribs with a slotted spoon and set aside. In a bowl, mix together onion, garlic, bay leaves, cumin, chile powder, cider vinegar, tomato ketchup, soy sauce, honey and tomatoes. Season with salt and pepper.

Stir tomato mixture into dish. Bring to a boil, reduce heat and simmer 5 minutes. Add ribs, turn to coat with sauce and cover. Return pan to oven and cook 30 minutes.

Makes 4 servings.

Variation: Use 4 pork chops instead of spareribs, if you prefer.

HARVEST CASSEROLE

2 tablespoons olive oil
4 pork blade chops
1 large onion, sliced
2 leeks, chopped
1 garlic clove, crushed
8 ozs. parsnips, cut into chunks
8 ozs. carrots, cut into chunks
1 teaspoon dried sage
2 tablespoons all-purpose flour
1¼ cups beef stock
1¼ cups apple juice
Salt and freshly ground pepper
2 small apples
1½ cups self-rising flour
1 teaspoon mixed dried herbs
¼ cup vegetable shortening

Preheat oven to 325F (165C). Heat oil in a large flameproof casserole dish. Add chops and cook 2 or 3 minutes on each side until browned. Remove from pan and drain on paper towels. Add onion, leeks and garlic and cook, stirring occasionally, 5 minutes, or until soft. Add parsnips, carrots and sage and cook 2 minutes. Add all-purpose flour and cook, stirring, 1 minute. Gradually stir in stock and apple juice. Season with salt and pepper and bring to a boil.

Replace chops, cover and bake 1¼ hours, or until pork is tender. Meanwhile, core and coarsely chop apples and set aside. Mix together self-rising flour, herbs, salt and pepper; cut in shortening. Add ¾ cup water and stir to a firm dough. Divide dough into 8 small dumplings. Stir apples into casserole. Place dumplings on top, return to oven and cook, uncovered, 20 minutes. Serve hot.

Makes 4 servings.

FRUITY HAM STEAKS

½-inch piece gingerroot, peeled and grated
2 tablespoons tomato ketchup
1 tablespoon light brown sugar
1 tablespoon light soy sauce
1 tablespoon malt vinegar
1 tablespoon lemon juice
2 tablespoons olive oil
4 ham steaks, each weighing 6 ozs.
1 green bell pepper, chopped
1 red bell pepper, chopped
1 onion, chopped
1 (8-oz.) can pineapple chunks in fruit juice,
   drained, with 2 tablespoons juice reserved
1 tablespoon cornstarch
Watercress to garnish

FRAGRANT HAM

1 (3-lb.) piece boneless, country-style ham
8 ozs. parsnips, halved lengthwise
1 lb. carrots, cut into chunks
1 lb. rutabaga, cut into chunks
2 stalks celery, cut into chunks
1 tablespoon brown sugar
1 tablespoon red wine vinegar
1 tablespoon black peppercorns
6 whole cloves
Oregano sprigs to garnish

In a bowl, mix together gingerroot, tomato ketchup, brown sugar, soy sauce, vinegar and lemon juice. Set aside. Heat oil in a flame-proof casserole dish. Add ham steaks and cook 5 minutes on each side.

Put ham into a large flameproof casserole dish. Cover with cold water and soak 1 hour. Drain and cover with fresh water.

Add remaining ingredients to dish. Bring to a boil, reduce heat, cover and simmer 1½ hours, or until ham is cooked through (170F/75C in center).

Remove steaks from dish and keep warm. Add bell peppers and onion to dish and cook, stirring occasionally, 5 minutes, or until soft. Stir in ketchup mixture and pineapple chunks. Blend reserved pineapple juice with cornstarch. Add to dish and bring to a boil, stirring. Return steaks to dish and simmer 5 minutes. Garnish and serve.

Makes 4 servings.

Lift out ham, slice and arrange on warmed serving plates. Remove vegetables with a slotted spoon, arrange around ham, garnish with oregano sprigs and serve.

Makes 6 to 8 servings.

STUFFED CABBAGE LEAVES

18 large cabbage leaves
2 onions, finely chopped
¼ cup finely chopped fresh parsley
2 garlic cloves, crushed
8 ozs. young spinach, shredded
8 ozs. lean ground pork
1 lb. pork sausage
¼ cup all-purpose flour
2 eggs, beaten
Salt and freshly ground pepper
12 slices bacon
2¼ cups chicken stock

Blanch cabbage leaves in boiling water 2 minutes. Remove and drain.

Preheat oven to 350F (180C). In a large bowl, mix together onions, parsley, garlic, spinach, ground pork and sausage. Add flour and eggs and mix well. Season with salt and pepper. Divide into 6 equal portions. Trim tough center core from each cabbage leaf. Arrange leaves in 6 piles of 3 leaves each.

Place a portion of filling on each pile of cabbage leaves. Fold each one into a package and wrap each one with 2 slices of bacon. Put into a casserole dish and add stock. Bring to a boil, cover and bake 1½ hours. Remove with a slotted spoon, add a little cooking liquid and serve.

Makes 6 servings.

TOAD IN THE HOLE

1 cup all-purpose flour
Pinch of salt
1 teaspoon mixed dried herbs
1 egg, beaten
1¼ cups milk
1 tablespoon sunflower oil
1 small onion, chopped
1 lb. sausage links

Preheat oven to 400F (205C). In a large bowl, mix together flour, salt and herbs. Make a well in center and add egg and half of the milk. Beat to a smooth batter. Stir in remaining milk and mix until smooth.

Heat oil in a shallow flameproof casserole dish. Add onion and cook, stirring occasionally, 3 minutes. Add sausages and cook until browned and cooked through. Drain off excess fat.

Pour batter into dish and bake 30 minutes, or until batter is risen and golden. Serve immediately.

Makes 4 servings.

SAUSAGE & PEPPERS

CHINESE SAUSAGE STIR-FRY

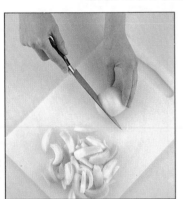

2 tablespoons olive oil
1½ lbs. hot, sweet or mixed Italian sausages
2 onions, halved lengthwise, then cut lengthwise
   into thin wedges.
4 to 6 garlic cloves, finely chopped
1 each large red, green and yellow bell peppers, cut
   in half lengthwise, then into strips
1 (8-oz.) can peeled tomatoes
1 tablespoon shredded fresh oregano or basil or 1
   teaspoon dried leaf oregano or basil
½ teaspoon crushed dried chiles
½ teaspoon dried leaf thyme
½ teaspoon rubbed sage
Salt and freshly ground black pepper
Oregano or basil leaves to garnish
Parmesan cheese to serve

2 tablespoons sesame oil or vegetable oil
½ lb. Chinese sausage (see Note) or sweet Italian-
   style sausage, cut diagonally into thin slices
1 onion, cut in half lengthwise and sliced
1 red bell pepper, diced
4 ozs. canned baby corn-on-the-cobs
2 zucchini, thinly sliced
4 ozs. snow peas
8 green onions, cut into 1-inch pieces
1 oz. bean sprouts, rinsed and drained
¼ cup cashew nuts or peanuts
2 tablespoons soy sauce
3 tablespoons dry sherry or rice wine
Rice or noodles to serve

Heat a wok until hot. Add olive oil and swirl to coat wok. Add sausages and cook over medium heat 8 to 10 minutes or until sausages are brown on all sides, turning and rotating sausages frequently during cooking. Remove sausages to a plate and pour off all but 2 tablespoons oil from the wok. Add onions and garlic and stir-fry 2 minutes or until golden. Add bell pepper strips and stir-fry 1 or 2 minutes or until just beginning to soften.

Heat a wok until hot. Add oil and swirl to coat wok. Add sausage slices and stir-fry 3 or 4 minutes or until browned and cooked. Add onion, bell pepper and baby corn and stir-fry 3 minutes. Add zucchini, snow peas and green onions and stir-fry 2 minutes.

Add tomatoes and their liquid, oregano, crushed chiles, thyme, sage, salt and pepper. Stir to break up the tomatoes and mix well. Return sausages to wok and cover with the vegetable mixture. Simmer 15 to 20 minutes or until vegetables are tender and sauce is thickened. Garnish with oregano leaves and shaved or grated Parmesan cheese. Serve with spaghetti.

Makes 6 servings.

Stir in the bean sprouts and nuts and stir-fry 1 or 2 minutes. Add soy sauce and dry sherry and stir-fry 1 minute or until vegetables are tender but still crisp and sausage slices completely cooked through. Serve with rice or noodles.

Makes 4 servings.

Note: Chinese sausage is available in Chinese groceries and some speciality shops and must be cooked before eating.

Vegetarian Main Courses

CHICKPEA & PEPPER OMELET

2 tablespoons olive oil
1 red onion, chopped
1 red bell pepper, chopped
2 garlic cloves, crushed
1 cup cooked chickpeas
1 teaspoon ground turmeric
2 tablespoons chopped fresh parsley
4 large eggs
Salt and pepper
Parsley sprigs and tomato wedges to garnish

In a nonstick skillet, heat oil. Add onion, bell pepper and garlic; cook 10 minutes or until light golden and softened. Add chickpeas, mashing them lightly. Stir in turmeric and parsley. Stir-fry 2 minutes. Lightly beat eggs with salt and pepper and stir into pan until evenly mixed.

Cook over medium heat 5 to 6 minutes or until cooked and browned underneath. Loosen around edges with a spatula. Carefully slip omelet out onto a plate. Invert pan over omelet and flip over so top is now on bottom. Cook 3 to 4 minutes longer or until golden on bottom. Turn out onto a plate. Cool to room temperature. Garnish with parsley and tomato wedges.

Makes 6 servings.

HAZELNUT CREPES WITH SPINACH

⅔ cup all-purpose flour
1 tablespoon hazelnuts, toasted and finely ground
Salt and pepper
1 egg, lightly beaten
1¼ cups milk
1 tablespoon butter or margarine, melted
6 ozs. fresh spinach, rinsed
¾ cup (6 ozs.) lowfat cream cheese
1 small garlic clove, crushed
1 tablespoon chopped fresh mixed herbs
2 tablespoons olive oil
1 teaspoon lemon juice
¼ teaspoon freshly grated nutmeg
Pinch of ground dried chiles

In a bowl, combine flour, hazelnuts and ½ teaspoon salt. Gradually beat in egg, milk and butter to form a thin batter; set aside 30 minutes. In a large pan, cook spinach with only the water that clings to leaves 1 minute or until just wilted. Drain well and squeeze out excess water. Chop finely and cool. Beat spinach with cheese, garlic, herbs, 1 tablespoon of the oil, lemon juice, spices, salt and pepper to form a paste.

Brush an omelet pan or small skillet with a little of the remaining oil. Place over medium heat. When hot, pour in a little batter, swirl mixture over bottom of pan and cook 1 to 2 minutes until browned on bottom. Turn over and cook other side 30 seconds or until golden. Transfer to a plate and keep warm. Repeat to make 12 crepes. Spread each with a little spinach and cheese mixture, then fold into quarters. Serve at once.

Makes 4 to 6 servings.

VEGETABLE GRATIN

⅔ cup long-grain rice
3 zucchini
1 red bell pepper
1 onion
6 ripe tomatoes
2 tablespoons olive oil
2 fresh thyme sprigs, chopped
2 fresh rosemary sprigs, chopped
2 bay leaves
1 teaspoon dried leaf oregano
1 teaspoon fennel seeds, toasted
⅔ cup vegetable stock
¾ cup shredded vegetarian Cheddar cheese

Preheat oven to 400F (205C). Into a small pan, put rice. Cover with cold water. Bring to a boil and cook 3 minutes. Drain well and transfer to a casserole dish. Cut zucchini into thick slices, cut bell pepper and onion into ½-inch pieces and chop tomatoes.

Into a large bowl, place prepared vegetables. Add oil and stir to coat vegetables with oil. Add thyme, rosemary, bay leaves, oregano and fennel seeds. Stir and spoon over rice. Pour stock over vegetables, cover with foil and bake 40 minutes. Remove foil, sprinkle with cheese and bake 10 to 15 minutes or until cheese is melted and all liquid is absorbed. Brown under a hot broiler, if desired, and serve hot.

Makes 6 servings.

MUSHROOM & BEAN CHILI

4 tablespoons olive oil
1 large eggplant, diced
6 ozs. button mushrooms, wiped
1 large onion, chopped
1 garlic clove, chopped
1½ teaspoons paprika
1 teaspoon chile powder
1 teaspoon ground coriander
½ teaspoon ground cumin
2 lbs. tomatoes, peeled and chopped
⅔ cup vegetable stock
10 tortilla chips
1 tablespoon tomato paste
1 (14-oz.) can red kidney beans
1 tablespoon chopped fresh cilantro
Salt and pepper

In a large pan, heat 2 tablespoons of the oil. Add eggplant; stir-fry 10 minutes or until browned. Remove from pan with a slotted spoon. Add 1 tablespoon of the oil to the pan, add mushrooms and stir-fry until browned. Remove with a slotted spoon. Add remaining oil to pan. Add onion, garlic and spices; cook 5 minutes. Add tomatoes and stock and cook, covered, 45 minutes.

Finely crush tortilla chips. Blend with 4 tablespoons water and tomato paste. Beat into chile sauce and add mushrooms and eggplant. Drain beans and add to pan with cilantro. Cover and cook 20 minutes longer. Season and serve with cooked rice and sour cream, if desired.

Makes 6 servings.

PARSNIP, PEAR & ALMOND SAUTÉ

12 pearl onions
3 tablespoons olive oil
1¼ lbs. baby parsnips, halved or quartered
1 garlic clove, chopped
2 teaspoons chopped fresh thyme
½ cup cider
⅔ cup vegetable stock
1 tablespoon brown sugar
2 teaspoons whole-grain mustard
2 small pears, cored and thickly sliced
½ cup blanched almonds, toasted
Salt and pepper

In a small pan, place onions. Cover with cold water and bring to a boil. Drain and refresh under cold water. Peel parsnips and cut in half. In a large skillet, heat 2 tablespoons of the oil. Add onions, parsnips, garlic and thyme; stir-fry 10 minutes or until browned. Add cider and boil rapidly 5 minutes. In a small bowl, blend stock, sugar and mustard together. Stir into pan. Cover and cook 10 to 12 minutes or until parsnips are tender.

Meanwhile, heat remaining oil in another skillet. Add pears; cook over high heat 1 minute on each side or until browned, then remove pears with a slotted spoon. Pour juices from parsnips into skillet. Boil rapidly 2 to 3 minutes or until thickened. Pour over parsnips, add pears and almonds. Heat through. Season with salt and pepper and serve at once.

Makes 4 servings.

BROCCOLI CAPONATA

2 tablespoons olive oil
1 red onion, chopped
1 red bell pepper, chopped
1 garlic clove, chopped
1 teaspoon chopped fresh thyme
⅓ cup dry red wine
1 lb. tomatoes, peeled and chopped
⅔ cup vegetable stock
1 tablespoon red-wine vinegar
1 tablespoon brown sugar
2⅔ cups chopped broccoli
2 tablespoons tomato paste
½ cup pitted green olives
¼ cup capers, drained
1 tablespoon shredded fresh basil

In a large pan, heat oil. Add onion, bell pepper, garlic and thyme; cook 6 to 8 minutes or until lightly browned. Add wine and boil rapidly 3 minutes. Add tomatoes, stock, vinegar and sugar. Stir well, then cover and simmer 20 minutes.

Steam broccoli over boiling water 5 minutes or until crisp-tender. Add tomato mixture, tomato paste, olives, capers and basil. Cook 3 to 4 minutes. Cool to room temperature and serve.

Makes 4 servings.

VEGETABLE & FRUIT CURRY

1½ teaspoons each coriander seeds and cumin seeds
4 tablespoons vegetable oil
1 large onion, chopped
2 carrots, chopped
2 potatoes, diced
3 garlic cloves, crushed, or 1 tablespoon garlic paste
2 teaspoons grated gingerroot
1 teaspoon each curry powder and turmeric
1 lb. tomatoes, peeled and chopped
2 cups vegetable stock
1 cup frozen green peas, thawed
1 apple, chopped
1 mango, chopped
⅔ cup cashews, toasted
1 oz. creamed coconut
1 tablespoon chopped fresh cilantro

In a small pan, roast coriander seeds and cumin seeds until browned. In a blender or spice grinder, grind seeds. In a large pan, heat 2 tablespoons of the oil. Add onion, carrots and potatoes; cook 10 minutes or until browned. In a medium-size pan, heat remaining oil. Add garlic, gingerroot, ground spices, curry powder and turmeric; cook 5 minutes. Add tomatoes. Cover and cook 10 minutes. Stir tomato mixture and stock into carrot mixture; simmer 20 minutes.

Add peas, apple and mango. Cook 5 minutes longer. Grind half the cashews and mix with creamed coconut in a small bowl. Stir in enough pan juices to form a paste. Carefully stir into curry until evenly combined. Heat through and serve at once, sprinkled with the whole cashews and cilantro.

Makes 4 to 6 servings.

TOMATO & BEAN TIAN

3 tablespoons olive oil
1 red onion, chopped
1 garlic clove, crushed
1 large red bell pepper, chopped
1 tablespoon chopped fresh thyme
2 teaspoons chopped fresh rosemary
1 (14-oz.) can chopped tomatoes
1 (15-oz.) can cannellino beans, drained
½ cup each fresh bread crumbs, chopped pine nuts
    and grated Parmesan cheese or shredded vegetarian
    Cheddar cheese
2 large zucchini, thinly sliced
2 beefsteak tomatoes, thinly sliced
Rosemary sprigs to garnish

Preheat oven to 375F (190C). In a saucepan, heat 2 tablespoons of the oil. Add onion, garlic, bell pepper, 2 teaspoons of the thyme and 1 teaspoon of the rosemary; cook 5 minutes. Add tomatoes. Cover and cook 20 minutes. Stir in beans and transfer to a shallow baking dish.

In a small bowl, mix bread crumbs, pine nuts and cheese together. Sprinkle half of the mixture over tomato layer. Arrange zucchini and beefsteak tomatoes in rows over the top. Sprinkle with remaining crumb mixture. Drizzle a little remaining oil and herbs over top, if desired. Cover with foil. Bake 30 minutes. Remove foil and bake 15 to 20 minutes or until golden. Garnish with rosemary sprigs and serve hot.

Makes 4 to 6 servings.

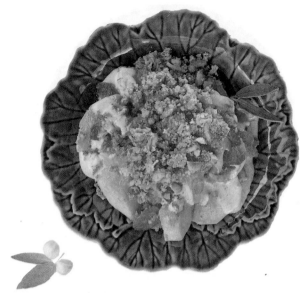

BUTTERNUT SQUASH CRUMBLE

CHEESE & EGG STRATA

1½ lbs. butternut squash (about 3 small squash)
1 small fennel bulb, trimmed
1 garlic clove, crushed
1 tablespoon chopped fresh sage
1 (14-oz.) can chopped tomatoes
⅔ cup whipping cream
Salt and pepper
1 cup whole-wheat flour
¼ cup butter or margarine, diced
⅓ cup macadamia nuts, chopped
¼ cup grated Parmesan cheese or vegetarian
   Cheddar cheese

2½ cups milk
1 bay leaf
2 cardamom pods, bruised
1 tablespoon butter
1 onion, thinly sliced
½ teaspoon chopped fresh thyme
½ cup sun-dried tomatoes in oil, drained and
   chopped
¼ cup Mascarpone cheese
2 cups shredded vegetarian Cheddar cheese
12 whole-wheat bread slices
3 eggs
Pinch of grated nutmeg
Salt and pepper

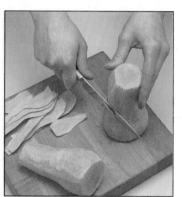

Preheat oven to 400F (205C). Peel squash, cut in half and scrape out and discard squash seeds. Cut flesh into ½-inch pieces. In a large baking dish, place squash pieces. Cut fennel crosswise into very thin slices. Scatter over squash with garlic and sage. Pour in tomatoes and cream and add a little salt and pepper.

Preheat oven to 400F (205C). Lightly oil a 9-cup deep, oval baking dish. Into a small pan, put milk, bay leaf and cardamom pods. Heat until almost boiling. Remove from heat and leave to infuse 10 minutes. Strain into a bowl. In a skillet, melt butter. Add onion and thyme; cook 10 minutes or until softened. Add tomatoes. Remove from heat, cool slightly and stir in Mascarpone cheese and ½ cup Cheddar cheese.

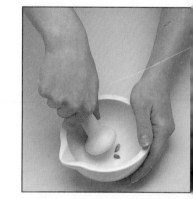

In a bowl, put flour. Cut in butter until the mixture resembles fine bread crumbs. Stir in nuts and cheese. Sprinkle topping over squash. Cover with foil. Bake 40 minutes. Remove foil and bake 15 to 20 minutes longer or until topping is golden and squash is tender.

Makes 6 servings.

Spread half of onion mixture over bottom of dish. Top with half of the bread and remaining onion mixture. Sprinkle with half of the remaining cheese. Top with remaining bread. Beat eggs, nutmeg, salt and pepper into milk. Pour into baking dish. Sprinkle remaining cheese over top. Place dish in a roasting pan. Pour in boiling water to come two-thirds of the way up side of dish. Cover with foil and bake 30 minutes. Remove foil and bake 20 minutes longer.

Makes 6 to 8 servings.

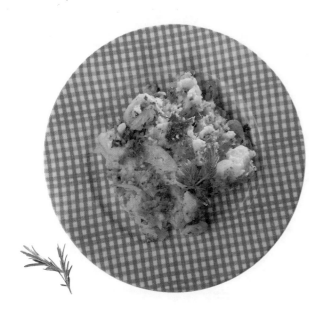

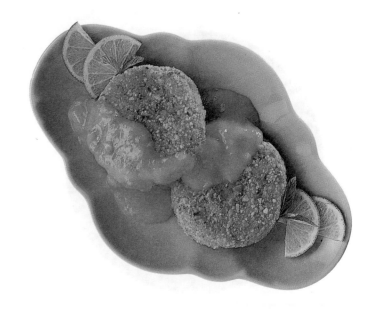

VEGETARIAN HASH POTATOES

1¼ lbs. potatoes, peeled
3 tablespoons butter or margarine
1 onion, thinly sliced
1 teaspoon chopped fresh sage
1 teaspoon chopped fresh rosemary
⅓ cup plain yogurt
⅓ cup shredded vegetarian Cheddar cheese
1 teaspoon whole-grain mustard
1 teaspoon Worcestershire sauce

Cut potatoes into chunks. In a pan, place potatoes. Cover with cold water and bring to a boil. Cook 15 to 20 minutes or until tender. Drain and mash into small pieces.

In a large, nonstick skillet, melt 1 tablespoon of the butter. Add onion and herbs; cook 10 minutes or until onion is soft and golden. In a small bowl, combine all remaining ingredients.

Add mashed potatoes to skillet. Stir in yogurt mixture, flattening mixture out to sides of pan. Cook over high heat 5 to 6 minutes or until golden on bottom. Using a spatula, turn potatoes, a little at a time, and brown other side. Serve from pan.

Makes 4 servings.

POTATO CAKES & MANGO SAUCE

½ lb. potatoes, peeled
1 (4-oz.) butternut squash, peeled
1 tablespoon butter or margarine, diced
1 egg yolk
⅓ cup shredded Cheddar cheese
1 tablespoon grated onion
2 teaspoons chopped fresh cilantro
All-purpose flour seasoned with salt and pepper
1 egg, beaten
¾ cup Brazil nuts, ground
1 small mango, chopped
1 green onion, chopped
1 small garlic clove, crushed
½ small fresh green chile, seeded and chopped
Juice of 1 lime
Vegetable oil for deep-frying

Cube potatoes and squash. In a pan of boiling water, cook until tender. Drain and mash well. Stir in butter, egg yolk and cheese until melted. Stir in onion and cilantro and season to taste. Leave until cold. Shape mixture into 8 small patties. Dust with seasoned flour, then dip into egg and then into ground nuts to coat on all sides.

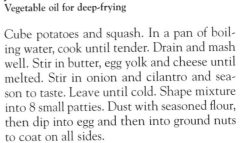

In a blender or food processor, place all remaining ingredients except oil. Purée until fairly smooth; stir in a little water if the sauce is too thick. In a nonstick skillet, heat ½ inch vegetable oil. Add potato cakes, in batches; fry 2 to 3 minutes on each side until golden. Drain well on paper towels. Serve hot with the mango sauce.

Makes 8 servings.

STIR-FRIED SPINACH & TOFU

1 tablespoon olive oil
2 stalks celery, sliced
10 green onions, sliced
1 (1-inch) piece gingerroot, peeled and thinly sliced
8 ozs. smoked tofu
6 ozs. snow peas
1 lb. spinach, torn
1 tablespoon black bean sauce
Freshly ground pepper
2 tablespoons toasted sesame seeds

Heat oil in a flameproof casserole dish. Add celery, green onions and gingerroot and stir-fry 3 or 4 minutes, or until soft.

Add tofu and snow peas and stir-fry 2 or 3 minutes. Gradually add spinach and stir-fry 8 to 10 minutes, or until wilted and tender.

Stir in black bean sauce and mix well. Season with pepper. Stir in sesame seeds and serve.

Makes 4 servings.

POLENTA WITH MUSHROOMS

3¾ cups vegetable stock
½ teaspoon salt
1 cup polenta
1 teaspoon chopped fresh thyme
½ cup freshly grated Parmesan cheese
2 tablespoons butter
½ oz. dried cep mushrooms
⅓ cup boiling water
¼ cup port wine
3 tablespoons virgin olive oil
1 garlic clove, crushed
1 shallot, finely chopped
5 cups sliced mixed fresh mushrooms, sliced
1 tablespoon chopped fresh parsley

In a large pan, bring 3¼ cups of the stock and the salt to a boil. Stir in polenta. Stir, cover and simmer 25 minutes, stirring frequently. Add thyme and cook 5 minutes. Stir in cheese and butter. Spoon polenta mixture into a lightly oiled, shallow pan. Smooth surface and let cool. Soak ceps in the boiling water 20 minutes. Into a pan, strain soaking liquid. Chop ceps. Add port and remaining ½ cup stock to pan. Boil rapidly until reduced to about ½ cup. Set aside.

Turn out polenta. Cut into 12 triangles. Brush with oil and broil 8 to 10 minutes on each side until golden. Meanwhile, in a large pan, heat oil. Add garlic, shallot and ceps; cook 5 minutes. Add sliced fresh mushrooms and stir-fry 3 to 4 minutes or until browned. Add reduced liquid, cover and cook 5 minutes. Add parsley. Serve broiled polenta triangles with mushroom sauce.

Makes 6 servings.

FENNEL & BEAN CASSEROLE

1¼ cups dried haricot beans, soaked overnight
1 tablespoon olive oil
2 onions, chopped
2 garlic cloves, crushed
1 head of celery, sliced
2 fennel bulbs, thinly sliced
2 tablespoons tomato paste
2 tablespoons chopped fresh oregano
1 tablespoon chopped fresh thyme
2 bay leaves
2 teaspoons each salt and sugar
2 (14-oz.) cans crushed tomatoes
Freshly ground pepper
6 slices day-old bread, made into crumbs
Thyme sprigs to garnish

Put haricot beans into a flameproof casserole dish. Cover with cold water. Bring to a boil and boil rapidly 10 minutes. Cover and simmer 1 hour. Drain and set aside. Heat oil in dish. Add onions and garlic and cook, stirring occasionally, 5 minutes, or until soft. Add beans, celery, fennel, tomato paste, half of the oregano, the thyme, bay leaves, salt, sugar and tomatoes. Season with pepper. Cover and simmer 30 minutes or until vegetables are tender.

Preheat oven to 425F (220C). Mix together bread crumbs and remaining oregano and scatter over top of bean mixture. Bake 15 to 20 minutes, or until bread crumbs are golden brown. Garnish with thyme sprigs and serve.

Makes 4 to 6 servings.

BAKED EGGS IN NESTS

1½ lbs. waxy potatoes, halved
8 ozs. broccoli flowerets
2 zucchini
2 leeks, thinly sliced
1 tablespoon Worcestershire sauce
Salt and freshly ground pepper
4 eggs

Cook potatoes in boiling salted water 5 to 10 minutes. Add broccoli and cook 5 minutes. Drain.

Coarsely grate potatoes. Using a vegetable peeler, cut zucchini lengthwise into ribbons. Mix together potatoes, broccoli, leeks, zucchini and Worcestershire sauce. Season with salt and pepper. Lightly oil a flameproof casserole dish and add vegetable mixture.

Make four wells in vegetable mixture and break an egg into each one. Cover and cook very gently 10 minutes, or until eggs have set. Serve immediately.

Makes 2 to 4 servings.

VEGETABLE & CHEESE BAKE

6 thick slices whole-wheat bread
2 zucchini, sliced
1 beefsteak tomato, chopped
6 ozs. mushrooms, chopped
1¾ cups milk
5 eggs, beaten
1 tablespoon chopped fresh chives
Salt and freshly ground pepper
1¼ cups (5 ozs.) shredded Cheddar cheese
Flat-leaf parsley sprigs, to garnish

Preheat oven to 400F (205C). Cut bread into strips. Arrange half of bread in a shallow ovenproof dish.

Spread zucchini, tomato and mushrooms over bread and top with remaining bread. In a large bowl, mix together milk and eggs. Add chives and season with salt and pepper.

Pour milk mixture over bread. Sprinkle cheese over top and bake 50 minutes, or until egg mixture has set and topping is golden brown. Garnish with flat-leaf parsley and serve immediately.

Makes 4 servings.

ZUCCHINI GOUGÈRE

2 tablespoons olive oil
5 zucchini, thinly sliced
10 ozs. button mushrooms
2 leeks, thinly sliced
2 teaspoons whole-grain mustard
1¼ cups crème fraîche
Salt and freshly ground pepper
CHOUX PASTRY:
¼ cup butter
2 cups all-purpose flour
2 eggs, beaten

To make choux pastry, melt butter in ⅔ cup water, then bring quickly to a boil. Remove from heat and immediately stir in flour.

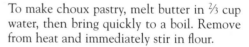
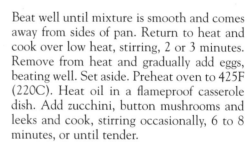

Beat well until mixture is smooth and comes away from sides of pan. Return to heat and cook over low heat, stirring, 2 or 3 minutes. Remove from heat and gradually add eggs, beating well. Set aside. Preheat oven to 425F (220C). Heat oil in a flameproof casserole dish. Add zucchini, button mushrooms and leeks and cook, stirring occasionally, 6 to 8 minutes, or until tender.

Stir in mustard and crème fraîche and season with salt and pepper. Put choux pastry in a pastry bag fitted with a plain ½-inch tip. Pipe small balls of pastry around edge of zucchini mixture. Bake 20 to 30 minutes, or until pastry is risen and golden. Serve hot.

Makes 4 to 6 servings.

LEEK STEW WITH DUMPLINGS

1½ lbs. leeks, halved lengthwise
12 ozs. potatoes, diced
8 ozs. Jerusalem artichokes, peeled and quartered
4½ cups vegetable stock
Salt
Fresh chives, to garnish
DUMPLINGS:
1 cup self-rising flour
2 tablespoons chopped fresh chives
2 tablespoons vegetable shortening

Cut leeks into 3-inch lengths. Put leeks, potatoes and artichokes in a large flameproof casserole dish.

Add stock and season with salt. Bring to a boil, reduce heat, cover and simmer 45 to 60 minutes or until tender. Meanwhile, to make dumplings, put flour, chives and salt in a large bowl; cut in shortening until mixture resembles coarse crumbs. Stir in ¼ cup water and stir to a dough. Knead lightly and rest 5 minutes.

Shape dough into 8 small dumplings. Place dumplings around outside of vegetable mixture. Cover and simmer 30 minutes. Garnish with chives and serve.

Makes 4 servings.

MOROCCAN CASSEROLE

2 tablespoon olive oil
1 large onion, chopped
1 large eggplant, cut into chunks
2 garlic cloves, crushed
1 teaspoon ground cumin
1 teaspoon turmeric
1 teaspoon ground ginger
1 teaspoon paprika
1 teaspoon ground allspice
3 (14-oz.) cans crushed tomatoes
1 (1-lb.) can chickpeas, drained
½ cup raisins
1 tablespoon chopped fresh cilantro
3 tablespoons chopped fresh parsley
Salt and freshly ground pepper

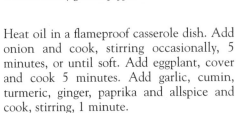

Heat oil in a flameproof casserole dish. Add onion and cook, stirring occasionally, 5 minutes, or until soft. Add eggplant, cover and cook 5 minutes. Add garlic, cumin, turmeric, ginger, paprika and allspice and cook, stirring, 1 minute.

Stir in tomatoes, chickpeas, raisins, cilantro and parsley. Season with salt and pepper. Bring to a boil, reduce heat and simmer 45 minutes or until vegetables are tender. Serve hot.

Makes 4 to 6 servings.

MIXED VEGETABLE RÖSTI

1 tablespoon olive oil
1 onion, sliced
8 ozs. green beans, trimmed
8 ozs. cauliflowerets
4 tomatoes, peeled and quartered
1 tablespoon chopped fresh parsley
Salt and freshly ground pepper
1½ lbs. potatoes, grated
1 cup (4 oz.) shredded mozzarella cheese

Heat oil in a flameproof casserole dish. Add onion and cook, stirring occasionally, 5 minutes, or until soft. Preheat oven to 400F (205C).

Add beans, cauliflower and tomatoes and cook, stirring occasionally, 10 minutes, or until tender. Stir in parsley and season with salt and pepper.

Spread potatoes over vegetables and top with cheese. Bake 30 minutes, or until potatoes are tender and cheese is melted and golden. Serve hot.

Makes 4 servings.

Note: Waxy potatoes should be used for this recipe.

VEGETABLE COBBLER

1 tablespoon olive oil
1 garlic clove, crushed
2 leeks, thinly sliced
2 teaspoons mustard seeds
8 ozs. mushrooms, sliced
8 ozs. broccoli flowerets
6 ozs. fresh or frozen green peas
1¼ cups half and half
Large pinch of freshly grated nutmeg
1 teaspoon prepared English mustard
1 tablespoon chopped fresh parsley
7 ozs. puff pastry, thawed if frozen
Milk for brushing

Heat oil in a flameproof casserole dish. Add garlic and leeks and cook until soft.

Add mustard seeds and cook until they start to pop. Add mushrooms, broccoli and peas. Cover and cook 8 to 10 minutes, or until tender. Remove from heat. Stir in half-and-half, nutmeg, mustard and parsley. Preheat oven to 425F (220C).

Roll out pastry on a lightly floured surface. Using a pastry cutter, cut out 12 (2-inch) rounds. Arrange on top of vegetable mixture. Brush with a little milk and bake 30 to 35 minutes, or until risen and golden. Serve hot.

Makes 4 to 6 servings.

NUT BAKE WITH TOMATOES

2 tablespoons butter
1 onion, finely chopped
1 large carrot, finely chopped
2 stalks celery, finely chopped
2½ cups finely chopped mixed nuts
2 cups fresh whole-wheat bread crumbs
2 teaspoons yeast extract (optional)
1¼ cups hot vegetable stock
2 teaspoons dried thyme
Salt and freshly ground pepper
2 beefsteak tomatoes, sliced
1 cup (4 oz.) shredded aged Cheddar cheese

Preheat oven to 350F (180C). Heat butter in a flameproof casserole dish.

Add onion, carrot and celery and cook over low heat, stirring occasionally, 10 minutes, or until soft. In a large bowl, mix together nuts and bread crumbs. Stir in cooked vegetables. If used, dissolve yeast extract in hot stock before stirring into nut mixture. Add thyme and season with salt and pepper. Mix well. Arrange half of the tomato slices in bottom of dish. Sprinkle with half of the cheese.

Spread half of the nut mixture on top. Add remaining tomato slices and cover with remaining nut mixture. Sprinkle with remaining cheese and bake 50 to 60 minutes, or until cheese is melted and golden. Serve hot.

Makes 4 servings.

SPANISH OMELET

2 tablespoons olive oil
1 onion, thinly sliced
12 ozs. potatoes, diced
1 red bell pepper, thinly sliced
1 green bell pepper, thinly sliced
6 eggs, beaten
1 tablespoon chopped fresh parsley
Salt and freshly ground pepper

Heat oil in a shallow flameproof casserole dish. Add onion and potatoes and cook, stirring occasionally, 6 to 8 minutes, or until potatoes are tender. Stir in bell peppers and cook 2 or 3 minutes.

Beat together eggs, parsley, salt and pepper and pour into dish. Cook over low heat 3 or 4 minutes, or until eggs have set on bottom. Preheat broiler.

Put omelet under broiler and cook 5 or 6 minutes, or until eggs have set. Cut into wedges and serve hot or at room temperature.

Makes 4 servings.

LENTIL & BEAN CHILE

1 tablespoon olive oil
1 onion, chopped
1 garlic clove, chopped
¾ cup green lentils
1¼ cups vegetable stock
1 teaspoon mild chile powder
1 (14-oz.) can crushed tomatoes
1 (15-oz.) can red kidney beans, drained
1 green bell pepper, chopped
Salt and freshly ground pepper
Chopped fresh flat-leaf parsley to garnish

Heat oil in a flameproof casserole dish. Add onion and garlic and cook until soft. Add lentils, stock, chile powder and tomatoes.

Cover and simmer 30 to 40 minutes, or until lentils are almost cooked.

Stir in kidney beans and bell pepper and simmer 10 to 15 minutes, or until lentils are tender and liquid has been absorbed. Season with salt and pepper. Garnish with chopped parsley and serve.

Makes 4 servings.

VEGETABLE CHILE

2 onions
5 large fresh red chiles, seeded and chopped
1 red bell pepper, chopped
1 large garlic clove, chopped
2 tablespoons dry white wine
Salt
1 tablespoon olive oil
1 green bell pepper, thinly sliced
1 tablespoon tomato paste
1 teaspoon ground cumin
1 (8-oz.) can red kidney beans, drained
Basil sprigs to garnish

Roughly chop one of the onions. Put into a food processor with chiles, red bell pepper, garlic, wine and salt.

Process 2 minutes or until puréed. Slice remaining onion. Heat oil in a flameproof casserole dish, add sliced onion and cook, stirring occasionally, 5 minutes, or until soft. Add puréed mixture, 2 tablespoons water and green bell pepper.

Bring to a boil, reduce heat, cover and simmer 30 minutes. Add tomato paste, cumin and kidney beans. Simmer 10 to 15 minutes. Garnish with basil and serve.

Makes 2 to 4 servings.

VEGETABLE FRICASSÉE

1¾ cups vegetable stock
12 ozs. rutabaga, cut into chunks
8 ozs. each carrots and potatoes, cut into chunks
1 leek, sliced
8 ozs. cauliflowerets
8 ozs. green beans
¼ cup butter
½ cup whole-wheat flour
⅔ cup milk
¾ cup chopped fresh parsley
1 teaspoon lemon juice
Salt and freshly ground pepper

Pour stock into a flameproof casserole dish and bring to a boil. Add rutabaga, carrots and potatoes.

Return to a boil and cook 5 minutes. Add leek, cauliflower and beans and cook 3 to 5 minutes. Drain vegetables, reserving stock. Heat butter in dish. Stir in flour and cook, stirring, 1 minutes. Gradually stir in milk and 1 cup of reserved stock, stirring constantly until smooth.

Reduce heat, stir in parsley and lemon juice and season with salt and pepper. Add vegetables and cook 4 or 5 minutes, to warm through. Serve hot.

Makes 4 servings.

MUSHROOM GRATIN

1 tablespoon butter
1 garlic clove, crushed
2 lbs. potatoes, thinly sliced
6 ozs. brown mushrooms, sliced
4 ozs. button mushrooms, sliced
Salt and freshly ground pepper
2 eggs, beaten
⅔ cup milk
⅔ cup crème fraîche
1½ cups (6 ozs.) shredded Gruyère cheese
Chopped fresh parsley to garnish

Preheat oven to 400F (205C). Rub an oven-proof dish with butter and garlic. Add half of the potatoes and mushrooms.

Top with remaining potatoes. Season generously with salt and pepper. Mix together eggs, milk and crème fraîche and pour over vegetables. Bake 1 hour.

Sprinkle cheese over top and bake 25 minutes, or until cheese is melted and golden and vegetables are tender. Garnish with parsley and serve.

Makes 4 servings.

MIXED VEGETABLE CURRY

3 tablespoons vegetable oil
1 onion, sliced
1 teaspoon ground cumin
1 teaspoon chile powder
2 teaspoons ground coriander
1 teaspoon ground turmeric
8 ozs. potaoes, diced
6 ozs. cauliflower, broken into flowerets
4 ozs. green beans, sliced
6 ozs. carrots, diced
4 tomatoes, peeled, chopped
1¼ cups hot vegetable stock
Onion rings to garnish

Heat oil in a large saucepan, add onion and cook 5 minutes until softened. Stir in cumin, chile powder, coriander and turmeric; cook 2 minutes. Add potatoes, cauliflower, green beans and carrots, tossing them in the spices until coated.

Add tomatoes and stock and cover. Bring to a boil, then reduce heat and simmer 10 to 12 minutes or until vegetables are just tender. Serve hot, garnished with onion rings.

Makes 4 servings.

Variation: Use any mixture of vegetables to make a total of 1½ lbs. – turnips, zucchini, eggplant, parsnips and leeks are all suitable.

FRESH HERB FRITTATA

6 eggs
2 egg whites
2 green onions, chopped
½ cup cottage cheese
½ cup fresh chopped mixed herbs
1 cup arugula leaves
Salt and pepper
¼ cup olive oil

In a bowl, beat eggs and egg whites together until thoroughly mixed. Stir in green onions, cheese and herbs. Roughly chop arugula leaves and add to mixture with salt and pepper.

Preheat broiler. In a nonstick skillet, heat oil. Pour in egg mixture, swirling to reach edges of pan. Cook, stirring, over medium-low heat about 3 minutes or until eggs are beginning to set.

Place pan under hot broiler 2 to 3 minutes or until set and lightly browned. Turn out onto a plate. Cut into wedges and serve warm or cold with a tomato and olive salad.

Makes 2 or 3 servings.

LENTIL-STUFFED PEPPERS

⅔ cup red split lentils
4 tablespoons vegetable oil
4 medium green or red bell peppers
1 teaspoon cumin seeds
2 onions, finely chopped
2 green chiles, seeded, chopped
1 (1-inch) piece fresh gingerroot, grated
1 tablespoon ground coriander
1¼ cups water
Salt and pepper to taste
2 tablespoons chopped cilantro
Cilantro leaves to garnish

Rinse lentils, then soak in cold water 30 minutes.

Heat half the oil in a skillet. Add peppers and cook 3 to 5 minutes, until golden brown. Drain on paper towels; cool. Add remaining oil to pan, add cumin seeds; cook until just beginning to pop. Add onions and chiles and cook, stirring, 8 minutes, until onions are soft and golden brown. Stir in gingerroot and ground coriander. Drain lentils; add to pan with 1¼ cups water. Stir well, then cover.

Cook over low heat 15 to 20 minutes, until tender and liquid has evaporated. Stir in salt, pepper and cilantro. Preheat oven to 350F (175C). Cut tops from peppers and remove seeds. Stuff peppers with lentil mixture and replace tops. Stand in a baking dish. Bake 15 to 20 minutes until peppers are soft. Serve hot, garnished with cilantro leaves.

Makes 4 servings.

SZECHUAN PANCAKES

2 cups all-purpose flour
2 teaspoons sesame oil
Strips of fresh green and red chile and celery leaves
  to garnish
FILLING:
2 tablespoons cornstarch
1 teaspoon Szechuan peppercorns, toasted and
  ground
Large pinch of salt
8 ozs. tofu, drained and cut into ¾-inch cubes
1 tablespoon sunflower oil
2 garlic cloves, finely chopped
2 tablespoons light soy sauce
6 ozs. vegetable chow-chow, shredded

Sift flour into a bowl and, using chopsticks or a fork, mix in ⅔ cup boiling water, to form a firm dough. Knead on a lightly floured surface until smooth. Divide dough into 8 and roll out each portion to form a 6-inch diameter pancake. Heat a nonstick skillet. Lightly brush pancakes on each side with oil and cook 1 or 2 minutes on each side. Drain on paper towels, layer between sheets of parchment paper and keep warm.

Place cornstarch, peppercorns and salt on a plate and toss tofu in the mixture until well coated. Heat oil in a nonstick or well-seasoned wok and stir-fry tofu and garlic 2 or 3 minutes or until browned. Add soy sauce and vegetable chow-chow and stir-fry 3 minutes. Place a little tofu mixture on each pancake and fold pancake around the filling. Garnish and serve.

Makes 4 servings.

CURRIED GARBANZO BEANS

1 cup dried garbanzo beans
Salt to taste
2 tablespoons vegetable oil
1 small onion, finely chopped
1 (1-inch) piece fresh gingerroot, grated
2 garlic cloves, crushed
½ teaspoon ground turmeric
1 teaspoon ground cumin
1 teaspoon garam masala
½ teaspoon chile powder
2 tablespoons chopped cilantro

Rinse garbanzo beans, put them in a bowl, cover with cold water and soak overnight.

Drain beans, add 2 cups cold water and salt. Boil 10 minutes, then reduce heat and simmer, partially covered 1 hour. In a separate pan, heat oil, add onion; cook about 8 minutes, until soft and golden brown.

Add gingerroot, garlic, turmeric, cumin, garam masala and chile powder; cook 1 minute. Stir in beans and their cooking water and bring to a boil. Cover and simmer 20 minutes, until beans are very tender, but still whole. Serve hot, sprinkled with chopped cilantro.

Makes 4 servings.

BEAN & CORN CHILE

2 teaspoons sunflower oil
2 onions, sliced
2 garlic cloves, crushed
1-2 teaspoons hot chile powder
1 teaspoon ground cumin
1 teaspoon ground coriander
3 stalks celery, sliced, leaves reserved garnish
6 ozs. mushrooms, sliced
⅔ cup vegetable stock
2 (8-oz.) cans whole-kernel corn, drained
1 (15-oz.) can each borlotti or pinto beans and red
 kidney beans, rinsed and drained
1 (14-oz.) can crushed tomatoes
2 tablespoons tomato paste
Salt and freshly ground pepper

In a large saucepan, heat oil and cook the onions and garlic 5 minutes. Add chile powder, cumin, coriander, celery and mushrooms and cook 5 minutes, stirring occasionally.

Add stock, corn, borlotti or pinto beans, kidney beans, tomatoes, tomato paste, salt and pepper and mix well. Bring slowly to a boil, reduce heat, cover and simmer 30 minutes, stirring occasionally. Garnish with the reserved celery leaves and serve with freshly cooked tagliatelle.

Makes 7¾ cups or 6 servings.

CHEESY STUFFED TOMATOES

8 tomatoes
2 tablespoons vegetable oil
1 small onion, finely chopped
1 garlic clove, crushed
1 (1-inch) piece fresh gingerroot, grated
1 teaspoon ground cumin
½ teaspoon ground turmeric
½ teaspoon red (cayenne) pepper
2 teaspoons ground coriander
Salt to taste
½ cup fresh farmers cheese
¼ cup shredded Cheddar cheese
1 tablespoon chopped cilantro

Cut a slice from the top of each tomato. Scoop out centers, discard seeds, then chop pulp and reserve. Turn tomatoes upside down on paper towels and drain.

Heat oil in a small skillet, add onion and cook 5 minutes or until soft, stirring occasionally. Stir in garlic and gingerroot and cook 1 minute. Stir in cumin, turmeric, cayenne, coriander and salt; cook 1 minute more.

Stir in tomato pulp and cook, uncovered, about 5 minutes, until thick. Preheat oven to 375F (190C). Stir farmers cheese and half the Cheddar cheese into spice mixture and spoon into tomato shells. Sprinkle remaining Cheddar cheese on top and place in a baking pan. Bake 10 to 15 minutes, until tops are golden brown and tomatoes are soft. Sprinkle with chopped cilantro and serve hot.

Makes 4 servings.

FASOULIA

¼ cup extra-virgin olive oil
1 garlic clove, crushed
3 large tomatoes, peeled and chopped
1⅓ cups dried haricot beans (8 ozs.), soaked overnight
1 bay leaf
1 fresh thyme sprig
Salt and pepper
Onion rings and fresh thyme sprigs to garnish

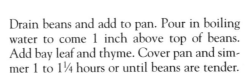

In a large saucepan, heat oil. Add garlic and tomatoes, and cook a few minutes or until tomatoes soften.

Drain beans and add to pan. Pour in boiling water to come 1 inch above top of beans. Add bay leaf and thyme. Cover pan and simmer 1 to 1¼ hours or until beans are tender.

The liquid should have reduced to form a thick sauce. If not, simmer uncovered a few minutes. Discard bay leaf and thyme. Season with salt and pepper. Transfer beans to a servings dish. Serve garnished with onion rings and thyme sprigs.

Makes 4 servings.

STUFFED EGGPLANT

2 eggplant (each about 8 ozs.)
2 garlic cloves, finely chopped
2 stalks lemon grass, chopped
2 tablespoons vegetable oil
1 small onion, finely chopped
6 ozs. boneless skinless chicken breasts, finely
 chopped
2 teaspoons fish sauce
25 Thai basil leaves
Freshly ground pepper
Thai basil leaves to garnish

Preheat broiler. Place eggplant under broiler and cook, turning as necessary, about 20 minutes until evenly charred.

Meanwhile, using a pestle and mortar, pound together garlic and lemon grass; set aside. Heat oil in a wok, add onion and cook, stirring occasionally, until lightly browned. Stir in garlic mixture, cook 1 to 2 minutes, then add chicken. Stir-fry 2 minutes. Stir in fish sauce, the 25 basil leaves and plenty of pepper.

Using a sharp knife, slice each charred eggplant in half lengthwise. Using a teaspoon, carefully scoop eggplant flesh into a bowl; keep skins warm. Using kitchen scissors, chop flesh. Add to chicken mixture in wok and stir ingredients together about 1 minute. Place eggplant skins on a large warmed plate and divide chicken mixture among them. Garnish with basil leaves.

Makes 4 servings.

SPICY TOFU

Vegetable oil for deep-frying
2 (8-oz.) cakes tofu, cut into small cubes
1 clove garlic, chopped
2 shallots, chopped
2-3 small red chiles, seeded and chopped
2 leeks, sliced
About ½ oz. black fungus, soaked and cut into small
pieces
Salt and freshly ground black pepper
½ teaspoon sugar
1 tablespoon rice vinegar
1 tablespoon crushed black bean sauce
About ¼ cup vegetarian stock or water
2 teaspoons cornstarch
½ teaspoon sesame oil
Chopped green onions to garnish

Heat oil in a wok or deep-fat fryer to 375F (190C) and deep-fry the tofu cubes until browned on all sides. Remove and drain. Pour off the excess oil, leaving about 1 tablespoon in the wok, stir-fry the garlic, shallots, and chiles about 30 seconds, then add the leeks and stir-fry 2-3 minutes.

Add tofu, black fungus, salt and pepper. Sir-fry 1 minute, then blend in sugar, vinegar, black bean sauce and stock or water. Bring to a boil and simmer 1-2 minutes. Mix cornstarch with 1 tablespoon water and stir into mixture. Cook, stirring, until thickened. Add sesame oil, garnish and serve.

Makes 4 servings.

Note: For a nonvegetarian dish, add about 6 ozs. chopped beef with the leeks in step 2, and increase seasonings by half.

PASTA & NOODLES

BUCATINI SICILIANA

12 ozs. bucatini
¼ cup olive oil
1 onion, chopped
2 garlic cloves, chopped
2 teaspoons capers
2 tablespoons sun-dried tomato paste
4 teaspoons pine nuts
½ cup fresh bread crumbs
1 tablespoon chopped fresh parsley
2 teaspoons chopped black olives

Bring a large saucepan of salted water to a boil. Add pasta and cook according to package instructions until just tender.

Meanwhile, heat 3 tablespoons of oil in a skillet. Add onion and garlic and cook over low heat 5 minutes or until soft. Add capers, tomato paste, ⅓ cup of water from saucepan of pasta and heat gently. Heat remaining oil in a skillet. When hot, add pine nuts and bread crumbs and cook, stirring, until crisp and golden. Stir in parsley.

Drain pasta and return to pan. Add caper mixture and toss to coat. Transfer to a warmed serving dish, sprinkle with bread crumb mixture and chopped olives and serve immediately.

Makes 4 servings.

Note: Bucatini is a long, thin, tubular type of pasta. If it is unavailable, spaghetti can be used instead.

PASTA WITH BROCCOLI

1 lb. broccoli
12 ozs. trumpet-shaped pasta, eg campanelle
⅓ cup olive oil
2 garlic cloves, finely chopped
6 anchovies in olive oil, drained and chopped
½ fresh red chile, cored, seeded and finely chopped
Salt and freshly ground pepper
Parmesan cheese to serve

Divide broccoli into small flowerets and slice stalks. Bring a large saucepan of salted water to a boil, add broccoli flowerets and stalks and cook 3 to 5 minutes or until just tender.

Remove broccoli with a slotted spoon and drain on paper towels. Add pasta to broccoli cooking water and cook according to package instructions until just tender. Meanwhile, heat half oil in a large skillet, add garlic and anchovies and cook, stirring, 1 minute.

Add chile and cook 1 minute. Gently stir in broccoli and season with salt and pepper. Drain pasta and add to broccoli mixture. Stir in remaining olive oil and cook, stirring, 1 minute. Transfer to a warmed serving dish. Use a vegetable peeler to shave Parmesan cheese on top of pasta and serve.

Makes 4 servings.

SPAGHETTI WITH GARLIC

5 tablespoons olive oil
Salt and freshly ground pepper
2 cloves garlic, finely chopped
1 red chile, seeded and chopped
14 ozs. dried spaghettini or spaghetti
2 tablespoons chopped fresh parsley

Heat oil in a medium saucepan. Add garlic and a pinch of salt and cook very gently until golden, stirring all the time. Do not allow the garlic to become too brown or it will taste bitter. Add chopped chile and cook 1 minute.

Bring a large pan of salted water to a boil and cook pasta according to package instructions until *al dente* (tender but firm to the bite). Drain well.

Toss pasta with the warm, not sizzling, garlic and chile oil and add plenty of black pepper and the parsley. Serve immediately.

Makes 6 servings.

PASTA CARBONARA

4 ozs. smoked lean bacon or pancetta in a piece
1 clove garlic, finely chopped
10 ozs. dried spaghetti or other ribbon pasta
3 eggs, beaten
Salt and freshly ground pepper
3 tablespoons freshly grated Parmesan cheese

Dice bacon and place in a medium saucepan with the garlic. Cook over medium heat until brown. Keep warm.

Bring a large saucepan of salted water to a boil and cook pasta according to package instructions until *al dente* (tender but still firm to the bite). Drain well. Quickly turn the spaghetti into the pan with the bacon.

Stir in eggs, a little salt, lots of pepper and half the cheese. Toss well to mix. The eggs should lightly cook with the heat from the spaghetti. Serve in warm bowls with the remaining cheese.

Makes 4 servings.

PASTA BOLOGNESE

3 ozs. pancetta or bacon in a piece, diced
1 medium onion, finely chopped
1 medium carrot, finely diced
1 celery stalk, finely chopped
8 ozs. lean ground beef
4 ozs. chicken livers, trimmed and chopped
1 medium potato, grated
2 tablespoons tomato paste
½ cup white wine
1 cup beef stock or water
Salt and freshly ground pepper
Freshly grated nutmeg
14 ozs. dried spaghetti, fettuccine or tagliatelle
Freshly grated Parmesan cheese to serve (optional)

Heat a saucepan over medium heat and add pancetta. Cook 2 to 3 minutes until browned. Add onion, carrot and celery and cook until browned. Stir in beef and cook over high heat, breaking it up with a wooden spoon. Stir in the chicken livers and cook them 2 to 3 minutes.

Add potato, tomato paste, mix well and pour in wine and stock. Season with salt, pepper and nutmeg. Bring to a boil, half-cover and simmer 35 minutes until reduced and thickened, stirring occasionally. Meanwhile, cook pasta in boiling salted water until tender. Drain well and toss with sauce. Serve with Parmesan cheese, if desired.

Makes 6 servings.

PASTA NAPOLETANA

2 lbs. fresh tomatoes, or 2 (14-oz.) cans plum
   tomatoes with juice, chopped
1 medium onion, finely chopped
1 medium carrot, finely diced
1 stalk celery, diced
⅔ cup dry white wine (optional)
Parsley sprig
Salt and freshly ground pepper
Pinch of sugar
1 tablespoon chopped fresh oregano
12 ozs. dried pasta of your choice
Freshly grated Parmesan cheese to serve (optional)

Put vegetables, wine, parsley, salt, pepper and sugar in a medium saucepan.

Bring to a boil and simmer, half-covered, 45 minutes until very thick, stirring occasionally. Pass mixture through a sieve or purée in a blender and sieve to remove the tomato seeds. Stir in the chopped oregano, then taste and adjust the seasoning, if necessary. Reheat gently.

Bring a large pan of salted water to a boil and cook pasta according to package instructions until *al dente* (tender but firm to the bite). Drain well and toss with the hot sauce. Serve at once, with grated Parmesan cheese if desired.

Makes 4 servings.

PENNE WITH LEEKS & RICOTTA

1 lb. leeks, rinsed
2-3 tablespoons hazelnut oil
1 garlic clove, sliced
4 cups dried penne or other pasta shape
Olive oil
1 cup ricotta cheese
¼ cup milk
⅓ cup freshly grated Pecorino cheese or Parmesan
  cheese
2 tablespoons mixed chopped fresh herbs
½ teaspoon grated lemon peel
½ teaspoon lemon juice
Salt and pepper
Parsley sprigs to garnish

Preheat oven to 425F (220C). Cut leeks into thick slices. Into a roasting pan, place leeks with 2 tablespoons of the oil and the garlic. Roast 25 minutes or until lightly browned. After 10 minutes, bring a large pan of water to a boil. Add pasta, a little olive oil and return to a boil. Reduce heat and simmer 10 minutes or until pasta is cooked but still firm to the bite.

Meanwhile, in a small pan, place all remaining ingredients. Stir over low heat until melted. Heat through 5 minutes without boiling. Drain pasta. Stir in a little more hazelnut oil and toss with cooked leeks. Stir in hot cheese mixture, season with salt and pepper and serve at once, garnished with parsley.

Makes 4 servings.

VEGETARIAN SPAGHETTI

2 tablespoons hazelnut oil
1 cup fresh bread crumbs
¾ lb. dried spaghetti
⅓ cup virgin olive oil
2 garlic cloves, sliced
Grated peel of 1 lemon
1½ teaspoons chopped fresh rosemary
3 cups thinly sliced zucchini
⅓ cup sliced drained sun-dried tomatoes in oil
2 tablespoons capers, drained
Juice of ½ lemon
Salt and pepper

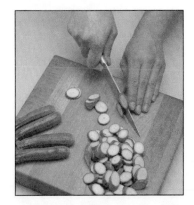

In a large nonstick skillet, heat hazelnut oil. Add bread crumbs; stir-fry over medium heat 3 to 4 minutes or until evenly browned. Remove from heat and set aside. In a pan of boiling water, cook spaghetti with a little olive oil, 8 to 10 minutes or until cooked but still firm to the bite.

In a large skillet, heat 1 teaspoon of the olive oil. Add garlic, lemon peel and rosemary. Cook 30 seconds or until beginning to brown. Add zucchini and stir-fry 3 to 4 minutes or until golden. Add tomatoes and capers; cook 1 minute. Stir in lemon juice, salt and pepper. Drain pasta. Add remaining olive oil and toss until well coated. Serve at once topped with zucchini mixture and the bread crumbs.

Makes 4 servings.

MACARONI WITH EGGPLANT

1 lb. eggplant, cut into ¼-inch strips
1 lb. macaroni
3 tablespoons olive oil
3 garlic cloves, finely chopped
1 lb. tomatoes, peeled, seeded and chopped
1 fresh hot red chile, seeded and chopped
4 ozs. Italian salami, cut into julienne strips
½ cup Italian-style ripe olives
2 tablespoons capers, drained and rinsed
¼ cup shredded fresh basil or oregano
1 cup crumbled feta cheese (4 ozs.)
¼ cup grated Parmesan cheese

Place eggplant strips into a colander and sprinkle with salt. Toss to mix and let stand, on a plate, 1 hour. Rinse with cold water and pat dry with paper towels.

In a large saucepan of boiling water, cook pasta according to package directions. Drain pasta and set aside. Heat a wok until very hot. Add oil and swirl to coat wok. Add eggplant and stir-fry 4 minutes or until browned. Drain on paper towels. Add garlic, tomatoes and chile and stir-fry 2 minutes or until juices are absorbed. Add salami, olives, capers, basil, eggplant and pasta and toss to coat well. Heat through. Stir in feta cheese and remove from heat. Serve with Parmesan cheese.

Makes 6 servings.

VEGETARIAN SPAGHETTI

2 tablespoons hazelnut oil
1 cup fresh bread crumbs
¾ lb. dried spaghetti
⅓ cup virgin olive oil
2 garlic cloves, sliced
Grated peel of 1 lemon
1½ teaspoons chopped fresh rosemary
3 cups thinly sliced zucchini
⅓ cup sliced drained sun-ried tomatoes in oil
2 tablespoons capers, drained
Juice of ½ lemon
Salt and pepper

In a large nonstick skillet, heat hazelnut oil. Add bread crumbs; stir-fry over medium heat 3 to 4 minutes or until evenly browned. Remove from heat and set aside. In a pan of boiling water, cook spaghetti with a little olive oil, 8 to 10 minutes or until cooked but still firm to the bite.

In a large skillet, heat 1 teaspoon of the olive oil. Add garlic, lemon peel and rosemary. Cook 30 seconds or until beginning to brown. Add zucchini and stir-fry 3 to 4 minutes or until golden. Add tomatoes and capers; cook 1 minute. Stir in lemon juice, salt and pepper. Drain pasta. Add remaining olive oil and toss until well coated. Serve at once topped with zucchini mixture and the bread crumbs.

Makes 4 servings.

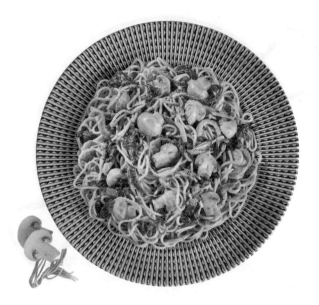

NOODLES WITH SPINACH

2 tablespoons olive oil
1 red onion, thinly sliced
10 ozs. button mushrooms, halved
12 ozs. spinach, torn
8 ozs. thread egg noodles
1 (8-oz.) package cream cheese with garlic and herbs
Salt and freshly ground pepper

Heat oil in a flameproof casserole dish. Add onion and cook, stirring occasionally, 5 minutes, or until soft. Add mushrooms and spinach and cook, stirring occasionally, 10 to 15 minutes, or until spinach is wilted and mushrooms tender.

Meanwhile, put noodles into a large bowl and cover with boiling water. Leave 4 or 5 minutes, or until tender. Drain. Add cheese to spinach mixture and heat gently, stirring, until melted.

Add noodles to vegetables and cheese, season with salt and pepper and mix well. Serve hot.

Makes 4 servings.

SEAFOOD LASAGNE

2 tablespoons olive oil
1 leek, thinly sliced
8 ozs. mushrooms, thinly sliced
8 ozs. haddock fillet, skinned and cubed
4 ozs. cooked, peeled shrimp
10 ozs. cod fillet, skinned and cubed
2 tablespoons lemon juice
Salt and freshly ground pepper
4 eggs, beaten
½ cup freshly grated Parmesan cheese
2¼ cups plain yogurt
6 wide fresh lasagne noodles
8 ozs. mozzarella cheese, sliced

Heat oil in a flameproof casserole dish and add leek and mushrooms.

Cook over low heat 10 minutes, stirring occasionally, until soft. Add haddock, shrimp, cod, lemon juice, salt and pepper and cook, stirring, 5 minutes. Preheat oven to 350F (180C). Mix together eggs, Parmesan cheese and yogurt. Stir two-thirds of egg mixture into fish mixture. Remove two-thirds of fish mixture from dish.

Cover fish mixture in dish with 2 lasagne noodles. Cover them with half of remaining fish mixture, then 2 more lasagne noodles. Spread remaining fish mixture over noodles. Cover with remaining noodles and pour reserved egg mixture over top. Cover with cheese and bake 40 to 50 minutes, or until topping is golden and pasta is tender.

Makes 6 to 8 servings.

FIDEUA

3-4 tablespoons olive oil
1¼ lbs. large raw shrimp
9 ozs. monkfish fillet, cut into pieces
Salt
1½ teaspoons paprika
1½ cups peeled, seeded and chopped beefsteak
  tomatoes
5½ cups fish stock
2 garlic cloves
1 tablespoon chopped fresh parsley
6-8 saffron threads, finely crushed
9 ozs. spaghettini, broken into pieces
Lemon wedges and sprigs of fresh parsley to garnish

Add more oil to pan, if necessary. Stir in paprika and cook 30 to 60 seconds, then add tomatoes. Cook about 5 minutes, stirring occasionally. Add stock and bring to a boil.

In a large paella pan or large skillet, heat 3 tablespoons oil. Add shrimp and cook, stirring, 2 to 3 minutes, then remove and set aside.

Using a mortar and pestle, pound garlic, parsley and saffron together. Stir in a little hot stock, then stir into pan and boil 2 minutes. Add spaghettini and boil until pasta has absorbed most of the stock and is just tender.

Add monkfish to pan and cook a few minutes or until lightly browned all over. Season with salt. Remove and set aside.

Arrange monkfish and shrimp in the spaghettini and cook until hot, then remove from heat. Cover pan and let stand 5 minutes before serving. Garnish with lemon wedges and parsley and serve from pan if a paella pan has been used.

Makes 4 servings.

SNAPPER WITH CAPELLINI

1 tablespoon olive oil
¼ cup unsalted butter
1 lb. red snapper or sea bass fillets, cut into 1-inch
  strips
Salt and freshly ground pepper
8 ozs. mushrooms, quartered
2 garlic cloves, finely chopped
⅔ cup dry white wine
2 tomatoes, peeled, seeded and chopped
Juice of 1 lemon
1 tablespoon tomato paste
4 green onions, thinly sliced
2 tablespoons thinly shredded fresh basil
1 lb. capellini or thin spaghetti
Basil sprigs to garnish

SPAGHETTI MARINARA

½ lb. spaghetti
1 tablespoon olive oil
1 small onion, finely chopped
1 garlic clove, crushed
1½ cups sliced button mushrooms
½ red or green bell pepper, diced
1¼ cups chopped canned tomatoes, sieved, with
  some liquid drained off
1 (7-oz.) can pink salmon, drained
¼ lb. cooked shelled shrimp
Pinch of dried leaf oregano
Salt and pepper

Cook pasta in boiling salted water according to package directions. Drain well.

Heat a wok until hot. Add oil and swirl to coat wok. Add half the butter and swirl to mix with oil. Add snapper and gently stir-fry 1 to 2 minutes or until just firm. Season with salt and pepper and, with a slotted spoon, remove to a bowl. Stir mushrooms into remaining oil and butter in the wok, then add garlic and stir-fry 1 minute. Add wine and stir to deglaze any bits stuck to wok. Bring to a boil and simmer 1 minute.

Meanwhile, in a saucepan, heat oil. Add onion, garlic, mushrooms and bell pepper and cook 3 to 4 minutes, until onion is softened. Add tomatoes and simmer 2 to 3 minutes longer. Remove any salmon bones and skin, then flake. Add to sauce with shrimp, oregano, salt and pepper.

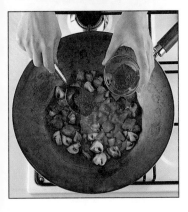

Stir in chopped tomatoes, lemon juice, tomato paste, green onions and basil. Stir in remaining butter in small pieces to thicken and smooth sauce. Return fish to sauce and cook gently 1 minute or until heated through. Meanwhile, in a large saucepan of boiling water, cook capellini or spaghetti according to package directions. Drain and divide among 4 plates. Top with fish strips and sauce and garnish with basil sprigs.

Makes 4 servings.

Return drained spaghetti to pan and mix together with sauce. Heat through before serving.

Makes 4 servings.

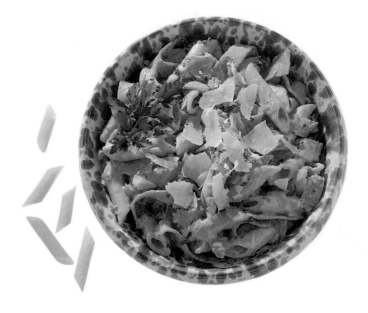

TUNA, TOMATO & PENNE

2 tablespoons olive oil
1 onion, chopped
2 garlic cloves, finely chopped
1 (28-oz.) can peeled tomatoes
1 tablespoon tomato paste
1 tablespoon chopped fresh oregano or 1 teaspoon
　dried leaf oregano
⅓ cup sun-dried tomatoes in oil, drained and
　chopped
Salt and freshly ground pepper
12 ozs. penne or rigatoni
⅓ cup ripe olives, coarsely chopped
2 tablespoons capers, drained
1 (7-oz.) can light tuna, drained
2 tablespoons chopped fresh parsley
Parmesan cheese to garnish

Heat a wok until hot. Add the oil and swirl to coat wok. Add onion and garlic and stir-fry 1 to 2 minutes or until beginning to soften. Add the tomatoes, stirring to break up the large pieces. Stir in the tomato paste, oregano and sun-dried tomatoes. Bring to a boil and simmer 10 to 12 minutes or until sauce is slightly thickened. Season with salt and pepper. Meanwhile, in a large saucepan of boiling water, cook penne according to package directions.

Stir olives, capers and tuna into sauce. Drain pasta and add to tomato sauce, stirring gently to mix well. Stir in chopped parsley and serve immediately from the wok, or spoon into 4 pasta bowls. Using a vegetable peeler, shave flakes of Parmesan cheese over each serving.

Makes 4 servings.

PENNE, VODKA & TOMATOES

1 lb. penne or rigatoni
2 tablespoons olive oil
1 onion, finely chopped
2 garlic cloves, finely chopped
1 (14-oz.) can plum tomatoes
½ teaspoon crushed dried chiles
4 ozs. thinly sliced ham, cut into strips
½ cup vodka
1 cup whipping cream
½ cup grated Parmesan cheese
¼ cup chopped parsley
Salt and freshly ground pepper

In a large saucepan of boiling water, cook pasta according to package directions.

Drain pasta and set aside. Heat a wok until hot. Add oil and swirl to coat wok. Add onion and garlic and stir-fry 2 minutes or until onion begins to soften. Add tomatoes and crushed chiles and bring to a boil. Reduce heat and simmer 10 minutes or until sauce thickens slightly.

Add ham and stir in vodka and simmer 5 minutes. Add cream and half of the cheese and simmer 3 minutes. Stir in pasta and parsley and toss to coat pasta. Season with salt and pepper and heat through. serve with remaining cheese.

Makes 4 to 6 servings.

PASTITSIO

2 tablespoons extra-virgin olive oil
1 onion, chopped
1 garlic clove, crushed
1 lb. ground beef
1¼ cups beef stock
2 teaspoons tomato paste
½ teaspoon ground cinnamon
1 teaspoon chopped fresh mint
Salt and pepper
½ lb. macaroni
¼ cup butter
½ cup all-purpose flour
2 cups milk
½ cup plain yogurt
1½ cups grated kefalotiri cheese (6 ozs.)

Preheat oven to 375F (190C). In a skillet, heat oil. Add onion and garlic and cook until soft. Add beef and stir until browned. Stir in stock, tomato paste, cinnamon, mint, salt and pepper. Simmer 10 to 15 minutes or until sauce is reduced. Meanwhile, in a pan of boiling water, cook macaroni 8 minutes or until tender. Drain, rinse with cold water and set aside.

In a saucepan, melt butter. Stir in flour and cook 1 minute. Gradually stir in milk and yogurt and simmer 5 minutes. Stir in half the cheese. Season with salt and pepper. Mix macaroni into cheese sauce. Spread half the macaroni mixture over bottom of a large gratin or soufflé dish. Cover with meat sauce, then top with remaining macaroni. Sprinkle remaining cheese over top. Bake 45 minutes or until browned.

Makes 4 to 6 servings.

RAINBOW MACARONI & CHEESE

¾ cup macaroni
6 tablespoons all-purpose flour
1¼ cups milk
1 tablespoon butter or margarine
Salt and pepper
⅓ cup frozen green peas
⅓ cup frozen whole-kernel corn
1 tomato, diced
¾ cup shredded Gouda or Edam cheese (3 ozs.)
½ cup whole-wheat bread crumbs

Cook macaroni in boiling salted water according to package directions until just tender to the bite. Drain.

In a medium-size saucepan, combine flour and a little of the milk until smooth. Gradually stir in remaining milk; add butter. Cook over medium heat, stirring constantly, until thickened. Season with a little salt and pepper. Reduce heat to low and add peas, corn, tomato and ½ cup of the cheese. Cook, stirring, 2 minutes. Meanwhile, preheat broiler.

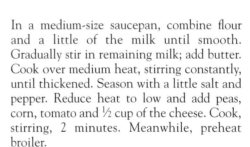

Stir in macaroni and heat through. Spoon mixture into 4 small ovenproof dishes or 1 large one. Mix together bread crumbs and remaining cheese, then sprinkle on top of macaroni mixture. Place under hot broiler 3 to 4 minutes, until browned. Serve immediately.

Makes 4 servings.

PASTA PRIMAVERA

1 lb. tagliatelle, linguine or thin spaghetti
2-4 tablespoons olive oil
8 ozs. asparagus, cut into 2-inch pieces
8 ozs. broccoli flowerets
2 yellow or green zucchini, sliced
4 ozs. snow peas, cut in half if large
2-4 garlic cloves, finely chopped
1 (14-oz.) can chopped tomatoes
2 tablespoons butter
4 ozs. fresh or frozen green peas
4-6 tablespoons shredded fresh basil
Shaved Parmesan cheese to serve

In a large saucepan of boiling water, cook pasta according to package directions.

Drain pasta, turn into a large bowl and toss with 1 tablespoon of the oil. Heat a wok until hot. Add remaining oil and swirl to coat wok. Add asparagus and broccoli and stir-fry 4 minutes or until crisp-tender. Remove to the bowl with pasta. Add zucchini and snow peas and stir-fry 1 or 2 minutes or until crisp-tender. Remove to bowl. Add garlic to oil remaining in wok and stir-fry 1 minute. Stir in chopped tomatoes and their juice and simmer 4 to 6 minutes or until slightly thickened.

Stir butter into tomato sauce and add reserved pasta and vegetables and basil. Toss to coat well. Stir and toss 1 minute to heat through. Serve with Parmesan cheese.

Makes 6 servings.

LAMB STEAKS WITH PASTA

4 thick lamb leg steaks
Salt and pepper
2 garlic cloves, sliced
⅔ cup water
1 (14-oz.) can chopped tomatoes
⅓ cup extra-virgin olive oil
1 tablespoon chopped fresh marjoram
1 tablespoon chopped fresh parsley
1¼ cups boiling water
10 ozs. orzo (rice-shaped pasta)
Salad leaves to serve

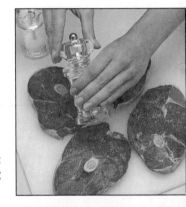

Preheat oven to 400F (205C). Season meat with salt and pepper. Place in a large roasting pan.

Scatter garlic over meat. Add the ⅔ cup water, tomatoes, olive oil, marjoram and parsley. Cook 40 minutes, basting occasionally and turning lamb over.

Add 1¼ cups boiling water and the pasta. Stir in more salt and pepper. Cook about 40 minutes or until pasta is cooked. If necessary, add more hot water. Serve with salad greens.

Makes 6 servings.

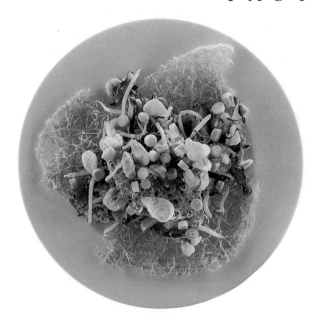

CRISPY NOODLES

6 ozs. rice vermicelli
6 pieces dried Chinese black mushrooms
4 ozs. lean pork
4 ozs. chicken breast
Vegetable oil for deep-frying
2 eggs
4 garlic cloves, finely chopped
3 shallots, thinly sliced
1 fresh red chile, seeded and sliced
1 fresh green chile, seeded and sliced
6 tablespoons lime juice
1 tablespoon fish sauce
1 tablespoon crushed palm sugar
1½ ozs. peeled cooked shrimp
4 ozs. bean sprouts
3 green onions, thickly sliced

Soak vermicelli in water 20 minutes, then sdrain and set aside. Soak mushrooms in water 20 minutes, drain, chop and set aside. Cut pork and chicken into cubes or 1-inch strips. Set aside.

For garnish, heat 2 teaspoons vegetable oil in a wok. In a small bowl, beat eggs with 2 tablespoons water, then drip small amounts in batches in tear shapes onto wok. Cook 1½ to 2 minutes until set. Remove using a thin spatula. Set aside.

Add enough oil to wok for deep-frying. Heat to 375F (190C). Add noodles in batches and fry until puffed, light golden-brown and crisp. Transfer to paper towels. Set aside.

Pour off oil leaving 3 tablespoons. Add garlic and shallots and cook, stirring occasionally, until lightly browned. Add pork, stir-fry 1 minute, then stir in chicken and stir-fry 2 minutes. Stir in chiles, mushrooms, lime juice, fish sauce and sugar.

Boil until liquid becomes slightly syrupy. Add shrimp, bean sprouts and noodles, tossing to coat with sauce without breaking up noodles. To serve, garnish with green onions and egg tear shapes.

Makes 4 servings.

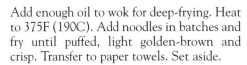

THAI FRIED NOODLES

3 tablespoons vegetable oil
4 garlic cloves, finely crushed
1 tablespoon fish sauce
3-4 tablespoons lime juice
1 teaspoon crushed palm sugar
2 eggs, beaten
12 ozs. rice vermicelli, soaked in water 20 minutes, drained
4 ozs. peeled shrimp
4 ozs. bean sprouts
4 green onions, sliced
2 tablespoons dried shrimp, ground, to garnish
Finely chopped roasted peanuts, cilantro leaves and lime slices to garnish

Heat oil in a wok, add garlic and cook, stirring occasionally, until golden. Stir in fish sauce, lime juice and sugar until sugar has dissolved. Quickly stir in eggs and cook for a few seconds. Stir in noodles to coat with garlic and egg, then add shrimps, ¾ of the bean sprouts and half of the green onions.

When noodles are tender, transfer contents of wok to a warmed serving dish. Garnish with remaining bean sprouts and green onions, dried shrimp, peanuts, cilantro leaves and lime slices.

Makes 4 servings.

PORK & NOODLE BALLS

3 garlic cloves, chopped
4 cilantro roots, chopped
1 cup ground lean pork (6 ozs.)
1 small egg, beaten
2 teaspoons fish sauce
Freshly ground pepper
About 2 ozs. egg thread noodles (1 coil)
Vegetable oil for deep-frying
Spicy Fish Sauce (page 311) to serve

Using a pestle and mortar or small food processor, pound or mix together garlic and cilantro roots. In a bowl, mix together pork, egg, fish sauce and pepper, then stir in garlic mixture.

Place noodles in a heatproof strainer and dip in boiling water 5 seconds if fresh, or about 2 minutes if dried, until separated. Remove and rinse immediately under cold running water. Form pork mixture into about 12 balls. Neatly and evenly wind 3 or 4 strands of noodles around each ball to cover completely.

Heat oil in a wok to 350F (175C). Using a slotted spoon, lower 4 to 6 balls into oil and cook about 3 minutes until golden-brown and pork is cooked through. Using a slotted spoon, transfer to paper towels to drain. Keep warm while cooking remaining balls. Serve hot with Spicy Fish Sauce.

Makes about 12 balls.

CRAB & EGGPLANT NOODLES

8 ozs. dark and white crabmeat
6 ozs. dried egg thread noodles
3 tablespoons vegetable oil
1 eggplant (about 8 ozs.), cut into about 2-inch x
    ¼-inch strips
2 garlic cloves, very finely chopped
1 (½-inch) slice galangal, finely chopped
1 fresh green chile, finely chopped
6 green onions, sliced
1 tablespoon fish sauce
2 teaspoons lime juice
1½ tablespoons chopped cilantro leaves

In a bowl, mash well dark crabmeat. Coarsely mash white crabmeat; set aside.

Add noodles to a pan of boiling salted water and cook about 4 minutes until just tender. Drain well. Meanwhile, in a wok, heat 2 tablespoons of the oil, add eggplant and stir-fry about 5 minutes until evenly browned. Using a slotted spoon, transfer to paper towels; set aside.

Add remaining oil to wok, heat, then one by one stir in garlic, galangal, chile and green onions. Add noodles, toss together 1 minute, then toss in crabmeat and eggplant. Sprinkle with fish sauce, lime juice and cilantro and toss to mix. Garnish with cilantro leaves.

Makes 3 servings.

PORK & SHRIMP NOODLES

7 ozs. bean thread noodles
6 dried Chinese black mushrooms
2 tablespoons vegetable oil
12 ozs. lean pork, very finely chopped
4 ozs. peeled cooked large shrimp
3 shallots, finely chopped
4 green onions, including some green tops, sliced
3 small inner celery stalks, thinly sliced
2 ozs. dried shrimp
2 tablespoons fish sauce
5 tablespoons lime juice
1½ teaspoons crushed palm sugar
2 fresh red chiles, seeded, chopped
¼ cup cilantro leaves, chopped
Whole cooked shrimp and cilantro leaves to garnish

Soak noodles 15 minutes, then drain. Meanwhile soak mushrooms in water 30 minutes. Drain and chop. In a wok, heat oil, add pork and stir-fry 2 to 3 minutes until cooked through. Using a slotted spoon, transfer to paper towels. Add noodles to a pan of boiling water and boil 5 minutes. Drain well and set aside.

Cut each large shrimp into 3 pieces, place in a bowl and add shallots, green onions, celery, mushrooms, noodles, pork and dried shrimp. Toss together. In a small bowl, mix together fish sauce, lime juice, sugar and chiles. Add cilantro leaves and toss ingredients together. Serve garnished with shrimp and cilantro leaves.

Makes 4 servings.

NOODLES WITH CHOP SUEY

1 tablespoon peanut oil
2 garlic cloves, finely chopped
1 green bell pepper, thinly sliced
1 red bell pepper, thinly sliced
8 ozs. shallots, chopped
2 small zucchini, cut into matchstick strips
2 large carrots, cut into matchstick strips
4 ozs. bean sprouts
2 teaspoons sugar
2 tablespoons light soy sauce
1/4 cup Chinese Vegetable Stock (see glossary)
Salt and freshly ground pepper
8 ozs. egg noodles

Heat the oil in a nonstick or well-seasoned wok and stir-fry garlic, green and red bell peppers, shallots, zucchini and carrots 2 or 3 minutes or until just softened. Add all remaining ingredients except noodles, bring to a boil, reduce heat and simmer 6 or 7 minutes.

Meanwhile, bring a large saucepan of water to a boil, add noodles and cook 5 minutes or until just tender. Drain well and transfer to warmed serving plates. Top with the vegetable mixture and serve.

Makes 4 servings.

COLD SPICY NOODLES

1 lb. soba (buckwheat) noodles or whole-wheat
  spaghetti
2 tablespoons sesame oil
2 garlic cloves, finely chopped
1 green bell pepper, thinly sliced
4 ozs. snow peas, sliced
4 ozs. daikon, thinly sliced
2 tablespoons light soy sauce
1 tablespoon cider vinegar
1-2 tablespoons Chinese chile sauce
2 teaspoons sugar
1/3 cup peanut butter or sesame butter
8-10 green onions, thinly sliced
Chopped peanuts or sesame seeds to garnish

In a large saucepan of boiling water, cook noodles according to package directions. Drain noodles, turn into a large bowl and toss with 1 tablespoon of the oil. Heat a wok until very hot. Add remaining oil and swirl to coat wok. Add garlic and stir-fry 5 to 10 seconds. Add bell pepper, snow peas and daikon. Stir-fry 1 minute until fragrant and peas are bright green.

Stir in soy sauce, vinegar, chile sauce, sugar, peanut butter and 1/4 cup hot water. Remove from heat and stir until peanut butter is smooth, adding more water if needed. Add reserved noodles and stir to combine. Turn into a bowl and cool. Stir in green onions and sprinkle with peanuts.

Makes 4 to 6 servings.

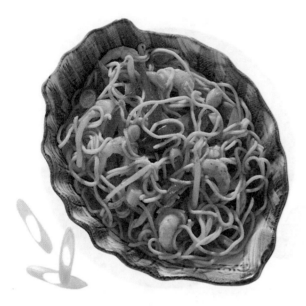

SINGAPORE NOODLES

8 ozs. thin round noodles
¼ cup vegetable oil
2 garlic cloves, chopped
1 (1-inch) piece gingerroot, peeled and finely
   chopped
1 fresh hot red chile, seeded and chopped
1 red bell pepper, thinly sliced
4 ozs. snow peas, sliced if large
4-6 green onions, thinly sliced
6 ozs. peeled cooked shrimp
4 ozs. bean sprouts
⅓ cup ketchup
1 teaspoon chile powder
1 teaspoon Chinese chile sauce

In a large saucepan of boiling water, cook noodles according to package directions. Drain noodles, turn into a large bowl and toss with 1 tablespoon of the oil. Heat a wok until hot. Add remaining oil and swirl to coat wok. Add garlic, gingerroot and chile and stir-fry 1 minute. Add bell pepper and snow peas and stir-fry 1 minute.

Add green onions, shrimp and bean sprouts. Stir in ketchup, chile powder, chile sauce and ½ cup water. Bring to a boil. Add noodles and stir-fry 2 minutes or until coated with sauce and heated through. Serve hot.

Makes 4 servings.

NOODLES WITH BROCCOLI

8 ozs. broccoli
2 tablespoons vegetable oil
3 garlic cloves, finely chopped
8 ozs. lean pork, finely chopped
1 lb. fresh rice noodles or 8 ozs. egg thread noodles
¼ cup roasted peanuts, chopped
2 teaspoons fish sauce
½ teaspoon crushed palm sugar
3 tablespoons water
1 fresh red chile, seeded and cut into thin slivers to
   garnish

Cut broccoli diagonally into ½-inch-wide pieces and cook in boiling salted water 2 minutes. Drain, refresh under cold running water and drain well; set aside.

Heat oil in a wok, add garlic and fry, stirring occasionally, until golden. Using a slotted spoon, transfer to paper towels; set aside. Add pork to wok and stir-fry 2 minutes. Add noodles, stir quickly, then add broccoli and peanuts and stir-fry 2 minutes. Stir in fish sauce, sugar and water. Stir briefly and serve garnished with reserved garlic and chile slivers.

Makes 4 servings.

CHOW MEIN

3 tablespoons soy sauce
2 tablespoons dry sherry or rice wine
1 teaspoon Chinese chile sauce
1 tablespoon sesame oil
2 tablespoons cornstarch
12 ozs. skinless boneless chicken breasts, shredded
8 ozs. Chinese long noodles or linguine
2 tablespoons vegetable oil
2 celery stalks, thinly sliced
6 ozs. button mushrooms
1 red or green bell pepper, thinly sliced
4 ozs. snow peas
4-6 green onions, thinly sliced
½ cup chicken stock or water
4 ozs. bean sprouts

In a shallow baking dish, combine soy sauce, sherry, chile sauce, sesame oil and cornstarch. Add chicken and stir to coat evenly. Let stand 20 minutes. In a large saucepan of boiling water, cook noodles according to package directions. Drain and set aside.

Heat a wok until hot. Add oil and swirl to coat wok. Add celery, mushrooms and bell pepper and stir-fry 3 minutes or until vegetables begin to soften. Add snow peas and green onions and stir-fry 1 minute. Remove to a bowl. Add chicken and marinade to oil remaining in wok. Stir-fry about 3 minutes or until chicken is no longer pink. Add stock and bring to a boil, then add reserved noodles and vegetables and bean sprouts. Stir-fry 2 minutes or until sauce thickens.

Makes 4 to 6 servings.

BEAN & MUSHROOM NOODLES

6 ozs. black-eyed peas
6 ozs. vermicelli rice noodles
1 tablespoon sunflower oil
2 garlic cloves, finely chopped
2 shallots, finely chopped
2 teaspoons fermented black beans
1 oz. dried Chinese mushrooms, soaked in hot water 20 minutes, drained and caps sliced
4 ozs. button mushrooms, sliced
4 ozs. oyster mushrooms, sliced
3 tablespoons light soy sauce
Salt and freshly ground pepper
¼ cup chopped fresh chives

Place peas in a saucepan, add enough water to cover and bring to a boil. Cover and simmer 45 minutes or until just softened. Drain and rinse in cold water. Bring a large saucepan of water to a boil. Turn off heat and add noodles. Loosen with chopsticks or 2 forks and leave to soak 3 minutes. Drain well and rinse in cold water.

Heat oil in a nonstick or well-seasoned wok and stir-fry garlic, shallots, black beans and mushrooms 2 or 3 minutes. Add black-eyed peas and stir-fry 1 minute. Add soy sauce, salt, pepper and noodles, mix well and simmer 2 or 3 minutes to warm through. Stir in chives, transfer to serving plates and serve with a salad.

Makes 4 servings.

RICE

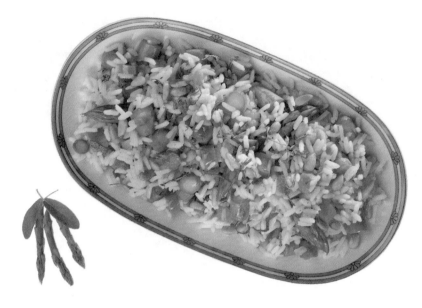

CHICKEN BIRYANI

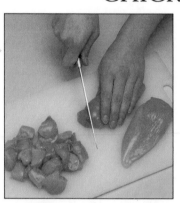

8 tablespoons vegetable oil
1 cinnamon stick
8 whole cloves
6 cardamom pods, bruised
1 (1-inch) piece gingerroot, finely chopped
1½ lbs. skinned and boned chicken, cubed
2 garlic cloves, crushed
1 teaspoon chile powder
1¼ cups plain yogurt
⅔ cup chicken stock
Pinch of saffron threads
¼ cup boiling water
2¼ cups basmati rice
¼ cup golden raisins
¼ cup slivered almonds
1 onion, sliced

Preheat oven to 375F (190C). In a Dutch oven, heat 4 tablespoons of the oil. Add spices and fry 15 seconds. Add chicken, garlic and chile powder and fry, stirring, 4 minutes. Add yogurt, 1 tablespoon at a time, stirring between each addition until yogurt is absorbed by spices. Add stock and simmer 20 to 25 minutes. Transfer to a bowl. In a small bowl, soak saffron in boiling water and set aside. Rinse rice under cold running water until water runs clear. In a medium-size saucepan, cook rice in 5 cups boiling salted water 3 minutes, then drain, if necessary.

Wash Dutch oven. Add 2 tablespoons of the oil. Spoon in a layer of rice, sprinkle with a little saffron water and cover with a layer of chicken. Repeat, ending with a layer of rice. Add any cooking juices left from chicken, cover tightly and cook 25 to 30 minutes. In a small pan, heat remaining oil. Fry golden raisins and almonds until golden; remove. Add onion; fry until crisp and golden. Sprinkle biryani with almonds, onion and golden raisins.

Makes 4 servings.

RICE WITH ASPARAGUS & NUTS

4 tablespoons butter or margarine
1 small onion, finely chopped
1 garlic clove, crushed
1¼ cups long-grain rice
2 cups vegetable stock
½ lb. asparagus spears, trimmed
3 tablespoons pine nuts
2 tablespoons chopped fresh sage
Salt and pepper

In a saucepan melt 1 tablespoon of the butter. Add onion and garlic; cook 5 minutes. Add rice and stir-fry 1 minute or until transparent and glossy. Pour in stock. Bring to a boil, stir once, cover and simmer 12 minutes.

Steam asparagus 3 minutes. Refresh under cold water, then drain and dry well. Coarsely chop. In a large pan, melt remaining butter. Add pine nuts; stir-fry over medium heat 3 to 4 minutes or until golden. Add sage and asparagus. Stir in cooked rice. Season with salt and pepper and heat through, stirring, 2 minutes. Serve at once.

Makes 6 servings.

JAMBALAYA

1 tablespoon olive oil
1 tablespoon butter or margarine
12 ozs. skinned and boned chicken
6 ozs. andouille or chorizo sausage
1 onion, thinly sliced
2 garlic cloves, sliced
1 red bell pepper, sliced
1 yellow bell pepper, sliced
1 green bell pepper, sliced
4 ozs. mushrooms, sliced
1 cup long-grain white rice
½ teaspoon ground allspice
1¼ cups chicken stock
⅔ cup white wine
4 ozs. shelled jumbo shrimp
Lime wedges and parsley to garnish

KEDGEREE

1¼ lbs. smoked haddock or salmon
½ cup long-grain rice
2 tablespoons lemon juice
⅔ cup half and half or sour cream
Pinch freshly grated nutmeg
Red (cayenne) pepper
2 hard-cooked eggs, shelled and chopped
4 tablespoons butter, diced
2 tablespoons chopped fresh parsley
Parsley sprigs and sliced hard-cooked eggs to garnish

In a large skillet, heat oil and butter. Cut chicken into thick strips. Fry until well browned, then remove from pan and set aside. Cut sausage into chunks. Fry 1 minute, stirring well, then, using a slotted spoon, add to chicken. Add onion and garlic; cook until slightly softened. Stir in bell peppers, mushrooms, rice and allspice. Cook, stirring, 1 minute longer.

In a large skillet that will take fish in a single layer, poach fish just covered by water about 10 minutes. Lift fish from cooking liquid and discard bones and skin. Flake flesh. Measure fish cooking liquid to twice volume of rice; top up with water if necessary. Into a saucepan, put liquid and rice. Bring to a boil. Add rice, and stir, then cover and simmer about 15 minutes until rice is tender and liquid absorbed. Meanwhile, preheat oven to 350F (175C). Butter a baking dish.

Pour in stock and wine. Bring to a boil. Return chicken and sausage to pan and simmer, uncovered, 15 to 20 minutes until the liquid is absorbed and rice is tender. Stir in shrimp. Cook 5 minutes longer, then season to taste. Garnish with lime wedges and parsley.

Makes 4 servings.

Remove rice from heat. Stir in lemon juice, cream, fish, nutmeg, and a pinch of cayenne. Gently fold in eggs. In an openproof serving dish, put rice mixture. Dot with butter and bake about 25 minutes. Stir chopped parsley into kedgeree and garnish with parsley sprigs and sliced hard-cooked egg. Sprinkle a little cayenne over top, if wished.

Makes 4 servings.

SHRIMP PASTE RICE

1¾ cups long-grain rice
2 tablespoons shrimp paste
1-inch piece gingerroot, peeled and grated
1 tablespoon peanut oil
1 teaspoon sesame oil
2 green onions, very finely chopped

Cook rice according to package directions until tender but firm to the bite.

Meanwhile, in a bowl, mix together shrimp paste, gingerroot, peanut oil and sesame oil. Transfer rice to a warmed serving bowl and stir in paste mixture. Sprinkle with finely chopped green onions.

Makes 4 servings.

GREEN FRIED RICE

¾ cup long-grain rice
3 eggs, beaten
4 tablespoons vegetable oil
8 ozs. spring greens or young spinach, ribs removed and finely sliced
1 garlic clove, finely chopped
4 green onions, finely chopped
½ cup ham, shredded

Cook rice according to package directions until tender but still firm to the bite. Use eggs to make an omelet; cut it into thin strips.

In a wok, heat 1 tablespoon vegetable oil, add greens or spinach and fry 1 minute; remove and keep warm. Add remaining oil to the wok, add garlic and green onions and stir-fry 1 minute, then stir in the rice. When mixed thoroughly, stir in ham, greens, omelet slices and salt.

Makes 4 servings.

CRAB FRIED RICE

¾ cup long-grain rice
3 eggs, beaten
1 (3-oz.) can crab meat
2 tablespoons vegetable oil
2⅓ cups bean sprouts
1 tablespoon light soy sauce
6 green onions, finely chopped
1 teaspoon sesame oil

Cook rice according to package directions until tender but still firm to the bite.

In a bowl, mix together eggs and crab meat with its liquid. Use to make an omelet, then cut it into strips.

In a wok, heat vegetable oil, add bean sprouts and fry 1 minute. Remove from wok and keep warm. Add rice to wok and stir-fry 3 minutes. Stir in soy sauce and cook 2 minutes. Stir in bean sprouts, omelet strips and green onions, and cook 2 or 3 minutes. Serve sprinkled with sesame oil.

Makes 4 servings.

VEGETABLE FRIED RICE

¾ long-grain rice
4 tablespoons vegetable oil
2 garlic cloves, finely chopped
½-inch piece gingerroot, peeled and grated
1 tablespoon Chinese winter pickle
6 tomatoes, seeded and chopped
1 large red bell pepper, diced
6 dried black winter mushrooms, soaked in hot water 25 minutes, drained, squeezed and diced
⅓ cup cooked or thawed frozen green peas
1 cup diced cucumber
2 tablespoons light soy sauce

Cook rice according to package directions until tender but still firm to the bite.

In a wok, heat oil, add garlic and gingerroot, fry 30 seconds, then add pickle, tomatoes, bell pepper and mushrooms, peas and cucumber. Stir-fry 4 minutes, then stir in soy sauce. Add rice, mix well and heat through 2 or 3 minutes.

Makes 4 servings.

EGG FRIED RICE

¾ cup long-grain rice
3 eggs, beaten
2 tablespoons vegetable oil
1 garlic clove, finely chopped
3 green onions, finely chopped
¾ cup cooked or thawed frozen green peas
1 tablespoon light soy sauce
1 teaspoon sea salt

Cook rice according to package directions until tender but still firm to the bite.

In a small saucepan, cook eggs over medium-low heat, stirring until lightly scrambled. Remove and keep warm.

In a wok, heat oil, add garlic, green onions and peas and stir-fry 1 minute. Stir in rice to mix thoroughly, then add soy sauce, eggs and salt. Stir to break up egg and mix thoroughly.

Makes 4 servings.

YANG CHOW FRIED RICE

¾ cup long-grain rice
3 tablespoons peanut oil
2 medium onions, finely sliced
3 slices gingerroot, peeled and finely chopped
½ cup ground pork
1 tablespoon light soy sauce
1 teaspoon brown sugar
2 eggs, beaten
½ teaspoon sea salt
Black pepper
3 dried black winter mushrooms, soaked in hot water 25 minutes, drained and squeezed
2 large tomatoes, peeled, seeded and chopped
⅓ cup cooked or thawed frozen green peas

Cook rice according to package directions until tender but still firm to the bite.

In a wok, heat oil, add onions and gingerroot and stir-fry 2 minutes. Stir in pork, continue stirring 3 minutes until crisp, then add soy sauce and sugar. Stir-fry 1 minute, then stir in rice. Remove to a warmed dish and keep warm. Pour eggs into wok, season with salt and pepper, then cook stirring 2 or 3 minutes until just beginning to set. Stir in mushrooms, tomatoes and peas. Cook 2 or 3 minutes, then stir in rice mixture.

Makes 4 servings.

MEXICAN RICE

1½ cups long-grain rice
2 tablespoons vegetable oil
1 large onion, chopped
2 garlic cloves, finely chopped
4-6 fresh hot red or green chiles
2 medium-size tomatoes, peeled, seeded and chopped
4 cups chicken stock
Salt and pepper
⅓ cup cooked or thawed frozen green peas
Cilantro sprigs to garnish

Put rice into a bowl, cover with boiling water and let stand 30 minutes. Drain. Pour into a strainer and let stand 1 hour to dry. Heat oil in a heavy skillet over low heat. Stir in rice until all grains are well coated with oil. Add onion, garlic and chiles. Cook until onion is transparent and rice is golden. Add tomatoes and stock; season with salt and pepper. Cover and simmer 20 to 3 minutes or until liquid has been absorbed and rice is tender and fluffy; add peas 5 minutes before end of cooking.

If a softer rice is preferred, stir in a little more stock after 20 minutes and continue cooking until additional liquid has been absorbed. Transfer to a warmed serving dish and garnish with cilantro.

Makes 6 to 8 servings.

RICE-FILLED TOMATOES

4 beefsteak tomatoes
Salt and freshly ground black pepper
About 1 cup cooked rice
1 tablespoon pine nuts
1 tablespoon raisins, soaked in hot water
1 stalk celery, finely chopped
2 tablespoons chopped fresh basil
2 teaspoons balsamic vinegar
2 tablespoons olive oil

Preheat oven to 325F (165C). Slice a lid off tomatoes; reserve. Scoop out flesh and sprinkle insides of tomatoes with salt. Invert and drain on paper towels 15 minutes.

Sieve tomato pulp and mix into the cooked rice with pine nuts, raisins, celery and half the basil. Season well and use this to fill the tomatoes. Replace lids and place tomatoes in an oiled shallow ovenproof dish. Bake 45 minutes.

Whisk the vinegar with the oil. Remove the tomatoes from the oven, take off the lids and drizzle each one with the oil and vinegar. Replace the lids and leave to cool. Serve at room temperature, garnished with the rest of the basil.

Makes 4 servings.

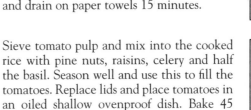

SWEET SAFFRON RICE

1½ cups basmati rice
1 teaspoon saffron threads
3 tablespoons boiling water
3 tablespoons vegetable oil
6 whole cloves
6 green cardamom pods, bruised
1 (3-inch) cinnamon stick
½ cup raisins
3 tablespoons sugar
Salt to taste
Flat-leaf parsley sprigs

Place rice in a sieve and rinse under cold running water until water runs clear.

Put rice in a bowl with 2½ cups water and soak 30 minutes. Put saffron in a small bowl, add boiling water and soak. Heat oil in a heavy saucepan, add cloves, cardamom pods and cinnamon and cook 1 minute. Drain rice and reserve the soaking water. Add rice to the pan and cook 2 to 3 minutes until opaque and light golden.

Stir in reserved water, saffron and its soaking water, raisins, sugar and salt. Bring to a boil, then reduce heat and cover. Simmer 12 to 15 minutes, stirring once or twice until liquid is absorbed and rice is very tender. Remove spices before serving. Serve hot, garnished with parsley.

Makes 4 servings.

Note: The whole spices in the rice are not meant to be eaten.

LEEK & MUSHROOM PILAF

¼ cup dried cep mushrooms
Pinch of saffron strands
⅔ cup boiling water
1¼ cups basmati rice
2 cups vegetable stock
2 tablespoons olive oil
3 large leeks
4 ozs. fresh mushrooms
Salt and pepper
Chives to garnish

In a small bowl, place ceps and saffron. Add boiling water. Let soak 10 minutes.

Rinse rice under cold running water several minutes until the water runs clear; drain well. In a saucepan, place rice. Add stock and cep mixture. Bring to a boil, stir once, cover and simmer 12 minutes.

Meanwhile, in a skillet, heat oil. Add leeks; cook 3 minutes. Add fresh mushrooms and stir-fry 3 minutes. Keep warm. As soon as rice is tender, stir it into mushroom mixture. heat through 1 to 2 minutes. Season, garnish with chives and serve at once.

Makes 6 servings.

MUSHROOM & RICE PATTIES

1¼ cups long-grain rice
1 tablespoon vegetable oil
⅓ cup very finely chopped onion
2½ cups finely chopped mushrooms (6 ozs.)
½ cup shredded Cheddar cheese (2 ozs.)
Salt and pepper
All-purpose flour
Cooked vegetables to serve

Cook rice according to package directions until very tender. Drain well if necessary, then put rice into a bowl. Mash to break up grains. Preheat oven to 400F (205C). Grease a baking sheet.

In a medium-size saucepan, heat oil. Add onion and mushrooms and cook until all liquid has evaporated from mushrooms. Stir into rice with cheese, salt and pepper.

With floured hands, form mixture into 8 patties. Place them on baking sheet. Bake 15 to 20 minutes, until golden. Serve with lightly cooked vegetables.

Makes 4 servings.

Variation: Serve with a salad, if preferred.

HOT DOG RISOTTO

2 tablespoons vegetable oil
1 large onion, chopped
1½ cups long-grain rice
1 red or green bell pepper, chopped
2 cups hot chicken stock
1 (7-oz.) can tomatoes
8 hot dogs
¾ cup frozen green peas
Salt and pepper
Tomato slices or wedges to garnish

In a large saucepan, heat oil. Add onion and cook until softened, stirring occasionally. Stir in rice and bell pepper, and cook 1 minute, stirring constantly.

Pour in stock. Push tomatoes through a strainer into pan. Bring mixture to a boil, then reduce heat, cover and simmer 15 to 20 minutes, until the rice is tender and all liquid has been absorbed.

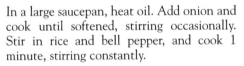

With a knife, cut hot dogs into ½-inch pieces. Add to risotto with peas, salt and pepper. Stir together over low heat 3 minutes longer. Serve hot, garnished with tomato slices or wedges.

Makes 4 servings.

BLACK-EYED PEAS & RICE

1⅓ cups dried black-eyed peas (8 ozs.)
1 tablespoon fresh lemon juice
2 tablespoons extra-virgin olive oil
1 large onion, finely chopped
1 garlic clove, crushed
½ cup long-grain rice
Salt and pepper
2 tablespoons white-wine vinegar
Chopped fresh herbs and green olives to garnish

Rinse and drain peas and place in a saucepan. Cover with cold water and bring to a boil and boil 2 minutes.

Drain peas, discarding water. Return peas to pan, cover with fresh water to come well above surface of peas. Add lemon juice. Bring to a boil. Cover, reduce heat and simmer 20 to 30 minutes or until peas are tender.

In another saucepan, heat oil and add onion and garlic and cook until soft. Add rice, stir to coat with oil, then add ¾ cup water and season with salt. Bring to a boil, cover pan and simmer 10 to 15 minutes or until rice is tender and water absorbed. Drain peas and mix with rice. Add vinegar, salt and pepper. Heat together 2 minutes. Serve garnished with chopped herbs and olives.

Makes 4 to 6 servings.

WOK-STYLE PAELLA

2 tablespoons olive oil
1 lb. chorizo sausage or hot Italian sausage, cut into
  1-inch slices
1 lb. skinless boneless chicken breasts, cut into
  1-inch slices
1 onion, chopped
2-3 garlic cloves, finely chopped
1 green or red bell pepper, diced
1 (14-oz.) can tomatoes
2⅔ cups long-grain rice
½ teaspoon crushed dried chiles
½ teaspoon dried leaf thyme
1 teaspoon crushed saffron threads
8 ozs. green beans, cut into 1-inch pieces
8 ozs. cooked peeled shrimp (optional)

Heat a wok until hot. Add oil and swirl to coat wok. Add sausage and stir-fry 4 or 5 minutes or until golden. Remove to a plate. Add chicken to oil in wok and stir-fry 3 or 4 minutes or until golden. Remove to a plate.

Add onion, garlic and bell pepper to drippings in wok and stir-fry 3 or 4 minutes or until crisp-tender. Stir in tomatoes, rice, 2 cups water, crushed chiles, thyme and saffron. Bring to a boil, stir in sausage and reduce heat to low. Cover tightly and cook 20 minutes until liquid is absorbed and rice is tender. Stir in chicken and green beans and cook, covered, 5 to 7 minutes or until beans are crisp-tender. Add shrimp if using and fluff with a fork. Cook, uncovered, 2 or 3 minutes.

Makes 6 to 8 servings.

RICE & BLACK BEANS

2 tablespoons olive oil
1 Spanish onion, chopped
2 garlic cloves, chopped
4 ozs. unsmoked slab bacon, chopped
1 small red bell pepper, chopped
1 teaspoon paprika
2 cups peeled, seeded and chopped beefsteak
  tomatoes
Salt and pepper
1⅓ cups short-grain white rice
Fresh herb sprigs to garnish
BLACK BEANS:
1⅓ cups dried black beans, soaked overnight and
  drained
½ Spanish onion
2 garlic cloves, crushed

To prepare the beans, put them in a saucepan with onion and garlic. Cover with water, bring to a boil and boil 10 minutes. Reduce heat, cover and simmer 1½ to 2 hours or until just tender. Meanwhile in a saucepan, heat oil. Add onion, garlic, bacon and bell pepper, and cook, stirring occasionally, until bacon begins to brown. Stir in paprika 30 to 60 seconds, then stir in tomatoes and cook about 5 minutes, stirring occasionally. Season with salt and pepper.

Drain beans. Discard onion and garlic. Stir rice and 2 cups water into pan with tomato mixture. Bring to a boil, stir, cover and simmer about 25 minutes or until liquid is absorbed and rice is tender. Stir in the beans. Taste for seasoning and serve garnished with herb sprigs.

Makes 4 to 6 servings.

SPICE RICE & PEPPERS

¼ cup olive oil
1⅓ cups long-grain white rice
2 garlic cloves
Salt
1 teaspoon each cumin seeds and coriander seeds
3 tablespoons tomato paste
2 teaspoons paprika
1 teaspoon chile powder
Pinch of saffron threads, crushed and dissolved in 2
  tablespoons boiling water
2½ cups boiling chicken stock, vegetable stock or
  water
3-4 red bell peppers, roasted, peeled and halved
Extra-virgin olive oil to serve, if desired
Fresh herbs, to garnish

In a paella pan or a wide, shallow saucepan, heat oil. Stir in rice and stir-fry 2 to 3 minutes. Meanwhile, using a mortar and pestle, grind together garlic, salt, cumin seeds and coriander seeds. Stir in tomato paste, paprika, chile powder and saffron liquid. Stir into rice. Stir in stock or water. Bring to a boil, then reduce heat, cover and simmer about 7 minutes.

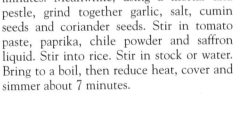

Arrange peppers around sides of pan. Simmer 7 to 10 minutes until rice is tender and plump and liquid is absorbed. Remove from heat and let stand 5 minutes. Drizzle extra-virgin oil over pepper, if desired, and garnish with herbs.

Makes 4 servings.

RICE WITH CHICKPEAS

12 ozs. chickpeas, soaked overnight and drained
Olive oil for frying
3 garlic cloves, finely chopped
1⅓ cups short-grain white rice
2½ cups chicken stock or water
1 recipe Tomato Sauce (page 307)
Chopped fresh herbs to garnish

Simmer chickpeas in plenty of water 1½ to 2 hours or until just tender.

Meanwhile, prepare the rice. In a saucepan, heat 2 tablespoons oil. Add garlic and fry 2 minutes. Stir in rice and stir-fry 3 to 4 minutes, then stir in 1¼ cups stock or water. Simmer 10 minutes, then add another 1¼ cups stock or water. Continue cooking 10 to 12 minutes or until liquid is absorbed and rice is tender. Cover and keep warm.

Drain chickpeas. In a skillet, heat about ½-inch layer of oil. Add chickpeas and fry, stirring frequently, until golden-brown. Stir into rice, then transfer to a warmed serving dish. Pour Tomato Sauce over chickpeas and rice. Garnish with herbs and serve.

Makes 4 servings.

ASIAN-STYLE FRIED RICE

1½ cups long-grain rice
3 tablespoons olive oil
2 garlic cloves, finely chopped
½-inch piece gingerroot, peeled and minced
2 tablespoons light soy sauce
1 teaspoon sugar
2 teaspoons nam pla (fish sauce)
½ teaspoon turmeric
4-6 green onions, thinly sliced
1 lb. cooked peeled small shrimp
1 (8-oz.) can unsweetened pineapple chunks, juice reserved
3 tablespoons chopped cilantro

In a large saucepan of boiling water, cook rice about 15 minutes or until just tender. Drain in a colander and rinse with cold water. Set aside. Heat a wok until hot. Add oil and swirl to coat wok. Add garlic and gingerroot and stir-fry 1 minute. Add soy sauce, sugar, nam pla, turmeric and green onions, stirring to dissolve sugar.

Stir in reserved rice, the shrimp and pineapple, tossing to mix. Stir-fry about 4 minutes or until rice is heated through. Stir in some reserved pineapple juice if rice begins to stick. Stir in cilantro and serve hot.

Makes 4 to 6 servings.

RICE WITH SHRIMP & TOFU

¾ cup long-grain white rice
3 tablespoons vegetable oil
3 garlic cloves, chopped
1 small onion, chopped
4 ozs. tofu, drained and cut into about ½-inch cubes
2 fresh small red chiles, seeded, finely chopped
1 tablespoonfish sauce
6 ozs. peeled shrimp
1 shallot, thinly sliced
Chile, unpeeled cooked shrimp and cilantro leaves to
  garnish

Cook rice. In a wok, heat oil, add garlic and onion and cook, stirring occasionally, 3 to 4 minutes until lightly browned. Add tofu and fry about 3 minutes until browned. Add chiles and stir-fry briefly. Stir in fish sauce and rice; cook, stirring 2 to 3 minutes, then stir in shrimp.

Add shallot, stir quickly to mix, then transfer rice mixture to a warmed serving dish. Garnish with chili, shrimp and cilantro leaves.

Makes 4 servings.

CHICKEN & MUSHROOM RICE

¾ cup long-grain white rice
2 tablespoons vegetable oil
1 small onion, finely chopped
2 garlic cloves, finely chopped
2 fresh red chiles, seeded, cut into slivers
8 ozs. boneless skinless chicken breasts, finely
  chopped
3 ozs. bamboo shoots, chopped
8 pieces dried Chinese black mushrooms, soaked 30
  minutes, drained and chopped
2 tablespoons dried shrimp
1 tablespoon fish sauce
About 25 Thai basil leaves
Thai basil leaves to garnish

Cook rice. Heat oil in a wok, add onion and garlic and cook, stirring occasionally, until golden. Add chiles and chicken and stir-fry 2 minutes.

Stir in bamboo shoots, mushrooms, dried shrimp and fish sauce. Stir-fry 2 minutes, then stir in rice and the 25 basil leaves. Garnish with additional basil leaves.

Makes 4 servings.

STEAMED CHICKEN & RICE

SEAFOOD FRIED RICE

Salt and freshly ground black pepper
1 teaspoon each sugar and sesame oil
1 tablespoon fish sauce
2 teaspoons chopped garlic
10 ozs. chicken thigh meat, boned and skinned, cut
   into bite-size pieces
3 tablespoons vegetable oil
4 shallots, finely chopped
2½ cups long grain rice
2 cups chicken broth
8 dried Chinese mushrooms, soaked and cut into
   small pieces
4 ozs. canned straw mushrooms, drained
1 tablespoon each soy sauce and oyster sauce
2 green onions, chopped
Cilantro leaves to garnish

In a bowl, mix salt, pepper, sugar, sesame oil, fish sauce and half the garlic. Add chicken and marinate 25-30 minutes. Heat about 2 tablespoons vegetable oil in a Dutch oven and stir-fry the remaining garlic and half of the chopped shallots about 1 minute. Add the rice and stir-fry about 5 minutes, then add the broth. Stir and bring to a boil, then reduce the heat to very low, cover and cook 8-10 minutes.

Heat remaining oil in a wok or saucepan and stir-fry remaining shallots until opaque. Add chicken pieces and stir-fry 2-3 minutes. Add mushrooms and soy sauce and cook, stirring, about 5 minutes. Uncover the rice and fluff up with a fork. Spoon chicken and mushroom mixture on top of the rice, add oyster sauce and green onions, cover and cook a further 5 minutes. Garnish with cilantro leaves and serve at once.

Makes 4-6 servings.

1 cup long grain rice
3 tablespoons vegetable oil
1 clove garlic, chopped
2 shallots, chopped
4 ozs. small cooked peeled shrimp
4 ozs. crabmeat, flaked
Salt and freshly ground black pepper
2-3 eggs, beaten
2 tablespoons fish or soy sauce
Chopped green onion to garnish

The day before, cook the rice, then refrigerate it, so that it is cold and dry when required.

Heat about 1 tablespoon oil in a wok or frying-pan over high heat and stir-fry the garlic and shallots about 30 seconds, then add the shrimp and crabmeat with salt and pepper. Stir-fry 2-3 minutes, remove from pan and set aside.

Heat remaining oil in the pan and lightly scramble beaten eggs. When just beginning to set hard, add the rice and stir-fry mixture 2-3 minutes. Add shrimp and crabmeat with the fish or soy sauce and blend well. Garnish with chopped green onion and serve at once.

Makes 4 servings.

GREEN RICE

1¼ cups long-grain white rice, rinsed
3½ cups Chinese Vegetable Stock (see glossary)
8 ozs. small broccoli flowerets
8 ozs. fresh spinach, tough ribs removed
1 tablespoon peanut oil
2 garlic cloves, finely chopped
1 fresh green chile, seeded and chopped
1 bunch green onions, finely chopped
1 (8-oz.) package frozen green peas
2 tablespoons light soy sauce
Salt and freshly ground pepper
¼ cup chopped fresh chives
Fresh chives to garnish

SPICY FRIED RICE

¾ cup long-grain white rice
2 tablespoons vegetable oil
1 large onion, finely chopped
3 garlic cloves, chopped
2 fresh green chiles, seeded, finely chopped
2 tablespoons ready-made Thai red curry paste
2 ozs. lean pork, very finely chopped
3 eggs, beaten
1 tablespoon fish sauce
⅓ cup cooked peeled shrimp
Thinly sliced red chile, shredded cilantro leaves and
    green onion brushes to garnish

Place rice and stock in a large saucepan, bring to a boil, reduce heat and simmer 25 minutes or until rice is cooked and liquid has been absorbed. Cook broccoli in a saucepan of boiling water 2 minutes. Drain and set aside. Blanch spinach in a saucepan of boiling water a few seconds or until just wilted. Drain well, shred and set aside.

Cook rice. Heat oil in a wok, add onion, garlic and chiles and cook, stirring occasionally, until onion has softened. Stir in curry paste and cook, stirring, 4 minutes. Add pork and stir-fry 2 to 3 minutes. Stir in rice to coat with ingredients, then push to side of wok.

Heat oil in a nonstick or well-seasoned wok and stir-fry garlic, chile, green onions and broccoli 1 minute. Add cooked rice, spinach, frozen peas and soy sauce. Season with salt and pepper and simmer 5 minutes. Stir in chopped chives. Garnish with chives and serve with a mixed salad.

Makes 4 servings.

Pour eggs into center of wok. When just beginning to set, stir into the rice, adding fish sauce at the same time. Stir in shrimp, then transfer rice mixture to a warmed serving dish and garnish with chile, cilantro and onion brushes.

Makes 4 servings.

233

LEMON VEGETABLE RICE

Juice of 2 lemons
2 tablespoons sugar
About 4 cups vegetable stock
1½ cups long-grain rice
½ teaspoon salt
1 cinnamon stick
5 whole cloves
2 tablespoons butter or margarine
1 teaspoon cumin seeds
1 small onion, thinly sliced
2 small zucchini
⅓ cup cashews, toasted
2 tablespoons chopped fresh mint
Lime wedges to garnish

In a 4-cup measure, mix lemon juice and sugar together. Make up to 2½ cups with vegetable stock. Pour mixture into a saucepan. Add rice, salt, cinnamon and cloves. Bring to a boil, stir once and simmer 10 minutes or until all liquid is absorbed. Remove from heat, cover with a tight-fitting lid, let sit undisturbed 10 minutes.

In a small skillet, melt butter. Add cumin seeds; stir-fry 1 to 3 minutes or until they start to pop. Add onion; cook 5 minutes. Cut zucchini into thin slices and add to skillet with cashews and mint. Stir-fry 2 to 3 minutes or until zucchini are tender. Stir in rice. Heat through 1 minute, then serve. Garnish with lime.

Makes 4 to 6 servings.

ASPARAGUS RISOTTO

5 cups vegetable stock
1 lb. thin asparagus
⅓ cup butter
1 onion, finely chopped
1½ cups Arborio rice
Pinch of saffron strands
Juice of 1 lemon
Salt and freshly ground pepper
Flat-leaf parsley and strips of lemon zest to garnish

In a large saucepan, heat stock until boiling. Keep at simmering point over low heat. Cut tips off asparagus and set aside.

Snap woody ends off asparagus stalks and peel off any tough skin. Cut stalks into 2-inch lengths. In a large heavy saucepan, heat 2 tablespoons of the butter. Add onion and cook, stirring occasionally, 5 minutes or until soft. Add rice and asparagus stalks and cook, stirring, 2 or 3 minutes. Add a ladleful of hot stock and cook over low heat, stirring frequently, until stock is absorbed. Continue to stir in stock in this way, a ladleful at a time.

When rice begins to look creamy, add saffron, lemon juice, salt and pepper. Continue adding stock and stirring until risotto is thick and creamy and rice is tender but not sticky. Meanwhile, put asparagus tips in a steamer and steam 5 minutes, or until tender. Just before serving, add asparagus tips and remaining butter to risotto and stir gently to combine. Garnish with parsley and lemon zest and serve.

Makes 6 servings.

VEGETABLE BIRYANI

2 tablespoons sunflower oil
1 lb. onions, sliced
3 carrots, diced
1 medium potato, diced
1 (1-inch) piece gingerroot, peeled and grated
2 garlic cloves, crushed
1 tablespoon hot curry paste
1 teaspoon turmeric
½ teaspoon ground cinnamon
1 cup long grain rice
4¼ cups hot vegetable stock
4 ozs. cauliflower flowerets
Salt and freshly ground pepper
4 ozs. frozen green peas
½ cup toasted cashew nuts
2 tablespoons chopped fresh cilantro

Heat half oil in a large flameproof casserole dish. Add half of the onions and cook, stirring occasionally, 10 to 15 minutes, or until crisp and golden. Remove with a slotted spoon, drain on paper towels and set aside. Heat remaining oil in dish and add carrots, potato and remaining onions. Stir in gingerroot, garlic, curry paste, turmeric and cinnamon and cook, stirring, 5 minutes.

Add rice and stir 1 minute. Pour in stock and bring to a boil. Stir in cauliflower, salt and pepper. Cover and simmer 15 minutes. Stir in peas, cashews and cilantro. Cover and cook 5 minutes or until rice is tender and liquid has been absorbed. Scatter reserved onions over top and serve.

Makes 4 servings.

SUN-DRIED TOMATO RISOTTO

¼ cup butter
1 tablespoon olive oil
2 red onions, chopped
12 sun-dried tomatoes, chopped
1 tablespoon pesto sauce
1 cup Arborio rice
4½ cups vegetable stock
8 ozs. mushrooms, sliced
Salt and freshly ground pepper
2 ozs. Parmesan cheese
Chopped fresh flat-leaf parsley to garnish

Heat butter and oil in a flameproof casserole dish. Add onions and cook, stirring occasionally, 5 minutes, or until soft.

Add sun-dried tomatoes and pesto sauce and cook 3 or 4 minutes. Add rice and cook, stirring, 1 minute. Stir in about one-third of stock and simmer, stirring occasionally, until most of liquid has been absorbed.

Stir in mushrooms and season with salt and pepper. Add half of the remaining stock and simmer, stirring occasionally. When most of liquid has been absorbed, stir in remaining stock and simmer until all liquid has been absorbed and rice is tender and creamy. Using a vegetable peeler, shave curls of Parmesan cheese over risotto, sprinkle with parsley and serve.

Makes 2 to 4 servings.

SUMMER RISOTTO

SPINACH RISOTTO CAKE

2 cups chicken stock
4 ozs. sugar snap peas
4 ozs. asparagus, cut into 2-inch lengths
4 ozs. green beans, cut into 2-inch lengths
½ cup dry white wine
1 tablespoon olive oil
4 green onions, chopped
1 garlic clove, crushed
1¼ cups Arborio rice
4 sun-dried tomatoes in oil, drained
¼ cup grated Pecorino cheese
2 ozs. prosciutto, roughly chopped
Salt and freshly ground pepper
Pecorino shavings and basil sprigs to garnish

Pinch of saffron threads
3¼ cups hot vegetable stock
¼ cup butter or margarine
1 large onion, finely chopped
1 garlic clove, crushed
1⅓ cups risotto rice
½ lb. spinach, trimmed
2 eggs, lightly beaten
¼ cup mascarpone cheese or dairy sour cream
¼ cup shredded vegetarian Cheddar cheese
1 tablespoon chopped fresh tarragon
Pinch of grated nutmeg
Salt and pepper

Put stock in a saucepan and bring to a boil. Add sugar snap peas, asparagus and green beans and cook 3 minutes. Remove with a slotted spoon and set aside. Add wine to stock and bring to a simmer. Heat olive oil in a large saucepan. Add green onions and garlic and cook over low heat 5 minutes or until soft. Add rice and cook, stirring, 2 minutes. Add a ladleful of simmering stock and cook, stirring, until absorbed. Continue adding stock, a ladleful at a time, as it is absorbed, stirring frequently.

Soak the saffron in hot stock 10 minutes. In a large skillet, melt butter. Add onion and garlic; cook 10 minutes. Add rice. Stir-fry 2 minutes. Add a little stock, simmer until absorbed and continue adding stock gradually until completely absorbed and rice is tender, about 25 minutes. Preheat oven to 400F (205C). Lightly grease an 8-inch springform pan.

Roughly chop sun-dried tomatoes. When rice has been cooking 15 minutes, add sugar snap peas, asparagus, beans, tomatoes and any remaining stock. Cook, stirring, until rice is tender and creamy. Stir in grated Pecorino and prosciutto and season with salt and pepper. Garnish with Pecorino shavings and basil and serve.

Makes 4 servings.

Note: Pecorino is a hard cheese from Italy. Replace it with Parmesan if it is unavailable.

In a large pan with only water that clings to leaves, cook spinach until just wilted. Drain well and squeeze out excess liquid. Chop finely. Beat remaining ingredients together until combined. Stir into cooked rice with spinach. Transfer to prepared pan. Smooth surface and bake 30 minutes or until set.

Makes 8 servings.

PIZZAS

PIZZA MARGHERITA

1 tablespoon active dried yeast
Pinch of sugar
3 cups bread flour, plus extra for dusting
3 tablespoons olive oil plus extra for drizzling
½ teaspoon salt
TOPPING:
8 tablespoons passata (strained crushed tomatoes)
4 ozs. part-skim mozzarella cheese, thinly sliced
Pinch of dried oregano
Fresh basil leaves, shredded
Salt and freshly ground black pepper

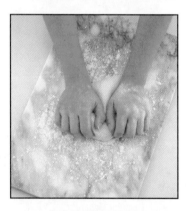

In a bowl, dissolve yeast and sugar in 1 cup warm water. Let stand 5 minutes. Sift flour into a bowl and make a well in center. Pour in yeast mixture, oil and salt; mix until dough comes together. On a floured surface, knead 10 minutes until smooth. Place in a clean oiled bowl, cover with a damp cloth towel and let rise until doubled in size.

Preheat oven to 475F (245C). Punch down dough and roll out, or stretch with your fingers, to a 12-inch circle on a large floured baking sheet. Spread passata over the dough, avoiding the edges. Scatter cheese, herbs, salt and pepper over the surface. Drizzle with oil. Bake 10 to 15 minutes until golden and crisp. Serve with salad.

Makes 4 servings.

ONION & ANCHOVY PIZZA

1 tablespoon active dried yeast
Pinch of sugar
3 cups bread flour
1 tablespoon olive oil
½ teaspoon salt
TOPPING:
1 tablespoon olive oil and sunflower oil, mixed
2 lbs. red onions, thinly sliced
2 tablespoons freshly squeezed lemon juice
2 tablespoons chopped fresh oregano and rosemary
8 anchovy fillets in oil, drained, rinsed and sliced lengthwise if desired, or 6 anchovies in salt, boned and rinsed.
10 ripe olives, stoned
Rosemary sprigs to garnish

In a bowl, dissolve yeast and sugar in 1 cup warm water. Let stand 5 minutes. Sift flour into a bowl and make a well in center. Pour in yeast mixture, oil and salt; mix until dough comes together. On a floured surface, knead 10 minutes until smooth. Place in a clean oiled bowl, cover with a damp cloth towel and let rise until doubled in size. To make topping, heat oil in a pan and stir in onions and lemon juice. Cover and cook over low heat until onions are soft. Add chopped herbs.

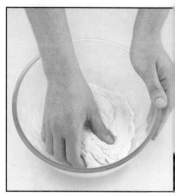

Preheat oven to 475F (245C). Punch down dough and stretch out to a 12-inch circle on a floured baking sheet. Spread onions evenly over the dough and scatter anchovy fillets and olives over onions. Bake 10 to 15 minutes until crisp and golden, sprinkling the rosemary sprigs over the top for the last 3 minutes. Serve with salad.

Makes 6 servings.

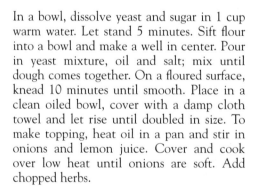

EGGPLANT PIZZA

12 ozs. eggplant
1 garlic clove, crushed
1 tablespoon lemon juice
1 tablespoon chopped fresh parsley
Salt and freshly ground pepper
1 quantity pizza dough (see opposite)
12 ozs. tomatoes, sliced
5 ozs. chorizo sausage, sliced
4 ozs. feta cheese, crumbled
1 tablespoon roughly chopped fresh oregano
1 tablespoon olive oil
Oregano leaves to garnish

Preheat oven to 350F (180C). Pierce eggplant all over with a skewer and put on a baking sheet.

Cook in oven 30 minutes or until soft. Halve eggplant and scoop soft flesh into a bowl. Stir in garlic, lemon juice, parsley, salt and pepper and let cool. Roll out pizza dough to fit a 12- x 9-inch jelly roll pan. Put dough in pan and pinch up edges to form a rim. Spread eggplant purée over dough.

Arrange tomato slices on top and season with salt and pepper. Arrange chorizo over tomatoes. Sprinkle with feta cheese and oregano. Leave 15 minutes. Preheat oven to 400F (200C). Drizzle pizza with olive oil and cook in oven 20 minutes. Cut into squares, garnish with oregano leaves and serve.

Makes 12 squares.

Note: The eggplant purée can be made in advance. It also makes a delicious dip.

ROASTED BELL PEPPER PIZZA

1 tablespoon sun-dried tomato paste
2 large red and 1 large yellow bell pepper, peeled and cut into strips
3 garlic cloves, finely chopped
1 tablespoon roughly chopped fresh parsley
Salt and freshly ground pepper
1 tablespoon olive oil
PIZZA DOUGH:
1½ cups white bread flour
¼ teaspoon salt
1 teaspoon fast-acting yeast
1 tablespoon olive oil

To make pizza dough, sift flour and salt into a warmed bowl. Stir in yeast.

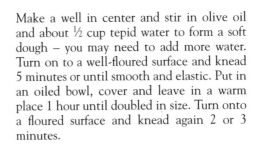

Make a well in center and stir in olive oil and about ½ cup tepid water to form a soft dough – you may need to add more water. Turn on to a well-floured surface and knead 5 minutes or until smooth and elastic. Put in an oiled bowl, cover and leave in a warm place 1 hour until doubled in size. Turn onto a floured surface and knead again 2 or 3 minutes.

Roll out dough to a circle approximately 10-inch in diameter and put on a lightly oiled baking sheet. Pinch up edges to form a rim. Spread sun-dried tomato paste over dough. Arrange bell pepper strips on top. Sprinkle with chopped garlic and parsley and season with salt and pepper. Leave 20 minutes. Preheat oven to 400F (200C). Drizzle pizza with oil and cook in oven 15 to 20 minutes. Cut into wedges and serve.

Makes 2 to 4 servings.

BELL PEPPER PIZZETTES

PIZZA DOUGH:
4 cups bread flour or all-purpose flour
Pinch of salt
1 (¼-oz.) package active dry yeast (about 1 tablespoon)
1 teaspoon sugar
Scant 1 cup warm water (110F/45C)
2 tablespoons extra-virgin olive oil
Oregano sprigs to garnish
TOPPING:
2 red or yellow bell peppers
3 tablespoons sun-dried tomato paste
¼ cup capers in wine vinegar, drained
2 tablespoons chopped fresh oregano or 2 teaspoons dried leaf oregano
Salt and freshly ground pepper

Sift flour and salt into a large bowl. In a small bowl, dissolve yeast and sugar in water. Let stand 5 to 10 minutes until frothy. Stir in olive oil. Using a wooden spoon, gradually stir yeast mixture into flour to give a soft, but not sticky, dough. Knead on a floured surface 5 minutes until smooth and elastic. Place in an oiled medium-size bowl, cover and let rise in a warm place 35 to 40 minutes until doubled in size.

Meanwhile, preheat broiler. Cook bell peppers under hot broiler about 10 minutes, turning occasionally, until skins are evenly blistered and charred. Transfer peppers to a plastic bag a few minutes, then peel away and discard skins. Cut peppers into strips. Set aside.

Preheat oven to 450F (230C). Oil 2 baking sheets. Turn out dough onto a lightly floured surface. Knead gently and cut into 16 equal pieces. Roll each piece into a small oval about ¼-inch thick.

Transfer to the baking sheets and prick dough with a fork. Divide sun-dried tomato paste, reserved peppers, capers and oregano among dough ovals. Season with salt and freshly ground pepper. Bake in preheated oven 8 to 10 minutes until golden. Serve hot or warm garnished with oregano sprigs.

Makes 16 pizzettes.

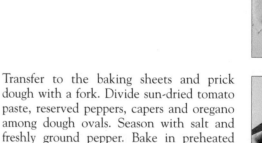

Red Onion & Gorgonzola Pizzettes In place of above topping, use 1½ cups (4 ozs.) crumbled Gorgonzola cheese, ½ chopped red onion and 2 tablespoons chopped thyme.

Shrimp & Fennel Pizzettes Replace bell peppers, capers and herbs with 1 small roasted fennel bulb, 4 ozs. cooked shrimp and 2 teaspoons fennel seeds. To roast fennel, brush with olive oil and place in a preheated 350F (175C) oven 35 to 40 minutes. Cool and chop.

PIZZA SWIRLS

2 cups bread flour
Pinch of salt
1 (¼-oz.) package active dry yeast
⅔ cup canned chopped tomatoes, drained
2 tablespoons tomato paste
1 garlic clove, crushed
1 teaspoon dried leaf oregano
1 (7-oz.) can tuna, drained and flaked
1 red or green bell pepper, finely chopped
1 small onion, finely chopped
¾ cup shredded mozzarella cheese (3 ozs.)

Into a bowl, sift flour and salt. Add yeast and ¾ cup plus 2 tablespoons warm water (130F/55C). Mix to a soft dough.

Turn out dough onto a lightly floured surface. Knead 10 minutes, until smooth. Roll out to a 16- x 8-inch rectangle. Mix tomatoes, tomato paste, garlic and oregano together. Spread over dough. Mix tuna with bell pepper and onion, then spoon over the tomato mixture. Sprinkle with cheese.

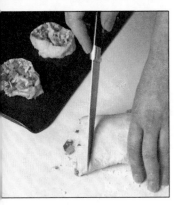

Grease a baking sheet. Roll up dough from a long side, then cut into ½-inch slices. Place slices, cut sides up, on baking sheets and leave in a warm place 15 minutes. Meanwhile, preheat oven to 375F (190C). Bake pizza swirls 15 minutes, until golden-brown. Serve warm.

Makes 25 to 30.

POTATO PIZZA

1 lb. potatoes, peeled
2 tablespoons butter or margarine
¼ cup whole-wheat flour
Salt
TOPPING:
1 tablespoon olive oil
1 small onion, sliced
1 (7-oz.) can chopped tomatoes
1 tablespoon tomato paste
 teaspoon dried leaf basil
⅔ cup sliced mushrooms
2 ozs. sliced pepperoni
½ green bell pepper, cut into thin strips
Lettuce leaves to serve (optional)

Preheat oven to 400F (205C). Grease a baking sheet. With a knife, cut potatoes into even-size pieces. In pan of lightly salted, boiling water, cook potatoes until tender. Drain well, then return to pan and mash. Beat in butter and flour, then season with salt. Mix to make a dough. Turn out dough onto baking sheet and with your fingers spread out to an 8-inch circle. Bake about 10 minutes, until the edge of pizza begins to crisp.

Meanwhile, in a small saucepan, heat oil. Add onion and cook over medium heat 2 to 3 minutes, until softened. Stir in tomatoes, tomato paste and basil, then simmer 5 minutes longer, until thickened. Spread sauce over potato base. Arrange mushrooms over sauce, then pepperoni. Place strips of bell pepper in a crisscross pattern over the pizza. Bake 20 minutes. Serve hot, cut into wedges. Serve with lettuce leaves, if desired.

Makes 3 to 4 servings.

BLUE CHEESE PIZZAS

½ cup pitted ripe olives
1 garlic clove, chopped
1 teaspoon chopped fresh thyme
1 tablespoon olive oil
1 recipe Pizza Dough (see opposite)
3 tablespoons butter
2 red onions, thinly sliced
½ teaspoon fennel seeds
1 teaspoon chopped fresh rosemary
3 ozs. blue cheese, crumbled
Grated peel of 1 lemon
Rosemary sprigs to garnish

In a blender or food processor, purée olives, garlic, thyme and oil to form a smooth paste.

Make Pizza Dough. Cover and let rise in a warm place 30 minutes. In a skillet, melt butter. Add onions; cook over low heat 20 to 25 minutes or until golden. Let cool. Preheat oven to 450F (230C); place a baking sheet or pizza stone on top shelf.

Divide pizza dough into 4 pieces. Roll out each piece on a lightly floured surface to a 5-inch circle. Spread olive paste and onion mixture over each circle. Sprinkle with fennel seeds and rosemary, then cheese. Sprinkle with lemon peel and transfer pizzas to hot baking sheet. Bake 10 to 12 minutes or until bubbly and golden. Serve hot, garnished with rosemary.

Makes 4 servings.

BROILED VEGETABLE PIZZA

1 red bell pepper, quartered
1 small zucchini, sliced
1 small eggplant, sliced
1 small onion, thinly sliced
6 large tomatoes, quartered and seeded
2 tablespoons prepared pesto sauce
Salt and pepper
1¼ cups shredded vegetarian mozzarella cheese
PIZZA DOUGH:
1⅔ cups all-purpose flour
½ teaspoon quick-rise dried yeast
½ teaspoon salt
½ cup warm water
1 tablespoon olive oil

To prepare dough: In a bowl, mix flour, yeast and salt together. Make a well in center; stir in water and oil to form a stiff dough. Knead 5 minutes. Place in a greased bowl, cover and let rise in a warm place 30 minutes or until doubled in size. Preheat oven to 450F (230C) and place a baking sheet or pizza stone on top shelf. Place pepper, zucchini, eggplant and onion on a rack in a baking sheet; brush with a little oil. Broil until charred on all sides.

Broil tomato quarters, skin-sides up, until blistered. Peel and discard skin and mash flesh with pesto sauce, salt and pepper. Roll out dough to a 9-inch circle. Spread tomato mixture over dough; arrange broiled vegetables over top. Sprinkle with cheese. Transfer to hot baking sheet or pizza stone. Bake 25 to 30 minutes until bubbly and golden.

Makes 4 servings.

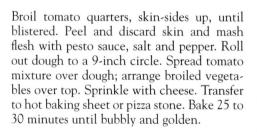

SAVORY
PIES &
PASTRIES

LEEK TART

¼ cup butter
4 leeks, halved lengthwise and thinly sliced
Salt and freshly ground pepper
4 egg yolks
1 cup milk or half and half
Leaves from 4 sprigs of tarragon, finely chopped
3 tablespoons freshly grated Parmesan cheese
  (optional)
PASTRY:
1½ cups all-purpose flour
⅓ cup butter, chilled, diced
1 egg yolk

Melt butter in a large saucepan, add leeks, salt and pepper and cook over low heat, stirring occasionally, 10 minutes or until soft.

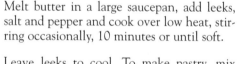

Leave leeks to cool. To make pastry, mix together flour, salt and pepper. Add butter and cut in until mixture resembles fine bread crumbs. Stir in egg yolk and enough cold water to make a firm but not dry dough. Cover and refrigerate 30 minutes. Thinly roll out pastry on a lightly floured surface and line an 8-inch tart pan. Prick bottom with a fork and line with foil. Fill with dried beans and refrigerate 20 minutes. Preheat oven to 400F (205C).

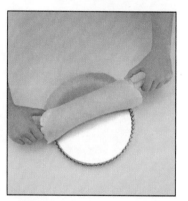

Bake pastry 10 minutes. Remove beans and foil and bake another 10 minutes. Reduce oven temperature to 350F (180C). Mix together egg yolks, milk or half and half, tarragon, salt and pepper and Parmesan cheese, if using. Arrange leeks in pastry and add egg mixture. Bake 30 to 40 minutes or until lightly set and golden. Serve warm or cold with a salad.

Makes 4 to 6 servings.

TURKEY & BROCCOLI QUICHES

1⅓ cups whole-wheat flour
Pinch of salt
⅓ cup butter or margarine, chilled
2 tablespoons vegetale oil
½ lb. boneless turkey breast meat
6 ozs. broccoli flowerets
½ cup shredded Gouda cheese (2 ozs.)
3 eggs
1¼ cups milk
Salt and pepper
Lettuce leaves to garnish

In a bowl, mix together flour and salt. Cut in butter until mixture resembles bread crumbs.

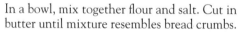

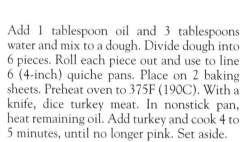

Add 1 tablespoon oil and 3 tablespoons water and mix to a dough. Divide dough into 6 pieces. Roll each piece out and use to line 6 (4-inch) quiche pans. Place on 2 baking sheets. Preheat oven to 375F (190C). With a knife, dice turkey meat. In nonstick pan, heat remaining oil. Add turkey and cook 4 to 5 minutes, until no longer pink. Set aside.

Trim broccoli into tiny flowerets. Blanch in boiling lightly salted water 2 minutes. Drain well. Divide cheese between pastry shells, then add turkey and broccoli. In a small bowl, beat eggs and milk together. Season with salt and pepper, then pour into quiches. Bake 25 to 30 minutes, until set. Remove from pans and serve warm or at room temperature. Garnish with lettuce leaves.

Makes 6 servings.

SALAMI PUFFS

6 ozs. puff pastry dough, thawed if frozen
8 slices Italian salami
¼ cup shredded Cheddar cheese (1 oz.)
1 egg, to glaze
Mâche leaves or parsley sprigs to garnish

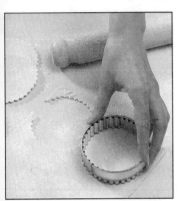

Preheat oven to 400F (205C). On a floured surface, roll out puff pastry dough to ⅛-inch thick. Using a 4-inch fluted cookie cutter, cut out 8 circles of dough.

Lay a slice of salami in center of each dough circle. Put a little cheese on each salami slice.

In a bowl, beat egg, then brush egg around edges of dough. Fold dough circle in half and press edges firmly to seal. Brush top of each puff with beaten egg. Bake 15 minutes, until well risen and golden-brown. Serve garnished with mâche leaves or parsley.

Makes 8.

SPANAKOPITTA

⅔ cup olive oil
1 onion, finely chopped
1 garlic clove, crushed
1 lb. frozen chopped spinach, thawed and well drained
2 tablespoons chopped fresh cilantro
½ teaspoon freshly grated nutmeg
4 ozs. feta cheese, crumbled
1 cup curd cheese
Salt and freshly ground pepper
8 sheets filo pastry, about 16- x 12-inch
Cilantro leaves to garnish

Preheat oven to 375F (190C). Brush a 12- x 9-inch baking sheet with oil.

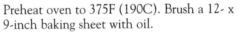

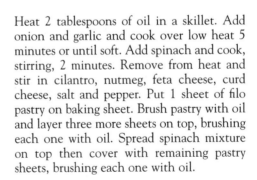

Heat 2 tablespoons of oil in a skillet. Add onion and garlic and cook over low heat 5 minutes or until soft. Add spinach and cook, stirring, 2 minutes. Remove from heat and stir in cilantro, nutmeg, feta cheese, curd cheese, salt and pepper. Put 1 sheet of filo pastry on baking sheet. Brush pastry with oil and layer three more sheets on top, brushing each one with oil. Spread spinach mixture on top then cover with remaining pastry sheets, brushing each one with oil.

Trim overhanging pastry then tuck in edges to seal. Brush top with oil. With a sharp knife, cut through top layers to mark 16 squares. Cook in oven 30 minutes or until golden brown and crisp. Leave in pan 10 minutes, then cut into marked squares. Garnish with cilantro leaves and serve hot or warm.

Makes 16 squares.

COULIBIAC

¼ cup long-grain rice
Salt and pepper
12 ozs. spinach, stems removed and torn
Pinch freshly grated nutmeg
6 tablespoons butter
1 onion, finely chopped
¾ cup plus 2 tablespoons milk
1 lb. salmon fillets
2 tablespoons all-purpose flour
¼ cup sour cream
1½ tablespoons chopped fresh parsley
1½ tablespoons snipped fresh chives
2 hard-cooked eggs, coarsely chopped
4 large sheets filo pastry dough

In a saucepan, melt 2 tablespoons butter. Stir in flour; cook 1 minute, then slowly pour in reserved milk, stirring. Bring to a boil, stirring, and simmer about 4 minutes, stirring occasionally. Remove from heat. Let cool slightly, then fold in salmon, cream, herbs, eggs, salt, and pepper. Let cool completely.

In a saucepan, bring ⅔ cup water to a boil. Add rice and salt, stir, and then return to a boil. Cover and cook 12 to 15 minutes until rice is tender and water absorbed. Meanwhile, wash but do not dry spinach. Put spinach into a saucepan and heat until there is no visible liquid. Turn into a colander and press out excess liquid. Season with salt, pepper, and nutmeg. Let cool.

Preheat oven to 400F (205C). Butter a baking sheet. In a saucepan, melt remaining butter. Cut filo pastry in half to make 8 sheets. Lay 1 sheet on baking sheet and brush lightly with melted butter, then repeat with 3 more sheets filo pastry; keep remaining filo pastry covered with damp cloth.

In a small pan, melt 2 tablespoons butter. Add onion and cook until softened but not browned. Stir into rice. Let cool. Pour milk into a shallow saucepan. Add salmon and bring to a boil, then poach 10 to 15 minutes or until only just cooked. Drain and reserve milk. Skin and flake fish.

Spoon rice onto filo pastry, leaving a 1-inch border. Cover with spinach, then fish mixture. Lay a sheet of filo pastry over filling, brush with butter, then repeat with remaining filo pastry. Press edges together, then bake in the oven about 25 minutes or until pastry is crisp and golden.

Makes 4 to 6 servings.

CRAB & RICOTTA TARTS

PASTRY DOUGH:
2 cups all-purpose flour
Pinch of salt
½ cup butter, chilled, diced
About ¼ cup water
FILLING:
8 ozs. crabmeat
1 cup ricotta cheese (8 ozs.)
3 green onions, finely chopped
2 whole eggs plus 1 yolk
2 tablespoons chopped Italian parsley
Few drops of hot pepper sauce
Salt and freshly ground pepper
Mixed lettuce leaves to serve
Italian parsley sprigs to garnish

Preheat oven to 400F (205C). Sift flour and salt into a small bowl. Rub in butter until mixture resembles bread crumbs. Stir in enough water to make a firm dough. Place dough on a floured surface and knead gently until smooth. Use to line 4 (3- to 4-inch) tart pans. Prick bottoms lightly and chill 20 minutes. Line tart shells with waxed paper and cover with dry beans. Bake in preheated oven 15 minutes, removing beans and paper after 10 minutes.

Remove tart shells from oven and reduce temperature to 350F (175C). To make filling, mix ingredients together in a bowl. Spoon into tart shells. Bake about 20 minutes until set and golden-brown. Serve warm or cold garnished with mixed lettuce leaves and parsley sprigs.

Makes 4 servings.

GOAT CHEESE & FIG TART

1¾ cups all-purpose flour
Pinch of salt
½ cup butter or margarine, chilled
1 egg yolk
2 tablespoons iced water
1 tablespoon olive oil
1 large onion, thinly sliced
2 teaspoons chopped fresh thyme
½ teaspoon fennel seeds
4 fresh figs
½ cup soft goat cheese
¼ cup freshly grated Parmesan cheese
⅔ cup dairy sour cream
1 large egg, lightly beaten

Preheat oven to 400F (205C). Into a bowl, sift flour and salt. Cut in butter until mixture resembles fine bread crumbs. Make a well in center and work in egg yolk and water to form a soft dough. On a floured surface, knead. Wrap and refrigerate 30 minutes. Thinly roll out dough and use to line a 9-inch tart pan. Prick bottom and refrigerate 20 minutes. Line with foil and pie weights. Bake blind 10 minutes. Remove foil and weights; bake 10 to 12 minutes or until crisp and golden.

In a skillet, heat oil. Add onion, thyme and fennel; cook 10 minutes. Chop 2 figs, add to pan and remove from heat. Beat goat cheese, Parmesan cheese, sour cream and egg together until smooth. Spread onion mixture into tart shell. Spoon in cheese mixture. Slice remaining figs and arrange around edge of tart. Bake 25 minutes or until set. Serve warm or cold.

Makes 8 servings.

SHRIMP & FETA TARTS

6 ozs. shelled cooked shrimp
4 ozs. feta cheese
Fresh basil leaves to garnish
PASTRY:
1½ cups all-purpose flour
½ teaspoon salt
3 tablespoons extra-virgin olive oil
1 egg, beaten
TOMATO SAUCE:
2 tablespoons extra-virgin olive oil
1 onion, chopped
1 garlic clove, crushed
½ (14-oz.) can chopped tomatoes
1 tablespoon chopped sun-dried tomato
2 teaspoons chopped fresh basil
Salt and pepper

To make pastry, into a bowl, sift flour and salt. With a fork, mix in olive oil, egg and 1 to 2 teaspoons water to make a firm dough. Knead lightly, wrap in plastic wrap and refrigerate 1 hour. To make Tomato Sauce, in a skillet, heat oil. Add onion and garlic and cook until soft. Add tomatoes. Cook 5 to 10 minutes or until sauce is very thick. Stir in basil, salt and pepper. Preheat oven to 400F (205C).

On a floured surface, roll out dough thinly. Line 4 (4-inch) loose-bottom tart pans with dough and press a piece of foil into each. Bake 10 minutes. Remove foil; bake 5 minutes. Divide shrimp among pastry cases. Crumble cheese over shrimp. Spread Tomato Sauce over cheese and shrimp. Bake 5 minutes. Serve garnished with basil leaves.

Makes 4 servings.

SEAFOOD PACKAGES

⅔ cup butter
¼ cup all-purpose flour
⅔ cup milk
2 tablespoons fresh lemon juice
1 garlic clove, crushed
1 tablespoon each chopped fresh mint, chopped fresh cilantro and chopped fresh parsley
Pinch of red (cayenne) pepper
Pinch of paprika
½ teaspoon ground cumin
Salt
3 ozs. cooked mussels
2 ozs. cooked shelled shrimp
2 ozs. cooked squid or white fish
6 sheets filo pastry, thawed if frozen

Preheat oven to 375F (190C). In a saucepan, melt 2 tablespoons of the butter. Stir in flour, then gradually stir in milk. Stirring, cook sauce until thick. Stir in lemon juice, garlic, mint, cilantro, parsley, cayenne, paprika, cumin and salt. Remove from heat. Gently stir in mussels, shrimp and squid or white fish.

Melt remaining butter. Brush over 1 sheet filo dough, place another sheet on top and butter it. Repeat with 2 more sheets of dough. Cut into 12 squares. Butter remaining 2 sheets of dough. Place one on top of the other. Cut in half. Pile the 4 sheets together; cut into 6 squares. Place some filling in middle of each square. Draw dough up and pinch together to form pouches. Place on a baking sheet. Bake 30 minutes or until brown and crisp.

Makes 18.

GOAT CHEESE TARTS

1-2 teaspoons extra-virgin olive oil
2 tablespoons butter
2 cups fresh bread crumbs
1 tablespoon sesame seeds
6 ozs. goat cheese
4 sun-dried tomatoes preserved in oil, drained
Salt and freshly ground pepper
4 basil leaves
1 teaspoon finely chopped mint
Mixed lettuce leaves and chives to garnish

Preheat oven to 400F (205C). Use olive oil to grease 4 (3- to 4-inch) tart pans.

Melt butter in a small saucepan, and stir in bread crumbs and sesame seeds. Divide among prepared tart pans, pressing firmly onto bottoms and sides. Bake in preheated oven 12 to 15 minutes until crisp and light golden. Carefully remove tart shells from pans and place on a baking sheet.

Divide goat cheese among tart shells and top each with a sun-dried tomato. Season with salt and freshly ground pepper. Return to oven 8 to 10 minutes to heat through. Put a basil leaf and a sprinkling of chopped mint on each tart and garnish with mixed lettuce leaves and chives.

Makes 4 servings.

LEEK & CHEESE PIE

1 lb. leeks, chopped
1 teaspoon salt
¼ cup butter
2 large onions, sliced
2 bunches green onions, sliced
1 cup (4 oz.) crumbled feta cheese
2 eggs, beaten
Freshly ground pepper
8 sheets filo pastry
¼ cup melted butter

Put leeks into a colander, sprinkle with salt and leave 30 minutes. Squeeze dry.

Heat butter in a flameproof casserole dish. Add onions and green onions and cook, stirring occasionally, 3 to 5 minutes, or until soft but not colored. Remove from heat and let cool 10 minutes. Preheat oven to 400F (205C). Add leeks, feta cheese and eggs to onion mixture, season with pepper and mix well.

Crumple sheets of filo pastry and arrange on top of leek mixture. Brush with melted butter and bake 30 to 35 minutes, or until pastry is golden brown. Serve.

Makes 4 to 6 servings.

Note: To prepare leeks, cut off dark green tops and root ends. Slice white part almost in half lengthwise, then rinse under cold running water to remove sand.

CHICKEN POTPIE

1½ lbs. chicken pieces
1 large onion, thickly sliced
⅓ cup dry white wine
¾ cup chicken stock
1 bouquet garni
2 tablespoons butter or margarine
2½ cups halved button mushrooms
¼ cup all-purpose flour
1 (8-oz.) whole-kernel corn, drained
2 tablespoons chopped fresh parsley
1 teaspoon fresh lemon juice
¼ cup whipping cream
2 lbs. potatoes
½ cup milk
¾ cup shredded Cheddar cheese
1 oz. salted potato chips

In a large pan, place chicken, onion, wine, stock and bouquet garni. Bring to a boil. Reduce heat and simmer 25 to 30 minutes or until chicken is tender. Drain liquid; reserve liquid and onion. Discard bouquet garni. Remove skin and bones from chicken; coarsely chop flesh. In a pan, melt butter. Add mushrooms; cook until softened. Stir in flour; cook 1 minute. Add reserved liquid and onion.

Bring to a boil, stirring constantly. Stir in chicken, corn, parsley, lemon juice and cream. Season to taste with salt and pepper. Boil potatoes until tender. Drain and mash with milk and ½ cup of the cheese; season to taste. Preheat broiler. Cover casserole with potatoes. Crush potato chips and mix with remaining cheese. Sprinkle over potatoes. Broil until golden.

Makes 4 servings.

CHICKEN & HAM POTPIE

2 tablespoons butter or margarine
½ lb. cooked ham, cut into 1-inch cubes
¾ lb. skinned and boned chicken, cut into 1-inch cubes
1 onion, chopped
1⅓ cups sliced leeks
6 ozs. button mushrooms
¼ cup all-purpose flour
1¼ cups chicken stock
⅔ cup half and half
Finely grated peel of ½ lemon
Salt and pepper
1 prepared flat pie crust
Milk for glazing
2 tablespoons grated Parmesan cheese

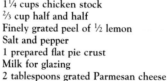

Preheat oven to 400F (205C). In a pan, melt butter, add ham and chicken and cook 2 to 3 minutes. Remove from pan and reserve. Add vegetables and cook 2 to 3 minutes or until softened. Return ham and chicken to pan. Stir in flour and cook 1 to 2 minutes. Remove from heat. Gradually stir in stock and half and half. Return to heat and cook, stirring, 2 minutes until thickened. Add lemon peel and season with salt and pepper.

Transfer chicken mixture to a deep 9-inch-round ovenproof dish. Cut off an 1-inch strip from pastry to fit edge of dish. Position dough strip on edge and brush with a little water. Cover with remaining pastry. Pinch edges together to seal. Brush pastry with milk to glaze. Sprinkle with cheese. Bake 25 minutes or until the pastry is golden-brown.

Makes 4 servings.

MUSHROOM TART

2 cups all-purpose flour
Pinch salt
½ cup butter, chilled, diced
About 5 tablespoons water
FILLING:
1 oz. dried porcini mushrooms
2 tablespoons butter
1 medium-size onion, finely chopped
4 ozs. button mushrooms, chopped
2 tablespoons finely chopped Italian parsley
1 tablespoon sun-dried tomato paste
¼ cup half and half
3 large eggs
¼ cup freshly grated Parmesan cheese (¾ oz.)
Salt and freshly ground pepper
Italian parsley sprig to garnish

Melt butter in a medium-size saucepan. Add onion and button mushrooms and cook 5 minutes to soften. Stir in porcini mushrooms, parsley and sun-dried tomato paste. Cook 2 minutes, then stir in half and half. Cook over low heat 8 to 10 minutes until liquid is reduced by half. Remove from heat and cool.

Sift flour and salt into a medium-size bowl. Rub butter in until mixture resembles bread crumbs. Stir in enough water to make a firm dough. Wrap in plastic wrap and refrigerate while preparing filling.

Roll out the dough and use to line greased pie pan. Prick bottom with a fork. Line pie shell with waxed paper and fill with dry beans. Bake in preheated oven 25 minutes, removing beans and paper last 5 minutes. Reduce temperature to 375F (190C).

Preheat oven to 400F (205C). Grease a 9-inch pie pan. Put porcini in a small bowl. Cover generously with warm water. Let soak 20 minutes, then drain and rinse to remove any grit. Dry on paper towels, then chop finely and set aside.

Beat eggs in a large bowl. Stir in mushroom mixture and cheese. Season with salt and freshly ground pepper, then pour into pie shell. Bake about 20 minutes until set. Serve warm or cold garnished with parsley sprig.

Makes 8 servings.

BELL PEPPER & ONION TART

2 cups bread flour
Salt and pepper
1 teaspoon active dry yeast
⅔ cup warm milk
1 egg yolk
4 tablespoons olive oil
1 lb. Spanish onions, halved and sliced
4 red bell peppers, sliced
4 yellow bell peppers, sliced
About ½ cup fresh thyme, oregano and parsley
  sprigs
16-20 canned anchovy fillets, drained

Into a bowl, sift flour and salt. Stir in yeast.

Stir milk into egg yolk, then slowly pour into flour, stirring constantly. Beat 5 to 10 minutes or until dough comes cleanly away from bowl.

Turn dough onto a lightly floured surface and knead until smooth and elastic. Form into a ball, place in an oiled bowl, cover and leave in a warm place about 1 hour until doubled in size.

Meanwhile, in a skillet, heat 3 tablespoons of the oil, add onions, peppers and herbs and cook over medium heat, stirring occasionally, 20 to 25 minutes or until vegetables are soft but not browned. Add a few tablespoons water if necessary to prevent browning. Season with salt and pepper and set aside.

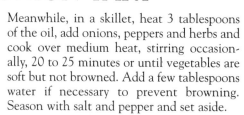

Preheat oven to 475F (240C). On a lightly floured surface, punch down and flatten dough. Roll out to a 12-inch circle. Carefully transfer to an oiled baking sheet. Turn up edge to make a rim. Prick well with a fork.

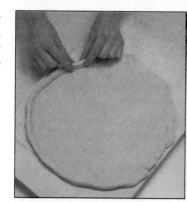

Spread vegetable mixture over dough, arrange anchovy fillets on top, drizzle with remaining oil and bake 25 to 30 minutes or until the dough is well risen, crisp and golden.

Makes 6 servings.

VEGETABLE FILO PACKAGES

4 small new potatoes, halved
8 baby carrots
8 baby zucchini, halved
8 asparagus tips
1 baby leek, sliced into 8 pieces
¼ cup butter or margarine, softened
1 tablespoon chopped fresh mint
¼ teaspoon ground cumin
Pinch red (cayenne) pepper
Salt and pepper
4 large sheets filo pastry
⅓ cup olive oil

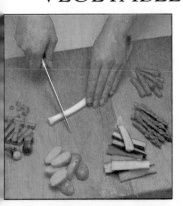

Preheat oven to 375F (190C); place a baking sheet on middle shelf.

In a large pan of boiling water, cook potatoes 6 to 8 minutes or until almost cooked. Blanch remaining vegetables 2 to 3 minutes, depending on size, until almost tender. Drain all vegetables. Cool in cold water. Drain and dry thoroughly. Cream together butter, mint, spices, salt and pepper. Take 1 large sheet of dough and, using a 10-inch plate or a pan lid as a template, carefully cut out a circle. Repeat to make 4 circles. Brush liberally with oil.

Place one-quarter of vegetables in a small pile on one side of dough circle. Dot with mint butter. Fold other side of dough over filling, pressing edges together to seal. Brush a little oil along edge and turn over a bit at a time to ensure filling is totally enclosed. Repeat to make 4 packages and transfer to heated cookie sheet. Carefully brush with remaining oil. Bake 12 to 15 minutes or until pastry is golden. Serve immediately.

Makes 4 servings.

MUSHROOM & CHEESE SQUARES

2 lbs. prepared puff pastry dough
¼ oz. dried cep mushrooms
⅔ cup boiling water
2 tablespoons olive oil
1 cup diced eggplant
3 cups finely chopped fresh mushrooms
1 garlic clove, crushed
1 teaspoon chopped fresh thyme
2 tablespoons tomato paste
Salt and pepper
⅓ cup diced goat cheese
1 egg, beaten
1 tablespoon milk

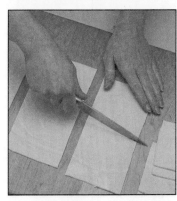

On a lightly floured surface, roll out dough into 2 (13- x 9-inch) rectangles. Cut out 6 (4-inch) squares from each rectangle. Cover and let rest 30 minutes. Into a bowl, place ceps. Add boiling water; let soak 20 minutes. Drain, reserving liquid. Chop and reserve ceps. In a large pan, heat 1 tablespoon of the oil. Add eggplant; stir-fry 3 to 4 minutes. Add ceps, fresh mushrooms, garlic and thyme; stir-fry 3 minutes. Add reserved cep liquid and boil rapidly 3 minutes. Stir in tomato paste, salt and pepper. Let cool.

Preheat oven to 425F (220C). Spread a large spoonful of mushroom mixture in center of 6 dough squares, leaving a narrow border around edges. Top with diced cheese. Dampen edges with a little water and top with remaining squares. Press edges together to seal and cut a small slit in top of each pie. In a small bowl, beat egg and milk together. Brush over each pie. Transfer to a baking sheet. Bake 15 to 18 minutes or until puffed and golden-brown.

Makes 6 servings.

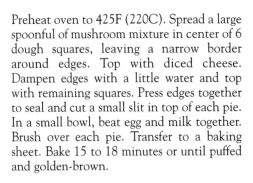

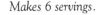

WINTER VEGETABLE PIE

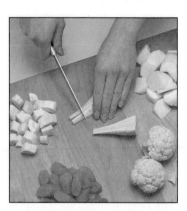

1¼ cups self-rising flour
Salt
8 tablespoons vegetable shortening
2 tablespoons chopped fresh mixed herbs
4-5 tablespoons iced water
2 tablespoons olive oil
6 ozs. pearl onions, halved
1 garlic clove, chopped
1¼ lbs. prepared mixed winter vegetables (carrots, turnips, parsnips, cauliflower flowerets)
4 ozs. button mushrooms
⅔ cup dry red wine
1½ cups vegetable stock (see below)
2 tablespoons tomato paste

Roll out dough to a ¼-inch rectangle. Cut out a pie top a little larger than dish. Cut remaining dough into strips, dampen and press around edge of dish. Dampen edge of dough. Place dough lid over pie and press edges to seal. Bake 30 minutes.

Makes 6 servings.

Into a large bowl, sift flour with 1 teaspoon salt. Cut in 2 tablespoons of the shortening. Stir in half the herbs and work in enough iced water to form a soft dough. Knead lightly. Wrap and refrigerate 30 minutes. Roll out dough to a rectangle about ½-inch thick. Dot top two-thirds with 2 tablespoons of the shortening. Bring the bottom third of dough up into middle and top third over this. Press edges to seal. Wrap and refrigerate 30 minutes. Repeat process twice and refrigerate a final 30 minutes.

Note: To make vegetable stock, cook 1 coarsely chopped onion and 1 trimmed and sliced leek in 2 teaspoons olive oil until softened. Add 2 chopped carrots, 1 diced large potato and 2 sliced celery stalks. Cook 5 minutes longer.

Preheat oven to 400F (205C). In a skillet, heat oil. Add onions, garlic and vegetables; cook 10 minutes. Add wine and boil 5 minutes. Add stock and tomato paste. Simmer 20 minutes. Transfer to a 5-cup-deep oval baking dish.

Add 4 coarsely chopped ripe tomatoes, 1½ cups quartered mushrooms, ⅓ cup rice, 2 parsley sprigs, 2 thyme sprigs, 1 bay leaf, 1 teaspoon salt, 6 white peppercorns and 5 cups water. Bring to a boil. Cover and simmer 30 minutes. Strain through a fine strainer.

POTATO & ONION TART

¾ cup all-purpose flour
Pinch of salt
½ cup unsalted butter, chilled
1 egg yolk
2 tablespoons iced water
FILLING:
1 lb. waxy potatoes
2 tablespoons butter or margarine
2 large onions, thinly sliced
1 teaspoon chopped fresh rosemary
½ teaspoon caraway seeds
¾ cup half and half
¼ cup shredded Cheddar cheese
Freshly grated nutmeg

Preheat oven to 400F (205C). Into a large bowl, sift flour and salt. Cut in butter until mixture resembles fine bread crumbs. Make a well in center. Work in egg yolk and water to form a soft dough. On a lightly floured surface, knead dough. Wrap and refrigerate 30 minutes. Roll out thinly and use to line a deep 9-inch fluted tart pan. Prick bottom. Refrigerate 20 minutes. Line with foil and pie weights. Bake blind 10 minutes. Remove weights and foil and bake 10 to 12 minutes or until crisp.

Increase oven temperature to 450F (230C). Boil potatoes 15 minutes or until just tender. Let cool, carefully peel and cut into very thin slices. Melt butter in a skillet. Add onions, rosemary and caraway seeds; cook 10 minutes or until golden. Spread onion mixture over pastry shell and top with potato slices. Beat remaining ingredients together. Pour over potatoes; bake on top rack 15 minutes or until golden.

Makes 6 to 8 servings.

OLIVE & MOZZARELLA PUFFS

½ cup pitted green olives
1 oz. mozzarella cheese
2 teaspoons chopped fresh parsley
½ teaspoon chopped fresh sage
Pinch of chile powder
1 sheet prepared puff pastry dough from a 17-oz. package, thawed if frozen
1 egg
Salt
Parsley leaves and extra olives to garnish

Preheat oven to 425F (220C); lightly oil a baking sheet. Very finely chop olives and cheese. Mix with herbs and chile powder to form a paste. Set aside.

On a lightly floured surface, roll out pastry dough. Using a 4-inch fluted cookie cutter, cut out 8 circles. Place 1 heaped teaspoon olive mixture in center of each circle. Lightly dampen edges of dough, fold in half to form semicircles, pressing edges together well to seal. Transfer to the baking sheet.

Beat egg with a little salt. Brush over pastries. Cut 2 small slashes in each one. Bake 12 to 15 minutes or until puffed and golden-brown. Serve warm or cold with a salad garnish.

Makes 8 servings.

Note: These make ideal buffet party nibbles. Make up double quantity of filling, cut dough into smaller circles to make bite-sized appetizers.

RATATOUILLE IN OLIVE TARTS

¼ cup olive oil
1 onion, chopped
1 garlic clove, crushed
1 eggplant, diced
1 zucchini, diced
1 red bell pepper, diced
3 tomatoes, peeled and roughly chopped
1 teaspoon dried herbes de Provence
Salt and freshly ground pepper
Mint sprigs and endive leaves, to garnish
PASTRY:
2 cups all-purpose flour, sifted
½ cup butter
1 oz. black olives, pitted and roughly chopped
1 egg, beaten
1 tablespoon olive oil

To make pastry, put flour, butter and a pinch of salt in a food processor and process until mixture resembles fine bread crumbs. Add olives and, with motor running, add egg and olive oil and process until mixture forms a ball. Remove from food processor. Wrap in plastic wrap and refrigerate 30 minutes.

Preheat oven to 400F (200C). Heat 2 tablespoons of olive oil in a skillet. Add onion and garlic and cook over low heat 5 minutes or until soft. Add eggplant, zucchini and bell pepper and cook 5 minutes.

Stir in tomatoes, herbes de Provence, salt and pepper. Cover and cook 10 minutes, stirring occasionally. Uncover and cook 15 minutes or until vegetables are tender but not too soft.

Meanwhile, prepare pastry cases. Thinly roll out pastry on a lightly floured surface. Cut out six circles of pastry to fit six 4-inch tartlet pans. Line pans with pastry, prick all over with a fork and press a square of foil into each one.

Bake pastry cases 15 minutes, then remove foil and bake another 10 to 15 minutes or until pastry is crisp. Reheat ratatouille, if necessary, and spoon into pastry cases. Drizzle with remaining olive oil, garnish with mint and endive leaves and serve.

Makes 6 servings.

CHICKEN PASTIES

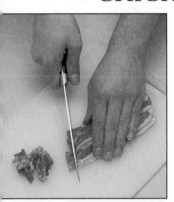

3 cups all-purpose flour
⅓ cup butter or margarine
⅓ cup vegetable shortening
1 tablespoon chopped fresh thyme
12 ozs. chicken breasts, ground
1 tablespoon vegetable oil
2 bacon slices, chopped
½ onion, chopped
1 large potato, diced
1 carrot, diced
1 cup chopped mushrooms
½ tablespoon all-purpose flour
⅔ cup chicken stock
Beaten egg or milk, for brushing
Parsley and thyme sprigs to garnish

Preheat oven to 375F (190C). Into a bowl, sift flour and a pinch of salt. Add butter and shortening; cut in until mixture resembles bread crumbs. Add chopped thyme and 3 tablespoons iced water. Mix together to form a dough. Wrap in plastic wrap; refrigerate 30 minutes. In a skillet, heat oil. Add bacon, onion, potato and carrot. Fry 2 to 3 minutes until onion starts to soften. Add chicken and mushrooms and cook, stirring, 3 to 4 minutes longer. Stir in flour; cook, stirring, 1 minute.

Gradually stir in stock. Return to heat and cook, stirring, until thickened. Season with salt and pepper; cool. On a floured surface, roll out dough. Cut out 8 (6-inch) circles. Place 2 tablespoons chicken mixture in center of each circle. Brush edges with beaten egg or milk and fold dough over to enclose filling. Pinch edges to seal. Glaze with egg or milk and place on a baking sheet. Bake 20 to 25 minutes or until golden.

Makes 4 servings.

GROUND MEAT PASTRIES

1 tablespoon pine nuts
¼ cup extra-virgin olive oil
1 onion, finely chopped
1 lb. lean ground beef
1 teaspoon ground cinnamon
1 tablespoon chopped fresh parsley
Salt and pepper
6 sheets filo pastry, thawed if frozen
1 recipe Tzatziki (page 25) to serve

In a skillet, fry pine nuts in a little oil until golden. Remove from pan and set aside.

In the same skillet, heat 2 tablespoons of the oil. Add onion and cook until soft. Stir in beef and cook, stirring, a few minutes or until brown all over. Add cinnamon, parsley, pine nuts, salt and pepper. Cook 10 minutes, then let cool.

Preheat oven to 350F (175C). Cut each sheet of dough into 3 long strips. Brush strips with remaining oil. Spread 1 teaspoon of filling in a line on one end of each strip, leaving a small margin on each side. Roll over twice and fold long sides over the edge, then continue rolling to make a tube. Place on a baking sheet. Bake 20 to 30 minutes or until crisp and golden. Serve with Tzatziki.

Makes 18.

LAMB PASTRIES

12 grape leaves, preserved in brine
¼ cup extra-virgin olive oil
Juice of ½ lemon
2 garlic cloves, crushed
1 tablespoon chopped fresh marjoram
Salt and pepper
6 thin lamb steaks or pieces of lamb fillet
6 sheets filo pastry
¼ cup butter, melted
Shredded nasturtium flowers and mint to garnish

Soak grape leaves in water 1 hour. In a saucepan of boiling water, cook grape leaves 5 minutes. Drain and dry on paper towels.

In a bowl, mix together olive oil, lemon juice, garlic, marjoram, salt and pepper. In a dish, place lamb, pour marinade over and let marinate in a cool place 1 hour.

Preheat oven to 375F (190C). Brush each sheet of dough with butter. Lay a grape leaf in middle of one end of each sheet. Place a lamb steak on top, then cover with another grape leaf. Fold sides of dough over lamb and roll up to form neat packages. Place on a baking sheet. Bake 20 to 30 minutes or until pastry is golden and crisp. Serve garnished with shredded nasturtium flowers and mint.

Makes 6 servings.

CRAB & GINGER TRIANGLES

1 (7-oz.) can crabmeat, drained
6 green onions, finely chopped
1 (1-inch) piece gingerroot, peeled and grated
2 teaspoons soy sauce
Salt and pepper
6 large sheets filo pastry, each about 14 inches square
6 tablespoons butter, melted
Green onion slivers or curls to garnish

In a bowl, mix together crabmeat, green onions, gingerroot, soy sauce, salt and pepper. Set aside.

Preheat oven to 350F (175C). Lightly grease a baking sheet. Work with 1 sheet of pastry at a time, keeping remainder covered with a damp cloth. Cut sheet of pastry in half. Brush each half with melted butter and fold in half lengthwise. Brush pastry all over with melted butter. Put a portion of crab mixture in 1 corner of 1 strip of pastry. Fold pastry and filling over at right angles to make a triangle, then continue folding in this way along strip of pastry to make a triangular package.

Repeat with remaining pastry and crab mixture. Brush each triangle with melted butter. Bake 20 to 25 minutes, until crisp and golden-brown. Serve warm, garnished with green onions slivers or curls.

Makes 12.

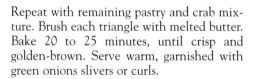

SALADS

TROPICAL SALAD

TUNISIAN ORANGE SALAD

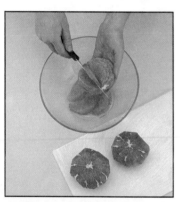

3 pink grapefruit
1 large papaya
3 avocados
3 tablespoons olive oil
2 teaspoons pink peppercorns, lightly crushed
Salt

Cut zest from pink grapefruit, removing white pith at the same time. Hold grapefruit over a bowl to catch juice and cut between membranes to remove segments.

Peel papaya, cut in half and scoop out seeds with a teaspoon. Cut flesh into thin slices. Halve avocados lengthwise, remove pits and peel. Cut flesh into thin slices.

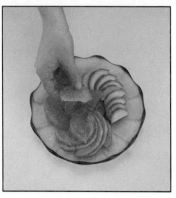

Arrange grapefruit segments, papaya slices and avocado slices on serving plates. Mix together 2 teaspoons reserved grapefruit juice, olive oil, crushed peppercorns and salt. Drizzle over fruit and serve at once.

Makes 6 servings.

4 small oranges
1 daikon
Mint sprigs to garnish
DRESSING:
1 tablespoon lemon juice
2 teaspoons orange-flower water
1 teaspoon sugar
¼ cup olive oil
Salt and freshly ground pepper
1 tablespoon chopped fresh mint

Cut peel off oranges, removing all pith. Thinly slice oranges.

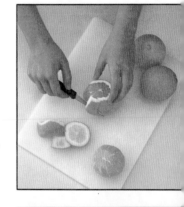

Peel daikon and thinly slice. Arrange orange and daikon slices on a large serving plate. To make dressing, whisk together lemon juice, orange-flower water, sugar, olive oil, salt and pepper.

Pour dressing over orange and daikon slices. Sprinkle with chopped mint and refrigerate. Garnish with mint sprigs and serve.

Makes 4 servings.

Note: A daikon is large white radish. If it is unavailable, this salad is also delicious made with sliced fennel.

BELL PEPPER SALAD

1 large red bell pepper
1 large green bell pepper
1 large yellow bell pepper
1 small red onion, sliced
16 ripe olives
2 teaspoons chopped basil or ⅔ teaspoon dried leaf
   basil
2 teaspoons chopped thyme or ⅔ teaspoon dried leaf
   thyme
DRESSING:
3 tablespoons extra-virgin olive oil
1 tablespoon red wine vinegar
1 garlic clove, finely chopped
Pinch of sugar
Salt and freshly ground pepper

SPINACH WITH GORGONZOLA

2 red bell peppers
About 4 ozs. young spinach leaves
1 head Belgium endive
1 ripe pear
⅓ cup crumbled Gorgonzola cheese
DRESSING:
3 tablespoons extra-virgin olive oil
1 tablespoon lemon juice
1 garlic clove, crushed
2 tablespoons chopped Italian parsley
Salt and freshly ground pepper

To make dressing, mix all ingredients together in a small bowl, or shake together in a jar with a tight-fitting lid. Set aside. Preheat broiler. Place whole peppers under hot broiler about 10 minutes, turning occasionally, until skins are evenly blistered and blackened. Transfer peppers to a plastic bag a few minutes, then peel away and discard skins.

Preheat broiler. Cook whole peppers under hot broiler about 10 minutes, turning occasionally, until skins are evenly blistered and blackened. Transfer peppers to a plastic bag a few minutes and then peel away and discard skins. Cut peppers in half, remove and discard seeds, and cut peppers into strips. Place in a salad bowl.

Cut peppers in half, remove and discard seeds and cut peppers into strips. Place in a salad bowl with onion and olives. Stir or shake dressing and pour over salad. Toss gently to mix and sprinkle with herbs.

Makes 4 servings.

Tear spinach leaves into bite-size pieces; slice endive. Peel core and slice pear. Add spinach, endive and pear to salad bowl. Mix all dressing ingredients together in a small bowl or put in a jar with a tight-fitting lid and shake until blended. Pour over salad and toss to mix. Scatter Gorgonzola cheese over salad and serve immediately.

Makes 4 to 6 servings.

BEAN & ONION SALAD

12 ozs. green beans
1 onion, thinly sliced
2 tablespoons capers in wine vinegar, drained
6 tablespoons extra-virgin olive oil
Juice of 1 lemon
½ teaspoon hot red pepper flakes
Pinch of 1 sugar
Salt and freshly ground pepper
2 teaspoons chopped Italian parsley
1 teaspoon chopped mint

Add beans to a saucepan of boiling salted water and cook 4 minutes until tender. Drain and refresh under cold running water. Place in a bowl with onion and capers.

Beat olive oil, lemon juice, red pepper flakes, sugar, salt and freshly ground pepper in a small bowl or shake together in a jar with a tight-fitting lid.

Pour over salad, add herbs and mix well.

Makes 4 to 6 servings.

ASPARAGUS & EGG SALAD

2 lbs. asparagus
Salt and freshly ground pepper
7 hard-cooked eggs
6 tablespoons olive oil
2 tablespoons white wine vinegar
2 small dill pickles, finely chopped
Freshly ground pepper
Chopped Italian parsley and Italian parsley sprig to garnish

Snap off and discard woody ends of asparagus stems. Using a small sharp knife, scrape stems. Rinse asparagus, then tie into small bundles using string.

Stand bundles in a deep pan of boiling salted water so tips are above water. Cover, making a dome of foil, if necessary. Boil 15 minutes until tips are crisp-tender. Drain, refresh under cold running water, drain, untie bundles and cool.

Finely chop 4 of the eggs and place in a bowl. Using a wooden spoon, gradually stir in oil, vinegar and pickles. Season with salt and freshly ground pepper. Set aside. Quarter remaining eggs and arrange with asparagus around edge of a serving plate. Pour egg sauce into center and sprinkle with chopped Italian parsley. Garnish with Italian parsley sprig.

Makes 4 to 6 servings.

TOMATO & RED ONION SALAD

4 beefsteak tomatoes, sliced
4 sun-dried tomatoes packed in oil, drained and
  chopped
1 red onion, chopped
Salt and freshly ground pepper
3 tablespoons extra-virgin olive oil
2 tablespoons oil from the sun-dried tomatoes
2 tablespoons red wine vinegar
Pinch of sugar
4 tablespoons chopped mixed fresh herbs such as
  basil, oregano, parsley, chives, dill and cilantro
Herb sprigs to garnish

Layer tomatoes, sun-dried tomatoes and onion in a shallow serving dish. Season with salt and freshly ground pepper.

Mix together remaining ingredients except herb sprigs in a small bowl, then pour over salad. Garnish with herb sprigs.

Makes 4 to 6 servings.

CAULIFLOWER INSALATA

1 cauliflower
⅓ cup pitted green olives, halved
⅓ cup pitted ripe olives, halved
2 tablespoons capers in wine vinegar, drained
1 red bell pepper packed in wine vinegar, drained
  and chopped
5 anchovy fillets canned in oil, drained and halved
  crosswise
6 tablespoons extra-virgin olive oil
1 tablespoon white wine vinegar
Salt and freshly ground pepper
3 small carrots

Break the cauliflower into flowerets.

Add cauliflower to a saucepan of boiling salted water and boil 4 to 5 minutes until crisp-tender. Drain, refresh under cold running water, drain again and cool. Put into a serving bowl with olives, capers, bell pepper and anchovies. Add oil and vinegar and season with salt and freshly ground pepper. Toss gently to mix and refrigerate at least 30 minutes.

Using a vegetable peeler, remove long thin slices from carrots. Place slices in a bowl of iced water 10 minutes to curl and crisp. Drain thoroughly and add to salad. Toss lightly to mix, then serve.

Makes 6 servings.

TRICOLOR SALAD

1 avocado
2 tablespoons lemon juice
2 large beefsteak tomatoes, sliced
6 ozs. Italian mozzarella cheese, preferably made
   from buffalo milk
Salt and freshly ground pepper
Few drops balsamic vinegar
¼ cup extra-virgin olive oil
6 fresh basil leaves, shredded
Basil sprigs to garnish

Seed and peel avocado, slice thinly and
brush with lemon juice.

Arrange tomatoes, cheese and avocado on a
large plate. Season with salt and freshly
ground pepper.

Drizzle balsamic vinegar and oil over salad;
sprinkle with shredded basil. Garnish with
basil sprigs.

Makes 4 to 6 servings.

ZUCCHINI & TOMATO SALAD

About 30 (2-inch-long) zucchini (about 1 lb. total)
12 ozs. small tomatoes, sliced
4 green onions, white part only, finely chopped
1 tablespoon chopped Italian parsley
Italian parsley sprig to garnish
DRESSING:
5 tablespoons extra-virgin olive oil
3 tablespoons white wine vinegar
2 garlic cloves, chopped
1 tablespoon chopped thyme or 1 teaspoon dried leaf
   thyme
1 teaspoon honey
Salt and freshly ground pepper

Add zucchini to a saucepan of boiling salted
water and cook 3 minutes. Drain well. Using
a small, sharp knife, cut a long lengthwise
slit in each zucchini, place in a serving dish.

To make dressing, mix ingredients together
in a small bowl or shake together in a jar
with a tight-fitting lid. Pour over hot
zucchini and leave until completely cold.
Add tomatoes, green onions and parsley to
dish. Toss to mix. Adjust seasoning before
serving. Garnish with Italian parsley sprig.

Makes 6 servings.

EGGPLANT & OLIVE SALAD

2 Japanese-type eggplants, diced
Peanut oil for deep-frying
6 tablespoons light olive oil
2 onions, chopped
1 garlic clove, chopped
4 celery stalks, sliced
2 small zucchini, sliced
1 tablespoon chopped rosemary
1 (14-oz.) can chopped plum tomatoes
1 tablespoon sun-dried tomato paste
2 teaspoons sugar
⅓ cup red wine vinegar
1 cup pitted mixed olives, halved
2 tablespoons capers in wine vinegar, drained
Salt and freshly ground pepper
Italian parsley sprig to garnish

Put eggplant in a colander, sprinkle with salt and drain 30 to 40 minutes. Rinse thoroughly to remove salt, drain and pat dry with paper towels. Heat peanut oil in a large skillet over high heat. Add eggplant and fry 4 to 5 minutes until an even golden-brown. Transfer eggplant to paper towels. Transfer to a serving dish and set aside. Heat olive oil in a large skillet over medium heat, add onions and garlic and cook 5 minutes to soften.

Add celery, zucchini and rosemary and cook 5 minutes. Stir in plum tomatoes, tomato paste, sugar and vinegar and cook, stirring frequently, 10 minutes until vinegar has evaporated. Transfer to serving dish and cool. Add olives and capers to serving dish. Season with salt and freshly ground pepper and toss well to mix. Cover and refrigerate before serving. Garnish with Italian parsley sprig.

Makes 4 to 6 servings.

ORIENTAL CARROT SALAD

¾ lbs. carrots
3 tablespoons peanut oil
½ teaspoon sesame oil
1 teaspoon grated peeled gingerroot
1 small garlic clove, sliced
1 dried red chile, seeded and crushed
2 tablespoons lemon juice
1 teaspoon sugar
⅓ cup peanuts, toasted and chopped
Salt and pepper
Cilantro leaves to garnish

Into a large bowl, finely grate carrot.

In a skillet, heat 1 tablespoon of the peanut oil and the sesame oil. Add gingerroot, garlic and chile; cook until just turning golden. Beat in remaining oil, lemon juice and sugar. Remove from heat.

Pour dressing over carrots. Add nuts and toss well until evenly combined. Cover and let marinate 30 minutes. Stir again, season to taste and serve garnished with cilantro leaves.

Makes 4 servings.

LETTUCE & EGG SALAD

ANCHOVY & PARMESAN SALAD

12 quail eggs or 3 chicken eggs
6 leaf lettuce hearts
3 cups watercress
3 green onions
1 oz. Parmesan cheese or vegetarian Cheddar cheese
½ cup coarsely shredded chervil
DRESSING:
3 tablespoons virgin olive oil
2 teaspoons Champagne vinegar
Salt and pepper

Simmer quail eggs 3 minutes or chicken eggs 12 minutes, then cool immediately in cold water. Peel and cut into halves or quarters.

Cut each lettuce head into quarters. Discard any thick stems from the watercress. Thinly slice the green onions. Divide lettuce quarters, watercress and onions among 4 serving plate. Using a vegetable peeler, shave a little Parmesan cheese or Cheddar cheese over each. Sprinkle with chervil. Garnish each salad with cooked eggs.

In a small bowl, blend dressing ingredients together until combined. Pour over salads and serve at once.

Makes 4 servings.

2 tablespoons olive oil
1 (2-oz.) can anchovies in olive oil
1 garlic clove
Pinch of cayenne pepper
4 slices white bread
9 ozs. mixed salad greens
2 ozs. Parmesan cheese
DRESSING:
1 tablespoon balsamic vinegar
1 teaspoon Dijon mustard
¼ cup olive oil
Freshly ground pepper

Preheat oven to 375F (190C). Brush a baking sheet with 1 tablespoon of the olive oil.

Drain anchovies, reserving oil. Using a pestle and mortar, or in a blender or food processor, pound together anchovies, garlic, cayenne and remaining olive oil. Remove crusts from bread. Spread one side of each slice of bread with anchovy paste. Cut bread into ½-inch cubes and arrange, paste side up, on baking sheet. Bake 8 to 10 minutes or until crisp. Let cool.

To make dressing, in a large bowl, mix together vinegar, mustard, olive oil, reserved oil from anchovies and pepper. Add salad leaves and toss to coat thoroughly. Arrange salad greens on serving plates. Scatter anchovy croûtons over salads. Using a vegetable peeler, shave curls of Parmesan cheese over salads and serve.

Makes 6 servings.

ROQUEFORT SALAD

½ cup walnut pieces
2 bunches watercress
4 ozs. Roquefort cheese
DRESSING:
1 tablespoon red wine vinegar
½ to 1 teaspoon Dijon mustard
¼ cup olive oil
Salt and freshly ground pepper

To make dressing, whisk together vinegar and mustard, then slowly pour in oil, whisking constantly. Season with salt and pepper and set aside.

Preheat broiler. Spread walnut pieces on a baking sheet and broil, turning occasionally, until crisp and evenly browned.

Put watercress into a serving bowl, crumble Roquefort cheese over watercress and sprinkle with toasted walnuts. Whisk dressing, pour over salad, toss and serve.

Makes 4 servings.

PANZANELLA SALAD

8 thick slices day-old Italian bread
10 plum tomatoes
½ small cucumber
½ small red onion
½ cup pitted ripe olives
2 tablespoons chopped fresh basil
Grated peel of 1 lemon
¼ cup virgin olive oil
2 teaspoons balsamic vinegar
Salt and pepper
Lemon slices and basil sprigs to garnish

Cut bread into small cubes. Place into a shallow dish. Pour over enough water to lightly moisten. Set aside 30 minutes.

Squeeze out all excess water and crumble bread into a large bowl. Cut tomatoes, cucumber, onion and olives into small pieces. Add to bread with basil and lemon peel. Stir well.

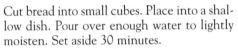
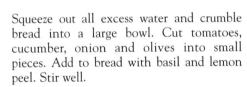

In a small bowl, heat oil and vinegar together. Pour over salad. Season with salt and pepper; toss salad until evenly combined. Cover and refrigerate at least 30 minutes; bring salad to room temperature before serving. Garnish with lemon slices and basil sprigs.

Makes 4 to 6 servings.

WARM SPINACH SALAD

1 lb. small spinach leaves
6 slices thick-cut lean bacon, cut into strips
2 slices bread, crusts removed
¼ cup olive oil
4 teaspoons red wine vinegar
1 teaspoon Dijon mustard
Salt and freshly ground pepper

Put spinach into a serving bowl. Heat a non-stick skillet, add bacon and cook until crisp and brown. Remove with a slotted spoon and drain on paper towels. Drain off fat from skillet.

Cut bread into cubes. Add 1 tablespoon of the oil to skillet, add bread and fry over medium to high heat until crisp and golden. Remove and drain on paper towels. Add to spinach with bacon.

Stir vinegar and mustard into skillet and bring to a boil. Add remaining oil, salt and pepper. Heat through and pour over salad. Toss and serve immediately.

Makes 4 servings.

VEGETARIAN CAESAR SALAD

2 tablespoons mayonnaise
1 tablespoon vodka
1 tablespoon lime juice
1 teaspoon Worcestershire sauce or 2 drops hot pepper sauce
⅔ cup light olive oil
1 tablespoon chopped fresh mint
1 tablespoon chopped fresh parsley
½ teaspoon ground cumin
¼ teaspoon chile powder
1 small garlic clove, crushed
2 (½-inch) slices day-old bread
2 romaine lettuce heads
¾ cup shredded vegetarian Cheddar cheese

Preheat oven to 375F (190C). In a small bowl, blend mayonnaise, vodka, lime juice, Worcestershire sauce or hot-pepper sauce together. Beat in ⅓ cup of the oil, a little at a time, until thickened slightly. Stir in half the herbs; set aside. Mix remaining oil, herbs, spices and garlic together. Brush over both sides of bread. Place on a wire rack. Bake 10 to 12 minutes. Turn bread and bake 10 to 12 minutes longer under crisp and golden on both sides. Cool slightly, then cut into cubes.

Just before serving, rinse lettuce, discarding outer leaves. Dry well. In a large bowl, place lettuce leaves. Stir in croûtons and cheese. Add dressing and toss well until evenly coated. Serve at once.

Makes 4 servings.

ROASTED VEGETABLE SALAD

2 Spanish onions, unpeeled
1 lb. small eggplants
2 red bell peppers
3 firm but ripe beefsteak tomatoes
8 garlic cloves
1½ teaspoons cumin seeds
Juice of 1 lemon
¼ cup extra-virgin olive oil
3 tablespoons white-wine vinegar
Salt
2 tablespoons finely chopped fresh parsley (optional)

Preheat oven to 350F (175C). Place onions on a baking sheet and bake 10 minutes. Add eggplants.

Bake another 10 minutes, then add peppers. Bake 10 minutes before adding tomatoes and 6 of the garlic cloves, then bake 15 minutes or until all vegetables are tender. If necessary, remove vegetables from oven as they are done. When vegetables are cool enough to handle, peel them with your fingers.

Remove and discard cores and seeds from peppers, then cut into strips. Halve tomatoes and discard seeds, then slice. Slice eggplants into strips and onions into rings. Arrange in a serving dish. Using a mortar and pestle, pound the roasted and the raw garlic and the cumin seeds to a paste. Beat in lemon juice, oil and vinegar. Add salt to taste. Pour over vegetables and sprinkle with parsley, if desired. Serve warm or cold.

Makes 4 servings.

VEGETABLE SALAD

1 lb. potatoes
1 large carrot, halved or quartered
⅓ cup shelled green peas
4 ozs. green beans
2 tablespoons chopped Spanish onion
1 small red bell pepper, chopped
4 small pickles, chopped
1½ tablespoons capers
8-12 anchovy-stuffed olives
⅔ cup mayonnaise
1 hard-cooked egg, sliced
Chopped fresh parsley to garnish

In a saucepan of lightly salted water, boil potatoes in their skins until tender. Cool, peel, then dice. Boil carrot, peas and beans separately in boiling salted water until tender; drain and cool. Dice carrot and cut beans into short pieces.

Into a bowl, put potatoes, carrot, peas and beans. Stir in onion, pepper, pickles, capers, olives and mayonnaise while vegetables are still warm. Refrigerate until chilled. Arrange egg and chopped parsley on top before serving.

Makes 4 servings.

SALADE NIÇOISE

8 ozs. small green beans
1 head lettuce
4 beefsteak tomatoes, cut into wedges
1 red bell pepper, chopped
3 hard-cooked eggs, quartered
1 (7-oz.) can tuna in olive oil, drained
Leaves from small bunch of flat-leaf parsley, coarsely
  chopped
16 pitted ripe olives
6-8 anchovy fillets, halved lengthwise
DRESSING:
½ cup olive oil
2 teaspoons wine vinegar
1-2 garlic cloves, crushed
Salt and freshly ground pepper

Cut beans crosswise in halves and cook in a saucepan of boiling salted water 10 minutes or until tender. Drain, rinse in cold water and drain again. Let cool. Tear lettuce into bite-size pieces and arrange on a large serving plate with beans, tomatoes, bell pepper, eggs and tuna.

Sprinkle with parsley and olives. Arrange anchovies on top in a lattice pattern. To make dressing, whisk together olive oil, vinegar, garlic, salt and pepper. Pour over salad and serve.

Makes 4 servings.

FRUITY CHEESE COLESLAW

1 red apple
1 tablespoon lemon juice
2 cups finely shredded white cabbage
2 celery stalks, finely sliced
4 ozs. seedless green grapes
4 ozs. seedless black grapes
2 ozs. Cheddar cheese
2 ozs. Gouda cheese
2 tablespoons vegetable oil
2 tablespoons plain yogurt
1 teaspoon honey

With a knife, core apple, then cut into small chunks. Toss in lemon juice to prevent browning.

Remove apple from juice (reserving juice). In a medium-size bowl, combine apple, cabbage, celery and grapes. Cut cheeses into small cubes, then add to other ingredients.

In a small bowl, mix together reserved lemon juice, oil, yogurt and honey. Beat until smooth, then fold into salad ingredients.

Makes 4 to 6 servings.

SQUID SALAD

1 lb. small or medium-size squid, prepared
1¼ cups dry white wine
1 shallot, chopped
Strip of lemon peel
1 garlic clove, chopped
1 red onion, chopped
¼ cup chopped mixed fresh herbs such as basil, tarragon and Italian parsley
Fresh herb sprigs to garnish
DRESSING:
5 tablespoons extra-virgin olive oil
2 tablespoons lemon juice
1 teaspoon balsamic vinegar
1 teaspoon Dijon-style mustard
Salt and freshly ground pepper

Put wine, shallot, lemon peel and garlic into a medium-size saucepan. Bring to a boil and boil 1 minute. Add the squid, in batches if necessary, and cook 5 to 7 minutes until firm but still tender. Using a slotted spoon, remove to a serving dish and cool.

Add onion and the herbs to the squid and toss to mix. To make dressing, mix all ingredients together in a small bowl, or shake together in a jar with a tight-fitting lid. Pour over salad and toss to mix. Cover and refrigerate at least 30 minutes before serving. garnish with fresh herb sprigs.

Makes 4 servings.

MINTY SEAFOOD SALAD

⅔ cup dry white wine
1 shallot, chopped
5 peppercorns
⅓ cup water
1 lb. shelled scallops, fresh or frozen and thawed
1 lb. cooked large shrimp
4 celery stalks
2 medium-size carrots
About 16 mint leaves
½ teaspoon finely grated lemon peel
DRESSING:
Juice of 2 lemons
½ cup extra-virgin olive oil
1 tablespoon white wine vinegar
2 tablespoons chopped Italian parsley
Salt and freshly ground pepper

Put white wine, shallot, peppercorns and water in a shallow pan. Heat until boiling then add scallops. Reduce heat and poach 5 to 6 minutes, until scallops are just firm and opaque. Using a slotted spoon transfer scallops to paper towels to drain and cool. Discard cooking liquid. Slice scallops in half horizontally. Put in a serving dish. Peel shrimp and add to dish.

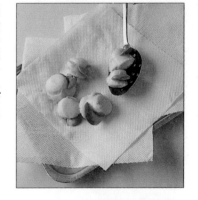

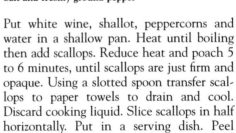

Cut celery and carrots into thin matchsticks and add to seafood with mint leaves and lemon peel. Toss lightly to mix. To make dressing, mix ingredients together in a small bowl or put in a jar with a tight-fitting lid and shake until blended. Pour over salad and toss. Cover and refrigerate 30 minutes before serving.

Makes 4 to 6 servings.

CRAB & AVOCADO SALAD

TUNA SALAD

12 ozs. crabmeat
1 tablespoon fresh lime juice
Grated zest of 1 lime
1 tablespoon chopped fresh cilantro
Salt and freshly ground pepper
2 ripe avocados
9 ozs. mixed salad greens
Lime slices and cilantro leaves to garnish
LIME DRESSING:
1 tablespoon fresh lime juice
⅓ cup olive oil
1 tablespoon chopped fresh cilantro
½ teaspoon sugar

3 small carrots, thickly sliced
1⅓ cups diced potatoes (about 8 ozs.)
1 (7-oz.) can tuna in olive oil, drained and flaked
1 (1¾-oz.) can anchovy fillets in oil, drained and chopped
About 12 pitted ripe olives, halved
2 tablespoons capers in wine vinegar, drained
2 hard-cooked eggs, quartered
¼ cup extra-virgin olive oil
Juice of 1 small lemon
1 garlic clove, crushed
Salt and freshly ground pepper
1 tablespoon chopped Italian parsley
Italian parsley sprigs to garnish

To make lime dressing, in a large bowl, mix together lime juice, olive oil, cilantro, sugar, salt and pepper. In another bowl, mix together crabmeat, lime juice, lime zest, cilantro, salt and pepper. Halve avocados lengthwise, remove pits and peel. Cut avocado flesh into ½-inch cubes.

Cook carrots in a saucepan of boiling salted water 4 minutes until tender. Cook potatoes in a separate saucepan of boiling salted water about 7 minutes until tender. Drain and refresh both vegetables under cold running water, then drain and cool completely.

Put salad leaves into bowl with dressing and toss to coat thoroughly. Arrange salad leaves on serving plates. Put a spoonful of crab mixture in center of each plate. Arrange diced avocado around crab mixture. Garnish with slices of lime and cilantro leaves and serve.

Makes 6 servings.

Put carrots, potatoes, tuna, anchovies, olives, capers and eggs into a large serving dish. Mix olive oil, lemon juice, garlic and salt and pepper together in a small bowl or put in a jar with a tight-fitting lid and shake until blended. Pour over salad, toss lightly to mix, then sprinkle with chopped Italian parsley. Garnish with Italian parsley sprigs.

Makes 4 servings.

MORTADELLA SALAD

1 (8-oz.) piece mortadella sausage
1 small red onion, sliced
½ each yellow and red bell peppers packed in wine
  vinegar, drained
3 small sweet dill pickles, sliced
6 radishes, sliced
12 pitted green olives, halved
6 leaves Romaine lettuce
DRESSING:
¼ cup extra-virgin olive oil
2 tablespoons red wine vinegar
1 teaspoon Dijon-style mustard
1 tablespoon chopped Italian parsley
Salt and freshly ground pepper

Cut mortadella into ½-inch cubes and place in a bowl with onion. Cut yellow and red bell peppers into strips and add to bowl with dill pickles, radishes and olives.

To make dressing, mix all ingredients together in a small bowl, or shake together in a jar with a tight-fitting lid. Pour over salad and toss to mix. Tear lettuce leaves into pieces and arrange on a serving plate. Place salad on top and serve at once.

Makes 4 to 6 servings.

SPICY THAI SALAD

2 teaspoons sesame oil
2 red chiles, seeded and chopped
1 garlic clove, crushed
Juice of 1 lime
2 teaspoons brown sugar
1 tablespoon fish sauce
1 stem lemon grass, chopped
2 tablespoons shredded basil
2 cups shredded cooked chicken
2 ozs. rice noodles
4 green onions, cut into matchstick strips
1 large carrot, cut into matchstick strips
1 yellow bell pepper, cut into matchstick strips
3 Napa cabbage leaves, shredded
2 tablespoons dry roasted peanuts, chopped

In a small pan, heat oil over high heat. Add chiles and garlic; cook, stirring, until softened. Remove from heat and stir in lime juice, sugar, fish sauce, lemon grass and basil. Pour mixture over shredded chicken and let stand 30 minutes.

Cook rice noodles according to package directions. Drain and rinse well in cold water. Drain well again. In a large bowl, mix together noodles, onions, carrot, bell pepper and cabbage. Spoon chicken and sauce over noodle mixture. Sprinkle with chopped peanuts.

Makes 4 servings.

CHICKEN SATÉ SALAD

2 tablespoons dry sherry
¼ cup crunchy peanut butter
1 (1-inch) piece gingerroot, finely chopped
2 tablespoons hoisin sauce
1 tablespoon fresh lemon juice
2 tablespoons dark soy sauce
⅔ cup chicken stock or water
¼ cup sunflower seeds
2 teaspoons sesame oil
2 tablespoons vegetable oil
Salt and pepper
1 head Romaine lettuce, separated into leaves
1 cup bean sprouts
4 ozs. green beans, cooked
4 skinned and boned chicken breasts halves

In a small bowl, mix together sherry, peanut butter, gingerroot, hoisin sauce, 2 teaspoons of the lemon juice and 1 tablespoon of the soy sauce. Slowly beat in stock or water; set aside. In a small pan over medium-high heat, put sunflower seeds. Cook, stirring constantly, about 1 minute or until seeds start to turn golden. Still stirring, add remaining 1 tablespoon soy sauce. The soy sauce will evaporate and coat the seeds. Turn seeds into a small bowl; cool. In a small bowl, mix together sesame oil, 1 tablespoon of the vegetable oil, remaining lemon juice, salt and pepper.

Into a bowl, place lettuce leaves and bean sprouts. Pour salad dressing over salad; toss to combine. Arrange lettuce mixture on 4 plates; set aside. Slice chicken into thin strips. In a skillet, heat remaining vegetable oil. Add chicken and stir-fry over high heat until chicken is golden-brown. Reduce heat and pour peanut butter mixture over chicken. Cook, stirring, until sauce is thick, adding more stock, if necessary. Spoon over lettuce; sprinkle with the sunflower seeds.

Makes 4 servings.

MEXICAN CHICKEN SALAD

⅔ cup canned kidney beans, drained
⅔ cup canned chickpeas, drained
1 red bell pepper, cut into strips
1 head leaf lettuce, shredded
1 tablespoon prepared mustard
2 teaspoons sugar
2 teaspoons red-wine vinegar
⅔ cup olive oil
Salt and pepper
4 teaspoons paprika
2 teaspoons red (cayenne) pepper
1 teaspoon chile powder
4 skinned and boned chicken breast halves, cut into strips
2 tablespoons vegetable oil

In a large bowl, mix together kidney beans, chickpeas, bell pepper and shredded lettuce. Arrange on 4 plates. In a bowl, beat together mustard, sugar and vinegar. Slowly drizzle in olive oil, whisking all the time to make a dressing the consistency of thin mayonnaise. Season with salt and pepper and set aside.

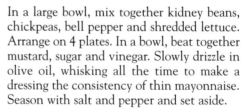

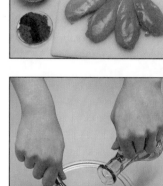

On a plate mix paprika, cayenne and chile powder. Add chicken strips; toss until evenly coated in the mixture. In a skillet, heat vegetable oil over medium-low heat. Add coated chicken; stir-fry 2 to 3 minutes or until cooked through. Spoon chicken over the salad, then add salad dressing. Serve immediately.

Makes 4 servings.

CURRIED CHICKEN SALAD

CHICKPEA SALAD

1 tablespoon olive oil
1 small onion, diced
2 teaspoons mild curry paste
1 (7-oz.) can chopped tomatoes
¼ cup dry white wine
2 tablespoons hot mango chutney, chopped if
  necessary
2 teaspoons apricot jam
2 teaspoons fresh lemon juice
⅔ cup mayonnaise
⅔ cup plain yogurt
1 lb. cooked chicken
2 cups cooked, long-grain rice
1 red bell pepper, diced
2 tablespoons chopped fresh mint
3 tablespoons prepared Italian salad dressing

1½ cups dried chickpeas, soaked overnight
1 tablespoon finely chopped fresh parsley
1½ teaspoons finely chopped fresh tarragon
4 green onions, finely chopped
Sliced green onion and flat-leaf parsley, to garnish
DRESSING:
2 garlic cloves, finely chopped
1 tablespoon red wine vinegar
2-3 teaspoons Dijon mustard
Salt and freshly ground pepper
¼ cup olive oil

Drain and rinse chickpeas. Put into a saucepan and cover with cold water.

In a small saucepan, heat oil. Add onion; cook until softened but not browned. Stir in curry paste, tomatoes and wine. Bring to a boil. Reduce heat and simmer 15 minutes. Stir in chutney, jam and lemon juice; cook, stirring occasionally, 5 minutes or until thick and syrupy.

Bring to a boil. reduce heat, cover and simmer 1 to 1½ hours or until chickpeas are tender. Meanwhile, make dressing. Mix together garlic, vinegar, mustard, salt and pepper. Slowly pour in oil, whisking constantly.

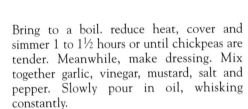

Remove from heat. Strain into a small bowl; set aside to cool. When completely cold, stir in mayonnaise and yogurt and mix well. Cut the chicken into large pieces and stir into sauce. In a medium-size bowl, combine rice, bell pepper, mint and dressing. Spoon rice mixture into a large serving dish; arrange chicken in center of rice.

Makes 4 servings.

Drain chickpeas and immediately toss with dressing, parsley, tarragon and green onions. Garnish with green onion slices and flat-leaf parsley and serve warm.

Makes 4 servings.

MEDITERRANEAN POTATO SALAD

POTATO SALAD

1 lb. new potatoes
4 ozs. green beans
1 fennel bulb
¼ cup pitted ripe olives
2 tablespoons capers, drained
2 tablespoons snipped fresh chives
2 teaspoons chopped fresh tarragon
¼ cup virgin olive oil
Juice of lemon
2 eggs
1 (14-oz.) can artichoke hearts, drained and halved

1½ lbs. small new potatoes
4-5 mint leaves, chopped
1 tablespoon chopped fresh chives
¼ shallot, finely chopped
Mint sprigs to garnish
DRESSING:
1 tablespoon wine vinegar
2 teaspoons Dijon mustard
Salt and freshly ground pepper
3 tablespoons olive oil

Cook potatoes in a saucepan of boiling salted water 15 minutes or until tender.

In a pan of lightly salted boiling water, cook potatoes 10 to 12 minutes or until just tender. Drain and place in a large bowl. Blanch beans in boiling water 1 to 2 minutes or until just tender. Drain and refresh under cold water. Pat dry. Very thinly slice fennel and halve olives. Add to potatoes with beans, capers and herbs. Stir in oil and lemon juice. Set aside until potatoes are cool.

Meanwhile, make dressing. Whisk together vinegar, mustard, salt and pepper. Slowly pour in oil, whisking constantly.

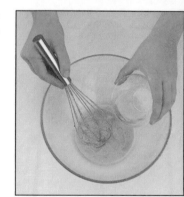

Meanwhile, hard cook eggs. Plunge into cold water, then peel. Rough chop and add to salad with the artichoke hearts. Toss well and serve at once.

Makes 4 to 6 servings.

Drain potatoes thoroughly, cut into halves or quarters, depending on size, then immediately toss with dressing, herbs and shallot. Let cool. Garnish with mint sprigs and serve.

Makes 4 servings.

THREE BEAN SALAD

3 ozs. dried flageolet beans
3 ozs. dried red kidney beans
2 fresh thyme sprigs
1 lb. fresh fava beans, shelled
1 small onion, finely chopped
Red bell pepper rings to garnish
DRESSING:
½ cup extra-virgin olive oil
Juice of 1 lemon
1 tablespoon chopped fresh mint
1 tablespoon chopped fresh parsley
Salt and pepper

Put flageolet and kidney beans on 2 separate bowls.

Cover each with water to come well above top of beans. Let soak at least 6 hours. Drain. Put flageolet and kidney beans in 2 separate saucepans each with a sprig of thyme. Cover with water, bring to a boil and boil briskly 10 minutes. Cover pans, reduce heat and simmer 1 to 1½ hours or until beans are tender. In a pan of boiling water, cook fava beans 5 to 10 minutes or until tender. Drain all the beans and put together into a bowl.

To make the dressing, in a bowl, mix together oil, lemon juice, mint, parsley, salt and pepper. Pour dressing over warm beans. Add chopped onion and mix well. Cover and refrigerate until chilled, then transfer to a serving dish. Serve garnished with bell pepper rings.

Makes 6 servings.

LENTIL SALAD

1¼ cups green lentils
¼ cup extra-virgin olive oil
1 onion, finely chopped
3 tomatoes, peeled and chopped
Salt and pepper
1 tablespoon chopped fresh parsley
2 tablespoons fresh lemon juice
Onion rings, chopped fresh parsley and lemon slices
   to garnish

Put lentils into a bowl, cover with cold water and let soak 3 to 4 hours. Drain well.

In a large saucepan, heat oil, add onion and cook until soft. Add tomatoes and cook 1 minute, then add lentils. Cover with water, cover pan and simmer 30 minutes, adding water if necessary, or until lentils are tender, yet still hold their shapes and all water has been absorbed.

Add salt, pepper, parsley, lemon juice and remaining oil to lentils. Mix carefully, then transfer to a serving dish and let cool. Serve garnished with onion rings, chopped parsley and lemon slices.

Makes 4 to 6 servings.

PEA TABBOULEH

1¼ cups bulgur wheat
⅔ cup olive oil
1 garlic clove, crushed
1 tablespoon red-wine vinegar
1 tablespoon chopped fresh cilantro
1 tablespoon chopped fresh mint
1 teaspoon ground coriander
½ teaspoon ground cumin
4 ozs. sugar snap peas
1 cup frozen green peas, thawed
1 large ripe peach, chopped
1 red onion, finely chopped
Salt and pepper

In a large bowl, cover bulgur wheat with plenty of cold water. Let soak 30 minutes. Drain well and squeeze out excess liquid. In a small bowl, mix together oil, garlic, vinegar, herbs and spices. Pour over bulgur wheat. Stir well, cover and set aside 30 minutes.

In a pan of boiling water, cook sugar snap peas 2 minutes and green peas 1 minute. Drain both and refresh under cold water. Pat all peas dry. Stir into bulgur wheat with the peach, onion, salt and pepper.

Makes 4 to 6 servings.

COUSCOUS SALAD

⅔ cup quick-cook couscous
1 fresh red chile
8 ozs. cherry tomatoes
1 bunch green onions
¼ cup extra-virgin olive oil
2 tablespoons lemon juice
¼ cup chopped fresh parsley
¼ cup chopped fresh cilantro
Salt and freshly ground pepper
Salad leaves to serve

Put couscous in a bowl and add ⅔ cup cold water. Leave 30 to 60 minutes or until water has been completely absorbed.

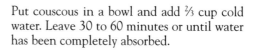

Meanwhile, cut chile in half and remove core and seeds. Finely chop chile. Cut cherry tomatoes in half and slice green onions. Gently fluff up couscous with a fork.

Add olive oil, lemon juice, parsley, cilantro, salt and pepper to couscous. Gently stir in chile, tomatoes and green onions. Let stand 1 hour. Line a serving dish with salad leaves, pile couscous in center and serve.

Makes 4 servings.

WILD & BROWN RICE SALAD

WARM PASTA SALAD

1 cup wild rice
1¼ cups brown rice
⅔ cup pecans
6 green onions, trimmed
⅓ cup dried cherries, cranberries or raisins
2 tablespoons chopped fresh cilantro
1 tablespoon chopped fresh parsley
DRESSING:
½ cup olive oil
2 teaspoons raspberry vinegar
¼ teaspoon honey or sugar
Salt and pepper

½ lb. mixed fresh mushrooms
¼ cup drained sun-dried tomatoes in oil, sliced
½ cup olive oil
2 garlic cloves, chopped
Grated peel of 1 lemon
1 tablespoon lemon juice
2 tablespoons chopped fresh mint
2½ cups dried penne
2 tomatoes, chopped
Salt and pepper

Thinly slice mushrooms. Into a large bowl, place mushrooms with sun-dried tomatoes.

In a pan of lightly salted boiling water, cook wild rice 35 to 40 minutes or until just tender. In another pan of lightly salted boiling water, cook brown rice 25 minutes or until just tender. Drain well. Place both rices in a large bowl.

In a skillet, heat 1 tablespoon of the oil. Add garlic; cook 1 minute until starting to turn golden. Remove pan from heat and stir in remaining oil, lemon peel, lemon juice and mint. Pour half over mushrooms and reserve the remainder. Stir mushrooms until well coated. Cover and refrigerate several hours to soften.

Preheat oven to 400F (205C). Roast pecans 5 to 6 minutes or until browned. Cool and coarsely chop. Set aside. Chop green onions. Add to rice with cherries and herbs. Stir well. Blend the dressing ingredients well together. Pour over salad, stir once, cover and let rice cool. Just before serving, toss in pecans and season with salt and pepper.

Makes 4 to 6 servings.

In a pan of lightly salted boiling water, cook pasta 10 minutes or until tender but firm to the bite. Drain well. Toss pasta with remaining dressing and stir into marinated mushrooms with tomatoes. Season with salt and pepper.

Makes 4 servings.

Note: Use a selection of button, oyster and shiitake mushrooms.

SESAME NOODLE SALAD

7 ozs. fine rice noodles
1 carrot
4 green onions, sliced
1 tablespoon toasted sesame seeds
Cilantro sprigs to garnish
SESAME DRESSING:
5 teaspoons sesame paste
5 teaspoons sesame oil
5 teaspoons soy sauce
2 tablespoons rice vinegar
1 teaspoon sugar
1 teaspoon grated gingerroot
Salt and freshly ground pepper

Soak noodles as directed on package, until soft. Drain and set aside.

Cut carrot into 1-inch-long matchsticks. Blanch in boiling water 1 minute. Drain, rinse in cold water, drain again and set aside.

To make sesame dressing, in a large bowl, mix together sesame paste, sesame oil, soy sauce, rice vinegar, sugar, gingerroot, salt and pepper. Add noodles and toss to coat thoroughly. Stir in carrot and green onions. Sprinkle with sesame seeds, garnish with cilantro sprigs and serve at once.

Makes 6 servings.

Variation: Add cooked, peeled large shrimp or diced ham before serving.

TORTELLONI SALAD

12 ozs. cheese- or meat-filled spinach tortelloni
½ cup olive oil
2 garlic cloves, finely chopped
8 ozs. asparagus, cut into 2-inch pieces
6 ozs. broccoli, cut into small flowerets
1 yellow bell pepper, thinly sliced
1 (6-oz.) jar marinated artichoke hearts, drained
1 red onion, thinly sliced
2 tablespoons capers, drained and rinsed
¼ cup Italian-style ripe olives
3 tablespoons red-wine vinegar
1 tablespoon Dijon-style mustard
Salt and freshly ground black pepper
3 tablespoons shredded fresh basil or parsley

In a large saucepan of boiling water, cook pasta according to package directions. Drain pasta, turn into a large bowl and toss with 1 tablespoon of the oil. Heat a wok until hot. Add 2 tablespoons oil and swirl to coat wok. Add garlic, asparagus and broccoli and stir-fry 4 minutes or until vegetables are crisp-tender. Add bell pepper and stir-fry 1 minute. Add vegetables to pasta and toss with artichoke hearts, onion, capers and olives. Cool to room temperature.

In a small bowl, whisk together vinegar, mustard, salt and pepper. Slowly whisk in remaining oil until creamy. Pour dressing over salad and toss gently to mix well. Serve at room temperature.

Makes 4 to 6 servings.

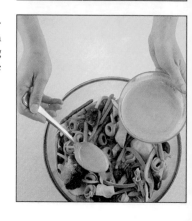

SIDE ORDERS

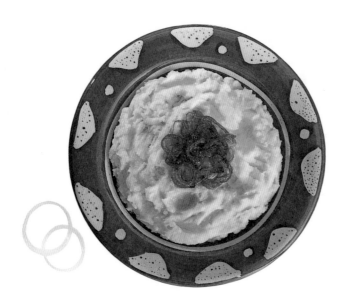

GARLIC & OLIVE OIL MASH

1 small garlic bulb
1 lb. baking potatoes, cut into chunks
5 tablespoons extra-virgin olive oil
¼ cup milk
Salt and freshly ground pepper
2 onions, finely sliced
1 tablespoon balsamic vinegar
1 tablespoon extra-virgin olive oil to serve

Preheat oven to 400F (200C). Cut top off garlic bulb. Wrap garlic loosely in foil and cook in oven 20 to 30 minutes or until soft.

Cook potatoes in a saucepan of boiling salted water 15 to 20 minutes or until soft. Drain thoroughly and return to pan. Heat milk until warm. Squeeze soft garlic cloves out of their skins and add to potatoes. Mash potatoes. Gradually stir in ¼ cup of oil, alternating with milk, until potatoes reach desired consistency. Season with salt and pepper.

Meanwhile, heat remaining oil in a skillet. Add onions and cook slowly, stirring frequently, 20 minutes or until soft and golden brown. Stir in balsamic vinegar. Top potatoes with fried onions, drizzle with olive oil and serve.

Makes 4 servings.

GARLIC-ROASTED POTATOES

2¼ lbs. new potatoes
12 unpeeled shallots
12 unpeeled garlic cloves
1 tablespoon chopped fresh sage
1 tablespoon chopped fresh thyme or rosemary
¼ cup hazelnut oil or olive oil
Salt and pepper

Preheat oven to 400F (205C). Rinse and dry potatoes and halve any large ones. Trim shallots, removing root ends. Combine with potatoes, garlic and herbs.

Into a roasting pan, place oil. Place in the oven 5 minutes until hot and starting to smoke. Add potato and shallot mixture, taking care not to splash the hot oil. Stir until potatoes, shallots, garlic and herbs are well coated.

Return to the oven and roast 50 to 60 minutes or until potatoes are tender, turning occasionally to brown evenly. Transfer to a hot serving dish and serve at once.

Makes 6 servings.

POTATOES WITH CHORIZO

¼ cup olive oil
4 ozs. chorizo, chopped
4 cups coarsely chopped potatoes (1½ lbs.)
1 Spanish onion, chopped
1 red bell pepper, seeded and chopped
2½ cups peeled, seeded and chopped beefsteak
  tomatoes
Salt and black pepper
Chicken stock, veal stock or water
Mint sprigs to garnish

In a large pan, heat oil. Add chorizo and cook, stirring occasionally, until lightly browned. Remove chorizo with a slotted spoon.

Add potatoes and onion and cook, stirring occasionally, 5 minutes. Stir in bell pepper and cook 5 minutes, then add tomatoes and return chorizo to pan. Season with salt and black pepper.

Just cover with stock or water and simmer about 15 minutes or until potatoes are tender and most of the liquid has been absorbed. Garnish with mint sprigs and serve.

Makes 4 servings.

POTATOES FORESTIÈRE

12 ozs. mixed mushrooms
1 lb. potatoes
Leaves from a bunch of parsley or basil
4 garlic cloves, crushed
Salt and freshly ground pepper
Flat-leaf parsley sprigs and basil leaves to garnish

Preheat oven to 350F (180C). Thinly slice mushrooms and potatoes.

Generously oil a baking dish that will hold potatoes and mushrooms in a layer no more than 1½ inches deep. In a large bowl, toss together mushrooms, potatoes, parsley or basil, garlic, salt and pepper.

Spread potato mixture in dish in an even layer and bake about 45 minutes or until potatoes are tender, turning mixture halfway through. Let stand a few minutes before serving. Garnish with flat-leaf parsley and basil and serve.

Makes 4 servings.

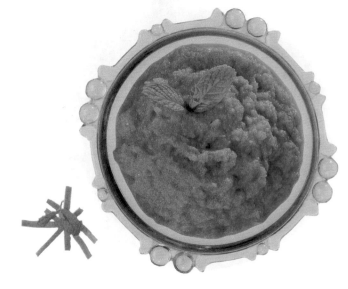

GRATIN SAVOYARD

PURÉED GINGER CARROTS

2 lbs. potatoes
1½ cups shredded Gruyère cheese
Freshly grated nutmeg
Salt and freshly ground pepper
About 1 cup chicken or vegetable stock
¼ cup butter
Flat-leaf parsley sprigs to garnish

Slice potatoes very thinly, keeping them in a bowl of cold water before slicing. Preheat oven to 400F (205C).

2½ lbs. carrots
⅔ cup vegetable stock
2 tablespoons hazelnut oil
1 large onion, chopped
1 garlic clove, chopped
2 teaspoons grated peeled gingerroot
1 teaspoon ground cumin
Pinch of freshly grated nutmeg
Salt and pepper
Mint sprigs to garnish

Roughly chop carrots. In a large pan, place carrots with stock. Slowly bring to a boil. Reduce heat, cover and simmer 20 minutes until or carrots are tender.

Grease a shallow baking dish. Layer potatoes in dish, sprinkling each layer with cheese, nutmeg, salt and pepper, and finishing with a layer of cheese.

In a skillet, heat 1 tablespoon of the oil. Add onion, garlic, gingerroot and cumin; cook 5 minutes or until soft. Transfer to a blender or food processor. Add cooked carrots and stock. Purée until smooth. Pass through a food mill or fine strainer if the purée is not completely smooth.

Add enough stock to come almost to the top of potatoes. Dot with butter. Bake 10 minutes. Reduce oven temperature to 350F (180C) and bake 50 minutes or until potatoes are tender and top is golden, and adding more stock if potatoes start to become dry. Garnish with parsley and serve.

Makes 4 servings.

Beat in remaining oil, freshly grated nutmeg, salt and pepper to taste. Serve hot, garnished with mint.

Makes 6 servings.

Note: This purée can easily be made ahead of time. To reheat, place in baking dish, cover with foil and bake 20 minutes at 400F (205C). Or, cover with vented plastic wrap and microwave on MEDIUM 6 to 8 minutes or until hot.

CAROTTES VICHY

1 lb. young carrots, thinly sliced diagonally
Salt
2 tablespoons unsalted butter
2 teaspoons sugar
1 tablespoon finely chopped fresh chervil or parsley
Chervil sprigs to garnish

Put carrots into a heavy saucepan and add enough water to just cover. Add a little salt.

Bring to a boil, reduce heat and simmer, uncovered, stirring occasionally, until carrots are tender and nearly all the water has evaporated.

Add butter and sugar and cook, shaking pan frequently, until carrots are lightly coated with glaze. Sprinkle with chervil or parsley, garnish with chervil sprigs and serve.

Makes 4 servings.

GLAZED BABY ONIONS

1¼ lbs. pickling onions
4 tablespoons unsalted butter
1 tablespoon sugar
Salt and freshly ground black pepper
⅓ cup chicken or vegetable stock

Peel onions by plunging them into boiling water 1 minute, then drain well and refresh under cold running water and peel off the skins.

Melt the butter in a heavy nonstick pan and add onions in a single layer. Sprinkle the sugar over them and add salt and pepper to taste. Cover and cook over very low heat 20 to 30 minutes until the onions are tender and caramelized, shaking pan often.

Add the stock, bring to a boil and simmer without the lid 5 minutes or until the sauce is syrupy. Serve immediately.

Makes 4 servings.

TOMATO & EGGPLANT GRATIN

HERBED PEAS

1 medium eggplant
Salt and freshly ground pepper
1 lb. ripe red tomatoes
2/3 cup olive oil
3 tablespoons freshly grated Parmesan cheese

Using a sharp knife, slice the eggplant into 1/8-inch slices. Sprinkle with salt and place in a colander to drain 30 minutes. Rinse well and pat dry with paper towels.

2 tablespoons olive oil
1 onion, finely chopped
2 garlic cloves, chopped
1 1/2 cups shelled fresh green peas
1/2 cup dry white wine
Bouquet garni of 2 fresh parsley sprigs, 1 fresh
    thyme sprig and 1 bay leaf
8 saffron threads
Salt and black pepper
Strips of red bell pepper and mint sprigs to garnish

Preheat oven to 400F (250C). Halve tomatoes. Heat oil in a frying pan and fry the eggplant slices in batches until golden brown. Drain on paper towels.

In a large pan, heat oil. Add onion and cook about 5 minutes, stirring occasionally, until soft but not colored. Add 1 garlic clove and cook 1 minute, then stir in peas, wine and bouquet garni. Heat until simmering, then cover and simmer about 15 minutes or until peas are tender. Discard bouquet garni.

Arrange the tomato halves and eggplant slices in a shallow ovenproof dish. Season with salt and pepper and sprinkle with Parmesan cheese. Bake 10 to 15 minutes until browned. Cool slightly and serve warm.

Makes 6 servings.

Using a mortar and pestle, crush together remaining garlic, the saffron and a pinch of salt to make a smooth paste. Stir in a little of the cooking liquid, then stir mixture into peas. Add black pepper and cook a few more minutes. Serve garnished with strips of bell pepper and mint sprigs.

Makes 4 servings.

TOMATOES WITH GARLIC CRUST

6 slices stale bread
1 (2-oz.) can anchovies in oil, drained
6 cloves garlic, finely chopped
3 tablespoons chopped fresh parsley
Salt and freshly ground pepper
1½ lbs. small plum tomatoes
3 tablespoons olive oil
Extra chopped fresh parsley to garnish

Preheat oven to 425F (220C). Tear up bread and place in a food processor with anchovies. Blend bread to crumbs, then dry-fry in a frying pan until crumbs are golden. Stir in garlic, parsley, salt and pepper.

Halve tomatoes and place cut side up, close together in a single layer in a shallow roasting tin or dish. Sprinkle the breadcrumb mixture evenly over tomatoes and drizzle with olive oil.

Bake about 20 minutes until crust is golden and tomatoes are soft. The tomatoes will slightly disintegrate under the crust. Garnish with more chopped parsley and serve at once.

Makes 6 servings.

OKRA & TOMATOES

1 lb. small okra
¼ cup olive oil
1 small onion, chopped
1 small leek, chopped
1 lb. tomatoes, peeled and chopped
1 oz. sun-dried tomatoes, chopped
1 garlic clove, crushed
1 tablespoon lemon juice
1 teaspoon sugar
Salt and freshly ground pepper
Oregano leaves to garnish

Cut stalks off okra but do not pierce pods. Wash pods, drain and pat dry.

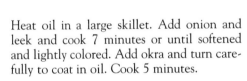

Heat oil in a large skillet. Add onion and leek and cook 7 minutes or until softened and lightly colored. Add okra and turn carefully to coat in oil. Cook 5 minutes.

Add tomatoes, sun-dried tomatoes, garlic, lemon juice, sugar, salt and pepper. Cover pan and simmer 10 minutes. Remove lid and cook 10 minutes or until okra is tender and sauce reduced and thickened. If sauce reduces too quickly, add a little water. Garnish with oregano leaves and serve hot or warm.

Makes 4 servings.

FENNEL & PARMESAN GRATIN

4 small fennel bulbs
3 tablespoons fresh lemon juice
¼ cup unsalted butter
1 tablespoon olive oil
½ cup freshly grated Parmesan cheese
Salt and freshly ground pepper
¼ cup sliced almonds, toasted

Trim feathery fronds from fennel and reserve. Cut fennel lengthwise into quarters.

Add fennel and lemon juice to a saucepan of boiling salted water and cook 15 minutes or until fennel is tender but still crisp. Drain, place on paper towels and drain thoroughly.

Preheat oven to 400F (205C). Arrange fennel in a single layer in a baking dish, dot with butter, drizzle with olive oil, sprinkle with cheese and season with plenty of pepper. Bake, uncovered, 20 to 25 minutes or until golden. Sprinkle with toasted almonds, garnish with reserved fennel fronds and serve.

Makes 4 servings.

ZUCCHINI GRATIN

2 lbs. zucchini, sliced
⅓ cup butter
1 lb. tomatoes, peeled, seeded and chopped
2 garlic cloves, chopped
2 tablespoons chopped fresh basil or parsley
Salt and freshly ground pepper
1 cup fresh bread crumbs
4-5 tablespoons finely grated Gruyère cheese
Basil sprigs to garnish

Put zucchini into a colander, sprinkle generously with salt and leave 1 hour. Rinse well, drain and dry thoroughly with paper towels.

Preheat oven to 400F (205C). Heat ¼ cup of the butter in a skillet, add zucchini and cook, stirring occasionally, 7 minutes or until browned. Remove with a slotted spoon and set aside.

Add tomatoes, garlic, basil or parsley, salt and pepper to skillet, bring to a boil, reduce heat and simmer until thickened. Stir in zucchini. Turn into a shallow baking dish. Mix together bread crumbs and cheese and sprinkle over zucchini. Dot with remaining butter and bake 25 minutes. Garnish with basil sprigs and serve.

Makes 4 to 6 servings.

FENNEL SICILIANO

3 fennel bulbs
1 cup fresh bread crumbs
1 oz. pine nuts
¼ cup raisins
1 teaspoon chopped fresh thyme
¼ cup grated Parmesan cheese
¼ cup olive oil
Salt and freshly ground pepper
Fennel leaves to garnish

Preheat oven to 375F (190C). Trim fennel and discard outer leaves, if necessary. Quarter bulbs and thinly slice.

Bring a saucepan of salted water to a boil. Add fennel and simmer 3 to 5 minutes or until just soft. Drain thoroughly. Brush an ovenproof dish with olive oil and arrange fennel slices in it in an even layer.

Mix together bread crumbs, pine nuts, raisins, thyme, Parmesan, olive oil, salt and pepper. Sprinkle mixture over fennel, making sure raisins are beneath surface. Cook in oven 20 to 30 minutes, or until golden. Garnish with fennel leaves and serve.

Makes 4 servings.

FAVA BEANS IN TOMATO SAUCE

6 tablespoons olive oil
2 garlic cloves, chopped
1 small onion, finely chopped
2 sage sprigs
2 lbs. fresh fava beans, shelled
1 (14-oz.) can chopped plum tomatoes
1 tablespoon sun-dried tomato paste
Salt and freshly ground pepper
Sage leaves to garnish

Heat oil in a large heavy saucepan. Add garlic, onion and sage sprigs and cook 4 to 5 minutes to soften.

Stir in beans, tomatoes and tomato paste and bring to a boil. Reduce heat, cover and cook 20 minutes, stirring frequently, until beans are tender. Discard sage sprigs and season with salt and freshly ground pepper. Serve hot garnished with sage leaves.

Makes 4 to 6 servings.

GREEN BEANS WITH ONION

1 lb. green beans
3 tablespoons extra-virgin olive oil
2 medium-size onions, chopped
1 garlic clove, crushed
4 teaspoons tomato paste
¾ cup water
1 tablespoon chopped fresh oregano
Salt and pepper
Finely chopped red bell pepper or oregano sprig to
  garnish

Trim ends from beans. In a large saucepan, heat oil. Add onions and garlic and cook 5 to 10 minutes or until soft.

Add beans to onion. Mix tomato paste with water. Pour tomato mixture over beans, then add more water, if necessary, to just cover beans.

Add oregano, salt and pepper. Cover pan and simmer 15 to 20 minutes or until beans are tender. Remove lid and boil to reduce the liquid. Serve garnished with chopped bell pepper or oregano sprig.

Makes 4 servings.

SPINACH WITH RAISINS

⅓ cup raisins
2 lbs. fresh spinach
3 tablespoons olive oil
1 garlic clove, finely chopped
3 tablespoons pine nuts
Salt and pepper
Croûtons to serve

Into a small bowl, put raisins. Cover with boiling water and let soak.

Rinse spinach well, then shake off surplus water but do not dry the leaves. Into a large saucepan, put spinach. Cover and cook until spinach wilts. Uncover and cook until excess moisture has evaporated. Chop coarsely. Drain raisins.

In a skillet, heat oil. Add garlic and pine nuts and fry, stirring occasionally, until beginning to color. Stir in spinach and raisins, season with salt and pepper and cook over low heat 5 minutes. Serve with croûtons sprinkled over the top.

Makes 4 servings.

FAVA BEANS WITH DILL

FAVA BEANS & ARTICHOKES

2 lbs. fresh fava beans
¼ cup extra-virgin olive oil
1 onion, finely chopped
1 garlic clove, crushed
2 tablespoons chopped fresh dill
Salt and pepper
Dill sprigs to garnish
Yogurt to serve

1½ lbs. fresh fava beans, shelled
1 (14-oz.) can artichoke hearts
1 tablespoon extra-virgin olive oil
1 teaspoon cornstarch
1 tablespoon fresh lemon juice
1 tablespoon chopped fresh parsley
Salt and pepper
Chopped fresh parsley to garnish

Shell fava beans. In a saucepan, heat oil. Add onion and garlic and cook over low heat until just beginning to color.

In a saucepan of boiling water, cook fava beans 10 minutes or until tender. Drain, reserving ¼ cup of the water.

Add fava beans and cook 2 to 3 minutes. Add enough hot water to just cover beans, stir in chopped dill and season with salt and pepper. Cook, covered, 10 minutes, or until beans are tender.

Drain and rinse artichoke hearts, then cut in half. In a saucepan, heat olive oil. Add fava beans and artichokes. In a small bowl, mix cornstarch and lemon juice and stir into reserved cooking water. Stir parsley, salt and pepper into cornstarch mixture.

When beans are tender, remove lid and cook briskly until liquid has almost evaporated. Garnish with dill sprigs and serve with yogurt.

Makes 6 servings.

Pour cornstarch mixture over beans and artichokes. Bring to a boil and cook until sauce is slightly thickened. Serve with more parsley sprinkled over the top.

Makes 6 servings.

SZECHUAN EGGPLANT

ZUCCHINI WITH GINGER

1 lb. small eggplants, cut into 1-inch cubes or thin
 slices
Salt
2 tablespoons peanut oil
2 garlic cloves, finely chopped
1-inch piece gingerroot, peeled and finely chopped
3-4 green onions, finely sliced
2 tablespoons dark soy sauce
1-2 tablespoons hot bean sauce or 1 teaspoon
 crushed dried chiles
1 tablespoon yellow bean paste (optional)
2 tablespoons dry sherry or rice wine
1 tablespoon cider vinegar
1 tablespoon sugar
Chopped parsley to garnish

2 tablespoons vegetable oil
Small piece gingerroot, peeled and sliced
1 teaspoon minced garlic
1 lb. zucchini, peeled and cut into small wedges
1 small carrot, sliced
2-3 tablespoons stock or water
2 ozs. straw mushrooms, halved lengthwise
1 tomato, sliced
2 green onions, cut into short lengths
Salt and freshly ground pepper
½ teaspoon sugar
1 tablespoon fish sauce

Place eggplant cubes in a plastic or stainless
steel colander or sieve, placed on a plate or
baking sheet. Sprinkle with salt and let stand
30 minutes. Rinse eggplant under cold running water and turn out onto layers of paper
towels; pat dry thoroughly. Heat wok until
very hot. Add oil and swirl to coat wok. Add
garlic, gingerroot and green onions and stir-
fry 1 or 2 minutes or until green onions begin
to soften. Add eggplant and stir-fry 2 or 3
minutes or until softened and beginning to
brown.

Heat oil in a wok or frying pan over high
heat and stir-fry ginger and garlic about 30
seconds until fragrant. Add the zucchini and
carrot and stir-fry about 2 minutes, then add
the broth or water to create steam, and cook,
stirring, 1-2 minutes.

Stir in remaining ingredients and ⅔ cup
water and bring to a boil. Reduce heat and
simmer 5 to 7 minutes or until eggplant is
very tender, stirring frequently. Increase heat
to high and stir-fry mixture until the liquid is
almost completely reduced. Spoon into a
serving dish and garnish with parsley.

Makes 4 to 6 servings.

Add straw mushrooms, tomato and green
onions with salt, pepper and sugar, blend
well and cook 1-2 minutes. Sprinkle with
fish sauce and serve at once.

Makes 4 servings.

Variation: Other fresh delicate vegetables,
such as asparagus, snow peas, green bell
peppers or cucumber can all be cooked in the
same way.

BROCCOLI & TOMATOES

2¼ lbs. tomatoes
3 tablespoons olive oil
1 garlic clove, crushed
2 teaspoons lemon juice
1 teaspoon hot pepper sauce
1 teaspoon balsamic vinegar
1 lb. broccoli
¼ cup sliced pitted ripe olives
¼ cup pine nuts, toasted
1 tablespoon chopped fresh parsley
¼ cup Parmesan shavings

Into a large heatproof bowl, place tomatoes. Pour boiling water over to cover.

Leave 1 minute, then drain. Refresh under cold water and pat dry. Peel and discard skins and seeds and finely chop flesh. In a large saucepan, heat oil. Add tomatoes, garlic, lemon juice, hot pepper sauce and vinegar. Bring to a boil, cover and cook 10 minutes. Uncover, increase heat and cook until slightly reduced and thickened.

Meanwhile, cut broccoli into flowerets. Steam 5 minutes. Add to sauce with olives, nuts and parsley and stir until combined. Transfer to a warmed serving dish. Sprinkle with Parmesan shavings and serve at once.

Makes 4 servings.

BROCCOLI WITH CHILES

1 lb. broccoli
Olive oil
2 garlic cloves, sliced
2 diced red chiles, seeded and crushed
Salt

With a sharp knife, cut thick broccoli stems in half or thirds lengthwise. Add all of broccoli to a saucepan of boiling salted water and boil 2 minutes, then drain and rinse under cold running water.

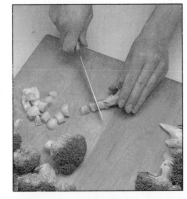

In a heavy skillet large enough to hold broccoli in a single layer, heat oil. Add garlic and chiles to pan. Cook over medium heat 3 to 4 minutes or until sizzling.

Add broccoli and turn to coat in oil and then reduce heat to very low. Pour in ½ cup water, add salt and cover tightly. Simmer about 20 minutes, turning broccoli carefully 2 or 3 times or until broccoli is tender. If necessary, uncover and boil off excess liquid. Serve hot or warm.

Makes 4 servings.

SPICY CAULIFLOWER

¼ cup whole blanched almonds
1 large cauliflower, separated into flowerets
¼ cup butter
1 onion, finely chopped
½ teaspoon chile powder
½ teaspoon turmeric
3-4 tablespoons lemon juice
½ cup dried bread crumbs
Salt and freshly ground pepper

Heat a wok until hot. Add almonds and dry-fry over medium heat until browned on all sides. Remove to a plate and cool. Chop almonds coarsely; set aside.

Half-fill the wok with water and over high heat, bring to a boil. Add cauliflower and simmer 2 minutes. Drain and rinse; set aside. Wipe wok dry and return to heat. Add butter to wok and swirl until melted. Add onion, chile powder and turmeric and stir-fry 2 or 3 minutes or until softened.

Add cauliflower and lemon juice and stir-fry 3 or 4 minutes or until crisp-tender. Add bread crumbs and chopped almonds and toss until cauliflowerets are well coated. Serve hot.

Makes 4 to 6 servings.

GINGERED BRUSSELS SPROUTS

2 tablespoons vegetable oil
1 onion, cut lengthwise in half and thinly sliced
1-2 garlic cloves, finely chopped
1 (1-inch) piece gingerroot, peeled and cut into julienne strips
2 lbs. Brussels sprouts, trimmed and shredded
1 tablespoon chopped stem ginger in syrup
Salt and red (cayenne) pepper

Heat a wok until hot. Add oil and swirl to coat wok. Add onion, garlic and gingerroot and stir-fry 1 minute. Stir in shredded sprouts and stem ginger and stir-fry 2 or 3 minutes.

Add 2 tablespoons water and cook, covered, 2 or 3 minutes, stirring once or twice. Uncover and add 1 tablespoon water if sprouts seem too dry. Season with salt and cayenne.

Makes 4 to 6 servings.

MUSHROOM CURRY

1 lb. button mushrooms
2 green chiles, seeded
2 teaspoons ground coriander
1 teaspoon ground cumin
½ teaspoon chile powder
2 garlic cloves, crushed
1 onion, cut into wedges
⅔ cup coconut milk
Salt to taste
2 tablespoons butter
Fresh bay leaves, to garnish if desired

Wipe mushrooms and trim stalks. Set aside.

Put chiles, coriander, cumin, chile powder, garlic, onion and coconut milk in a blender or food processor fitted with the metal blade and blend until smooth. Season to taste with salt.

Melt butter in a saucepan, add mushrooms and cook 3 to 4 minutes until golden brown. Add spice mixture, reduce heat and simmer, uncovered, 10 minutes, or until mushrooms are tender. Serve hot, garnished with bay leaves, if desired.

Makes 4 servings.

BELL PEPPERS & CAULIFLOWER

¼ cup vegetable oil
1 large onion, sliced
2 garlic cloves, crushed
2 green chiles, seeded, chopped
1 cauliflower, cut into small flowerets
½ teaspoon ground turmeric
1 teaspoon garam masala
¼ cup water
1 green bell pepper
1 red bell pepper
1 orange or yellow bell pepper
Salt and pepper to taste
1 tablespoon chopped cilantro (fresh coriander) to garnish

Heat oil in a large saucepan, add onion and cook over medium heat 8 minutes, or until soft and golden brown. Stir in garlic, chiles and cauliflowerets and cook 5 minutes, stirring occasionally. Stir in turmeric and garam masala; cook 1 minute.

Reduce heat and add water. Cover and cook 10 to 15 minutes, until cauliflower is almost tender. Meanwhile, cut peppers in half lengthwise; remove stalks and seeds and thinly slice peppers. Add to pan and cook another 3 to 5 minutes, until softened. Season with salt and pepper. Serve hot, garnished with chopped cilantro.

Makes 4 servings.

EGGPLANT IN SPICY SAUCE

CAULIFLOWER & COCONUT

1 lb. eggplant, cut into small strips
2-3 tablespoons vegetable oil
1 clove garlic, chopped
2 shallots, finely chopped
Salt and freshly ground black pepper
½ teaspoon sugar
2-3 small hot red chiles, seeded and chopped
2 tomatoes, cut into wedges
1 tablespoon soy sauce
1 teaspoon chile sauce
1 tablespoon rice vinegar
About ½ cup vegetarian stock
2 teaspoons cornstarch
½ teaspoon sesame oil
Cilantro leaves to garnish

1 cauliflower
2 tablespoons light olive oil
1 teaspoon sesame oil
1 red chile, seeded and sliced
1 (½-inch) piece gingerroot, finely chopped
2 shallots, thinly sliced
⅓ cup shredded coconut
1 tablespoon light soy sauce
1 teaspoon sherry vinegar

Trim and discard cauliflower leaves and cut out central core. Cut flowerets into bite-size pieces. Steam 5 to 6 minutes or until crisp-tender.

Stir-fry the eggplant in a dry wok or frying pan 3-4 minutes or until soft and a small amount of natural juice has appeared. Remove and set aside. Add the oil and heat. Stir-fry garlic and shallots about 30 seconds. Add the eggplant, salt, pepper, sugar and chiles and stir-fry 2-3 minutes.

Meanwhile, in a nonstick skillet, heat 1 tablespoon of the olive oil and the sesame oil. Add chile, gingerroot and shallots; cook 5 minutes or until softened.

Add the tomatoes, soy sauce, chile sauce, vinegar and stock, blend well and bring to a boil. Reduce heat and simmer 3-4 minutes. Mix cornstarch with 1 tablespoon water and stir into sauce. Cook, stirring, until thickened. Blend in sesame oil, garnish and serve.

Makes 4 servings.

Variation: For nonvegetarians, fish sauce or shrimp paste can be used instead of soy sauce. Chicken stock can be used instead of the vegetarian stock.

Add coconut. Stir-fry over medium heat 3 to 4 minutes or until golden. Stir in cauliflower, remaining oil, soy sauce and vinegar. Serve hot or warm.

Makes 4 servings.

STIR-FRIED VEGETABLES

2 tablespoons vegetable oil
1 clove garlic, chopped
1 teaspoon chopped gingerroot
1 carrot, sliced
4 ozs. baby corn cobs, halved
1-2 young leeks, sliced
1-2 bok choy (Chinese cabbage), cut into small
   pieces
4 ozs. snow peas
4 ozs. bean sprouts
Salt and freshly ground black pepper
1 tablespoon soy sauce
2 teaspoons cornstarch
½ teaspoon sesame oil (optional)

Heat oil in a wok or frying-pan over high heat and stir-fry garlic and ginger about 30 seconds. Add the carrot, baby corn, leeks, bok choy and snow peas and stir-fry about 2 minutes.

Add bean sprouts and stir-fry 1 minute. Add salt, pepper and soy sauce and stir-fry 2 minutes. Mix cornstarch with 1 tablespoon water and stir into the gravy. Cook, stirring, until thickened. Finally blend in sesame oil, if using, then serve vegetables hot or cold.

Makes 4-6 servings.

Variation: Fish or oyster sauce can be used instead of soy sauce a nonvegetarians.

SPICED CABBAGE

14 peppercorns
2 tablespoons coconut cream
2 shallots, chopped
4 ozs. lean pork, finely chopped
About 1 lb. white cabbage, finely sliced
1¼ cups coconut milk
1 tablespoon fish sauce
1 fresh red chile, very finely chopped

In a wok, heat peppercorns about 3 minutes, until aroma changes. Stir in coconut cream, heat 2 to 3 minutes, then stir in shallots.

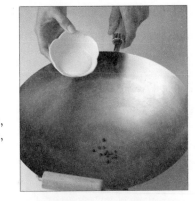

Stir-fry 2 to 3 minutes, then stir in pork and cabbage. Cook, stirring occasionally, 3 minutes. Add coconut milk and bring just to a boil. Reduce heat, cover and simmer 5 minutes.

Uncover and cook about 10 minutes until cabbage is crisp-tender. Stir in fish sauce. Sprinkle with chopped chile.

Makes 4 to 5 servings.

POLENTA WITH VEGETABLES

Salt and freshly ground pepper
Scant 1 cup polenta
1 tablespoon butter
1 small eggplant, thinly sliced
1 zucchini, thinly sliced
½ cup olive oil
1 red bell pepper, quartered
Basil sprigs to garnish

MIXED VEGETABLES

2-3 tablespoons vegetable oil
12 ozs. bok choy (Chinese leaves), cut into large
  pieces
4-6 dried Chinese mushrooms, soaked and sliced
2 ozs. bean thread vermicelli, soaked and cut into
  short lengths
2 ozs. dried bean curd sticks, soaked and cut into
  short sections
2 ozs. dried lily buds, soaked
4 ozs. sliced bamboo shoots, drained
4 ozs. broccoli flowerets
Salt and freshly ground black pepper
2 tablespoons soy sauce
½ teaspoon sesame oil

Put 2½ cups water in a saucepan and bring to a boil. Add a pinch of salt then pour in polenta in a fine, steady stream, stirring vigorously with a wooden spoon.

Heat oil in a Dutch oven over high heat and stir-fry the bok choy 2-3 minutes.

Simmer 5 to 10 minutes, stirring frequently until polenta is thick and no longer grainy. Remove pan from heat and stir in butter and black pepper. Turn polenta on to an oiled baking sheet or wooden board and spread out to a thickness of ¼ to ½ inch. Cool, cover and refrigerate 1 hour. With a 2½- to 3-inch pastry cutter, cut into eight circles. Preheat broiler. Brush eggplant and zucchini with oil and broil until browned on both sides. Keep warm.

Broil bell pepper quarters and peel. Keep warm. Brush polenta circles with oil and broil 3 or 4 minutes on each side until browned and crisp. Place a polenta circle on each of four serving plates and arrange vegetable slices on top. Season with salt and pepper and top with a polenta circle. Garnish with basil and serve.

Makes 4 servings.

Add the soaked mushrooms, vermicelli, bean curd sticks, lily buds, bamboo shoots and broccoli and stir-fry 2 minutes, then add salt, pepper, soy sauce and some of the mushroom soaking water. bring to a boil, cover and simmer 2-3 minutes. Blend in the sesame oil. Serve hot straight from the pot.

Makes 4-6 servings.

BAKED MIXED VEGETABLES

2¼ cups thinly sliced eggplants (1 lb.)
Salt and black pepper
⅔ cup olive oil
3 garlic cloves, crushed
3 cups peeled, seeded and chopped beefsteak
  tomatoes
1 tablespoon tomato paste
2 Spanish onions, thinly sliced
1 green bell pepper, sliced
1 lb. potatoes, boiled and sliced
½ cup fresh bread crumbs

VEGETABLES IN SPICY SAUCE

2-3 tablespoons vegetable oil
1 (8-oz.) cake tofu, cut into small cubes
½ teaspoon minced garlic
2 shallots, sliced
1 tablespoon curry powder
2 tablespoons soy sauce
1 tablespoon chopped lemon grass
1 tablespoon chopped gingerroot
1 teaspoon chile sauce (optional)
1 cup coconut milk
½ teaspoon salt
1 tablespoon sugar
2 small carrots and 1 onion, sliced
4-6 ozs. cauliflower flowerets
8 ozs. green beans, trimmed and cut in half
2 firm tomatoes, cut into wedges

In a colander, sprinkle eggplant slices with salt and leave 30 minutes. Rinse under cold running water and dry well on paper towels. Meanwhile, in a saucepan, heat 1 tablespoon of the oil. Add garlic and fry gently without browning. Add tomatoes, tomato paste, salt and black pepper. Cover and simmer 15 minutes. Meanwhile, preheat oven to 400F (205C). In a skillet, heat 4 tablespoons of the oil.

Heat oil in a wok or large fry-pan and fry the tofu until browned on all sides. Remove and drain. Stir-fry the garlic and shallots in the same oil about 1 minute, then add curry powder, soy sauce, lemon grass, ginger and chile sauce, if using, and cook 1 minute. Add the coconut milk, salt and sugar and bring to a boil.

Add onions and bell pepper and cook 15 minutes, stirring occasionally. Using a slotted spoon, remove from pan; set aside. Add remaining oil to pan. Add eggplant slices in batches and fry until golden. Drain on paper towels. Layer all the vegetables in a baking dish, season each layer with salt and black pepper and moisten with the tomato sauce. Finish with tomato sauce. Sprinkle with bread crumbs. Bake about 20 minutes or until golden.

Makes 4 to 6 servings.

Add the carrots, onion, cauliflower, beans and tofu and stir-fry 3-4 minutes, then add the tomatoes. Blend well and cook 2 minutes. Serve at once.

Makes 4-6 servings.

Variation: For nonvegetarians, either fish sauce or oyster sauce can be used instead of soy sauce this dish.

PEPERONATA

2 green bell peppers
1 red bell pepper
⅓ cup olive oil
1 onion, coarsely chopped
1 garlic clove, crushed
1½ lbs. tomatoes, peeled, seeded and chopped
Pinch of sugar
Salt and freshly ground pepper
1 tablespoon chopped Italian parsley
Italian parsley sprig to garnish

Preheat broiler. Place whole peppers under hot broiler about 10 minutes, turning occasionally, until skins are evenly blistered and blackened.

Transfer to a plastic bag a few minutes, then peel away and discard skins. Cut peppers in half, remove and discard seeds and cut peppers into strips. Heat oil in a large skillet over medium heat. Add onion and garlic and cook 3 minutes to soften. Stir in tomatoes and sugar and cook 10 to 12 minutes until thickened.

Add pepper strips and simmer 5 minutes until peppers are soft. Season with salt and freshly ground pepper and serve hot sprinkled with chopped Italian parsley and garnished with Italian parsley sprig.

Makes 4 servings.

CHAR-BROILED ARTICHOKES

⅓ cup olive oil
1 garlic clove, crushed
2 tablespoons chopped fresh parsley
Salt and freshly ground pepper
6 baby artichokes
Flat-leaf parsley sprigs to garnish
RED BELL PEPPER SAUCE:
1 tablespoon olive oil
1 small onion, chopped
2 red bell peppers, diced
1 cup vegetable stock

Mix together olive oil, garlic, parsley, salt and pepper. Set aside.

To make red bell pepper sauce, heat oil in a saucepan. Add onion and cook 5 minutes or until soft. Add red bell peppers and cook over low heat 5 minutes. Pour in stock, bring to a boil, reduce heat and simmer 10 minutes. Push through a sieve or purée in a food processor or blender. Season with salt and pepper.

Trim bases of artichokes and remove any tough outer leaves. Cut artichokes in half lengthwise and immediately brush with seasoned oil. Preheat a ridged broiler pan, add artichokes and cook over a medium heat 10 minutes, turning once, until browned on both sides. Reheat sauce. Drizzle artichokes with remaining seasoned oil, garnish with parsley and serve with red bell pepper sauce.

Makes 3 or 4 servings.

RATATOUILLE

2 eggplant, sliced
3 zucchini, sliced
3-4 tablespoons olive oil
1 Spanish onion, very thinly sliced
3 garlic cloves, crushed
2 large red bell peppers, thinly sliced
4 ripe beefsteak tomatoes, peeled, seeded and
    chopped
Leaves from a few sprigs of thyme, marjoram and
    oregano
Salt and freshly ground pepper
2 tablespoons each chopped fresh parsley and basil

Put eggplant and zucchini in a colander, sprinkle generously with salt and let stand 1 hour.

Rinse well, drain and dry thoroughly with paper towels. Heat 2 tablespoons of the oil in a heavy Dutch oven, add eggplant and cook, stirring occasionally, a few minutes. Add 1 tablespoon more oil, onion and garlic and cook, stirring occasionally, 2 minutes. Add bell peppers and cook, stirring occasionally, 2 minutes.

Add zucchini to pan with more oil if necessary. Cook, stirring occasionally, 2 or 3 minutes, then add tomatoes, thyme, marjoram and oregano. Season lightly with salt and pepper, cover and cook over very low heat 30 to 40 minutes, stirring occasionally. Stir in parsley and basil and cook, uncovered, 5 to 10 minutes or until liquid has evaporated. Serve warm or cold.

Makes 4 servings.

ZUCCHINI WITH CHEESE

1½ lbs. zucchini
2 tablespoons extra-virgin olive oil
1 large onion, chopped
1 teaspoon chopped fresh mint
2 eggs
1½ cups grated kefaloriri cheese (6 ozs.)
¼ teaspoon grated nutmeg
Salt and pepper

Preheat oven to 350F (175C). Trim zucchini ends, then cut into ½-inch slices. Put zucchini slices into a steamer above boiling water and steam a few minutes or until crisp-tender. Cook in batches, if necessary.

In a skillet, heat oil, add onion and cook until soft. Mix zucchini and mint with onion, then put in a baking dish.

In a bowl, beat eggs with cheese, nutmeg, salt and pepper, then pour over the zucchini. Bake 20 minutes, or until top is lightly browned.

Makes 4 servings.

Variation: This dish may also be made with summer squash.

FUNGHETTO

1 eggplant (about 8 ozs.), diced
2 cups thinly sliced zucchini (about 8 ozs.)
Salt
½ oz. dried porcini mushrooms
2 tablespoons butter
¼ cup olive oil
2 garlic cloves, crushed
4 cups sliced button or oyster mushrooms or a
  mixture (8 ozs.)
2 tablespoons rosemary leaves
2 tablespoons chopped Italian parsley
Freshly ground pepper
Rosemary sprig to garnish

Put eggplant and zucchini into a colander. Sprinkle with salt and drain 30 minutes.

Rinse thoroughly to remove salt and drain on paper towels. Put dried mushrooms into a small bowl. Cover with warm water and soak 20 minutes. Strain, reserving 3 tablespoons soaking liquid. Rinse thoroughly and chop.

Heat butter and oil in a large heavy skillet. Add garlic and sauté 1 minute. Add eggplant, zucchini, fresh and dried mushrooms and rosemary. Sauté 3 to 4 minutes. Stir in reserved porcini soaking liquor and the parsley, reduce heat and cook 20 minutes until vegetables are soft and liquid evaporated. Season with salt and freshly ground pepper. Garnish with rosemary sprig.

Makes 4 to 6 servings.

ZUCCHINI WITH GARLIC

6 medium-size zucchini
1 cup corn oil or peanut oil
1 cup light olive oil
2 garlic cloves, finely chopped
⅓ cup red wine vinegar
1 to 2 tablespoons chopped dill
Salt and freshly ground pepper
12 mint leaves

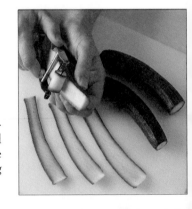

Preheat oven to 375F (190C). Using a vegetable peeler and pressing quite firmly, peel along the length of the zucchini to remove long thick strips. Divide between 2 baking sheets; bake 20 minutes until crisp-tender.

Transfer zucchini to paper towels to drain 30 minutes. Preheat the oils together in a saucepan or deep-fryer to 375F (190C). Line a baking sheet with paper towels. Fry zucchini slices in batches in the hot oil 2 to 3 minutes until light golden-brown. Transfer to paper towels to drain. When all the zucchini are cooked and drained transfer to a serving dish.

Add garlic, wine vinegar, dill, salt and freshly ground pepper to zucchini. Toss gently to mix. Cover and refrigerate at least 2 hours. Serve sprinkled with mint leaves.

Makes 6 servings.

SAUCES & SALAD DRESSINGS

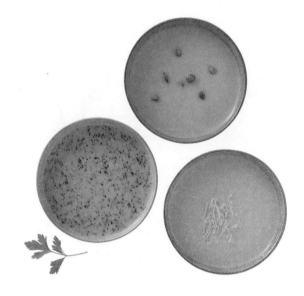

BASIC WHITE SAUCE

WHITE SAUCE VARIATIONS

2 tablespoons margarine
¼ cup all-purpose flour
1¼ cups low-fat milk
Salt and pepper

In a saucepan over low heat, melt low-fat margarine. Stir in flour and cook 1 minute, stirring.

CHEESE SAUCE

Follow recipe for Basic White Sauce. Before seasoning with salt and pepper, stir in ½ cup shredded Cheddar cheese and 1 teaspoon prepared mustard. Serve with fish, poultry, ham, vegetables, or egg dishes.

Remove pan from heat and gradually stir or whisk in the milk. Return pan to heat. Bring slowly to a boil, stirring or whisking, and continue to cook until mixtures thickens.

PARSLEY SAUCE

Follow recipe for Basic White Sauce. After seasoning with salt and pepper, stir in 2 tablespoons finely chopped fresh parsley. Serve with fish or ham.

Simmer 3 minutes. Remove pan from heat and season with salt and pepper. Serve with meat, poultry, fish, or vegetables.

Makes 1¼ cups.

CAPER SAUCE

Follow recipe for Basic White Sauce. Before seasoning with salt and pepper, stir in 2 tablespoons capers and 2 teaspoons vinegar from jar of capers. Reheat gently before serving. Serve with lamb or fish.

TARRAGON SAUCE

2 tablespoons margarine
¼ cup all-purpose flour
1¼ cups chicken stock
⅔ cup milk
2 tablespoons tarragon vinegar
Few sprigs tarragon
2 teaspoons Dijon mustard
½ cup shredded Cheddar cheese
Salt and pepper

In a saucepan over low heat, melt margarine. Stir in flour and cook 1 minute, stirring. Remove pan from heat and gradually stir or whisk in stock, milk, and vinegar.

Return pan to heat. Bring slowly to a boil, stirring or whisking, then continue to cook until mixture thickens. Simmer 3 minutes. Finely chop tarragon.

Stir tarragon into sauce along with mustard, cheese, salt, and pepper and reheat gently, but do not let sauce boil. Serve with chicken or turkey.

Makes 2¼ cups.

BECHAMEL SAUCE

1 small onion or shallot
1 small carrot
½ stalk celery
1 bay leaf
6 black peppercorns
Several sprigs parsley
1¼ cups milk
2 tablespoons margarine
¼ cup all-purpose flour
Salt and pepper

Slice onion or shallot and carrot. Chop celery roughly. Put vegetables, bay leaf, peppercorns, and parsley into a saucepan with milk and bring slowly to a boil.

Remove pan from heat, cover, and set aside to infuse 30 minutes. Strain into a measuring cup, reserving milk. In a saucepan over low heat, melt margarine. Stir in flour and cook 1 minute, stirring.

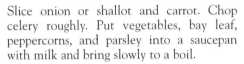

Remove pan from heat and gradually stir or whisk in flavored milk. Bring slowly to a boil, stirring or whisking, then continue to cook until mixture thickens. Simmer 3 minutes. Remove pan from heat and season with salt and pepper. Serve with poultry, fish, vegetables, or egg dishes.

Makes 1¼ cups.

SPICY ZUCCHINI SAUCE

2 zucchini
1 green bell pepper
1 small onion
1 garlic clove
2 tablespoons margarine
1 teaspoon ground coriander
½ teaspoon ground cumin
½ teaspoon chile powder
¼ teaspoon red (cayenne) pepper
¼ teaspoon turmeric
⅔ cup vegetable stock
Salt and pepper

Trim the zucchini, then coarsely grate them.

Seed and finely chop bell pepper. Finely chop onion and crush garlic. In a saucepan over low heat, melt margarine. Add zucchini, bell pepper, onion, and garlic and cook 5 minutes, stirring.

Stir in spices, stock, salt, and pepper and mix well. Bring slowly to a boil, then cover and simmer 25 minutes, stirring occasionally. Remove pan from heat and set aside to cool. When slightly cool, in a blender or food processor, purée mixture until smooth. Return sauce to clean saucepan. Reheat gently and adjust seasoning before serving. Serve with shellfish, fish, or meat.

Makes 2 cups.

BROCCOLI & CHEESE SAUCE

8 ozs. broccoli
1 tablespoon cornstarch
1 cup dry white wine
1 garlic clove
⅔ cup low-fat cream cheese
Salt and pepper

Trim broccoli, then cook in a saucepan of boiling water 10 minutes or until tender. Drain, reserving 2 tablespoons of the cooking liquid. Cool broccoli, then, in a blender or food processor, purée with reserved liquid until smooth. Set puréed broccoli aside.

In a saucepan, blend cornstarch and wine. Crush garlic and add to wine mixture. Bring slowly to a boil, stirring constantly, until mixture thickens. Simmer 3 minutes.

Remove pan from heat and stir in cream cheese, puréed broccoli, salt and pepper. Return pan to heat and mix together well. Reheat gently. Adjust seasoning before serving. Serve hot or cold with poultry, beef, or fish.

Makes 2¼ cups.

YELLOW BELL PEPPER SAUCE

2 yellow bell peppers, chopped
½ mild green chile, seeded and finely chopped
1 tablespoon chopped mixed fresh herbs, such as
   parsley, thyme, rosemary, and chives
1¼ cups vegetable stock
2 tablespoons medium-dry white wine
Salt and pepper
1 tablespoon cornstarch

Put peppers, chile, herbs, stock, wine, salt, and pepper into a saucepan and mix together well.

Bring slowly to a boil, then cover and simmer 10 minutes, stirring occasionally. Remove pan from heat and set aside to cool. When slightly cool, in a blender or food processor, purée mixture until smooth. Return sauce to clean saucepan. In a small bowl, blend cornstarch with 2 tablespoons water.

Stir cornstarch mixture into pepper sauce and heat gently until sauce thickens, stirring constantly. Simmer 3 minutes. Remove pan from heat and adjust seasoning before serving. Serve with lamb or vegetables, such as asparagus, broccoli, or corn.

Makes 2 cups.

TOMATO SAUCE

2 tablespoons olive oil
½ Spanish onion, finely chopped
½ garlic clove, chopped
1 red bell pepper, seeded and chopped
6 cups peeled, seeded and chopped beefsteak
   tomatoes
Sugar or tomato paste (optional)
Salt and black pepper

In a skillet, heat oil. Add onion and cook over low heat 5 minutes.

Stir in garlic and bell pepper and cook 10 minutes, stirring occasionally.

Stir tomatoes into pan. Simmer 20 to 30 minutes, stirring occasionally, until thickened. Add sugar or tomato paste, if desired, and season with salt and black pepper. Process in a blender or food processor with the metal blade until puréed, or press through a non-metallic strainer, if desired.

Makes 4 to 6 servings.

GOOSEBERRY SAUCE

1 lb. gooseberries
Finely grated zest and juice of 1 orange
2 tablespoons margarine
2 tablespoons light brown sugar
¼ teaspoon grated nutmeg

Place gooseberries into a saucepan. Add orange zest and juice and ⅔ cup water, mixing together well. Bring the mixture slowly to a boil, then reduce heat, cover saucepan, and simmer 5 to 10 minutes or until gooseberries are soft, stirring occasionally.

Remove pan from heat and set aside to cool. When slightly cool, in a blender or food processor, pur´´e gooseberries until smooth. Return mixture to clean saucepan.

Stir in margarine, sugar and nutmeg. Bring slowly to a boil, stirring, then simmer 1 minute. Serve with oily fish such as mackerel.

Makes 2 cups.

APPLESAUCE WITH MINT

1 small onion
1 lb. cooking appples
Small bunch fresh mint
2 tablespoons sugar

Using a sharp knife, finely chop onion. Peel, core, and slice apples. Put onion, apples, and 2 tablespoons water into a saucepan.

Cover saucepan and simmer until apples and onion are soft, stirring occasionally. Remove pan from heat and mash apples and onion lightly together.

Using a sharp knife, finely chop mint. Add mint to saucepan with sugar, mixing together well. Reheat sauce gently, stirring until sugar dissolves. Serve hot or cold with lamb or pork.

Makes 1⅔ cups.

PLUM SAUCE

12 ozs. red dessert plums
Finely grated zest and juice of 1 orange
¼ cup sugar
½ teaspoon ground cinnamon
1 tablespoon brandy

Halve and pit plums. Place plums into a saucepan and add ⅔ cup cold water.

Bring slowly to a boil, then reduce heat, cover, and simmer until plums are soft, stirring occasionally. Remove pan from heat and set aside to cool. When slightly cool, in a blender or food processor, purée plums and cooking liquid until smooth.

Return sauce to clean saucepan and stir in orange zest, orange juice, sugar, cinnamon, and brandy, mixing together well. Reheat sauce gently before serving or serve sauce cold. Serve with lamb, pork, or beef.

Makes 2¼ cups.

SWEET & SOUR SAUCE

8 ozs. carrots
6 green onions
1 garlic clove
1 (1-inch) piece gingerroot
2 teaspoons olive oil
1 cup unsweetened applesauce
2 cups beef stock
⅔ cup red wine
3 tablespoons lemon juice
2 tablespoons honey
2 tablespoons soy sauce
Salt and pepper
1 tablespoon cornstarch

Grate carrots coarsely and finely chop green onions. Crush garlic. Peel and grate ginger or finely chop. In a saucepan, heat oil 1 minute. Add carrots, green onions, garlic, and gingerroot and cook 5 minutes, stirring. Stir in applesauce, stock, wine, lemon juice, honey, soy sauce, salt, and pepper and mix together well. Bring slowly to a boil, then cover and simmer 1 hour, stirring occasionally. Remove pan from heat and press the sauce through a nylon strainer. Discard pulp and return sauce to clean saucepan.

In a small bowl, blend cornstarch with 1 tablespoon water. Stir cornstarch mixture into sauce and bring slowly to a boil, stirring constantly. Simmer 3 minutes and adjust seasoning before serving. Serve with lamb, pork, fresh vegetables, or mixed beans.

Makes 2¾ cups.

CURRY SAUCE

1 onion
1 garlic clove
2 teaspoon sunflower oil
8 ozs. potatoes
1 (8-oz.) can crushed tomatoes
1¼ cups vegetable stock
1 tablespoon curry powder
1 teaspoon ground bay leaves
Salt and pepper
⅓ cup golden raisins

Finely chop onion and crush garlic. In a saucepan, heat oil 1 minute. Add onion and garlic and cook 5 minutes, stirring.

Peel and coarsely grate potatoes. Add potatoes, tomatoes, stock, curry powder, ground bay leaves, salt, and pepper to saucepan and mix together well. Bring slowly to a boil, then cover and simmer 30 minutes, stirring occasionally. Remove pan from heat and set aside to cool. When slightly cool, in a blender or food processor, purée sauce until smooth.

Return sauce to clean saucepan and add golden raisins. Reheat gently and adjust seasoning before serving. Serve with vegetables or egg dishes.

Makes 3¼ cups.

Variation: The golden raisins can be added with potatoes and tomatoes and puréed, if preferred.

PINEAPPLE-CHUTNEY SAUCE

2 garlic cloves
1 (8-oz.) can sliced pineapple packed in fruit juice
1 (8-oz.) can crushed tomatoes
3 tablespoons cider vinegar
2 tablespoons light brown sugar
2 tablespoons mango chutney
2 teaspoons Worcestershire sauce
½ teaspoon Dijon mustard
½ teaspoon apple pie spice
Few drops hot-pepper sauce
Salt and pepper
1 tablespoon cornstarch

Crush garlic and coarsely chop pineapple.

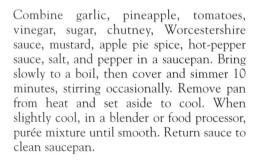

Combine garlic, pineapple, tomatoes, vinegar, sugar, chutney, Worcestershire sauce, mustard, apple pie spice, hot-pepper sauce, salt, and pepper in a saucepan. Bring slowly to a boil, then cover and simmer 10 minutes, stirring occasionally. Remove pan from heat and set aside to cool. When slightly cool, in a blender or food processor, purée mixture until smooth. Return sauce to clean saucepan.

In a small bowl, blend cornstarch with 1 tablespoon water. Stir cornstarch mixture into sauce and bring slowly to a boil, stirring constantly. Simmer 3 minutes, stirring occasionally and adjust seasoning before serving. Serve with grilled or broiled meats, such as steaks, chops, or chicken.

Makes 1¾ cups.

SPICY FISH SAUCE

2 cloves garlic
2 small red or green chiles, seeded and chopped
1 tablespoon sugar
2 tablespoons lime juice
2 tablespoons fish sauce

Using a pestle and mortar, pound garlic and chiles until finely ground. If you do not have a pestle and mortar, just finely mince the garlic and chiles.

Place mixture in a bowl and add sugar, lime juice, fish sauce and 2-3 tablespoons water. Blend well. Serve in small dipping saucers.

Makes 4 servings.

Note: This sauce is known as *nuoc cham*. You can make a large quantity of the base for later use by boiling the lime juice, fish sauce and water with sugar in a pan. It will keep for months in a tightly sealed jar or bottle in the refrigerator. Add freshly minced garlic and chiles for serving.

SALSA FRESCA

4 large tomatoes, coarsely chopped
1 tablespoon finely chopped cilantro
½ small onion, finely chopped
2 green chiles, finely chopped
Juice of ½ lemon
½ teaspoon salt
1 teaspoon freshly ground pepper

Mix all ingredients together and let stand 15 minutes before serving. Serve as an accompaniment to any bean, rice or meat dish.

Makes 1¼ cups.

Note: Fresh salsa does not keep long, so if there is any left, cook it in a little olive oil and serve as a sauce.

MELBA SAUCE

1 lb. raspberries
1 cup powdered sugar
3 tablespoons medium-dry white wine
1 teaspoon arrowroot

Into a saucepan, put raspberries with 2 table-spoons water. Cover and cook raspberries gently until they are soft. Remove pan from heat and set aside to cool.

When slightly cool, strain raspberries through a nylon strainer, discarding seeds. Sift powdered sugar, then place in saucepan with raspberry sauce and wine, mixing together well. Heat sauce gently until sugar dissolves, then bring to a boil. Remove pan from heat. In a small bowl, blend arrowroot with 1 tablespoon water.

Stir arrowroot mixture into raspberry sauce. Reheat gently until sauce thickens, stirring constantly. Serve hot or cold with peaches, ice cream, or sorbet.

Makes 2¼ cups.

APRICOT SAUCE

8 ozs. dried apricots
¼ cup sugar
1¼ cups dry white wine

Chop apricots roughly. Into a saucepan, place sugar with ⅔ cup water. Heat mixture gently until sugar dissolves.

Stir in apricots and wine, mixing together well. Bring slowly to a boil, then cover and simmer 20 minutes, stirring occasionally. Remove pan from heat and set aside to cool.

When slightly cool, in a blender or food processor, purée mixture until smooth. Return sauce to saucepan and reheat gently before serving. Serve with baked desserts, crêpes, or baked fruit, such as baked pears.

Makes 2¼ cups.

HOT LEMON SAUCE

Grated peel and juice of 3 lemons
⅓ cup butter
⅓ cup superfine sugar
1 teaspoon cornstarch

In a saucepan, combine lemon peel and juice, butter and sugar. Stir over gentle heat until butter melts and sugar dissolves.

Mix cornstarch and a small amount of water to a smooth paste; stir into lemon mixture. Bring sauce to a boil, stirring constantly.

Simmer 1 to 2 minutes, stirring constantly. Keep warm until ready to serve.

Makes 4 to 6 servings.

Note: Serve with Austrian Cheesecake, page 380, if desired.

DARK CHOCOLATE SAUCE

6 ozs. semisweet chocolate
½ cup strong coffee or water
¼ cup superfine sugar

Break chocolate in pieces and put into top of a double boiler or a bowl set over a pan of simmering water. Add coffee or water and sugar.

Stir over medium heat until chocolate melts and sauce is smooth and creamy. Serve hot or cold.

Makes 4 to 6 servings.

Note: Serve with White & Dark Chocolate Terrine, page 391, or Chocolate Profiteroles, page 390, if desired.

THOUSAND ISLAND DRESSING

1 medium-size dill pickle
2 tablespoons chopped red bell pepper
2 tablespoons chopped green bell pepper
1¼ cups reduced-calorie mayonnaise
¼ cup low-fat plain yogurt
2 tablespoons tomato ketchup
1 tablespoons chopped fresh parsley
Salt and pepper

Using a sharp knife, chop pickle finely. In a bowl, mix together pickle and red and green bell peppers.

Stir in mayonnaise, yogurt, tomato ketchup, parsley, salt, and pepper and mix together thoroughly. Cover and leave in a cool place 30 minutes before serving to let flavors develop.

Serve with a fresh mixed seafood salad.

Makes 2½ cups.

Variation: Add 2 cold hard-boiled eggs, mashed or finely chopped, to dressing.

MILD CURRY MAYONNAISE

6 green onions
1 tablespoon low-fat margarine
2 tablespoons mango chutney
1 tablespoon mild curry powder
1 tablespoon shredded coconut
1¼ cups low-fat or nonfat mayonnaise
⅔ cup low-fat plain yogurt
Salt and pepper

Using a sharp knife, trim and chop green onions finely. In a saucepan over low heat, melt margarine. Add green onions and cook 5 minutes, stirring.

Remove pan from heat and stir in chutney, curry powder, and coconut, mixing together well. Set aside to cool.

When cool, mix with mayonnaise, yogurt, salt, and pepper. Cover and leave the sauce in a cool place 30 minutes before serving to let flavors develop. Serve with potato salad or coleslaw.

Makes 2 cups.

HERBY CHEESE DRESSING

1 garlic clove
1 cup low-fat cream cheese
⅔ cup sour cream
2 tablespoons chopped fresh mixed herbs, such as
   parsley, chives, rosemary, and thyme
1 tablespoons lemon juice
Salt and pepper

Peel and crush garlic. Into a bowl, put garlic, cream cheese, cream, herbs, lemon juice, salt, and pepper.

Whisk ingredients together until thoroughly mixed. Cover and leave dressing in a cool place 30 minutes before serving to let flavors develop.

Adjust seasoning before serving. Serve with fresh salad leaves, raw or cooked vegetables, a pasta salad, or a beef salad.

Makes 1½ cups.

ORANGE-CINNAMON DRESSING

⅔ cup unsweetened orange juice
6 tablespoons white-wine vinegar
¼ cup sunflower oil
Finely grated zest and juice of 1 orange
1 teaspoon ground cinnamon
Salt and pepper

Into a bowl, put orange juice, vinegar, oil, orange zest and squeezed juice, cinnamon, salt, and pepper. Beat ingredients together until thoroughly mixed.

Alternatively, place all ingredients in a clean jelly jar. Screw top on jar and shake until all ingredients are thoroughly mixed together.

Adjust seasoning before serving. Serve with fresh salad leaves, pasta salad, cooked or raw vegetables, or cold, sliced pork.

Makes 1¼ cups.

Variation: Use all freshly squeezed orange juice extra flavor.

CILANTRO & LIME DRESSING

⅔ cup white grape juice
6 tablespoons white-wine vinegar
¼ cup sunflower oil
2 tablespoons chopped fresh cilantro
Finely grated zest of 1 lime
Juice of 2 limes
1 teaspoon sugar
Salt and pepper

Into a bowl, put grape juice, vinegar, oil, cilantro, lime rind, lime juice, sugar, salt, and pepper.

Beat ingredients together until thoroughly mixed. Alternatively, put all ingredients in a clean jelly jar. Screw top on jar and shake until all ingredients are thoroughly mixed together.

Adjust seasoning before serving. Serve with fresh salad leaves, fish, or cold, sliced cooked meats.

Makes 1½ cups.

Variation: In place of the lime zest and juice, use lemon or orange zest and a mixture of chopped fresh herbs, such as parsley, thyme, and basil.

FRESH TARRAGON DRESSING

¾ cup low-fat cream cheese
⅔ cup half and half or low-fat yogurt
2 tablespoons chopped fresh tarragon
1 tablespoon tarragon vinegar
Salt and pepper

Into a bowl, put cream cheese and half and half or yogurt and mix together well.

Stir in tarragon, vinegar, salt, and pepper, mixing together well. Cover and leave dressing in a cool place 30 minutes before serving to let flavors develop. Adjust seasoning before serving.

Serve with asparagus or hot or cold sliced cooked meats, such as chicken or turkey.

Makes 1⅓ cups.

Variation: Use low-fat milk in place of the half and half or yogurt, for a lower-calorie/lower-fat dressing.

BREADS

CHAPATI

1¼ cups all-purpose flour
1¼ cups whole-wheat flour
Salt to taste
About ¾ cup water
¼ cup butter or ghee, melted, plus extra for serving

Sift together flours and salt into a medium bowl, add any bran remaining in sifter. Mix in enough water to make a soft dough.

Knead dough on a lightly floured surface about 5 minutes, until smooth and pliable, then with wet hands, knead dough 1 minute more to make it extra smooth. Wrap in plastic wrap; refrigerate 30 minutes. Divide dough into 12 pieces and roll each out on a lightly floured surface to a 5-inch round.

Heat a griddle or heavy skillet over medium heat; cook rounds one at a time, floured side down, 1 to 2 minutes, until beginning to bubble on surface. Turn over and cook 30 to 60 seconds, pressing with a folded dry cloth during cooking to make them puff up. Wrap chapatis in a dry cloth as they are ready. Serve warm, brushed with extra melted butter.

Makes 12.

NAAN

4 cups all-purpose flour
1 teaspoon baking powder
½ teaspoon baking soda
Salt to taste
1 egg, beaten
6 tablespoons plain yogurt
3 tablespoons butter or ghee, melted
About 1 cup milk
1 tablespoon poppy seeds

Sift together flour, baking powder, baking soda and salt into a medium bowl.

Stir in egg, yogurt and 2 tablespoons butter. Gradually mix in enough milk to make a soft dough. Cover bowl with a damp cloth and put in a warm place 2 hours. Preheat oven to 400F (205C). Knead dough on a lightly floured surface for 2 to 3 minutes until smooth, then divide dough into 8 pieces.

Roll each piece into a ball, then roll out to make ovals about 6 inches long, pulling ends to stretch dough into shape. Brush ovals with water and place wet side down on greased baking sheets. Brush dry side with melted butter; sprinkle with poppy seeds. Bake 8 to 10 minutes, until puffy and golden brown.

Makes 8.

TOMATO & ONION BREAD

4 cups bread flour or all-purpose flour
Pinch of salt
1 (¼-oz.) package active dry yeast (about 1
    tablespoon)
1 teaspoon sugar
Scant 1 cup warm water (110F/45C)
4 tablespoons extra-virgin olive oil
1 onion, finely chopped
1 garlic clove, crushed
4 ozs. sun-dried tomatoes preserved in oil, drained
9 large basil leaves
Freshly ground pepper
Milk to glaze
1 teaspoon coarse sea salt
Basil leaves to garnish

Sift flour and salt into a large bowl. In a small bowl, dissolve yeast and sugar in warm water. Let stand 5 to 10 minutes until frothy.

Stir 3 tablespoons of the olive oil into yeast mixture. Using a wooden spoon, gradually stir yeast mixture into flour to give a soft, but not sticky, dough. Knead on a lightly floured surface 5 minutes until smooth and elastic. Put dough into an oiled medium-size bowl, cover and let rise in a warm place 35 to 40 minutes until doubled in size.

Oil a baking sheet. Heat remaining 1 table-spoon oil in a skillet, add onion and garlic, and cook 3 minutes until softened. Remove skillet from heat and set aside. Turn out dough onto a lightly floured surface and cut in half. Roll out to give 2 rectangles each about 12- x 9-inches. Transfer 1 piece to the baking sheet and prick surface with a fork.

Spread cooked onion mixture over pricked dough, leaving a ½-inch border around the edge. Arrange sun-dried tomatoes and basil leaves over onion and season with freshly ground pepper. Moisten edges of dough with a little cold water and cover with second sheet of dough.

Crimp dough edges to seal. Using a sharp knife mark a lattice pattern on surface of dough. Brush with a little milk to glaze and sprinkle with coarse sea salt. Let rise 20 minutes. Preheat oven to 450F (230C). Bake loaf in preheated oven about 25 minutes until golden-brown and underside is firm and lightly colored. Serve warm or cold, on its own as part of the antipasti. Cut into pieces and garnish with basil leaves.

Makes 1 large loaf.

WALNUT BREAD

1 (¼-oz.) package active dry yeast
1 tablespoon honey
⅔ cup warm milk (110F/45C)
3 cups bread flour or all-purpose flour
3 cups whole-wheat flour
1½ teaspoons salt
2 tablespoons butter, diced
1¼ cups chopped walnuts
2 teaspoons fennel seeds, lightly crushed
½ teaspoon grated nutmeg
About 1 cup warm water
Milk to glaze

In a small bowl, dissolve yeast and honey in milk. Let stand 5 to 10 minutes until frothy.

Sift flours and salt into a large bowl. Rub butter into flour. Stir in walnuts, 1 teaspoon of the fennel seeds and the grated nutmeg.

Using a wooden spoon, stir yeast mixture into flour mixture, then gradually beat in enough water to form a soft, but not sticky, dough.

Knead dough on a lightly floured surface 5 minutes until elastic. Put dough into an oiled large bowl, cover and let rise in a warm place 35 to 40 minutes until doubled in size. Turn out onto a lightly floured surface and knead 5 minutes.

Preheat oven to 425F (220C). Oil a 6-inch round pan. Divide dough into 7 equal pieces and shape into balls. Arrange balls in oiled pan. Brush tops with milk and sprinkle with remaining 1 teaspoon fennel seeds. Let rise in a warm place 25 minutes. Bake in preheated oven about 45 minutes until browned and bottom sounds hollow when tapped.

Turn bread out onto wire rack and cool. Serve as part of the antipasti.

Makes 1 large loaf.

Note: This bread is delicious served with cheese and fish dishes, for soaking up olive oil dressings and is particularly good toasted.

FOCACCIA

4 cups bread flour or all-purpose flour
Pinch of salt
1 (¼-oz.) package active dry yeast (about 1 tablespoon)
1 teaspoon sugar
1 cup warm milk (110F/45C)
¼ cup extra-virgin olive oil, plus extra for brushing
2 teaspoons rosemary
Coarse sea salt

Sift flour and salt into a large bowl.

In a small bowl, dissolve yeast and sugar in milk. Let stand 5 to 10 minutes until frothy. Stir in the ¼ cup olive oil. Using a wooden spoon, gradually beat yeast mixture into flour mixture to give a soft, but not sticky, dough. Knead on a lightly floured surface 5 minutes until smooth and elastic. Place in an oiled medium-size bowl, cover and let rise in a warm place about 40 minutes until doubled in size. Turn out onto a lightly floured surface and knead 5 minutes.

Oil a baking sheet. Roll out dough to a large circle about ½-inch thick and transfer to baking sheet. Brush dough with olive oil, sprinkle with rosemary and sea salt and lightly press into surface. With your finger make deep indentations over surface. Let rise 25 minutes. Preheat oven to 450F (230C). Bake in preheated oven 20 to 25 minutes until golden. Brush again with olive oil. Serve warm.

Makes 1 loaf.

SAVORY PASTRIES

1 recipe Pizza Dough (page 239)
Vegetable oil for deep-frying
FILLING:
3 tablespoons sun-dried tomato paste
2 tablespoons Tapénade, page 24
6 ozs. mozzarella cheese, thinly sliced
Freshly ground pepper
1 egg white, lightly beaten
Italian parsley sprigs to garnish

Make dough and let rise until doubled in size. On a lightly floured surface, roll out dough to ¼-inch thick. Cut out circles using a 4-inch plain round cutter. Spread a little sun-dried tomato paste and Tapénade onto each round of dough. Cut cheese slices in half and place a piece on each dough circle. Season with freshly ground pepper.

Brush edges of dough circles with a little egg white, then fold dough over filling to make half-moon shapes; press edges together to seal. Half-fill a deep-fat fryer with oil. Preheat to 350F (175C). Deep-fry a few pastries at a time, 2 to 3 minutes, turning once, until golden. Using a slotted spoon, transfer to paper towels to drain. Serve hot garnished with parley sprigs.

Makes about 12.

LEEK & BACON KNOTS

1 leek, finely chopped
¼ cup butter, chilled
6 ozs. bacon slices, chopped
2 cups bread flour
2 cups whole-wheat flour
1 teaspoon salt
1 teaspoon sugar
2 teaspoons active dry yeast
⅔ cup lukewarm milk (130F/55C)
¾ cup lukewarm water (130F/55C)
TO FINISH:
1 egg, beaten, and sesame seeds

Into a skillet, put leek and half the butter. Cook over low heat until leek is softened.

Remove leek from pan and cool. In same skillet, cook bacon until slightly crisp. Let cool. Into a bowl, sift bread flour. Stir in whole-wheat flour, salt, sugar and yeast. Cut in remaining butter. Stir in leek and bacon. Make a well in center. Pour in milk and water. Stir until a soft dough is formed. Turn dough out onto a floured surface and knead about 10 minutes, until smooth. Put in an oiled bowl, cover and leave in a warm place until doubled in bulk.

Grease 2 baking sheets. Turn dough onto a floured surface and knead 3 to 4 minutes, until smooth. Divide into 12 pieces, then roll each into a rope about 12 inches long. Tie each one in a knot and place on baking sheets. Cover with plastic wrap and leave in a warm place until doubled in size. Preheat oven to 425F (220C). Brush rolls with egg and sprinkle with sesame seeds. Bake 15 minutes, until golden. Cool on a wire rack.

Makes 12.

CHEESE BUNS

7 cups bread flour
1 envelope active dry yeast (about 1 tablespoon)
2 teaspoons salt
2 teaspoons sugar
2 tablespoons extra-virgin olive oil
About 2 cups warm water
Sesame seeds, to garnish
CHEESE FILLING:
12 ozs. kefalotiri cheese, grated
4 ozs. haloumi cheese, finely chopped
1 tablespoon all-purpose flour
1 teaspoon baking powder
1 tablespoon chopped fresh mint
¼ teaspoon freshly grated nutmeg
4 eggs, beaten

To make the filling, into a bowl, put cheeses. Add flour, baking powder, mint and nutmeg to cheese. Stir in most of beaten egg, reserving extra egg, to make a stiff paste. To make the dough, into a bowl, sift flour. Stir in yeast, salt and sugar. Add oil and mix in enough warm water to make a soft dough. Turn dough out onto a floured surface and knead 10 minutes or until smooth and elastic. Divide into 16 pieces; roll out each piece to a 4-inch circle.

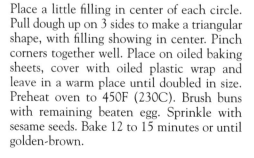

Place a little filling in center of each circle. Pull dough up on 3 sides to make a triangular shape, with filling showing in center. Pinch corners together well. Place on oiled baking sheets, cover with oiled plastic wrap and leave in a warm place until doubled in size. Preheat oven to 450F (230C). Brush buns with remaining beaten egg. Sprinkle with sesame seeds. Bake 12 to 15 minutes or until golden-brown.

Makes 16.

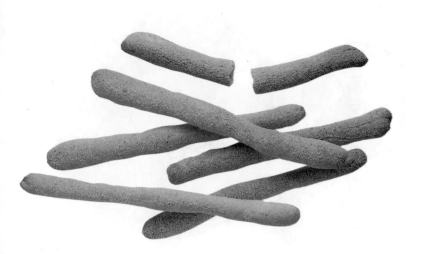

BREADSTICKS

4 cups bread flour or all-purpose flour
½ teaspoon salt
¼ cup grated Parmesan cheese or Provolone cheese
1 (¼-oz.) package active dry yeast (about 1 tablespoon)
1 teaspoon sugar
1¼ cups warm water (110F/45C)
2 tablespoons extra-virgin olive oil, plus extra for oiling
¾ cup polenta or coarse cornmeal

Lightly oil a baking sheet. Roll out dough to a large rectangle and transfer to the baking sheet. Brush surface with a little oil, cover loosely with plastic wrap and let rise in a warm place 35 to 40 minutes until doubled in size. Preheat oven to 450F (230C). Lightly oil 2 more baking sheets. Cut dough into 24 equal pieces. Sprinkle polenta or cornmeal onto work surface. Using your hands, roll each piece of dough into a long thin rope about 9 inches long, coating thoroughly in polenta or cornmeal.

Sift flour and salt into a large bowl. Stir in cheese. In a small bowl, dissolve yeast and sugar in warm water. Let stand 5 to 10 minutes until frothy.

Arrange slightly apart on the baking sheets and bake in preheated oven 15 to 20 minutes until golden and crisp. Cool on wire racks. Serve warm or cold as part of the antipasti.

Makes 24 breadsticks.

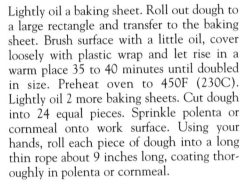

Stir the 2 tablespoons olive oil into yeast mixture. Using a wooden spoon, gradually beat yeast mixture into flour to give a soft dough. Knead dough on a floured surface 5 minutes until smooth and elastic.

Variation: Replace polenta or cornmeal with 3 ounces sesame seeds.

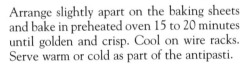

OLIVE BREAD

⅓ cup extra-virgin olive oil
1 onion, finely chopped
7 cups bread flour
1 envelope active dry yeast (about 1 tablespoon)
2 teaspoons salt
About 1 cup warm water
1⅓ cups ripe olives, pitted and chopped

In a skillet, heat oil. Add onion and cook until soft. Let cool. Into a large bowl, sift flour. Stir in yeast and salt. Add 2 table-spoons of the cooking oil and mix in enough water to make a soft dough. Turn dough out onto a floured surface.

Knead dough thoroughly 10 minutes or until smooth and elastic. Knead in 1 tablespoon of the cooking oil, the fried onion, reserving remaining oil, and chopped olives. Cut dough in half and shape into 2 round loaves. Place on lightly oiled baking sheets.

Cover with oiled plastic wrap and leave in a warm place 1 hour, or until doubled in size. Preheat oven to 350F (175C). Brush loaves with a little of the cooking oil. Bake loaves 30 to 40 minutes or until bottom of each sounds hollow when tapped. Brush tops of loaves with remaining oil. Return to the oven 2 minutes, then transfer to wire racks to cool.

Makes 2 loaves.

PITTA BREAD

7 cups bread flour
1 envelope active dry yeast (about 1 tablespoon)
2 teaspoons salt
2 tablespoons extra-virgin olive oil

Into a large bowl, sift flour. Stir in yeast and salt. Add oil and mix in enough water to make a soft dough. Turn dough out onto a floured surface.

Knead dough thoroughly 10 minutes or until smooth and elastic. Cut into 12 equal-size pieces. Roll each piece into a ball, then roll out to an oval shape 7 inches long. Place on floured trays, cover with a cloth and leave in a warm place 1 hour or until doubled in size.

Preheat oven to 475F (240C). Oil 2 baking sheets and place in the oven to heat. Place 3 pitta breads on each baking sheets and sprinkle with water. Bake 5 minutes or until puffed and lightly browned. Remove from baking sheets and wrap in a cloth while baking remaining bread.

Makes 12.

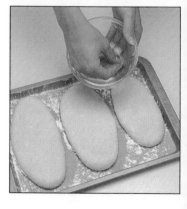

PISSALADIÈRE

¼ cup olive oil, plus extra for brushing
2 lbs. Spanish onions, thinly sliced
1 large garlic clove, crushed
Salt and freshly ground pepper
1 (2-oz.) can anchovies in olive oil
12 large pitted ripe olives, halved
1 teaspoon herbes de Provence
Basil sprigs, to garnish
CRUST:
2 cups bread flour
1 teaspoon herbes de Provence
1 teaspoon fast-acting yeast
1 teaspoon salt

Turn dough out on a lightly floured surface and knead until firm and elastic. Lightly oil a 13 x 9-inch baking pan. Roll out dough to fit pan and put into pan, pushing dough up sides and into corners.

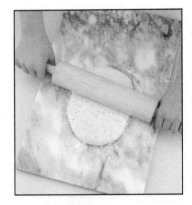

Heat oil in a large, heavy skillet, add onions, garlic, salt and pepper and cook gently, stirring occasionally, 25 to 30 minutes, until onions are soft and golden. Let cool.

Brush dough with oil, cover and let rise 30 minutes or until dough is lightly puffy. Preheat oven to 425F (220C).

Meanwhile, make crust. Stir together flour, herbs, yeast, salt and pepper. Slowly stir in about ¾ cup warm water (105F/40C) to make a smooth dough.

Spread onions over dough. Drain anchovies, reserving oil. Cut anchovies lengthwise in half and arrange in lattice pattern on top of onions. Arrange olives on top, sprinkle with herbs and drizzle with anchovy oil. Bake on top shelf of oven 20 to 25 minutes. Cut into squares, garnish with basil sprigs and serve warm or room temperature.

Makes 4 to 6 servings.

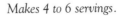

SPANISH COUNTRY BREAD

2 cups bread flour
2 teaspoons salt
1 envelope active dry yeast (about 1 tablespoon)
¾ cup warm water
Olive oil for brushing
Cornmeal for sprinkling

Into a large bowl, sift flour and salt. Stir in yeast and form a well in center. Slowly pour water into well, stirring with a wooden spoon, to make a dough. Beat well until dough comes away from sides of bowl.

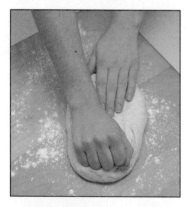

Turn dough out onto a lightly floured surface and knead 10 to 15 minutes or until smooth and elastic; add a little more flour if dough is sticky. Put dough in an oiled bowl, cover and leave in a warm place, about 2½ hours or until doubled in volume. Lightly sprinkle a baking sheet with cornmeal. Turn dough onto lightly floured surface and punch down, then roll to a 16- x 6-inch rectangle. Roll up like a jellyroll and pinch seam to seal.

Place roll, seam-side down, on baking sheet. Using a very sharp knife, make 3 diagonal slashes on roll at equal distances. Brush top lightly with water. Leave in a warm place about 1 hour or until doubled in volume. Preheat oven to 450F (230C). Place a pan of water in the bottom of oven. Brush loaf again with water and bake 5 minutes. Remove pan of water. Brush loaf once more with water. Bake about 20 minutes or until loaf sounds hollow when tapped on bottom.

Makes 1 loaf.

CHEESE & CHIVE BRAID

4 cups bread flour
1 teaspoon salt
1 teaspoon sugar
1½ teaspoons active dry yeast
2 tablespoons butter, chilled
1 cup shredded Cheddar cheese (4 ozs.)
3 tablespoons snipped fresh chives
4 green onions, chopped
⅔ cup lukewarm milk (130F/55C)
¾ cup lukewarm water (130F/55C)
Beaten egg, to glaze

Into a bowl, sift flour. Stir in salt, sugar and yeast. Cut in butter.

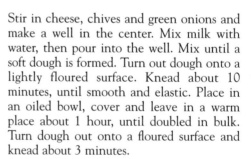

Stir in cheese, chives and green onions and make a well in the center. Mix milk with water, then pour into the well. Mix until a soft dough is formed. Turn out dough onto a lightly floured surface. Knead about 10 minutes, until smooth and elastic. Place in an oiled bowl, cover and leave in a warm place about 1 hour, until doubled in bulk. Turn dough out onto a floured surface and knead about 3 minutes.

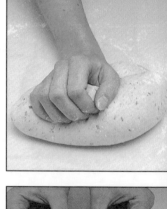

Divide dough into 3 pieces. Roll each one out to a long rope and braid together, pinching ends to seal. Place on a baking sheet, cover with oiled plastic wrap and leave in a warm place about 45 minutes, until doubled in bulk. Preheat oven to 425F (220C). Brush with beaten egg and bake 20 minutes. Reduce temperature to 350F (175C) and bake 15 minutes longer, until golden brown and the bottom sounds hollow when tapped. Serve warm or cold with cheese and a salad.

Makes about 10 slices.

EASTER BREAD

7 cups bread flour
1 envelope active dry yeast (about 1 tablespoon)
¼ cup superfine sugar
2 teaspoons caraway seeds
½ cup butter, melted
2 eggs, beaten
1 cup warm milk
1 egg, beaten, for glazing
2 tablespoons slivered almonds to decorate

Into a large bowl, sift flour. Stir in yeast, sugar and caraway seeds. Stir in butter, eggs and milk. Mix together, then turn dough out onto a floured surface.

Knead dough thoroughly 10 minutes or until smooth and elastic. Cut dough in half and divide each half into 3 pieces. Roll each piece into a rope 20 inches long. Braid 3 ropes, then shape the braid into a ring, pressing the ends together firmly. Braid remaining 3 ropes. Place the 2 rings on oiled baking sheets. Cover with a cloth and leave in a warm place 1 hour or until doubled in size. Preheat oven to 375F (190C).

Brush loaves with beaten egg. Scatter slivered almonds over the top. Bake 40 minutes or until loaves are lightly browned and sound hollow when tapped on the bottoms. Leave on wire racks to cool. Serve sliced and buttered.

Makes 2 loaves.

Note: Traditionally these loaves have red-dyed eggs tucked into the braids before baking.

PARATHAS

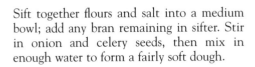

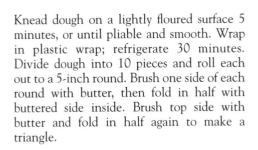

½ cup all-purpose flour
⅔ cup whole-wheat flour
Salt to taste
½ teaspoon onion seeds
½ teaspoon celery seeds
About ⅔ cup water
1 cup butter or ghee, melted
Celery leaves to garnish

Sift together flours and salt into a medium bowl; add any bran remaining in sifter. Stir in onion and celery seeds, then mix in enough water to form a fairly soft dough.

Knead dough on a lightly floured surface 5 minutes, or until pliable and smooth. Wrap in plastic wrap; refrigerate 30 minutes. Divide dough into 10 pieces and roll each out to a 5-inch round. Brush one side of each round with butter, then fold in half with buttered side inside. Brush top side with butter and fold in half again to make a triangle.

Roll out triangles on a lightly floured surface until both straight sides measure about 5 inches. Heat a griddle or heavy skillet and brush with butter. Cook 2 or 3 parathas at a time 1 minute, brush with butter, then turn over and cook 1 to 2 minutes more, until cooked. Stack on a plate, cover with a dry cloth while cooking remaining bread. Serve warm, garnished with celery leaves.

Makes 10.

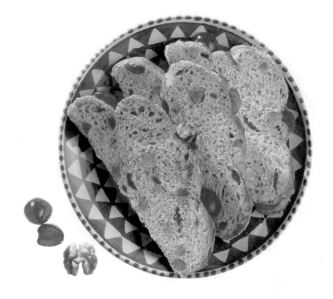

CARAWAY KUGELHOPF

2 cups all-purpose flour
¼ cup sugar
2 teaspoons active dry yeast
2 tablespoons caraway seeds
¼ cup lukewarm water (130F/55C)
½ cup unsalted butter, melted
3 eggs, at room temperature, beaten
Powdered sugar to finish

Grease an 8-inch kugelhopf mold. Into a bowl, sift flour. Stir in sugar, yeast and caraway seeds.

Make a well in center. Stir in water, butter and eggs. Beat vigorously until smooth. Cover bowl with plastic wrap and leave in a warm place until doubled in bulk. Stir mixture and pour into prepared mold. Cover with plastic wrap and leave to rise again until doubled in bulk.

Preheat oven to 400F (205C). Bake kugelhopf 20 minutes. Reduce temperature to 375F (190C) and bake 10 minutes longer, until well risen and golden-brown. Cool in the mold 10 minutes, then turn out kugelhopf and transfer to a wire rack. Dust lightly with powdered sugar. Serve sliced with butter while still slightly warm.

Makes 8 to 10 slices.

CHERRY-NUT BREAD

3 cups bread flour
½ teaspoon salt
1 teaspoon sugar
2 teaspoons active dry yeast
¼ cup butter, chilled
⅓ cup candied cherries, chopped
½ cup chopped walnuts
⅔ cup lukewarm milk (130F/55C)
⅓ cup lukewarm water (130F/55C)
1 egg, beaten
TOPPING:
½ cup powdered sugar, sifted
2 tablespoons candied cherries
⅓ cup walnut halves

Grease and flour a baking sheet. Into a bowl, sift flour. Stir in salt, sugar and yeast. Cut in butter, and add chopped cherries and walnuts. Make a well in center. Pour in milk, water and egg. Mix to a soft dough. Turn dough out onto a floured surface and knead 10 minutes, until smooth. Put in an oiled bowl, cover and leave in a warm place until doubled in bulk. Turn dough out onto a floured surface, knead lightly and divide into 5 pieces. Roll each out to a rope 12 inches long.

Braid 3 ropes together and place on prepared baking sheet. Twist the remaining 2 ropes together and place on top. Cover with oiled plastic wrap. Leave in a warm place until doubled in bulk. Preheat oven to 425F (220C). Bake 10 minutes, then reduce heat to 375F (190C) and bake 20 minutes longer. Cool. Mix powdered sugar and enough water to make a thin frosting; drizzle over loaf. Decorate with cherries and walnuts.

Makes about 12 slices.

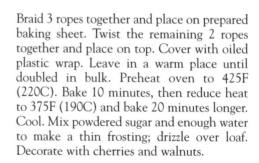

CHELSEA BUNS

2 cups bread flour
2 teaspoons active dry yeast
1 teaspoon sugar
½ teaspoon salt
2 tablespoons unsalted butter, chilled
½ cup lukewarm milk (130F/55C)
1 egg, beaten
FILLING:
¼ cup unsalted butter, softened
⅓ cup packed light brown sugar
¾ cup chopped mixed dried fruit
1 teaspoon apple pie spice
½ cup powdered sugar to finish

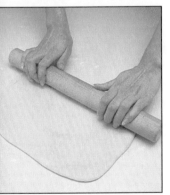

Butter an 8-inch square cake pan. Into a bowl, sift. Stir in yeast, sugar and salt. Cut in butter. Make a well in center. Pour in milk and egg and beat vigorously to make a soft dough. On a floured surface, knead dough 5 to 10 minutes, until smooth. Put dough in an oiled bowl, cover and leave in a warm place about 1 hour, until doubled in bulk. Turn dough out onto a floured surface. Knead lightly. Roll out to a 12- x 9-inch rectangle.

Spread with butter, then sprinkle with brown sugar, fruit and spice. Roll up from a long side and cut into 9 pieces. Place in pan, cut sides up. Cover with oiled plastic wrap. Leave in a warm place 45 minutes, until almost doubled in bulk. Preheat oven to 375F (190C). Bake 30 minutes, until golden. Cool in pan 10 minutes, then turn out and transfer in one piece to a wire rack to cool. Mix powdered sugar with enough water to make a thin glaze. Brush over buns. Leave to cool.

Makes 9.

LEMON & CURRANT BRIOCHES

2 cups bread flour
2 teaspoons active dry yeast
½ teaspoon salt
1 tablespoon sugar
⅓ cup dried currants
Grated zest of 1 lemon
2 tablespoons lukewarm water (130F/55C)
2 eggs, at room temperature, beaten
¼ cup unsalted butter, melted
1 egg, beaten, to glaze

Butter 12 individual brioche molds. Into a bowl, sift flour. Stir in yeast, salt, sugar, currants and lemon zest.

Make a well in center. Pour in water, eggs and melted butter and beat vigorously to make a soft dough. Turn dough out onto a lightly floured surface and knead 5 minutes, until smooth and elastic. Put dough in an oiled bowl, cover and leave in a warm place 1 hour, until doubled in bulk. Turn dough out onto a lightly floured surface, reknead and roll into a rope shape. Cut into 12 equal pieces. Shape three quarters of each piece into a ball and place in prepared molds.

With a floured finger, press a hole in center of each. Shape remaining dough into little plugs, then press into holes, flattening the tops slightly. Place molds on a baking sheet. Cover with oiled plastic wrap and leave in a warm place until dough comes almost to top of molds. Preheat oven to 425F (220C). Brush brioches with beaten egg. Bake 15 minutes, until golden-brown. Serve warm.

Makes 12.

CRUMPETS

4 cups bread flour
1 teaspoon salt
1 teaspoon sugar
2 teaspoons active dry yeast
2½ cups lukewarm milk (130F/55C)
⅔ cup lukewarm water (130F/55C)
Vegetable oil for cooking
Butter and jam to serve

Into a bowl, sift flour. Stir in salt, sugar and yeast.

Make a well in center of flour and pour in milk and water. With a wooden spoon, gradually work flour into liquid, then beat vigorously to make a smooth batter. Cover bowl with a cloth and leave in a warm place 1 hour or until batter has doubled in bulk.

Thoroughly grease a heavy skillet or griddle and several crumpet rings or round cookie cutters. Arrange as many rings as possible in pan. Heat pan, then pour in enough batter to half fill each ring. Cook crumpets 5–6 minutes, until bubbles appear and burst on the surface. Remove rings and turn crumpets over. Cook on other side 2–3 minutes longer. Return rings to skillet to heat and repeat with remaining batter. Serve crumpets hot, generously buttered, with jam.

Makes about 16.

DEVONSHIRE SPLITS

¼ cup unsalted butter
2 tablespoons sugar
⅔ cup milk
⅔ cup water
4 cups bread flour
2 teaspoons active dry yeast
½ teaspoon salt
FILLING:
⅓ cup strawberry jam
1¼ cups whipping cream, whipped
Powdered sugar for dusting

In a saucepan, heat butter, sugar, milk and water until sugar has dissolved.

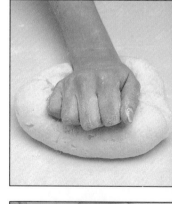

Let mixture stand until lukewarm (130F/55C). Into a bowl, sift flour. Stir in yeast and salt. Make a well in center, then pour in liquid and mix vigorously to make a soft dough. On a lightly floured surface, turn out dough and knead until smooth. Place in an oiled bowl, cover and leave in a warm place until doubled in bulk. Grease 2 baking sheets.

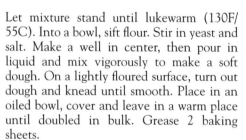

Turn dough out onto a floured surface. Divide into 16 pieces. Knead each piece lightly and shape into a ball. Place on baking sheets, flattening each ball slightly. Cover with oiled plastic wrap and leave in a warm place about 40 minutes, until well risen. Preheat oven to 425F (220C). Bake about 15 minutes, until bottoms sound hollow when tapped. Cool on a wire rack. Split and fill with jam and cream. Dust lightly with powdered sugar.

Makes 16.

SWEET PASTRIES

PECAN PIE

1 recipe Shortcrust Pastry (page 336)
3 eggs
2 cups packed light-brown sugar
1 tablespoon honey
2 tablespoons butter, melted
2 tablespoons whipping cream
Pinch of salt
1½ cups pecans, coarsely chopped
Powdered sugar to finish

Prepare pastry as directed and line a 10-inch flan pan. Bake blind as directed. Leave oven temperature at 375F (190C).

In a large bowl, whisk eggs and brown sugar until pale and thick. Stir in honey, butter, whipping cream and salt and mix thoroughly. Fold in chopped pecans.

Pour mixture evenly into baked pastry shell and bake 20 minutes. Lower oven temperature to 325F (165C) and bake 45 to 50 minutes more, until set. Dust with powdered sugar and serve warm or chilled.

Makes 6 servings.

Variation: Substitute walnuts for pecans, if desired.

ORANGE MERINGUE PIE

1 recipe Shortcrust Pastry (page 336)
¼ cup cornstarch
1¼ cups water
2 tablespoons butter
Grated peel and juice of 2 small oranges
Juice of 1 small lime
2 eggs, separated
¾ cup superfine sugar
Orange and lime twists and mint leaves to garnish, if desired

Preheat oven to 375F (190C). Prepare pastry as directed and line a 10-inch flan pan. Bake blind as directed. Lower oven temperature to 325F (165C).

In a bowl, mix cornstarch and a small amount of water to a smooth paste. Stir in remaining water, then pour into a saucepan and add butter. Bring to a boil, stirring constantly. Simmer 2 to 3 minutes, stirring constantly, and remove from heat. Beat in citrus juices and grated orange peel, egg yolks and ⅓ of sugar. Spoon into baked pastry shell and cool slightly.

In a large bowl, whisk egg whites until stiff but not dry. Add ½ of remaining sugar and whisk again until mixture holds its shape. Fold in remaining sugar. Using a pastry bag fitted with a star nozzle, pipe meringue on top of flan to cover filling and pastry. Bake 2 to 3 minutes, until meringue is set and lightly golden. Serve warm or cold, garnished with orange and lime twists and mint leaves, if desired.

Makes 6 to 8 servings.

TARTE AU CITRON

3 eggs
1 egg yolk
¾ cup granulated sugar
Grated zest and juice of 3 lemons
Grated zest and juice of 1 orange
½ cup powdered sugar, plus extra for dusting
Shredded zest of 1 lemon
Lemon twists and chervil sprigs to decorate
PÂTE SUCRÉE:
¾ cup all-purpose flour
Pinch of salt
¼ cup sugar
½ cup unsalted butter, softened
2 egg yolks

Prick bottom of pastry case with a fork, line with waxed paper or foil and fill with dried beans. Put tart pan on a baking sheet and bake 10 to 12 minutes. Reduce oven temperature to 375F (190C). Remove paper and beans and bake 5 minutes or until golden. Transfer pan to a wire rack and let cool. Leave oven on.

To make pâte sucrée, sift flour and salt onto a marble slab or a work surface and make a well in center. Put sugar, butter and egg yolks into well and pinch them together to form a paste, then lightly draw in flour, adding about 1 tablespoon cold water to make a soft but firm dough. Cover and refrigerate 2 hours.

Mix together eggs, egg yolk, granulated sugar and grated lemon and orange zests and juices. Return tart pan to baking sheet and ladle in filling. Bake 25 to 30 minutes or until set. Transfer pan to a wire rack, cool slightly, then remove outer ring of tart pan. Leave tart to cool completely.

Roll out pastry on a lightly floured surface and use to line a 9½-inch loose-bottomed fluted tart pan, pressing pastry well into sides and bottom. Run rolling pin over top of pan to cut off excess pastry. Refrigerate 20 minutes. Preheat oven to 400F (205C).

Put powdered sugar and ⅔ cup water in a small pan and heat gently, stirring, until dissolved. Boil 2 minutes, then add shredded lemon zest and simmer until shiny. Remove with a slotted spoon and let cool on waxed paper. Just before serving, dust tart thickly with sifted powdered sugar and sprinkle with candied lemon zest. Garnish with lemon twists and chervil sprigs and serve with cream, if desired.

Makes 6 to 8 servings.

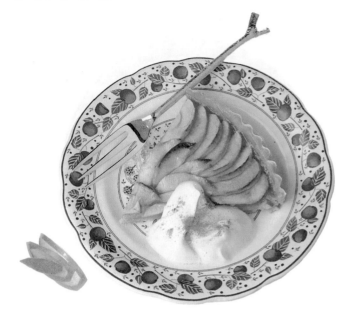

RED FRUIT TART

9½-inch loose-bottomed fluted tart pan lined with
    pâte sucrée (page 333)
About 26 each raspberries, halved strawberries and
    pitted cherries
3 tablespoons red fruit jam
1 tablespoon fresh lemon juice
Raspberries and raspberry leaves to decorate
CRÈME PÂTISSIÈRE:
⅔ cup milk
⅔ cup half-and-half
1 vanilla bean
3 egg yolks
¼ cup sugar
1 tablespoon all-purpose flour
1½ tablespoons cornstarch
1 tablespoon unsalted butter

To make crème pâtissière, place milk, half-and-half and vanilla bean into a saucepan and heat gently to simmering point. Remove from heat, cover and leave 30 minutes. Whisk egg yolks and sugar until pale and very thick. Stir in flour and cornstarch. Remove vanilla bean from milk and return almost to a boil. Slowly whisk into egg mixture. Return to pan and bring to a boil, whisking. Simmer 2 or 3 minutes. Remove from heat, stir in butter and pour into a bowl. Let cool, stirring occasionally. Cover and refrigerate. Preheat oven to 400F (205C).

Prick pastry case with a fork, line with waxed paper or foil and fill with dried beans. Bake 10 to 12 minutes. Reduce oven temperature to 375F (190C). Remove paper and beans and bake 8 to 10 minutes. Cool on a wire rack. Fill pastry case with crème pâtissière and arrange fruit on top. Put jam and lemon juice in a pan and heat gently, to soften. Strain and brush over fruit. Let cool, decorate and serve.

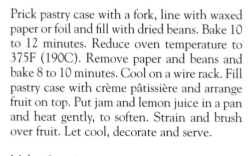

Makes 6 servings.

FRENCH APPLE TART

1 cup all-purpose flour
1 teaspoon sugar
⅓ cup low-fat margarine
2 lbs. Granny Smith apples
2 tablespoons water
Grated peel and juice of 1 lemon
4 tablespoons apricot jam
½ lb. Golden Delicious apples

Preheat oven to 350F (175C). Into a bowl, sift flour. Mix in sugar. Rub or cut in ¼ cup of the margarine until mixture resembles coarse crumbs. Add enough water to make a soft dough. On a lightly floured surface, roll out dough.

Use dough to line an 8-inch loose-bottomed tart pan. With a fork, prick bottom of dough all over. Bake blind 10 minutes. Peel, core and slice Granny Smith apples. Into a saucepan, place apple slices with remaining margarine and the 2 tablespoons water. Cover and simmer 15 minutes or until apples are soft. Add lemon peel and 3 tablespoons of the jam. Cook, stirring occasionally, 15 minutes or until thickened. Into pastry shell, spoon apple purée. Let cool. Peel, core and slice Golden Delicious apples thinly.

Arrange apple slices in an overlapping circle around edge of tart and in the center. Brush with lemon juice. Bake 30 to 40 minutes or until brown on top. Heat remaining jam and brush over tart to glaze. Serve warm or cold with yogurt sprinkled with cinnamon.

Makes 6 servings.

FIG & ORANGE TART

8 ozs. no-soak dried figs, roughly chopped
Juice of 2 oranges
⅓ cup butter diced
2 eggs, beaten
2 tablespoons pine nuts
Powdered sugar for dusting
Orange segments to decorate
PASTRY:
1¼ cups all-purpose flour
⅓ cup butter
2 tablespoons powdered sugar
1 egg yolk

To make pastry, sift flour into a bowl. Rub in butter until mixture resembles fine bread crumbs.

Stir in powdered sugar. Add egg yolk and 1 teaspoon of water. Stir with a knife to form a smooth dough. Knead lightly, wrap in plastic wrap and refrigerate 30 minutes. On a lightly floured surface, roll out dough to fit a 8-inch loose-bottomed tart pan. Line tart pan with pastry and refrigerate again 20 to 30 minutes. Preheat oven to 375F (190C). Prick pastry all over with a fork then line with foil and fill with baking beans. Bake blind 10 to 15 minutes or until pastry has set.

Remove baking beans and foil and bake another 10 to 15 minutes or until firm and golden brown. Put figs and orange juice in a saucepan. Cook 5 to 10 minutes, stirring, until thickened. Remove from heat, add butter and stir until melted. Beat in eggs. Pour mixture into pastry case and scatter with pine nuts. Bake 15 minutes or until just set. Dust with powdered sugar, decorate with orange segments and serve warm or cold.

Makes 6 servings.

PLUM-CUSTARD TART

1 lb. plums
½ cup all-purpose flour
½ cup whole-wheat flour
¼ cup margarine
1¼ cups milk
2 eggs
¼ cup sugar
Few drops almond essence

Preheat oven to 350F (175C). Cut plums into quarters; set aside. Into a bowl, sift flours. Rub or cut in margarine until mixture resembles coarse crumbs.

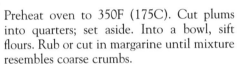

Stir in enough water to make a soft dough. On a lightly floured surface, roll out dough and use to line an 8-inch quiche dish. With a fork, prick bottom of dough. Line with foil and fill with dried beans or pie weights and bake 10 minutes. Remove foil and beans. Place plums in bottom of pastry shell.

In a bowl, beat together milk, eggs, sugar and almond extract. Pour mixture over plums. Bake 45 minutes or until custard is set and golden. Serve warm or cold.

Makes 6 servings.

Note: Almond extract is strong in flavor so use it sparingly.

TARTE TATIN

½ cup unsalted butter, softened
½ cup sugar
About 3 lbs. firm, well-flavored apples, peeled, cored
    and cut into wedges
Juice of 1 lemon
Strips of lemon zest and mint sprigs, to decorate
SHORTCRUST PASTRY:
2 cups all-purpose flour
1 tablespoon sugar
½ cup butter, diced
2-3 tablespoons crème fraîche (or milk)

Sprinkle with lemon juice and cook over medium to high heat, shaking pan occasionally, 20 to 30 minutes or until apples are lightly caramelized. If a lot of juice is produced, pour it off into a saucepan, boil to a thick syrup and pour back over apples.

To make pastry, combine flour and sugar in a bowl. Add butter and rub or cut in until mixture resembles fine bread crumbs. Add enough crème fraîche to form a dough. Form into a ball, cover and refrigerate at least 30 minutes.

Preheat oven to 425F (220C). Roll out pastry on a lightly floured surface until slightly larger than pan. Lay pastry on top of apples, tucking edge of pastry down side of pan.

Spread butter over bottom of a heavy 9½-inch cake pan or ovenproof skillet. Sprinkle with sugar and arrange apples on top, rounded-side down.

Prick pastry lightly with a fork and put pan on a baking sheet. Bake 20 minutes or until pastry is golden. Turn tart onto a warmed serving plate, decorate with lemon zest and mint sprigs and serve.

Makes 6 to 8 servings.

Note: Be careful when turning out the tart as the syrup will be very hot and can burn.

PRUNE & ALMOND TART

8 ozs. pitted prunes
¼ cup brandy
Pie crust for 9-inch pie, thawed if frozen
½ cup unsalted butter, softened
½ cup powdered sugar
3 eggs, beaten
½ cup all-purpose flour
½ cup ground almonds
½ cup sliced almonds

Put prunes and brandy into a bowl and soak overnight. Roll out pastry slightly and use to line a 10-inch tart dish.

Trim pastry and prick bottom all over with a fork. Drain prunes and arrange in pastry shell. Preheat oven to 400F (205C). In a bowl, beat together butter and powdered sugar. Beat in eggs and fold in flour and ground almonds. Spread mixture evenly over prunes.

Sprinkle sliced almonds over top. Bake 40 to 45 minutes, or until filling is risen and golden brown. Serve warm.

Makes 6 to 8 servings.

TIA MARIA CHOUX RING

1 recipe Choux Pastry (page 343)
2 tablespoons all-purpose flour
2 tablespoons cornstarch
¼ cup sugar
1¼ cups milk
3 egg yolks
⅔ cup whipping cream
½ teaspoon coffee extract
2¼ teaspoons Tia Maria
¾ cup powdered sugar, sifted

Preheat oven to 425F (220C). Spoon pastry into a pastry bag fitted with a ½-inch plain tip.

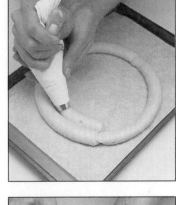

Pipe a double 8-inch circle onto a paper-lined baking sheet. Bake choux ring 20 minutes. Reduce temperature to 350F (175C) and bake 10 to 15 minutes longer, until golden-brown. Split horizontally, then cool on a wire rack. Into a bowl, sift flour and cornstarch. Stir in sugar and 2 tablespoons milk to make a thick paste. Beat in egg yolks. In a saucepan, heat remaining milk to just below boiling point. Pour onto egg mixture, stirring constantly.

Strain mixture back into saucepan, then cook over low heat, stirring constantly, until thickened. Cover closely with plastic wrap and refrigerate until chilled. In a bowl, whip cream until stiff peaks form and fold into custard. Stir in 2 teaspoons of the coffee extract and Tia Maria. Sandwich choux rings together with coffee filling. In a bowl, mix together powdered sugar, remaining ¼ teaspoon coffee extract and about 1 tablespoon water. Spoon over cake and let set.

Makes 8 servings.

NUTTY FILO FINGERS

1¼ cups skinned hazelnuts, very finely ground
¼ cup granulated sugar
1 tablespoon orange-flower water
⅓ cup unsalted butter
6 large sheets filo pastry
Sugar for dusting

Preheat oven to 350F (175C). Grease 2 baking sheets. In a bowl, mix together ground hazelnuts, sugar and orange-flower water.

In a saucepan, melt butter. Cut each sheet of dough into 4 rectangles. Pile on top of each other and cover with a towel to prevent drying out. Working with 1 pile of dough rectangles at a time, brush each piece of dough with melted butter.

Spread 1 teaspoon of filling along a short end. Fold long sides in, folding slightly over filling. Roll up from filling end. Place on a prepared baking sheet with seam underneath. Brush with melted butter. Repeat with remaining pastry rectangles and filling. Bake 20 minutes, or until very lightly colored. Transfer to wire racks to cool; sprinkle with sugar.

Makes 24.

FILO FRUIT PASTRIES

1 Granny Smith apple
2 teaspoons lemon juice
2 kiwifruit
1 peach
⅓ cup raisins
1 teaspoon apple-pie spice
8 sheets filo pastry dough
¼ cup margarine, melted
1 tablespoon powdered sugar
Strawberry slices, to decorate (optional)

Preheat oven to 400F (205C). To prepare filling, into a bowl, peel, core and coarsely grate apple. Sprinkle with lemon juice to prevent browning.

Peel kiwifruit, then chop roughly and add to apple. Peel, pit and chop peach roughly, then add to apple with raisins and spice. Stir well to mix. Set aside. To make each filo package, cut each filo sheet in half crosswise to make 2 (4-inch) squares (total of 16 squares). Brush 2 squares of dough lightly with melted margarine, then place one on top of the other diagonally. Place some fruit filling in the center of the dough and then fold over all the sides like a package.

Place seam-edge down on a greased baking sheet. Brush lightly with melted margarine. Repeat with remaining dough squares and filling, to make 8 packages. Bake 30 minutes or until golden and crisp. Sift powdered sugar over pastries just before serving and decorate with a few slices of strawberry, if desired. Serve hot or cold.

Makes 8 servings.

MANGO & LYCHEE TURNOVERS

1 tablespoon cornstarch
1 tablespoon granulated sugar
3 tablespoons water
3 tablespoons unsweetened orange juice
1 teaspoon lemon juice
1 teaspoon grated nutmeg
1 mango
10 lychees
8 sheets filo pastry dough
¼ cup margarine, melted
1 tablespoon powdered sugar

Preheat oven to 400F (205C). In a saucepan, blend cornstarch, granulated sugar and water. Stir in juices and nutmeg.

Over low heat, cook, stirring, until mixture thickens. Simmer sauce 3 minutes; set aside to cool. Peel, pit and coarsely chop mango and lychees. Add fruit to cooled sauce, mixing well. To make each turnover, cut each filo sheet to make 2 (4-inch) squares (total of 16 squares). Brush 2 squares of dough lightly with melted margarine and place one on top of the other. Place some filling in the center of the dough, fold diagonally in half and press edges to seal.

Onto a greased baking sheet, place turnover. Brush lightly with melted margarine. Repeat with remaining dough and filling to make 8 turnovers. Bake 30 minutes or until golden and crisp. Sift powdered sugar over turnovers and serve warm.

Makes 8 servings.

KADAIFI

1 cup finely chopped walnuts
1 cup finely chopped almonds
¼ cup superfine sugar
½ teaspoon ground cinnamon
14 ozs. kadaifi pastry dough (see Note)
¼ cup butter
SYRUP:
1 cup granulated sugar
1¼ cups water
1 tablespoon fresh lemon juice
1 tablespoon orange-flower water

Preheat oven to 350F (175C). Butter a 13- x 9-inch baking pan. In a bowl, mix together walnuts, almonds, sugar and cinnamon.

Tease dough out to an 18- x 15-inch rectangle. Cut into 18 pieces, each 5- x 3-inch. Place 1 tablespoon of nut mixture on short end of each rectangle of dough. Roll up, enclosing filling. Place rolls in prepared pan. In a small saucepan, melt butter, then pour it over the rolls. Bake 25 to 30 minutes or until golden and crisp. Cool 15 minutes.

To make the syrup, put sugar, water and lemon juice in a saucepan. Heat gently until sugar has dissolved, then boil 5 minutes or until slightly thickened. Add orange-flower water, then pour syrup over pastry rolls.

Makes 18.

Note: Kadaifi is a white shredded raw pastry dough available from delicatessens and Greek specialty stores. It has to be teased into shape rather than rolled.

CHEESE & HONEY TRIANGLES

1 (8-oz.) package cream cheese, softened
2 tablespoons creamed honey
1 egg yolk
¼ cup butter
6 sheets filo pastry
Powdered sugar for dusting

Preheat oven to 375F (190C). Butter a baking sheet. In a bowl, beat together cream cheese, honey and egg yolk.

In a small saucepan, melt butter. Brush a sheet of filo dough with melted butter. Cover with a second sheet of dough and brush with butter. Cover with a third sheet of dough. Cut dough layers in half across. Cut each half crosswise into 4 strips. Repeat with remaining 3 sheets of dough.

Place a spoonful of cream cheese mixture on corner of a filo dough strip. Fold dough and filling over at right angles to make a triangle and continue folding in this way along strip of dough to form a neat triangular package. Place on baking sheet and brush with melted butter. Repeat with remaining dough strips and filling. Bake 10 minutes until crisp. Dust lightly with powdered sugar.

Makes 16.

WALNUT PASTRIES

2½ cups all-purpose flour
¾ cup butter, chilled
⅓ cup powdered sugar
1 egg yolk
3 tablespoons superfine sugar
⅓ cup water
1 cup coarsely chopped walnuts
½ cup chopped mixed citrus peel
¼ teaspoon freshly grated nutmeg
3 tablespoons rosewater
Extra powdered sugar for coating

Into a bowl, sift flour. Cut in butter until mixture resembles bread crumbs.

Sift powdered sugar over flour mixture. Stir in powdered sugar, egg yolk and a little water to make a firm dough. Cover and refrigerate 30 minutes. Preheat oven to 350F (175C). Butter a baking sheet. To make the syrup, in a saucepan, put superfine sugar and the water. Heat over low heat until sugar has dissolved. Bring to a boil and boil a few minutes until syrup has reduced and thickened slightly.

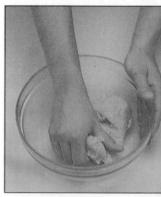

In a bowl, mix together walnuts, citrus peel and nutmeg. Stir in syrup. On a floured surface, thinly roll out pastry. Cut out 4-inch circles. Place a teaspoon of walnut mixture on each circle. Fold in half, pressing edges together. Bake in the oven 20 to 30 minutes until pale golden. Brush with rosewater. Coat liberally with powdered sugar.

Makes about 20.

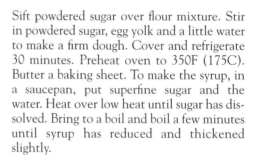

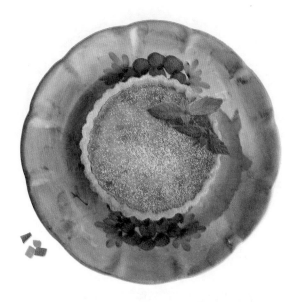

SERPENT CAKE

Powdered sugar for dusting
12 sheets filo pastry, about 16 x 12 inches
⅓ cup unsalted butter, melted
Ground cinnamon for dusting
ALMOND PASTE:
2 cups ground almonds
¾ cup powdered sugar
Grated zest and juice of ½ orange
¼ cup softened butter

To make almond paste, mix together ground almonds, powdered sugar, orange zest, orange juice and butter. Cover and refrigerate 30 minutes, or until firm.

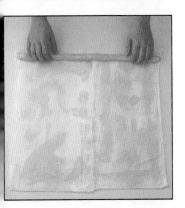

Preheat oven to 350F (180C). Dust a work surface with powdered sugar. Divide almond paste into three and roll each piece into a sausage 20-inch long. Brush two sheets of filo pastry with melted butter and place side by side, with long sides overlapping slightly. Place two more buttered sheets on top. Lay a roll of almond paste along one of long sides and roll up. Brush with butter and roll into a tight coil. Place coil on a baking sheet.

Make two more rolls in same way. Join them to coil, continuing shape and sealing joins with water. Bake 20 to 30 minutes or until crisp and golden. Invert on to another baking sheet and return to oven until crisp. Invert onto a serving dish and let cool. Dust with powdered sugar. Decorate with stripes of ground cinnamon and serve.

Makes 6 servings.

Note: This cake does not keep well and is best eaten on day it is made.

CANDIED FRUIT TARTS

1 cup ricotta cheese
3 egg yolks
¼ cup sugar
1 tablespoon brandy
Grated zest of 1 lemon
1 tablespoon lemon juice
4 ozs. crystallized fruit, finely chopped
Powdered sugar for dusting
Mint sprigs, to decorate
PASTRY:
1½ cups all-purpose flour
⅓ cup butter
⅓ cup shortening

To make pastry, sift flour into a bowl. Add butter and shortening.

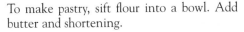

Rub in butter and shortening until mixture resembles fine bread crumbs. Stir in 2 tablespoons of cold water and use a knife to mix to a smooth dough. Knead lightly, wrap in plastic wrap and refrigerate 30 minutes. Preheat oven to 350F (180C). On a lightly floured surface, roll out pastry until ⅛-inch thick. Cut out four circles to fit four 4-inch tart pans.

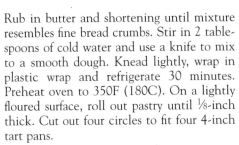

Put ricotta cheese, egg yolks, sugar, brandy and lemon zest and juice in a bowl. Beat together until smooth then stir in crystallized fruit. Divide mixture among pastry cases. Bake 30 to 40 minutes or until filling is set and golden. Let cool. Dust with powdered sugar, decorate with mint sprigs and serve cold.

Makes 4 servings.

MAIDS OF HONOR

PALMIERS

1½ recipes Pie Crust Dough (page 346)
½ cup cottage cheese
¼ cup butter, softened
¼ cup sugar
Shredded zest and juice of ½ lemon
¼ cup ground blanched almonds
½ teaspoon grated nutmeg
2 teaspoons brandy
⅓ cup dried currants
Sugar for sprinkling

½ lb. puff pastry dough, thawed if frozen
¼ cup sugar, plus extra for rolling out
FILLING:
½ cup whipping cream
4 teaspoons red jelly (such as red currant jelly)

Roll out pastry and use to line 12 tartlet pans. Refrigerate 30 minutes.

Preheat oven to 425F (220C). On a surface sprinkled with sugar, roll out dough to a 12-inch square. Sprinkle dough with half of the sugar. Fold sides of dough into center, sprinkle with half of remaining sugar, then fold sides into center again.

Preheat oven to 375F (190C). Press cottage cheese through a strainer into a bowl. Add butter and beat until well blended. Add sugar, lemon zest and juice, ground almonds, nutmeg and brandy. Mix thoroughly. Stir in currants.

Sprinkle dough with remaining sugar and fold in half down center. Press lightly together to seal the edges. Cut dough into 24 slices. Place slices, cut edges down, on dampened baking sheets. With palm of your hand, press to flatten slightly. Bake 10 minutes, or until crisp and a light golden-brown. Turn over and bake 2 to 3 minutes more, until second side is golden-brown. Remove from baking sheets immediately and cool on wire racks.

Spoon batter into prepared dough cases. Bake 20 to 30 minutes, until risen and golden-brown. Sprinkle with sugar. Transfer to a wire rack to cool.

Makes 12.

In a bowl, whip cream until soft peaks form. Spread a little jelly on 12 of the palmiers. Spread cream over jelly, then top with remaining 12 palmiers.

Makes 12.

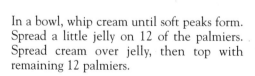

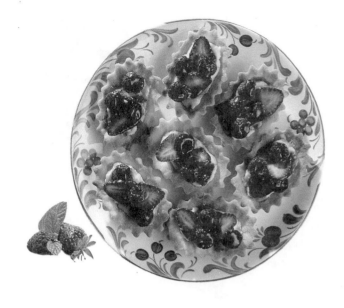

RASPBERRY ECLAIRS

CHOUX PASTRY:
½ cup unsalted butter
⅔ cup water
⅓ cup all-purpose flour, sifted
2 eggs, beaten
FILLING:
¾ cup whipping cream
1 tablespoon powdered sugar
6 ozs. raspberries
FROSTING:
¾ cup powdered sugar, sifted
2 teaspoons lemon juice
Pink food coloring (optional)

SUMMER FRUIT TARTLETS

1¾ cups all-purpose flour, sifted
½ cup ground blanched almonds
½ cup powdered sugar, sifted
½ cup butter, chilled
1 egg yolk
1 tablespoon milk
FILLING:
1 cup cream cheese (8 ozs.), softened
Sugar to taste
¾ lb. fresh summer fruits, such as red and black
   currants, raspberries and wild strawberries
Red currant jelly or other red jelly, heated, to glaze

Preheat oven to 425F (220C). Into a saucepan, put butter and water, and bring to a boil. Add flour all at once and beat thoroughly until mixture leaves the side of the pan. Cool slightly, then vigorously beat in eggs, one at a time. Spoon dough into a pastry bag fitted with a plain ½-inch tip and pipe 20 to 24 (3-inch) strips onto dampened baking sheets. Bake 10 minutes. Reduce temperature to 375F (190C); bake 20 minutes more, until golden.

In a bowl, mix together flour, ground almonds and powdered sugar. Cut in butter until mixture resembles bread crumbs. Add egg yolk and milk; work in with a spatula, then with fingers until dough binds together. Wrap dough in plastic wrap and refrigerate 30 minutes. Preheat oven to 400F (205C). On a floured surface, roll out dough to about ⅛-inch thick. Line 12 deep tartlet pans or individual brioche molds with dough; prick bottoms.

Slit the side of each eclair, then leave on wire racks to cool. To make filling, in a bowl, whip cream and powdered sugar until stiff peaks form. Put into a pastry bag fitted with a ⅛-inch tip. Pipe the filling into each eclair. Put a few raspberries in each eclair. To make frosting, in a small bowl, mix powdered sugar with lemon juice and enough water to make smooth paste. Add pink coloring, if desired. Spread frosting over eclairs and let set.

Makes 20 to 24.

Press a piece of foil into each dough case. Covering the edges. Bake 10 to 15 minutes, until light golden-brown. Remove foil and bake 2 to 3 minutes longer. Transfer to a wire rack to cool. To make filling, in a bowl, mix cream cheese and sugar together. Put a spoonful of filling in each pastry shell. Arrange fruit on top, then brush with glaze and serve at once.

Makes 12.

INDIVIDUAL PEAR PUFFS

8 ozs. fresh or frozen puff pastry
2 large ripe pears
1 egg yolk
1 tablespoon milk
Superfine sugar
Fresh herbs to garnish, if desired
Poire William liqueur, if desired

Preheat oven to 425F (220C). Thaw pastry, if frozen, and roll out to a rectangle about ¼ inch thick. Using half a pear as a guide, cut out pastry pear shapes ½ inch larger than pears, then cut around pear leaving a pear-shaped frame.

Roll out solid pear shape to same size as frame, dampen edges with water and fit frame on top. Press edges together lightly. Prepare 3 more pastry pear shapes in same way. Peel and halve pears. Core pears and cut crosswise in thin slices. Place in pastry shapes.

Place pear puffs on a baking sheet. In a small bowl, beat egg yolk and milk and brush edges of pastry. Bake 15 to 20 minutes, until pears are tender and pastry edges are puffed up and golden. Remove from oven, sprinkle with sugar and broil 1 minute. Transfer to serving plates. Garnish with fresh herbs, if desired. If desired, heat liqueur in a small saucepan, light and pour flaming over puffs. Serve at once.

Makes 4 servings.

STRAWBERRY MILLE-FEUILLE

13 ozs. fresh or frozen puff pastry
1 lb. strawberries
1¼ cups whipping cream
1-2 drops vanilla extract
Sugar to taste
¼ cup plus 1 tablespoon red currant jelly
2 tablespoons water

Thaw pastry, if frozen. Preheat oven to 425F (220C). Roll out pastry to a thin rectangle and cut in 3 equal sections.

Place sections on baking sheets and prick all over with a fork. Bake 15 to 20 minutes, until golden-brown and crisp. Cool on a wire rack. When cold, trim edges with a very sharp knife to make even. Reserve trimmings. Cut ½ of strawberries in half, using even-sized ones. Slice remainder. In a bowl, whip cream until fairly stiff and flavor with vanilla and sugar. Fold sliced strawberries into whipped cream.

Place 1 pastry slice on a serving plate and spread with ½ of whipped cream mixture. Lay another slice on top and spread with remaining cream mixture. Top with remaining slice. In a small saucepan, heat jelly and water gently until jelly has dissolved. Brush top slice with jelly and arrange halved strawberries on top. Brush with remainder of jelly. Crush reserved pastry trimmings and press into sides of mille-feuille.

Makes 6 to 8 servings.

MINCEMEAT JALOUSIE

2 eating apples
2 bananas
Juice and grated peel of ½ lemon and 1 orange
⅓ cup grapes
⅔ cup currants
½ cup golden raisins
½ cup dark raisins
¼ cup almonds, coarsely chopped
⅓ cup walnuts, coarsely chopped
⅓ cup sugar
2 tablespoons brandy
3 tablespoons butter, melted
⅔ (17¼-oz.) package frozen puff pastry, thawed
1 tablespoon milk
1 tablespoon superfine sugar
Whipped cream and apple slices to serve, if desired

To prepare mincemeat, peel, core and chop apples. Peel and chop bananas. In a large bowl, quickly toss prepared fruit in lemon juice. Halve and seed grapes and add to fruit with orange juice and lemon and orange peels. Add currants and raisins. Add chopped nuts, sugar and brandy to mixture and mix well. Stir in melted butter.

Dampen a baking sheet. Roll out pastry to a 12- x 5-inch rectangle. Cut in half.

Place 1 pastry half on dampened baking sheet and spread about ½ of mincemeat on top to within 1 inch of edges. Reserve remaining mincemeat for another use. Moisten edges with water. Roll out remaining pastry ½ inch larger all around than other piece. Fold in half lengthwise and make cuts down from folded edge, ½ inch apart to within 1 inch of edge. Open and lifting carefully, place over mincemeat and pastry.

Press edges of pastry together and flute edges. Chill jalousie 30 minutes. Preheat oven to 425F (220C). Brush jalousie lightly with milk and sprinkle with sugar. Bake 30 to 35 minutes, until pastry is puffed up and golden.

If pastry starts to brown too quickly, cover with foil. Garnish with apple slices and fresh herbs, if desired. Serve with whipped cream, if desired.

Makes 6 servings.

CLEMENTINE TARTLETS

1 recipe Shortcrust Pastry (page 336)
Juice of 2 oranges and 1 lemon
2¼ cups superfine sugar
4 clementines
2 eggs plus 2 extra yolks
8 tablespoons butter, softened
1 tablespoon ground almonds
2 to 3 tablespoons Grand Marnier or Cointreau

Prepare pastry as directed and line 6 (5-inch) tartlet pans. Bake blind 10 to 15 minutes as directed. Leave oven temperature at 375F (190C).

In a saucepan, combine orange and lemon juices and 1¼ cups of sugar. Cook over medium heat until sugar has dissolved, then boil syrup 15 minutes. Peel clementines and cut in slices. Cut slices in half and add to syrup. Simmer gently 2 to 3 minutes. Using a slotted spoon, transfer clementines to a plate and boil syrup until very thick and syrupy. Set aside. In a bowl, beat eggs, extra yolks and remaining sugar until well mixed. Beat in butter, ground almonds and liqueur.

Divide mixture among baked pastry shells and bake about 8 minutes, until set and golden; cool. When cold, brush top of tartlets with thick syrup and arrange clementine slices on top. Brush with more syrup, then chill.

Makes 6 servings.

Variation: Use strawberries or blackberries instead of clementines, but immerse in syrup only for a few seconds.

FRANGIPANE TARTLETS

PIE-CRUST DOUGH:
1 cup all-purpose flour
Pinch of salt
¼ cup butter or margarine, chilled
FILLING:
2 tablespoons apricot jam
¼ cup butter, softened
¼ cup sugar
1 egg
½ teaspoon almond extract
1 tablespoon all-purpose flour, sifted
½ cup ground blanched almonds
¼ cup sliced almonds
GLAZE:
2 tablespoons apricot jam

Preheat oven to 375F (190C). Into a bowl, sift flour and salt. Cut in butter until mixture resembles bread crumbs. Add 1 or 2 table-spoons water to make soft dough. On a floured surface, roll out dough about ⅛-inch thick. Line 12 tartlet pans with dough. Put a little apricot jam in bottom of each. To make filling, in a bowl, beat butter and sugar until creamy. Mix egg and almond extract together, then add to creamed mixture with flour and ground almonds. Mix well to form a smooth paste.

Spoon paste into dough cases. Arrange a few sliced almonds on top of each. Bake 15 to 20 minutes, until golden. To make glaze, in a saucepan, melt jam with 2 teaspoons cold water. Bring to a boil, then strain and reheat. Brush over hot tartlets. Transfer tartlets to a wire rack to cool.

Makes 12.

PEAR & DATE RECTANGLES

1 lb. pears
2 tablespoons water
⅓ cup sugar
1 teaspoon ground cinnamon
⅔ cup dried dates, chopped
12 sheets filo pastry dough
¼ cup low-fat margarine, melted
2 tablespoons honey, warmed

Preheat oven to 300F (150C). Peel, core and slice pears. Into a saucepan, place pear slices and water. Cover and cook over low heat until just softened. Add sugar, cinnamon and dates, mix well and cool slightly. Trim filo pastry into sheets measuring 11 x 7-inches.

Place 1 sheet of dough into the bottom of an 11- x 7-inch baking pan. Brush lightly with melted margarine. Place another sheet of dough on top, brush lightly with melted margarine and repeat with another 2 sheets of dough. Place half the fruit mixture on top. Place 4 sheets of dough on top of fruit, brushing each sheet lightly with melted margarine.

Repeat with remaining fruit mixture and dough sheets, brushing each sheet with melted margarine. Cut through the layers to make 12 rectangles. Bake about 1 hour or until golden on top. Spoon warm honey evenly over rectangles. Let stand 5 minutes.

Makes 12 servings.

APRICOT & HAZELNUT GALETTE

½ cup hazelnuts, skins removed
⅓ cup butter, softened
⅓ cup superfine sugar
1 cup all-purpose flour
8 ozs. fresh apricots, halved, pitted
3 tablespoons water
1¼ cups whipping cream
Powdered sugar
Additional toasted hazelnuts and apricot slices to garnish, if desired

Toast hazelnuts under broiler to brown evenly. Reserve 8 nuts and grind remainder finely in a coffee grinder. Preheat oven to 350F (175C). Lightly grease 2 baking sheets.

In a bowl, beat butter and ⅔ of superfine sugar until light and fluffy. Fold in ground nuts and flour, then beat to a firm dough. Knead lightly on a lightly floured surface, wrap in foil and chill 30 minutes. Unwrap dough and cut in half. Roll each half out to an 8-inch circle. Carefully place on greased baking sheets and bake about 20 minutes, until golden. Cut 1 circle in 8 wedges and cool all pastry on wire racks.

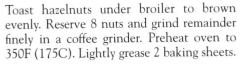

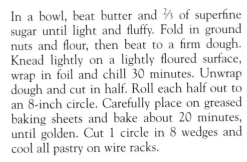

Poach apricots and remaining superfine sugar gently in water, until just soft; cool. In a bowl, whip cream until stiff. Transfer pastry circle to a serving plate and spread with ½ of whipped cream. Remove apricots from pan with a slotted spoon and arrange over whipped cream. Top with pastry wedges and dust lightly with powdered sugar. Using a pastry tube fitted with a star nozzle, pipe a rosette of remaining whipped cream onto each wedge and decorate with hazelnuts. Serve within 1 hour, garnished with additional hazelnuts and apricot slices, if desired.

Makes 8 servings.

RASPBERRY & APPLE STRUDEL

½ lb. cooking apples, peeled, cored and sliced
½ lb. raspberries
2 tablespoons water
¼ cup granulated sugar
½ lb. chopped mixed nuts
1 teaspoon ground cinnamon
8 sheets filo pastry dough
¼ cup margarine, melted
1 tablespoon powdered sugar

Preheat oven to 375F (190C). Grease a baking sheet. Into a saucepan, put apples, raspberries and water. Cover and simmer until just soft. Stir in granulated sugar and cool. Stir in nuts and cinnamon.

Place one sheet of pastry dough on a sheet of parchment paper. Brush dough lightly with margarine. Place another sheet of dough on top, then layer remaining sheets of dough on top of one another, brushing each one lightly with margarine. Spoon fruit mixture over dough leaving a 1-inch border uncovered all around edge. Fold these edges over fruit mixture.

With a long side toward you, using parchment paper, roll up strudel. Carefully place it on greased baking sheet, seam-side down. Brush lightly with margarine. Bake about 40 minutes or until browned. Sift with powdered sugar.

Makes 8 servings.

LEMON CUSTARD SLICES

½ lb. puff pastry dough, thawed if frozen
FILLING:
3 tablespoons cornstarch
¼ cup sugar
⅔ cup milk
Juice of 1 lemon
Shredded zest of ½ lemon
1 egg yolk
½ cup whipping cream
TO DECORATE:
½ cup powdered sugar, sifted
2 kiwifruit, peeled and sliced

Preheat oven to 450F (225C). On a lightly floured surface, roll out dough to a 12- x 10-inch rectangle. With a sharp, floured knife, cut dough into 8 rectangles. Prick all over with a fork. Place rectangles on a dampened baking sheet. Bake 10 to 15 minutes, until well risen and golden-brown. Transfer to a wire rack to cool. Split rectangles in half.

To make filling, in a saucepan, blend cornstarch with sugar and milk. Bring to a boil, stirring, until mixture thickens. Stir in lemon juice and zest. Beat in egg yolk. Cover and refrigerate until chilled. Beat in cream. In small bowl, mix powdered sugar with about 2 tablespoons water to make a smooth paste. Spread over 8 pastry slices. Let set. Spread custard over remaining pastry slices. Top with iced slices. Decorate with kiwifruit.

Makes 8.

CREAM CHEESE STRUDEL

¾ cup chopped hazelnuts
1 (8-oz.) package cream cheese, softened
2 tablespoons superfine sugar
1 egg
Grated peel of 1 lemon
5 sheets filo pastry, thawed if frozen
4 tablespoons butter, melted
BLACK CURRANT AND CASSIS SAUCE
8 ozs. fresh or frozen black currants
¼ cup superfine sugar
2 tablespoons crème de cassis

Preheat over to 400F (205C). Generously grease a baking sheet. Toast hazelnuts to brown evenly; cool.

In a bowl, beat cream cheese, sugar, egg and lemon peel until smooth. Beat in toasted hazelnuts. Place 1 sheet of pastry on greased baking sheet, keeping remainder covered with a damp tea towel. Brush with melted butter and place another sheet on top. Layer all 5 sheets of pastry, brushing each one with melted butter.

Spoon cream cheese mixture down center of pastry and fold short ends over filling. Roll up pastry around filling and turn over on baking sheet. Brush top with butter and bake 25 to 30 minutes, until golden-brown and flaky. To make the sauce, in a saucepan over medium heat, cook blackcurrants, sugar and ¼ cup water until currants are tender. Drain, reserving juice. Push currants through a sieve. Stir in liqueur and enough juice to desired consistency. Cool.

Makes 4 to 6 servings.

NECTARINE BAKLAVA

10 sheets filo pastry, thawed if frozen
⅔ cup butter, melted
1¾ cups chopped mixed nuts
1½ teaspoons ground cinnamon
½ cup superfine sugar
Grated peel and juice of 2 lemons
1 tablespoon orange flower water
4 nectarines
Powdered sugar
Nectarine slices and fresh herbs to garnish, if desired

Preheat oven to 350F (175C). Cut pastry sheets in half, then cut each half in quarters.

Working quickly, brush 1 cut sheet of pastry with melted butter. Line 8 individual 4-inch pans with 1 piece of pastry. Brush 3 more cut sheets with butter and lay cut pieces into pans, overlapping each other at different angles. In a bowl, combine nuts, cinnamon and ½ of sugar; spread ½ of nut mixture over pastry. Cover with 2 more layers of pastry, each brushed with butter, then top with remaining nut mixture. Cover with remaining pastry, brushed with butter.

Press down pastry in pans and bake 20 to 25 minutes, until golden-brown. Meanwhile, in a saucepan, combine remaining sugar and lemon juice. Cook, over low heat, until sugar dissolves. Stir in lemon peel and orange flower water. Bring to a boil and simmer 3 minutes; cool slightly. Slice nectarines into syrup, turning carefully to coat. Spoon into center of pastries and dust edges with powdered sugar. Serve lukewarm or cold, when pastries have absorbed some syrup.

Makes 8 servings.

APRICOPITA

2 lbs. fresh apricots
Seeds from 5 cardamom pods
½ cup superfine sugar
¼ teaspoon vanilla essence
6 tablespoons butter, melted
12 sheets filo pastry
3 eggs whites
3 tablespoons light brown sugar
1¼ cups ground blanched almonds
Powdered sugar

Into a bowl, put apricots. Cover with boiling water and leave 2 minutes, then drain. Cover with cold water, leave 2 minutes and drain again.

Peel skins off apricots. Cut in half and remove pits. Put apricots in a saucepan with cardamom seeds, superfine sugar and vanilla essence. Cook gently until apricots are soft. In a blender or food processor fitted with the metal blade, purée the apricots. Preheat oven to 375F (190C). Brush a 13- x 9-inch baking pan with melted butter. Brush a sheet of dough with butter and lay it in pan. Repeat with 3 more sheets. Spread apricot purée on top. Cover with 4 more layers of buttered dough sheets.

In a bowl, whisk egg whites until stiff but not dry. Whisk in brown sugar. Fold in ground almonds. Spread meringue on dough. Cover gently with 4 more sheets of buttered dough. Tuck top layer of dough down sides. With a sharp knife, cut diamond shapes in dough, down to meringue layer. Dust with powdered sugar, then bake 40 to 50 minutes or until browned and crisp. Serve warm or cold, cut into diamonds, and dusted with more sugar.

Makes 6 to 8 servings.

BAKLAVA

1 cup blanched almonds
1 cup walnuts
⅓ cup pistachio nuts
⅓ cup packed brown sugar
1 teaspoon ground cinnamon
¼ teaspoon freshly grated nutmeg
¼ cup butter
8 sheets filo pastry
SYRUP:
1 cup granulated sugar
⅔ cup water
1 tablespoon fresh lemon juice
1 tablespoon orange-flower water

To make syrup, in a saucepan, heat sugar, water and lemon juice until sugar dissolves. Boil gently 5 minutes or until syrupy. Add orange-flower water and boil 2 minutes. Cool completely. In a food processor fitted with the metal blade, process ⅓ of all nuts until finely chopped. Coarsely chop remaining nuts. In a bowl, mix together nuts, brown sugar, cinnamon and nutmeg. Butter a 13- x 9-inch baking pan. Preheat oven to 350F (175C). In a saucepan, melt butter.

Cut dough sheets in half across. Brush one halved sheet with butter and place on bottom of roasting pan. Repeat with 3 more sheets. Spread one-third of nut mixture over the top, then repeat the layers twice more, ending with a layer of dough. With a sharp knife, cut top layer of dough into diamonds. Bake in oven 30 to 40 minutes until crisp and golden. Pour cold syrup over the top. When cold, trim edges and cut into diamond shapes.

Makes about 20.

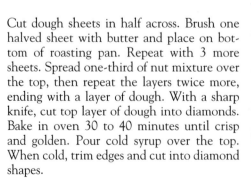

HOT PUDDINGS

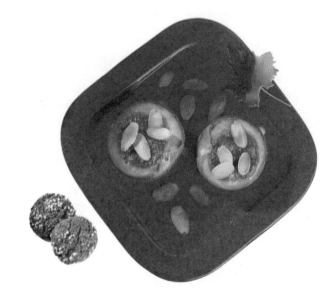

ROAST FIGS

AMARETTI-STUFFED PEACHES

12 figs
3 tablespoons sugar
1 tablespoon orange juice
⅔ cup walnut halves
1 tablespoon honey
Regular plain yogurt to serve

Preheat oven to 400F (200C). Butter a shallow flameproof dish. Put figs side by side in dish.

4 large peaches
2 ozs. amaretti biscuits
1 egg yolk
4 teaspoons sugar
2 tablespoons softened butter
1 cup sweet white wine
Toasted flaked almonds and vine leaves, to decorate

Preheat oven to 375F (190C). Butter an ovenproof dish. Cut peaches in half and remove pits.

Sprinkle with 2 tablespoons of sugar and orange juice. Cook in oven 20 minutes, basting from time to time with cooking juices. Add walnuts and sprinkle with remaining sugar.

Scoop out a little flesh from each peach half and place in a bowl. Crush amaretti biscuits and add to bowl. Stir in egg yolk, sugar and butter and mix well. Put some filling in each peach half, forming it into a smooth mound.

Reduce oven temperature to 300F (150C) and cook another 10 minutes. Remove figs and walnuts with a slotted spoon and arrange on a serving dish. Add honey to cooking juices and warm through over low heat. Spoon syrup over figs and serve warm or cold with yogurt.

Makes 4 servings.

Put peaches in dish and pour in wine. Cook in oven 30 to 40 minutes or until peaches are tender and filling is firm. Transfer to serving plates, sprinkle with toasted almonds and decorate with vine leaves. Spoon cooking juices around and serve.

Makes 4 servings.

Note: Be careful not to cook peaches for too long – they should retain their shape.

PINEAPPLE ALASKA

RED BERRY SOUFFLÉ

1 large ripe pineapple with leaves
1 to 2 tablespoons kirsch
1 quart vanilla ice cream
3 egg whites
¾ cup plus 1 tablespoon superfine sugar

Cut pineapple in half lengthwise. Using a grapefruit knife, cut out pulp. Discard core, then cut pulp in chunks and place in a bowl. Sprinkle with kirsch, cover with plastic wrap and chill pulp and pineapple shells overnight.

Place pineapple chunks in shells and pack ice cream on top. Freeze about 2 hours, until very firm. Preheat oven to 400F (205C). Whisk egg whites in a bowl until stiff. Whisk in ¼ cup plus 2 tablespoons of sugar, then whisk 1 minute more. Fold in ¼ cup plus 2 tablespoons of sugar.

Pile meringue over ice cream, completely covering ice cream. Make small peaks in meringue with a flat-bladed knife. Place pineapple shells on a baking sheet and sprinkle with remaining sugar. Bake about 8 minutes, until meringue is set and brown. Serve immediately.

Makes 6 servings.

Variation: Prepare this dessert using a fruit sorbet instead of vanilla ice cream.

2 tablespoons butter
½ cup plus 1 tablespoon superfine sugar
1¾ cups mixed red berries, thawed if frozen
1 tablespoon strawberry liqueur or crème de cassis
5 egg whites
Powdered sugar to serve

Preheat oven to 350F (175C). Butter a 4-cup soufflé dish, then dust with 1 tablespoon of superfine sugar.

In a blender or food processor, process remaining superfine sugar, berries and liqueur to a purée. Pour into a bowl. In a separate bowl, whisk egg whites until stiff but not dry. Fold 1 tablespoon of whipped egg whites into purée. Pour purée onto whipped egg whites and, using a metal spoon, carefully fold in.

Spoon mixture into prepared soufflé dish. Place dish on a baking sheet and bake 25 to 30 minutes, until risen and just set. Dust with powdered sugar and serve immediately.

Makes 6 servings.

Note: If desired, spoon mixture into 6 individual soufflé dishes and bake 15 to 20 minutes.

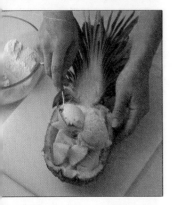

CRUNCHY MARASCHINO PEACHES

6 medium-size peaches
¼ cup maraschino or other cherry liqueur
1¼ cups whipping cream
⅓ cup packed light-brown sugar
Fresh sweet cherries and leaves to garnish, if desired

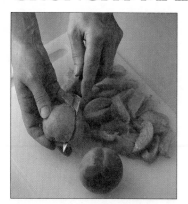

Blanch peaches in boiling water 1 minute. Drain and peel. Cut pulp in thick slices. Discard pits.

Place peach slices in an oval flameproof dish, filling dish evenly. Pour liqueur over peaches. In a bowl, whip cream until stiff and drop spoonfuls on top of peaches. Gently spread whipped cream evenly. Cover dish with plastic wrap and refrigerate at least 4 hours.

To serve, preheat broiler. Remove plastic wrap from dish and sprinkle brown sugar evenly over whipped cream. Broil until sugar has dissolved and caramelized. Garnish with fresh cherries and leaves, if desired. Serve at once.

Makes 6 servings.

FIGS WITH CINNAMON CREAM

9 large ripe figs
¼ cup unsalted butter
4 teaspoons brandy
1 tablespoon brown sugar
Almond slices to decorate
CINNAMON CREAM:
⅔ cup whipping cream
1 teaspoon ground cinnamon
1 tablespoon brandy
2 teaspoons honey

To prepare Cinnamon Cream, in a small bowl, combine all ingredients. Cover and refrigerate 30 minutes to allow flavors to develop.

Preheat broiler. Halve figs and thread onto 6 skewers. In a small pan, melt butter. Stir in brandy.

Brush figs with brandy butter and sprinkle with a little sugar. Broil 4 to 5 minutes or until bubbling and golden. Whip Cinnamon Cream until just soft peaks form, decorate with almond slices and serve with broiled figs.

Makes 6 servings.

BANANAS WITH RUM & LIME

¼ cup butter
¼ cup packed light brown sugar
½ teaspoon ground cinnamon
4 bananas, cut into ½-inch pieces
⅓ cup light rum
Grated peel and juice of 1 lime or lemon
2 tablespoons chopped almonds
Shaved fresh coconut or toasted shredded coconut to
  decorate

Heat a wok until hot. Add butter and swirl to melt and coat wok. Stir in sugar and cinnamon and cook 1 minute until sugar melts and mixture bubbles.

Add bananas and gently stir-fry 1 or 2 minutes, tossing to coat all pieces and heat through. Add rum and, with a match, ignite rum. Shake wok gently until flames subside. Add lime peel, lime juice and almonds. Spoon into dishes and top with coconut.

Makes 4 servings.

TOFFEE PEARS & PECANS

4 pears, peeled, cut in half lengthwise and cored
2 tablespoons lemon juice
5 tablespoons butter
½ cup packed brown sugar
1 teaspoon ground cinnamon
½ teaspoon ground ginger
1 cup pecan halves
1 cup whipping cream
Vanilla extract

Cut pear halves into ¼-inch-thick slices. Sprinkle with lemon juice.

Heat a wok until hot. Add 2 tablespoons of the butter and 3 tablespoons of the brown sugar and swirl to coat wok. Stir until sugar melts and bubbles. Add pear slices, spices and pecans and stir-fry gently 4 to 6 minutes or until pear slices are crisp-tender. Remove pear mixture to a shallow serving dish.

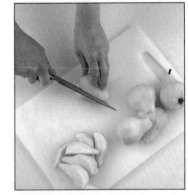

Add remaining butter and sugar to wok and stir 2 minutes or until sugar dissolves and sauce boils. Stir in cream and bring to a boil. Simmer 3 minutes or until sauce thickens. Remove from heat, add a little vanilla and pour over pear mixture. Serve warm or at room temperature.

Makes 4 to 6 servings.

BLACKBERRY-APPLE COBBLER

1 lb. cooking apples
8 ozs. blackberries
2 tablespoons water
⅓ cup sugar
2 cups self-rising flour
Pinch of salt
2 teaspoons apple-pie spice
3 tablespoons margarine
⅔ cup milk

Preheat oven to 425F (220C). Peel, core and slice apples and place in a saucepan with blackberries and water. Cover and simmer until just soft, stirring occasionally. Mix in ¼ cup sugar; pour into a 7-cup baking dish.

Sift flour into a bowl with salt and mixed spice. Rub or cut in margarine until mixture resembles coarse crumbs, then stir in remaining sugar. Add enough milk to make a soft dough. Roll out dough on a lightly floured surface and cut out 12 (2-inch) rounds.

Place rounds around edge of dish on top of fruit, overlapping them slightly. Brush rounds with a little milk. Bake 15 to 20 minutes or until browned.

Makes 6 servings.

CHERRY CLAFOUTI

1½ lbs. pitted dark sweet cherries, thawed and drained if frozen
¾ cup all-purpose flour
Pinch of salt
3 eggs
⅓ cup superfine sugar
2 cups milk
1 tablespoon cherry brandy or kirsch
Powdered sugar

Preheat oven to 400F (205C). Butter an oval baking dish and place cherries in it.

Sift flour and salt into a small bowl. In a large bowl, beat eggs and sugar until creamy, then fold in flour and salt. In a saucepan, warm milk slightly over low heat and stir milk and cherry brandy or kirsch into egg mixture. Beat well until batter is smooth, then pour batter over cherries.

Bake 30 minutes, until set and golden. Serve warm dusted with powdered sugar.

Makes 6 servings.

Note: Fresh cherries can taste a little bland when cooked. Add 1 to 2 drops almond extract to improve the flavor, if desired.

PEAR CRUMBLE

1 (14-oz.) cans pear halves packed in fruit juice
1 tablespoon granulated sugar
2 teaspoons ground cinnamon
1¼ cups whole-wheat flour
¼ cup packed brown sugar
⅓ cup margarine

Preheat oven to 400F (205C). Into a bowl, drain pears, reserving juice. Chop pears roughly. Mix sugar with 1 teaspoon of the cinnamon and mix with pears.

In a bowl, mix together remaining cinnamon, flour and brown sugar. Rub or cut in margarine until mixture resembles coarse crumbs.

In a 5-cup baking dish, layer crumble mixture and pear mixture, pouring pear juice over fruit. Finish with a crumble layer. Bake 30 minutes or until golden on top. Serve hot or cold.

Makes 6 servings.

BAKED STUFFED APPLES

3 tablespoons dark raisins
3 tablespoons golden raisins
¼ cup plus 1 tablespoon ginger wine, Madeira or
  sweet sherry
4 large baking apples
¾ cup toasted sliced almonds
1-2 tablespoons orange marmalade
Chilled whipped cream to serve

Preheat oven to 350F (175C). In a small bowl, combine raisins and ginger wine, Madeira or sweet sherry. Let stand several hours.

Wash and dry apples; do not peel. Core apples and score a line around middle of each apple. Place in an ovenproof dish. Drain raisins, reserving liquid. In a bowl, mix raisins, almonds and marmalade and fill apple cavities with fruit and nut mixture, pushing mixture down firmly. Pour strained liquid over apples.

Bake apples 45 minutes to 1 hour, until soft. Spoon a dollop of whipped cream on top of each apple and serve immediately.

Makes 4 servings.

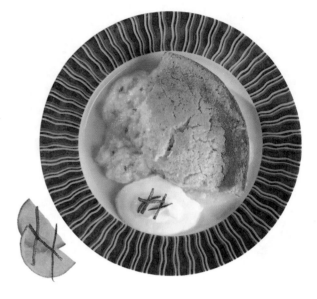

RICE PUDDING WITH PEACHES

3¾ cups whole milk
6 cardamom pods
½ cup short grain rice
½ cup pistachio nuts, chopped
½ cup packed light brown sugar
¼ cup butter, diced
2 egg yolks
1 (14-oz.) can peach halves, drained

Pour milk into a flameproof casserole dish. Add cardamom pods, bring to a boil, reduce heat and simmer 5 minutes. Remove cardamom pods. Stir in rice.

Return to a boil, reduce heat and simmer, stirring frequently, 15 to 20 minutes, or until rice is tender and most of liquid has been absorbed. Remove from heat and stir in pistachio nuts, half of the brown sugar, the butter and egg yolks. Let cool slightly. Preheat oven to 325F (165C).

Remove half of mixture from dish and set aside. Arrange peaches on top of rice in dish and cover with remaining rice. Bake 25 minutes. Preheat broiler. Sprinkle pudding with remaining sugar and broil until sugar melts and turns a deep golden brown. Serve warm.

Makes 6 to 8 servings.

SAUCY LIME PUDDING

¼ cup unsalted butter, softened
¼ cup sugar
Grated zest and juice of 3 limes
2 eggs, separated
½ cup self-rising flour
1¼ cups milk

Preheat oven to 325F (160C). In a large bowl, beat together butter, sugar and lime zest until light and fluffy. Stir in egg yolks and carefully fold in flour. Stir in milk and lime juice.

Whisk egg whites until they form stiff peaks. Fold into lime mixture. Lightly butter an ovenproof dish.

Pour lime mixture into dish and bake 40 to 50 minutes, or until risen and golden. Serve warm.

Makes 4 to 6 servings.

BREAD & FRUIT PUDDING

¾ cup raisins and currants, mixed
8 thin slices white bread, buttered
2 tablespoons candied fruit, chopped
Superfine sugar
CUSTARD:
1 egg yolk
1¼ cups milk
⅔ cup half and half
1 vanilla bean
1 teaspoon superfine sugar

In a bowl, cover raisins and currants with water; let stand to swell. Preheat oven to 350F (175C). Grease an oval baking dish.

Cut crusts from bread and sandwich 4 slices together. Cut in 4 squares and place in greased dish. Drain fruit and sprinkle fruit and chopped candied fruit over bread. Top with remaining bread, buttered side up.

To prepare custard, place egg yolk in a large glass measure. In a saucepan, combine milk, half and half, vanilla bean and sugar and bring almost to boiling point. Pour over egg, stir, then strain into dish, pouring down sides so top slices of bread are not soaked. Let stand 30 minutes. Sprinkle with sugar and place in a roasting pan. Pour in enough boiling water to come halfway up sides of dish and bake 45 to 50 minutes, until top is golden-brown. Serve immediately.

Makes 4 servings.

QUEEN OF PUDDINGS

2¼ cups milk
¼ cup butter
2 cups cake crumbs
Grated zest of 1 lemon
Grated zest of 1 orange
¼ cup sugar
4 egg yolks, beaten
2 egg whites, beaten until stiff
¼ cup strawberry jelly
4 ozs. strawberries, sliced
Powdered sugar for dusting
MERINGUE:
2 egg whites
¼ cup sugar

Preheat oven to 325F (165C). Put milk and butter into a flameproof casserole dish and heat gently until butter melts. Stir in cake crumbs and lemon and orange zests. Whisk in sugar and egg yolks. Fold in egg whites. Put dish in a deep roasting pan and pour in enough boiling water to come halfway up side of dish. Bake 45 to 50 minutes or until set. Mix together jelly and strawberries and spread over top of pudding.

Remove pudding from water. To make meringue, beat egg whites until they form stiff peaks. Beat in sugar. Put mixture in a pastry bag with a star tip and pipe in a lattice pattern on top of pudding. Dust with powdered sugar and bake 30 minutes. Serve warm.

Makes 4 to 6 servings.

Note: Queen of Puddings is a classic English dessert.

MANGO WITH STICKY RICE

1¼ cups sticky rice, soaked overnight in cold water
1 cup coconut milk
Pinch of salt
2-4 tablespoons sugar or to taste
2 large ripe mangoes, peeled and halved
3 tablespoons coconut cream
Mint leaves to decorate

Drain and rinse rice thoroughly. Place in a steaming basket lined with a double thickness of cheesecloth. Steam over simmering water 30 minutes. Remove from heat.

In a medium-size bowl, stir together coconut milk, salt and sugar to taste until sugar has dissolved. Stir in warm rice. Set aside 30 minutes.

Thinly slice mangoes by cutting lengthwise through flesh to the seed. Discard the seeds. Spoon rice into mounds in centers of 4 plates and arrange mango slices around. Pour coconut cream over rice. Decorate with mint leaves.

Makes 4 servings.

SUMMER FRUIT GRATIN

2 large peaches, peeled and sliced
½ cup raspberries
¾ cup sliced strawberries
About ⅓ cup red currants and blueberries or black currants
2 tablespoons kirsch or Cointreau (optional)
2 tablespoons granulated sugar
1¼ cups crème fraîche or whipping cream
½ cup packed light brown sugar

Divide fruit among four heatproof serving dishes. Sprinkle with kirsch or Cointreau, if using, and granulated sugar.

Whip crème fraîche or cream until it forms soft peaks. Spread over fruit and refrigerate at least 1 hour.

Preheat broiler to very hot. Sprinkle a thick even layer of brown sugar over crème fraîche or cream. Broil until sugar is bubbling and caramelized. Serve immediately.

Makes 4 servings.

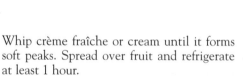

ZABAGLIONE

4 egg yolks
2½ ozs. vanilla sugar
½ cup Marsala
Lady fingers, to serve

With an electric whisk, whisk the egg yolks and sugar together in a large heatproof bowl until pale and fluffy. Place bowl over a pan of gently simmering water. Mix in the Marsala.

Start whisking slowly. Gradually whisk faster until the mixture doubles in volume and becomes very thick and glossy. Take care not to overheat or the mixture will scramble.

Spoon the zabaglione into heatproof glasses or ramekins and serve immediately with lady fingers.

Makes 6 servings.

Note: To make vanilla sugar, simply store a vanilla bean in a jar of sugar and leave at least 2 to 3 weeks for it to flavor the sugar.

CARAMEL SESAME BANANAS

4 bananas
Juice of 1 lemon
4 ozs. sugar
2 tablespoons sesame seeds
Mint sprigs and lemon slices to decorate

Peel bananas and cut into 2-inch pieces. Place in a bowl, add lemon juice and stir to coat.

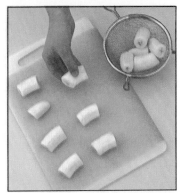

Place sugar and ¼ cup water in a saucepan and heat gently, stirring, until the sugar dissolves. Bring to a boil and cook 5 or 6 minutes or until the mixture caramelizes and turns golden brown. Drain bananas well and arrange on parchment paper.

Drizzle caramel over the bananas, working quickly as the caramel sets within a few seconds. Sprinkle with sesame seeds. Allow to cool 5 minutes, then carefully peel away from paper, decorate and serve.

Makes 4 servings.

Note: Tossing the banana in lemon juice prevents it from turning brown.

FRIED CUSTARD

About 3 tablespoons sugar
3 eggs
½ cup all-purpose flour
1 cup whipping cream
1 cup milk
Few drops of vanilla extract
1½ cups cake crumbs, preferably lemon cake
Vegetable oil for deep-frying
Orange slices and zest to decorate

Lightly flour an 11- x 7-inch baking pan. In a bowl, beat together sugar and 2 eggs until pale. Gradually stir in flour.

In a heavy, preferably nonstick, saucepan, heat cream, milk and vanilla extract to a boil. Slowly pour into the egg mixture, stirring. Return to heat and simmer, stirring, until thickened; do not boil. Pour onto baking pan to make an even layer about ½-inch thick, then cool. Cover and refrigerate at least 1 hour. Cut cold custard mixture into 1-inch squares, rectangles or diamonds.

Beat remaining egg. Dip shapes first in beaten egg, then in the crumbs. Half fill a deep-fryer or pan with vegetable oil and heat to 375F (190C). Add coated shapes in batches and cook about 1½ minutes or until golden and crisp on outside; keep oil temperature up because the cubes should cook very quickly. Using a slotted spoon, transfer to paper towels, drain quickly and serve immediately. Decorate with orange slices and zest.

Makes 4 to 6 servings.

SOUFFLÉ OMELET

3 eggs, separated
1 tablespoon half and half
2 teaspoons superfine sugar
1 tablespoon butter
2 tablespoons raspbery jam
Powdered sugar
Fresh raspberries and leaves to garnish if desired

Preheat oven to 400F (205C). In a bowl, beat egg yolks, half and half and superfine sugar lightly. In a large bowl, whisk egg whites until stiff. Add egg yolk mixture to whisked egg whites and carefully fold together.

In an omelet pan, melt butter over medium heat and pour egg mixture into pan. Spread evenly and cook about 1 minute, until brown underneath. Bake in oven 5 minutes, until top is set. Meanwhile, heat 2 metal skewers either in a gas flame or under a broiler until they are red hot and glowing.

Warm jam slightly. Remove omelet from oven and quickly spread with jam. Fold over and transfer to a serving plate. Sift powdered sugar thickly over omelet. Holding hot skewers with thick oven gloves, mark a criss-cross pattern in powdered sugar by pressing in skewers. Garnish with fresh raspberries and leaves, if desired, and serve immediately.

Makes 2 servings.

APPLE PANCAKES

1 cup all-purpose flour, sifted with pinch of salt
½ cup milk combined with ½ cup water
2 eggs
1 tablespoon vegetable oil
3 eating apples
2 teaspoons lemon juice
1 tablespoon brandy
2 teaspoons superfine sugar

In a food processor fitted with the metal blade, process flour and salt, ½ of milk and water and eggs. Blend well, add remaining milk and water and oil and blend again. Let stand 30 minutes. Process again before using.

Peel and core apples and slice very finely onto a plate. Sprinkle with lemon juice and brandy. Heat a 6- or 7-inch heavy-bottom skillet and grease lightly. Pour in 1 tablespoon of batter and roll pan to spread evenly. Place a few apple slices over pancake, then spoon a little more batter over apples. Cook 2 to 3 minutes, until batter is almost set. Place pan under a broiler to finish cooking batter.

Turn pancake out onto a plate and sprinkle with sugar. Prepare remaining pancakes. Garnish with sliced apple and mint leaves, if desired. Serve immediately.

Makes 4 servings.

Variation: Beer or cider can be used instead of milk.

Note: Mixing milk and water helps to lighten pancake batter.

PEKING APPLES

1 egg
½ cup water
1 cup all-purpose flour
4 crisp eating apples
2½ cups vegetable oil
SYRUP:
1 tablespoon vegetable oil
2 tablespoons water
6 tablespoons brown sugar
2 tablespoons corn syrup
Iced water to set

In a large bowl, stir the egg and water into the flour to make a thick batter. Peel, core and thickly slice apples. Dip each apple slice in the batter to evenly coat; allow excess to drain off. In a wok, heat oil until smoking. Add apple pieces in batches and deep-fry 3 minutes until golden brown. Using a slotted spoon, remove to paper towels to drain.

To make syrup, in a small saucepan, gently heat oil, water and sugar, stirring until sugar has dissolved. Simmer 5 minutes, stirring. Stir in corn syrup and boil 5 to 10 minutes until thick and syrupy. Reduce heat to very low. Dip each piece of apple into syrup to coat then place in ice cold water a few seconds. Remove to a serving dish. Repeat with remaining apple. Serve immediately.

Makes 4 servings.

FRUIT FRITTERS

4 baking or crisp tart eating apples
2-3 tablespoons calvados or cognac
3 tablespoons superfine sugar
1 cup all-purpose flour
Pinch of salt
2 eggs, separated
⅔ cup milk
1 tablespoon vegetable oil
Vegetable oil for deep-frying
Powdered sugar
Edible flowers to garnish if desired

Peel, core and cut apples in rings.

In a shallow dish, mix calvados or cognac with ½ of sugar. Add apples, turning to coat. Let stand 30 minutes. Sift flour and salt into a large bowl and mix in remaining sugar. Make a well in center and drop in egg yolks. Using a wooden spoon, draw flour into yolks while gradually adding milk. Beat to a smooth batter, then let stand 30 minutes. In a separate bowl, whisk egg whites until stiff and fold into batter with 1 tablespoon oil.

Heat oil for deep frying to 385F (195C). Drain fruit and dip each ring into batter to coat. Deep-fry a few at a time, turning once, until puffed up and golden-brown. Drain on paper towels. Sprinkle with powdered sugar. Garnish with edible flowers, if desired. Serve hot.

Makes 4 servings.

Variation: Use pineapple, pears or bananas in place of apples, soaking fruit in an appropriate liqueur 30 minutes.

FRUIT-FILLED WHITE CRÊPES

3 egg whites, lightly beaten
¼ cup cornstarch
1 teaspoon sunflower oil
Mint sprigs to decorate
FILLING:
4 slices fresh pineapple, chopped
2 kiwi fruit, peeled and quartered
½ mango, peeled, pitted and sliced
½ papaya, peeled, seeded and chopped
2 tablespoons dry sherry
1 tablespoon brown sugar
1 whole cinnamon stick, broken
2 star anise

Place all the filling ingredients in a nonstick or well-seasoned wok and mix gently. Bring to a boil, reduce heat and simmer very gently 10 minutes. Remove and discard cinnamon stick and star anise. Set aside. Meanwhile, make the crêpes. Put egg whites and cornstarch in a bowl and stir in 8 teaspoons water, mixing well to form a smooth paste.

Brush a nonstick or well-seasoned crêpe pan with a little oil and heat. Pour in a quarter of the mixture, tilting pan to cover the bottom. Cook 1 minute on one side only, until set. Drain on paper towels, layer with parchment paper and keep warm while making the remaining 3 crepes. Lay crêpes cooked-side up, fill with the fruit and fold crêpes over the filling. Decorate and serve.

Makes 4 servings.

MINCEMEAT CRÊPE GÂTEAU

1 recipe Pancakes (page 363)
1 (12-oz.) jar prepared mincemeat
1 eating apple
1 tablespoon brandy
Grated peel of 1 orange
Juice of ½ lemon
1 cup sliced almonds
¼ cup apricot jam, sieved
Orange slices and fresh herbs to garnish, if desired

Prepare pancakes as directed. Preheat oven to 350F (175C). Grease an 8-inch round baking dish. Spoon mincemeat into a saucepan. Peel, core and chop apple and add to mincemeat.

Heat through, stirring occasionally, until apple is tender. Remove from heat and stir in brandy, orange peel, lemon juice and ¾ of almonds. Place 1 pancake in greased dish and spread with a small amount of mincemeat mixture. Layer gâteau, alternating pancakes and mincemeat, ending with a pancake.

In a small saucepan, warm apricot jam and pour over gâteau. Sprinkle with remaining almonds and bake 15 minutes. Cut in wedges and garnish with orange slices and fresh herbs, if desired. Serve at once.

Makes 6 servings.

HOT ORANGE CAKE

8 tablespoons butter, softened
½ cup superfine sugar
2 large eggs, separated
1 cup self-rising flour
Greated peel and juice of 3 small oranges
1 cup whipping cream
Powdered sugar and fresh orange sections to decorate

Preheat oven to 350F (175C). In a large bowl, cream butter and superfine sugar until light and fluffy. Beat egg yolks into mixture with 1 tablespoon of flour and grated peel and juice of 1 orange.

In a separate bowl, whisk egg whites until stiff but not dry; fold into creamed mixture with remaining flour. Spoon into a deep 8-inch nonstick cake pan. Bake 20 to 30 minutes, until golden-brown and springy to touch.

Meanwhile, in a bowl, whip cream and remaining orange juice and peel until stiff. Leave cake in pan 2 to 3 minutes, then turn out and cut in half crosswise. Working quickly, spread bottom with whipped cream and cover with top half of cake. Dust thickly with powdered sugar and arrange orange sections on top. Serve at once.

Makes 6 servings.

Note: The whipped cream will melt, so serve as quickly as possible.

APRICOT UPSIDE-DOWN CAKE

1 (14-oz.) can apricot halves packed in fruit juice
6 candied cherries
½ cup margarine
⅓ cup packed brown sugar
2 eggs, beaten
2 cups self-rising flour
5 tablespoons milk
Vanilla frozen yogurt to serve

Preheat oven to 350F (175C). Grease a 9-inch cake pan. Drain apricots and halve cherries. Arrange cherries cut-side down in greased pan. Place apricot halves over cherries.

In a bowl, cream together margarine and sugar until light and fluffy. Gradually add eggs, beating well after each addition. Using a large metal spoon, fold in flour and milk to make a soft batter.

Spread mixture over apricots. Bake 45 minutes or until cake springs back when lightly pressed. Turn out cake on a wire rack, then place on a plate, bottom-side up. Serve with frozen yogurt.

Makes 8 servings.

COCONUT CUSTARDS

2 egg yolks
3 eggs
2 cups coconut milk
⅓ cup sugar
Few drops rosewater or jasmine extract
Toasted coconut to decorate

Preheat oven to 350F (175C). Place 4 individual heatproof custard cups in a baking pan.

In a medium-size bowl, stir together egg yolks, eggs, coconut milk, sugar and rosewater or jasmine extract until sugar dissolves. Pour through a strainer into cups. Pour boiling water into baking pan to surround cups.

Bake about 20 minutes until a knife inserted off-center in custard comes out clean. Remove from baking pan and cook slightly before unmolding. Serve warm or cold. Decorate with toasted coconut.

Makes 4 servings.

CABINET PUDDING

⅓ cup raisins
2 tablespoons rum, brandy or water
10 ozs. chocolate or plain sponge cake or ratafias
½ cup superfine sugar
1 cup chopped mixed nuts
4 eggs
2 cups milk
¼ cup sliced almonds
RASPBERRY SAUCE:
1¾ cups fresh or frozen raspberries
2 tablespoons lemon juice
¼-⅓ cup superfine sugar
⅓ cup framboise liqueur or water

Soak raisins in rum or brandy at least 1 hour.

Preheat oven to 350F (175C). Lightly butter an oval baking dish. Break up sponge cake coarsely and place in buttered dish. Add raisins and soaking liquid, then sprinkle with about ¼ of sugar and all chopped mixed nuts. In a bowl, beat eggs with remaining sugar and whisk in milk. Pour into dish. Sprinkle with almonds.

Place dish in a roasting pan and add boiling water to come halfway up sides. Bake 1 to 1½ hours, until custard is lightly set. To make Raspberry Sauce, combine all ingredients in a saucepan and bring slowly to a boil. Simmer a few minutes. Using a wooden spoon, press through a nylon sieve. Serve pudding hot with sauce. Decorate with fresh raspberries, if desired.

Makes 6 servings.

COFFEE BRÛLÉE

8 egg yolks
½ cup sugar
1 cup whole milk
2 cups whipping cream
1 teaspoon coffee flavoring
Summer berries to decorate
TOPPING:
¼ cup sugar

In a large bowl, beat together egg yolks and sugar until light and foamy.

Put milk, cream and coffee flavoring in a flameproof casserole dish. Simmer but do not boil. Remove from heat and let cool. Preheat oven to 300F (150C). Pour milk mixture into egg yolk mixture and stir well. Pour into a measuring cup and allow froth to rise to surface. Skim off froth. Pour mixture back into dish.

Put a piece of waxed paper in a roasting pan. Put dish on top of paper. Pour enough boiling water into pan to come halfway up side of dish. Bake 45 minutes or until mixture has set. Let cool slightly, then refrigerate. To make topping, preheat broiler. Sprinkle top of custard with sugar and broil until sugar melts and turns a deep golden-brown. Decorate with summer berries and serve.

Makes 6 servings.

STEAMED RAISIN PUDDING

1 cup self-rising flour
3 tablespoons cornstarch
1 teaspoon baking powder
½ cup superfine sugar
8 tablespoons butter, softened
Grated peel and juice of 1 orange
2 eggs
¾ cup golden raisins
⅓ cup chopped mixed candied citrus peel
Milk, if needed
1 recipe Black Currant & Cassis Sauce (page 349)

Butter a 3¾-cup bowl or an 8-inch ring mold. Sift flour, cornstarch and baking powder onto a plate.

In a large bowl, cream sugar, butter and grated orange peel until light and fluffy. In a separate bowl, beat eggs with orange juice; beat gradually into butter mixture with 1 tablespoon of flour mixture. Fold in remaining flour with raisins and candied peel. Mixture should be a soft dropping consistency; if too stiff, add a small amount of milk.

Spoon mixture into prepared bowl or mold and cover with a piece of buttered foil pleated in middle. Tie securely around rim of bowl or mold and set in a saucepan of gently boiling water to come halfway up sides. Steam 1½ to 2 hours. Meanwhile, prepare Black Currant & Cassis Sauce as directed. Turn out pudding and serve warm with sauce.

Makes 6 servings.

STEAMED FRUIT DUMPLINGS

1 small banana, chopped
Grated zest and juice of 1 small lemon
1 oz. dried mango or dried apricots, chopped
8 pitted dates, chopped
1 oz. ground almonds
Large pinch ground cinnamon
12 round wonton skins
1 egg white, lightly beaten
2 teaspoons powdered sugar
Strips of dried mango and date and mint sprigs, to decorate

Place banana, lemon zest and juice, mango, dates, almonds and cinnamon in a food processor and blend until smooth.

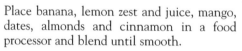

Divide fruit mixture among wonton skins, placing it in the center of each one. Brush edges of the wonton skins with egg white, fold in half to form crescent shapes and press edges together to seal.

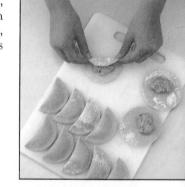

Bring a wok or large saucepan of water to a boil. Place dumplings on a sheet of parchment paper in a steamer and place over the water. Cover and steam 10 minutes or until soft. Dust with powdered sugar, decorate and serve.

Serves 4.

HOT CHOCOLATE SOUFFLÉ

2 tablespoons superfine sugar
4 ozs. semisweet chocolate
2 tablespoons brandy or coffee
4 eggs, separated, plus 2 extra whites
1 recipe Dark Chocolate Sauce (page 313), if
  desired, and powdered sugar to serve

Preheat oven to 400F (205C). Butter a 4-cup soufflé dish and dust with 1 tablespoon of superfine sugar. Break chocolate in pieces. In top of a double boiler or a bowl set over a pan of simmering water, place chocolate pieces and brandy or coffee.

Cook over medium heat, stirring until smooth. Remove from heat and beat in remaining superfine sugar and egg yolks. In a bowl, whisk egg whites until stiff but not dry. Fold 1 tablespoon into chocolate mixture. Scrape chocolate mixture into egg whites and, using a metal spoon, quickly fold together.

Pour into buttered soufflé dish and place on a baking sheet. Bake 15 to 18 minutes, until risen and just set. Meanwhile prepare Dark Chocolate Sauce, if desired, according to directions. Dust soufflé with powdered sugar and serve immediately with sauce, if desired.

Makes 4 servings.

Note: Take care when melting chocolate not to overheat it. It loses its gloss and becomes very thick, making it difficult to combine with other ingredients.

LEMON BELVOIR PUDDING

8 tablespoons butter, softened
½ cup superfine sugar
2 large egg yolks
2½ cups fresh bread crumbs
Grated peel and juice of 2 lemons
1 teaspoon baking powder
1 recipe Hot Lemon Sauce (page 313)
Powdered sugar
Lemon peel strips and fresh herbs to garnish, if
  desired

Generously butter a 4-cup charlotte mold. In a large bowl, cream butter and sugar until light and fluffy.

Beat in egg yolks and bread crumbs. When well mixed, stir in lemon peel and juice and baking powder. Spoon into buttered mold and cover top with a piece of foil pleated in middle. Tie securely around mold, then set mold in a saucepan of enough gently boiling water to come halfway up sides.

Steam 45 minutes to 1 hour. Check water in pan occasionally and add more boiling water as necessary. Meanwhile, prepare Hot Lemon Sauce as directed. Turn out pudding and dust with powdered sugar. Garnish with lemon peel strips and fresh herbs, if desired, and serve pudding hot with sauce.

Makes 4 servings.

Note: A charlotte mold is a plain cylindrical mold.

ROUND CHRISTMAS PUDDING

3 cups mixed dried fruit
½ cup chopped prunes
⅓ cup chopped glacé cherries
½ cup chopped almonds
¼ cup grated carrot
¼ cup grated cooking apple
Finely grated peel and juice 1 orange
1 tablespoon molasses
1 tablespoon brandy
⅓ cup stout
1 egg, beaten
¼ cup butter, melted
⅓ cup dark-brown sugar
¾ teaspoon ground allspice
½ cup all-purpose flour
1 cup soft white bread crumbs
Holly sprigs to decorate
Additional brandy

Combine mixed fruit, prunes, cherries, almonds, carrot, apple, orange peel and juice, molasses, brandy and stout. Stir in egg, butter, brown sugar, allspice, flour and bread crumbs. Cover with plastic wrap and refrigerate. Using a 5-inch buttered spherical mold or a rice steamer mold lined with a double thickness of foil, fill each half of mold with mixture. Place 2 halves together, securing mold tightly.

Half-fill a saucepan with water. Bring to a boil and place mold in so water comes just below seam of mold. Cover and simmer 6 hours. Cool in mold, then turn out. When cold, wrap in foil. To reheat, unwrap and replace in mold. Cook as before in simmering water 2 to 3 hours. Decorate with holly. Warm brandy, spoon over pudding and light.

Makes 8 servings.

CARROT PUDDING

½ cup margarine
⅓ cup packed brown sugar
2 eggs, beaten
1½ cups self-rising flour, sifted
1 cup coarsely grated carrots
⅓ cup golden raisins
3 tablespoons milk

Grease a deep 5-cup heatproof bowl. In a bowl, cream together margarine and sugar until light and fluffy. Gradually add beaten eggs, beating well after each addition.

Using a metal spoon, stir in flour, carrots, raisins and milk, mixing gently to combine. Spoon batter into greased bowl and level surface.

Cover with a double layer of parchment paper and secure with string. Place bowl in a saucepan of gently boiling water that comes half-way up bowl. Steam 1½ hours. To serve, turn out onto a plate.

Serves 8.

COLD DESSERTS

PEARS WITH CHOCOLATE SAUCE

CARAMEL ORANGES

½ cup ricotta cheese
½ cup hazelnuts, finely ground
2 tablespoons honey
2 small egg yolks
Seeds from 1 cardamom pod, crushed
4 large pears
Mint sprigs to decorate
CHOCOLATE SAUCE:
4 ozs. semisweet chocolate
3 tablespoons unsalted butter
2 tablespoons brandy
2 tablespoons dairy sour cream

In a bowl, cream together cheese, hazelnuts, honey, egg yolks and cardamom seeds.

4 large oranges
½ cup sugar
1¼ cups fresh orange juice
1 tablespoon orange liqueur

Remove the peel from the oranges, then remove pith as you would an apple, being careful not to leave any of the white pith behind. Cut the peel into fine julienned strips.

Preheat oven to 375F (190C). Cut a thin slice from bottom of each pear. Using a corer or small spoon, carefully scoop out core as far up inside pear as possible, without damaging skin. Fill cavities with ricotta mixture, pressing in well; smooth bottoms flat. Peel pears and place in a small roasting pan. Cover with foil. Bake 45 to 50 minutes until pears are tender.

Slice each orange horizontally into rounds and re-form into oranges with the help of a wooden pick. Place in a serving dish. Put the sugar into a heavy pan and add ¼ cup of the orange juice. Heat gently to allow the sugar to melt and dissolve slowly, then boil until it turns a rich golden brown. Remove from heat and add the remaining orange juice, taking care as it will splutter.

Just before pears are cooked, into a small pan, place the chocolate, butter, brandy and sour cream. Heat gently until melted, stir well and keep warm. Transfer cooked pears to serving plates. Slice in half to reveal filling and top with sauce. Serve immediately, decorated with mint.

Makes 4 servings.

Return to heat again, add the peel and stir until caramel has dissolved. Bring to a boil and boil until reduced and syrupy. Cool, then stir in the liqueur. Pour mixture over the oranges and serve.

Makes 4 servings.

MELON & BERRIES

¾ lb. mixed fresh berries (raspberries, strawberries,
  blackberries, blueberries)
½ cup Muscat dessert wine
1 teaspoon chopped preserved stem ginger
2 teaspoons stem ginger syrup (from jar)
1 teaspoon shredded fresh mint
2 small cantaloupe melons
Mint leaves to decorate

Rinse and dry berries; hull and halve as
necessary. Arrange in a bowl. Pour wine, ginger, ginger syrup and mint over berries. Stir
well, cover and refrigerate 2 hours.

With a sharp knife, cut melons in half, cutting into flesh in a zigzag pattern all the way
around centers of each fruit to form attractive edges. Carefully scoop out and discard
seeds. Fill each hollow with a large spoonful
of chilled berries. Pour in juices, decorate
with mint leaves.

Makes 4 servings.

FRUIT & ELDERBERRY CREAM

½ cup whipping cream
½ cup plain yogurt
2 tablespoons elderberry syrup
1 small ripe mango
1 small ripe papaya
1 large ripe peach
1 large apple
4 ozs. strawberries
4-oz. bunch seedless grapes
Freshly grated nutmeg and fresh mint, to decorate

In a bowl, whip cream. Gently fold in yogurt
and elderberry syrup. Cover and refrigerate
until required.

Peel mango. Cut down each side of pit and
cut the flesh into thin slices. Peel and halve
the papaya. Scoop out and discard seeds and
cut flesh into thin strips. Halve and pit
peach. Cut into thin wedges. Quarter and
core apple. Cut into thin wedges. Hull and
halve strawberries.

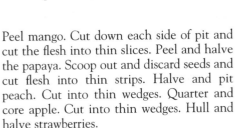

Arrange all prepared fruit and the grapes on
a large platter. Place bowl of elderberry
cream in center. Sprinkle a little nutmeg
over cream and serve the fruit decorated
with the mint.

Makes 8 servings.

Note: Use any fruit liqueur as an alternative
to elderberry syrup, if desired. Sprinkle apple
and peach with lemon juice if not serving
immediately.

CLEMENTINE & DATE SALAD

8 clementines
2 teaspoons orange-flower water
¾ cup dates
¼ cup pistachio nuts
Clementine leaves to decorate

Peel clementines. Cut them into slices, reserving any juice.

Arrange clementine slices on serving plates. Add reserved juice and sprinkle with orange-flower water.

Remove pits from dates. Chop dates. Roughly chop pistachio nuts. Scatter dates and nuts over clementines. Decorate with clementine leaves and serve.

Makes 4 to 6 servings.

PEARS IN RED WINE

4 firm pears, peeled, with stalks left on
4 whole cloves
8 pitted prunes
2½ cups red wine
1-2 tablespoons sugar
1½ cinnamon sticks
1 vanilla bean
2 tablespoons crème de cassis
Orange slices and bay leaves to decorate

Preheat oven to 250F (120C). Insert 1 clove into each pear and put into a Dutch oven with prunes.

Put wine, sugar, cinnamon sticks and vanilla into a saucepan and bring to a boil over low heat, stirring until sugar has dissolved. Pour over pears, cover and bake 3 hours, turning and basting pears twice.

Transfer pears and prunes to a serving dish, standing pears upright. Remove vanilla bean. Add cassis to cooking liquid and boil rapidly until lightly syrupy. Add sauce and let cool. Refrigerate before serving. Slice pears and arrange on serving plates. Decorate with orange slices and bay leaves and serve.

Makes 4 servings.

APRICOT DESSERT

1¾ cups dried apricots
1 cup water
1 cup superfine sugar
2 cups water
½ pint (1 cup) whipping cream
⅓ cup blanched almonds, chopped, toasted

Put apricots and 1 cup water in a medium saucepan; bring to a boil. Reduce heat, cover and simmer about 25 minutes, or until very soft.

Meanwhile, put sugar and 2 cups water in a heavy saucepan and heat gently, stirring occasionally, until sugar has dissolved. Increase heat, bring to a boil and boil 3 minutes, or until syrupy. Drain apricots and purée in a blender or food processor fitted with the metal blade. Add syrup and process again.

Pour into a bowl and cool, then refrigerate at least 1 hour. Whip cream until soft peaks form, fold half into apricot purée, leaving it slightly marbled, and spoon into serving dishes. Chill 30 minutes, then top with remaining cream and scatter with chopped almonds.

Makes 4 to 6 servings.

RHUBARB MERINGUE

1 lb. rhubarb, sliced
4 bananas, sliced
¼ cup packed light brown sugar
½ teaspoon ground cinnamon
Grated zest and juice of 3 oranges
MERINGUE:
3 egg whites
¾ cup sugar

Preheat oven to 350F (180C). Put rhubarb and bananas in an ovenproof dish. Sprinkle with brown sugar, cinnamon and orange zest. Add orange juice, making sure fruit is evenly coated.

Cover with a lid or piece of foil and bake 15 to 20 minutes or until fruit is tender. Meanwhile, to make meringue, beat egg whites until they form stiff peaks. Beat in sugar.

Put meringue into a pastry bag with a star tip and pipe over fruit. Return to oven and cook 20 minutes or until meringue is crisp and golden. Serve warm or cold.

Makes 4 to 6 servings.

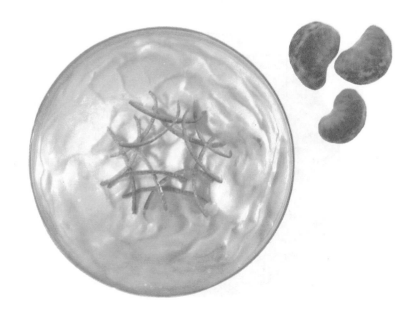

TANGERINE SYLLABUB

Grated peel and juice of 3 tangerines
Grated peel and juice of 1 lemon
⅓ cup superfine sugar
⅓ cup cream sherry
1¼ cups whipping cream
Additional grated peel to decorate if desired

In a bowl, combine tangerine and lemon peels and juices, sugar and sherry. Chill at least 1 hour to infuse.

In a large bowl, whip cream while gradually pouring in tangerine mixture. Whip until mixture is thick enough to form soft peaks.

Pour mixture into a glass serving bowl or individual dessert dishes and chill at least 2 hours before serving. Decorate with additional grated peel, if desired.

Makes 4 to 6 servings.

Notes: Use a sharp grater to grate tangerine peel, otherwise peel tends to tear. Warm citrus fruits slightly before squeezing and they will yield more juice.

SUMMER PUDDINGS

8 ozs. red currants
8 ozs. black currants
Juice of ½ orange
½ cup superfine sugar
1⅔ cups fresh raspberries
12-16 thin slices white bread
Additional red currants to garnish, if desired.

In a saucepan, combine currants, orange juice and sugar. Cook over low heat, stirring occasionally, until currants are juicy and just tender. Gently stir in raspberries; cool.

Cut crusts from bread. From 6 slices, line 6 ramekin dishes or dariole molds, overlapping bread to line dishes completely. From remaining bread, cut circles same size as top of small ramekin dishes or dariole molds. Strain fruit, reserving juice, and spoon fruit into bread-lined dishes, pressing down quite firmly. Cover with bread circles. Pour some of reserved juice into dishes to soak bread. Place a small weight on top of each pudding.

Chill puddings and remaining juice several hours or overnight. To serve, turn puddings out onto individual plates and spoon a small amount of reserved juices over them. Garnish with additional red currants, if desired.

Makes 6 servings.

MIXED CURRANT SENSATION

DRIED FRUIT SALAD

4 ozs. black currants
4 ozs. red currants
4 ozs. white currants
1 tablespoon honey
5 tablespoons water
1 tablespoon unflavored gelatin powder
1¾ cups cold custard (page 387)
1¼ cups half and half
¼ cup mixed chopped nuts

⅔ cup orange juice
⅓ cup light brown sugar
1 tablespoon orange liqueur
2¼ cups mixed dried fruit, eg apricots, peaches,
    pitted dates, figs, pears
⅓ cup raisins
¼ cup blanched almonds
1 tablespoon chopped pistachio nuts
Regular plain yogurt and ground cinnamon to serve

Reserve a few currants decoration. In a saucepan, place remaining currants, honey and 2 tablespoons of the water. Heat gently until just soft. Set aside to cool completely.

Put orange juice in a saucepan and heat until warm. Add sugar and heat, stirring, until dissolved.

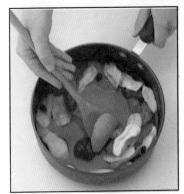

In a small bowl, sprinkle gelatin over remaining 3 tablespoons water. Let stand 2 to 3 minutes to soften. Place bowl in a saucepan of hot water and stir until dissolved. Cool. Into a blender or food processor, place currants and their juice, gelatin, custard and half and half. Purée until well mixed.

Remove from heat and stir in orange liqueur and ¾ cup cold water. Add mixed fruit, raisins and orange juice mixture. Turn fruit in liquid. Transfer to a bowl and add more water, if necessary, to cover.

Into individual serving dishes, pour mixture. Cover and refrigerate until set. When ready to serve, sprinkle chopped nuts over each dessert and decorate with the reserved currants. Serve cold.

Makes 6 servings.

Note: Desserts set more quickly if placed in a container full of cold water and ice cubes.

Cover bowl and leave in a cool place 24 hours. Add almonds and pistachio nuts and stir to mix with fruit. Serve with yogurt, sprinkled with cinnamon.

Makes 4 servings.

GOOSEBERRY-YOGURT SNOW

12 ozs. gooseberries
2 tablespoons water
⅓ cup sugar
1¾ cups low-fat plain yogurt
Mint sprigs, to decorate

Into a saucepan, place gooseberries and water. Cook gently over medium heat until soft, stirring occasionally.

Into gooseberries, stir sugar until dissolved. Let cool. In a blender or food processor, purée cooled gooseberries with juice and yogurt.

Pour mixture into 6 serving dishes. Cover and refrigerate until ready to serve. To serve, decorate with mint sprigs.

Makes 6 servings.

Variation: Bottled gooseberries in syrup may be used instead of fresh gooseberries; omit ¼ cup sugar and blend gooseberries with remaining sugar and yogurt.

MANGO MOUSSE

1 (16-oz.) can mangoes
Juice of ½ lemon
1-2 tablespoons superfine sugar
1 (¼-oz.) envelope unflavored gelatin (1 tablespoon)
¼ cup plus 1 tablespoon water
1¼ cups whipping cream
Fresh mango slices and lemon peel strips to decorate

Drain mangoes well. In a blender or food processor fitted with the metal blade, process mangoes and lemon juice to a purée. Sweeten to taste with sugar.

In a small bowl, sprinkle gelatin over water and let stand 2 to 3 minutes, until softened. Set bowl of gelatin in a saucepan of hot water and stir until dissolved. Stir gelatin into purée, then chill until almost set. In a bowl, whip cream lightly and gently fold into mango mixture.

Pour mixture into a glass serving bowl or individual serving dishes and refrigerate until set. Decorate with fresh mango slices and lemon peel strips to serve.

Makes 4 servings.

Note: When folding whipped cream and/or egg whites into gelatin mixture, the gelatin mixture must be almost set. If folded in too soon, the mixture will separate with the gelatin on bottom and froth on top.

RICOTTA & COFFEE DESSERT

12 ozs. reduced-fat ricotta cheese, softened
12 ozs. reduced-fat cream cheese, softened
1 tablespoon rum
2 tablespoons brandy or Tia Maria
1 teaspoon vanilla extract
2 tablespoons finely ground Italian roast coffee beans
3 tablespoons powdered sugar
⅔ cup whipping cream
2 ozs. chocolate, cut into shavings, to decorate

Sieve ricotta and cream cheese together, then beat with a wooden spoon. Do not attempt to do this in a food processor.

Beat in the rum, brandy, vanilla and ground coffee. Taste and add sugar. Carefully spoon mixture into small freezerproof dishes or demitasse cups, piling the mixture high. Place in freezer 30 minutes and transfer to the refrigerator to soften slightly about 10 minutes before serving it. The dessert should be only just frozen or very chilled.

Just before serving, whisk the whipping cream to soft peaks and spoon a dollop on top of each dessert, then sprinkle with chocolate shavings. Place on saucers and serve at once.

Makes 6 servings.

MINTY CHOCOLATE MOUSSE

6 ozs. semisweet chocolate
1¼ cups whipping cream
1 egg
Pinch of salt
Few drops peppermint extract
Coarsely graped semisweet chocolate to decorate
SUGARED MINT LEAVES:
Mint leaves
1 small egg white
Superfine sugar

Break up chocolate in small pieces and place in a blender or food processor fitted with the metal blade.

In a small saucepan, heat whipping cream until almost boiling. Pour cream over chocolate and blend 1 minute. Add egg, salt and peppermint extract and blend 1 minute more. Pour into individual ramekin dishes or chocolate cups, if desired, and refrigerate overnight.

To prepare decoration, wash and dry mint leaves. In a shallow bowl, lightly whisk egg white and dip in mint leaves to cover. Dip leaves into sugar, shake off any excess and let stand on waxed paper until hardened. To serve, decorate mousses with sugared mint leaves and grated chocolate, if desired.

Makes 4 to 6 servings.

Note: Peppermint extract has a very strong flavor; use it sparingly.

FEATHER-LIGHT TIRAMISU

3 tablespoons very strong cold espresso coffee
1 teaspoon vanilla extract
1 tablespoon brandy or rum
⅓ cup vanilla sugar (page 361)
2 egg whites
8 ozs. reduced-fat cream cheese, softened
½ cup reduced-fat crème fraîche or plain yogurt
18 lady fingers
2 ozs. dark chocolate, grated

In a bowl, mix together coffee, vanilla and brandy. In another bowl, beat sugar and cream cheese together. Whisk crème fraîche until just holding its shape and fold into the cream cheese mixture.

In a clean bowl, whisk the egg whites until forming soft peaks, then fold into the cheese and cream mixture.

Break half the lady fingers into pieces and place on the bottom of 6 glasses. Drizzle with half the coffee mixture. Spoon on half the cream mixture and sprinkle with half the grated chocolate. Repeat with remaining ingredients, finishing with grated chocolate. Chill until firm and serve within 1 day.

Makes 6 servings.

AUSTRIAN CHEESECAKE

4 tablespoons butter, softened
⅔ cup superfine sugar
1 cup + 1 tablespoon cottage cheese, sieved
2 eggs, separated
½ cup ground almonds
⅓ cup fine semolina
Grated peel and juice of 1 small lemon
Powdered sugar
1 recipe Raspberry Sauce (page 367) or Hot Lemon Sauce (page 313)

Preheat oven to 375F (190C). Butter a deep 8-inch cake pan and dust with flour. In a large bowl, cream butter, sugar and cottage cheese until soft and fluffy.

Beat egg yolks into cheese mixture, then fold in ground almonds, semolina and lemon peel and juice. In a separate bowl, whisk egg whites until stiff and carefully fold into cottage cheese mixture.

Turn mixture into buttered pan and bake about 50 minutes, until golden-brown and springy to touch. Cool 20 minutes in pan, then turn out and dust with powdered sugar. Prepare Raspberry Sauce or Hot Lemon Sauce as directed. Serve cheesecake warm or cold with sauce.

Makes 6 servings.

Note: If desired, place a paper doily on cheesecake, then dust with powdered sugar. Remove doily and serve.

RICE & FRUIT MOLD

½ cup plus 1 tablespoon uncooked white short-grain rice
3¾ cups milk
Superfine sugar to taste
Grated peel and juice of 1 orange
1 (¼-oz.) envelope unflavored gelatin (1 tablespoon)
8 ozs. mixed fresh fruit such as grapes, bananas and strawberries
2 tablespoons whipping cream
2 egg whites
1 recipe Raspberry Sauce (page 367), if desired

In a saucepan, combine rice and milk. Simmer 40 minutes to 1 hour, until creamy. Sweeten rice with sugar and stir in orange peel.

In a small bowl, sprinkle gelatin over orange juice and let stand 2 to 3 minutes, until softened. Set bowl of gelatin in a saucepan of hot water and stir until dissolved. Stir gelatin into rice; cool. Halve and seed grapes, finely slice bananas and cut strawberries in quarters. Reserve a few strawberries and grapes for decoration. Fold remaining fruit into rice. In a bowl, whip cream lightly.

In a separate bowl, whisk egg whites until stiff. Fold whipped cream, then egg whites into rice mixture. Turn rice into a glass serving bowl or a lightly oiled ring mold and refrigerate until set. Meanwhile, prepare Raspberry Sauce, if desired, as directed. To serve, turn dessert out of mold onto a serving plate and garnish with reserved fruit. Serve with sauce, if desired.

Makes 4 to 6 servings.

PORT GELATIN

Peel and juice of ½ orange
Peel and juice of 1 lemon
2½ cups ruby port
⅓ cup superfine sugar
1 (3-inch) cinnamon stick
1⅔ (¼-oz.) envelopes unflavored gelatin
 (1 tablespoon plus 2 teaspoons)
FROSTED FRUIT:
1 egg white
Small bunches of red currants and seedless grapes
Superfine sugar

Using a vegetable peeler, thinly peel orange and lemon. In a saucepan, combine fruit peel, port, lemon juice and squeezed lemon shell.

Add sugar and cinnamon stick and heat gently until sugar dissolves. Let stand 20 minutes to infuse. In a small bowl, sprinkle gelatin into orange juice and let stand 2 to 3 minutes, until softened. Set bowl of gelatin in a saucepan of hot water and stir until dissolved. Stir gelatin into port, then strain mixture through a fine sieve into a wetted 3¼-cup mold.

Chill until set. To prepare frosted fruit, lightly whisk egg white in a shallow dish. Wash and dry fruit. Dip into whisked egg white and then into sugar to coat thoroughly. Place on waxed paper to dry. To serve, turn out mold onto a serving dish and decorate with frosted fruit.

Makes 4 to 6 servings.

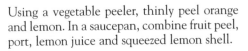

NECTARINE MERINGUE NESTS

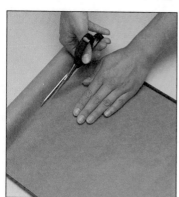

3 egg whites
¾ cup sugar
½ cup cream cheese
⅔ nonfat plain yogurt
3 nectarines
4 ozs. black currants
2 tablespoons apricot jam
1 tablespoon water

Preheat oven to 300F (150C). Line a large baking sheet with parchment paper. In a large bowl, beat egg whites until stiff but not dry. Gradually beat in sugar until mixture is stiff and glossy.

Into a pastry bag fitted with a star tip, spoon meringue. Onto the lined baking sheet, pipe meringue mixture into 6 (4-inch) rounds, leaving a gap between them. Pipe remaining meringue in stars around edge of each round to form an attractive border. Bake meringue nests 1 to 1½ hours or until crisp on the outside. Cool on a wire rack. In a bowl, stir together cream cheese and yogurt, mixing well. Peel and pit nectarines and slice thinly. Remove stems from black currants. Rinse well and drain.

In a saucepan, gently heat apricot jam with water until melted. To fill each meringue nest: place some cream cheese mixture in the nest. Top with sliced nectarines and black currants, then brush with melted jam to glaze. Refrigerate until ready to serve.

Makes 6 servings.

LEMON-ORANGE CUPS

4 large oranges
Grated peel of 1 lemon
⅓ cup light whipping cream
½ cup nonfat yogurt
Julienne strips of lemon and orange peel to decorate

With a sharp knife, cut each orange in half crosswise. Remove flesh and chop finely, then place in a bowl. Drain shells upside down on a wire rack.

Mix lemon peel and chopped orange flesh. Whip cream lightly. Mix whipped cream with yogurt. To chopped oranges, add cream mixture and stir gently to mix. Thinly slice bottom off each orange shell so they sit level on a plate.

Fill all the shells with orange mixture, then place on a serving plate. Refrigerate filled orange shells up to 30 minutes. To serve, decorate with lemon and orange peels.

Makes 6 servings.

STRAWBERRY YOGURT MOLDS

2 cups strawberry-flavored yogurt
1 (¼-oz.) envelope unflavored gelatin (1 tablespoon)
3 tablespoons water
1 pint strawberries

Pour yogurt into a bowl and chill.

In a small bowl, sprinkle gelatin over water and let stand 2 to 3 minutes, until softened. Set bowl of gelatin in a saucepan of hot water and stir until dissolved. Whisk into chilled yogurt, then pour into a wetted mold or 4 wetted individual molds. Chill until set.

To serve, slice strawberries. Turn out mold onto a serving plate and surround with sliced strawberries.

Makes 4 servings.

Note: For a softer texture, increase quantity of yogurt to 2½ cups and set in a bowl rather than a mold.

ENGLISH TRIFLE

2 eggs
2 egg yolks
1 tablespoon plus 2 teaspoons superfine sugar
1¼ cups milk
1 teaspoon vanilla extract
2 tablespoons Madeira wine
1 tablespoon brandy
20 sponge fingers
2 tablespoons raspberry jam
1½ cups raspberries, thawed if frozen
1¼ cups whipping cream
Angelica leaves to decorate

To prepare custard, whisk whole eggs, egg yolks and sugar in a bowl until well blended. In a saucepan, bring milk and vanilla to boil. Pour over eggs in bowl, stirring thoroughly. Rinse out saucepan and strain custard through a sieve back into saucepan. Stirring continuously, cook over a gentle heat until thick but do not boil. Let stand until cold. In a small bowl, mix wine and brandy. Dip 1 sponge finger at a time into wine mixture. Spread with some jam and sandwich together with another dipped sponge finger. Place in bottom of a glass dish.

Repeat with remaining sponge fingers to cover bottom of dish. Pour remaining wine mixture over sponge fingers and cover with ⅔ of raspberries. In a bowl, whip cream until soft peaks form. Fold ⅔ of whipped cream into cold custard until well blended and smooth. Pour custard over raspberries in bowl. Place remaining whipped cream in a pastry bag fitted with a star nozzle. Pipe a border and decorate with angelica leaves and remaining raspberries. Chill until needed.

Makes 8 servings.

COEURS À LA CRÈME

1 cup ricotta or cottage cheese
1 tablespoon plus 2 teaspoons superfine sugar
1 teaspoon lemon juice
1¼ cups whipping cream
2 egg whites
Fresh fruit or 1 recipe Raspberry Sauce (page 367) or Black Currant & Cassis Sauce (page 349) and whipped cream to serve, if desired

Line 4 heart-shaped molds with muslin. Press cheese through sieve into a bowl. Stir in sugar and lemon juice.

In a separate bowl, whip cream until stiff. Stir into cheese mixture. Whisk egg whites until stiff, then fold into the cheese mixture.

Spoon cheese mixture into the molds, place on a plate overnight to drain. To serve, unmold onto individual plates and gently remove the muslin. Serve hearts with fresh fruit or sauce and whipped cream, if desired.

Makes 4 to 6 servings.

ORANGE CARAMEL CREAM

½ cup granulated sugar
3 tablespoons water
3 eggs
2 tablespoons plus 2 teaspoons superfine sugar
1¼ cups milk
1 tablespoon orange flower water
1 orange
Fresh herbs to decorate, if desired

Preheat oven to 350F (175C). Warm 4 china ramekin dishes or 4 dariole molds. In a saucepan, combine granulated sugar and water and cook over low heat, stirring to dissolve sugar. Increase heat and boil steadily, without stirring, to a rich brown caramel.

Divide caramel among dishes or molds and tip to cover bottom and sides with caramel. Set aside. In a bowl, beat eggs and superfine sugar. In a saucepan, heat milk until almost boiling, then pour over egg mixture, beating constantly. Stir in orange flower water.

Strain mixture into dishes or molds. Grate orange peel finely and section orange; reserve orange sections. Divide orange peel among dishes and stir in. Place dishes in a roasting pan. Pour in boiling water to come halfway up sides, then bake about 20 minutes, until set. Cool in dishes and chill until needed. Turn out onto serving plates and decorate with reserved orange sections and fresh herbs, if desired.

Makes 4 servings.

APPLE CHARLOTTE

1½ lbs. tart eating apples
½ cup packed light-brown sugar
8 tablespoons butter
Grated peel of 1 lemon
2½ cups coarse fresh bread crumbs
Apple slices and fresh mint to decorate, if desired

Peel, core and slice apples. In a saucepan, place sliced apples, ⅓ cup of brown sugar, 2 tablespoons of butter and grated lemon peel. Simmer, covered, over low heat until soft. Beat until puréed.

In a skillet, melt remaining butter and sauté bread crumbs until golden-brown, stirring constantly to prevent burning. Stir in remaining brown sugar and cool.

Spoon ½ of apple mixture into 4 serving dishes and cover with ½ of crumb mixture. Top with remaining apples and crumbs and chill 2 hours before serving. Decorate with apple slices and fresh mint, if desired.

Makes 4 servings.

Note: To prevent brown sugar from hardening when stored, place a slice of apple in the container with it, and the brown sugar will stay soft.

CHARLOTTE RUSSE

16 ladyfingers
1 (¼-oz.) envelope unflavored gelatin (1 tablespoon)
3 tablespoons water
4 egg yolks
⅓ cup superfine sugar
2½ cups whipping cream
1 vanilla bean, split open
1¼ cups dairy sour cream
Additional whipped cream and 1¼ cups fresh raspberries to decorate

Line bottom of a 4¼-cup charlotte mold with waxed paper. Stand ladyfingers, pressing against each other, around sides of mold and trim to fit.

In a small bowl, sprinkle gelatin over water and let stand 2 to 3 minutes, until softened. In a bowl, whisk egg yolks and sugar until thick and mousse-like. In a saucepan, place 1½ cups of whipping cream and vanilla bean and bring almost to a boil. Strain over egg mixture, stirring well. Pour back into saucepan and stir over low heat until mixture has thickened slightly; do not boil.

Strain into a clean bowl and add gelatin. Stir until dissolved. Cool, then set bowl in a larger bowl of iced water and stir until mixture thickens. Whip remaining cream with sour cream and fold into mixture. Pour into prepared mold, cover with plastic wrap and chill overnight. To serve, turn out onto a serving plate. Remove waxed paper and decorate with additional whipped cream and raspberries. Tie ribbon around pudding.

Makes 6 to 8 servings.

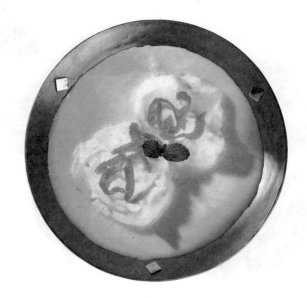

PETITS POTS AU CHOCOLAT

2½ cups half and half or milk
1 vanilla bean
Butter for greasing
1 egg
5 egg yolks
3 tablespoons sugar
8 ozs. semisweet chocolate, chopped
1 tablespoon instant coffee granules
Whipped cream and chocolate shavings to decorate

Put half and half or milk and vanilla bean into a small saucepan and bring almost to a boil over low heat. Cover, remove from heat and let stand 15 minutes.

Preheat oven to 300F (150C). Butter 6 to 8 custard cups or ramekins and put into a roasting pan. Whisk together egg, egg yolks and sugar in a large bowl until thick and pale. Remove vanilla bean from half-and-half and return half and half almost to a boil.

Remove half and half from heat, add chocolate and coffee and stir until dissolved. Stir into egg mixture. Strain into cups, pour boiling water into pan to come halfway up sides of cups and bake about 1 hour, until very lightly set. Transfer cups to a wire rack and let cool. Chill. Decorate with whipped cream and chocolate shavings and serve.

Makes 6 to 8 servings.

OEUFS À LA NEIGE

3 eggs, separated
½ cup sugar
2 egg yolks
2 cups milk
1-2 tablespoons Cointreau, orange flower water or
   rose water
Strips of orange zest and mint sprigs to decorate

Bring a large skillet of water to a boil. Meanwhile, whisk egg whites until stiff but not dry. Gradually whisk in half the sugar until mixture is stiff and shiny.

Reduce heat beneath pan so water is barely simmering. Float spoonfuls of egg white onto water, a few at a time so they are not crowded, and poach 2 or 3 minutes, turning halfway through. Remove with a slotted spoon, transfer to a tilted tray and leave to drain. Whisk all 5 egg yolks with remaining sugar until thick and pale. Put milk into a saucepan and bring almost to a boil.

Stir a little milk into egg yolk mixture then, over low heat, stir back into milk. Cook over low heat, stirring, until slightly thickened; do not boil. Let cool, stirring occasionally. Refrigerate if not serving immediately. Just before serving, add Cointreau or flower water and pour custard into shallow serving bowls. Float meringues on top, decorate with orange zest and mint and serve.

Makes 4 to 6 servings.

PEACH TRIFLE

3 tablespoons reduced-sugar strawberry jam
5 slices pound cake
1 (14-oz.) can peach slices packed in fruit juice
2 tablespoons sweet sherry
1 (½-oz.) package sugar-free strawberry gelatin
1 cup boiling water
1¼ cups cold water
1 tablespoon cornstarch
1 tablespoon sugar
Pinch of salt
3 egg yolks
2 cups skim milk
⅔ cup light whipping cream, lightly whipped
Fresh fruit to decorate

Spread jam on cake; cut into fingers.

Place in a glass serving dish. Drain peaches, reserving juice. Mix together peach juice and sherry and pour over cake. Arrange peach slices over cake. Dissolve gelatin in boiling water, then stir in cold water. Cool and then pour gelatin mixture over cake. Cover and refrigerate until set. Meanwhile, to make custard, blend cornstarch, sugar, salt and egg yolks with 3 tablespoons milk. In a saucepan heat remaining milk until hot, then pour over cornstarch mixture, stirring well.

Return mixture to saucepan and bring to a boil, stirring, until thickened. Boil 1 minute, stirring. Pour into a bowl to cool, covered with a damp cloth. When cool, spread it over gelatin; top with cream and fruit.

Makes 6 servings.

Variation: Sprinkle chopped nuts over the top, but remember this adds calories.

RASPBERRY & HAZELNUT ROLL

1⅔ cups hazelnuts
5 eggs, separated
⅔ cup superfine sugar
Powdered sugar
1¾ cups whipping cream
2¼ cups raspberries
Additional raspberries and mint leaves to garnish if desired

Preheat oven to 350F (175C). Line a jelly-roll pan with a double thickness of foil and oil thoroughly. In a food processor fitted with the metal blade, process hazelnuts until finely ground.

In a large bowl, whisk egg yolks and superfine sugar until thick and mousse-like. Fold in ground hazelnuts. In a separate bowl, whisk egg whites until stiff but not dry. Fold carefully into nut mixture, then pour into prepared pan and spread evenly. Bake 15 to 20 minutes, until risen and firm to touch. Cover immediately with a damp tea towel and let stand overnight. The next day, turn out cake onto a sheet of foil thickly dusted with powdered sugar. Peel off foil.

In a bowl, whip 1¼ cups of cream to stiff peaks. In a separate bowl, lightly crush ½ of raspberries, then fold into whipped cream. Spread raspberry cream over cake. Dot 2¼ cups raspberries over raspberry cream, then roll up cake using foil to help. Transfer to a serving plate. Whip remaining cream until thick. Slice roll and serve with whipped cream. Garnish individual servings with additional raspberries and mint leaves, if desired.

Makes 6 servings.

GÂTEAU GRENOBLE

⅓ cup hazelnuts, skinned
4 eggs, separated, plus 1 extra white
½ cup plus 1 tablespoon superfine sugar
3 ozs. semisweet chocolate
2½ cups walnuts, finely chopped
Whipped cream to serve
Additional chopped walnuts and mint leaves to garnish if desired

Preheat oven to 300F (150C). Generously butter an 8- x 4-inch loaf pan. Grind hazelnuts in a coffee grinder. In a large bowl, beat egg yolks, then gradually beat in ½ cup of sugar, until mixture is light and fluffy.

In top of a double boiler or a bowl set over a pan of simmering water, melt chocolate and stir into yolk mixture with hazelnuts and walnuts. In a large bowl, whisk egg whites until stiff but not dry. Sprinkle in remaining sugar and whisk again until mixture is glossy; fold 2 to 3 tablespoons into chocolate mixture.

Carefully fold remaining egg white into chocolate mixture. (This is quite hard to do as chocolate mixture is very stiff; keep cutting and folding until it is incorporated.) Pour into buttered pan and place in a roasting pan. Add boiling water to come halfway up dish. Cover and bake 1½ hours; cool. Slice and serve with whipped cream. Sprinkle additional chopped walnuts on whipped cream and garnish with mint leaves, if desired.

Makes 6 servings.

COFFEE-BRANDY CAKE

1 recipe Victoria Sponge Cake (page 403)
2 tablespoons brandy
1 tablespoon superfine sugar
1¼ cups hot strong coffee
1¼ cups whipping cream
1 tablespoon powdered sugar
½ cup sliced almonds, toasted

Prepare sponge cake as directed and bake in a 2½-cup greased bowl. Cool in bowl.

When cake is cold, stir brandy and superfine sugar into hot coffee and pour over cake while still in bowl. Place a saucer over bowl and chill overnight.

About 2 hours before serving, run a knife around edges of cake, then turn out on a serving plate. In a bowl, whip cream and powdered sugar until very stiff and spread evenly over cake, covering completely; chill. Just before serving, stick toasted almonds into surface of whipped cream all over cake.

Makes 4 to 6 servings.

Variation: Using a pastry bag fitted with a star nozzle, pipe rosettes of whipped cream all over cake and decorate with sliced almonds and tiny edible flowers.

FRUIT-FILLED CAKE

4 eggs
½ cup granulated sugar
1 cup all-purpose flour
¾ cup light whipping cream
¼ lb. black grapes
½ small cantaloupe melon
2 kiwifruit
1 tablespoon powdered sugar

Preheat oven to 375F (190C). Grease an 8-inch deep cake pan. Into a large bowl, put eggs and granulated sugar. Beat until thick, pale and creamy. Sift flour over mixture. Using a metal spoon, fold in gently.

Pour batter into prepared pan, tilting pan to level surface. Bake 25 to 30 minutes until firm to touch. Turn out of pan and cool on a wire rack. In a bowl, whip cream until stiff. Prepare fruit. Halve and seed grapes. Peel, seed and dice melon. Peel and slice kiwifruit. In a bowl, gently mix fruit together. To assemble cake, cut the cake horizontally into 3 layers. Place bottom slice on a serving plate, cut-side up. Spread one third of the cream over bottom, then arrange some fruit on top.

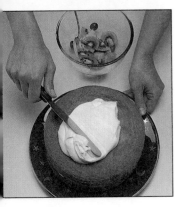

Place a sponge cake on top and spread this with another third of cream. Arrange fruit on top. Place remaining sponge cake slice on top, cut-side down. Spread or pipe remaining cream over top and arrange remaining fruit decoratively over cream. Sift powdered sugar over top. Serve immediately.

Makes 10 servings.

COCONUT LAYER CAKE

½ cup all-purpose flour
1⅔ cups coconut milk
6 egg yolks, beaten
½ cup sugar
Seeds from 4 green cardamom pods, crushed
Pinch of freshly grated nutmeg
½ cup butter, melted
Plain yogurt and sliced bananas, to serve

Put flour in a medium bowl, whisk in coconut milk, egg yolks, sugar, cardamom seeds and nutmeg, then let batter stand 30 minutes.

Preheat oven to 425F (220C). Butter a 6-inch soufflé dish. Add 1 tablespoon butter to dish and heat in oven 5 minutes. Pour in 6 tablespoons of batter and bake 10 to 15 minutes, until firm to the touch and lightly browned. Brush with butter. Continue adding another three layers, brushing each cooked layer with butter before adding batter. Bake each layer 10 to 15 minutes.

Put soufflé dish in a baking pan half-filled with boiling water, then continue adding another three layers in same way as before. When last layer is cooked, remove dish from oven and cool. Run a knife around edge of dish to loosen cake and turn out onto a serving plate. Serve warm, with yogurt and sliced bananas.

Makes 4 to 6 servings.

CHOCOLATE CHERRY SLICE

CHOCOLATE PROFITEROLES

6 (1-oz.) squares semisweet chocolate
4 eggs
¼ cup superfine sugar
⅓ cup all-purpose flour
1 cup unsweetened marron purée
4 (1-oz.) squares semisweet chocolate, melted
1¼ cups whipping cream
3 tablespoons cherry jam
1 cup sweet cherries, pitted, halved

Preheat oven to 350F (175C). Line a 13- x 9-inch jelly-roll pan with waxed paper. Break up chocolate; place in a bowl over a saucepan of hand-hot water. Stir occasionally until melted and smooth.

In a bowl, whisk eggs and sugar until thick and pale. Stir in chocolate. Sift in flour and fold in gently. Pour mixture into prepared pan and shake to level. Bake in oven 20 to 25 minutes or until firm to touch. Remove from oven. Cover with a damp tea towel and let stand until cold. To prepare filling, process marron in a food processor fitted with a metal blade to a purée. Add chocolate and process until smooth. In a small bowl, whip cream until thick. Place ⅓ of whipped cream into a pastry bag fitted with small star nozzle. Fold remaining whipped cream into chocolate mixture.

Remove cake from pan. Remove paper, trim edges and cut into 3 short strips across width. Spread 2 strips of cake with jam. Cover each with ⅓ of filling. Spread smoothly. Arrange ⅓ of cherry halves on each and stack layers on a serving plate. Top with remaining cake layer. Spread top and sides of cake evenly with remaining filling and pipe scrolls of whipping cream around top edge. Decorate with remaining cherry halves. Chill until needed.
Makes 10 servings.

4 tablespoons butter, cut in small pieces
⅔ cup water
½ cup plus 2 tablespoons all-purpose flour, sifted
2 eggs, beaten
1¼ cups whipping cream
1 recipe Dark Chocolate Sauce (page 313) to serve

Preheat oven to 400F (205C). Line baking sheets with parchment paper. To prepare choux pastry, combine butter and water in a saucepan and cook over medium heat until butter melts. Bring to a boil and remove from heat. Add flour and beat with a wooden spoon until mixture leaves sides of pan.

Beat in eggs gradually, until mixture is smooth and shiny. Using a pastry bag fitted with a plain nozzle, pipe walnut-size balls onto prepared baking sheets. Bake 20 to 25 minutes, until brown, puffed up and just crisp on outside. Make a small hole in side of each profiterole to allow steam to escape and keep profiterole crisp.

Cool profiteroles on a wire rack. To serve, whip cream until stiff. Enlarge hole in side of each profiterole and, using a pastry bag fitted with a plain nozzle, pipe cream into them. Prepare Dark Chocolate Sauce as directed. To serve, pour hot sauce over profiteroles.

Makes 4 servings.

WHITE & DARK CHOCOLATE TERRINE

WHITE CHOCOLATE MOUSSE:
9 ozs. white chocolate
½ (¼-oz.) envelope unflavored gelatin (1½ teaspoons)
1 tablespoon light corn syrup
2 egg yolks
⅔ cup whipping cream
⅔ cup dairy sour cream
DARK CHOCOLATE MOUSSE:
6 ozs. semisweet chocolate
¼ cup strong coffee
⅔ (¼-oz.) envelope unflavored gelatin (2 teaspoons)
8 tablespoons butter, cubed
2 egg yolks
1¼ cups whipping cream
Whipped cream and grated chocolate to decorate

Line an 8- x 4-inch loaf pan with plastic wrap to overlap edges. To prepare white chocolate mousse, break white chocolate in small pieces and set aside. In a small bowl, sprinkle gelatin over 2 tablespoons of water and let stand 2 to 3 minutes, until softened. In a saucepan, combine 3 tablespoons water and corn syrup and bring to boil. Remove from heat and stir in gelatin until dissolved. Add chocolate pieces and beat until chocolate is melted and mixture is smooth.

Beat in egg yolks, 1 at a time. In a bowl, whip whipping cream and sour cream lightly and fold into chocolate mixture. Pour into prepared loaf pan and refrigerate until set.

To prepare dark chocolate mousse, in top of a double boiler or bowl set over a pan of simmering water, melt chocolate with coffee. In a small bowl, sprinkle gelatin over 3 tablespoons water and let stand 2 to 3 minutes, until softened. Set bowl of gelatin in a saucepan of hot water and stir until dissolved. Stir gelatin and butter into chocolate mixture and beat until butter has melted and mixture is smooth. Cool, then beat in egg yolks. In a bowl, whip cream lightly and fold into chocolate mixture.

Pour dark chocolate mixture over set white chocolate mousse. Refrigerate until set, then cover with overlapping plastic wrap and refrigerate overnight.

To serve, unfold plastic wrap from top and turn out onto a serving dish. Carefully peel off plastic wrap. Decorate with whipped cream and grated chocolate, if desired, and cut in slices.

Makes 8 to 10 servings.

KIWIFRUIT ICE

6 kiwifruit
1 tablespoon lemon juice
½ cup sugar
1¼ cups water
4 ripe passion fruit
Cookies to serve (optional)

Slice kiwifruit into a blender or food processor; add lemon juice. Blend until smooth; set aside.

Into a saucepan, put sugar and water. Cook, stirring, until sugar dissolves, then boil 10 minutes. Stir in kiwifruit purée and set aside to cool. Place cooled mixture into a chilled, shallow plastic container. Cover and freeze 1½ to 2 hours or until the mixture is mushy in consistency. Turn out mixture into a chilled bowl.

Cut each passion fruit in half and scoop out flesh. Add to frozen mixture. Beat with a fork or electric mixer until smooth. Return mixture to container, cover and freeze until firm. Transfer to the refrigerator about 15 minutes before serving to soften. Serve in scoops in individual dishes or glasses, accompanied by cookies, if desired.

Makes 6 servings.

BANANA & RUM ICE CREAM

1 lb. bananas
1¼ cups milk
1¼ cups nonfat plain yogurt
3 tablespoons rum
5 tablespoons honey
¼ cup chopped walnuts
Cookies to serve (optional)

Peel bananas. Into a large bowl, put bananas, then mash with a fork.

Add milk, yogurt, rum, honey and walnuts and beat well to mix. Pour mixture into a chilled, shallow plastic container. Cover and freeze 1½ to 2 hours or until the mixture is mushy in consistency. Into a chilled bowl, turn out mixture. Beat with a fork or whisk until smooth.

Return mixture to container, cover and freeze until firm. Transfer to the refrigerator 30 minutes before serving to soften. Serve in scoops in individual glasses with cookies, if desired.

Makes 6 servings.

MOCHA ESPRESSO ICE CREAM

2 cups milk
⅔ cup whipping cream
⅓ cup medium-ground espresso coffee beans
3 ozs. semisweet chocolate, chopped
6 egg yolks
¾ cup sugar
Chocolate shavings to decorate

Into a small saucepan, place milk, cream, ground coffee and 2 ounces of the chocolate. Heat slowly until almost boiling. Remove from heat and set aside 30 minutes for the flavors to infuse.

In a large bowl, beat egg yolks and sugar together until thick and pale. Gradually beat in mocha mixture and transfer to a clean saucepan. Heat gently, stirring, until mixture thickens, but do not boil. Refrigerate until chilled.

Transfer mixture to a freezerproof container and freeze. Beat to mix and break up ice crystals after about 1 hour and again at hourly intervals until almost firm. Stir in remaining chocolate, cover and let freeze completely. Remove from freezer 20 minutes before serving to soften. Decorate with chocolate shavings.

Makes 4 servings.

STRAWBERRY SORBET

1¼ cups sugar
1 lb. fresh strawberries
1 tablespoon balsamic vinegar

Pour 1 cup water into a saucepan and add the sugar. Cook, stirring, to dissolve sugar, then bring to a boil and boil 1 minute. Cool, then chill in refrigerator. Meanwhile, wash and hull the strawberries. Purée in a blender or food processor until smooth, and pass through a sieve, if desired. Chill the purée.

Stir the syrup into the chilled strawberry purée and add the balsamic vinegar. Freeze in an ice cream maker for the best results.

Alternatively, pour mixture into a shallow freezer tray and freeze until the sorbet is frozen around the edges. Mash well with a fork, beat and refreeze until almost solid. Repeat this twice more. Serve in chilled glass dishes.

Makes 6 servings.

ORANGE SORBET

10 large oranges
1 cup sugar
2 tablespoons orange flower water

Pare the peel from the oranges with a vegetable peeler, avoiding any white pith. Chop roughly. Squeeze the juice from the oranges and strain through a sieve.

Pour ¾ cup water into a saucepan, add the sugar and cook, stirring, to dissolve. Stir in the orange peel, juice, and the orange flower water. Boil rapidly 1 minute. Cool, then chill in refrigerator. Strain the syrup.

Freeze in an ice cream maker for the best results. Alternatively, pour into a shallow freezer tray and freeze until the sorbet is frozen around the edges. Mash well with a fork, beat and refreeze until almost solid. Repeat this twice more. Serve in chilled glass dishes

Makes 4 servings.

NUTTY-CRUMB CREAM

½ cup hazelnuts
1¼ cups fresh whole-wheat bread crumbs
2 tablespoons light-brown sugar
2 egg whites
⅓ cup superfine sugar
1¼ cups whipping cream
1-2 drops vanilla extract
Fresh flower buds or leaves to decorate if desired

Toast hazelnuts under broiler evenly. Cool, then grind coarsely in a coffee grinder or a food processor fitted with the metal blade. In a bowl, mix ground nuts with bread crumbs and brown sugar.

Spread crumb mixture evenly on a baking sheet. Broil, turning and shaking, until brown; cool. Whisk egg whites in a large bowl, until stiff. Sprinkle in sugar and whisk 2 minutes more. Whip cream and vanilla to soft peaks, then fold into egg whites with all but 1 tablespoon of browned crumb mixture.

Spoon mixture into 6 dessert dishes and chill until ready to serve. Sprinkle with reserved crumb mixture just before serving. Decorate with fresh flower buds or leaves, if desired.

Makes 6 servings.

Note: This mixture makes a delicious ice cream. Pour finished cream into a plastic container and freeze.

LARGE CAKES

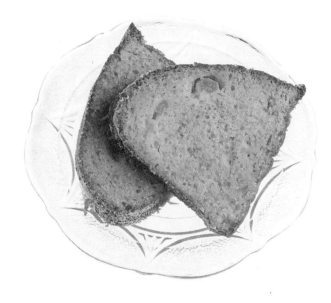

TOFFEE DATE CAKE

1⅔ cups chopped dates
1¼ cups boiling water
½ cup butter, softened
¾ cup sugar
3 eggs, beaten
2 cups self-rising flour, sifted
½ teaspoon ground cinnamon
1 teaspoon baking soda
1 teaspoon vanilla extract
TOPPING:
½ cup packed brown sugar
¼ cup butter
3 tablespoons whipping cream

Cover dates with the boiling water.

Preheat oven to 350F (175C). Grease a 9-inch springform pan. In a bowl, beat butter and sugar until light and fluffy. Gradually beat in eggs. Fold in flour and cinnamon. Add baking soda and vanilla to dates and water. Pour onto creamed mixture; stir until thoroughly mixed. Pour into prepared pan. Bake 1 to 1¼ hours, until well risen and firm to the touch. Meanwhile, preheat broiler.

To make topping, into a saucepan, put brown sugar, butter and cream. Heat gently until sugar is melted. Bring to a boil, then simmer 3 minutes. Pour topping over cake and put under the broiler until topping is bubbling. Cool in pan until toffee is set. Turn out cake, then transfer to a wire rack to cool completely.

Makes 8 to 10 slices.

PEACH & ORANGE CAKE

½ cup canned peach slices
¾ cup butter
1¼ cups sugar
Grated zest of 1 orange
4 eggs, beaten
⅔ cup dairy sour cream
2 cups all-purpose flour
½ teaspoon baking soda
TO FINISH:
Powdered sugar
Grated zest of 1 orange

Preheat oven to 350F (175C). Grease a kugelhopf mold and dust with flour. Drain peach slices and coarsely chop.

In a bowl, beat butter and sugar until light and fluffy. Add orange zest and gradually beat in eggs. Fold in peaches and sour cream. Sift flour and baking soda onto batter. Fold in gently and spread into prepared pan, smoothing the top with a metal spatula. Bake 45 to 50 minutes, until well risen and golden-brown.

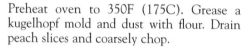

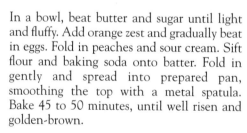

Cool in pan 10 minutes, then turn out cake and transfer to a wire rack to cool completely. Sift powdered sugar over cake. Decorate with orange zest.

Makes 8 to 10 slices.

HONEY SPICE CAKE

⅔ cup butter or margarine
¾ cup packed light brown sugar
½ cup honey
1 tablespoon water
1¾ cups self-rising flour
1½ teaspoons apple-pie spice
2 eggs, beaten
FROSTING:
2¼ cups powdered sugar
About 3 tablespoons water

Preheat oven to 350F (175C). Grease a fluted ring mold with a 3¾-cup capacity. Into a saucepan, put butter, sugar, honey and water.

Heat gently until butter has melted and sugar has dissolved. Remove from heat and cool 10 minutes. Into a bowl, sift flour and apple pie spice. Pour in melted mixture and eggs; beat well until smooth. Pour batter into prepared pan. Bake 40 to 50 minutes, until well risen and a skewer inserted into center comes out clean. Cool cake in pan 2 to 3 minutes, then turn out cake and transfer to a wire rack to cool completely.

To make frosting, into a bowl, sift powdered sugar. Stir in enough water to make a smooth frosting. Carefully spoon frosting over cake so cake is evenly covered.

Makes 8 to 10 slices.

CHOCOLATE MARBLE CAKE

2 ozs. semisweet chocolate
1 tablespoon strong coffee
2 cups self-rising flour
1 teaspoon baking powder
1 cup margarine, softened
1¼ cups sugar
4 eggs, beaten
½ cup ground blanched almonds
2 tablespoons milk
FROSTING:
4½ ozs. semisweet chocolate
2 tablespoons butter
2 tablespoons water

Preheat oven to 350F (175C). Grease a ring mold with a 7½-cup capacity. In a heatproof bowl set over a pan of simmering water, break chocolate and add coffee. Heat until melted. Let cool. Into a bowl, sift flour and baking powder. Add margarine, sugar, eggs, ground almonds and milk. Beat well until smooth. Spoon half the batter evenly into prepared pan. Stir cooled, soft chocolate into the remaining batter, then spoon into pan. Draw a knife through batter in a spiral. Smooth the surface.

Bake 50 to 60 minutes, until well risen and a skewer inserted into center comes out clean. Cool in pan 5 minutes, then turn out cake and transfer to a wire rack to cool completely. To make frosting, into a heatproof bowl set over a pan of simmering water, put chocolate, butter and water; heat until melted. Stir frosting and pour over cake on a rack, working quickly to coat top and sides. Let set before serving.

Makes 10 to 12 slices.

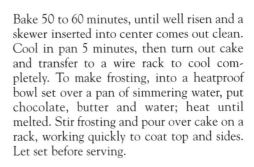

LEMON CRUNCH CAKE

½ cup butter or margarine, softened
¾ cup sugar
2 eggs, beaten
Finely grated zest of 1 lemon
1½ cups self-rising flour, sifted
¼ cup milk
TOPPING:
Juice of 1 lemon
½ cup sugar

GINGER CAKE

2 cups self-rising flour
1 tablespoon ground ginger
1 teaspoon ground cinnamon
½ teaspoon baking soda
½ cup butter or margarine, chilled
¾ cup packed light brown sugar
2 eggs
5 teaspoons light corn syrup
5 teaspoons milk
TOPPING:
3 pieces stem ginger
¾ cup powdered sugar
4 teaspoons stem ginger syrup

Preheat oven to 350F (175C). Grease a 9- x 7-inch or an 8-inch square baking pan and line with waxed paper. In a bowl, beat together butter and sugar until light and fluffy.

Preheat oven to 325F (165C). Grease an 11- x 7-inch baking pan and line with waxed paper. Into a bowl, sift flour, ginger, cinnamon and baking soda. Cut in butter, then stir in sugar. In another bowl, beat together eggs, syrup and milk. Pour into dry ingredients and beat until smooth and glossy. Pour batter into pan. Bake 45 to 50 minutes, until well risen and firm to the touch. Cool in pan 30 minutes, then transfer to a wire rack to cool completely.

Gradually beat in eggs. Stir in lemon zest. Fold in sifted flour, alternately with milk. Pour batter into prepared pan and level surface with a metal spatula. Bake about 50 minutes, until well risen and pale golden.

While cake is baking, make topping. In a bowl, mix together lemon juice and sugar. Spoon topping over hot cake. Leave cake in pan until completely cold, then turn out cake and cut into squares or diamonds.

Makes 12 squares or diamonds.

Cut each piece of stem ginger into quarters and arrange on top of cake. In a bowl, mix together powdered sugar, ginger syrup and enough water to make a smooth frosting. Put frosting into a waxed-paper pastry bag and drizzle frosting over top of cake. Let set. Cut cake into squares.

Makes 12 pieces.

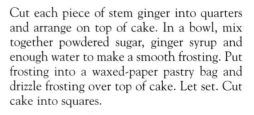

JEWEL-TOPPED MADEIRA CAKE

1 cup butter, softened
1¼ cups sugar
Grated zest of 1 lemon
4 eggs, beaten
2 cups self-rising flour, sifted
3 tablespoons milk
TOPPING:
2⅔ tablespoons honey
½ lb. glacé fruits and angelica

Preheat oven to 325F (165C). Grease and line an 8-inch springform cake pan with waxed paper. In a bowl, beat together butter, sugar and lemon zest until light and fluffy. Gradually beat in eggs. Fold in flour, alternately with milk. Spoon batter into prepared pan. Bake 1½ to 1¾ hours, until a skewer inserted into center of cake comes out clean.

Cool cake in pan 5 minutes, then turn out onto a wire rack to cool completely. In a saucepan, gently heat honey. Brush over cake and arrange fruits and angelica on top.

Makes 8 to 10 slices.

Variation: A traditional Madeira cake has thin sliced candied peel on top. This should be placed on cake after it has been baking about 1 hour.

COCONUT & CHERRY CAKE

1 cup butter, softened
1¼ cups sugar
4 eggs and 1 egg yolk
2 cups self-rising flour, sifted
⅔ cup shredded coconut
1 cup candied cherries, quartered
TOPPING:
1 egg white
½ cup powdered sugar, sifted
1¼ cups unsweetened thin coconut slices

Preheat oven to 350F (175C). Grease an 8-inch springform cake pan and line with waxed paper.

In a bowl, beat butter and sugar until light and fluffy. In another bowl, beat together eggs and egg yolk. Gradually beat into creamed mixture. Fold in flour, coconut and cherries. Spoon mixture into prepared pan. Bake 45 to 50 minutes, until just firm to the touch. To make the topping, in a bowl, beat egg white until soft peaks form; gradually beat in powdered sugar until stiff peaks form.

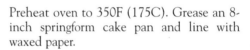

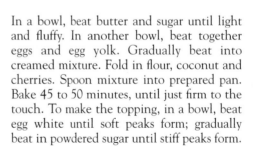

Spread topping over top of cake. Sprinkle with coconut. Return cake to oven and bake 20 minutes, until golden-brown and a skewer inserted into center comes out clean. Cover lightly with foil if topping is browning too quickly. Cool cake in pan 10 minutes, then remove from pan, peel off lining paper and transfer to a wire rack to cool.

Makes 8 to 10 slices.

Note: Thin, dried slices of unsweetened coconut are available in natural food stores.

RUM TRUFFLE CAKE

7 (1-oz.) squares semi-sweet chocolate
½ cup unsalted butter
¼ cup dark rum
3 eggs, separated
½ cup superfine sugar
¾ cup all-purpose flour
½ cup ground almonds
FILLING & ICING:
7 (1-oz.) squares semi-sweet chocolate
1¼ cups whipping cream
1 tablespoon dark rum
2 (1-oz.) squares white chocolate, grated

Preheat oven to 350F (175C). Butter and flour a 2½-inch deep 8-inch-round cake pan. Line bottom with a circle of waxed paper. Place chocolate and butter in a bowl over hand-hot water. Stir occasionally until melted. Add rum and stir well.

Place egg yolks and sugar in a bowl over a saucepan of simmering water. Whisk until thick and pale. Remove bowl from saucepan. Continue to whisk until mixture leaves a trail when whisk has been lifted. Stir chocolate mixture into egg yolk mixture until evenly blended. In a small bowl, mix flour and ground almonds. Add to chocolate mixture; fold in carefully using a spatula.

In a bowl, whisk egg whites until stiff. Fold ⅓ at a time into chocolate mixture until all egg whites are incorporated. Pour mixture into prepared pan. Bake in oven 45 to 55 minutes or until firm to touch in center. Turn out of pan and cool on a wire rack.

To prepare filling, melt 4 squares of chocolate with ¼ cup of whipping cream in a bowl set over hot water. Stir in rum until well blended. Let stand until cool. To prepare icing, whip ½ cup of whipping cream in a bowl until thick. Add ½ of rum-chocolate to whipped cream and fold in until smooth.

Cut cake in half. Sandwich together with chocolate icing and spread remainder over top and sides. Chill cake and remaining rum-chocolate mixture in bowl. Melt remaining chocolate with whipping cream in a bowl set over hot water. Stir until smooth and cool until thick. Spread chocolate mixture over cake to cover evenly. Shape rum-chocolate mixture into 16 truffles. Coat in grated white chocolate. Arrange truffles on top of cake and chill to set.

Makes 10 servings.

LEMON-POPPY SEED CAKE

4 eggs, separated
½ cup sugar
Grated peel and juice of 1 lemon
¾ cup blanched, finely ground almonds
¾ cup dried bread crumbs
1 tablespoon poppy seeds
2 tablespoons brandy
Mint leaves and lemon peel to decorate
RASPBERRY SAUCE:
½ lb. fresh raspberries
1 tablespoon honey
½ teaspoon ground cinnamon

APPLE CAKE

2 cups plus 2 tablespoons self-rising flour
¾ teaspoon ground cinnamon
⅓ cup sugar
Finely grated zest and juice 1 lemon
2 eggs, beaten
3 tablespoons sweet sherry
⅔ cup olive oil
1 lb. Granny Smith apples

Preheat oven to 350F (175C). Grease and line the bottom of an 8-inch springform pan with waxed paper. In a large bowl, beat egg yolks, sugar, lemon peel and lemon juice together until pale and creamy. In another bowl, beat egg whites until stiff. Fold in with almonds, bread crumbs and poppy seeds until evenly combined. Transfer to prepared pan. Bake 40 minutes or until golden and firm to the touch. Remove from oven and stab all over with a wooden pick. Pour brandy over cake and let cool.

Preheat oven to 350F (175C). Grease a 7-inch pan. In a bowl, stir together flour, cinnamon, sugar and lemon zest. Make a well in the center and gradually add eggs, sherry, olive oil and lemon juice, stirring to make a smooth batter.

Reserve 12 raspberries for decoration. In a blender or food processor, purée remaining raspberries until smooth. Pass through a fine strainer to remove seeds. Beat in honey and cinnamon. Serve cake cut into wedges, topped with the sauce. Decorate with reserved raspberries, mint and lemon peel.

Makes 6 servings.

Note: Frozen raspberries can be substituted for fresh.

With a sharp knife, peel, core and chop apples. Fold into cake batter, then spoon batter into prepared pan. Bake 40 to 45 minutes or until golden-brown and firm to the touch in center. Cool in pan a few minutes, then turn out onto a wire rack to cool completely.

Makes 8 servings.

WALNUT GÂTEAU

1 cup pitted dates, chopped
1 cup boiling water
8 tablespoons butter, softened
1 egg
1 cup superfine sugar
Few drops vanilla extract
1½ cups all-purpose flour
1 teaspoon baking soda
1 teaspoon baking powder
1 teaspoon salt
½ cup walnuts, chopped
BUTTERSCOTCH ICING:
2 tablespoons whipping cream
1 tablespoon butter
2 tablespoons light-brown sugar

Preheat oven to 350F (175C). Grease an 8- x 4-inch loaf pan. Place dates in a bowl and cover with boiling water; cool. In a bowl, cream butter, egg, sugar and vanilla until light and fluffy. Sift dry ingredients into mixture and fold in with dates and soaking liquid. Fold in chopped walnuts and pour into greased pan. Bake 1 to 1½ hours, until spongy to touch. Turn out of pan.

To prepare icing, combine all ingredients in a small saucepan. Cook over medium heat, stirring constantly. Bring to a boil and pour over cake. Serve at once.

Makes 6 to 8 servings.

Note: To prevent dates sticking when chopping, dip the knife in hot water.

ORANGE & ALMOND CAKE

½ cup butter
Grated zest of 1 orange
½ cup sugar
2 eggs, beaten
1 cup semolina
1 cup ground almonds
1 teaspoon baking powder
3 tablespoons orange juice
Strips of pared orange zest, to decorate
SYRUP:
1 cup orange juice
½ cup sugar
2 teaspoons orange-flower water

Preheat oven to 350F (180C). Butter and line bottom of an 8-inch cake pan.

Beat together butter, orange zest and sugar until light and creamy. Gradually beat in eggs. Mix together semolina, ground almonds and baking powder and fold half into creamed mixture with half orange juice. Fold in remaining semolina mixture and orange juice. Spoon mixture into prepared pan and bake 30 to 40 minutes or until well risen – a skewer inserted into center should come out clean.

Let cool in pan a few minutes. Meanwhile, make syrup. Put orange juice and sugar in a saucepan. Heat gently until sugar has dissolved. Bring to a boil, reduce heat and simmer 4 minutes. Stir in orange-flower water. Turn cake out on to a deep serving plate and spoon syrup on top. Decorate with orange zest and serve warm or cold.

Makes 8 servings.

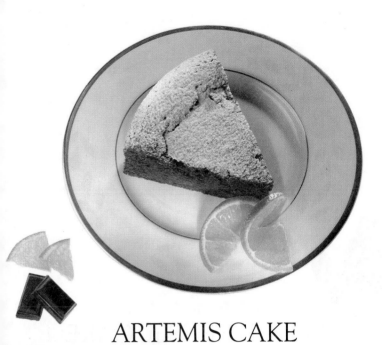

ARTEMIS CAKE

14 ozs. semisweet chocolate
5 eggs, separated
1 cup butter, softened
¾ cup powdered sugar, sifted
2 tablespoons all-purpose flour, sifted
1 teaspoon ground cinnamon
Extra powdered sugar to decorate

Preheat oven to 350C (175C). Butter and line an 8-inch cake pan with waxed paper (preferably a loose-bottomed pan). Into a bowl, break chocolate. Stand bowl over a pan of hot water until melted. Leave until almost cold.

In a bowl, whisk egg whites until stiff but not dry. In another bowl, beat butter and powdered sugar until light and creamy. Beat in egg yolks. Stir in chocolate. It does not need to be thoroughly mixed.

Stir in flour and cinnamon, then fold in egg whites. Pour mixture into prepared pan. Bake 45 minutes or until firm to the touch. Leave in pan until almost cool, then transfer to a wire rack. Sift powdered sugar over the top and place on a serving plate.

Makes 8 servings.

VICTORIA SPONGE CAKE

8 tablespoons margarine or butter, softened
½ cup superfine sugar
2 large eggs, beaten
1 cup self-rising flour
Milk, if necessary
Whipped cream and sliced strawberries and kiwifruit
  to serve
Additional strawberries and leaves to garnish, if
  desired

Preheat oven to 350F (175C). Grease 2 (8-inch) round cake pans.

In a bowl, cream margarine and sugar until light and fluffy. Beat eggs into creamed margarine and sugar, a little at a time. Sift flour into mixture and fold in, using a metal spoon. Mixture should be a soft dropping consistency; add a little milk, if necessary. Spoon into greased pan. Bake about 20 to 25 minutes, until golden and spongy to touch. Turn out and cool on a wire rack.

Spread ½ of whipped cream on top of 1 cake and arrange ½ of fruit on whipped cream. Top with remaining cake. Spread or pipe remaining whipped cream on top of cake and arrange remaining fruit on whipped cream. Garnish with additional strawberries and leave, if desired.

Makes 6 servings.

Variation: Flavor with a few drops of vanilla extract or 1 tablespoon grated orange or lemon peel. Beat into mixture before adding flour.

GLACÉ FRUIT CAKE

2½ cups mixed glacé fruit, chopped
¾ cup dried apricots, chopped
1 cup chopped pecans
Finely grated peel and juice 1 lemon
3 cups all-purpose flour
1 teaspoon baking powder
1½ teaspoons ground mixed spice
1⅔ cups ground almonds
1¾ cups superfine sugar
1½ cups butter, softened
4 eggs
¼ cup apricot jam
2 teaspoons water
Mixed glacé fruit and nuts

Preheat oven to 275F (135C). Line a 2½-inch deep 8-inch-square cake pan or a 2½-inch deep 9-inch-round pan with a double thickness of greased waxed paper, extending greased waxed paper above edge of pan. Place pan on baking sheet lined with a double thickness of waxed paper. Combine glacé fruit, apricots, nuts and lemon peel and juice. Sift flour, baking powder and mixed spice into a bowl. Mix in ground almonds, sugar, butter and eggs, then beat 2 to 3 minutes or until smooth and glossy. Stir in fruit and nuts.

Spoon mixture into prepared pan. Smooth top and bake 2¼ to 2½ hours or until cake feels firm and springy. Cool in pan, then turn out and wrap in foil. In a saucepan, bring jam and water to a boil, stirring constantly, then sieve. Brush top of cake with jam. Arrange fruit and nuts over top and brush with remaining jam. Let stand until set.

Makes 30 servings.

APPLE STREUSEL CAKE

1½ cups self-rising flour
1 teaspoon baking powder
½ cup margarine, softened
½ cup sugar
2 eggs, beaten
1-2 tablespoons milk
TOPPING:
1 cup self-rising flour
1 teaspoon ground cinnamon
6 tablespoons butter
⅓ cup granulated sugar
1 lb. Granny Smith apples
A little lemon juice
Powdered sugar to finish

Preheat oven to 350F (175C). Grease a 9-inch springform pan. To make topping, into a bowl, sift flour and cinnamon. Cut in butter until mixture resembles coarse crumbs. Stir in granulated sugar; set aside. Peel, core and thinly slice apples. Toss in a little lemon juice.

In another bowl, sift flour and baking powder. Add margarine, sugar and eggs. Beat well until mixture is smooth, adding just enough milk to make a good consistency. Spoon into prepared pan. Cover with apple slices and sprinkle with streusel topping. Bake 1 hour, until firm to the touch and golden-brown. Cool in pan before opening sides. Dust with powdered sugar.

Makes 8 to 10 slices.

Note: Keep cake 24 hours before serving.

DUNDEE CAKE

1 cup butter, softened
1½ cups packed brown sugar
4 eggs, beaten
2½ cups all-purpose flour, sifted
¼ cup milk
½ cup ground blanched almonds
¾ cup dried currants
¾ cup golden raisins
¾ cup dark raisins
⅓ cup chopped mixed candied citrus peel
⅓ cup candied cherries, halved
Grated zests of 1 small orange and 1 small lemon
½ teaspoon baking soda, dissolved in 1 teaspoon
  milk
⅓ cup whole blanched almonds

Preheat oven to 325F (165C). Grease and line an 8-inch springform cake pan with waxed paper. In a bowl, beat butter and sugar until light and fluffy. Gradually beat in eggs. Fold in flour alternately with milk. Carefully fold in ground almonds, currants, golden raisins, raisins, peel, cherries and orange and lemon zests. Add baking soda dissolved in milk. Stir to mix.

Pour batter into prepared pan. Smooth top with a metal spatula. Arrange blanched almonds in concentric circles over top of cake. Bake 2½ to 3 hours, until a skewer inserted into center of the cake comes out clean. Cool in pan 30 minutes, then turn out cake, peel off lining paper and transfer to a wire rack to cool completely.

Makes about 12 slices.

HALVA CAKE

½ cup butter
½ cup superfine sugar
Grated zest of 1 orange
Juice of ½ lemon
2 eggs, beaten
1 cup semolina
2 teaspoons baking powder
1 cup ground blanched almonds
1 teaspoon ground cinnamon
SYRUP:
¾ cup superfine sugar
Juice of ½ lemon
Juice of ½ orange
½ cup water
2 tablespoons candied orange peel, to decorate

Preheat oven to 425F (220C). Butter a ring mold. In a food processor fitted with the metal blade, put butter, sugar, orange zest, juice, eggs, semolina, baking powder, ground almonds and cinnamon. Process until well mixed. Turn mixture into prepared mold. Bake 10 minutes, then reduce heat to 350F (175C) and bake 25 minutes, or until a wooden pick inserted into cake comes out clean. Cool in the mold a few minutes, then turn out into a warm, deep plate.

Meanwhile, make the syrup. Into a pan, put sugar, lemon juice, orange juice and the water. Heat gently until sugar has dissolved, then bring to a boil and simmer 4 minutes. Stir in candied peel. As soon as cake is turned out, bring syrup to the boil, then spoon over cake so peel is arranged decoratively over the cake.

Makes 8 servings.

CHRISTMAS CAKE

CAKE:
6¾ cups mixed dried fruit
¾ cup quartered glacé cherries
½ cup cut mixed peel
¾ cup flaked almonds
Finely grated peel and juice 1 orange
½ cup brandy or sherry
3 cups all-purpose flour
1 tablespoon ground mixed spice
⅔ cup ground almonds
1½ cups dark-brown sugar
1½ cups butter, softened
2 tablespoons molasses
5 eggs
DECORATION:
3 tablespoons apricot jam, boiled, sieved
1¾ lb. marzipan
2-lb. ready-to-roll fondant icing (sugar paste)
Red and green food colorings

Preheat oven to 275F (135C). Line a 2½-inch-deep 8-inch-square or 2½-inch deep 9-inch-round cake pan with a double thickness of greased parchment paper, extending parchment paper above sides of pan. Place pan on a double parchment paper-lined baking sheet. In a large bowl, combine dried fruit, cherries, mixed peel and flaked almonds until well mixed. Add orange peel and juice and brandy or sherry; mix well.

In another bowl, combine flour, mixed spice, ground almonds, brown sugar, butter, molasses and eggs with a wooden spoon, then beat until smooth and glossy. Add mixed fruit to cake mixture; stir until evenly mixed.

Spoon mixture into prepared pan. Level top with back of a metal spoon, making a slight depression in center. Bake in oven 3¼ to 3½ hours. Test with a skewer; when inserted in center, skewer should come out clean. Cool in pan. Invert cake, remove paper and place on a cake plate.

Brush top and side of cake with apricot jam. Knead marzipan and roll out to ¼-inch thickness. Cover top and sides of cake; trim to fit at bottom. Roll out fondant icing on a lightly sugared surface. Cover cake. Press icing over top and down side of cake. Trim off excess icing at bottom.

Knead trimmings together; color ⅓ red and remainder green with food colorings. Make tiny berries with some of the red icing. Roll and cut out holly leaves from green icing. Mark in veins with knife; let stand until set. Arrange on top of cake with berries. Cut out 'NOEL' from red icing and place on cake. Let cake stand until dry. Tie with ribbon.

Makes 40 servings.

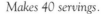

SMALL CAKES

QUEEN CAKES

1/3 cup dried currants
1 cup self-rising flour
1/4 cup butter, softened
1/4 cup sugar
1 egg
Finely shredded zest of 1 lemon
1 tablespoon whipping cream

Preheat oven to 350F (175C). Thoroughly butter 9 individual brioche molds. Put currants into bottoms of molds. Stand molds on a baking sheet.

Into a bowl, sift flour, then set aside. In another bowl, beat butter and sugar until creamy. Mix together egg and lemon zest, then gradually beat into creamed mixture. Add half the flour and fold in lightly. Add remaining flour and the whipping cream and mix to a smooth consistency.

Spoon batter into brioche molds on top of currants. Bake 15 to 20 minutes, until golden. Turn out of molds while still hot. Leave on a wire rack to cool completely. Serve currant sides up.

Makes 9.

Note: If you do not have brioche molds, use paper cupcake cups placed in muffin pans.

LEMON BUTTERFLY CUPCAKES

1/3 cup butter, softened
1/3 cup sugar
1 egg, beaten
1 cup self-rising flour
Shredded zest of 1/2 lemon
3-6 tablespoons milk
FROSTING:
1/4 cup butter, softened
3/4 cup powdered sugar, sifted
1 tablespoon lemon juice
TO DECORATE:
A few black and green grapes

Preheat oven to 375F (190C). Put 12 paper cupcake cups into a muffin pan.

In a bowl, beat butter and sugar until creamy. Gradually add egg to creamed mixture, beating well after each addition. Add half of the flour and the lemon zest and fold in lightly. Add remaining flour and enough milk to make a thick batter. Spoon mixture into paper cups. Bake 15 to 20 minutes, until well risen and brown. Cool on a wire rack.

When cupcakes are cool, cut a shallow cone from center of each one; reserve. To make frosting, in a bowl, beat together butter and powdered sugar until creamy. Add lemon juice and beat until smooth and well blended. Fill hollow in top of each cupcake with frosting. Cut the reserved cones in half and arrange in frosting to resemble wings. Cut grapes into quarters and use them to decorate cupcakes.

Makes 12.

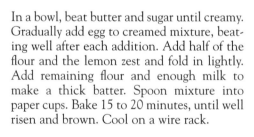

BLACK CURRANT WHIRLS

1 cup butter, softened
1/3 cup powdered sugar, sifted
Few drops almond extract
2 cups all-purpose flour
2 tablespoons black currant jam
TO FINISH:
Powdered sugar for dusting

Preheat oven to 350F (175C). Arrange 12 paper cupcake cups in a muffin pan. In a bowl, beat butter with powdered sugar and almond extract until creamy. Sift flour onto mixture and beat until smooth.

Spoon batter into a pastry bag fitted with a large star tip. Pipe whirls into paper cups, covering bottoms. Pipe a ring around edge to leave a slight hollow in center.

Bake 20 minutes, until set and very lightly browned. Transfer from muffin pan to a wire rack to cool. Put a little jam in center of each whirl. Dust lightly with powdered sugar.

Makes 12.

STRAWBERRY-ROSE MERINGUES

MERINGUES:
2 egg whites
1/2 cup sugar
FILLING:
2/3 cup whipping cream
4 medium-size strawberries
2 teaspoons powdered sugar
2 teaspoons rosewater
TO DECORATE:
12 strawberries

Preheat oven to 250F (120C). Line 2 baking sheets with parchment paper.

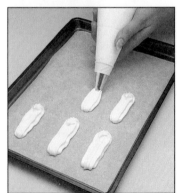

To make meringues, in a bowl, beat egg whites until soft peaks form. Slowly beat in sugar until stiff peaks form. Spoon meringue into a pastry bag fitted with a large star tip. Pipe 24 (3-inch) strips onto prepared baking sheets. Bake 1 hour, until dry and crisp. Cool on wire racks.

To make filling, in a bowl, whip cream until stiff peaks form. In a food processor or blender, process strawberries until smooth. Press through a strainer into a bowl. Stir in powdered sugar and rosewater. Add cream and mix well together. Sandwich meringues together with strawberry cream. Decorate with strawberries and serve at once.

Makes 12.

HONEY MADELEINES

¼ cup butter
2 eggs
¼ cup sugar
1 tablespoon honey
½ cup all-purpose flour
½ teaspoon baking powder
Powdered sugar for sifting

Preheat oven to 375F (190C). Lightly butter 12 madeleine molds. In a small saucepan over low heat, melt the ¼ cup butter. Cool.

In a bowl, beat eggs and sugar until pale and thick. Stir in melted butter and honey. Sift flour and baking powder onto egg mixture, then fold in.

Spoon mixture into prepared molds. Bake 10 minutes, until light golden-brown. Leave in molds 2 minutes, then turn out and transfer to a wire rack to cool. Dust lightly with powdered sugar.

Makes 12.

Note: If you do not have madeleine molds, these light cakes can be made in tartlet pans.

CHOCOLATE BROWNIES

½ cup all-purpose flour
¼ cup unsweetened cocoa powder
½ cup butter
1¼ cups sugar
1 teaspoon vanilla extract
2 eggs, beaten
½ cup chopped walnuts
FROSTING:
4 ozs. semisweet chocolate
⅔ cup dairy sour cream

Preheat oven to 325F (165C). Butter an 8-inch square cake pan. Onto a plate, sift flour and cocoa powder.

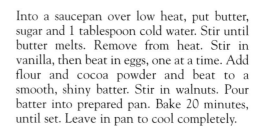

Into a saucepan over low heat, put butter, sugar and 1 tablespoon cold water. Stir until butter melts. Remove from heat. Stir in vanilla, then beat in eggs, one at a time. Add flour and cocoa powder and beat to a smooth, shiny batter. Stir in walnuts. Pour batter into prepared pan. Bake 20 minutes, until set. Leave in pan to cool completely.

To make frosting, into a heatproof bowl over a pan of simmering water, break chocolate. Heat until chocolate is melted. Stir until smooth, then remove from heat. Stir in sour cream and beat until evenly blended. Spoon topping over brownies and make a swirling pattern with a spatula. Leave in a cool place to set. Cut into squares and remove from pan.

Makes 9 large or 16 small brownies.

SPONGE DROPS

½ cup all-purpose flour
2 large eggs
¼ cup sugar
Sugar for sprinkling
FILLING:
⅔ cup whipping cream
4 teaspoons red jam

Preheat oven to 375F (190C). Grease several baking sheets and line with waxed paper. Into a bowl, sift flour. In another bowl, beat together eggs and sugar until pale and thick.

Sift flour again onto egg mixture, then fold in very gently. Spoon batter into a pastry bag fitted with a 1-inch plain tip. Pipe batter onto prepared baking sheets in 1½-inch circles. Sprinkle each circle with sugar. Bake 10 minutes, until light golden. Slide paper with sponge drops still attached off baking sheet onto a damp dish towel. Cool completely.

In a bowl, whip cream until stiff peaks form. Remove sponge drops from paper. Sandwich together in pairs with a little jam and whipped cream.

Makes 18.

GINGER BRANDY SNAPS

¼ cup unsalted butter
¼ cup packed dark brown sugar
2 tablespoons light corn syrup
½ cup all-purpose flour
½ teaspoon ground ginger
1 teaspoon brandy
FILLING:
1¼ cups whipping cream
1 tablespoon stem ginger syrup
6 pieces stem ginger

Preheat oven to 350F (175C).

Grease several baking sheets. Butter the handles of 3 or 4 wooden spoons. Into a saucepan over medium heat, put butter, brown sugar and syrup. Heat until butter melts. Cool slightly. Sift flour and ginger onto melted ingredients and stir in with brandy. Drop teaspoonfuls of mixture, well spaced out, onto baking sheets. Bake 7 to 10 minutes, until brandy snaps are golden.

Quickly remove brandy snaps from baking sheets and roll around spoon handles, leaving them in place until set. Slide off spoons and leave on wire racks until completely cool. In a bowl, beat cream with ginger syrup until stiff peaks form. Spoon cream into a pastry bag fitted with a small star tip. Pipe into each end of brandy snaps. Slice stem ginger pieces and use to decorate brandy snaps. Refrigerate until ready to serve.

Makes about 18.

CUPCAKES

1 cup self-rising flour
½ cup sugar
½ cup margarine, softened
2 eggs
2 tablespoons milk
1 teaspoon vanilla extract
FROSTING:
1½ cups powdered sugar
3-4 teaspoons water
Few drops of food coloring (optional)
Jellybeans or other candies to decorate

Preheat oven to 350F (175C). In a medium-size bowl, beat together all cake ingredients until blended.

Using 2 spoons, divide batter among 20 paper cupcake cups placed in 2 (12-cup) muffin pans; put water in unused cups. Bake 15 minutes, until golden. Transfer to a wire rack to cool.

To make frosting, into a bowl, sift powdered sugar, then mix in just enough water to give a smooth consistency for coating. Tint some frosting with a small amount of coloring, if desired. Frost cupcakes and decorate as desired, while frosting is still soft. Let set before serving.

Makes 20.

CHERRY-NUT ROCKS

⅔ cup candied cherries
½ cup walnuts
2 cups all-purpose flour
2 teaspoons baking powder
½ teaspoon apple-pie spice
1 cup packed brown sugar
¾ cup butter, chilled
1 egg, beaten
1-2 tablespoons milk (optional)

Preheat oven to 375F (190C). Grease a baking sheet. With a sharp knife, cut cherries into quarters. Coarsely chop walnuts.

Into a bowl, sift flour, baking powder and apple pie spice. Stir in sugar. Cut in butter until mixture resembles bread crumbs. Stir in cherries and nuts. Stir egg into flour mixture to form a stiff dough. Add a little milk, if necessary.

Using 2 forks, pile the mixture in rocky heaps on baking sheet. Bake 15 to 20 minutes, until golden-brown and firm to the touch. Cool on baking sheet 2 minutes, then, using a metal spatula, transfer to a wire rack to cool completely.

Makes 10 to 12.

WELSH CAKES

2 cups self-rising flour
Pinch of salt
¼ cup vegetable shortening
¼ cup margarine, chilled
⅔ cup sugar
⅔ cup dried currants
1 egg, beaten
1 tablespoon milk (optional)
Sugar for dusting

Into a bowl, sift flour and salt. Cut in shortening and margarine until mixture resembles bread crumbs. Stir in sugar and currants.

Add egg and a little milk, if necessary, to make a soft, but not sticky dough. On a floured surface, roll out dough to ¼-inch thick. Using a 2½-inch plain or fluted round cookie cutter, cut out about 16 circles.

Heat a greased griddle or heavy-bottomed skillet. Cook cakes, over low heat, about 3 minutes on each side until golden-brown. Dust with sugar.

Makes about 16.

BLACKBERRY MUFFINS

2½ cups all-purpose flour
1 tablespoon baking powder
½ cup sugar
1 egg
1⅓ cups milk
6 tablespoons vegetable oil
1 teaspoon vanilla extract
6 ozs. blackberries
2 tablespoons granulated brown sugar

Preheat oven to 400F (205C). Grease a 12-cup muffin pan. Into a bowl, sift flour and baking powder. Stir in sugar.

In another bowl, beat together egg, milk, oil and vanilla. Add to dry ingredients all at once. Stir just until blended. Gently stir in blackberries.

Spoon batter into prepared muffin pan. Sprinkle with brown sugar. Bake 15 to 20 minutes, until well risen and golden-brown. Cool in pan 5 minutes, then turn out muffins onto a wire rack to cool completely.

Makes 12.

SCONES

CHOCOLATE-NUT MUFFINS

2 cups self-rising flour, plus extra for dusting
1 teaspoon baking powder
¼ cup butter, chilled
5 teaspoons sugar
⅔ cup milk
TO SERVE:
Butter or whipped cream and jam

Preheat oven to 425F (220C). Dust a baking sheet with flour. Into a bowl, sift flour and baking powder, then stir to mix. Cut in butter, then stir in sugar.

4 ozs. semisweet chocolate
2 cups all-purpose flour
1 tablespoon baking powder
½ teaspoon ground cinnamon
⅓ cup packed brown sugar
1 cup coarsely chopped walnuts
1 cup milk
¼ cup vegetable oil
1 teaspoon vanilla extract
1 egg

Preheat oven to 400F (205C). Grease a 12-cup muffin pan.

Make a well in the center of the mixture and pour in milk. Using a knife, mix together until dough is soft, but not sticky. Turn out dough onto a floured surface and knead lightly. Pat dough out to ½-inch thick.

Into a heatproof bowl set over a pan of simmering water, break chocolate and heat until melted. Remove from heat.

Using a 2-inch round cookie cutter, cut out 12 scones. Arrange on prepared baking sheet and dust the tops with flour. Bake 10 to 12 minutes, until well risen and light brown. Transfer to a wire rack and cover with a cloth while cooling. Serve with butter or whipped cream and jam.

Makes 12.

Variation: For Cheese Scones, omit sugar and stir in ½ cup shredded Cheddar cheese.

Into bowl of chocolate, sift flour, baking powder and cinnamon. Add sugar and nuts. In another bowl, mix together milk, oil, vanilla and egg. Add to dry ingredients and stir just until blended. Spoon batter into prepared pan. Bake 15 to 20 minutes, until well risen and firm to the touch. Cool in pan 5 minutes, then turn out muffins onto a wire rack to cool completely.

Makes 12.

NUTTY BROWNIES

1¼ cups self-rising flour
1 cup packed light brown sugar
¾ cup lightly toasted, chopped hazelnuts or pecans
½ cup butter
4 ozs. semisweet chocolate, broken into small pieces
2 eggs, beaten
5 tablespoons milk
1 teaspoon vanilla extract

Preheat oven to 350F (175C). Grease an 8-inch square cake pan. In a medium-size bowl, put flour, sugar and three-quarters of the nuts. Mix together.

In a small saucepan, melt butter and chocolate over low heat. Cool slightly.

Into another bowl, put eggs, milk and vanilla and beat together. Add to flour mixture with melted butter and chocolate. Beat until combined. Pour into prepared pan, scatter nuts over top and bake 25 to 30 minutes, until firm. Cool on a wire rack, then cut into 12 pieces.

Makes 12.

ORANGE MUFFINS

2½ cups all-purpose flour
1 tablespoon baking powder
Pinch of salt
½ cup packed light brown sugar
Grated zest and juice of 1 orange
2 eggs
1 cup milk
¼ cup butter, melted
1 cup semisweet chocolate pieces

Preheat oven to 400F (205C). Grease a 12-cup muffin pan or line with paper cupcake cups. Into a medium-size bowl, sift flour, baking powder and salt. Stir in sugar and orange zest.

In another bowl, beat together orange juice, eggs, milk and butter. Pour onto dry ingredients. Add chocolate pieces and stir together just until blended. Do not overmix.

Spoon batter into muffin pan, filling each cup about two-thirds full; put water in any unfilled cups so they do not burn during baking. Bake 20 to 25 minutes, until golden-brown. Cool on a wire rack.

Makes 10 to 12.

STRAWBERRY SHORTCAKE

2 cups all-purpose flour
1 tablespoon baking powder
5 teaspoons sugar
⅓ cup butter, chilled
⅓ cup milk
FILLING:
1½ lbs. strawberries
¼ cup sugar
1¼ cups whipping cream

Preheat oven to 425F (220C). Grease a baking sheet. Into a bowl, sift flour and baking powder.

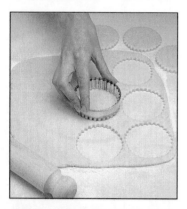

Stir in sugar. Cut in butter until mixture resembles bread crumbs. Pour in milk and mix to form a soft dough. Turn out dough onto a lightly floured surface, then roll out to ¼-inch thick. Cut into 8 (3-inch) circles. Place on prepared baking sheet. Bake 10 to 12 minutes, until golden-brown. Slice most of strawberries, reserving a few for decoration. In a bowl, mix together sliced strawberries and sugar. In another bowl, whip cream until soft peaks form.

Split shortcakes in half while still warm. Spread bottom halves with ⅔ of cream. Cover cream with sliced strawberries and top with other shortcake halves. Add a swirl of cream to each one and decorate with reserved strawberries.

Makes 8.

TINY CHOCOLATE LOGS

3 eggs
2 tablespoons plus 2 teaspoons superfine sugar
¼ cup all-purpose flour
1 tablespoon cocoa powder
Powdered sugar, if desired
Marzipan toadstools and holly sprigs to decorate
FILLING:
1¼ cups whipping cream
4 (1-oz.) squares semisweet chocolate

Preheat oven to 400F (205C). Line a 1-inch deep 12-inch baking sheet with waxed paper. Place eggs and sugar in a bowl set over a saucepan of simmering water. Whisk until thick and pale.

Remove bowl from saucepan; continue whisking until mixture leaves a trail. Sift in flour and cocoa; fold in carefully until mixture is evenly blended. Pour mixture onto prepared baking sheet; spread carefully to edges. Bake in oven 8 to 10 minutes or until firm to touch. Cool a few minutes and remove cake. Remove waxed paper, trim edges and cut cake in half. To prepare filling, place ¼ cup whipping cream and chocolate broken into pieces in a bowl set over saucepan of hot water. Stir occasionally until melted. Whip remaining cream until almost thick.

When chocolate has cooled, fold it carefully into whipped cream. Using ⅓ of chocolate cream, spread evenly over each cake. Roll each in a firm roll from long edge. Wrap in plastic wrap and chill 20 minutes or until firm. Cut each roll in 6 lengths. Spread each with remaining chocolate cream using a small palette knife; mark cream in lines. Sprinkle with powdered sugar, if desired. Decorate, then refrigerate until ready to serve.

Makes 12 servings.

COOKIES

ALMOND MACAROONS

2 egg whites
¾ cup ground blanched almonds
½ cup sugar
2 teaspoons cornstarch
¼ teaspoon almond extract
12 blanched almonds halves

Preheat oven to 350F (175C). Line 2 baking sheets with parchment paper or waxed paper. Reserve 2 teaspoons egg white. In a large bowl, put remaining egg whites and beat until soft peaks form.

Fold in ground almonds, sugar, cornstarch and almond extract until mixture is smooth. Put 6 spoonfuls of mixture onto each baking sheet and flatten slightly. Place an almond half in center of each macaroon. Brush lightly with reserved egg white.

Bake 20 minutes, until very lightly browned. Cool on baking sheets. When cold, remove macaroons from paper.

Makes 12.

LINZER HEARTS

½ cup butter, softened
¼ cup sugar
1 egg, beaten
¼ teaspoon almond extract
1¾ cups all-purpose flour
3 tablespoons cornstarch
½ teaspoon baking powder
FILLING:
6 tablespoons seedless raspberry jam
TO FINISH:
Powdered sugar for sifting

In a bowl, beat butter and sugar together until creamy. Gradually beat in egg, then beat in almond extract.

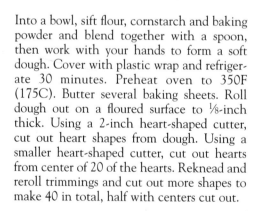

Into a bowl, sift flour, cornstarch and baking powder and blend together with a spoon, then work with your hands to form a soft dough. Cover with plastic wrap and refrigerate 30 minutes. Preheat oven to 350F (175C). Butter several baking sheets. Roll dough out on a floured surface to ⅛-inch thick. Using a 2-inch heart-shaped cutter, cut out heart shapes from dough. Using a smaller heart-shaped cutter, cut out hearts from center of 20 of the hearts. Reknead and reroll trimmings and cut out more shapes to make 40 in total, half with centers cut out.

Bake 15 minutes, until very lightly browned. Remove from baking sheets to wire racks to cool. Dust cookies with cut-out centers with powdered sugar. Spread whole hearts with raspberry jam, then top with cut-out cookies.

Makes 20.

JUMBLES

⅔ cup butter, softened
½ cup plus 2 tablespoons sugar
1 egg, beaten
2 cups all-purpose flour
½ cup ground blanched almonds
Shredded zest of 1 lemon
GLAZE:
2 tablespoons honey
2 tablespoons brown sugar

In a bowl, beat butter with sugar until creamy. Gradually beat in egg.

Sift flour onto creamed mixture. Add ground almonds and lemon zest. Mix well to make a firm dough. Knead lightly, then wrap in plastic wrap and refrigerate 30 minutes. Meanwhile, preheat oven to 350F (175C). Grease several baking sheets. Divide dough into 32 equal pieces. Roll each piece into a pencil-thin strip 4 inches long. Twist into an S-shape and place on a baking sheet. Bake 15 minutes, until very lightly browned.

To glaze, in small saucepan, warm honey. Brush warm jumbles with honey, then sprinkle with brown sugar. Return to oven 2 minutes. Cool on baking sheets a few minutes, then remove to wire racks to cool completely.

Makes 32.

COFFEE-WALNUT COOKIES

2 cups all-purpose flour, sifted
1 cup butter, softened
1 cup powdered sugar, sifted
1 egg yolk
1 teaspoon vanilla extract
1¼ cups coarsely chopped walnuts
2 tablespoons medium-ground coffee beans
1¼ cups walnut pieces

Preheat oven to 350F (175C). Butter several baking sheets.

Into a bowl, sift flour. Add butter, powdered sugar, egg yolk and vanilla. Mix well, then mix in the chopped walnuts and coffee with your hands.

Place heaped teaspoonfuls of mixture on prepared baking sheets. Flatten slightly and top each mound with a walnut piece. Bake 12 to 15 minutes, until just starting to color. Cool on baking sheets a few minutes, then transfer to wire racks to cool completely.

Makes 28 to 30.

SPICED APRICOT SQUARES

2 cups all-purpose flour
1 teaspoon apple-pie spice
1 cup ground blanched almonds
1 egg, beaten
1½ cups sugar
¾ cup butter, softened
⅓ cup apricot jam
TO FINISH:
Powdered sugar for sifting

Into a bowl, sift flour and spice. Add ground almonds, egg, sugar and butter. Mix well until thoroughly combined. Knead lightly. Wrap in plastic wrap and refrigerate at least 30 minutes.

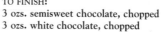

Butter an 11- x 7-inch baking pan. Into pan, press half of the dough. Spread apricot jam over dough. On a floured surface, lightly knead remaining dough. Roll out and cut into thin strips. Arrange strips over jam to form a close lattice pattern. Refrigerate 30 minutes. Preheat oven to 350F (175C).

Bake 30 to 40 minutes, until lightly browned. Cool cookies in pan, then sift powdered sugar over top. Cut into 24 squares or bars.

Makes 24.

FLORENTINES

¼ cup unsalted butter
⅓ cup whipping cream
⅓ cup sugar
Finely shredded zest of 1 lemon
1 teaspoon lemon juice
½ cup all-purpose flour, sifted
½ cup slivered blanched almonds
¾ cup chopped mixed candied citrus peel
⅓ cup chopped candied cherries
2 tablespoons golden raisins
2 tablespoons chopped angelica
TO FINISH:
3 ozs. semisweet chocolate, chopped
3 ozs. white chocolate, chopped

Preheat oven to 350F (175C). Grease several baking sheets. Line with parchment paper. Into a saucepan, put butter, cream, sugar, lemon zest and juice. Stir over medium heat until butter melts. Remove from heat and stir in flour, almonds, mixed peel, cherries, golden raisins and angelica. Drop teaspoonfuls of mixture onto baking sheets, spacing well apart. Using a fork dipped in cold water, flatten each mound to a circle about 2½ inches in diameter.

Bake 10 to 12 minutes, until lightly browned around edges. Cool on baking sheets a few minutes, then remove with a spatula to wire racks to cool completely. Melt semisweet and white chocolate separately in 2 heatproof bowls placed over pans of simmering water. Spread flat sides of half the florentines with semisweet chocolate and the remaining florentines with white chocolate. Using a fork, mark chocolate into wavy lines. Leave to set, chocolate sides up.

Makes 28.

LEMON SHORTBREAD

½ cup butter, softened
¼ cup sugar
1¾ cups all-purpose flour
¼ teaspoon grated nutmeg
2 tablespoons cornstarch
Shredded zest of 1 lemon
TO FINISH:
Sugar and grated nutmeg for sprinkling

In a bowl, beat butter with sugar until creamy. Into another bowl, sift flour and nutmeg, then add cornstarch and lemon zest. Blend in creamed butter and sugar with a spoon, then work with your hands to form a soft dough.

On a lightly floured surface, knead until smooth. Roll out to a smooth circle, about 6 inches in diameter. Very lightly flour a 7-inch shortbread mold. Place shortbread, smooth side down, in mold. Press out to fit mold exactly. Very carefully unmold shortbread onto a baking sheet. Refrigerate 1 hour. (If you do not have a shortbread mold, shape dough into a neat circle. Place on baking sheet, prick well with a fork, then pinch edge to decorate.)

Preheat oven to 325F (165C). Bake shortbread 35 to 40 minutes, until cooked through, but still pale in color. As soon as shortbread is removed from oven, sprinkle lightly with sugar and nutmeg. Cool on baking sheet about 20 minutes, then very carefully transfer to a wire rack to cool completely.

Makes 1.

ORANGE-GLAZED SHORTIES

1 cup butter, softened
⅓ cup powdered sugar, sifted
Shredded zest of 1 orange
½ teaspoon ground coriander
2 cups all-purpose flour
GLAZE:
2 teaspoons apricot jam, heated and strained
3 tablespoons powdered sugar, sifted
1 tablespoon orange juice

Butter several baking sheets and dust lightly with flour.

In a bowl, beat butter with powdered sugar until very light and creamy. Stir in the orange zest. Into another bowl, sift the coriander and flour, then work into creamy mixture with a wooden spoon to form a soft dough. Put dough into a pastry bag fitted with a large star tip. Pipe rings of dough onto prepared baking sheets. Refrigerate 30 minutes. Preheat oven to 350F (175C). Bake cookies 20 minutes, until very lightly browned.

To glaze, brush each shortie with a little apricot jam. In a small bowl, mix together the powdered sugar and orange juice and brush over cookies. Return cookies to oven 2 to 3 minutes, until glaze is set. Cool on baking sheets a few minutes, then transfer to wire racks to cool completely.

Makes 25 to 28.

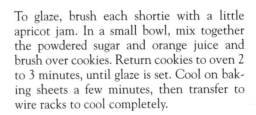

DOUBLE CHOCOLATE COOKIES

½ cup butter
¼ cup granulated sugar
⅓ cup packed brown sugar
1 egg, beaten
½ teaspoon vanilla extract
1 cup plus 2 tablespoons all-purpose flour
2 tablespoons unsweetened cocoa powder
½ teaspoon baking soda
5 ozs. white chocolate pieces, cut into pieces

Preheat oven to 350F (175C). Butter several baking sheets.

In a bowl, beat butter with sugars until creamy. Gradually beat in egg and vanilla extract. Into another bowl, sift flour, cocoa powder and baking soda. Mix well, then stir in chocolate pieces.

Drop teaspoonfuls of dough, well spaced out, onto prepared baking sheets. Bake 10 to 12 minutes, until firm. Cool on baking sheets a few minutes, then remove to wire racks to cool completely.

Makes about 48.

EASTER COOKIES

⅔ cup walnuts
½ cup sunflower oil
½ cup superfine sugar
2 tablespoons dried currants
1 egg
1½ cups all-purpose flour
1 teaspoon baking powder
¼ teaspoon vanilla extract
Powdered sugar

Preheat oven to 350F (175C). Grease 2 baking sheets. In a food processor, chop walnuts finely. In a bowl, mix together walnuts, sunflower oil, sugar, currants and egg.

Sift in flour and baking powder. Add vanilla extract. Stir together to form a firm paste, adding more flour if too soft.

Roll mixture into small walnut-size balls, flatten slightly and place on prepared baking sheets. Bake 10 minutes, or until crisp and golden. Transfer to wire racks to cool. Dust with powdered sugar as they cool.

Makes about 14.

FESTIVAL CRESCENTS

4½ ozs. hazelnuts
1¼ cups unsalted butter, softened
¼ cup superfine sugar
1 egg yolk
2 tablespoons brandy
½ cup cornstarch
2½ cups all-purpose flour
Orange-flower water
Powdered sugar

In a food processor, chop nuts finely, without reducing to ground hazelnuts. Preheat oven to 350F (175C). Butter 2 or 3 baking sheets.

In a bowl, cream butter and superfine sugar until pale and fluffy. Beat in egg yolk and brandy. Stir in hazelnuts. Sift cornstarch and flour over mixture. Stir in, adding more flour, if necessary, to make a firm dough. With floured hands, break off small pieces of dough and roll into 3-inch pieces, tapering into pointed ends. Shape into crescents; place on baking sheets. Bake 20 to 25 minutes or until firm. Reduce heat if cookies brown. Transfer to wire racks to cool.

Into a small bowl, pour orange-flower water. Into a large bowl, put powdered sugar. Dip crescents very briefly into orange-flower water, then into powdered sugar, to coat completely. Pack loosely in a pan to avoid cookies sticking together.

Makes about 40.

DOMINO COOKIES

2 cups self-rising flour
½ cup butter, chilled
½ cup sugar
Finely grated zest of 1 lemon
1 small egg, beaten
1 cup semisweet chocolate pieces

Preheat oven to 350F (175C). Into a bowl, sift flour. Cut in butter until mixture resembles bread crumbs. Stir in sugar and lemon zest, then mix in egg to form a dough. Turn out dough onto a floured surface and knead until smooth.

Grease 2 baking sheets. Roll out dough to a rectangle about ¼-inch thick. With a knife, cut into 3- x 1½-inch bars. With a metal spatula, transfer to baking sheets.

With a knife, mark each cookie crosswise across center. Arrange chocolate pieces on each to resemble domino dots. Bake 12 to 15 minutes, until light brown around edges. Cool slightly on baking sheets, then, with a metal spatula, transfer to a wire rack to cool completely.

Makes about 20.

CHOCOLATE CIGARETTES

2 egg whites
1/3 cup plus 1 tablespoon superfine sugar
1/4 cup plus 3 tablespoons all-purpose flour
2 teaspoons cocoa powder
1/4 cup unsalted butter, melted
2 (1-oz.) squares white chocolate, melted
Holly sprigs to decorate

Preheat oven to 400F (205C). Line 2 baking sheets with waxed paper. In a bowl, whisk egg whites until stiff. Add sugar gradually, whisking well after each addition. Sift flour and cocoa over surface of mixture. Add butter and fold in carefully until mixture is evenly blended.

Place 2 spoonfuls of mixture onto each prepared baking sheet, spacing well apart. Spread each in a thin round. Bake 1 sheet at a time in oven 3 to 4 minutes. Loosen each round with a palette knife, then return to oven 1 minute.

Remove 1 chocolate round at a time and quickly roll around a greased pencil or wooden spoon handle to form a tube. Slip off and cool cigarette on a wire rack. Repeat with remaining rounds. Cook second tray of rounds, then repeat to make cigarettes. Dip both ends of each cigarette into melted chocolate. Let set on waxed paper-lined baking sheet. Store in an airtight container until needed. Decorate with holly sprigs.

Makes 25 pieces.

VANILLA RINGS

1/2 cup butter, softened
1/3 cup superfine sugar
1/2 teaspoon vanilla extract
1 egg yolk
1 1/2 cups all-purpose flour
1/2 teaspoon baking powder
1 1/2 teaspoons ouzo, or other aniseed liqueur
2 tablespoons chopped blanched almonds

Preheat oven to 350F (175C). Grease 2 baking sheets. In a bowl, cream together butter and sugar until light and fluffy.

Beat in vanilla extract and egg yolk. Sift flour and baking powder over mixture, then add ouzo and mix to a smooth dough. Break off walnut-size pieces of dough.

Roll the pieces into short ropes and join the ends to make rings. Place on prepared baking sheets and sprinkle chopped almonds over the rings. Bake 5 to 20 minutes or until pale gold. Transfer to wire racks to cool.

Makes about 16.

CINNAMON COOKIES

1 cup margarine, softened
½ cup sugar
1 teaspoon vanilla extract
3 cups all-purpose flour
2 teaspoons ground cinnamon
1½ cups powdered sugar

Grease 2 baking sheets. Beat together margarine, sugar and vanilla. Stir in flour and 1 teaspoon of the cinnamon to make a soft dough. Cover and refrigerate 1 hour.

Preheat oven to 350F (175C). Form mixture in 1-inch balls and place on prepared baking sheets, leaving space between cookies.

Bake 15 minutes or until lightly browned on bottom. Remove from oven, cool on baking sheets for a few minutes, then transfer to a wire rack to cool. Mix together powdered sugar and remaining cinnamon; sift over cookies.

Makes 24 cookies.

CREME DE MENTHE COOKIES

8 (1-oz.) squares semisweet chocolate
2 tablespoons butter
2 cups graham cracker crumbs
¾ cup plain cake crumbs
Superfine sugar for sprinkling
Mint sprigs to decorate
FILLING:
¼ cup unsalted butter
¾ cup powdered sugar, sieved
2 teaspoons Crème de Menthe

To prepare filling, beat butter in a bowl with a wooden spoon or electric mixer until soft and smooth. Gradually beat in powdered sugar and Crème de Menthe until light and fluffy.

Break up chocolate and place in a bowl with butter over a saucepan of hand-hot water. Stir occasionally until melted. Add graham cracker and cake crumbs; stir until evenly mixed and mixture forms a ball. Sprinkle a 10-inch square of foil with superfine sugar.

Roll out chocolate mixture on foil in an 8-inch square. Spread filling evenly over chocolate mixture to within ½ inch of edges. Roll up carefully from long edge in a smooth roll using foil. Wrap in foil and chill until firm. Cut in thin slices when needed. Decorate with mint sprigs.

Makes 20 servings.

COCONUT CRISPS

⅔ cup butter or margarine, softened
1 egg
½ teaspoon vanilla extract
½ cup packed light brown sugar
1 cup shredded coconut
⅔ cup rolled oats
1 cup self-rising flour
2 cups cornflakes, lightly crushed

Preheat oven to 325F (165C). Grease 2 baking sheets. Into a medium-size bowl, put butter, egg, vanilla and sugar. Beat until creamy.

Stir in coconut, oats and flour, and mix to form a dough. Roll dough into about 25 balls, each the size of a large walnut.

Put crushed cornflakes on a plate. Lightly press dough balls in cornflakes to coat all over. Place on baking sheets. Bake about 15 minutes, until lightly browned. Transfer to a wire rack to cool.

Makes about 25.

CHEESE THINS

1 cup all-purpose flour
½ teaspoon salt
½ teaspoon pepper
½ teaspoon dry mustard
½ cup butter
1 cup shredded Cheddar cheese (4 ozs.)
1 tablespoon plus 1 teaspoon regular oats
1 teaspoon cayenne pepper
1 egg white
Fennel sprigs to garnish

Preheat oven to 425F (220C). Lightly grease 2 baking sheets. Sift flour, salt, pepper and mustard into a bowl.

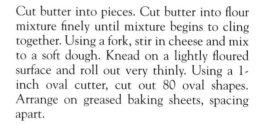

Cut butter into pieces. Cut butter into flour mixture finely until mixture begins to cling together. Using a fork, stir in cheese and mix to a soft dough. Knead on a lightly floured surface and roll out very thinly. Using a 1-inch oval cutter, cut out 80 oval shapes. Arrange on greased baking sheets, spacing apart.

In a small bowl, mix oatmeal and cayenne. Brush each oval with egg white and sprinkle with oatmeal mixture. Beat in oven to 5 to 6 minutes or until pale in color. Cool on baking sheets a few minutes, then remove carefully with a palette knife. Arrange on a plate to serve. Garnish with fennel sprigs.

Makes 80 pieces.

FOOD FOR CHILDREN

PLAYING CARD SANDWICHES

4 slices whole-wheat bread, crusts removed
4 slices white bread, crusts removed
Margarine or butter, softened
SALMON FILLING:
1 tablespoon mayonnaise
2 teaspoons lemon juice
1 (3½-oz.) can red salmon, drained, skin and bones removed
½ carton radish or mustard sprouts, trimmed
EGG FILLING:
2 eggs, hard-cooked
1 tablespoon mayonnaise
2 green onions, finely chopped

With a knife, cut each slice of bread into quarters. Cut out playing card symbols from centers of half of the quarters. To make Salmon Filling, in a small bowl, beat mayonnaise and lemon juice together. Stir in salmon until combined, then stir in sprouts. Lightly spread margarine over whole squares of whole-wheat bread. Spread Salmon Filling on top, then cover with cut-out whole-wheat quarters.

To make Egg Filling, in a small bowl, mash eggs into small pieces with a fork. Stir in mayonnaise and onions. Make up egg sandwiches like salmon sandwiches, using the white bread.

Makes 16 sandwiches.

ZOO FRENCH TOAST

6 slices bread
1 large egg
3 tablespoons milk
3 tablespoons butter

With cookie cutters, cut bread into animal shapes.

In a shallow dish, beat egg and milk together.

In a large skillet, melt butter. Dip bread shapes in egg mixture, coating each side. Place egg-coated shapes in skillet and cook on each side until golden. Serve at once.

Makes about 12 pieces.

FUN FISH CAKES

½ lb. potatoes, peeled
Salt
2 tablespoons butter or margarine
1 egg yolk
1 tablespoon snipped fresh chives
1 (7-oz.) can tuna in water, drained
1 egg, beaten
¾ cup dry bread crumbs
Vegetable oil for cooking
4 green peas
1 small tomato
Fresh chives to garnish

Preheat the oven to 400F (205C). Grease a baking sheet. Cut the potatoes into pieces.

In a pan of lightly salted boiling water, boil potatoes just until tender. Drain potatoes. Return to pan and dry over low heat a few moments. Add butter and egg yolk, then mash together. Stir in chives and tuna. Divide mixture into 6 equal portions. With floured hands, shape portions into flat pear shapes. Shape the thinner end of the fish cakes to form a V-shape, like the tail of a fish.

Into a shallow dish, put beaten egg. Gently add fish cakes to egg and brush tops with egg. Coat in bread crumbs, then place on baking sheet. Brush with a little oil. Bake 20 to 25 minutes, until crisp and golden. To serve, place a pea on each fish for an eye and add a small sliver of tomato for the mouth. Garnish with chives and serve hot.

Makes 6 servings.

CHEESY MICE

4 eggs, hard-cooked
¼ cup finely grated Cheddar cheese (1 ounce)
2 tablespoons low-fat cream cheese
8 radishes
16 dried currants
2 ozs. Edam cheese, cut into small chunks
Radish or mustard sprouts to garnish

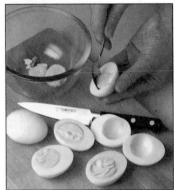

With a sharp knife, carefully halve eggs lengthwise and scoop out the yolks. Put yolks into a small bowl.

Add cheeses. Mix together until smooth. Spoon into egg whites and smooth the surface.

Place filled egg halves upside down. To assemble each mouse, cut slits at the pointed end of eggs, then insert small slices of radish for ears, currants for eyes and small pieces of radish for noses. Attach the radish roots for tails. To serve place 2 mice on each plate. Arrange small chunks of cheese in front of mice. Garnish with sprouts.

Makes 4 servings.

SALAMI PASTA

2 tablespoons olive oil
1 onion, finely chopped
1 garlic clove, crushed
1 red bell pepper, finely sliced
1 (14-oz.) can chopped tomatoes
½ teaspoon sugar
½ teaspoon dried leaf oregano
Salt and pepper
4 cups pasta shapes
4 ozs. salami stick, sliced
½ cup shredded Cheddar cheese (2 ozs.)

In a medium-size saucepan, heat oil. Add onion and cook over medium heat 3 to 4 minutes, until softened.

Add garlic and bell pepper, and cook a few minutes longer. Stir in tomatoes, sugar, oregano, salt and pepper. Cover and simmer 10 minutes, stirring occasionally.

Meanwhile, cook pasta in boiling salted water according to package directions just until tender to the bite. Drain well, then return to saucepan. Stir in salami and tomato sauce, then heat through. Serve sprinkled with cheese.

Makes 4 servings.

SURPRISE HAMBURGERS

1¼ lbs. lean ground beef
1 small onion, finely chopped
1 teaspoon Italian seasoning
⅔ cup rolled oats
1 egg, beaten
Salt and pepper
1 (3-oz.) piece cheese, such as Gouda
1 tablespoon vegetable oil
Grated carrots, lettuce leaves and onion rings, to serve

Into a bowl, put beef, onion, herbs and oats. Mix together to break up beef. Add egg, salt and pepper; stir until combined.

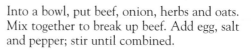

With floured hands, divide mixture into 6 balls, then flatten each on a board or flat surface. With a knife, cut cheese into 6 pieces. Place a piece in middle of each meat patty. Preheat broiler.

Carefully enclose each cheese piece in meat mixture, then form into patties. Brush with oil, place under a medium-hot broiler and broil 4 to 5 minutes on each side, until browned. Serve with carrots, lettuce leaves and onion rings.

Makes 6 servings.

TWICE-BAKED POTATOES

4 baking potatoes
Vegetable oil for brushing
2 tablespoons butter or margarine
3 eggs, separated
¾ cup shredded Cheddar cheese
Salt and pepper
Cherry tomatoes, lettuce leaves and bell pepper
  strips to serve

Preheat oven to 400F (205C). With a fork, prick potatoes all over. Brush skins lightly with oil. Bake 45 to 60 minutes, until softened.

With a knife, cut off tops of potatoes. Scoop out cooked centers and put into a bowl, making sure skins are not pierced. Mash potatoes with butter, then beat in egg yolks, cheese, salt and pepper.

Beat egg whites until stiff but not dry, then fold into mashed potatoes. Spoon back into potato skins. Bake 10 to 15 minutes longer, until puffed and golden on top. Serve with cherry tomatoes, lettuce leaves and bell pepper strips.

Makes 4 servings.

Variations: Stir in ¼ cup chopped cooked ham, or 1 tablespoon chopped sweet pickle, if desired.

CHICKEN FRIED RICE

1½ cups long-grain brown rice
3 tablespoons vegetable oil
1 egg
1 tablespoon water
1 small onion, finely chopped
1 red bell pepper, chopped
1½ cups shredded cooked chicken (8 ozs.)
⅓ cup frozen green peas, thawed
⅓ cup frozen whole-kernel corn, thawed
1 tablespoon soy sauce
Green onions to garnish

Cook rice in boiling water according to package directions until tender; drain, if necessary

In a medium-size skillet, heat 2 tablespoons of the oil. Beat egg with water, then add to skillet and cook until set. Turn out omelet onto a board, then roll up and cut into thin strips; set aside. In a large skillet, heat remaining oil. Add onion and bell pepper, and cook 2 to 3 minutes.

Stir in rice and stir-fry over low heat 3 to 4 minutes. Add chicken, peas, corn and soy sauce and continue stir-frying 3 minutes longer. Add omelet strips to fried rice and toss together before serving. Garnish with green onions.

Makes 4 servings.

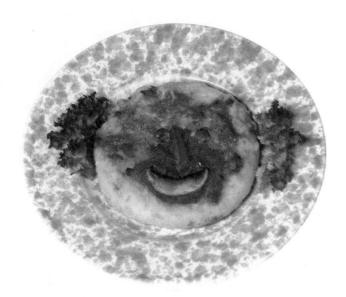

FUNNY FACE PIZZAS

2 teaspoons vegetable oil
½ small onion
1 (7-oz.) can chopped tomatoes
1 tablespoon tomato paste
3 cups self-rising flour
⅓ cup margarine, chilled
1 cup shredded mild Cheddar cheese (4 ozs.)
1 egg
⅔ cup milk
24 green peas
3 large button mushrooms
Red, orange or yellow bell pepper
Leaf lettuce to garnish

In a small saucepan, heat oil. Add onion and cook until softened. Stir in tomatoes and tomato paste; cook over medium heat 10 minutes, until thickened. Preheat oven to 400F (205C). Grease 2 baking sheets. Into a bowl, sift flour. Cut in margarine until mixture resembles bread crumbs, then stir in half the cheese. Beat egg with milk. Add to bowl and mix to form a smooth ball of dough. Divide dough into 12 pieces. Roll out each piece to a 3-inch circle. Place 6 on each baking sheet.

Spread tomato sauce over each dough circle. Place remaining cheese on one edge of each pizza for hair. Add peas to resemble eyes. Slice mushrooms, discarding stems. Place a slice on each pizza for the mouth. Cut bell pepper into strips and arrange on each pizza to look like a nose. Bake pizzas 12 to 15 minutes, until the edges are golden. Garnish with lettuce.

Makes 12 servings.

RAINBOW POPS

½ cup orange juice
3 ozs. fresh raspberries or strawberries
1 teaspoon sugar
¼ cup grape juice

Into a plastic mold or individual molds, pour orange juice. Place in freezer and leave until frozen.

Put raspberries or strawberries, sugar and ¼ cup cold water into a food processor or blender and process until smooth. Pour through a strainer, then pour over frozen orange juice. Return to freezer about 1 hour, until almost frozen.

Mix grape juice with ¼ cup cold water, then pour over strawberry or raspberry layer. Insert the holders and put back into freezer until solid. To unmold, dip each mold in a bowl of hot water for a few seconds, then pull off. Serve at once.

Makes about 4, depending on size of molds.

TEDDY BEAR PUDDINGS

JELLY WOBBLES

½ lb. strawberries, rinsed and hulled
1¼ cups thick plain yogurt
1 tablespoon honey
8 thin oval cookies
8 seedless grapes
2 candied cherries, halved
2 slices kiwifruit, halved

In a bowl, mash the strawberries slightly (do not make them completely smooth).

In a small bowl, whisk yogurt with honey until smooth and creamy. Add to the mashed strawberries and mix well. Divide the mixture among 4 serving dishes. Decorate by placing the cookies in position for ears.

Use grapes for eyes and cherry halves for noses. Press kiwifruit halves into puddings for mouths.

Makes 4 servings.

Variations: Instead of using strawberries, cook 1 cup dried apricots until soft; purée and mix into yogurt. Or, mash 2 small, ripe bananas and add to yogurt.

4 oranges
¼ cup sugar
⅔ cup water
5 teaspoons unflavored gelatin powder
⅔ cup plain yogurt
1 (11-oz.) can mandarin oranges in natural juice, drained

Using a vegetable peeler, pare the peel from 2 oranges and put into a saucepan with sugar and water. Bring to a boil, then simmer until the sugar has dissolved. Let stand a few minutes. Squeeze juice from all oranges and reserve.

Into a medium-size bowl, strain sugar syrup, discarding orange peel. Into a small heat-proof bowl, measure 3 tablespoons cold water. Sprinkle with gelatin; let stand 5 minutes to soften. Stand bowl in a pan of simmering water until gelatin dissolves. Add to strained liquid. Cool, then add orange juice and refrigerate until beginning to set.

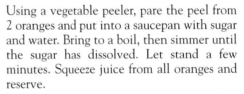

Beat in yogurt and pour into 4 or 5 small molds. Return to refrigerator 2 to 3 hours, until set. To release desserts from molds, dip each mold briefly in hot water and turn out into small dishes. Decorate with mandarin oranges.

Makes 4 to 5 servings.

OWL MADELEINES

½ cup margarine, softened
½ cup sugar
1 cup self-rising flour
2 eggs, beaten
½ teaspoon vanilla extract
⅔ cup shredded coconut
¼ cup strawberry or raspberry jam
2 tablespoons butter, softened
⅓ cup powdered sugar
16 chocolate buttons or drops
2 candied cherries

Grease 8 dariole molds, muffin cups or ramekins. Into a medium-size bowl, put margarine, sugar, flour, eggs and vanilla. Beat until smooth.

Preheat oven to 350F (175C). Spoon cake batter into molds or cups, filling each one half full. If using dariole molds or ramekins, place on a baking sheet after filling. Bake 15 to 18 minutes, until cakes feel firm when pressed. Remove from oven, run a round-bladed knife around inside of cups, then turn out cakes and transfer to a wire rack to cool. Trim so all cakes are the same height.

In a small plate, spread out coconut. In a small saucepan, melt jam with 1 tablespoon water. Push a skewer into each cake. Brush with melted jam, then roll in coconut until well coated. Put cakes, narrow ends up, on a plate. Beat butter and powdered sugar together. Use this mixture to attach 2 chocolate buttons to each cake for eyes. Pipe a spot of frosting in center of each eye. Complete owls with cherry pieces for beaks.

Makes 8.

MERRY MICE CAKES

1 cup self-rising flour
¼ cup unsweetened cocoa powder
½ cup margarine, softened
¾ cup packed light brown sugar
2 eggs, beaten
2 tablespoons milk
DECORATIONS:
1 cup powdered sugar, sifted
6 tablespoons butter, softened
Chocolate buttons
Gumdrops
Licorice strands and candies

Preheat oven to 350F (175C). Into a bowl put all cake ingredients. Beat until smooth.

Divide cake batter evenly among 20 paper cupcake cups placed in 2 (12-cup) muffin pans; place water in unused cups. Bake about 15 minutes, until firm to the touch. Cool on a wire rack. Trim tops to flatten if there are peaks.

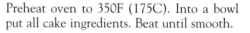

To decorate, in a small bowl, beat powdered sugar and butter together until light and fluffy. Spread over tops of cakes. Attach 2 chocolate buttons on each cake for ears, and place a gumdrop for a nose. Cut slices of licorice candies to make eyes. Cut pieces of licorice strands to make whiskers and insert 3 on each side of candy nose.

Makes 20.

PARTY PIECES

DEEP-FRIED FISH BALLS

1 lb. firm white fish fillet, skinned
4 ozs. potato flour
¼ cup coconut milk or water
Salt and freshly ground black pepper
1 tablespoon chopped cilantro leaves
½ teaspoon minced garlic
1 egg, beaten
Flour for dusting and oil for deep-frying
Lettuce leaves, to garnish
Spicy Fish Sauce (page 311)

Remove bones from fish, then cut into small pieces. Using a pestle and mortar, pound to a paste with potato flour and coconut milk, adding the coconut milk a little at a time.

In a medium bowl, mix the fish paste with the salt, pepper, chopped cilantro, garlic and egg. Blend well, then shape the mixture into about 20-24 small balls, dusting with flour.

Heat the oil in a wok, frying pan or deep-fat fryer to 350F (180C) and deep-fry the fish balls, in batches, 3-4 minutes or until golden brown. Remove and drain. Serve on a bed of lettuce leaves with the Spicy Fish Sauce as a dip.

Makes 8-10 servings.

Variation: Other types of seafood such as shrimp, squid and crabmeat can be cooked in the same way.

PEARL PATTIES & SHERRY DIP

¾ cup long-grain white rice
12 ozs. extra-lean ground beef
2 green onions, finely chopped
1 garlic clove, crushed
1 tablespoon dark soy sauce
1 tablespoon dry sherry
2 teaspoons cornstarch
DIP:
2 tablespoons dry sherry
2 tablespoons dark soy sauce
1 teaspoon sugar
1 garlic clove, crushed

Place rice in a bowl, add enough water to cover and soak 1 hour. Drain well and dry on a clean cloth. Mix together beef, green onions, garlic, soy sauce, sherry and cornstarch to form a firm mixture. Divide into 16 portions and shape into 1½-inch diameter patties.

Press each patty into the rice to coat on both sides. Bring a wok or large saucepan of water to a boil. Arrange patties on a layer of parchment paper in a steamer, making sure they don't overlap – you will probably need 2 steamers. Place over water, cover and steam 20 minutes. Mix together ingredients for dip and serve with the patties.

Makes 4 servings.

CHICKEN APRICOT BAGS

½ tablespoon vegetable oil, for frying, plus extra for brushing
½ onion, finely chopped
½ cup finely chopped dried apricots
1 cup finely diced cooked chicken
¼ cup plain yogurt
2 tablespoons chopped fresh cilantro
Salt and pepper
3 sheets filo pastry dough
Watercress to garnish

Preheat oven to 375F (190C). In a small pan, heat the ½ tablespoon oil. Add onion; cook 3 to 4 minutes or until softened. Add chopped apricots and cook 2 minutes.

Into a bowl, put onion mixture. Add chicken, yogurt, cilantro, salt and pepper; mix well. Cut each sheet of filo pastry dough in half, then cut each half into quarters to make 16 (4-inch) squares.

Brush each dough square with a little oil. Place a spoonful of chicken mixture in center. Gather up corners of the square and pinch together to form a loose bag. Place filo bags on 2 baking sheets. Bake 10 to 12 minutes or until the dough is crisp and golden. Serve warm. Garnish with watercress.

Makes 16 appetizers.

OLIVE PASTE TOASTS

4 large thick slices rustic bread
3 tablespoons extra-virgin olive oil
½ garlic clove, crushed
Red bell pepper strips and thyme sprigs to garnish
OLIVE PASTE:
1¼ cups pitted ripe olives (6 ozs.)
2 tablespoons extra-virgin olive oil
Few drops of balsamic vinegar
Freshly ground pepper

Preheat oven to 400F (205C). To make Olive Paste, put ingredients in a food processor or blender and process until fairly smooth. Transfer to a bowl and set aside.

Cut each slice of bread into 3 strips. Place on a baking sheet and bake in preheated oven 10 to 12 minutes until golden and crisp. Meanwhile, warm oil with garlic in a small saucepan.

Drizzle oil and garlic over toasted bread. Spread with Olive Paste and serve at once garnished with bell pepper strips and thyme sprigs.

Makes 4 to 6 servings.

Note: Olive Paste can be made in advance or in larger quantities. Put into jars, add olive oil to cover and seal. Cover jars and keep in refrigerator up to 1 month.

PARMESAN BEIGNETS

¼ cup butter
½ cup plus 2 tablespoons all-purpose flour, sifted
2 eggs, beaten
1 teaspoon chopped fresh parsley
½ cup grated Parmesan cheese (1½ ozs.)
¼ cup shredded Cheddar cheese (1 oz.)
Salt and pepper
Vegetable oil for deep-frying
Parsley sprigs to garnish

In a large pan, melt butter. Add ⅔ cup water and bring to a boil.

Add flour, all at once, and beat thoroughly until mixture leaves the side of the pan. Cool slightly, then vigorously beat in eggs, a little at a time. Stir in parsley, cheeses, salt and pepper. Continue beating until cheeses have melted.

One-third fill a deep-fat fryer with vegetable oil and heat to 360F (180C). Carefully drop 4 or 5 walnut-size spoonfuls of dough into hot oil. Deep-fry 2 to 3 minutes, until puffed and golden-brown. Drain well on paper towels and keep warm until all the beignets are fried. Serve garnished with parsley sprigs.

Makes about 16.

DEVILED HAM TOASTS

¼ lb. lean cooked ham
1 tablespoon Worcestershire sauce
Red (cayenne) pepper, to taste
2 teaspoons Dijon-style mustard
6 slices bread
¼ cup butter, softened
3 pimento-stuffed olives, sliced, and watercress sprigs to garnish

With a sharp knife, chop ham very finely, or mince. In a bowl, mix together ham, Worcestershire sauce, cayenne and mustard.

Toast bread. Using a 2-inch plain, round cookie cutter, cut out 2 circles from each slice of toast. Butter each circle of toast using 2 tablespoons of the butter and keep warm. In a saucepan, melt remaining butter. Add ham mixture. Cook, stirring, over low heat until mixture is hot.

Spread ham mixture over toast circles. Garnish with olives and arrange on a serving plate with watercress sprigs. Serve at once.

Makes 12.

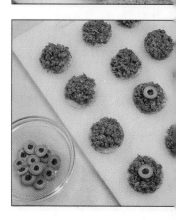

BACON AIGRETTES

4 slices bacon
1 tablespoon chopped fresh parsley
½ teaspoon ground black pepper
½ teaspoon Dijon-style mustard
Oil for frying
CHOUX PASTRY:
⅔ cup water
¼ cup butter
½ cup all-purpose flour
2 eggs
DIP:
⅔ cup plain yogurt
1 tablespoon chopped chives
1 tablespoon mango chutney

Cook bacon until crisp and chop finely. In a bowl, mix together bacon, parsley, pepper and mustard. To prepare pastry, in a saucepan, heat water and butter until melted. Bring to a boil, remove pan from heat and immediately add all flour, beating vigorously to form a paste. Return to heat for a few seconds, stirring until paste forms a ball. Add eggs 1 at a time, beating until paste is very smooth and glossy. Stir in bacon mixture until well blended.

Half-fill a deep saucepan with oil. Heat to 360F (180C), or test by dropping small pieces of paste into oil. If it sizzles on contact, oil is hot enough. Drop teaspoonfuls of mixture into hot oil. Fry 3 to 4 minutes, turning once, or until puffed and golden brown. Drain on paper towels. Arrange on a serving dish. To prepare dip, mix yogurt, chives and chutney in a bowl. Serve with Bacon Aigrettes.

Makes 35 to 40.

ASPARAGUS IN CHICORY LEAVES

8 ozs. asparagus spears, trimmed
3 heads chicory
1 (8-oz.) pkg. cream cheese
3 slices proscuitto or Parma ham
Tangerine wedges and dill sprigs to garnish
MARINADE:
1 tangerine
½ clove garlic, crushed
¼ teaspoon salt
¼ teaspoon ground black pepper
½ teaspoon Dijon-style mustard
2 teaspoons honey
1 tablespoon plus 1 teaspoon olive oil
2 teaspoons chopped fresh tarragon

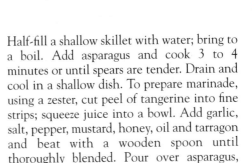

Half-fill a shallow skillet with water; bring to a boil. Add asparagus and cook 3 to 4 minutes or until spears are tender. Drain and cool in a shallow dish. To prepare marinade, using a zester, cut peel of tangerine into fine strips; squeeze juice into a bowl. Add garlic, salt, pepper, mustard, honey, oil and tarragon and beat with a wooden spoon until thoroughly blended. Pour over asparagus, cover and chill for at least 1 hour.

Separate chicory leaves and cut in 1-inch lengths. Spread a little cream cheese onto each leaf. Cut asparagus spears in 1-inch lengths; place a piece of asparagus onto each chicory leaf. Cut proscuitto or ham in thin strips and wrap a piece around each chicory leaf. Garnish with tangerine wedges and dill sprigs.

Makes 48.

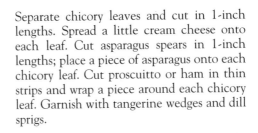

CURRIED VEGETABLE ENVELOPES

OYSTERS WITH EGGPLANT

2 ozs. puff pastry, thawed
1 egg, beaten
1 teaspoon cumin seeds
Lime twists and herb sprigs to garnish
FILLING:
1 tablespoon butter
1 leek, finely chopped
1 clove garlic, crushed
1 teaspoon ground cumin
1 teaspoon garam masala
2 teaspoons mango chutney
½ teaspoon finely grated lime peel
2 teaspoons lime juice
½ cup cooked diced potato

1 cup diced eggplant
Salt
6 large slices white bread
¼ cup butter
2 tablespoons snipped chives
2 teaspoons chopped fresh oregano
4 button mushrooms, finely chopped
½ teaspoon ground black pepper
2 teaspoons fromage frais
12 fresh oysters in shells
¾ cup soft bread crumbs

Place eggplant in a bowl. Sprinkle with salt. Cover and let stand 30 minutes.

Preheat oven to 425F (220C). To prepare filling, melt butter in small saucepan. Add leek and garlic. Cook quickly, stirring, 1 minute. Add cumin, garam masala, chutney and lime peel and juice. Stir well. Cook gently 1 to 2 minutes. Add potatoes, mix well and cool. Roll out puff pastry very thinly to a 12- x 8-inch rectangle. Cut in 2-inch squares. Brush edge with beaten egg and place a little filling in center of each square.

Preheat oven to 425F (220C). Cut crusts off bread. Roll slices flat with a rolling pin. Cut in 24 (2-inch) rounds using a daisy cutter. Spread both sides with some butter and press into muffin pans. Bake in oven 5 minutes or until lightly browned.

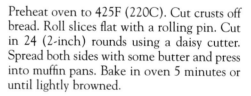

Draw all corners to center and seal joins like a tiny envelope. Arrange on a baking sheet. Brush envelopes with egg to glaze and sprinkle with cumin seeds. Bake in oven 5 to 8 minutes or until well risen and golden brown. Garnish with lime twists and herb sprigs.

Makes 24.

Drain and rinse eggplant. Dry on paper towels. Melt remaining butter in a saucepan. Add eggplant, chives, chopped oregano, mushrooms, pepper and some salt. Fry quickly, stirring occasionally, until eggplant is tender. Stir in fromage frais. Scrub oyster shells. Open and remove oysters. Cut each in half and place a half into each bread cup. Top with eggplant mixture and sprinkle with bread crumbs. Return to oven 10 minutes or until bread crumbs are lightly browned.

Makes 24.

440

OATIE BRIE CUBES

1½ cups soft bread crumbs
¼ cup regular oatmeal
½ teaspoon salt
½ teaspoon ground black pepper
½ teaspoon dry mustard
2 eggs
8 ozs. firm Brie or Camembert cheese
Oil for frying
Bay leaves, cranberries and lime wedges to garnish
DIP:
¾ cup cranberries
Grated peel and juice 1 lime
1 tablespoon superfine sugar

In a bowl, mix bread crumbs, oatmeal, salt, pepper and mustard.

Beat eggs in a small bowl. Cut cheese in bite-sized cubes. Place 1 cube at time into beaten eggs, then coat evenly in oatmeal mixture. Repeat to coat all cheese cubes. Repeat to coat cheese cubes a second time in eggs and oatmeal mixture. Chill until needed.

To prepare dip, place cranberries and lime peel and juice in a saucepan. Bring to a boil, cover and cook 1 to 2 minutes until cranberries are tender. In a food processor fitted with a metal blade, process cranberry mixture and sugar until smooth. Pour into a small serving dish. Half-fill a saucepan with oil. Heat to 350F (175C) or when a cheese cube sizzles immediately. Fry about 6 cheese cubes at a time until pale golden. Drain on paper towels. Serve with dip.

Makes 20.

CRAB & FENNEL PUFFS

1 recipe Choux Pastry (page 390)
1 egg yolk, beaten
2 teaspoons sesame seeds
Fennel sprigs and radish slices to garnish
Cayenne pepper
FILLING:
1 tablespoon butter
3 tablespoons finely chopped green onions
3 tablespoons finely chopped fennel
⅓ cup white crab meat
¼ cup dark crab meat
½ teaspoon finely grated lemon peel
¼ teaspoon ground black pepper
1 tablespoon sour cream
Cayenne pepper

Preheat oven to 425F (220C). Grease 2 baking sheets. Place pastry in a piping bag fitted with a ½-inch plain nozzle. Pipe about 40 small rounds of pastry, spacing apart, onto greased baking sheets. Brush with egg yolk and sprinkle with sesame seeds. Bake in oven 15 to 20 minutes or until crisp and golden brown. Cool on a wire rack.

To prepare filling, melt butter in a small saucepan. Add green onion and fennel. Cook 1 to 2 minutes or until tender. Remove pan from heat. Stir in light and dark crab meat, lemon peel, pepper and sour cream until well blended. Cut each pastry ball across top. Fill each with crab filling and dust with cayenne pepper. Arrange on a serving plate. Garnish with fennel sprigs and radish slices.

Makes 40.

SESAME SHRIMP TOASTS

8-10 ozs. raw peeled shrimp, chopped
½ teaspoon minced garlic
½ teaspoon finely chopped ginger root
2 shallots or 1 small onion, finely chopped
1 egg, beaten
Salt and freshly ground black pepper
1 tablespoon cornstarch
1 French baguette
3-4 tablespoons white sesame seeds
Oil for deep-frying
Chopped fresh cilantro leaves, to garnish

In a bowl, mix the shrimp, garlic, ginger, shallots, egg, salt, pepper and cornstarch and chill in the refrigerator for at least 2 hours.

Cut the bread into ½-inch slices and spread thickly with shrimp mixture on one side, then press that side down onto the sesame seeds so that the entire surface is covered by the seeds, making sure the seeds are firmly pressed into the shrimp mixture.

Heat the oil in a wok or deep-fat fryer to 350F (180C) and deep-fry the toasts, in batches, spread-side down, 2-3 minutes until they start to turn golden brown around the edges. Remove and drain on paper towels. Serve hot, garnished with chopped cilantro leaves.

Makes 6-8 servings.

CRISPY PESTO SHRIMP

12 cooked peeled jumbo shrimp
6 large slices white bread
¼ cup butter
1 clove garlic
1 tablespoon plus 1 teaspoon pesto sauce
1 teaspoon finely grated lemon peel
¼ teaspoon salt
¼ teaspoon ground black pepper
Lemon triangles and lemon balm leaves to garnish

Cut each shrimp in half across width. Cut crusts off bread. Using a rolling pin, roll each slice flat.

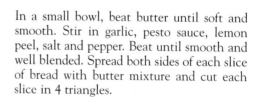

In a small bowl, beat butter until soft and smooth. Stir in garlic, pesto sauce, lemon peel, salt and pepper. Beat until smooth and well blended. Spread both sides of each slice of bread with butter mixture and cut each slice in 4 triangles.

Place a shrimp in center of each bread triangle. Fold 2 points to center and secure with a wooden pick. Arrange on a grid in a grill pan and broil under a moderately hot grill until bread is lightly browned. Garnish with lemon triangles and lemon balm leaves and serve hot.

Makes 24.

FESTIVE DIP SELECTION

1 small eggplant
2 cloves garlic
½ cup sour cream
Salt
Ground black pepper
1 tablespoon chopped fresh rosemary
1 (8-oz.) package cream cheese
2 tablespoons fromage frais
¼ cup chopped fresh mixed herbs such as parsley,
    basil, thyme, oregano and chervil
⅔ cup red lentils
1¾ cups water
⅔ cup plain yogurt
Mixed vegetable sticks (zucchini, bell peppers, celery,
    cucumbers, carrots) baby sweet corn, cherry
    tomatoes and radishes

Preheat oven to 425F (220C) or use a hot grill. Bake or grill eggplant until skin has charred and flesh is tender, turning once. Cut eggplant in half, scoop out flesh, cool. Using a food processor fitted with a metal blade, process eggplant, 1 clove of garlic, sour cream, salt and pepper to taste and rosemary until mixture is smooth and creamy. Spoon into a serving bowl. Place cream cheese, fromage frais, herbs and salt and pepper to taste in a bowl. Beat until soft and well blended. Spoon into a serving dish.

In a saucepan, bring lentils and water to a boil, then simmer gently until all water has been absorbed. Cool. In food processor, process lentils, remaining garlic, salt, pepper and yogurt until creamy and smooth. Spoon into a serving dish. Serve dips with mixed vegetables.

Each dip makes 6 to 8 servings.

CURRY WHIRLS

1¼ cups all-purpose flour
1 teaspoon curry powder
½ teaspoon salt
½ teaspoon pepper
½ teaspoon dry mustard
½ cup butter
2 tablespoons Parmesan cheese
1 egg, beaten
1 teaspoon coriander seeds

Preheat oven to 425F (220C). Lightly grease several baking sheets. In a bowl, sift flour, curry powder, salt, pepper and mustard. Cut butter in pieces. Cut butter into flour mixture finely to resemble bread crumbs.

Using a fork, stir in Parmesan cheese and egg until mixture clings together. Mix to a soft dough. Place mixture in a pastry bag fitted with a star nozzle. Pipe about 40 swirls of mixture onto lightly greased baking sheets, spacing apart.

Sprinkle each swirl with coriander seeds and bake in oven 10 to 15 minutes or until lightly browned at edges. Cool on a wire rack. Arrange on a plate to serve.

Makes 40.

STUFFED LEAVES

10 small spinach leaves
10 small lettuce leaves
10 small radicchio leaves
FILLING:
5 slices bacon
1 tablespoon plus 1 teaspoon chopped pickled
 vegetables
2 ozs. Neufchâtel cheese
¼ cup cooked white long-grain rice
1 teaspoon Dijon-style mustard
½ teaspoon salt
½ teaspoon ground black pepper
1 small red bell pepper, seeded
1 small yellow bell pepper, seeded

Bring a saucepan of water to a boil. Add spinach leaves. Bring back to boil, remove quickly and refresh leaves in cold water. Drain thoroughly and dry on paper towels. Repeat with remaining leaves. In a skillet, cook bacon until crisp. Chop bacon and pickled vegetables finely. Place Neufchâtel cheese in a bowl; beat until smooth. Add bacon, pickled vegetables, rice, mustard, salt and pepper. Stir until well blended.

Spread leaves out flat on a board. Place 1 teaspoonful of mixture on each leaf. Roll up and secure each with a wooden pick. Cut bell peppers in thin rings; cut rings in 4 pieces. Arrange stuffed leaves on a serving plate. Garnish with bell peppers.

Makes 30.

FETA CHEESE KEBABS

7 ozs. feta cheese
¼ red bell pepper
¼ yellow bell pepper
1 zucchini
¼ eggplant
Thyme sprigs and pink peppercorns
MARINADE:
2 tablespoons olive oil
1 tablespoon raspberry vinegar
1 teaspoon honey
½ teaspoon Dijon-style mustard
2 teaspoons chopped fresh thyme
¼ teaspoon salt
½ teaspoon ground black pepper

To prepare marinade, combine olive oil, vinegar, peppercorns, honey, mustard, thyme, salt and pepper in a large bowl with a wooden spoon until thoroughly blended. Cut feta cheese, bell peppers, zucchini and eggplant in bite-sized pieces. Add to marinade; stir well to coat evenly. Cover with plastic wrap and refrigerate at least 1 hour.

Thread 1 piece of each ingredient onto wooden picks. Just before serving, broil under a hot grill 2 to 3 minutes or until vegetables are just tender. Garnish with thyme sprigs and peppercorns.

Makes 24.

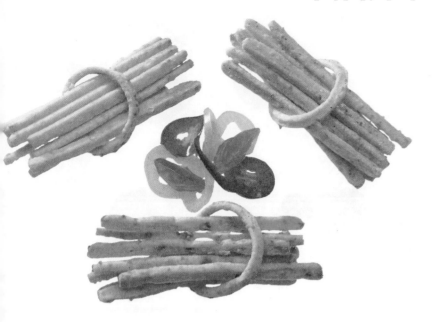

CHEESE STRAWS

COCKTAIL PINWHEELS

CHEESE PASTRY:
2 cups all-purpose flour
½ teaspoon salt
½ teaspoon cayenne pepper
½ teaspoon dry mustard
½ cup butter
1 cup shredded Cheddar cheese (4 ozs.)
1 egg, beaten
FLAVORINGS:
1 tablespoon plus 1 teaspoon finely chopped red and
  yellow bell peppers
1 clove garlic, crushed
1 tablespoon plus 1 teaspoon chopped fresh basil
1 tablespoon plus 1 teaspoon chopped fresh parsley
Red and yellow bell pepper twists and bay leaves to
  garnish

2¼ cups all-purpose flour
½ teaspoon salt
½ teaspoon cayenne pepper
1 teaspoon dry mustard
¾ cup butter
1 cup shredded Cheddar cheese (4 ozs.)
1 egg, beaten
Parsley sprigs to garnish
1 teaspoon sesame seeds
1 teaspoon poppy seeds
1 teaspoon curry paste
2 teaspoons tomato paste

In a bowl, sift flour, salt, cayenne and mustard. Cut butter in pieces. Cut butter into flour mixture to resemble bread crumbs.

Preheat oven to 400F (205C). Grease several baking sheets. In a bowl, sift flour, salt, cayenne and mustard. Cut butter into pieces. Cut butter into flour mixture finely to resemble bread crumbs. Using a fork, stir in cheese and egg until mixture clings together. Knead to a smooth dough. Cut pastry in 4 pieces. Flavor 1 piece with peppers, 1 with garlic, 1 with basil and remaining piece with parsley, kneading each piece lightly. Roll out 1 piece at a time to a 4-inch-wide strip that is ¼-inch thick.

Using a fork, stir in cheese and egg until mixture clings together. Knead in a smooth dough. Cut pastry in 4 pieces. Knead sesame seeds into 1 piece and poppy seeds into another. Form both in 6-inch rolls. Wrap separately in plastic wrap. Roll remaining 2 pieces of pastry in 8- x 6-inch rectangles. Spread 1 piece with curry paste and other with tomato paste. Roll up each from long edge in 2 firm rolls. Wrap in plastic wrap. Chill until firm or freeze until needed.

Using a knife, cut in ¼-inch strips. Arrange in a straight line on greased baking sheets. Knead each of flavored trimmings together, re-roll and cut out rings using a 2-inch and 1½-inch plain cutter. Place on baking sheets. Bake in oven 5 to 8 minutes or until golden. Cool on wire racks. Serve straws in bundles threaded through pastry rings. Garnish with bell pepper twists and bay leaves.

Makes 100.

Preheat oven to 400F (205C). Line several baking sheets with parchment paper. Cut each roll in thin slices and arrange a little apart on prepared baking sheets. Bake for 6 to 8 minutes or until golden. Cool, then transfer to wire racks. Garnish with parsley sprigs.

Makes 96.

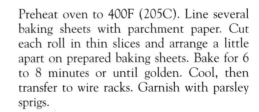

HERBED CRÊPE PINWHEELS

½ cup all-purpose flour
Salt and freshly ground black pepper
1 egg
¼ cup milk
1 tablespoon fresh chopped basil
Oil
8 large spinach leaves
½ (8-oz.) package cream cheese with herbs and
  garlic, softened
8 thin slices proscuitto

Sift flour, salt and pepper into a bowl. Mix in egg and ½ of milk with a wooden spoon; beat until smooth. Stir in remaining milk and basil. Beat until well blended.

Heat a little oil in a small skillet. Add 1 spoonful of batter; swirl pan to coat thinly. Cook until crêpe is pale golden on both sides, turning only once. Place on paper towels. Repeat to make 8 crêpes. In a saucepan, cook spinach leaves 1 minute in boiling salted water. Drain and cool.

Cover 1 crêpe with a spinach leaf, spread with some cream cheese and cover with a slice of proscuitto or Parma ham. Roll up firmly and wrap in plastic wrap. Repeat to make 8 crêpe rolls. Just before serving, cut each roll in ½-inch slices. Arrange on a serving plate. Garnish with cherry tomato wedges and herb sprigs.

Makes 48.

PARTY QUICHES

½ cup all-purpose flour
¼ teaspoon salt
2 teaspoons butter
2-3 teaspoons cold water
Red bell pepper rings and fennel sprigs to garnish
FILLING:
1 egg
2 tablespoons half and half
¼ teaspoon salt
¼ teaspoon pepper
¼ teaspoon dry mustard
2 teaspoons finely chopped bell peppers
2 teaspoons chopped button mushrooms
2 teaspoons chopped crispy bacon
2 teaspoons chopped fresh herbs

Sift flour and salt into a bowl. Cut butter in pieces. Cut butter into flour mixture finely until mixture resembles bread crumbs. Using a fork, stir in water until mixture begins to bind together. Knead to a firm dough. Roll out pastry thinly on a lightly floured surface. Line 24 tiny pastry boat molds or tiny round tart pans with pastry. Prick pastry and chill 1 hour. Preheat oven to 425F (220C). Bake pastry molds in oven 5 minutes, then remove from oven.

To prepare filling, place egg, half and half, salt, pepper and mustard into a bowl. Whisk until well blended. Half-fill each pastry with egg mixture, then fill with chopped bell peppers, mushrooms, bacon and herbs. Return to oven 5 to 6 minutes or until filling has set. Cool slightly, then slip pastry out of molds. Serve warm or cold. Garnish with bell pepper rings and fennel sprigs.

Makes 24.

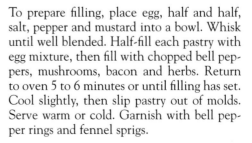

CRISPY BACON PINWHEELS

¾ cup shredded Cheddar cheese (3 ozs.)
¼ teaspoon salt
¼ teaspoon pepper
½ teaspoon Dijon-style mustard
2 tablespoons plain yogurt
6 large slices white bread
3 tablespoons butter
6 slices bacon
Celery leaves and radish slices to garnish

In a bowl, mix cheese, salt, pepper, mustard and yogurt. Cut crusts off bread; roll slices flat with a rolling pin.

Spread each slice with butter and invert. Spread unbuttered sides evenly with cheese mixture and roll each up in a firm roll. Stretch each bacon slice with a knife and cut in 3 pieces. Cut each bread roll in 3 rolls and wrap a piece of bacon around each roll. Secure with a wooden pick. Cover with plastic wrap and chill until needed.

Just before serving, broil bacon rolls under a hot grill until bacon is crisp and golden brown. Cool slightly, remove wooden picks and cut each roll in 3 slices. Garnish with celery and radish slices.

Makes 54.

MARINATED MUSHROOMS

1 large pink grapefruit
⅓ cup ginger wine
2 teaspoons mint jelly
½ teaspoon salt
½ teaspoon ground black pepper
1 teaspoon Dijon-style mustard
48 button mushrooms
Mint leaves to garnish

Using a sharp knife, cut away grapefruit peel including white pith from flesh, allowing juice to fall into a small saucepan. Cut out segments in between membranes and place on a plate. Squeeze remaining juice from membranes into saucepan.

Stir in ginger wine, mint jelly, salt, pepper and mustard. Bring to a boil. Stir in mushrooms. Pour into a bowl and refrigerate until cold.

Cut grapefruit segments in bite-sized pieces. Reserve several grapefruit pieces for garnish. Thread mushrooms and grapefruit onto 24 wooden picks. Garnish with mint leaves and reserved grapefruit pieces.

Makes 24.

AVOCADO SALMON ROLLS

3 ozs. smoked salmon slices
3 slices rye bread
1 tablespoon butter
Lemon twists and dill sprigs to garnish
FILLING:
2 ozs. cream cheese
½ avocado, mashed
2 teaspoons chopped fresh dill
1 small tomato, peeled, seeded, chopped
¼ teaspoon ground black pepper

To prepare filling, beat cream cheese in a bowl until soft. Stir avocado into cream cheese until evenly blended. Add dill, chopped tomato and pepper and stir gently.

Place filling in a pastry bag fitted with a ½-inch plain nozzle. Cut smoked salmon in 20 (1½- x 1-inch) rectangles. Pipe a length of cheese mixture across top of short edge of each salmon rectangle and roll up.

Spread rye bread with butter. Cut in 20 rectangles to fit salmon rolls. Place salmon rolls on each piece of bread. Garnish with lemon twists and dill sprigs.

Makes 20.

FILLED BUTTON RAREBIT

1 cup soft white bread crumbs
¼ cup chopped ham
1 tablespoon chopped fresh parsley
1 tablespoon fromage frais
24 button mushrooms
4 large slices white bread
2 tablespoons margarine
Celery leaves and parsley to garnish
TOPPING:
1 tablespoon cider
¾ cup shredded Cheddar cheese (3 ozs.)
1 teaspoon Worcestershire sauce
¼ teaspoon salt
¼ teaspoon ground black pepper
¼ teaspoon dry mustard

Preheat oven to 425F (220C). To prepare filling, mix bread crumbs, ham, parsley and fromage frais in a bowl. Remove stalks from mushrooms, chop finely and stir into filling. Press filling into center of each mushroom. Cut out 24 rounds of bread to match size of mushrooms using a plain cutter. Spread both sides with margarine and place a mushroom on top of each bread round. Arrange on a baking sheet. Bake in oven 5 minutes, then remove.

To prepare topping, place cider in a saucepan. Bring to a boil. Remove saucepan from heat and stir in cheese, Worcestershire sauce, salt, pepper and mustard. Beat well. Spoon a little cheese mixture over top of each filled mushroom. Return to oven and bake 3 to 4 minutes or until cheese has melted and browned slightly. Arrange on a serving dish. Garnish with celery leaves and parsley.

Makes 24.

DRINKS

STRAWBERRY-YOGURT WHIZZ

½ lb. strawberries
1¼ cups milk
1¼ cups natural or strawberry-flavored yogurt
2 scoops vanilla ice cream or frozen yogurt
1 kiwi fruit (optional), sliced

Reserve 4 strawberries for decoration; cap remaining strawberries.

Use a hand blender or food processor to blend milk, yogurt, strawberries and ice cream until smooth.

Into 3 or 4 glasses, pour strawberry drink. Decorate with reserved strawberries and slices of kiwi fruit, if using.

Makes 3 or 4 servings.

MALTED MILKSHAKES

1 (12-oz.) can evaporated milk
2 cups milk
3 tablespoons unsweetened cocoa powder
2 teaspoons light brown sugar
¼ cup malt-flavored drink powder
8 scoops vanilla ice cream
4 chocolate candy sticks

Put 4 glass tumblers into refrigerator to chill 30 minutes.

Use a hand blender or food processor to blend both milks, cocoa powder, sugar, malt-flavored drink powder and half the ice cream 2 minutes, until frothy; if necessary, do in 2 batches.

Pour malted mixture into chilled glasses. Top each drink with a scoop of ice cream and a chocolate candy stick. Serve with straws.

Makes 4 servings.

APPLE ZING

2 ripe pears, peeled and cored
2 cups apple juice
Crushed ice
2½ cups chilled ginger ale
Apple slices or mint sprigs to decorate

Use a hand blender or food processor to blend the pears and apple juice until smooth.

Into 4 tall glasses, spoon crushed ice. Pour apple juice mixture over ice.

Fill glasses with ginger ale, then decorate with apple slices or mint sprigs. Serve immediately.

Makes 4 servings.

SPANISH HOT CHOCOLATE

3 ozs. semisweet chocolate, broken into pieces
2 cups milk
Cinnamon sticks and orange zest to decorate

Into the top of a double boiler or a bowl placed over a saucepan of hot water, place chocolate and heat until melted.

In a saucepan, heat milk to a boil. Using a wooden spoon, slowly stir a little boiling milk into chocolate.

Using a wire whisk, whisk in remaining milk and continue to whisk until mixture is frothy. Pour into heatproof glasses or cups and decorate with cinnamon sticks and orange zest.

Makes 2 servings.

Variation: Rub cubed sugar over a whole orange to remove the zest, then add the sugar to the hot chocolate.

OLD-FASHIONED LEMONADE

GRAPEFRUIT BARLEY WATER

3 lemons
½ cup sugar
Ice
Mint sprigs
Lemon slices

⅓ cup pearl barley
¼ cup sugar
2 pink grapefruit
Mint leaves

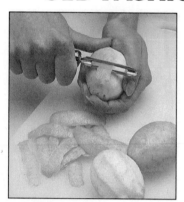

Using a vegetable peeler, thinly pare peel from lemons and put in a heatproof bowl or large pitcher with sugar. Squeeze juice from lemons into a bowl and set aside.

Into a saucepan, put barley. Just cover with cold water and bring to a boil. Pour barley into a strainer and rinse under cold water.

Bring 3¼ cups water to a boil and pour over lemon peel and sugar. Stir to dissolve sugar, then let cool completely. Add lemon juice and strain into a pitcher. Refrigerate until chilled. Serve in ice-filled tumblers, decorated with mint and lemon slices.

Makes 6 servings.

Return barley to saucepan. Add 2½ cups cold water and bring to a boil again. Cover and simmer 1 hour. Strain liquid into a pitcher, stir in the sugar and leave until completely cold.

Variations: To make Pink Lemonade, add just enough pink grenadine syrup to each glass to give lemonade a pale pink color. Omit mint and lemon slices and decorate each glass with a cherry.

To make Orangeade, use 3 oranges and 1 lemon instead of 3 lemons. Omit mint and lemon slices and decorate with orange slices.

Squeeze juice from grapefruit and add to cooled barley water. Refrigerate until chilled. Serve decorated with mint leaves.

Makes about 2½ cups.

Variation: To make Lemon Barley Water, use 2 lemons instead of grapefruit.

FRAGRANT LEMON DRINK

Grated peel and juice of 2 lemons
¼ cup superfine sugar
1 cup packed lemon balm leaves
Crushed ice
About 4 cups iced water
Lemon peel and lemon balm leaves to decorate

Put lemon peel and juice, sugar and lemon balm leaves in a blender or food processor fitted with the metal blade; process until smooth. Strain into a pitcher and chill.

Fill glasses with crushed ice, add a little lemon concentrate and top with iced water, to taste. Serve at once, decorated with lemon peel and lemon balm leaves.

Makes about 5 cups.

Note: Lemon peel spirals: cut a long strip of peel from a lemon using a zester. Wind strip of peel around a skewer or chopstick, fasten securely to prevent it from unwinding and blanch in boiling water a few seconds. Rinse in cold water and remove skewer.

SPICED TEA

1 tablespoon plus 2 teaspoons black peppercorns
1 tablespoon cardamom seeds
1 tablespoon whole cloves
1 (1½-inch) cinnamon stick
⅓ cup ground ginger
Hot tea
Boiling water
Milk and sugar to taste

Put peppercorns, cardamom seeds, cloves and cinnamon in a mortar and grind to a fine powder with a pestle. Add ginger and grind again a few seconds to mix. Add about ½ teaspoon of spice mixture to a pot of tea; leave in a warm place 1 to 2 minutes to brew. Serve hot, with milk and sugar.

Makes about 8 tablespoons spice mix, enough for 16 pots of tea.

Note: Store remaining spice mixture in an airtight container, in a dark cupboard to preserve its flavor. It will keep 2 to 3 months.

CAFE DE OLLA

5 cups water
1 (1-inch) piece cinnamon stick
2 whole cloves
¼ cup packed brown sugar
¼ cup freshly ground coffee

Put water, cinnamon and cloves into a saucepan, and bring to a boil. Reduce heat, add sugar and stir until dissolved. Stir in coffee and simmer 2 minutes.

Turn off heat and let stand, covered, about 5 minutes or until all coffee has settled. Strain into individual mugs.

Makes 4 servings.

INDIAN SUMMER PUNCH

1 tablespoon fennel seeds
Seeds from 6 green cardamom pods
3 whole cloves
4 black peppercorns
½ cup ground almonds
¼ cup shelled pistachio nuts
½ cup shelled sunflower seeds
1¼ cups boiling water
½ cup superfine sugar
3 cups cold milk
Apple slices and fennel sprigs to decorate

Put fennel seeds, cardamom seeds, cloves and peppercorns in a mortar and grind to a fine powder with a pestle, or use a coffee grinder.

Put almonds, pistachios and sunflower seeds in a small bowl; add 6 tablespoons of the boiling water. Soak 20 minutes, then drain. Put in a blender or food processor fitted with the metal blade; add remaining boiling water and process until smooth.

Add spices and sugar; process again. Strain through a cheesecloth, squeezing paste to extract as much liquid as possible. Discard paste, cover and refrigerate liquid at least 1 hour, then mix with milk and serve in tall glasses over ice, decorated with apple slices and fennel sprigs.

Makes about 6 cups.

ICED ROSE TEA

3 tablespoons Ceylon breakfast tea or to taste
4¼ cups lukewarm water
Sugar to taste
Few drops rosewater to taste
12 ice cubes
6 mint sprigs
Fresh rose petals

Into a bowl, put tea. Pour warm water over tea and let stand overnight.

Strain tea into a large pitcher. Stir in sugar and rosewater, then add ice cubes. Place a mint sprig and a few rose petals in each of 6 glasses. Pour tea on top.

Makes 6 servings.

Variations: For Vanilla Iced Tea, omit rosewater. Instead, put a vanilla bean in the bowl with tea to soak overnight. Remove it before serving.

For Mint Tea, omit the rosewater and rose petals. Put a mint sprig in bowl with tea to soak overnight. Remove it before serving. Place a fresh mint sprig in each glass.

SUMMER TEA CUP

1 Lapsang Souchong tea bag
2½ cups boiling water
4 teaspoons brown sugar
1¼ cups pineapple juice
⅓ cup white rum
2½ cups ginger ale
Ice cubes
Pieces fresh pineapple

In a heatproof bowl, place tea bag and boiling water.

Leave tea to steep 5 minutes, then remove tea bag. Stir in brown sugar and leave until cold. Stir pineapple juice and rum into tea.

Just before serving, pour ginger ale into tea. Add ice cubes. Place a few pieces of pineapple in each glass and pour in the chilled tea.

Makes about 6¾ cups.

TEQUILA SUNRISE

¼ cup tequila
⅔ cup orange juice
1 tablespoon grenadine
1 teaspoon fresh lime juice
Crushed ice
Maraschino cherry to decorate

MARGARITA

1 lime, halved
Salt
Crushed ice
¼ cup tequila
1 tablespoon orange-flavored liqueur
Wedge of lime to serve

Pour tequila, orange juice, grenadine and lime juice into a blender; mix well. Spoon crushed ice into a chilled tall glass.

Rub rim of a chilled cocktail glass with one of lime halves, then dip rim into salt. Add crushed ice to a cocktail shaker. Squeeze juice from remaining lime half.

Strain tequila mixture over ice. Decorate with a maraschino cherry on a wooden pick.

Makes 1 serving.

Add lime juice, tequila and liqueur to shaker. Shake or stir well. Strain into glass. Serve with a wedge of lime to squeeze into drink.

Makes 1 serving.

TENNIS CUP

CHRISTMAS EVE MULL

1 cup sugar
⅔ cup water
1 lemon
2 oranges
2 (750-ml.) bottles red or white wine
2½ cups soda water
TO DECORATE:
Thin cucumber and orange slices
Borage flowers or violets, if available

Into a saucepan, put sugar and water. Cook over low heat, stirring, until sugar has dissolved. Bring to a boil, then boil until syrup reaches 220F (105C) on a candy thermometer.

With a vegetable peeler, thinly pare peel from lemon and oranges. Add to syrup and simmer gently 10 minutes. Set aside until completely cold.

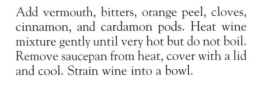

Squeeze juice from lemon and oranges and strain into syrup, then pour in the wine and refrigerate until chilled. Just before serving, add soda water. Pour into glasses. Decorate with cucumber and orange slices and borage sprigs or violets.

Makes about 9 cups.

3¼ cups white wine
3¼ cups red wine
1¼ cups sweet red vermouth
1 tablespoon Angostura bitters
6 strips orange peel
8 whole cloves
1 cinnamon stick
8 cardamon pods, crushed
1 tablespoon dark raisins
½ cup superfine sugar
Lemon, orange and apple slices

Pour white and red wines into a large stainless steel or enamel saucepan.

Add vermouth, bitters, orange peel, cloves, cinnamon, and cardamon pods. Heat wine mixture gently until very hot but do not boil. Remove saucepan from heat, cover with a lid and cool. Strain wine into a bowl.

Just before serving, return wine to a clean saucepan. Add raisins and sugar. Heat gently until sugar has dissolved and wine is hot enough to drink. Add fruit slices and serve in heatproof mugs.

Makes 16 servings.

HOT BUTTERED RUM

4 sticks cinnamon
1 tablespoon+1 teaspoon light-brown sugar
½ cup dark rum
2⅔ cups apple cider
2 tablespoons butter
1 teaspoon ground mace
4 lemon slices

Evenly divide cinnamon sticks, brown sugar and rum among 4 warm heatproof glasses or mugs.

In a saucepan, heat apple cider until very hot but not boiling. Fill each glass or mug to top with apple cider.

Add a dot of butter to each. Sprinkle with mace and add a lemon slice. Stir well and serve.

Makes 4 servings.

ROSÉ GLOW

¼ cup sweet red vermouth
¼ cup cherry brandy liqueur
¼ cup brandy
1 kiwifruit, peeled, sliced
8 maraschino cherries, halved
Orange, lemon and lime slices
1 bottle rosé wine
Ice cubes
Mint and borage sprigs
Rose petals, if desired
1 bottle sparkling white wine

In a large punch bowl, pour vermouth, cherry brandy and brandy. Add kiwifruit, cherries and citrus fruit slices. Stir to mix well.

Just before serving, pour in rosé wine. Add ice cubes, mint and borage sprigs and rose petals, if desired.

At the last minute, add sparkling wine and serve in punch glasses or cups, including some fruit and ice.

Makes 10 servings.

CHOCOLATES & CANDIES

CHOCOLATE TRUFFLE CUPS

16 (1-oz.) squares white chocolate
¼ cup unsalted butter, melted
2 tablespoons whipping cream
1 tablespoon +1 teaspoon cherry brandy
1 tablespoon +1 teaspoon Chartreuse liqueur
1 tablespoon +1 teaspoon apricot brandy
Pink, green and yellow food colorings
6 pistachio nuts, chopped

Break up chocolate and place in a bowl set over a saucepan of hand-hot water. Stir occasionally until melted. Remove bowl from saucepan and cool. Place 36 foil cups on a tray. Spoon a little chocolate into each.

Using a fine brush, coat inside of each cup and refrigerate to set. Add melted butter and cream to remaining chocolate and stir until smooth. Divide mixture evenly among 3 bowls. Flavor 1 with cherry brandy and tint pink with food coloring; stir until well blended. Repeat to flavor and color 1 chocolate with Chartreuse and green food coloring and remaining chocolate with apricot brandy and yellow and pink food coloring.

When chocolate mixtures are set enough to peak softly, place each into a pastry bag fitted with a small star nozzle. Pipe swirls of each flavored chocolate into 12 chocolate cups. Sprinkle with pistachio nuts and let set. Pack into pretty boxes, baskets or dishes and cover with pretty paper and ribbon.

Makes 36.

CHOCOLATE DECORATIONS

4 (1-oz.) squares semisweet chocolate
8 (1-oz.) squares white chocolate
Pink, green and yellow oil-based or powdered food colorings
Pink, green and yellow fine ribbon

Break up each chocolate and place in separate bowls set over saucepans of hand-hot water. Stir occasionally until melted. Divide ½ of white chocolate into 3 bowls. Color each pink, green and yellow with food colorings.

Draw around novelty cookie cutters on parchment paper. Half-fill 2 small pastry bags with dark chocolate. Snip a small point off 1 bag and pipe a fine outline of chocolate following shapes. Fill center of each shape with remaining dark chocolate, snipping a larger point off end so that shapes look over-filled and rounded.

Repeat to make different shaped chocolate decorations, using white and some colored chocolate as above. Let stand until hard. Carefully peel off paper, taking care not to mark surface. Sandwich matching shapes together with melted chocolate, placing ribbon loops in between. Decorate shapes with piped colored chocolate using a small pastry bag with end snipped off. Pipe lines, dots, zig-zags, lattice or write Christmas messages. Allow all decorations to dry before hanging.

Makes about 20 decorations.

FONDANT SWEETS

8 ozs. ready-to-roll fondant icing (sugar paste)
Pink, green, yellow, violet and orange food colorings
FLAVORINGS:
3 pieces marrons glacés
3 pieces crystallized ginger
½ teaspoon peppermint oil
1 teaspoon finely grated orange peel
1 teaspoon finely grated lemon peel
1 teaspoon finely grated lime peel

Cut fondant in 6 pieces. Tint 5 pieces very pale pink, green, yellow, violet and orange.

Cut 2 marrons glacés and pink fondant in 8 pieces. Wrap each piece of marron glacé in pink fondant and shape in a smooth ball. Repeat with violet fondant and crystallized ginger to make oval shaped sweets. Decorate tops with remaining marron glacé and crystallized ginger.

Flavor white fondant with a few drops of peppermint oil. Roll out to ¼-inch thickness. Using a small round or crescent cutter, cut out about 8 to 10 shapes. Knead orange peel into orange fondant, lemon peel into yellow fondant and lime peel into green fondant. Shape each piece in tiny pinwheels, squares or diamond shapes. Place all fondants on a parchment paper-lined baking sheet to dry out completely.

Makes 40 pieces.

HAND-DIPPED CHOCOLATES

3 ozs. ready-to-roll fondant icing (sugar paste)
Rose and violet flavorings
Pink and violet food colorings
2 ozs. white marzipan
6 Brazil nuts
6 whole almonds
6 (1-oz.) squares semisweet chocolate
6 (1-oz.) squares white chocolate
6 (1-oz.) squares milk chocolate
6 maraschino cherries and 6 crème de menthe cherries
Crystallized rose and violet petals

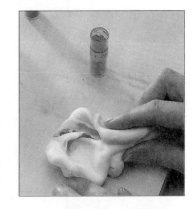

Cut fondant in 2 pieces. Flavor 1 piece rose and color pale pink. Flavor remaining piece violet and color pale mauve.

Roll out fondant to ½-inch thickness. Cut in shapes using cocktail cutters. Place on a waxed paper-lined baking sheet. Shape marzipan in various shapes by rolling bite-sized pieces between hands in balls, logs or ovals. Arrange on a baking sheet. Let dry several hours or overnight. Toast nuts until golden brown.

Melt each chocolate in different bowls over hand-hot water, stirring until melted. Using a fork, dip 1 center at a time into chocolate. Tap to remove excess and place chocolate on parchment paper-lined baking sheets. Leave plain, mark top with a fork or decorate rose and violet centers with crystallized petals. Continue to dip all centers, using white, dark or milk chocolate. Using a pastry bag, pipe some chocolates with threads of chocolate.

Makes 30.

THAI SWEETMEATS

2 ozs. split mung beans, rinsed
½ cup shredded coconut
1 egg, separated
½ cup palm sugar, crushed
¾ cup water
Few drops of jasmine extract

PISTACHIO HALVA

1¼ cups shelled pistachios
1 cup boiling water
2 tablespoons milk
½ cup sugar
1½ tablespoons butter or ghee
1 teaspoon vanilla extract

Put mung beans into a medium-size saucepan, and add enough water to cover by 1½ inches. Bring to a boil, reduce heat and simmer 30 to 45 minutes until tender. Drain through a strainer, then mash thoroughly.

Put pistachios in a bowl, top with boiling water and soak 30 minutes. Grease and line an 8-inch square pan with waxed paper.

Using your fingers, mix coconut and egg yolk with mung beans to make a firm paste. Divide into pieces about the size of a small walnut and shape into egg-shaped balls using a spoon. Put sugar and water into a small saucepan over low heat, and heat, stirring, until sugar has dissolved. Increase heat and bring to a boil. Add jasmine extract to taste and keep hot at just below a simmer.

Drain pistachios thoroughly and put in a blender or food processor fitted with the metal blade. Add milk and process until finely chopped, scraping mixture down from sides once or twice. Stir in sugar. Heat a large non-stick skillet, add butter and melt over medium-low heat. Add nut paste and cook about 15 minutes, stirring constantly, until mixture is very thick.

Using a fork, beat egg white well in a small bowl. Using two forks, dip each ball into egg white, then lower balls into syrup. Cook in syrup 2 to 3 minutes. Using a slotted spoon, transfer to a plate. When all balls have been cooked, spoon over a little syrup. Let stand until cold.

Makes about 16.

Stir in vanilla extract, then spoon into prepared pan and spread evenly. Cool completely, then cut into 20 squares using a sharp knife.

Makes about 20 squares.

Note: This halva will keep 2 to 3 weeks, covered and stored in the refrigerator.

TOASTED ALMOND TOFFEE

2 cups sugar
1 cup water
2 cups nonfat dry milk powder
1 teaspoon vanilla extract
¼ cup flaked almonds, toasted

Grease and line an 8-inch square pan with waxed paper. Put sugar and water in a large heavy saucepan. Heat gently, stirring occasionally, until sugar is dissolved.

Increase heat and bring to a boil, and boil over medium-high heat until a few drops of mixture will form a soft ball in cold water. Stir in milk powder and cook 3 to 4 minutes more, stirring all the time, until mixture begins to dry on spoon. Stir in vanilla.

Pour into prepared pan and spread evenly. Scatter almonds over top and press into surface. Leave to cool slightly, then cut into 25 squares with a sharp knife while still warm. Leave in pan until cold and firm.

Makes 25 squares.

CASHEW NUT FUDGE

1½ cups unsalted cashew nuts
1½ cups boiling water
2 tablespoons milk
⅔ cup sugar
1 tablespoon butter or ghee
1 teaspoon vanilla extract
Few sheets of silver leaf

Put cashew nuts in a bowl, top with boiling water and soak 1 hour. Grease and line an 8-inch square pan with waxed paper.

Drain cashew nuts thoroughly and put in a blender or food processor fitted with the metal blade. Add milk and process until smooth, scraping mixture down from side once or twice. Stir in sugar. Heat a large non-stick skillet, add butter and melt over medium-low heat. Add nut paste and cook about 20 minutes, stirring constantly, until mixture is very thick.

Stir in vanilla extract, then spoon into prepared pan and spread evenly. Cool completely, then press silver leaf onto surface. Cut fudge into about 25 diamond shapes using a wet sharp knife.

Makes about 25 pieces.

Note: This fudge will keep for two to three weeks if stored in an airtight container.

PEANUT BRITTLE

1 heaped cup shelled unsalted peanuts
1¾ cups sugar
¼ cup water
3 tablespoons light corn syrup
2 tablespoons butter
Pinch of baking soda

Preheat oven to 275F (135C). Lightly oil an 8-inch square cake pan; set aside. On a baking sheet, toast peanuts about 15 minutes.

In a heavy-bottomed, medium-size saucepan, combine sugar, water and corn syrup. Cook over medium heat, stirring, until sugar dissolves. Stir in butter, then bring to a boil. Boil rapidly until mixture reaches 300F (150C) on a candy thermometer, or a small amount forms a brittle thread when dropped into a cup of cold water.

Remove saucepan from heat. Stir in baking soda and toasted peanuts. Pour into oiled pan, stretch slightly with forks, if needed, and cool. When almost set, with an oiled knife, mark into squares. Let set completely. Break into pieces and wrap in colored cellophane, if desired. Store in an airtight container until ready to serve.

Makes about 25 pieces.

CHOCOLATE BALLS

½ cup butter
3 tablespoons light corn syrup
4 ozs. semisweet chocolate
¾ cup chopped dried apricots
1 heaped cup muesli-type cereal
Hot chocolate drink mix

Into a saucepan over low heat, put butter and corn syrup. Heat, stirring, until butter melts.

Break in chocolate and melt. Beat together until smooth. Add apricots and cereal; mix together well. Set aside to cool. When cool, refrigerate about 1 hour.

Roll teaspoons of chocolate mixture into balls. Toss in hot chocolate drink mix. Place in petits fours cases. Return to refrigerator until firm.

Makes about 20.

PRESERVES

LEMON CURD

4 lemons
1¾ cups sugar
1½ cups butter
4 eggs, beaten

Into a heatproof bowl, finely grate zest of lemons. Squeeze lemons and pour juice into bowl. Stir in sugar. Cut butter into small pieces and add to other ingredients.

Set bowl over a saucepan one-quarter filled with simmering water and stir until butter has melted and sugar dissolved. Strain eggs into lemon mixture.

Cook gently, stirring frequently, 10 to 15 minutes, until mixture is thick and creamy. Pour into clean, warm jars and seal while hot. Keep in the refrigerator.

Makes about 1½ lbs.

Variations: For Lime Curd, use limes instead of lemons. For Lemon & Elderflower Curd, add 2 handfuls of elderberry flower, well shaken, after adding butter.

APPLE BUTTER

5 cups dry cider
2½ lbs. Golden Delicious apples
1 lb. Granny Smith apples
Sugar
Grated zest and juice of ½ orange
Grated zest and juice of ½ lemon
½ teaspoon ground cinnamon
½ teaspoon ground cloves

Into a large saucepan, put cider. Boil rapidly until reduced by ⅓. With a knife, peel, core and slice apples, then add to pan.

If necessary, add enough water to just cover apples. Half cover pan and simmer until apples are very soft and pulpy and well reduced. Stir occasionally and crush pulp down in pan as it cooks. Measure pulp and process to a purée if it is lumpy. Return to saucepan. Add 1½ cups sugar for every 2½ cups apple pulp. Stir in orange and lemon zests and juices, cinnamon and cloves.

Cook gently until sugar has dissolved. Simmer, stirring frequently, until most moisture has been driven off. The mixture is ready when a spoon drawn across the surface leaves an impression. Spoon into clean, warm jars and store in the refrigerator. Once a jar is opened, apple butter should be consumed within 3 to 4 days.

Makes 4 or 5 small jars.

CUMBERLAND RUM BUTTER

½ cup butter, softened
1½ cups packed dark brown sugar
¼ teaspoon ground cinnamon
2 tablespoons dark rum
TO SERVE:
Hot toast, muffins or crumpets
TO DECORATE:
Orange zest

Into a bowl, put butter and beat until soft. Gradually beat in sugar.

Gradually beat in the cinnamon and rum. Pile mixture into a small dish. Cover and refrigerate until firm. Decorate with orange zest. Serve with hot toast, muffins or crumpets.

Makes 6 to 8 servings.

Variation: For Anchovy Butter, instead of sugar, cinnamon and rum, work 1½ ozs. drained, canned anchovies into butter. Serve on toast.

ROSE PETAL JAM

½ lb. fragrant, red rose petals
2 cups sugar
4½ cups water
Juice of 2 lemons

Cut off white area from bottom of each petal. Into a bowl, put petals and sprinkle with enough of the sugar to cover them. Leave overnight.

In a saucepan, put remaining sugar, the water and lemon juice. Heat gently until sugar has dissolved. Stir in rose petals and simmer 20 minutes. Bring to a boil and boil 5 minutes, until mixture thickens.

Pour jam into clean, warm jars. Cover and label. Store in a cool place.

Makes about 1 lb.

SPICED CITRUS SLICES

3 thin-skinned oranges
4 thin-skinned lemons
5 limes
2½ cups white wine vinegar
4½ cups sugar
2 (2-inch) cinnamon sticks
2 teaspoons whole cloves
6 blades mace

Scrub fruit thoroughly. Cut each fruit in ⅛-inch thick slices. Lay slices in a stainless steel or enamel saucepan and just cover with water. Bring to a boil, cover and cook very gently about 10 minutes or until peel is tender. Drain slices and reserve liquor.

In another saucepan, gently heat vinegar, sugar and spices, stirring occasionally, until sugar has dissolved. Bring to a boil. Lay fruit slices in syrup. Add reserved liquor to cover fruit, if necessary, and cook very gently 15 minutes or until peel looks transparent.

Meanwhile, sterilize 3 small jars and lids. Arrange fruit slices in warm jars, alternating slices or packing each separately. Bring syrup to a boil. Immediately fill each jar to top and seal with lids. When cold, label and store in a cool place.

Makes 3 small jars.

CHARTREUSE FRUITS

10 fresh lychees or 1 (15-oz.) can lychees
2 cups fresh sweet cherries or 1 (15-oz.) can
  cherries
1 cup sugar
1¼ cups Chartreuse or Benedictine liqueur

Sterilize 3 or 4 small jars and lids and keep warm. Peel lychees and carefully remove pits, keeping fruit whole. Remove cherry stalks and pits. Wash cherries or drain canned fruit and dry on paper towels. Pierce skins of cherries all over with a clean needle or fine skewer.

Arrange 1 layer of cherries in 1 warm jar and sprinkle with a layer of sugar. Arrange 1 layer of lychees on top and sprinkle with more sugar. Continue to layer cherries, sugar and lychees until jar is loosely filled to neck of jar. Do not pack fruit tightly. Sprinkle with a final layer of sugar.

Fill jar to top with liqueur and seal with a clean lid. Repeat to fill more small jars with remaining fruit, sugar and liqueur. Store in a cool dry place up to 6 months.

Makes 3 or 4 small jars.

SATSUMA & PINE NUT CONSERVE

9 satsumas (2 lb. total)
About 2½ cups water
4 cups sugar
¼ cup orange flower water
½ cup pine nuts

Scrub satsumas well. Using a potato peeler or sharp knife, pare peel from satsumas, not including white pith. Cut peel in fine strips. Place in a large saucepan with ⅔ cup of water. Bring to a boil, cover and cook gently 1 hour or until tender.

Cut satsumas in half. Squeeze juice into a 2-cup glass measure. Add enough water to make 1¾ cups, if necessary. Reserve all seeds and place in a piece of muslin; tie securely with a string. Place in a saucepan with satsuma peel. Bring to a boil. Cover and simmer 1 hour. Strain liquid from satsuma peel into saucepan with peel. Stir in sugar and juice. Bring to a boil, stirring constantly, until sugar has dissolved.

Boil rapidly 5 to 10 minutes until setting point is reached. To test, spoon some conserve onto a cold plate. Let stand a few minutes, then push with your finger. If surface wrinkles, setting point has been reached. Add orange flower water and pine nuts. Bring to a boil and boil 2 minutes. Cool 30 minutes. Meanwhile, sterilize 3 jars and lids. Stir conserve, then pour into warm jars. Cover each with paraffin and seal with lids. Store in a dry cool place.

Makes 3 jars.

BRANDIED MINCEMEAT

6 cups raisins
3⅓ cups currants
1 cup dried apricots
¾ cup dates
1 cup candied peel
¾ cup whole almonds
1 lb. cooking apples, peeled, cored
Finely grated peel and juice 2 lemons
2¼ cups light-brown sugar
1 cup unsalted butter, melted
1 tablespoon ground mixed spice
⅔ cup brandy

In a large bowl, place raisins and currants. Chop or mince apricots, dates, candied peel, almonds and apples. Add chopped fruit and nuts and lemon peel and juice to raisins and currants. Mix well. Stir in brown sugar, butter, mixed spice and brandy. Stir mixture until evenly blended. Cover with plastic wrap and refrigerate 2 days.

Sterilize 6 (1-pint) jars and lids and keep warm. Stir mincemeat thoroughly, then spoon into hot jars, filling each to top. Cover each with paraffin and seal with lids.

Makes 6 (1-pint) jars.

MANGO CHUTNEY

LIME PICKLE

4 lbs. green mangoes, peeled and cubed
2 limes, sliced into semi-circles
3 fresh red chiles, cored, seeded and finely chopped
3 cups+2 tablespoons white wine vinegar
1 tablespoon ground toasted cardamom seeds
1 teaspoon ground toasted cumin seeds
1 teaspoon ground turmeric
1½ teaspoons salt
1 lb. light brown sugar

Put mangoes, limes, chiles and vinegar into a nonreactive pan. Bring to a boil then lower heat and simmer, uncovered, for 10-15 minutes until mangoes are just tender.

Add spices, salt and sugar. Stir until sugar has dissolved, then increase heat and bring to a boil. Lower heat again and simmer, uncovered, for 50-60 minutes, stirring occasionally, until most of the liquid has evaporated and the chutney is quite thick.

Ladle chutney into hot, very clean jars. Cover top of each jar of chutney with a disc of waxed paper, waxed side down. Close jars with nonreactive lids. Leave chutney for 1 month before using.

Makes about 3 lbs.

12 limes
¼ cup coarse sea salt
1 tablespoon fenugreek seeds
1 tablespoon mustard seeds
2 tablespoons chile powder
1 tablespoon ground turmeric
1 cup vegetable oil
Cilantro leaves to garnish

Cut each lime lengthways into 8 thin wedges. Place in a large sterilized bowl, sprinkle with salt and set aside.

Put fenugreek and mustard seeds in a skillet and dry roast them over medium heat 1 to 2 minutes, until they begin to pop. Put them in a mortar and grind them to a fine powder with a pestle.

Add chile powder and turmeric and mix well. Sprinkle spice mixture over limes and stir gently. Pour over oil and cover with a dry cloth. Leave in a sunny place 10 to 12 days, until limes have been softened. Pack in sterilized jars, then seal and store in a cool, dark place. Serve at room temperature.

Makes about 6 cups.

Variation: To make lemon pickle, substitute 8 lemons for the limes.

SPICED OLIVES

1 lb. green or ripe olives
1 fresh oregano sprig
1 fresh thyme sprig
1 teaspoon finely chopped fresh rosemary
2 bay leaves
1 teaspoon fennel seeds, bruised
1 teaspoon finely crushed cumin seeds
1 fresh red chile, seeded and chopped
4 garlic cloves, crushed
Olive oil

MARINATED FETA CHEESE

¾ lb. feta cheese
2 garlic cloves
½ teaspoon mixed peppercorns
8 coriander seeds
1 bay leaf
Fresh oregano and thyme sprigs
Olive oil, to cover
Bread, toasted, cut into squares, to serve

With a sharp knife, cut feta cheese into cubes. Cut garlic into thick slivers.

Using a small sharp knife, make a lengthwise slit through to pit of each olive. Put olives into a bowl. Stir in oregano, thyme, rosemary, bay leaves, fennel seeds, cumin seeds, chile and garlic.

With a mortar and pestle, lightly crush peppercorns and coriander seeds.

Into a jar with a tight-fitting lid, pack olive mixture. Add enough oil to cover olives, seal and leave at least 3 days, shaking jar occasionally, before using.

Makes 6 servings.

Into a jar with a tight-fitting lid, pack cubes of cheese with the bay leaf, interspersing layers of cheese with garlic, peppercorns, coriander and oregano or thyme. Pour in enough olive oil to cover cheese. Cover and refrigerate 2 weeks. Serve on hot toast, sprinkled with a little of the oil from the jar.

Makes 6 servings.

MEDITERRANEAN INGREDIENTS

Balsamic vinegar: This Italian vinegar is more expensive than wine vinegars but has a rich, sweet, aromatic flavor so is used much more sparingly. The more mature vinegars, which can be very expensive, are more concentrated and often a few drops are all that are required to flavor a dressing.

Bresaola: Sold thinly sliced, bresaola is raw beef that has been salted and airdried in the same way as prosciutto (see below).

Bulgar wheat: Also spelled bulghar and burghul, this is made from wheat grains that are cracked by boiling, then dried. It only needs to be rehydrated by soaking in water 10-20 minutes before it is ready for use.

Cous cous: A staple in North African countries, cous cous is really a form of pasta, not a grain. Fine grains of semolina are dampened then rolled in flour. Most of the cous cous now sold has already been cooked and only needs to be moistened and reheated, usually by steaming, and the grains separated.

Dolcelatte: This is a factory version of gorgonzola (see below). It has a creamier flavor.

Feta cheese: A white, salty cheese, stored in brine. Traditionally, feta comes from Greece and Cyprus and is made from unpasteurized ewes' milk, but today it is often made elsewhere from cows' milk.

Filo (phyllo) pastry: When using filo pastry it is important to keep the sheets in a pile between two dish cloths or closely covered with plastic wrap and to work with one piece at a time, otherwise the pastry will become dry and brittle.

Garlic: The smell and taste of garlic is one of the most characteristic features of the food of the Mediterranean. For the best flavor, use garlic that is as fresh as possible and if there is a green shoot in a clove, discard the shoot. Buy garlic bulbs loose, rather than in cardboard boxes, or woven into a string. Store in a cool airy dry place away from direct light.

Gorgonzola cheese: A mild, blue-veined Italian cheese with a pleasantly sharp flavor.

Haloumi cheese: A Greek soft to semi-soft goats' milk cheese that is quite salty, yet mild. It is generally served broiled or fried.

Kefalotori cheese: A strong Greek cheese that is good for grating. If you can't find it, use Parmesan or mature, well-flavored Cheddar instead.

Mascarpone cheese: A very rich, thick velvety Italian cheese that is often served sweetened and flavored with liqueurs as a dessert but its luxurious flavor and texture are very good in savory dishes as well.

Mortadella: The largest Italian sausage. The best are made from pure pork but others may contain some beef or offal. The spices and flavorings can vary, the most usual being black peppercorns, coriander seeds and pistachio nuts.

Mozzarella cheese: Today most of the mozzarella we buy is made from cows' milk. This is fine for cooked dishes, but for salads or for eating on its own it is worth paying for the authentic full-flavored, more creamy textured mozzarella di bufala.

Olives: These come in many different varieties and colors and may be cured in brine, packed in oil or flavored with herbs, spices or lemon. Color differences are linked to the degree of ripeness – a progression from green through yellow or greeny-brown to red, violet, then purple and black.

Olive oil: Each country, even regions within a country, have their own olive oils and these give the dishes in which they are used their distinctive flavor. Extra virgin oils have the strongest, finest flavor and are usually used for dressings; virgin oils are one step down in the hierarchy and can be used in special dishes; olive oils are the everyday cooking oil.

Orange flower water: A clear, delightfully scented liquid that is distiled from orange blossoms. It is widely used to flavor sweet dishes around the southern Mediterranean, Turkey and Greece, and in southern France. It is particularly good with its own fruit, the orange, whether in sweet or savory dishes.

Parmesan cheese: The most famous matured hard cheese of Italy, Parmesan is most often used for grating over pasta, risottos, sauces and other cooked dishes, but it is also superb as a table cheese. Always buy Parmesan in a piece to be cut or grated as needed. Ready-grated Parmesan cheese is available but simply does not compare in flavor.

Pasta: Unless you are going to prepare your own pasta, dried pasta is usually preferable to commercial "fresh" pastas, which can be starchy and rather heavy. If making pasta at home, try to buy special "type 00" flour, which is available in Italian delicatessens and some large stores. Alternatively, use strong bread flour.

Pine nuts: These are not really nuts but are the kernels from the cones of the stone pine. They are expensive but have a distinctive almost resinous flavor for which their really is no substitute.

Prosciutto: Salted and air-dried raw ham. Parma ham is the most famous, but other regions have their own versions.

Rice: Locally grown short grain rice gives a characteristic texture to Spanish paellas, Turkish pilaus and Italian risottos. Risotto, or arborio, rice is now widely available and is the only one to use for a genuine risotto; it can also be used for paellas. For pilaus and other Mediterranean rice dishes, use long grain rice, or basmati rice.

Ricotta cheese: This is a fresh, soft Italian cheese that is made from the whey that is the by-product of other cheeses. Ricotta has a mild, delicate flavor and should be used soon after purchase.

Rose water: Made from distiled fragrant rose petals, rose water is used in many North African, Middle Eastern, Turkish and Greek pastries and sweet dishes, particularly milk-based desserts. In North Africa, rose water is also sometimes added to savory dishes.

Saffron: For preference, use pure saffron threads rather than powder as this may be adulterated. A mere pinch of saffron is all that is needed to flavor a dish for four to six people.

Tahini: This a paste made from ground toasted sesame seeds. Tahini separates if left to stand for a while and must be stirred thoroughly before using; the jar can be inverted for a while to make blending easier. Keep tahini in a cool place, but preferably not the refrigerator, because this makes blending more difficult.

EASTERN INGREDIENTS

Bean curd: Low in fat and high in protein, bean curd is made from yellow soya beans and has a mild flavor.

Chinese beef stock: Put into a large saucepan 2 lbs. lean stewing beef, trimmed and cut into 2-inch pieces, 1 (1-inch) piece fresh gingerroot, peeled, 1 garlic clove, 2 shallots, 1 stalk celery, 2 carrots, 2 tablespoons dark soy sauce, a large pinch of salt and a large pinch of freshly ground black pepper. Add 3½ pints (9 cups) cold water. Bring to a boil. Skim scum from surface, cover pan and simmer gently 2 hours. Leave to cool. Line a sieve with clean muslin and place over a large bowl. Ladle stock through sieve and discard beef and vegetables. Cover and chill. Skim fat from surface. Refrigerate for up to 3 days or freeze for up to 3 months. Makes 3 pints (7½ cups).

Chinese vegetable stock: Put 1 lemon grass stalk, broken, 2 slices fresh gingerroot, 1 garlic clove, 2 green onions, 4 ozs. carrots, sliced, 2 stalks celery, 4 ozs. bean sprouts, a large pinch of salt and a large pinch of ground white pepper in a large saucepan. Add 3½ pints (9 cups) cold water and bring to a boil. Skim scum from the surface then cover pan and simmer gently 45 minutes. Leave to cool. Line a sieve with clean muslin and place over a large bowl. Ladle stock through sieve and discard vegetables. Cover and refrigerate for up to 3 days or freeze for up to 3 months. Makes 2½ pints (6 cups).

Cilantro: Fresh cilantro looks like fine flat-leaf parsley but it has a more pungent, distinctive smell and taste.

Coconut milk and cream: This is not the liquid from inside a coconut, but is extracted from shredded coconut flesh that has been soaked in water. Soak the shredded flesh of 1 medium coconut in 10 fl oz (1¼ cups) boiling water 30 minutes Tip into a sieve lined with muslin or fine cotton and squeeze this fabric hard to extract as much liquid as possible. Coconut milk can also be made by putting 8 ozs. (2⅔ cups) desiccated coconut in a blender with 10 fl oz (1¼ cups) boiling water. Mix together 1 minute then soak and strain as above. Home-made coconut milk should be stored in the refrigerator. Ready prepared coconut milk is sold canned (which affects the flavor) and in pouches. Coconut cream is the layer that forms on top of the coconut milk.

Dried mushrooms: There are several types of Eastern dried mushrooms, all of which add a distinctive flavor and aroma to dishes, but the most commonly used is the Chinese black mushroom. They need to be soaked in hot water about 20 minutes then drained and the tough stalks discarded.

Fish sauce (nam pla): A clear brown liquid, rich in protein and B vitamins, this is South East Asia's answer to soy sauce and the essential Thai seasoning. It enriches without tasting too fishy or salty when mixed with other ingredients or when cooked.

Five-spice powder: The Chinese spice mixture made from ground star anise, Szechuan peppercorns, fennel, cloves and cinnamon. Five-spice powder adds a warm, spicy, fragrant flavor to recipes.

Galangal (galangale, laos): A root that is similar in appearance to ginger but the skin is thinner, paler and more translucent. The flavor is also similar to ginger but with distinctive, seductive citrus-pine undertones. A whole root can be kept wrapped in paper in the refrigerator for up to two weeks, or it can be frozen.

Allow to thaw just enough for the required amount to be sliced or grated off, then return the root to the freezer.

Hoisin sauce: A reddish brown sauce based on soya beans and flavored with garlic, chiles and a combination of spices. Brands vary in flavor, but hoisin sauce is usually quite sweet and can range from the thickness of a soft jelly to a runny sauce.

Kaffir limes: These are slightly smaller than ordinary limes and have dark green, knobbly rind. The smell and taste of the zest resemble aromatic limes with a hint of lemon. The zest of ordinary limes can be substituted.

Kaffir lime leaves: The smooth, dark green leaves give an aromatic, clean, citrus-pine flavor and smell. They keep well in a cool place and can be frozen. Use 1½ teaspoons grated ordinary lime zest if kaffir lime leaves are unavailable.

Lemon grass: A long, slim bulb with a lemon-citrus flavor. To use, cut off the root tip, peel off the tough outer layers and cut away the top part of the stalk. Then chop the remaining bulb very finely. Lemon grass can be kept in a cool place for several days, or it can be chopped and frozen. If lemon grass is unavailable, use the grated zest of half a lemon in place of one stalk.

Lily buds: Also known as golden needles, these are the dried buds of the tiger lily flower. They should be soaked in warm water about 30 minutes, then rinsed in fresh water and the hard tip discarded before use.

Noodles: There are many varieties and thicknesses. Egg noodles, whether fresh or dried, need to be cooked in a similar way to pasta before using. Rice noodles are also known as rice sticks and come in three different widths, large, medium and small. There are also fine strands of rice vermicelli. Rice noodles only need to be soaked in hot water to separate and soften them.

Oyster sauce: Used in Chinese cooking this thick brown sauce is made from concentrated oysters, soy sauce and brine. Nowadays, cornstarch and coloring are also often added.

Plum sauce: A thick, sweet condiment made from plums, apricots, garlic, vinegar and seasonings. It is used in cooking and as a dip.

Preserved vegetables: Mixed pickled mustard greens and root vegetables are available in cans and jars. They have a crunchy texture and hot, spicy flavor. They are salty and need to be rinsed before use. Once opened, jars should be covered and stored in the refrigerator and canned vegetables should be transferred to a glass or pottery container.

Rice: For authentic-tasting savory Thai dishes, use Thai fragrant, or jasmine, rice; for other savory Eastern recipes use long grain rice for everyday meals. Short grain glutinous rice is used for particular desserts.

Rice vinegar: This is fermented from rice and is much less acidic than Western vinegars. Chinese rice vinegar many be "black" with a rich, smoky, complex flavor and is usually used for dips; clear pale red, when it is slightly tart; and white and mild. Japanese rice vinegar is subtle, with a clean, elegant flavor. Cider or sherry vinegar can be substituted for rice vinegar.

Rice wine: Chinese rice wine is similar to sherry in color, bouquet and alcohol content (18%). It is made from glutinous rice, yeast and spring water. Dry sherry can be substituted.

Sesame oil: A thick, rich oil made from toasted sesame seeds with a strong nutty flavor. The darker the oil, the stronger the flavor. Lighter oils can be used for cooking but full-flavored ones are reserved for use as a seasoning when the cooking is complete.

Shrimp paste: Made from fermented dried shrimp with salt, this highly pungent paste is used sparingly.

Soy sauce: The essential ingredient in Chinese cooking, soy sauce is made from soya beans, flour and water, fermented together and aged several months. Light soy sauce is more full flavored and quite salty; dark soy sauce, which has caramel added, is thicker and sweeter. Additional salt is often unnecessary.

Fragrant curry paste: This Indian mix is often described as mild as well as fragrant and is available in jars. Fragrant curry powder can be substituted if liked.

Garam masala: A prepared mixture of Indian spices, garam masala can be bought readily in jars and packages.

Tamarind: Sold in sticky brown blocks, tamarind provides a sharp, slightly fruity taste. To make tamarind water, break off a 1-oz. piece and pour over 10 fl oz. (1¼ cups) boiling water. Break up the lump then let stand about 30 minutes, stirring occasionally. Strain off the tamarind water, pressing on the pulp, and discard the remaining debris. Keep the water in a jar in the refrigerator. Ready-to-use tamarind syrup is sometimes available and is usually more concentrated than homemade tamarind water.

Thai curry pastes: Red and green Thai curry pastes are readily available in jars and packages. The red varieties are more mild than green pastes, and have a more mellow flavor, but brands vary in their strengths so add cautiously.

INDEX